MR. RHEE'S BRILLIANT MATH SERIES

PRAXIS MATHEMATICS

CONTENT KNOWLEDGE 5161

PREP

By Brian Rhee

Complete Review of All Topics

6 Full-Length Practice Tests

Detailed Solutions for All Questions

Legal Notice

Praxis® is a registered trademark of Educational Testing Service (ETS), which was not involved in the production of this publication nor endorses this book.

Published by: Solomon Academy
First Edition
ISBN: 9781096383543

About Author

Brian(Yeon) Rhee obtained a Masters of Arts Degree in Statistics at Columbia University, NY. He served as the Mathematical Statistician at the Bureau of Labor Statistics, DC. He is the Head Academic Director at Solomon Academy due to his devotion to the community coupled with his passion for teaching. His mission is to help students of all confidence level excel in academia to build a strong foundation in character, knowledge, and wisdom. Now, Solomon academy is known as the best academy specialized in Math in Northern Virginia.

Brian Rhee has published more than nineteen books. The titles of his books are Praxis Mathematics Content Knowledge 5161 Prep, New TJHSST Math Workbook, 7 full-length practice tests for the AP Calculus AB/BC Multiple choice sections, AP Calculus, SAT 1 Math, SAT 2 Math level 2, 12 full-length practice tests for the SAT 2 Math Level 2, SHSAT/TJHSST Math workbook, and IAAT (Iowa Algebra Aptitude Test) Volume 1 and 2, NNAT 2 Level B Grade 1, CogAT form 7 Level 8, CogAT form 7 Level 9, and five arithmetic workbooks for grade 1 through grade 6. He's currently working on other math books which will be introduced in the near future.

Brian Rhee has more than twenty years of teaching experience in math. He has been one of the most popular tutors among TJHSST (Thomas Jefferson High School For Science and Technology) students. Currently, he is developing many online math courses with www.masterprep.net for AP Calculus AB and BC, SAT 2 Math level 2 test, and other various math subjects.

SOLOMON ACADEMY

Solomon Academy is a prestigious institution of learning with numerous qualified teachers of various fields of education. Our mission is to thoroughly teach students of all ages and confidence levels, elevate skills to the highest standard of education, and provide them with all the tools and materials to succeed.

5723 Centre Square Drive
Centreville, VA 20120
Tel: 703-988-0019

Email: solomonacademyva@gmail.com
info@solomonacademy.net

CLASSES OFFERED

MATHEMATICS	TESTING	ENGLISH
1st-6th grade math	CogAt	1st-6th Reading
Algebra 1, 2	IAAT and SOL 7	1st-6th Writing
Geometry	TJHSST Prep	Essay Writing
Pre-Calculus	SAT/ACT Prep	SAT Writing
AP Calculus AB/BC	SAT 2 Subject Tests	
AP Statistics	MathCounts	
Multivariate Calculus	AMC 10/12	

LEARN FROM THE AUTHOR

Private sessions with Brian Rhee is also available on the following subjects: Praxis CK 5161, Praxis CK 5169, TJ Math, SAT Math, SAT 2 Subject Math Level 2, Pre-Calculus, AP Calculus AB/BC, AP Statistics, IB SL/HL, Multivariate Calculus, Linear Algebra, AMC 8/10/12, and AIME.

Feel free to contact me at solomonacademyva@gmail.com

Contents

Chapter 1 Introduction **11**
1.1 About the Praxis Mathematics CK 5161 11
1.2 Graphing Calculator 11
1.3 Scoring 11
1.4 Content Categories 12
1.5 Questions Types 12
1.6 Notations, Definitions, and Formulas 14
Chapter 2 Number and Quantity **17**
2.1 The Real Number System 17
2.2 The Closure Properties of Numbers 18
2.3 Prime Factorization 19
2.4 Greatest Common Factor and Least Common Multiple 20
2.5 Divisibility Rules 20
2.6 Order of Operations 21
2.7 Scientific Notation 21
2.8 Ratios, Rates, and Proportions 21
2.9 Properties of Exponents 22
2.10 Properties of Logarithms 22
2.11 Simplifying Radicals 23
2.12 Complex Numbers 23
2.13 Powers of i 24
2.14 Absolute Value of Complex Numbers 24
2.15 Operations on Complex Numbers 25
2.16 Properties of Conjugates 26
2.17 Matrices 27
2.18 Adding and Subtracting Two Matrices 27
2.19 Multiplying Two Matrices 28
2.20 Transformation using Matrices 29
2.21 Matrix Algebra 30
2.22 Evaluating Determinants 30
2.23 The Area of a Triangle using 3×3 Determinant 31
2.24 The Inverse of a 2×2 Matrix 32
Chapter 3 Algebra **33**
3.1 Linear Function 33
3.2 Linear Inequalities 34
3.3 Solving Systems of Equations using Substitution and Elimination methods 35
3.4 Solving Systems of with Three Variables 37
3.5 Solving Systems of Equations using Cramer's rule 39
3.6 Solving systems of linear equations using matrix algebra 41

3.7 Graphing Systems of Linear Inequalities . . . 42
3.8 Optimal solution of a linear programming problem . . . 42
3.9 Quadratic Functions and Quadratic Equations . . . 44
3.10 The Discriminant . . . 46
3.11 Solving Quadratic Inequalities . . . 46
3.12 Operations on Polynomial Functions . . . 47
3.13 Special Product Patterns . . . 48
3.14 Finding the Real Zeros of a Polynomial Function . . . 48
3.15 Remainder Theorem . . . 49
3.16 Factor Theorem . . . 50
3.17 Rational Zeros Theorem . . . 51
3.18 Conjugate Pairs Theorem . . . 52
3.19 Writing a Polynomial Function with the Given Zeros . . . 52
3.20 Graphing Cubic Functions using Multiplicity . . . 54
3.21 Solving Polynomial and Rational Inequalities . . . 55
3.22 Simplifying Rational Expressions . . . 56
3.23 Solving Rational and Radical Equations . . . 57

Chapter 4 Functions **59**

4.1 Definition of Function . . . 59
4.2 Vertical Line Test . . . 60
4.3 Operations on Functions . . . 60
4.4 Odd and Even Functions . . . 62
4.5 Piecewise Functions . . . 63
4.6 Inverse Functions . . . 64
4.7 Horizontal Line Test . . . 64
4.8 Graphing the Inverse Functions . . . 66
4.9 Graphs of Parent Functions . . . 67
4.10 Transformations . . . 68
4.11 Order of Transformations . . . 69
4.12 Graph of $y = |f(x)|$ . . . 70
4.13 Rational Functions . . . 71
4.14 Finding Vertical Asymptotes . . . 72
4.15 Finding Horizontal Asymptotes . . . 72
4.16 Graphing Simple Rational Functions . . . 74
4.17 Graphing Simple Rational Functions with a Hole . . . 75
4.18 Graphing complicated Rational Functions . . . 75
4.19 Graphs of Exponential and Logarithmic Functions . . . 77
4.20 Solving Exponential and Logarithmic Equations . . . 80
4.21 Exponential Growth and Decay . . . 81
4.22 Compound Interest . . . 82

Chapter 5 Trigonometry **83**

5.1 Angles . . . 83
5.2 Arc length and Area of a sector . . . 85
5.3 Definitions of Six Trigonometric Functions . . . 86
5.4 Finding the Exact Value of Trigonometric Functions . . . 87
5.5 Pythagorean Identities . . . 89
5.6 Even-Odd Properties . . . 89
5.7 Cofunctions Identities . . . 90
5.8 Graphs of Six Trigonometric Functions . . . 91
5.9 Finding amplitude, period, horizontal translation, and vertical translation . . . 92

5.10 Angle Formulas 96
5.11 The Inverse Trigonometric Functions 99
5.12 Solving Trigonometric Equations 101
5.13 The Area of a SAS Triangle 103
5.14 Solving Triangles 103
5.15 The Law of Sines 104
5.16 The Law of Cosines 105
5.17 Polar Coordinates 106
5.18 Converting from Polar Coordinates to Rectangular Coordinates 107
5.19 Converting from Rectangular Coordinates to Polar Coordinates 108
5.20 Converting between Polar and Rectangular Equations 109
5.21 Cartesian and Polar Form of Complex Numbers 110
5.22 Converting Cartesian Forms to Polar Forms 111
5.23 Multiplying and Dividing in Polar Form 112
5.24 De Moivre's Theorem 112
5.25 Finding **n**th Roots of Complex Numbers 113
5.26 Vectors 115
5.27 Algebraic Operations on Vectors 116
5.28 Drawing the resultant vectors 117

Chapter 6 Calculus **119**

6.1 Definition of Limit 119
6.2 One-Sided Limits 120
6.3 Properties of Limits 122
6.4 Limit of a Rational Function 122
6.5 Special Limits 124
6.6 Limits at Infinity 125
6.7 Finding Horizontal Asymptote of a Rational Function 126
6.8 Continuity 128
6.9 Types of Discontinuities 128
6.10 The Intermediate Value Theorem 129
6.11 Rate of Change and Instantaneous Rate of Change 130
6.12 Writing an Equation of the Tangent line 131
6.13 Definition of the Derivative Function 131
6.14 Differentiability 132
6.15 The Graph of the Derivative Function 133
6.16 Differentiation Rules 134
6.17 Product Rule and Quotient Rule 135
6.18 Derivatives of Six Trigonometric Functions 135
6.19 The Chain Rule 137
6.20 Implicit Differentiation 139
6.21 Higher Derivatives 141
6.22 Velocity and Acceleration 141
6.23 L'Hospital's Rule 143
6.24 Related Rates 145
6.25 The Mean Value Theorem 148
6.26 Increasing and Decreasing Test 149
6.27 Concavity Test 149
6.28 Finding a Local Maximum and a Local Minimum 150
6.29 Optimization Problems 151
6.30 Basic Indefinite Integrals 153

6.31 Numerical Approximations of a Definite Integral . . . 154
6.32 The Fundamental Theorem of Calculus . . . 157
6.33 U-Substitution Rule . . . 159
6.34 Integration by parts . . . 160
6.35 Area Between Curves . . . 162
6.36 Average Value of a Function . . . 164
6.37 Volume by the Disk Method . . . 165
6.38 Volume by the Washer Method . . . 167
6.39 The Limit of a Sequence . . . 168
6.40 Convergence of Series . . . 169
Chapter 7 Geometry **173**
7.1 Angles . . . 173
7.2 Parallel Lines and Transversals . . . 174
7.3 Names of Triangles . . . 175
7.4 Theorems of Triangles . . . 176
7.5 Proving Triangles are Congruent . . . 177
7.6 Perpendicular Bisector Theorem and Angle Bisector Theorem . . . 177
7.7 Bisectors of a Triangle . . . 178
7.8 Properties of Regular Polygons . . . 180
7.9 Pythagorean Theorem and Special Right Triangles . . . 181
7.10 Properties of Quadrilaterals . . . 182
7.11 Similar Polygons . . . 184
7.12 Reflection, Rotation, Translation, and Dilation . . . 185
7.13 Symmetry . . . 186
7.14 Properties and Theorems of Circles . . . 187
7.15 Perimeter, Area, and Volume . . . 189
7.16 Identifying Conic Sections . . . 191
7.17 Circles . . . 192
7.18 Ellipses . . . 192
7.19 Parabolas . . . 194
7.20 Hyperbolas . . . 195
7.21 Solving Systems of Nonlinear Equations . . . 198
Chapter 8 Probability and Statistics **201**
8.1 Probability . . . 201
8.2 Complementary and Independent Events . . . 202
8.3 Laws of Probability . . . 202
8.4 Key Statistical Concepts . . . 204
8.5 Display of Numerical Data . . . 205
8.6 Measuring the Center of Data . . . 208
8.7 Comparing the Mean and Median of a Distribution . . . 208
8.8 Measuring the Spread of Data . . . 209
8.9 Properties of the Standard Deviation . . . 210
8.10 Random Variables . . . 211
8.11 Normal Distributions . . . 212
8.12 The Standard Normal Distribution(**Z**-distribution) . . . 213
8.13 Determining whether two variables are related . . . 215
8.14 Facts about Correlation, r . . . 216
8.15 Least Squares Regression Line . . . 217
8.16 How Good is our Least Square Regression Line? . . . 218
8.17 Observational studies and Experiments . . . 219

8.18 Sampling from a Population . . . 220
8.19 Sampling Distribution of a Sample Mean . . . 220
Chapter 9 Discrete Mathematics **221**
9.1 Sequences . . . 221
9.2 Arithmetic Sequences and Geometric Sequences . . . 222
9.3 Series . . . 223
9.4 Arithmetic Series and Geometric Series . . . 224
9.5 Properties of Sigma Notation . . . 226
9.6 Converse, Inverse, and Contrapositive . . . 227
9.7 Equivalence Relations . . . 228
9.8 Counting . . . 228
9.9 The Fundamental Counting Principle . . . 229
9.10 Permutation and Combination . . . 230
9.11 The Binomial Theorem . . . 232
Practice Test 1 **235**
Practice Test 1 Solutions . . . 246
Practice Test 2 **267**
Practice Test 2 Solutions . . . 278
Practice Test 3 **297**
Practice Test 3 Solutions . . . 308
Practice Test 4 **329**
Practice Test 4 Solutions . . . 340
Practice Test 5 **361**
Practice Test 5 Solutions . . . 373
Practice Test 6 **393**
Practice Test 6 Solutions . . . 404

Chapter 1

Introduction

1.1 About the Praxis Mathematics CK 5161

The Praxis Mathematics: Content Knowledge test (test code 5161) is designed to access the mathematical knowledge and skills necessary for entry-level teachers in secondary school mathematics. Candidates are required to understand mathematical concepts, and solve problems using extensive knowledge from different areas of mathematics. Candidates who take the Praxis Mathematics CK 5161 test completed a bachelor's program in mathematics or mathematics education.

The Praxis Mathematics CK 5161 test is a computer-delivered test. It consists of 60 questions. Of the 60 questions, only 50 questions are scored. 10 questions are pretest questions. These questions are used to evaluate whether they should appear on future test based on candidates responses. There is **NO** penalty for guessing wrong answers. The time limit on the test is 150 minutes (2 hours and 30 minutes).

1.2 Graphing Calculator

As of September 1, 2018, the Praxis Mathematics CK 5161 test provides an on-screen graphing calculator, which is the TI-84 Plus CE graphing calculator. A tutorial is available at https://www.ets.org so that you may practice using the on-screen graphing calculator.

1.3 Scoring

The raw score is the number of questions answered correctly on the test. The minimum passing score is 32 (64%) out of 50 raw-score points which corresponds to 160 on a 100-200 scale. For the practice tests in this book, the minimum passing score is 39 (65%) out of 60 raw-score points.

The minimum scores considered passing vary from state to state. Here is a list of state passing scores as of May 1, 2018.

AK - 160	AL - 145	AR - 160	CO - 152	CT - 160
DC - 160	DE - 160	HI - 160	IA - 135	ID - 160
KS - 152	KY - 160	LA - 160	MD - 160	ME - 160
MS - 160	MT - 160	NC - 160	ND - 160	NE - 146
NH - 160	NJ - 160	NV - 160	PA - 160	RI - 160
SC - 160	SD - 160	TN - 160	UT - 160	VA - 160
VT - 160	WI - 160	WV - 160	WY - 160	AS - 160
GU - 160	MP - 136	VI - 160		

1.4 Content Categories

The Praxis Mathematics CK 5161 test has two content categories.

Content Category	Number of Questions	Percent of Test
Number and Quantity, Algebra, Functions, and Calculus	41	68%
Geometry, Probability and Statistics, and Discrete Mathematics	19	32%

1.5 Questions Types

The Praxis Mathematics CK 5161 test has four types of questions: Multiple-choice (select one answer choice) questions, multiple-choice (select one or more answer choices) questions, numeric-entry (fill in a numeric answer) questions, and numeric-entry (fill in a fraction answer) questions.

Multiple-Choice (Select one answer choice) Questions

The equation $x^2 + y^2 + 4x - 2y - 3 = 0$ represents a circle. What is the center of the circle?

(A) $(-2, -1)$

(B) $(-2, 1)$

(C) $(2, -1)$

(D) $(2, 1)$

Multiple-Choice (Select one or more answer choices) Questions

For the following question, select all the answer choices that apply.

a	$\lim_{x\to a^-} f(x)$	$\lim_{x\to a^+} f(x)$	$f(a)$
1	2	2	3
2	$-\infty$	∞	undefined
3	1	1	1
4	∞	∞	undefined

According to the table shown above, Which of the following statements are true about the function f ?

Select all that apply.

(A) f has a hole at $x = 1$.

(B) f has vertical asymptotes at $x = 2$ and $x = 4$.

(C) f has a horizontal asymptote at $y = 1$.

(D) f is continuous at $x = 3$.

Numeric-Entry (Fill in a numeric answer) Questions

For the following question, enter your answer in the answer box.

If x is a positive integer greater than 1 for which $\sqrt{x}$ and $\sqrt[3]{x}$ are both integers, what is the smallest possible value of x ?

$x =$ [ ]

Numeric-Entry (Fill in a fraction answer) Questions

For the following question, enter your answer in the answer box.

If you toss a coin three times, what is the probability that two heads will be shown?

Give your answer as a fraction.

$\frac{\square}{\square}$

1.6 Notations, Definitions, and Formulas

NOTATIONS

(a, b)	$\{x : a \leq x < b\}$
$[a, b)$	$\{x : a < x < b\}$
$(a, b]$	$\{x : a < x \leq b\}$
$[a, b]$	$\{x : a \leq x \leq b\}$
$\gcd(m, n)$	**greatest common divisor** of two integers m and n
$\text{lcm}(m, n)$	**least common divisor** of two integers m and n
$[\,x\,]$	**greatest integer** m such that $m \leq x$
$m \equiv k (\text{mod } n)$	m and k are **congruent modulo** $\boldsymbol{n}$ (m and k have the same remainder when divided by n, or equivalently, $m - k$ is a multiple of n)
f^{-1}	**inverse** of an invertible function f; (**not** to be read as $\dfrac{1}{f}$)
$\lim\limits_{x \to a^+} f(x)$	**right-hand limit** of $f(x)$; limit of $f(x)$ as x approaches a from the right
$\lim\limits_{x \to a^-} f(x)$	**left-hand limit** of $f(x)$; limit of $f(x)$ as x approaches a from the left
$\varnothing$	the empty set
$x \in S$	x is an element of set S
$S \subset T$	set S is a proper subset of set T
$S \subseteq T$	either set S is a proper subset of set T or $S = T$
$\overline{S}$	complement of set S; the set of all elements not in S that are in some specified universal set
$T \setminus S$	relative complement of set S in set T, i.e., the set of all elements of T that are not elements of S
$S \cup T$	union of sets S and T
$S \cap T$	intersection of sets S and T

DEFINITIONS

A relation $\Re$ on a set S

reflexive if $x \Re x$ for all $x \in S$

symmetric if $x \Re y \Rightarrow y \Re x$ for all $x, y \in S$

transitive if $(x \Re y$ and $y \Re z) \Rightarrow x \Re z$ for all $x, y, z \in S$

antisymmetric if $(x \Re y$ and $y \Re x) \Rightarrow x = y$ for all $x, y \in S$

An equivalence relation is a reflexive, symmetric, and transitive relation.

FORMULAS

Sum

$$\sin(x \pm y) = \sin x \cos y \pm \cos x \sin y$$
$$\cos(x \pm y) = \cos x \cos y \mp \sin x \sin y$$
$$\tan(x \pm y) = \frac{\tan x \pm \tan y}{1 \mp \tan x \tan y}$$

Half-angle (sign depends on the quadrant of $\frac{\theta}{2}$)

$$\sin\frac{\theta}{2} = \pm\sqrt{\frac{1-\cos\theta}{2}}$$
$$\cos\frac{\theta}{2} = \pm\sqrt{\frac{1+\cos\theta}{2}}$$

Range of Inverse Trigonometric Functions

$\sin^{-1} x$	$\left[-\frac{\pi}{2}, \frac{\pi}{2}\right]$
$\cos^{-1} x$	$[0, \pi]$
$\tan^{-1} x$	$\left(-\frac{\pi}{2}, \frac{\pi}{2}\right)$

Law of Sines

$$\frac{\sin A}{a} = \frac{\sin B}{b} = \frac{\sin C}{c}$$

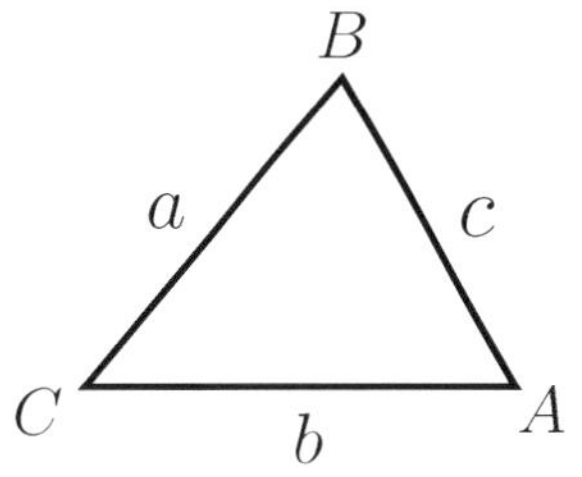

Law of Cosines

$$c^2 = a^2 + b^2 - 2ab(\cos C)$$

DeMoivre's Theorem

$$\Big(r(\cos\theta + i\sin\theta)\Big)^k = r^k\Big(\cos(k\theta) + i\sin(k\theta)\Big)$$

Coordinate Transformation

Rectangular (x, y) to polar (r, θ): $r^2 = x^2 + y^2$; $\tan\theta = \dfrac{y}{x}$ if $x \neq 0$

Polar (r, θ) to rectangular (x, y): $x = r\cos\theta$; $y = r\sin\theta$

Distance from point (x_1, y_1) to line $Ax + by + C = 0$

$$d = \frac{|Ax_1 + By_1 + C|}{\sqrt{A^2 + B^2}}$$

Volume

Sphere with radius r:	$V = \dfrac{4}{3}\pi r^3$
Right circular cone with height h and base of radius r:	$V = \dfrac{1}{3}\pi r^2 h$
Right circular cylinder with height h and base of radius r:	$V = \pi r^2 h$
Pyramid with height h and base of area B:	$V = \dfrac{1}{3}Bh$
Right prism with height h and base of area B:	$V = Bh$

Surface Area

Sphere with radius r:	$A = 4\pi r^2$
Right circular cone with radius r and slant height s:	$A = \pi rs + \pi r^2$

Differentiation

$$\Big(f(x)g(x)\Big)' = f'(x)g(x) + f(x)g'(x)$$

$$\Big(f(g(x))\Big)' = f'(g(x))g'(x)$$

$$\left(\frac{f(x)}{g(x)}\right)' = \frac{f'(x)g(x) - f(x)g'(x)}{\big(g(x)\big)^2} \quad \text{if } g(x) \neq 0$$

Integration by Parts

$$\int u\,dv = uv - \int v\,du$$

Chapter 2

Number and Quantity

2.1 The Real Number System

In mathematics, a real number is a value of a continuous quantity that can represent a distance along a line. There are five subsets of real numbers: Natural numbers, whole numbers, integers, rational numbers, and irrational numbers.

The Real Number System

	Definition	Example
Natural numbers	Counting numbers	$1, 2, 3, 4 \cdots$
Whole numbers	Natural numbers together with zero	$0, 1, 2, 3, \cdots$
Integers	Whole numbers plus negatives	$\cdots, -2, -1, 0, 1, 2, \cdots$
Rational numbers	Numbers can be expressed as fractions	0.25 or $\frac{1}{4}$
Irrational numbers	Numbers cannot be expressed as fractions	$\sqrt{2}$, e, π
Real numbers	All of the rational and irrational numbers	All points on the number line

2.2 The Closure Properties of Numbers

The Closure Property

A set has the closure property under a particular operation if the result of the operation is always an element in the set. If a set has the closure property under a particular operation, the we say that the set is **closed** under the operation.

	Closed under
Nature numbers	Addition and multiplication
Whole numbers	Addition and multiplication
Integers	Addition, subtraction, and multiplication
Rational numbers	Addition, subtraction, and multiplication
Irrational numbers	None
Real numbers	Addition, subtraction, and multiplication

Tips

1. Whole numbers, integers, rational numbers, and real numbers are NOT closed under division because division by 0 is undefined.
2. The sum or product of two rational numbers is rational.
3. The sum a rational number and an irrational number is irrational.
4. The product of a nonzero rational number and an irrational number is irrational.
5. The sum or product of two irrational number can be rational or irrational.

Basic Number Properties

- Commutative property: $a + b = b + a$, and $ab = ba$
- Associate property: $a + (b + c) = (a + b) + c$, and $a(bc) = (ab)c$
- Distributive property: $a(b + c) = ab + ac$

2.3 Prime Factorization

Prime Factorization

Factors

Factors are the numbers that you multiply to get another number. For instance, $10 = 1 \times 10$ and $10 = 2 \times 5$. Thus, the factors of 10 are 1, 2, 5, and 10.

Prime numbers

A prime number is a whole number that has only two factors: 1 and itself. The prime numbers less than 60 are 2, 3, 5, 7, 11, 13, 17, 19, 23, 29, 31, 37, 41, 43, 47, 53, and 59. It is worth noting that 2 is the first, smallest, and only even prime number among the prime numbers. A composite number is a number that has more than two factors. For instance, 4 has three factors: 1, 2, and 4. Thus, 4 is a composite number.

Prime factorization

A prime factorization of a number is a process of writing the number as the product of all its prime factors. Since 12 can be written as $12 = 2 \times 2 \times 3$, the prime factorization of 12 is $2^2 \times 3$.

The prime factorization is useful when you count the total number of factors of a number. If a prime factorization of a number, n, is $n = 2^a \times 3^b \times 5^c$, the total number of factors of n is $(a + 1) \times (b + 1) \times (c + 1)$. For instance, a prime factorization of 72 is $72 = 2^3 \times 3^2$. Thus, the total number of factors of 72 is $(3 + 1) \times (2 + 1) = 12$.

Example **Finding the number of factors**

How many factors does 42 have?

Solution The prime factorization of 42 is $42 = 2^1 \times 3^1 \times 7^1$. Thus, the total number of factors of 42 is $(1 + 1) \times (1 + 1) \times (1 + 1) = 8$. Or, you can find the total number factors of 42 by listing them out. The factors of 42 are 1, 2, 3, 6, 7, 14, 21, and 42.

2.4 Greatest Common Factor and Least Common Multiple

GCF and LCM

The GCF(greatest common factor) is the largest value that divides into both numbers without a remainder. To find the GCF, multiply the prime factors that are common to both prime factorizations of the two numbers. For instance,

$$24 = 2^3 \times 3$$
$$36 = 2^2 \times 3^2$$
$$GCF(24, 36) = 2^2 \times 3 = 12$$

The LCM(least common multiple) is the smallest value that two or more numbers multiply into. To find the LCM, multiply the largest multiple of each prime that appears at least once. For instance,

$$24 = 2^3 \times 3$$
$$36 = 2^2 \times 3^2$$
$$LCM(24, 36) = 2^3 \times 3^2 = 72$$

2.5 Divisibility Rules

Divisibility Rules

A number is divisibly by

- 2: If the last digit is even.
- 3: If the sum of the digits is divisible by 3.
- 4: If the last two digits is divisible by 4.
- 5: If the last digit is either 5 or 0.
- 6: If the number is divisible by 2 and 3.
- 8: If the last thee digits is divisible by 8.
- 9: If the sum of the digits is divisible by 9.
- 10: If the last digit is 0.
- 11: Take the alternating sum of the digits in the number, read from left to right. If it is 0 or divisible by 11, so is the original number. For instance, 8173 has alternating sum of digits $8 - 1 + 7 - 3 = 11$. Since 11 is divisible by 11, so is 8173.

2.6 Order of Operations

Order of Operations

PEMDAS is an acronym for the words parenthesis, exponents, multiplication, division, addition, subtraction. Given two or more operations in a single expression, the order of the letters in PEMDAS tells you what to calculate first, second, third and so on, until the calculation is complete. The order of operations(PEMDAS) suggests to first perform any calculations inside parentheses. Afterwards, evaluate any exponents. Next, perform all multiplications and divisions working from left to right. Finally, perform addition and subtraction from left to right.

2.7 Scientific Notation

Scientific Notation

Scientific notation is the process of writing large or small numbers in the form of $c \times 10^n$ where $1 \leq c < 10$, and n is an integer. In other words, c must be greater than or equal to 1 but less than 10. In general, positive n values give a large number while negative n values produce small fractional values. It is important to understand how to convert numbers written in standard notation to scientific notation and vice versa.

To convert standard notation to scientific notation, set the decimal point to create a number that satisfies the definition of c. For example, the c value of 12,400 is 1.24. Since 12,400 is a large number and the decimal point moved 4 places to the left, the scientific notation is written as $12,400 = 1.24 \times 10,000 = 1.24 \times 10^4$. For smaller numbers such as 0.000000024, the c value is 2.4. Since the number is small and the decimal point moved 8 places to the right, the scientific notation is written as $0.000000024 = \frac{2.4}{100,000,000} = 2.4 \times 10^{-8}$

2.8 Ratios, Rates, and Proportions

Ratios, Rates, and Proportions

A **ratio** is a fraction that compares two quantities measured in the same units. The ratio of a to b can be written as $a : b$ or $\frac{a}{b}$. If the ratio of a number of apples to that of oranges in a store is $3 : 4$ or $\frac{3}{4}$, it means that there are 3 apples to every 4 oranges in the store.

A **rate** is a ratio that compares two quantities measured in different units. A rate is usually expressed as a unit rate. A unit rate is a rate per one unit of a given quantity. The rate of a per b can be written as $\frac{a}{b}$. If a car travels 100 miles in 2 hours, the car travels at a rate of 50 miles per hour.

A **proportions** is an equation that states that two ratios are equal A proportion can be written as

$$a : b = c : d \quad \text{or} \quad \frac{a}{b} = \frac{c}{d}$$

The proportion above reads a is to b as c is to d.

2.9 Properties of Exponents

Properties of Exponents

The table below summarizes the properties of exponents.

Properties of Exponents	Example
1. $a^m \cdot a^n = a^{m+n}$	1. $2^4 \cdot 2^6 = 2^{10}$
2. $\frac{a^m}{a^n} = a^{m-n}$	2. $\frac{2^{10}}{2^3} = 2^{10-3} = 2^7$
3. $(a^m)^n = a^{mn} = (a^n)^m$	3. $(2^3)^4 = 2^{12} = (2^4)^3$
4. $a^0 = 1$	4. $(-2)^0 = 1$, $(3)^0 = 1$, $(100)^0 = 1$
5. $a^{-1} = \frac{1}{a}$	5. $2^{-1} = \frac{1}{2}$
6. $a^{\frac{1}{n}} = \sqrt[n]{a}$	6. $2^{\frac{1}{2}} = \sqrt{2}$, $x^{\frac{1}{3}} = \sqrt[3]{x}$
7. $a^{\frac{m}{n}} = (a^m)^{\frac{1}{n}} = \sqrt[n]{a^m}$	7. $2^{\frac{3}{2}} = \sqrt[2]{2^3}$, $x^{\frac{3}{4}} = \sqrt[4]{x^3}$
8. $a^{-\frac{m}{n}} = (a^{\frac{m}{n}})^{-1} = \frac{1}{\sqrt[n]{a^m}}$	8. $2^{-\frac{3}{4}} = (2^{\frac{3}{4}})^{-1} = \frac{1}{\sqrt[4]{2^3}}$
9. $(ab)^n = a^n b^n$	9. $(2 \cdot 3)^6 = 2^6 \cdot 3^6$, $(2x)^2 = 2^2 x^2$
10. $\left(\frac{a}{b}\right)^n = \frac{a^n}{b^n}$	10. $(\frac{2}{x})^3 = \frac{2^3}{x^3}$
11. $\frac{b^{-n}}{a^{-m}} = \frac{a^m}{b^n}$	11. $\frac{y^{-3}}{x^{-2}} = \frac{x^2}{y^3}$

2.10 Properties of Logarithms

Properties of Logarithms

The table below summarizes the properties of logarithms.

Properties of Logarithms	Example
1. $\log_a 0 =$ undefined	1. $\log_a 0 =$ undefined
2. $\log_a 1 = 0$	2. $\log_2 1 = 0$
3. $\log_a a = 1$	3. $\log_2 2 = 1$
4. $\log_a x^n = n \log_a x$	4. $\log_2 125 = \log_2 5^3 = 3 \log_2 5$
5. $\log_{a^n} x = \frac{1}{n} \log_a x$	5. $\log_8 5 = \log_{2^3} 5 = \frac{1}{3} \log_2 5$
6. $\log_a x = \frac{\log_c x}{\log_c a}$	6. $\log_2 3 = \frac{\log_{10} 3}{\log_{10} 2} = \frac{\ln 3}{\ln 2}$
7. $\log_a xy = \log_a x + \log_a y$	7. $\log_2 15 = \log_2(3 \cdot 5) = \log_2 3 + \log_2 5$
8. $\log_a \frac{x}{y} = \log_a x - \log_a y$	8. $\log_2 \frac{5}{3} = \log_2 5 - \log_2 3$
9. $a^{\log_a x} = x^{\log_a a} = x$	9. $2^{\log_2 3} = 3^{\log_2 2} = 3^1 = 3$

Tips

1. The common logarithm is the logarithm with base 10, which is denoted by either $\log_{10} x$ or $\log x$.
2. e is an irrational number and is approximately $2.718\cdots$. The natural logarithm of x can be expressed as either $\log_e x$ or $\ln x$.

2.11 Simplifying Radicals

Simplifying Radicals

$$\sqrt[n]{ab} = \sqrt[n]{a}\sqrt[n]{b}, \qquad \sqrt[n]{\frac{a}{b}} = \frac{\sqrt[n]{a}}{\sqrt[n]{b}}$$

2.12 Complex Numbers

Definition of Complex Numbers

The equation $x^2 = -1$ does not have real solutions because the square of a real number x is either 0 or positive, never negative. In order to provide a solution to $x^2 = -1$, complex numbers are created.

A complex number z is written in the form $z = a + bi$, where a and b are real numbers, and i is an imaginary unit which satisfies $i^2 = -1$. The number a is the real part of the complex number denoted by $a = Re(z)$ and the number b is the imaginary part of the complex number denoted by $b = Im(z)$. For instance, $z = 2 + 3i$, $Re(z) = 2$ and $Im(z) = 3$.

Tips

1. The imaginary unit, denoted as i, is defined as $i = \sqrt{-1}$. Thus, $i^2 = -1$.
2. The property of the square root of a negative number is as follows:
$$\sqrt{-3} = \sqrt{-1 \cdot 3} = \sqrt{-1}\sqrt{3} = i\sqrt{3}$$

Example **Solving a quadratic equation**

Solve $(x+1)^2 = -3$

Solution The equation $(x+1)^2 = -3$ means that the square of a number $x + 1$ is equal to -3. Since the square of a real number cannot be negative, the solutions to $(x+1)^2 = -3$ involve complex numbers.

$(x+1)^2 = -1 \cdot 3$	Since $i^2 = -1$
$(x+1)^2 = 3i^2$	Take the square root of both sides
$x + 1 = \pm i\sqrt{3}$	Subtract 1 from each side
$x = -1 \pm i\sqrt{3}$	

Therefore, the solutions to $(x+1)^2 = -3$ is $x = -1 + i\sqrt{3}$ or $x = -1 - i\sqrt{3}$.

2.13 Powers of i

Powers of i

The table below shows the powers of i, which repeat in a pattern: i, -1, $-i$, and 1.

Powers of i	i	i^2	i^3	i^4	i^5	i^6	i^7	i^8	$\cdots$	i^{12}	$\cdots$	i^{4n}
Value	i	-1	$-i$	1	i	-1	$-i$	1	$\cdots$	1	$\cdots$	1

Tips

1. $i^3 = i^2 \cdot i = -1 \cdot i = -i.$ $\qquad i^7 = i^4 \cdot i^3 = 1 \cdot i^3 = 1 \cdot -i = -i.$
2. $i^{4n} = 1$ means that if the power of i is a multiple of 4, the value is always equal to 1. For instance, $i^4 = 1$, $i^8 = 1$, $i^{12} = 1$, and $i^{1000} = 1$.

Example **Evaluating powers of i**

Evaluate i^{123}.

Solution The closest multiple of 4 which is smaller than 123 is 120. Since $i^{4n} = i^{120} = 1$,

$$i^{123} = i^{120} \cdot i^3 = 1 \cdot i^3 = -i$$

Therefore, the value of i^{123} is $-i$.

2.14 Absolute Value of Complex Numbers

Absolute Value(Modulus) of Complex Numbers

A complex number can be plotted in the complex plane, where the horizontal axis is the real axis and the vertical axis is the imaginary axis. Two complex numbers, $z_1 = 3 + 4i$, and $z_2 = -2 - 3i$, are plotted in the complex plane as shown in Figure 1.

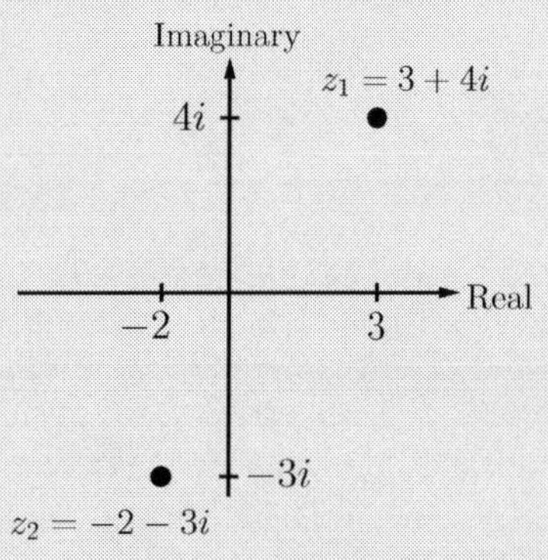

Figure 1

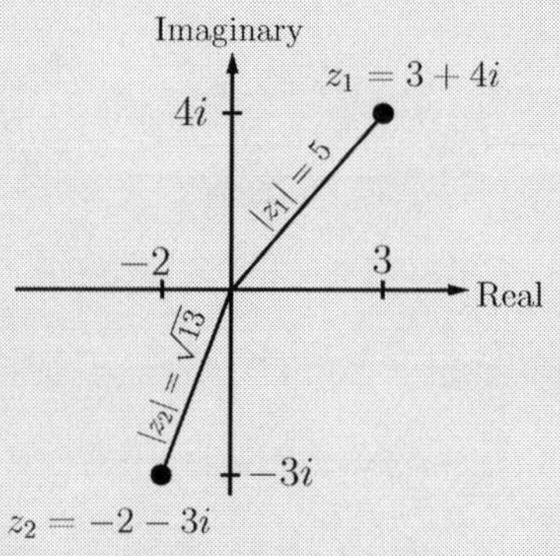

Figure 2

The absolute value of a complex number $a + bi$, denoted by $|z|$, is the distance from the origin to the complex number in the complex plane. The formula for finding the absolute value of a complex number $a + bi$ is as follows:

$$\text{If } z = a + bi, \qquad |z| = \sqrt{a^2 + b^2}$$

The absolute value of $z_1 = 3 + 4i$ and $z_2 = -2 - 3i$ are shown in Figure 2 and are calculated below.

$$|z_1| = |3 + 4i| = \sqrt{3^2 + 4^2} = 5$$
$$|z_2| = |-2 - 3i| = \sqrt{(-2)^2 + (-3)^2} = \sqrt{13}$$

Tips Note that $|a + bi| \neq \sqrt{a^2 + (bi)^2}$. For instance, $|3 + 4i| \neq \sqrt{3^2 + (4i)^2} = \sqrt{-7}$.

2.15 Operations on Complex Numbers

Operations on Complex Numbers

There are five operations for complex numbers: Equality, addition, subtraction, multiplication, and division.

1. Equality of complex numbers: Two complex numbers are equal if and only if their real parts are equal and their imaginary parts are equal.

$$a + bi = c + di \qquad \text{if and only if } a = c \text{ and } b = d$$

2. Addition of complex numbers: Add real parts and imaginary parts of the complex numbers.

$$4 + 3i + 1 + 2i = (4 + 1) + (3i + 2i) = 5 + 5i$$

3. Subtraction of complex numbers: Subtract real parts and imaginary parts of the complex numbers.

$$4 + 3i - (1 + 2i) = (4 - 1) + (3i - 2i) = 3 + i$$

4. Multiplication of complex numbers: Use FOIL (First, Outer, Inner, Last) method.

$$\begin{aligned}(4 + 3i) \cdot (1 + 2i) &= 4 + 8i + 3i + 6i^2 && \text{Since } i^2 = -1 \\ &= (4 - 6) + (8i + 3i) \\ &= -2 + 11i\end{aligned}$$

5. Division of complex numbers: Multiply the numerator and denominator of the quotient by the

conjugate of the denominator. If $z = x + yi$, the conjugate of z, denoted by z^*, is $z^* = x - yi$.

$$\begin{aligned}\frac{4+3i}{1-2i} &= \frac{4+3i}{1-2i}\cdot\frac{1+2i}{1+2i} && \text{Since the conjugate of } 1-2i \text{ is } 1+2i\\ &= \frac{(4+3i)(1+2i)}{(1-2i)(1+2i)} && \text{Use FOIL method}\\ &= \frac{-2+11i}{1-4i^2} && \text{Since } i^2=-1\\ &= \frac{-2+11i}{5}\end{aligned}$$

Tips

1. The product of a complex number and its conjugate is a nonnegative real number. Let $z = x + yi$ and its conjugate $z^* = x - yi$.

$$\begin{aligned}zz^* &= (x+yi)(x-yi) && \text{Use FOIL method}\\ &= x^2+y^2\end{aligned}$$

2. The conjugate of bi is $-bi$. For instance, the conjugate of $3i$ is $-3i$.

$$z = 3i = 0 + 3i \quad\Longrightarrow\quad z^* = 0 - 3i = -3i$$

2.16 Properties of Conjugates

Properties of Conjugates

1. $(z^*)^* = z$
2. $(z_1 \pm z_2)^* = z_1^* \pm z_2^*$
3. $(z_1 z_2)^* = z_1^* \times z_2^*$
4. $\left(\dfrac{z_1}{z_2}\right)^* = \dfrac{z_1^*}{z_2^*}$
5. $(z^n)^* = (z^*)^n$, where n is an integer.
6. $z + z^*$ and zz^* are real.

2.17 Matrices

Matrices

A matrix is a rectangular array of numbers arranged in rows and columns. For instance, matrix **A** shown below has two rows and three columns. So, the dimensions of matrix **A** is 2×3(read "two by three").

$$\mathbf{A} = \begin{bmatrix} a_{11} & a_{12} & a_{13} \\ a_{21} & a_{22} & a_{23} \end{bmatrix} = \begin{bmatrix} 3 & 6 & 1 \\ 4 & 3 & 5 \end{bmatrix}$$

The individual items in an $m \times n$ matrix denoted by a_{ij} are called its elements or entries. In matrix **A** above, $a_{23} = 5$.

2.18 Adding and Subtracting Two Matrices

Addition and Subtraction of Matrices

In order to add or subtract two matrices, they must have the same dimensions and simply add or subtract corresponding elements. For instance,

$$\mathbf{A} + \mathbf{B} = \begin{bmatrix} 3 & 6 & 1 \\ 4 & 3 & 5 \end{bmatrix} + \begin{bmatrix} 1 & 6 & 3 \\ 2 & 5 & 1 \end{bmatrix} = \begin{bmatrix} 4 & 12 & 4 \\ 6 & 8 & 6 \end{bmatrix}$$

$$\mathbf{A} - \mathbf{B} = \begin{bmatrix} 3 & 6 & 1 \\ 4 & 3 & 5 \end{bmatrix} - \begin{bmatrix} 1 & 6 & 3 \\ 2 & 5 & 1 \end{bmatrix} = \begin{bmatrix} 2 & 0 & -2 \\ 2 & -2 & 4 \end{bmatrix}$$

Multiples of Matrices

If a scalar C is multiplied by a matrix **A**, the result is matrix $C\mathbf{A}$ obtained by multiplying every element of **A** by C. For instance,

$$3\mathbf{A} = 3 \begin{bmatrix} 3 & 6 & 1 \\ 4 & 3 & 5 \end{bmatrix} = \begin{bmatrix} 9 & 18 & 3 \\ 12 & 9 & 15 \end{bmatrix}$$

2.19 Multiplying Two Matrices

Matrix Product

The product of an $m \times n$ matrix $\mathbf{A}$ with an $n \times p$ matrix $\mathbf{B}$ is the $m \times p$ $\mathbf{AB}$ matrix where the element in the ith row and jth column is the sum of the products of the elements in the ith row of matrix $\mathbf{A}$ and with the corresponding elements in the jth column of matrix $\mathbf{B}$. For instance,

$$\text{If } \mathbf{A} = \begin{bmatrix} a & b \\ c & d \end{bmatrix} \text{ and } \mathbf{B} = \begin{bmatrix} p & q \\ r & s \end{bmatrix}, \text{ then } \mathbf{C} = \mathbf{AB} = \begin{bmatrix} ap+br & aq+bs \\ cp+dr & cq+ds \end{bmatrix}$$

Example Product of two matrices

For $\mathbf{A} = \begin{bmatrix} 1 & 2 & 3 \end{bmatrix}$ and $\mathbf{B} = \begin{bmatrix} 2 \\ 4 \\ 6 \end{bmatrix}$,

(a) Find $\mathbf{AB}$.

(b) Find $\mathbf{BA}$.

Solution

(a) $\mathbf{A}$ is 1×3 and $\mathbf{B}$ is 3×1. Thus, $\mathbf{AB}$ is 1×1.

$$\mathbf{AB} = \begin{bmatrix} 1 & 2 & 3 \end{bmatrix} \begin{bmatrix} 2 \\ 4 \\ 6 \end{bmatrix} = \begin{bmatrix} 1 \times 2 + 2 \times 4 + 3 \times 6 \end{bmatrix} = \begin{bmatrix} 28 \end{bmatrix}$$

(b) $\mathbf{B}$ is 3×1 and $\mathbf{A}$ is 1×3. Thus, $\mathbf{BA}$ is 3×3.

$$\mathbf{BA} = \begin{bmatrix} 2 \\ 4 \\ 6 \end{bmatrix} \begin{bmatrix} 1 & 2 & 3 \end{bmatrix} = \begin{bmatrix} 2 & 4 & 6 \\ 4 & 8 & 12 \\ 6 & 12 & 18 \end{bmatrix}$$

Tips: In general, the **commutative property** of multiplication for matrices does not work; that is $\mathbf{AB} \neq \mathbf{BA}$.

2.20 Transformation using Matrices

Transformation Matrices

Suppose a triangle has vertices (a, b), (c, d), and (e, f). A vertex matrix for the triangle is given by

$$\begin{bmatrix} a & c & e \\ b & d & f \end{bmatrix}$$

To obtain an image of the triangle after transformation, multiply the vertex matrix by the following standard matrix.

1. Reflection about the x-axis: $\begin{bmatrix} 1 & 0 \\ 0 & -1 \end{bmatrix} \begin{bmatrix} a & c & e \\ b & d & f \end{bmatrix}$
2. Reflection about the y-axis: $\begin{bmatrix} -1 & 0 \\ 0 & 1 \end{bmatrix} \begin{bmatrix} a & c & e \\ b & d & f \end{bmatrix}$
3. Reflection about the origin: $\begin{bmatrix} -1 & 0 \\ 0 & -1 \end{bmatrix} \begin{bmatrix} a & c & e \\ b & d & f \end{bmatrix}$
4. Reflection about the line $y = x$: $\begin{bmatrix} 0 & 1 \\ 1 & 0 \end{bmatrix} \begin{bmatrix} a & c & e \\ b & d & f \end{bmatrix}$
5. Reflection about the line $y = -x$: $\begin{bmatrix} 0 & -1 \\ -1 & 0 \end{bmatrix} \begin{bmatrix} a & c & e \\ b & d & f \end{bmatrix}$
6. Dilation with factor k: $\begin{bmatrix} k & 0 \\ 0 & k \end{bmatrix} \begin{bmatrix} a & c & e \\ b & d & f \end{bmatrix}$
7. Rotation $\theta°$ counterclockwise about the origin: $\begin{bmatrix} \cos\theta & -\sin\theta \\ \sin\theta & \cos\theta \end{bmatrix} \begin{bmatrix} a & c & e \\ b & d & f \end{bmatrix}$
8. Rotation $\theta°$ clockwise about the origin: $\begin{bmatrix} \cos\theta & \sin\theta \\ -\sin\theta & \cos\theta \end{bmatrix} \begin{bmatrix} a & c & e \\ b & d & f \end{bmatrix}$
9. Shift right h units, and up k units: $\begin{bmatrix} 1 & 0 & h \\ 0 & 1 & k \\ 0 & 0 & 1 \end{bmatrix} \begin{bmatrix} a & c & e \\ b & d & f \\ 1 & 1 & 1 \end{bmatrix}$

Tips: Notice that translation(shifting either right, left, up, or down) **cannot** be represented by a 2×2 standard matrix.

2.21 Matrix Algebra

Matrix Algebra

A zero matrix $\mathbf{0}$ is a matrix where all elements are zero. For instance, the 2×2 zero matrix is $\mathbf{0} = \left[\begin{smallmatrix} 0 & 0 \\ 0 & 0 \end{smallmatrix}\right]$. The identity matrix $\mathbf{I}$ of size n is the $n \times n$ matrix with ones on the main diagonal and zeros elsewhere. For instance, the 2×2 identity matrix is $\mathbf{I} = \left[\begin{smallmatrix} 1 & 0 \\ 0 & 1 \end{smallmatrix}\right]$.

1. $\mathbf{A}+\mathbf{B}=\mathbf{B}+\mathbf{A}$
2. $(\mathbf{A}+\mathbf{B})+\mathbf{C}=\mathbf{A}+(\mathbf{B}+\mathbf{C})$
3. $\mathbf{A}+\mathbf{0}=\mathbf{0}+\mathbf{A}=\mathbf{A}$
4. $\mathbf{A}+(-\mathbf{A})=(-\mathbf{A})+\mathbf{A}=\mathbf{0}$
5. If $\mathbf{I} = \begin{bmatrix} 1 & 0 \\ 0 & 1 \end{bmatrix}$, then $\mathbf{AI} = \mathbf{IA} = \mathbf{A}$
6. $\mathbf{A}^n$ for $n \geq 2$ can be determined that $\mathbf{A}$ is a square and n is an integer.

Tips $\mathbf{A}^2 = \mathbf{A} \times \mathbf{A}$ and $\mathbf{A}^3 = \mathbf{A} \times \mathbf{A} \times \mathbf{A}$

2.22 Evaluating Determinants

The Determinant of a Matrix

The determinant $|\mathbf{A}|$ of a 2×2 matrix $\mathbf{A} = \begin{bmatrix} a & b \\ c & d \end{bmatrix}$ is defined as $|\mathbf{A}| = ad - bc$.

The determinant $|\mathbf{A}|$ of a 3×3 matrix $\mathbf{A} = \begin{bmatrix} a & b & c \\ d & e & f \\ g & h & i \end{bmatrix}$ is defined as

$$|\mathbf{A}| = \begin{vmatrix} a & b & c \\ d & e & f \\ g & h & i \end{vmatrix} = a\begin{vmatrix} e & f \\ h & i \end{vmatrix} - b\begin{vmatrix} d & f \\ g & i \end{vmatrix} + c\begin{vmatrix} d & e \\ g & h \end{vmatrix}$$

Example **Evaluating the determinant of a matrix**

Find the determinant of $\mathbf{A}=\begin{bmatrix}2&3\\1&2\end{bmatrix}$ and $\mathbf{B}=\begin{bmatrix}2&3&1\\1&3&2\\3&1&2\end{bmatrix}$

Solution

$$|\mathbf{A}|=\begin{vmatrix}2&3\\1&2\end{vmatrix}=2(2)-3(1)=1$$

$$|\mathbf{B}|=\begin{vmatrix}2&3&1\\1&3&2\\3&1&2\end{vmatrix}=2\begin{vmatrix}3&2\\1&2\end{vmatrix}-3\begin{vmatrix}1&2\\3&2\end{vmatrix}+1\begin{vmatrix}1&3\\3&1\end{vmatrix}=2(6-2)-3(2-6)+1(1-9)=12$$

2.23 The Area of a Triangle using 3×3 Determinant

Area of a Triangle

The area of a triangle with vertices (a,b), (c,d), and (e,f) is given by

$$\text{Area}=\pm\frac{1}{2}\begin{vmatrix}a&b&1\\c&d&1\\e&f&1\end{vmatrix}$$

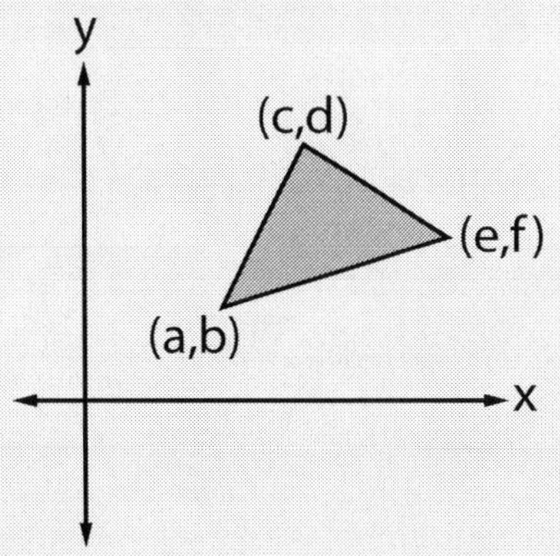

where the symbol $\pm$ indicates that the appropriate sign should be chosen to yield a positive value.

2.24 The Inverse of a 2×2 Matrix

The Inverse of a 2×2 Matrix

The multiplication inverse of $\mathbf{A}$, $\mathbf{A}^{-1}$, satisfies $\mathbf{A}^{-1}\mathbf{A} = \mathbf{A}\mathbf{A}^{-1} = \mathbf{I}$ if it exists.

$$\text{If } \mathbf{A} = \begin{bmatrix} a & b \\ c & d \end{bmatrix}, \text{ then } \mathbf{A}^{-1} = \frac{1}{|\mathbf{A}|}\begin{bmatrix} d & -b \\ -c & a \end{bmatrix}$$

where $|\mathbf{A}|$ is the determinant of $\mathbf{A}$. Notice that $\mathbf{A}^{-1}$ exists when $|A| = ad - bc \neq 0$. We say that $\mathbf{A}^{-1}$ is **invertible** or **non-singular** if $ad - bc \neq 0$.

Tips

1. A matrix that does not have an inverse is said to be **singular**.
2. A 3×3 matrix does not an inverse if the determine is zero.

Example Finding the inverse of a 2 × 2 matrix

If $\mathbf{A} = \begin{bmatrix} 5 & -3 \\ 4 & -2 \end{bmatrix}$, find $\mathbf{A}^{-1}$.

Solution

$$|\mathbf{A}| = \begin{vmatrix} 5 & -3 \\ 4 & -2 \end{vmatrix} = 5 \times (-2) - (-3 \times 4) = -10 - (-12) = 2.$$

$$\mathbf{A}^{-1} = \frac{1}{|\mathbf{A}|}\begin{bmatrix} -2 & 3 \\ -4 & 5 \end{bmatrix} = \frac{1}{2}\begin{bmatrix} -2 & 3 \\ -4 & 5 \end{bmatrix} = \begin{bmatrix} -1 & \frac{3}{2} \\ -2 & \frac{5}{2} \end{bmatrix}$$

Example Determining a value to make a 3 × 3 matrix singular

Find the value of k so that $\mathbf{A} = \begin{bmatrix} 1 & 2 & k \\ 4 & 5 & 6 \\ 5 & 7 & 9 \end{bmatrix}$ does not have an inverse.

Solution Matrix $\mathbf{A}$ does not have the inverse. So the determinant must be zero.

$$|\mathbf{A}| = \begin{vmatrix} 1 & 2 & k \\ 4 & 5 & 6 \\ 5 & 7 & 9 \end{vmatrix} = 1\begin{vmatrix} 5 & 6 \\ 7 & 9 \end{vmatrix} - 2\begin{vmatrix} 4 & 6 \\ 5 & 9 \end{vmatrix} + k\begin{vmatrix} 4 & 5 \\ 5 & 7 \end{vmatrix} = 1(45 - 42) - 2(36 - 30) + k(28 - 25) = 0.$$

Since $3 - 12 + 3k = 0$, $k = 3$.

Chapter 3

Algebra

3.1 Linear Function

Linear functions

The **slope**, m, of a line is a number that describes the steepness of the line. The larger the absolute value of the slope, $|m|$, the steeper the line is (closer to y-axis). If a line passes through the points (x_1, y_1) and (x_2, y_2), the slope m is defined as

$$m = \frac{\text{Rise}}{\text{Run}} = \frac{y_2 - y_1}{x_2 - x_1}$$

If the points (x_1, y_1) and (x_2, y_2) are given, the following formulas are useful in solving math problems.

Midpoint Formula:	$\left(\frac{x_1 + x_2}{2}, \frac{y_1 + y_2}{2}\right)$
Distance Formula:	$D = \sqrt{(x_2 - x_1)^2 + (y_2 - y_1)^2}$

An equation of a line can be written in three different forms.

1. **Slope-intercept form:** $y = mx + b$, where m is slope and b is y-intercept.
2. **Point-slope form:** If the slope of a line is m and the line passes through the point (x_1, y_1),

$$y - y_1 = m(x - x_1)$$

3. **Standard form:** $Ax + By = C$, where A, B, and C are integers.

Below summarizes the lines by slope.

- Lines that rise from left to right have positive slope.
- Lines that fall from left to right have negative slope.

- Horizontal lines have zero slope (example: $y = 2$).
- Vertical lines have undefined slope (example: $x = 2$).
- Parallel lines have the same slope.
- Perpendicular lines have negative reciprocal slopes (product of the slopes equals -1).

The x-intercept of a line is a point where the line crosses x-axis. **The y-intercept** of a line is a point where the line crosses y-axis.

To find the x-intercept of a line	$\Longrightarrow$	Substitute 0 for y and solve for x
To find the y-intercept of a line	$\Longrightarrow$	Substitute 0 for x and solve for y

3.2 Linear Inequalities

Linear Inequalities

A linear inequality in two variables is an inequality that can be written in one of the following forms:

$$y < ax + b, \qquad y \le ax + b, \qquad y > ax + b, \qquad y \ge ax + b,$$

An ordered pair (x, y) is a solution of a linear inequality if the inequality is true when the values of x and y are substituted into the inequality. For instance, $(2, 4)$ is a solution of $y > x + 1$ because $4 > 2 + 1$ is a true statement.

Graphing a linear inequality

The graph of a linear inequality in two variables is a half-plane. To graph a linear inequality, follow these steps:

1. Graph the boundary line of the inequality. Use a dashed line for $<$ or $>$ and a solid line for $\le$ or $\ge$.
2. For $<$ or $\ge$, shade the lower half-plane. For $>$ or $\ge$, shade the upper half-plane.

For instance, the graph of $y \ge 2x + 1$ is a upper half-plane that lies above the solid line $y = 2x + 1$ as shown below.

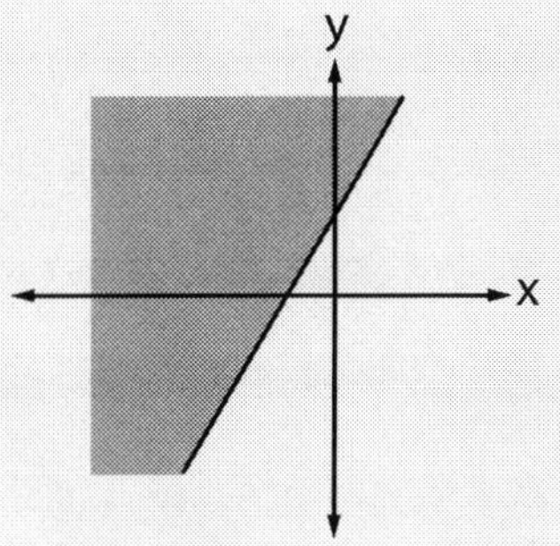

3.3 Solving Systems of Equations using Substitution and Elimination methods

Solving Systems of Two Linear Equations

A system means more than one. A linear equation represents a line. Thus, a **system of linear equations** represents more than one line. Below is an example of a system of linear equations.

$$2x - y = 5$$
$$3x + y = 10$$

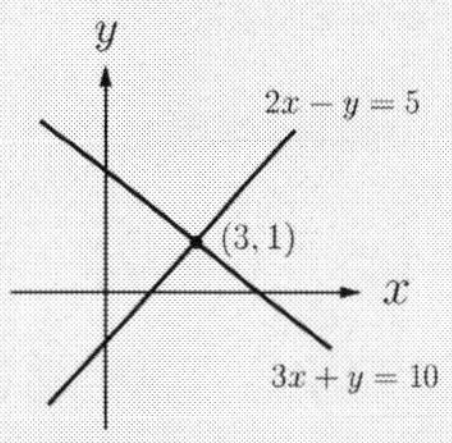

A solution to a system of linear equations is an ordered pair (x, y) that satisfies all equations in the system. In other words, a solution to a system of linear equation is an intersection point that lies on both lines. In the figure above, $(3, 1)$ is an ordered pair that satisfies both equations,

$$\begin{aligned} 2x - y = 5 &\implies 2(3) - 1 = 5 \\ 3x + y = 10 &\implies 3(3) + 1 = 10 \end{aligned}$$

and is the intersection point of both lines.

Solving a system of linear equations means finding the x and y coordinates of the intersection point of the lines. There are two methods to solve a system of linear equations: **substitution** and **linear combinations**.

1. Substitution method
In the example above, write y in terms of x in the first equation. $2x - y = 5 \Longrightarrow y = 2x - 5$. Substitute $2x - 5$ for y in the second equation.

$$\begin{aligned} 3x + y = 10 \implies 3x + (2x - 5) &= 10 \\ 5x - 5 &= 10 \\ x &= 3 \implies y = 2x - 5 = 2(3) - 5 = 1 \end{aligned}$$

The solution to the system using the substitute method is $(3,1)$.

2. Linear combinations(or Elimination) method
In the example above, the coefficient of the y variable in each equation is the opposite. Thus, adding the two equations eliminates the y variables. Then, solve for x.

$$\begin{aligned} 2x - y &= 15 \\ 3x + y &= 10 \qquad \text{Add two equations} \\ \hline 5x \quad &= 15 \\ x &= 3 \end{aligned}$$

Substitute 3 for x in the first equation and solve for y. Thus, $y = 5$. Therefore, the solution to the system using the linear combinations method is $(3,1)$.

Number of Solutions in a System of Two Linear Equations

The number of solutions in a system of linear equations is equal to the number of intersection points that lie on both equations. The table below summarizes the relationship between the graph of a system of linear equations and the number of solutions.

Graph	Description	Number of intersection points	Number of solutions
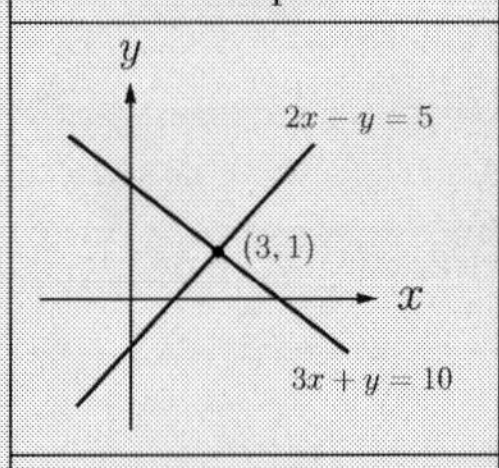	Two lines intersect in one point.	1	One solution
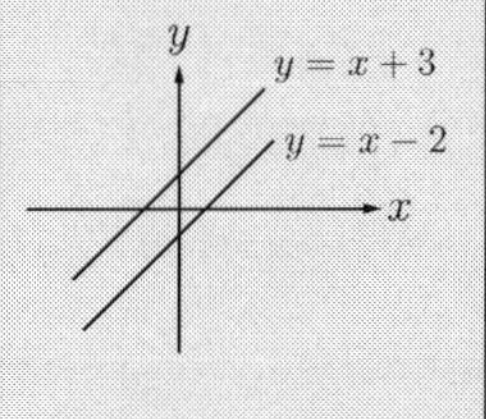	Two lines are parallel. There is no intersection point.	0	No solutions
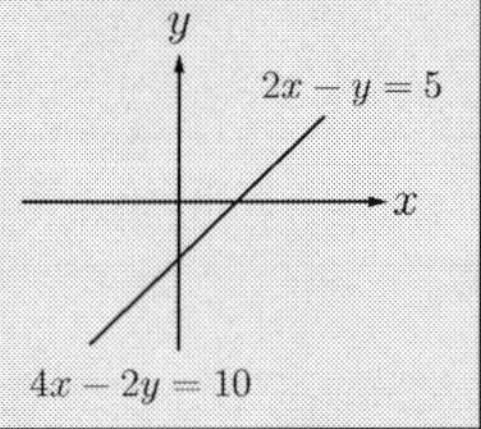	Two lines are the same line.	Infinitely many	Infinite solutions

$$ax + by = c$$
$$dx + ey = f$$

If the system of linear equations is given above, algebraically, the number of solutions can be determined by the following rules.

Tips Case 1: If $\frac{a}{d} \neq \frac{b}{e}$, the two lines intersect in one point. Thus, there is one solution.

Case 2: If $\frac{a}{d} = \frac{b}{e} \neq \frac{c}{f}$, the two lines are parallel. Thus, there are no solutions.

Case 3: If $\frac{a}{d} = \frac{b}{e} = \frac{c}{f}$, the two lines are the same line. Thus, there are an infinite number of solutions.

3.4 Solving Systems of with Three Variables

Solving Systems of Three Equations with Three Variables

Each equation with three variables represents a plane in space. A system of three equations with three variables represents three planes in space. Thus, the solution (x, y, z) to the system of three equations with three variables is the intersection point(s) of the three planes. The solution (x, y, z) is called an **ordered triple**.

Number of solutions in a system of three equations with three variables:

- A unique solution (a consistent system with independent equations)
- Infinitely many solution (a consistent system with dependent equations)
- No solution (an inconsistent system)

To find a solutions in a system of three equations with three variables, perform the following operations:

1. Interchange any two equations of the system.
2. Multiply or divide each side of an equation by the same nonzero constant.
3. Replace any equation in the system by the sum or difference of that equation and a nonzero multiple of any other equation in the system.

Example Solving the consistent system with a unique solution

Solve the system of equations with three variables using the elimination method.

$$\begin{aligned} 2x - y - z &= 7 &\quad (1)\\ 3x + y + z &= 8 &\quad (2)\\ x - 2y + z &= -1 &\quad (3) \end{aligned}$$

Solution First, add two equations (1) and (2) to eliminate the variable z.

$$\begin{aligned} 2x - y - z &= 7 \\ 3x + y + z &= 8 \qquad \text{Add two equations} \\ \hline 5x \qquad &= 15 \\ x &= 3 \end{aligned}$$

Then, add two equations (1) and (3) to eliminate the variable z.

$$\begin{aligned} 2x - y - z &= 7 \\ x - 2y + z &= -1 \qquad \text{Add two equations} \\ \hline 3x - 3y \quad &= 6 \\ x - y &= 2 \end{aligned}$$

Since $x = 3$ and $x - y = 2$, $y = 1$. Substituting $x = 3$ and $y = 1$ into equation (1) gives $z = -2$. Thus, the solution to the system with three variables is $(3, 1, -2)$. The system is a consistent with a unique solution.

3.5 Solving Systems of Equations using Cramer's rule

Solving Systems of Equations using Cramer's rule

Cramer's rule for two equations with two variables

The solution to the system of equations

$$\begin{aligned} ax + by &= c \\ dx + ey &= f \end{aligned}$$

is given by

$$x = \frac{\begin{vmatrix} c & b \\ f & e \end{vmatrix}}{\begin{vmatrix} a & b \\ d & e \end{vmatrix}} \qquad y = \frac{\begin{vmatrix} a & c \\ d & f \end{vmatrix}}{\begin{vmatrix} a & b \\ d & e \end{vmatrix}}$$

Cramer's rule for three equations with three variables

The solution to the system of equations with three variables

$$\begin{aligned} ax + by + cz &= j \\ dx + ey + fz &= k \\ gx + hy + iz &= l \end{aligned}$$

is given by

$$x = \frac{\begin{vmatrix} j & b & c \\ k & e & f \\ l & h & i \end{vmatrix}}{\begin{vmatrix} a & b & c \\ d & e & f \\ g & h & i \end{vmatrix}} \qquad y = \frac{\begin{vmatrix} a & j & c \\ d & k & f \\ g & l & i \end{vmatrix}}{\begin{vmatrix} a & b & c \\ d & e & f \\ g & h & i \end{vmatrix}} \qquad z = \frac{\begin{vmatrix} a & b & j \\ d & e & k \\ g & h & l \end{vmatrix}}{\begin{vmatrix} a & b & c \\ d & e & f \\ g & h & i \end{vmatrix}}$$

Example Solving the system using Cramer's rule

Solve the system of equations using Cramer's rule.

$$\begin{aligned} 2x + y - z &= 3 \\ -x + 2y + 4z &= -3 \\ x - 2y - 3z &= 4 \end{aligned}$$

Solution
Let's evaluate the following determinants.

$$\begin{aligned} D_x = \begin{vmatrix} 3 & 1 & -1 \\ -3 & 2 & 4 \\ 4 & -2 & -3 \end{vmatrix} &= 3\begin{vmatrix} 2 & 4 \\ -2 & -3 \end{vmatrix} - 1\begin{vmatrix} -3 & 4 \\ 4 & -3 \end{vmatrix} + (-1)\begin{vmatrix} -3 & 2 \\ 4 & -2 \end{vmatrix} \\ &= 3(2) - 1(-7) + (-1)(-2) \\ &= 15 \end{aligned}$$

$$\begin{aligned} D_y = \begin{vmatrix} 2 & 3 & -1 \\ -1 & -3 & 4 \\ 1 & 4 & -3 \end{vmatrix} &= 2\begin{vmatrix} -3 & 4 \\ 4 & -3 \end{vmatrix} - 3\begin{vmatrix} -1 & 4 \\ 1 & -3 \end{vmatrix} + (-1)\begin{vmatrix} -1 & -3 \\ 1 & 4 \end{vmatrix} \\ &= 2(-7) - 3(-1) + (-1)(-1) \\ &= -10 \end{aligned}$$

$$\begin{aligned} D_z = \begin{vmatrix} 2 & 1 & 3 \\ -1 & 2 & -3 \\ 1 & -2 & 4 \end{vmatrix} &= 2\begin{vmatrix} 2 & -3 \\ -2 & 4 \end{vmatrix} - 1\begin{vmatrix} -1 & -3 \\ 1 & 4 \end{vmatrix} + 3\begin{vmatrix} -1 & 2 \\ 1 & -2 \end{vmatrix} \\ &= 2(2) - 1(-1) + 3(0) \\ &= 5 \end{aligned}$$

$$\begin{aligned} D = \begin{vmatrix} 2 & 1 & -1 \\ -1 & 2 & 4 \\ 1 & -2 & -3 \end{vmatrix} &= 2\begin{vmatrix} 2 & 4 \\ -2 & -3 \end{vmatrix} - 1\begin{vmatrix} -1 & 4 \\ 1 & -3 \end{vmatrix} + (-1)\begin{vmatrix} -1 & 2 \\ 1 & -2 \end{vmatrix} \\ &= 2(2) - 1(-1) + (-1)(0) \\ &= 5 \end{aligned}$$

Thus, the solution to the system using Cramer's rule is

$$x = \frac{D_x}{D} = \frac{15}{5} = 3 \qquad y = \frac{D_y}{D} = \frac{-10}{5} = -2 \qquad z = \frac{D_z}{D} = \frac{5}{5} = 1$$

3.6 Solving systems of linear equations using matrix algebra

Solving systems of linear equations

A system of linear equations can be written in the matrix form $\mathbf{AX} = \mathbf{B}$ where $|\mathbf{A}| \neq 0$ and $\mathbf{A}$ is invertible. The solution to the system is $\mathbf{X} = \mathbf{A}^{-1}\mathbf{B}$ as shown above.

$$\begin{aligned} \mathbf{AX} &= \mathbf{B} \\ \mathbf{A}^{-1}\mathbf{AX} &= \mathbf{A}^{-1}\mathbf{B} && \text{Multiply both sides by } \mathbf{A}^{-1} \\ \mathbf{IX} &= \mathbf{A}^{-1}\mathbf{B} && \text{where } \mathbf{I} \text{ is the identity matrix} \\ \mathbf{X} &= \mathbf{A}^{-1}\mathbf{B} \end{aligned}$$

Tips $\mathbf{A}^{-1}\mathbf{A} = \mathbf{I}$

Example Solving the system using matrix algebra

Use the matrix algebra to solve the following system.

$$\begin{aligned} 5x - 3y &= 2 \\ 4x - 2y &= 4 \end{aligned}$$

Solution The system of linear equations above can be converted into matrix equation $\mathbf{AX} = \mathbf{B}$.

$$\begin{bmatrix} 5 & -3 \\ 4 & -2 \end{bmatrix} \begin{bmatrix} x \\ y \end{bmatrix} = \begin{bmatrix} 2 \\ 4 \end{bmatrix}$$

where $\mathbf{A} = \begin{bmatrix} 5 & -3 \\ 4 & -2 \end{bmatrix}$, $\mathbf{X} = \begin{bmatrix} x \\ y \end{bmatrix}$, and $\mathbf{B} = \begin{bmatrix} 2 \\ 4 \end{bmatrix}$.

Since $\mathbf{A}^{-1} = \begin{bmatrix} -1 & \frac{3}{2} \\ -2 & \frac{5}{2} \end{bmatrix}$ and the general solution is $\mathbf{X} = \mathbf{A}^{-1}\mathbf{B}$,

$$\mathbf{X} = \mathbf{A}^{-1}\mathbf{B} = \begin{bmatrix} -1 & \frac{3}{2} \\ -2 & \frac{5}{2} \end{bmatrix} \begin{bmatrix} 2 \\ 4 \end{bmatrix} = \begin{bmatrix} 4 \\ 6 \end{bmatrix} \Longrightarrow \begin{bmatrix} x \\ y \end{bmatrix} = \begin{bmatrix} 4 \\ 6 \end{bmatrix}$$

Therefore, $x = 4$ and $y = 6$.

3.7 Graphing Systems of Linear Inequalities

Graphing Systems of Linear Inequalities

Each graph of linear inequality is a half-plane. The graph of the system of inequalities is the region common to all of the half-planes.

For instance, the graph of a system of inequalities is given by

$$x \geq 0$$
$$y \geq 0$$
$$y \leq -2x + 12$$
$$y \leq \frac{1}{3}x + 5$$

is shown below.

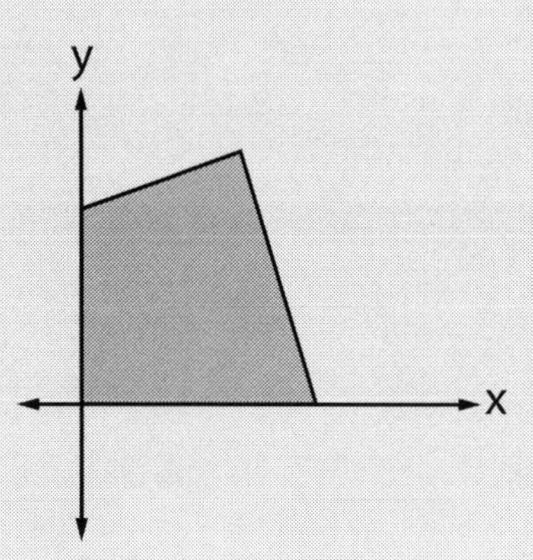

3.8 Optimal solution of a linear programming problem

Linear Programming

Linear programming is the process of optimizing a linear objective function subject to a system of linear inequalities called **constraints**. The graph of the system of constraints is called the **feasible region.**

Optimal solution of a linear programming problem

If an object function has a maximum or a minimum value, then it must occur at a vertex of the feasible region. In addition, the objective function will have both a maximum and a minimum value if the feasible region is bounded.

Example Solving a linear programming problem

Find the maximum value and the minimum value of the objective function $C = 2x + 3y$ subject to the following constraints.

$$\begin{aligned} &x \geq 0 \\ &y \geq 0 \\ &y \leq -2x + 12 \\ &y \leq \frac{1}{3}x + 5 \end{aligned}$$

Solution The feasible region determined by the constraints is shown below.

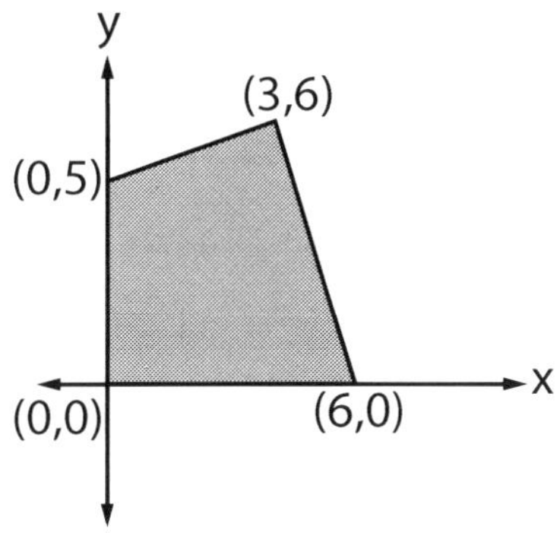

The four vertices are $(0,0)$, $(0,5)$, $(3,6)$, and $(6,0)$. In order to find the maximum and minimum value of $C = 2x + 3y$, evaluate C at each of the four vertices.

$$\begin{aligned} &\text{At } (0,0): \quad C = 2(0) + 3(0) = 0 \\ &\text{At } (0,5): \quad C = 2(0) + 3(5) = 15 \\ &\text{At } (3,6): \quad C = 2(3) + 3(6) = 24 \\ &\text{At } (6,0): \quad C = 2(6) + 3(0) = 12 \end{aligned}$$

Thus, the maximum value of $C = 2x + 3y$ is 24, and the minimum value of $C = 2x + 3y$ is 0.

3.9 Quadratic Functions and Quadratic Equations

Quadratic Functions and Quadratic Equations

A quadratic function is a polynomial function of degree 2 and can be expressed in three forms.

Standard form: $y = ax^2 + bx + c$

Vertex form: $y = a(x-h)^2 + k$, Vertex (h, k)

Factored form: $y = a(x-p)(x-q)$, where p and q are x-intercepts.

The graph of a quadratic function is a parabola. Depending on the value of the **leading coefficient**, $a\ (a \neq 0)$, the graph of a quadratic function either opens up or opens down.

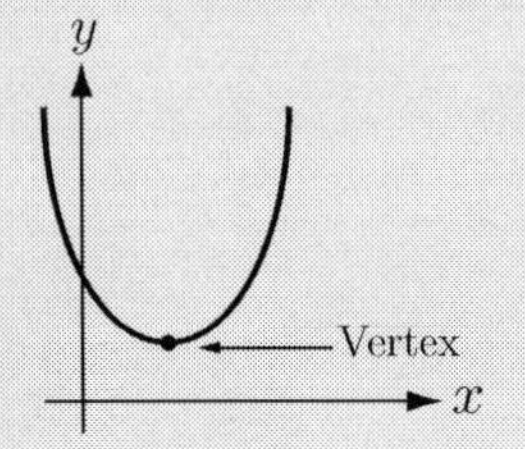

Figure 1: If $a > 0$, opens up

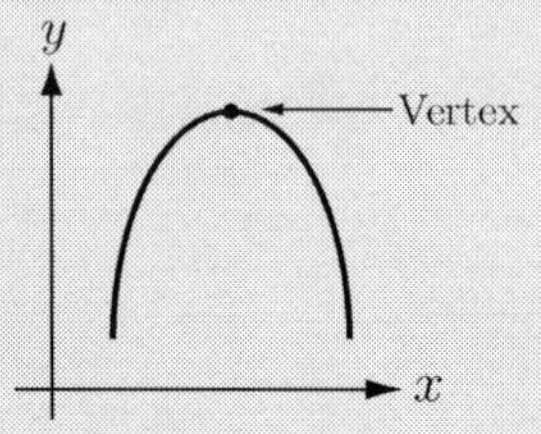

Figure 2: If $a < 0$, opens down

The vertex is the minimum point when the parabola opens up as shown in Figure 1 and the maximum point when the parabola opens down as shown in Figure 2.

Below are ways to find the x-coordinate of the vertex from each form.

$$\text{Standard form: } y = ax^2 + bx + c \implies x = -\frac{b}{2a}$$

$$\text{Vertex form: } y = a(x-h)^2 + k \implies x = h$$

$$\text{Factored form: } y = a(x-p)(x-q) \implies x = \frac{p+q}{2}$$

To evaluate the y-coordinate of the vertex, substitute the value of the x-coordinate in each form.

The x-intercept and y-intercept of quadratic functions

- To solve for the x-intercept: substitute 0 for y. Then, quadratic functions become quadratic equations as shown below.

$$\text{Standard form: } y = ax^2 + bx + c \implies ax^2 + bx + c = 0$$

$$\text{Vertex form: } y = a(x-h)^2 + k \implies a(x-h)^2 + k = 0$$

$$\text{Factored form: } y = a(x-p)(x-q) \implies a(x-p)(x-q) = 0$$

- To solve for the y-intercept: substitute 0 for x and evaluate the y-intercept.

Solving Quadratic Equations

Solving a quadratic equation is finding the x-intercept(s) of the quadratic function. There are three common methods to solve a quadratic equation: **Factoring**, **Completing the square**, and **Quadratic formula**.

1. Factoring
Factoring is an important tool that is required for solving a quadratic equation. Factoring is the opposite of expanding. Factoring a quadratic expression is to write the expression as a product of two linear terms. Below is an example.

$$(x-2)(x-3) \xrightarrow{\text{Expanding}} x^2-5x+6$$
$$x^2-5x+6 \xrightarrow{\text{Factoring}} (x-2)(x-3)$$

If a quadratic equation can be expressed as $x^2+(p+q)x+pq=0$, it can be factored as $(x+p)(x+q)=0$. For instance,

$$x^2-5x+6=0 \implies x^2+(-2+-3)x+(-2)(-3)=0 \implies (x-2)(x-3)=0$$

Once a quadratic equation is written in a factored form, use the **zero product property** to solve the equation.

$$\text{Zero product property:} \qquad \text{If } ab=0, \text{ then } a=0 \text{ or } b=0$$

Thus, the solutions to $(x-2)(x-3)=0$ is

$$(x-2)(x-3)=0 \implies (x-2)=0 \text{ or } (x-3)=0 \implies x=2 \text{ or } x=3$$

2. Completing the square
Equations of the form $ax^2+bx+c=0$ can be converted to the form $(x+p)^2=q$ from which the solutions are easy to obtain. For instance,

$$x^2+2x-2=0 \implies x^2+2x=2 \implies x^2+2x+1=3 \implies (x+1)^2=3$$

3. The Quadratic Formula
The quadratic formula is a general formula for solving quadratic equations. The solutions to the quadratic equation $ax^2+bx+c=0$ are as follows:

$$x=\frac{-b\pm\sqrt{b^2-4ac}}{2a}$$

3.10 The Discriminant

The Discriminant of a Quadratic

In the quadratic formula, the quantity $b^2 - 4ac$ under the square root sign is called **discriminant**. The symbol D is used to represent the discriminant.

- If $D > 0$, there are two distinct real roots.
- If $D = 0$, there are two identical real roots(repeated or double roots).
- If $D < 0$, there are no real roots.

3.11 Solving Quadratic Inequalities

Solving Quadratic Inequalities

Solving a quadratic inequality means finding the x-values for which the graph of a quadratic function lies above or below the x-axis. A quadratic inequality can be solved algebraically. However, solving a quadratic inequality **graphically** is highly recommended.

In order to solve $ax^2 + bx + c > 0$ (or $ax^2 + bx + c \geq 0$) graphically,

Step 1 Find the x-intercepts of $y = ax^2 + bx + c$: Let $y = 0$ and solve for x using factoring or the quadratic formula.

Step 2 Graph $y = ax^2 + bx + c$.

Step 3 From the graph in step 2, find the x-values for which the graph lies **above** (or on and above) the x-axis.

In order to solve $ax^2 + bx + c < 0$ (or $ax^2 + bx + c \leq 0$) graphically,

Step 1 Find the x-intercepts of $y = ax^2 + bx + c$: Let $y = 0$ and solve for x using factoring or the quadratic formula.

Step 2 Graph $y = ax^2 + bx + c$.

Step 3 From the graph in step 2, find the x-values for which the graph lies **below** (or on and below) the x-axis.

Example **Solving a quadratic inequality graphically**

Solve $x^2 - 5x + 6 \geq 0$

Solution Substitute 0 for y in $y = x^2 - 5x + 6$ and solve $x^2 - 5x + 6 = 0$ using factoring.

$$(x-2)(x-3) = 0 \implies (x-2) = 0 \quad \text{or} \quad (x-3) = 0 \implies x = 2 \quad \text{or} \quad x = 3$$

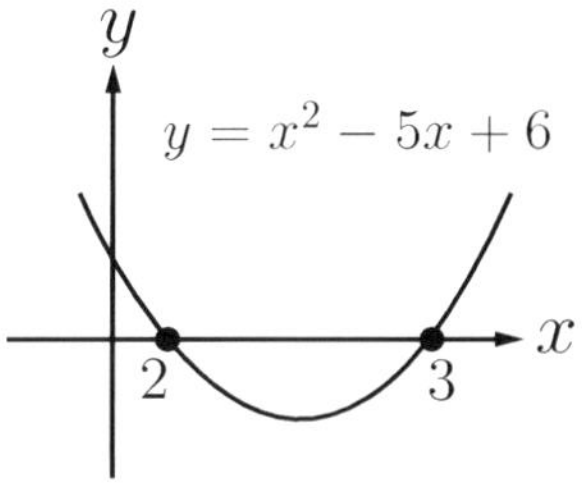

Figure 3

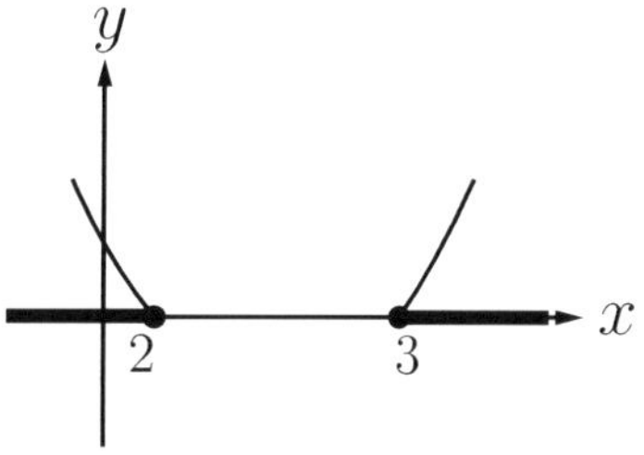

Figure 4

As shown in Figure 3, the x-intercepts of $y = x^2 - 5x + 6$ are 2, and 3. Since the graph lies on and above the x-axis to the left of $x = 2$ and to the right of $x = 3$ as shown in Figure 4, the solution to $x^2 - 5x + 6 \geq 0$ is $x \leq 2$ or $x \geq 3$.

3.12 Operations on Polynomial Functions

Operations on Polynomial Functions

Polynomial functions can be added, subtracted, and multiplied. Let $f(x) = x^2 + 1$ and $g(x) = x - 3$.

- The sum of $f(x)$ and $g(x)$: $f(x) + g(x) = x^2 + 1 + x - 3 = x^2 + x - 2$
- The difference of $f(x)$ and $g(x)$: $f(x) - g(x) = x^2 + 1 - (x - 3) = x^2 - x + 4$
- The product of $f(x)$ and $g(x)$: use the distributive property.

$$f(x) \cdot g(x) = (x^2 + 1)(x - 3) = x^3 - 3x^2 + x - 3$$

3.13 Special Product Patterns

Special Product Patterns

- **Sum and Difference**

$$(a+b)(a-b)=a^2-b^2$$

- **Square of a binomial**

$$(a+b)^2=a^2+2ab+b^2$$
$$(a-b)^2=a^2-2ab+b^2$$

- **Sum and difference of two cubes**

$$a^3+b^3=(a+b)(a^2-ab+b^2)$$
$$a^3-b^3=(a-b)(a^2+ab+b^2)$$

- **Cube of a binomial**

$$(a+b)^3=a^3+3a^2b+3ab^2+b^3$$
$$(a-b)^3=a^3-3a^2b+3ab^2-b^3$$

3.14 Finding the Real Zeros of a Polynomial Function

Finding the Real Zeros of a Polynomial Function

A polynomial function $f(x)$ crosses the x-axis at three points as shown below.

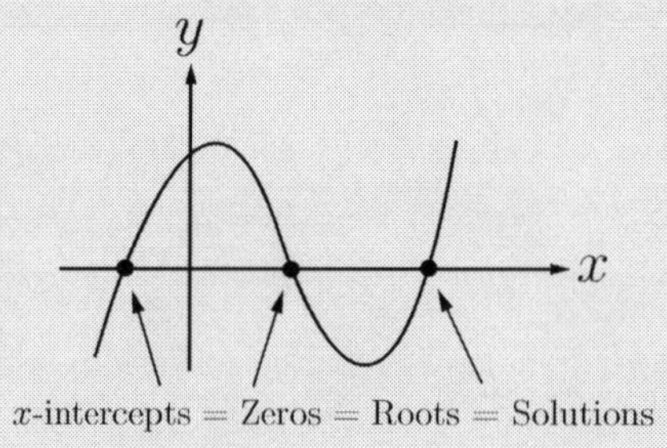

These three points are called either the x-intercepts, zeros, roots, or solutions. That is, they are the values of x that make $f(x)=0$.

Finding the real zeros of a polynomial function of degree 3 or higher is very complicated because there is no general formula like the quadratic formula available.

However, the remainder theorem, factor theorem, and rational zeros theorem are very useful to find the real zeros of a polynomial function.

3.15 Remainder Theorem

1. Remainder Theorem

If a polynomial function $f(x)$ is divided by $x - k$, the remainder is $f(k)$.

Tips

1. In order to evaluate the remainder, use either polynomial long division, synthetic division, or the remainder theorem. However, the remainder theorem is the easiest to use.
2. In order to determine the quotient polynomial when a polynomial function $f(x)$ is divided by $x - c$, use polynomial division or synthetic division. The remainder theorem doesn't tell you about the quotient polynomial.

	Quotient	Remainder
Polynomial long division	✓	✓
Synthetic division	✓	✓
Remainder theorem	Not available	✓

Example Finding the quotient and remainder

If $f(x) = x^3 - 2x^2 + 3x + 2$ is divided by $x - 1$, find the quotient and remainder.

Solution Since we are trying to find the quotient and the remainder, we can use either polynomial long division as shown in Figure 1, or synthetic division as shown in Figure 2. However, synthetic division is easier and faster to find the quotient and remainder.

$$\begin{array}{rl} x^2 - x + 2 & \longleftarrow \text{Quotient} \\ x - 1\,\overline{)\,x^3 - 2x^2 + 3x + 2} & \\ -x^3 + x^2 & \\ \hline -x^2 + 3x & \\ x^2 - x & \\ \hline 2x + 2 & \\ -2x + 2 & \\ \hline \text{Remainder} \longrightarrow 4 & \end{array}$$

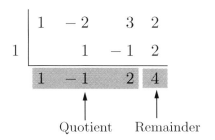

Fig. 1: Polynomial long division

$$\begin{array}{r|rrrr} & 1 & -2 & 3 & 2 \\ 1 & & 1 & -1 & 2 \\ \hline & 1 & -1 & 2 & 4 \end{array}$$

Quotient: $1 \quad -1 \quad 2$ Remainder: 4

Fig. 2: Synthetic division

Therefore, the quotient polynomial is $x^2 - x + 2$ and the remainder is 4.

3.16 Factor Theorem

2. Factor Theorem

- If $x - k$ is a factor of $f(x)$, then the remainder $r = f(k) = 0$.
- If the remainder $r = f(k) = 0$, then k is a zero of $f(x)$ and $x - k$ is a factor of $f(x)$.

Tips The factor theorem states a relationship between a zero and a factor such that if a function has a zero k, then the function has a factor of $x - k$.

Example **Finding a factor of a polynomial function**

Determine whether the function $f(x) = x^3 - 7x + 6$ has the factor $x - 2$.

Solution Use the factor theorem to determine whether $x - 2$ is the factor of $f(x)$. Substitute 2 for x in $f(x)$ to see if the remainder $r = f(2)$ is equal to 0.

$$f(x) = x^3 - 7x + 6 \qquad \text{Substitute 2 for } x$$
$$f(2) = 2^3 - 7(2) + 6 = 0$$

Since the remainder $r = f(2) = 0$, $x - 2$ is a factor of $f(x) = x^3 - 7x + 6$.

3.17 Rational Zeros Theorem

3. Rational Zeros Theorem

The rational zeros theorem provides a list of all possible rational zeros of a polynomial function with integer coefficients. Out of all possible rational zeros, use the factor theorem or synthetic division to find the real zeros of the polynomial function.

The rational zeros theorem states that for the polynomial function with integer coefficients, $f(x) = a_n x^n + a_{n-1}x^{n-1} + \cdots + a_1 x + a_0$, the possible rational zeros are as follows:

$$\text{Possible rational zeros} = \pm\frac{\text{factors of } a_o}{\text{factors of } a_n}$$

where a_n is the leading coefficient and a_0 is the constant.

For instance, if $f(x) = 2x^3 - 11x^2 + 13x - 4$, the possible rational zeros are shown below.

$$\begin{aligned}\text{Possible rational zeros} &= \pm\frac{\text{factors of } 4}{\text{factors of } 2}\\ &= \pm\frac{\{1,2,4\}}{\{1,2\}}\\ &= \pm1,\ \pm2,\ \pm4,\ \pm\frac{1}{2}\end{aligned}$$

There are 8 possible rational zeros. Use the factor theorem to find one real zero of $f(x)$.

$$f(-1) = -30 \neq 0, \qquad f(1) = 0$$

$f(1) = 0$ means that 1 is a zero of $f(x)$. Let's use synthetic division to factor $f(x)$.

$$\begin{array}{c|cccc} & 2 & -11 & 13 & -4 \\ 1 & & 2 & -9 & 4 \\ \hline & 2 & -9 & 4 & 0 \end{array}$$

Since the quotient polynomial is $2x^2 - 9x + 4$, the function $f(x)$ can be factored as follows:

$$\begin{aligned}2x^3 - 11x^2 + 13x - 4 &= (x-1)(2x^2 - 9x + 4) && \text{Factor } 2x^2 - 9x + 4\\ &= (x-1)(x-4)(2x-1)\end{aligned}$$

Therefore, the real zeros of $f(x)$ are 1, 4, and $\frac{1}{2}$.

Tips: If a polynomial function has a rational zero, the zero is one of the possible rational zeros suggested by the rational zeros theorem. However, if a polynomial function does not have any rational zeros, the rational zeros theorem does not help you find complex zeros.

3.18 Conjugate Pairs Theorem

Conjugate Pairs Theorem

The conjugate pairs theorem states that complex zeros and irrational zeros always occur in conjugate pairs.

If $a + bi$ is a zero of f, $\implies$ $a - bi$ is also a zero of f.

If $a + \sqrt{b}$ is a zero of f, $\implies$ $a - \sqrt{b}$ is also a zero of f.

3.19 Writing a Polynomial Function with the Given Zeros

Writing a Polynomial Function with the Given Zeros

By the factor theorem, if 2 is a zero of f, then $x - 2$ is a factor of f. In order to write a polynomial function with the given zeros, convert each zero to a factor and expand. For instance,

Given zeros: 2, and 3 $\implies$ $y = (x-2)(x-3) = x^2 - 5x + 6$

Given zeros: $1+\sqrt{2}$, and $1-\sqrt{2}$ $\implies$

$$\begin{aligned} y &= (x-(1+\sqrt{2}))(x-(1-\sqrt{2})) \\ &= ((x-1)-\sqrt{2})((x-1)+\sqrt{2}) \\ &= (x-1)^2 - 2 \\ &= x^2 - 2x - 1 \end{aligned}$$

Vieta's Formulas

When irrational zeros or complex zeros are given, use Vieta's formula to easily write a quadratic function with leading coefficient 1. Vieta's formulas relate the coefficients of a polynomial to the sum and product of its zeros and are described below. For a quadratic function $f(x) = x^2 + bx + c$, let z_1 and z_2 be the zeros of f.

$z_1 + z_2 = -b$ Sum of zeros equals the opposite of the coefficient of x

$z_1 z_2 = c$ Product of zeros equals the constant term

For instance, when irrational zeros, $1+\sqrt{2}$ and $1-\sqrt{2}$, are given,

Sum of zeros: $(1+\sqrt{2}) + (1-\sqrt{2}) = 2$ $\xrightarrow{\text{Opposite}}$ -2 (Coefficient of x)

Product of zeros: $(1+\sqrt{2})(1-\sqrt{2}) = -1$ $\xrightarrow{\text{Same}}$ -1 (Constant term)

Thus, the quadratic function whose zeros are $1+\sqrt{2}$ and $1-\sqrt{2}$ is $x^2 - 2x - 1$.

Tips

1. In order to expand the expression $((x-1)-\sqrt{2})((x-1)+\sqrt{2})$ shown above, use $(a-b)(a+b)=a^2-b^2$ formula.
2. In order to use Vieta's formulas, two zeros must be the same type: rational zeros, irrational zeros, or complex zeros.

Example **Writing a polynomial function with given zeros**

If zeros of the polynomial function f are 1 and $2+i$, write a cubic function with leading coefficient 1.

Solution According to the conjugate pairs theorem, $2-i$, is also a zero of f. Thus, 1, $2+i$, and $2-i$ are zeros of f. Since complex zeros are given, use Vieta's formulas to write a quadratic function with leading coefficient 1.

$$\text{Sum of zeros: } (2+i)+(2-i)=4 \xrightarrow{\text{Opposite}} -4 \text{ (Coefficient of } x\text{)}$$

$$\text{Product of zeros: } (2+i)(2-i)=5 \xrightarrow{\text{Same}} 5 \text{ (Constant term)}$$

The quadratic function whose zeros are $2+i$ and $2-i$ is x^2-4x+5. Since 1 is a zero of f, $x-1$ is a factor of f. Thus,

$$\begin{aligned} f(x) &= (x-1)(x^2-4x+5) \\ &= x^3-5x^2+9x-5 \end{aligned}$$

Therefore, the cubic function whose zeros are 1, $2+i$, and $2-i$ is $f(x)=x^3-5x^2+9x-5$.

3.20 Graphing Cubic Functions using Multiplicity

Graphing Cubic Functions

A polynomial function of degree 3, $f(x) = ax^3 + bx^2 + cx + d$, is a cubic function, where a is the leading coefficient and is nonzero. Depending on the values of a, either positive or negative, the graph of the cubic function varies.

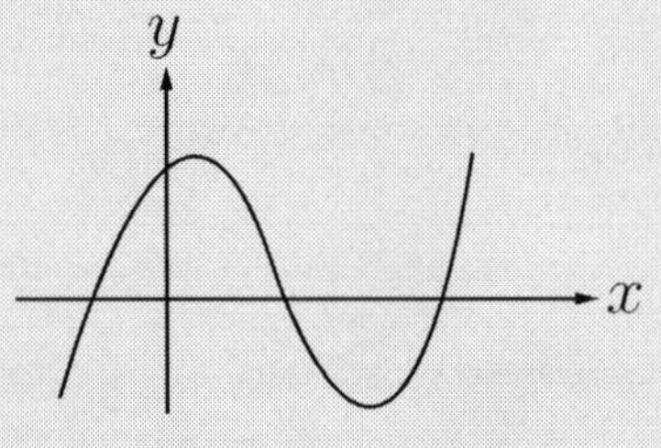

Figure 1: If $a > 0$

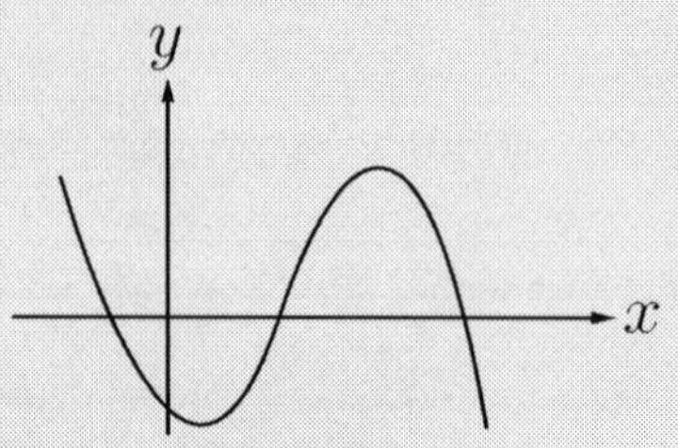

Figure 2: If $a < 0$

If $a > 0$, the graph of a cubic function shown in Figure 1 goes up as x increases and goes down as x decreases. Whereas, if $a < 0$, the graph of a cubic function shown in Figure 2 goes down as x increases and goes up as x decreases.

Zeros of odd or even multiplicity

If $(x-c)^m$ is a factor of a polynomial function f, c is called a zero of multiplicity of m. Depending on the value of m, either odd or even, the graph of f either crosses or touches the x-axis at $x = c$.

$$\text{If } m = \text{odd} \implies \text{graph of } f \text{ crosses the } x\text{-axis at } x = c.$$
$$\text{If } m = \text{even} \implies \text{graph of } f \text{ touches the } x\text{-axis at } x = c.$$

For instance, let $f(x) = -5(x-1)^2(x-3)$. Since the leading coefficient is -5, the shape of the graph of f is similar to the graph in Figure 2.

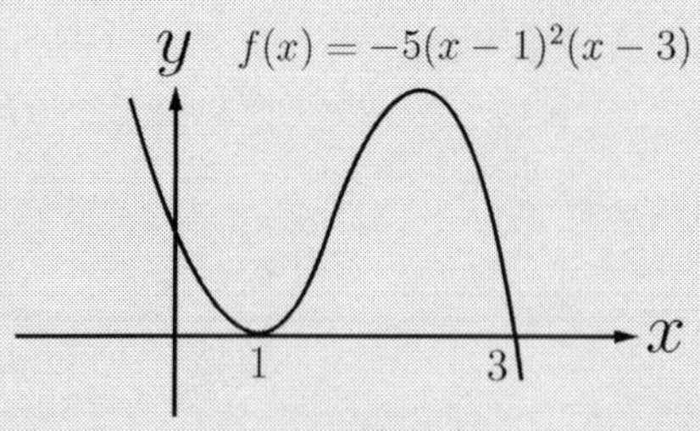

Figure 3

Since $(x-1)^2$ is a factor of f, 1 is a zero of multiplicity 2. Thus, the graph of f touches the x-axis at $x = 1$. Additionally, $(x-3)$ is a factor of f. Thus, 3 is a zero of multiplicity 1 and the graph of f crosses the x-axis at $x = 3$. The graph of f is shown in Figure 3 above.

3.21 Solving Polynomial and Rational Inequalities

Solving Polynomial Inequalities

Solving a polynomial inequality means finding the x-values for which the graph of the polynomial function f lies above or below the x-axis. A polynomial inequality can be solved algebraically. However, solving a polynomial inequality **graphically** is highly recommended.

Let the polynomial inequality be $(x-1)(x-2)(x-3) > 0$. First, graph the polynomial function $f(x) = (x-1)(x-2)(x-3)$ with the leading coefficient 1. Since 1, 2, and 3 are zeros of multiplicity 1, the graph of f crosses the x-axis at $x = 1$, $x = 2$, and $x = 3$ as shown in Figure 2.

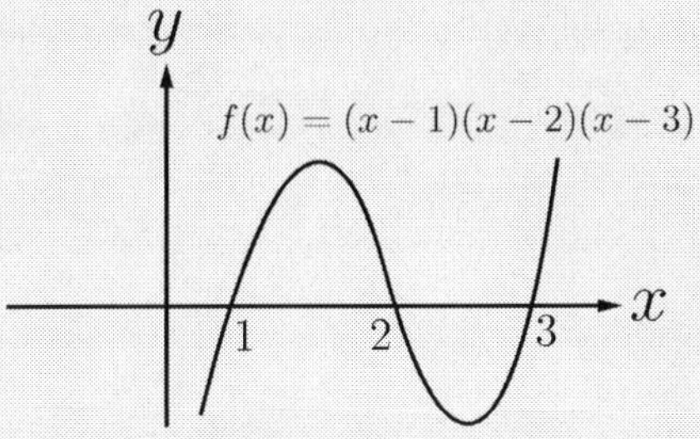

Figure 1

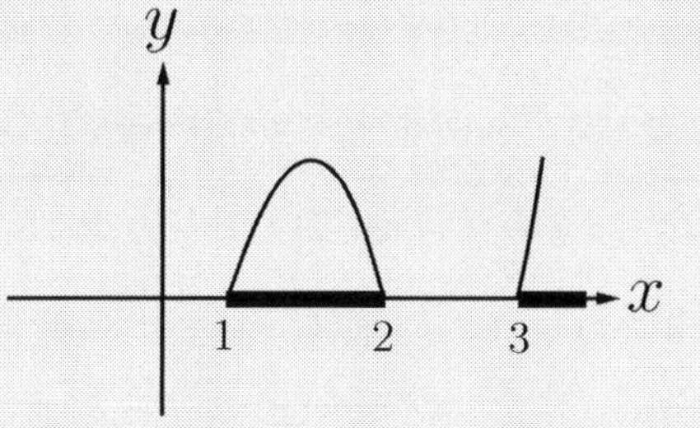

Figure 2

As shown in Figure 2, the graph of f lies above the x-axis when $1 < x < 2$ or $x > 3$. Therefore, the solution to $(x-1)(x-2)(x-3) > 0$ is $1 < x < 2$ or $x > 3$.

Solving Rational Inequalities

Solving a rational inequality means finding the x-values for which the graph of the rational function f lies above or below the x-axis. A rational inequality can be solved graphically. However, solving a rational inequality **algebraically** is highly recommended. The following guideline will help you solve the rational inequality algebraically.

1. Find the zeros and values of x at which the rational expression is undefined.
2. Use the number obtained in previous step to separate the real numbers line into several intervals.
3. Choose a test number in each interval and determine whether the rational inequality is positive or negative.

For instance, $f(x) = \dfrac{x-1}{x+2} > 0$.

1. The zero of $f(x)$ and value of x at which $f(x)$ is undefined are $x = 1$ and $x = -2$.

2. Use $x = 1$ and $x = -2$ to separate the real numbers line into three intervals as shown below.

$$x < -2, \qquad -2 < x < 1, \qquad x > 1$$

3. Choose a test number in each interval and determine whether $f(x) = \dfrac{x-1}{x+2} > 0$.

Interval	Test number	$f(x)$	Positive/Negative
$x < -2$	-3	$f(x) = \frac{-}{-} = +$	Positive
$-2 < x < 1$	0	$f(x) = \frac{-}{+} = -$	Negative
$x > 1$	2	$f(x) = \frac{+}{+} = +$	Positive

Therefore, the solution to $f(x) = \dfrac{x-1}{x+2} > 0$ is $x < -2$ or $x > 1$.

3.22 Simplifying Rational Expressions

Simplifying Rational Expressions

To multiply two rational expressions, factor the numerator and denominator of each rational expression. Then, cancels out any common factors to both the numerator and denominator. For instance,

$$\frac{x-1}{x^2-4} \cdot \frac{x+2}{x-1} = \frac{\cancel{(x-1)}}{\cancel{(x+2)}(x-2)} \cdot \frac{\cancel{(x+2)}}{\cancel{(x-1)}} = \frac{1}{x-2}$$

To divide two rational expressions, multiply the first rational expression by the reciprocal of the second rational expression. For instance,

$$\frac{x-1}{x+2} \div \frac{x-1}{x^2+5x+6} = \frac{\cancel{(x-1)}}{\cancel{(x+2)}} \cdot \frac{\cancel{(x+2)}(x+3)}{\cancel{(x-1)}} = x+3$$

To add (or subtract) two rational expressions with like denominators, simply add (or subtract) their numerators and put the result over the common denominator. For instance,

$$\frac{2}{x-3} + \frac{x}{x-3} = \frac{x+2}{x-3}$$

To add (or subtract) two rational expressions with unlike denominators, find the least common denominator of the rational expressions. Then, rewrite each expression as an equivalent expression using the least common denominator. Finally, add (or subtract) their numerators and put the result over the least common denominator. For instance,

$$\frac{3}{x+1} + \frac{2}{x-2} = \frac{3(x-2)}{(x+1)(x-2)} + \frac{2(x+1)}{(x+1)(x-2)} = \frac{5x-4}{(x+1)(x-2)}$$

3.23 Solving Rational and Radical Equations

Solving Rational Equations

To solve a rational equation, multiply each side of the equation by the least common denominator (LCD) of the rational expressions. Then, simplify and solve the resulting polynomial equation. Once you get the solution of the rational equation, you need to substitute the solution in the original equation to check the solution. If the solution doesn't make the equation true, it is called an **extraneous solution**, and is disregarded. Below shows how to solve a rational equation.

$$\frac{x-1}{x-2}+\frac{2}{x-4}=\frac{4}{x^2-6x+8}$$

$$(x-2)(x-4)\left(\frac{x-1}{x-2}+\frac{2}{x-4}\right)=\left(\frac{4}{x^2-6x+8}\right)(x-2)(x-4) \qquad \text{LCD: } (x-2)(x-4)$$

$$(x-1)(x-4)+2(x-2)=4$$

$$x^2-3x-4=0$$

$$(x+1)(x-4)=0$$

$$x=-1 \quad \text{or} \quad x=4$$

Substitute -1 and 4 for x in the original equation to check the solutions. Thus, the only solution to the rational equation is $x=-1$.

Solving Radical Equations

An equation that contains a radical ($\sqrt{x}$) is called a radical equation. Often, solving a radical equation involves squaring a binomial. The binomial expansion formulas are shown below.

$$(x+y)^2=x^2+2xy+y^2 \qquad \text{Common mistake: } (x+y)^2\neq x^2+y^2$$

$$(x-y)^2=x^2-2xy+y^2 \qquad \text{Common mistake: } (x-y)^2\neq x^2-y^2$$

To solve a radical equation, square both sides of the equation to eliminate the square root. Then, solve for the variable. Once you get the solution of the radical equation, you need to substitute the solution in the original equation to check the solution. If the solution doesn't make the equation true, it is called an **extraneous solution**, and is disregarded. Below shows how to solve the radical equation $x - 1 = \sqrt{x+5}$.

$$\begin{aligned}
x - 1 &= \sqrt{x+5} && \text{Square both sides}\\
(x-1)^2 &= x+5 && \text{Use the binomial expansion formula}\\
x^2 - 2x + 1 &= x + 5 && \text{Subtract } x+5 \text{ from each side}\\
x^2 - 3x - 4 &= 0 && \text{Factor the quadratic expression}\\
(x+1)(x-4) &= 0 && \text{Use the zero product property: If } ab = 0, \text{ then } a = 0 \text{ or } b = 0.\\
x = -1 \quad &\text{or} \quad x = 4
\end{aligned}$$

Substitute -1 and 4 for x in the original equation to check the solutions.

$$(-1) - 1 = \sqrt{-1+5} \qquad\qquad (4) - 1 = \sqrt{4+5}$$
$$-2 \neq 2 \quad \text{(Not a solution)} \qquad\qquad 3 = 3 \quad \checkmark \text{ (Solution)}$$

Chapter 4

Functions

4.1 Definition of Function

Definition of Function

A relation is a set of ordered pairs. A function is a special relation where each x-value is related to exactly one corresponding y-value, or where x-values are not repeated. For instance, a set $A=\{(-1,-2),(0,-1),(2,1),(4,3)\}$ is a relation because set A is a set of ordered pairs. Also, set A is a function because the x-values, -1, 0, 2, and 4, are not repeated. The set of the x-values and the y-values in set A are called the **domain** and the **range** of the function, respectively. Thus, the domain of the function is $\{-1,0,2,4\}$ and the range of the function is $\{-2,-1,1,3\}$.

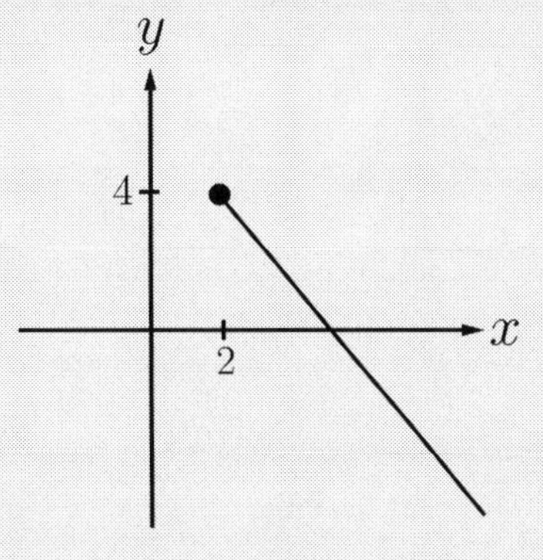

Domain of the graph of a function shown above is $\{x|x \geq 2\}$ or $[2,\infty)$, and Range is $\{y|y \leq 4\}$ or $(-\infty,4]$.

Tips: If set $B=\{(1,3),(2,5),(1,2),(3,5)\}$, set B is a relation, but not a function because the x-value, 1, is repeated twice.

Function Notation and Value of Function

Functions are often denoted by f or g. The function can be written as $f : x \mapsto f(x)$ or $y = f(x)$. The value of function f at x is denoted by $f(x)$. In order to evaluate the value of function f at $x = 2$, $f(2)$, substitute 2 for x. For instance, if $f(x) = x^2 + 1$, $f(2) = 2^2 + 1 = 5$.

Tips

1. When substituting a negative numerical value in a function, make sure to use parentheses to avoid a mistake. If $f(x) = x^2 + 1$, $f(-2) = (-2)^2 + 1 = 5$.
2. To evaluate $f(x+1)$ when $f(x) = x^2 + 1$, substitute $x + 1$ for x in $f(x)$.

$$f(x+1) = (x+1)^2 + 1 = x^2 + 2x + 2$$

4.2 Vertical Line Test

Vertical Line Test

The vertical line test is a graphical way to determine if a graph represents a function or not. If all vertical lines intersect the graph at most one point, the graph in Figure 1 represents a function. Otherwise, the graph does not represent a function as shown in Figure 2.

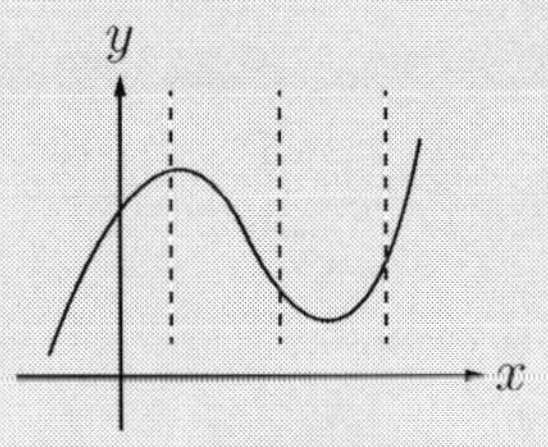

Figure 1

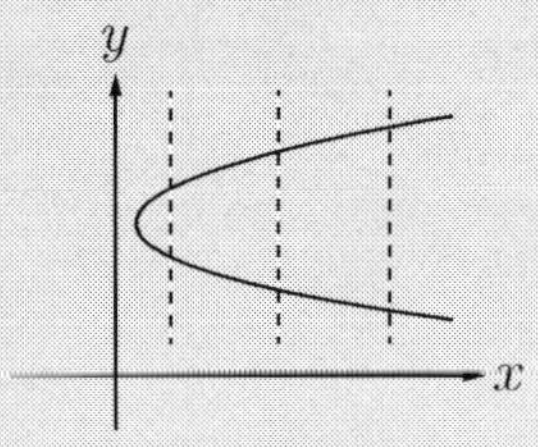

Figure 2

4.3 Operations on Functions

Operations on Functions

Functions can be added, subtracted, multiplied, divided, or combined to create a new function. Below are types of operations on functions. Let $f(x) = x^2 + 1$ and $g(x) = x - 3$.

- The sum of $f(x)$ and $g(x)$: $f(x) + g(x) = x^2 + 1 + x - 3 = x^2 + x - 2$
- The difference of $f(x)$ and $g(x)$: $f(x) - g(x) = x^2 + 1 - (x - 3) = x^2 - x + 4$
- The product of $f(x)$ and $g(x)$: use the distributive property.

$$f(x) \cdot g(x) = (x^2 + 1)(x - 3) = x^3 - 3x^2 + x - 3$$

- The quotient of $f(x)$ and $g(x)$.

$$\frac{f(x)}{g(x)} = \frac{x^2+1}{x-3}, \text{ where } x-3 \neq 0$$

- The composition function: $(f \circ g)(x)$ or $f\big(g(x)\big)$.

$$\begin{aligned}(f \circ g)(x) &= f\big(g(x)\big) = f(x-3)\\ &= (x-3)^2 + 1 = x^2 - 6x + 9 + 1\\ &= x^2 - 6x + 10\end{aligned}$$

Tips

1. The quotient of $f(x)$ and $g(x)$, or $\frac{f(x)}{g(x)} = \frac{x^2+1}{x-3}$ is a rational function. In order for the rational function to be defined, the denominator, $g(x) = x-3$, cannot be zero. Otherwise, it will be undefined. The rational function $\frac{x^2+1}{x-3}$ has a vertical asymptote at $x = 3$.
2. $(f \circ g)(x)$ or $f\big(g(x)\big)$ is read as f composed with g. This operation substitutes $g(x)$ for x in $f(x)$.

Example Finding vertical asymptotes

If $f(x) = \dfrac{x-3}{x^2-4}$, find the vertical asymptotes, if any.

Solution Set the denominator x^2-4 equal to zero and solve for x: $x^2 - 4 = 0$. Thus, $x = \pm 2$. Therefore, the rational function $f(x) = \dfrac{x-3}{x^2-4}$ has two vertical asymptotes at $x = 2$ and $x = -2$.

Example Evaluating a composition function

If $f(x) = x^2 - 3$ and $g(x) = 3x - 2$, evaluate $f\big(g(2)\big)$.

Solution Since $g(2) = 3(2) - 2 = 4$, substitute $g(2) = 4$ for x in $f(x)$.

$$\begin{aligned}f\big(g(2)\big) &= f(4) && \text{Substitute } g(2) = 4 \text{ for } x \text{ in } f(x)\\ &= (4)^2 - 3\\ &= 13\end{aligned}$$

Therefore, the value of $f(g(2))$ is 13.

4.4 Odd and Even Functions

Odd and Even Functions

Let $f(x)$ be a function. $f(x)$ is an odd function when $f(-x) = -f(x)$ for all values of x. Any odd function is symmetric with respect to the origin. Whereas, $f(x)$ is an even function when $f(-x) = f(x)$ for all values of x. Any even function is symmetric with respect to the y-axis.

	Odd functions	Even functions
Definition	$f(-x) = -f(x)$	$f(-x) = f(x)$
Graph	Symmetric with respect to the origin	Symmetric with respect to the y-axis
Example	$x^3,\ \sin x,\ \tan x$	$x^2,\ \cos x$

Tips Not all functions are either odd or even. Some functions are neither.

Example **Determining odd and even functions**

If $f(x) = x^3 - 2x + 3$, determine whether function $f(x)$ is odd, even, or neither.

Solution Evaluate $f(-x)$ and $-f(x)$.

$$\begin{aligned} f(x) &= x^3 - 2x + 3 \\ f(-x) &= (-x)^3 - 2(-x) + 3 = -x^3 + 2x + 3 \\ -f(x) &= -(x^3 - 2x + 3) = -x^3 + 2x - 3 \end{aligned}$$

Since $f(-x) \neq -f(x)$ and $f(-x) \neq f(x)$, $f(x)$ does not satisfy the definition of an odd function or an even function. Therefore, $f(x)$ is neither.

4.5 Piecewise Functions

Piecewise Functions

A piecewise function is defined by multiple functions with different domains. For instance, the piecewise function $f(x)$ below

$$f(x) = \begin{cases} 3x - 3, & x < 2 \\ -2x + 8, & x \geq 2 \end{cases}$$

is defined by two different functions: $g(x) = 3x - 3$, $x < 2$ in Figure 3, and $h(x) = -2x + 8$, $x \geq 2$ in Figure 4.

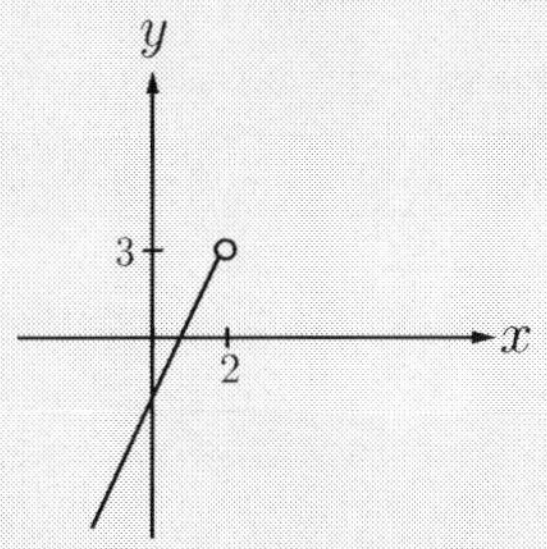

Fig. 3: $g(x) = 3x - 3$, $x < 2$

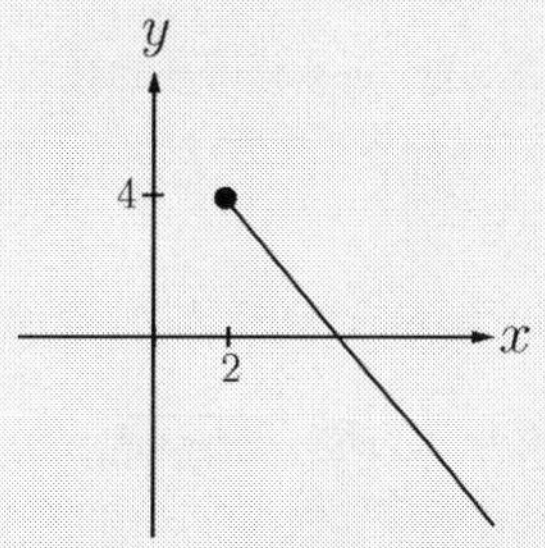

Fig. 4: $h(x) = -2x + 8$, $x \geq 2$

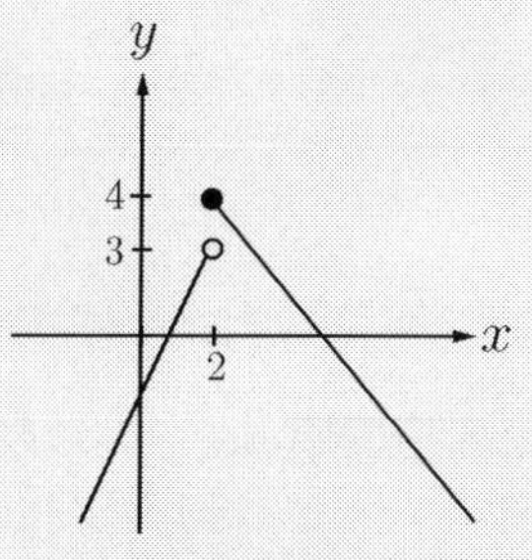

Fig. 5: Piecewise function $f(x)$

As shown in Figure 5, the graph of the piecewise function, $f(x)$, consists of the graphs of $g(x)$ and $h(x)$. The domain and range of the piecewise function $f(x)$ are (∞, ∞) and $(-\infty, 4]$, respectively.

Tips: In order to evaluate the piecewise function at $x = a$, or $f(a)$, check the conditions on the right side of the piecewise function to see where $x = a$ belongs to. For instance, to evaluate $f(1)$, use the equation $3x - 3$ for f because $x = 1$ belongs to $x < 2$. Thus, $f(1) = 3(1) - 3 = 0$.

Example **Evaluating piecewise functions**

$$f(x) = \begin{cases} x^2 - 3, & x < -1 \\ x + 4, & x \geq -1 \end{cases}$$

For the following function f above, evaluate $f(-2)$ and $f(3)$.

Solution In order to evaluate the piecewise function at $x = -2$ and $x = 3$, check the conditions on the right side of the piecewise function to see where $x = -2$ and $x = 3$ belong. Since $x = -2$ satisfies the condition $x < -1$, the equation for f is $x^2 - 3$. Thus, $f(-2) = (-2)^2 - 3 = 1$. Likewise, $x = 3$ satisfies the condition $x \geq -1$, the equation for f is $x + 4$. Thus, $f(3) = 3 + 4 = 7$.

4.6 Inverse Functions

Inverse Functions

Addition and subtraction can be considered as an example of do and undo processes. For instance, you start with a number, x. If you add 2 to x, then subtract 2 from the result, you will get the original number x as shown below.

$$x \xrightarrow{\text{Add 2}} x+2 \xrightarrow{\text{Subtract 2}} x$$

In mathematics, a function, f, and its inverse function, f^{-1}, are considered as do and undo functions. Thus, when a function, f, is composed with its inverse, f^{-1}, or vice versa, the result is x.

$$f(f^{-1}(x)) = x, \qquad f^{-1}(f(x)) = x$$

Tips

1. The inverse of f is denoted by f^{-1}. Note that the -1 used in f^{-1} is not an exponent. Thus, the inverse function of $f(x)$, $f^{-1}(x)$, is not the reciprocal of $f(x)$. In other words, $f^{-1}(x) \neq \frac{1}{f(x)}$. For instance, if $f(x) = x^3 + 5$, $f^{-1}(x) \neq \frac{1}{x^3+5}$.
2. The domain of f is the range of f^{-1}. Whereas, the range of f is the domain of f^{-1}.

4.7 Horizontal Line Test

Horizontal Line Test

The horizontal line test is a graphical way to determine if a function has an inverse function or not. If all horizontal lines intersect the graph at most one point, the function has an inverse function as shown in Figure 6. Otherwise, the function does not have an inverse function as shown in Figure 7.

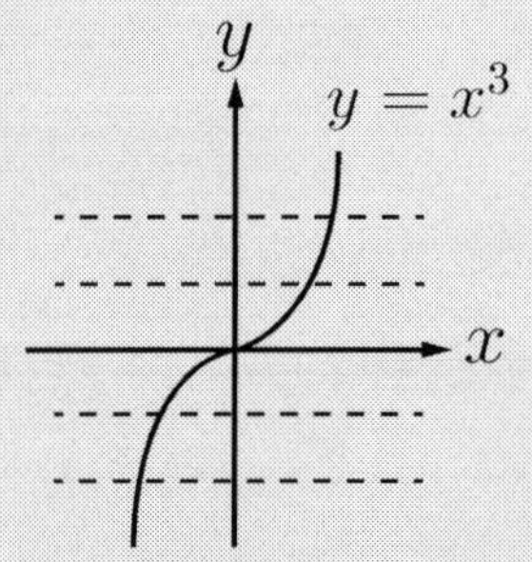

Figure 6: f has an inverse function

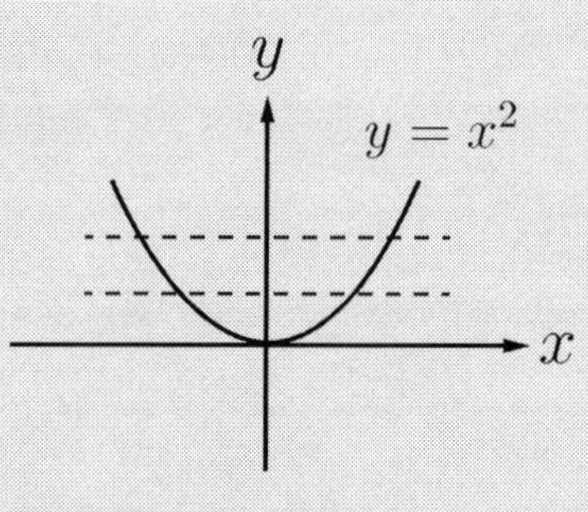

Figure 7: f does not have an inverse function

Tips

As shown in Figure 6, if every horizontal line intersects the graph of the function f at most one point, f is said to be **one-to-one**. All one-to-one functions have inverse functions.

Finding Inverse Functions

There are four steps to find the inverse of a function.

Step 1: Replace $f(x)$ with the y variable.

Step 2: Switch the x and y variables.

Step 3: Solve for y.

Step 4: [Optional] Replace the y variable with $f^{-1}(x)$.

Tips: Perform the horizontal line test to determine if a function has an inverse function. If the function passes the horizontal line test, follow the four steps shown above to find the inverse function.

Example **Finding the inverse function**

Find the inverse function of $f(x) = x^3 + 5$.

Solution Replace $f(x)$ with the y variable so that $f(x) = x^3 + 5$ becomes $y = x^3 + 5$. Next, switch the x and y variables and solve for y.

$$y = x^3 + 5 \qquad \text{Switch the } x \text{ and } y \text{ variables}$$
$$x = y^3 + 5 \qquad \text{Subtract 5 from each side}$$
$$x - 5 = y^3 \qquad \text{Take the cube root of each side}$$
$$y = \sqrt[3]{x-5}$$

Therefore, the inverse function of $f(x) = x^3 + 5$ is $y = \sqrt[3]{x-5}$.

4.8 Graphing the Inverse Functions

Graphing the Inverse Functions

The graph of the function $f(x) = \sqrt{x} + 2$ is shown in Figure 8. The graph of the inverse function is obtained by reflecting the graph of $f(x)$ about the line $y = x$ as shown in Figure 9. In other words, the graph of $f(x)$ and its inverse function $f^{-1}(x)$ are symmetric with respect to the line $y = x$.

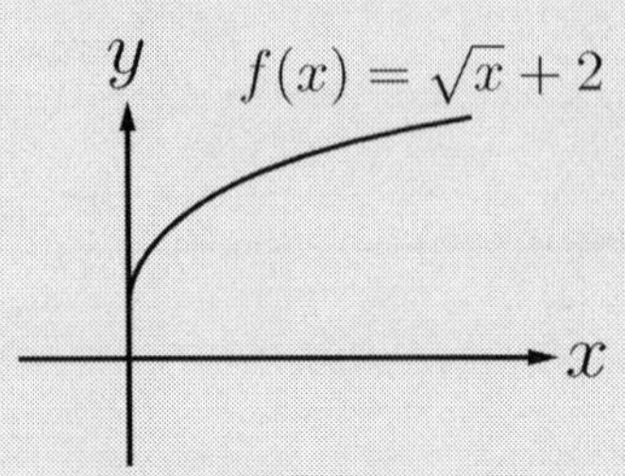

Figure 8: The graph of $f(x)$

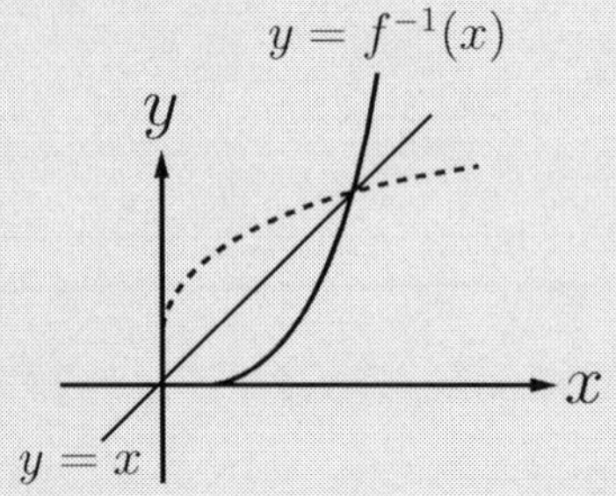

Figure 9: The graph of $f^{-1}(x)$

Example Finding the inverse function

Find the inverse function of $f(x) = \sqrt{x} + 2$ and state the domain and range of the inverse function.

Solution The graph of $f(x) = \sqrt{x} + 2$ shown in Figure 8 suggests that the domain and range of the function are $x \geq 0$ and $y \geq 2$, respectively. Since the domain of a function is the range of the inverse function, and the range of a function is the domain of the inverse function, the domain and range of the inverse function are $x \geq 2$ and $y \geq 0$, respectively. The graph of the inverse function is shown in Figure 9.

In order to find the inverse function algebraically, switch the x and y variables and solve for y.

$y = \sqrt{x} + 2$	Switch the x and y variables
$x = \sqrt{y} + 2$	Subtract 2 from each side
$x - 2 = \sqrt{y}$	Square both sides
$y = (x-2)^2$	Replace y with $f^{-1}(x)$
$f^{-1}(x) = (x-2)^2, \quad x \geq 2$	Since the domain of $f^{-1}(x)$ is $x \geq 2$

Therefore, the inverse function is $f^{-1}(x) = (x-2)^2$, $x \geq 2$.

4.9 Graphs of Parent Functions

Graphs of Parent Functions

A family of functions is a group of functions that all have a similar shape. A parent function is the simplest function and is used as a reference to graph more complicated functions in the family. The table below summarizes the graph, domain, and range of each parent function.

Parent function	Graph	Parent function	Graph
Constant $y = k$ Domain: $(-\infty, \infty)$ Range: $y = k$	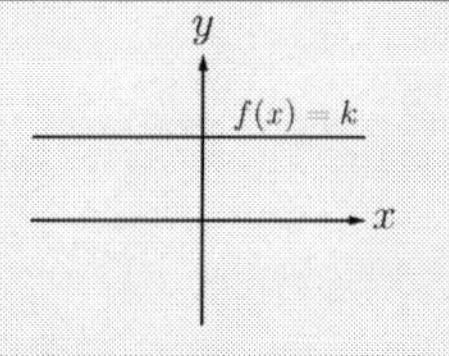	Greatest integer $y = [x]$ Domain: $(-\infty, \infty)$ Range: All integers	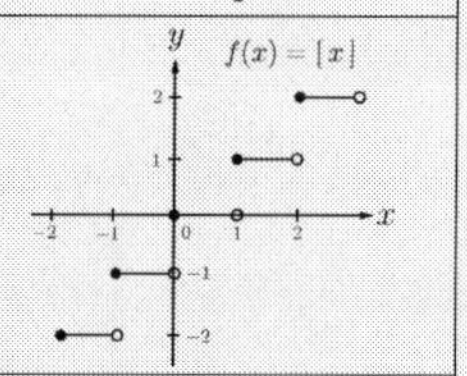
Linear $y = x$ Domain: $(-\infty, \infty)$ Range: $(-\infty, \infty)$	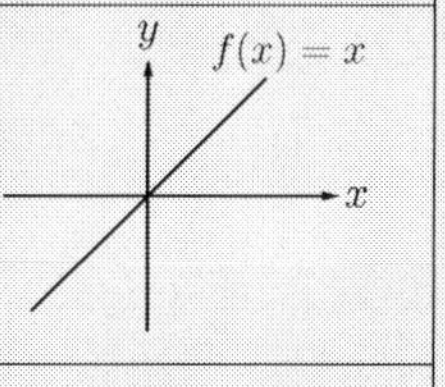	Absolute value $y = \|x\|$ Domain: $(-\infty, \infty)$ Range: $[0, \infty)$	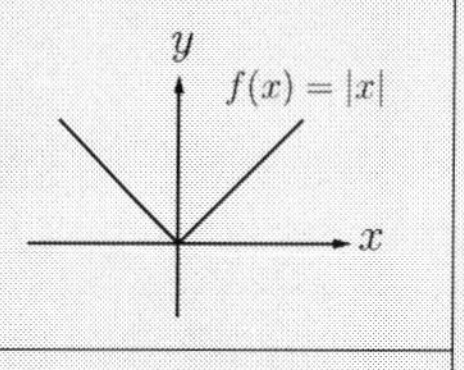
Quadratic $y = x^2$ Domain: $(-\infty, \infty)$ Range: $[0, \infty)$	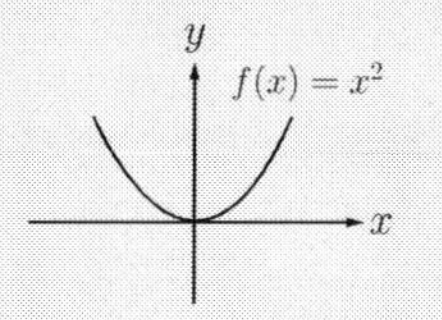	Square root $y = \sqrt{x}$ Domain: $[0, \infty)$ Range: $[0, \infty)$	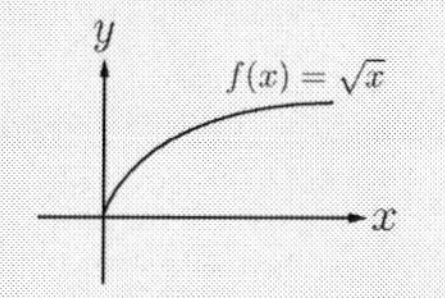
Cubic $y = x^3$ Domain: $(-\infty, \infty)$ Range: $(-\infty, \infty)$	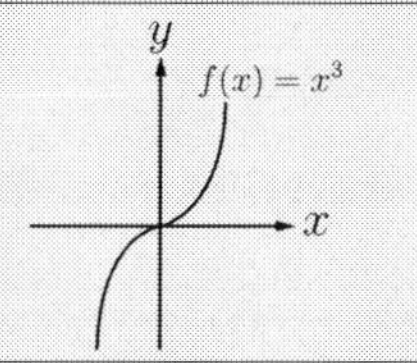	Cube root $y = \sqrt[3]{x}$ Domain: $(-\infty, \infty)$ Range: $(-\infty, \infty)$	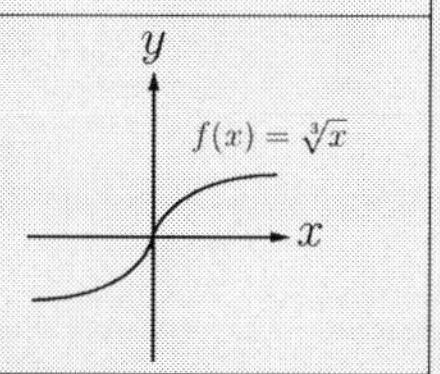
Rational 1 $y = \dfrac{1}{x}$ Domain: $x \neq 0$ Range: $y \neq 0$	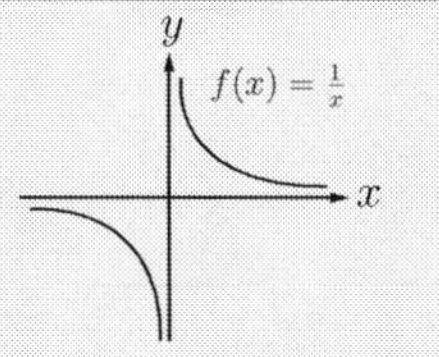	Rational 2 $y = \dfrac{1}{x^2}$ Domain: $x \neq 0$ Range: $(0, \infty)$	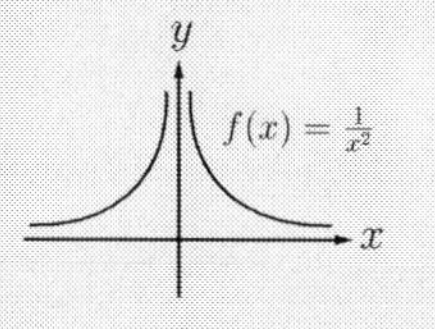
Exponential $y = a^x,\ a > 1$ Domain: $(-\infty, \infty)$ Range: $(0, \infty)$	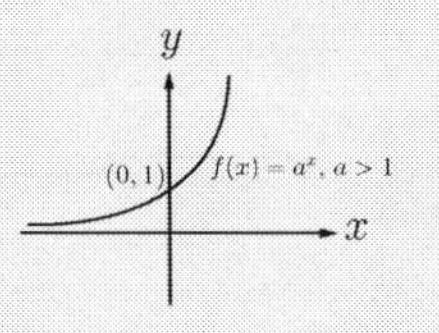	Logarithmic $y = \log_a x,\ a > 1$ Domain: $(0, \infty)$ Range: $(-\infty, \infty)$	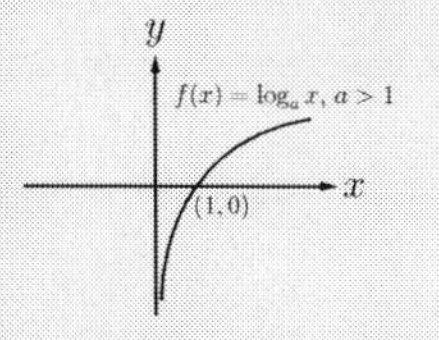

4.10 Transformations

Transformations

The general shape of each parent function can be moved or resized by transformations. For instance, the three functions shown below

$$y = x^2, \qquad y = (x-1)^2, \qquad y = \frac{1}{2}x^2 + 3$$

are in the family of quadratic functions and have the same shape. After moving or resizing the graph of the parent function, $y = x^2$, we can obtain the graphs of $y = (x-1)^2$ and $y = \frac{1}{2}x^2 + 3$.

Transformations consist of horizontal and vertical shifts, horizontal and vertical stretches and compressions, and reflections about the x-axis and y-axis. The table below summarizes the transformations.

Transformation	Function Notation	Effect on the graph of $f(x)$
Horizontal shift	$y = f(x-1)$	Move the graph of $f(x)$ right 1 unit
	$y = f(x+2)$	Move the graph of $f(x)$ left 2 units
Vertical shift	$y = f(x) + 3$	Move the graph of $f(x)$ up 3 units
	$y = f(x) - 4$	Move the graph of $f(x)$ down 4 units
Horizontal stretch and compression	$y = f(2x)$	Horizontal compression of the graph of $f(x)$ by a factor of $\frac{1}{2}$
	$y = f(\frac{1}{3}x)$	Horizontal stretch of the graph of $f(x)$ by a factor of 3
Vertical stretch and compression	$y = 3f(x)$	Vertical stretch of the graph of $f(x)$ by a factor of 3
	$y = \frac{1}{2}f(x)$	Vertical compression of the graph of $f(x)$ by a factor of $\frac{1}{2}$
Reflection about the x-axis, y-axis, and origin	$y = -f(x)$	Reflect the graph of $f(x)$ about the x-axis
	$y = f(-x)$	Reflect the graph of $f(x)$ about the y-axis
	$y = -f(-x)$	Reflect the graph of $f(x)$ about the origin

Tips

1. Translation means moving right, left, up, or down. Sometimes, horizontal shifts or vertical shifts are referred to as translations.
2. Horizontal shifts, written in the form $f(x-h)$, do the opposite of what they look like they should do. $f(x-1)$ means to move the graph of $f(x)$ right 1 unit. Whereas, $f(x+2)$ means to move the graph of $f(x)$ left 2 units.
3. Horizontal stretches and compressions, written in the form $f(cx)$, also do the opposite of what they look like they should do. $f(2x)$ means a horizontal compression of the graph of $f(x)$ by a factor of $\frac{1}{2}$. Whereas, $f(\frac{1}{3}x)$ means a horizontal stretch of the graph of $f(x)$ by a factor of 3.

4.11 Order of Transformations

Order of Transformations

In order to graph a function involving more than one transformation, use the order of transformations.

1. Horizontal shift
2. Horizontal and vertical stretch and compression
3. Reflection about x-axis and y-axis
4. Vertical shift

The order of transformations suggests to first perform the horizontal shift. Afterwards, perform the horizontal and vertical stretch and compression. Next, perform the reflection about the x-axis and y-axis. Finally, perform the vertical shift.

Example Graphing the function by transformations

Graph $f(x) = -\sqrt{x-1}+2$ and state the domain and range of the function.

Solution If $f(x) = \sqrt{x}$, $-f(x-1)+2$ in function notation represents $-\sqrt{x-1}+2$. The function notation $-f(x-1)+2$ suggests that the graph of $-\sqrt{x-1}+2$ involves a horizontal shift, reflection about the x-axis, and a vertical shift from the graph of the parent function $y = \sqrt{x}$. Thus, perform the horizontal shift first. Next, perform the reflection about the x-axis, and lastly, perform the vertical shift.

Let's start with the graph of $f(x) = \sqrt{x}$.

$f(x) = \sqrt{x}$	The graph of the parent function as shown in Fig. 1
$f(x-1) = \sqrt{x-1}$	Move the graph of $\sqrt{x}$ right 1 unit as shown in Fig. 2
$-f(x-1) = -\sqrt{x-1}$	Reflect the graph of $\sqrt{x-1}$ about the x-axis as shown in Fig. 3
$-f(x-1)+2 = -\sqrt{x-1}+2$	Move the graph of $-\sqrt{x-1}$ up 2 units as shown in Fig. 4

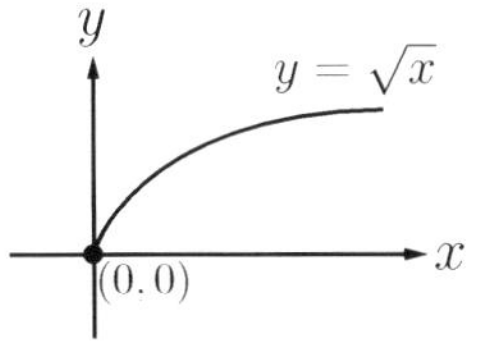

Fig. 1

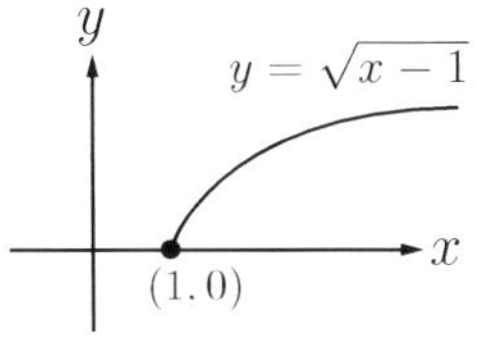

Fig. 2

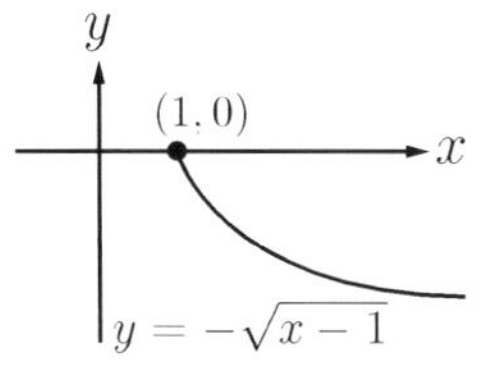

Fig. 3

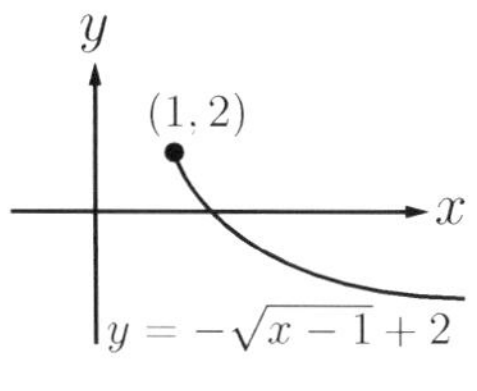

Fig. 4

As shown in Fig. 4, the domain of the function is $[1, \infty)$, and the range of the function is $(-\infty, 2]$.

4.12 Graph of $y = |f(x)|$

Graph of $y = |f(x)|$

In order to graph the function $y = |f(x)|$, reflect the part of the graph of $y = f(x)$ that lies below the x-axis about the x-axis. For instance, in order to graph $y = |x^2 - 3|$, start with the graph of $y = x^2 - 3$ as shown in Figure 5. Determine the part of the graph that lies below the x-axis as shown in Figure 6. Lastly, reflect the part of the graph that lies below the x-axis about the x-axis as shown in Figure 7.

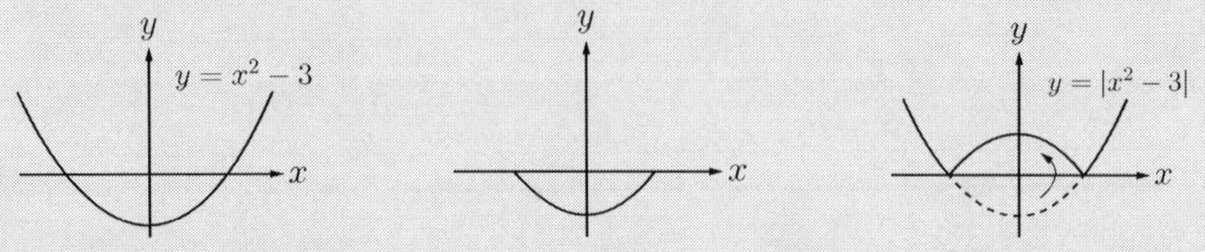

Fig 5: $y = x^2 - 3$ Fig 6: Part below the x-axis Fig 7: $y = |x^2 - 3|$

Tips: In general, the graph of $y = |f(x)|$ is **NOT** a reflection of the entire graph of $y = f(x)$ about the x-axis nor about the y-axis.

Example Graphing $y = |f(x)|$

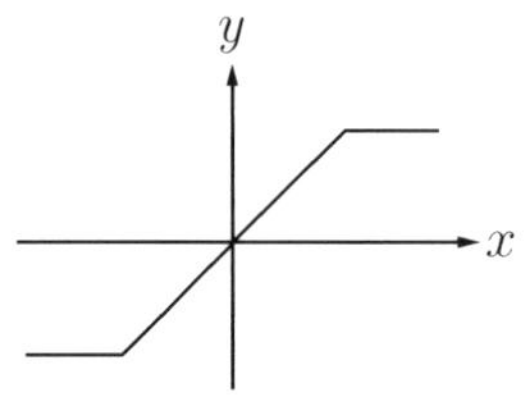

The graph of $y = f(x)$ is given above. Graph $y = |f(x)|$.

Solution The function $f(x)$ is an odd function since the graph of $y = f(x)$ is symmetric with respect to the origin. To graph $y = |f(x)|$, reflect the part of the graph of $y = f(x)$ that lies below the x-axis about the x-axis. The graph of $y = |f(x)|$ is shown below.

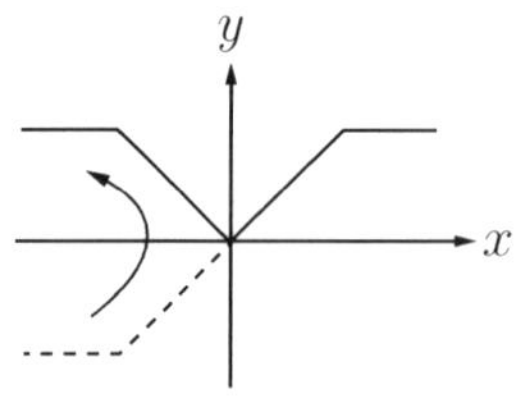

Graph of $y = |f(x)|$

Since the graph of $y = |f(x)|$ is symmetric with respect to the y-axis, the function $y = |f(x)|$ is an even function.

4.13 Rational Functions

Rational Functions

A rational function $f(x)$ is a function that is expressed in the form

$$f(x) = \frac{p(x)}{q(x)}$$

where p and q are polynomial functions and q is not the zero polynomial function. The domain of a rational function f is a set of x-values for which the denominator q is not zero.

An asymptote is a line that the graph of a function approaches but never touches. There are three kinds of asymptotes: horizontal, vertical, and slant (or oblique) asymptotes. In general, a rational function has either a vertical asymptote or a horizontal asymptote or both.

A horizontal asymptote is a horizontal line that the graph of a function approaches as $x \to \infty$ (read as x approaches ∞) or as $x \to -\infty$. A vertical asymptote is a vertical line near which the values of f approach ∞ (increases without bound) or $-\infty$ (decreases without bound).

For instance, $f(x) = \dfrac{1}{x-2} + 1$ is a rational function whose graph is shown below.

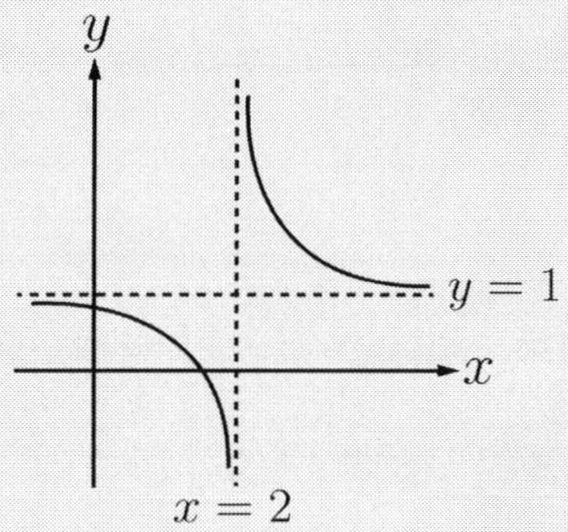

The horizontal asymptote of f is $y = 1$ because the values of f approach 1 as $x \to \infty$ or $x \to -\infty$. Whereas, the vertical asymptote is $x = 2$ because the values of f approach ∞ or $-\infty$ as $x \to 2$.

Tips: Since the values of f approach 1 as $x \to \infty$, this can be denoted by $\lim_{x\to\infty} f(x) = 1$. In general, $\lim_{x\to\infty} f(x)$, the limit of a function f at infinity, means to find the horizontal asymptote of f.

4.14 Finding Vertical Asymptotes

Finding Vertical Asymptotes

A rational function $f(x) = \frac{p(x)}{q(x)}$ has a vertical asymptote at $x = c$ if c is a real zero of the denominator $q(x)$.

For instance, let $f(x) = \frac{2x}{x^2-9}$. The zeros of the denominator of $x^2 - 9$ are 3 or -3. Thus, the rational function f has the vertical asymptotes at $x = 3$ and $x = -3$.

Tips: If the denominator of a rational function has no real zeros, the rational function does not have a vertical asymptote. For instance, let $f(x) = \frac{1}{x^2+1}$. Since the zeros of $x^2 + 1$ are i and $-i$, the rational function f does not have a vertical asymptote.

4.15 Finding Horizontal Asymptotes

Finding Horizontal Asymptotes $\left(\lim_{x\to\infty} f(x)\right)$

For the rational function

$$f(x) = \frac{p(x)}{q(x)} = \frac{ax^m + \cdots}{bx^n + \cdots}$$

where m is the degree of the numerator and n is the degree of the denominator, a horizontal asymptote can be determined by the following three cases.

- Case 1: If $n < m$, there is no horizontal asymptote. Whereas, there is a slant (or oblique) asymptote.
- Case 2: If $n = m$, f has a horizontal asymptote of $y = \dfrac{a}{b}$, where a and b are the leading coefficients of the numerator and denominator.
- Case 3: If $n > m$, f has a horizontal asymptote of $y = 0$.

For instance, for the rational function $f(x) = \frac{1}{x} = \frac{1\cdot x^0}{x^1}$ whose graph is shown below,

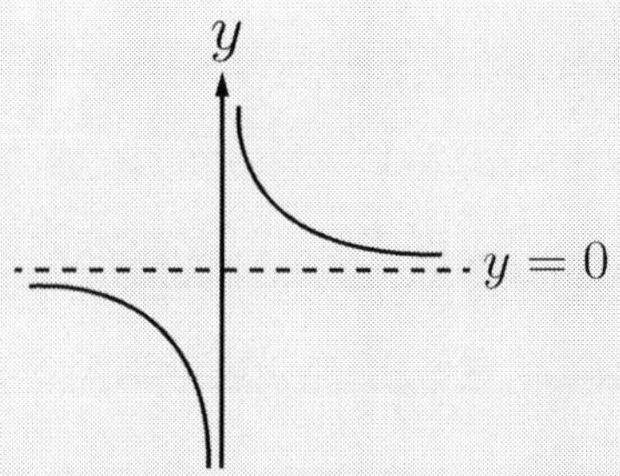

the degree of numerator is 0 and the degree of the denominator is 1. Thus, the rational function has the horizontal asymptote of $y = 0$, which can be denoted by $\lim_{x\to\infty} \frac{1}{x} = 0$ and $\lim_{x\to-\infty} \frac{1}{x} = 0$.

Example   Finding vertical asymptotes

Find the domain and vertical asymptotes of the following rational function.

$$y = \frac{2x+1}{x^2-5x+6}$$

Solution In order to find the domain and vertical asymptotes, set the denominator equal to zero and solve for x. The solutions to $x^2 - 5x + 6 = 0$ will be the values that are excluded in the domain, and will be the vertical asymptotes.

$$\begin{aligned} x^2 - 5x + 6 &= 0 && \text{Factor} \\ (x-2)(x-3) &= 0 && \text{Solve} \\ x = 2 \quad &\text{or} \quad x = 3 \end{aligned}$$

Therefore, the domain of the rational function is $x \neq 2$ and $x \neq 3$, and the vertical asymptotes are $x = 2$ and $x = 3$.

Example   Finding horizontal asymptotes

Find the horizontal asymptotes of each rational function.

(a) $f(x) = \dfrac{1-3x}{2x^2+3x}$

(b) $f(x) = \dfrac{-x^3+1}{x^2-2x+2}$

(c) $f(x) = \dfrac{2x^2 - 2x + 3}{2 - 4x + 3x^2}$

Solution

(a) The numerator is a first degree polynomial ($m = 1$) and the denominator is a second degree polynomial ($n = 2$). Since $n > m$, the horizontal asymptote of f is $y = 0$.

(b) The numerator is a third degree polynomial ($m = 3$) and the denominator is a second degree polynomial ($n = 2$). Since $n < m$, there is no horizontal asymptote.

(c) $f(x) = \dfrac{2x^2 - 2x + 3}{2 - 4x + 3x^2} = \dfrac{2x^2 - 2x + 3}{3x^2 - 4x + 2}$. Both the numerator and the denominator are 2nd degree polynomials. Thus, the horizontal asymptote of f is the ratio of the leading coefficients, or $y = \frac{2}{3}$.

4.16 Graphing Simple Rational Functions

Graphing Simple Rational Functions

For a rational function $f(x) = \dfrac{a}{x-h} + k$, the vertical asymptote of f is $x = h$ (set the denominator $x - h$ equal to zero and solve for x) and the horizontal asymptote of f is $y = k$. Depending on the value of a, either positive or negative, the graph of f varies as shown in Figures 2 and 3.

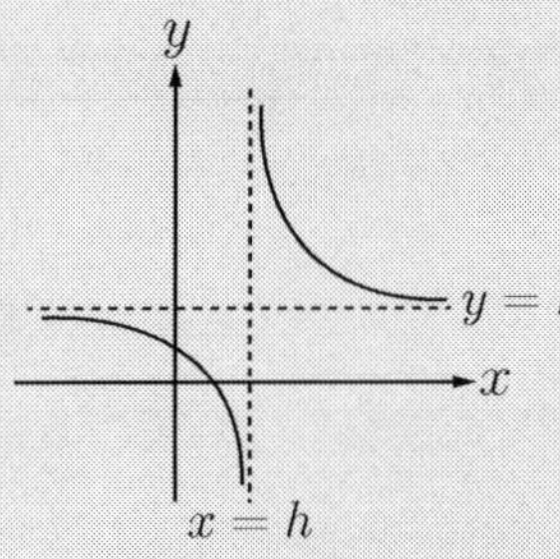

Figure 2: If $a > 0$

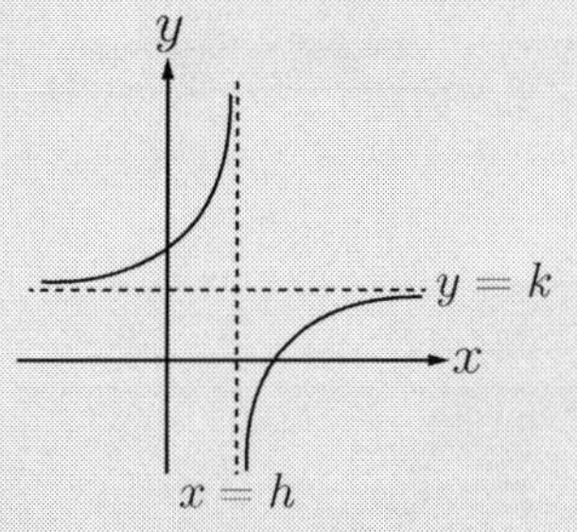

Figure 3: If $a < 0$

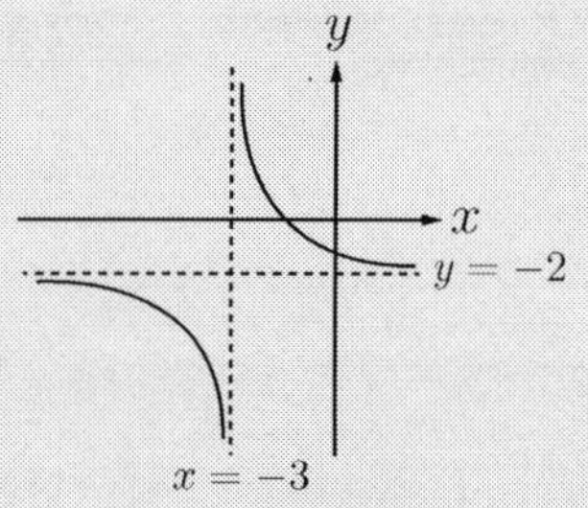

Figure 4: Graph of $\frac{1}{x+3} - 2$

For instance, for the rational function $f(x) = \dfrac{1}{x+3} - 2$, the vertical asymptote of f is $x = -3$ (set the denominator $x + 3$ equal to zero and solve for x), and the horizontal asymptote of y is $y = -2$. The graph of f is shown in Figure 4.

4.17 Graphing Simple Rational Functions with a Hole

Graphing Simple Rational Functions with a Hole

A hole in the graph of a rational function is produced by cancelling out the common factor $x - c$ from both the numerator and the denominator. A hole is a point at which f has no value and is plotted using an open circle.

For instance, let $f(x) = \frac{x-4}{(x-2)(x-4)}$. f has the common factor $x - 4$ from both the numerator and the denominator. Thus, cancelling out $x - 4$ produces a hole in the graph of f at $x = 4$. Since f simplifies to $\frac{1}{x-2}$, the vertical asymptote of f is $x = 2$ and the horizontal asymptote of f is $y = 0$. The graph of f is shown below.

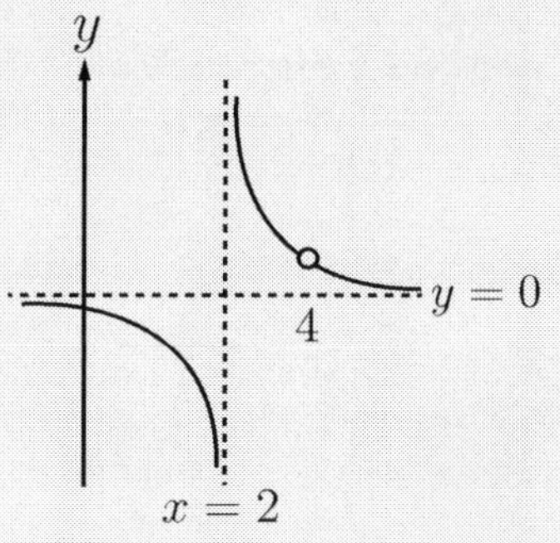

4.18 Graphing complicated Rational Functions

Graphing complicated Rational Functions

For a rational function $f(x) = \dfrac{p(x)}{q(x)}$, where the degree of $q(x)$ is 2 or higher, the following guidelines will help you sketch the graph of $f(x)$.

1. Find the vertical and horizontal asymptotes.
2. Find the x- and y-intercepts.
3. Check end behaviors of $f(x)$ near the vertical asymptotes.

For instance, $f(x) = \dfrac{x-1}{x^2-9}$ has vertical asymptotes at $x = \pm 3$ and a horizontal asymptote at $y = 0$. The x- and y-intercepts of $f(x)$ are 1 and $\frac{1}{9}$, respectively.

Factor $f(x) = \dfrac{x-1}{x^2-9} = \dfrac{x-1}{(x+3)(x-3)}$ and check the end behaviors near vertical asymptotes as shown in the table below.

Near vertical asymptotes	End behaviors
At $x = 3.01$	$y = \frac{+}{+\cdot+} = \infty$
At $x = 2.99$	$y = \frac{+}{+\cdot-} = -\infty$
At $x = -2.99$	$y = \frac{-}{+\cdot-} = \infty$
At $x = -3.01$	$y = \frac{-}{-\cdot-} = -\infty$

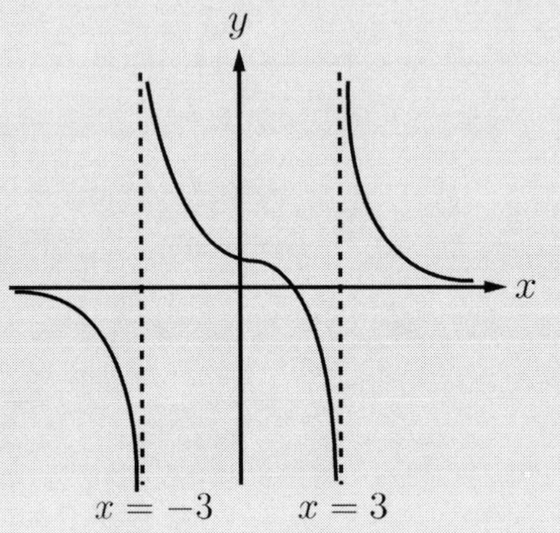

4.19 Graphs of Exponential and Logarithmic Functions

Graphs of Exponential and Logarithmic Functions

The exponential functions, $y = a^x$, and logarithmic functions, $y = \log_a x$, are inverses of each other. For instance, the inverse function of 3^x is $\log_3 x$. The following two equations relate exponents to logarithms or vice versa and are used to find the inverse function of an exponential function or a logarithmic function.

$$a^x = y \quad \Longleftrightarrow \quad x = \log_a y$$

Note that the two equations above are equivalent.

Since exponential functions and logarithmic functions are inverse functions, their graphs are symmetric with respect to the line $y = x$ as shown in Figures 1 and 2.

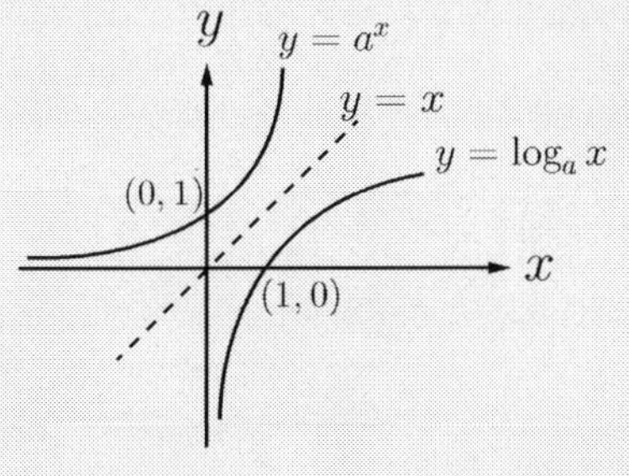

Figure 1: when $a > 1$

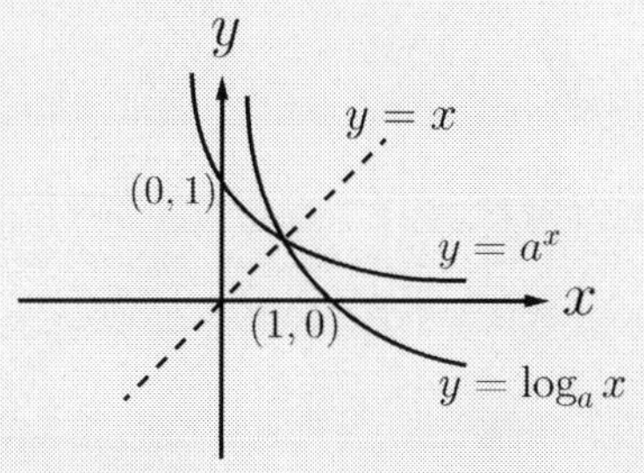

Figure 2: when $0 < a < 1$

Tips: The graphs of all exponential functions pass through the point $(0, 1)$. Whereas, the graphs of all logarithmic functions pass through the point $(1, 0)$.

Domain of a Logarithmic function

For a logarithmic function $y = \log_a h(x)$, where $h(x)$ is an algebraic expression or the argument of a logarithmic function, the domain of a logarithmic function is a set of all x-values for which $h(x) > 0$. In other words, solve the inequality $h(x) > 0$ to find the domain of a logarithmic function. For instance,

$$\log_2(x-2) \implies \text{Solve } x - 2 > 0 \implies \text{Domain: } x > 2$$
$$\log_3(6-2x) \implies \text{Solve } 6 - 2x > 0 \implies \text{Domain: } x < 3$$
$$\log_{10}(x^2-2x) \implies \text{Solve } x^2 - 2x > 0 \implies \text{Domain: } x < 0 \text{ or } x > 2$$

Properties of Exponents

The table below summarizes the properties of exponents.

Properties of Exponents	Example
1. $a^m \cdot a^n = a^{m+n}$	1. $2^4 \cdot 2^6 = 2^{10}$
2. $\frac{a^m}{a^n} = a^{m-n}$	2. $\frac{2^{10}}{2^3} = 2^{10-3} = 2^7$
3. $(a^m)^n = a^{mn} = (a^n)^m$	3. $(2^3)^4 = 2^{12} = (2^4)^3$
4. $a^0 = 1$	4. $(-2)^0 = 1$, $(3)^0 = 1$, $(100)^0 = 1$
5. $a^{-1} = \frac{1}{a}$	5. $2^{-1} = \frac{1}{2}$
6. $a^{\frac{1}{n}} = \sqrt[n]{a}$	6. $2^{\frac{1}{2}} = \sqrt{2}$, $x^{\frac{1}{3}} = \sqrt[3]{x}$
7. $a^{\frac{m}{n}} = (a^m)^{\frac{1}{n}} = \sqrt[n]{a^m}$	7. $2^{\frac{3}{2}} = \sqrt[2]{2^3}$, $x^{\frac{3}{4}} = \sqrt[4]{x^3}$
8. $a^{-\frac{m}{n}} = (a^{\frac{m}{n}})^{-1} = \frac{1}{\sqrt[n]{a^m}}$	8. $2^{-\frac{3}{4}} = (2^{\frac{3}{4}})^{-1} = \frac{1}{\sqrt[4]{2^3}}$
9. $(ab)^n = a^n b^n$	9. $(2 \cdot 3)^6 = 2^6 \cdot 3^6$, $(2x)^2 = 2^2 x^2$
10. $\left(\frac{a}{b}\right)^n = \frac{a^n}{b^n}$	10. $(\frac{2}{x})^3 = \frac{2^3}{x^3}$
11. $\frac{b^{-n}}{a^{-m}} = \frac{a^m}{b^n}$	11. $\frac{y^{-3}}{x^{-2}} = \frac{x^2}{y^3}$

Properties of Logarithms

The table below summarizes the properties of logarithms.

Properties of Logarithms	Example
1. $\log_a 0 =$ undefined	1. $\log_a 0 =$ undefined
2. $\log_a 1 = 0$	2. $\log_2 1 = 0$
3. $\log_a a = 1$	3. $\log_2 2 = 1$
4. $\log_a x^n = n \log_a x$	4. $\log_2 125 = \log_2 5^3 = 3 \log_2 5$
5. $\log_{a^n} x = \frac{1}{n} \log_a x$	5. $\log_8 5 = \log_{2^3} 5 = \frac{1}{3} \log_2 5$
6. $\log_a x = \frac{\log_c x}{\log_c a}$	6. $\log_2 3 = \frac{\log_{10} 3}{\log_{10} 2} = \frac{\ln 3}{\ln 2}$
7. $\log_a xy = \log_a x + \log_a y$	7. $\log_2 15 = \log_2(3 \cdot 5) = \log_2 3 + \log_2 5$
8. $\log_a \frac{x}{y} = \log_a x - \log_a y$	8. $\log_2 \frac{5}{3} = \log_2 5 - \log_2 3$
9. $a^{\log_a x} = x^{\log_a a} = x$	9. $2^{\log_2 3} = 3^{\log_2 2} = 3^1 = 3$

Tips

1. The common logarithm is the logarithm with base 10, which is denoted by either $\log_{10} x$ or $\log x$.
2. e is an irrational number and is approximately $2.718\cdots$. The natural logarithm of x can be expressed as either $\log_e x$ or $\ln x$.

Example Finding the domain of a logarithmic function

Find the domain of $y = \log_3(4 - x^2)$.

Solution The domain of the logarithmic function $y = \log_3(4 - x^2)$ is a set of all x-values for which $4 - x^2 > 0$. Thus,

$4 - x^2 > 0$	Subtract 4 from each side
$-x^2 > -4$	Multiply each side by -1 and reverse the inequality symbol
$x^2 < 4$	Solve the inequality
$-2 < x < 2$	

Therefore, the domain of $y = \log_3(4 - x^2)$ is $-2 < x < 2$ or $(-2, 2)$.

Example Finding the inverse function of an exponential function

Find the inverse function of $y = 3^{x-1} + 2$.

Solution In order to find the inverse function, switch the x and y variables and solve for y.

$y = 3^{x-1} + 2$	Switch the x and y variables
$x = 3^{y-1} + 2$	Subtract 2 from each side
$3^{y-1} = x - 2$	Convert the equation to a logarithmic equation
$y - 1 = \log_3(x - 2)$	Add 1 to each side
$y = \log_3(x - 2) + 1$	

Therefore, the inverse function of $y = 3^{x-1} + 2$ is $f^{-1}(x) = \log_3(x - 2) + 1$.

Example Writing a logarithmic expression

If $\log 2 = x$ and $\log 3 = y$, write $\log 72$ in terms of x and y.

Solution Since the prime factorization of $72 = 2^3 \cdot 3^2$,

$\log 72 = \log(2^3 \cdot 3^2)$	Use $\log_a xy = \log_a x + \log_a y$
$= \log 2^3 + \log 3^2$	Use $\log_a x^n = n \log_a x$
$= 3 \log 2 + 2 \log 3$	Since $\log 2 = x$ and $\log 3 = y$
$= 3x + 2y$	

Therefore, $\log 72$ can be written as $3x + 2y$.

4.20 Solving Exponential and Logarithmic Equations

Solving Exponential and Logarithmic Equations

Below shows how to solve an exponential equation and a logarithmic equation.

- When each side of an equation (either exponential or logarithmic) has the same base.

$$\text{If } a^x = a^y \implies x = y \qquad \text{e.g. If } 2^x = 2^3, \text{ then } x = 3$$
$$\text{If } \log_a x = \log_a y \implies x = y \qquad \text{e.g. If } \log_2 x = \log_2 5, \text{ then } x = 5$$

- When each side of an equation (either exponential or logarithmic) has a different base, convert the exponential equation to a logarithmic equation or vice versa.

$$\text{If } a^x = b \implies x = \log_a b \qquad \text{e.g. If } 2^x = 7, \text{ then } x = \log_2 7$$
$$\text{If } \log_a x = b \implies x = a^b \qquad \text{e.g. If } \log_2 x = 3, \text{ then } x = 2^3$$

Tips

Always check you solutions whenever you solve the following types of equations because some solutions may be extraneous.

- Radical equations: e.g. $x - 1 = \sqrt{x+5}$
- Rational equations: e.g. $\dfrac{1}{x-1} = \dfrac{2}{x(x-1)}$
- Logarithmic equations: e.g. $\ln(x+1) + \ln(x-2) = \ln 4$

Example **Solving an exponential equation**

If $2^x = 3^y$, find the value of $\frac{x}{y}$.

Solution Since each side of equation has a different base (left side has the base 2 and right side has the base 3), convert the exponential equation to a logarithmic equation.

$$
\begin{aligned}
2^x &= 3^y && \text{Convert the equation to a logarithmic equation} \\
x &= \log_2 3^y && \text{Use } \log_a x^n = n \log_a x \\
x &= y \log_2 3 && \text{Divide each side by } y \\
\frac{x}{y} &= \log_2 3
\end{aligned}
$$

Therefore, the value of $\frac{x}{y}$ is $\log_2 3 \approx 1.585$.

Example **Solving a logarithmic equation**

Solve: $\ln(x+1) + \ln(x-2) = \ln 4$

Solution Express the left side as a single logarithm and solve for x.

$\ln(x+1) + \ln(x-2) = \ln 4$	Express the left side as a single logarithm
$\ln\left[(x+1)(x-2)\right] = \ln 4$	Since each side has the same base, e
$(x+1)(x-2) = 4$	Subtract 4 from each side
$x^2 - x - 6 = 0$	Use the factoring method
$(x+2)(x-3) = 0$	Use the zero product property
$x = -2 \quad \text{or} \quad x = 3$	

Substitute -2 and 3 for x in the original equation to check the solutions.

$$\ln(-2+1) + \ln(-2-2) = \ln 4$$
$$\text{undefined} \neq \ln 4 \qquad \text{(Not a solution)}$$

$$\ln(3+1) + \ln(3-2) = \ln 4$$
$$\ln 4 = \ln 4 \qquad \checkmark \text{ (Solution)}$$

Therefore, the only solution to $\ln(x+1) + \ln(x-2) = \ln 4$ is $x = 3$.

4.21 Exponential Growth and Decay

Exponential Growth and Decay

Exponential growth:	$A(t) = A_0(1+r)^t$
Exponential decay:	$A(t) = A_0(1-r)^t$

where A_0 is the initial amount at time $t = 0$ and r is the growth or decay rate (the percent changed to a decimal).

4.22 Compound Interest

Compound Interest

If an initial amount P is invested at an annual interest rate (expressed as a decimal) r compounded n times per year, the amount of money A accumulated in t years is as follows:

$$A = P\left(1 + \frac{r}{n}\right)^{nt}$$

For instance, the initial amount of \$1000 is deposited into a savings account which yields an annual interest of 4%. The amounts after 3 years if the interest is compounded annually, quarterly, and monthly are shown below.

- Annually compounded:

$$A = \$1000\left(1 + \frac{0.04}{1}\right)^{1\cdot 3} = \$1124.86$$

- Quarterly compounded:

$$A = \$1000\left(1 + \frac{0.04}{4}\right)^{4\cdot 3} = \$1126.83$$

- Monthly compounded:

$$A = \$1000\left(1 + \frac{0.04}{12}\right)^{12\cdot 3} = \$1127.27$$

If the interest rate is compounded continuously, the compound interest formula above becomes

$$A = Pe^{rt}$$

Thus, the amount after 3 years is $A = \$1000e^{(0.04)(3)} = \$1127.5$.

Tips $\quad \lim_{x\to\infty}\left(1 + \frac{1}{x}\right)^{x} = e \quad$ or $\quad \lim_{x\to 0}(1 + x)^{\frac{1}{x}} = e$

Chapter 5

Trigonometry

5.1 Angles

Angles

Two rays form an angle. One ray is called the **initial side** and the other ray is called the **terminal side**. An angle θ is in **standard position** if its vertex is at the origin and the initial side is on the positive x-axis shown in Figure 1.

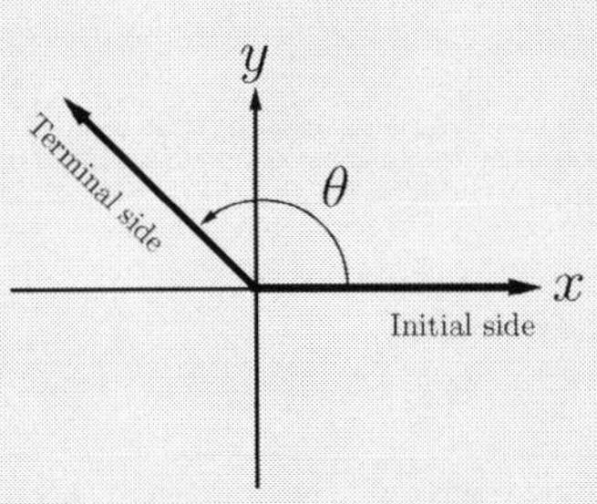

Fig. 1: Standard position

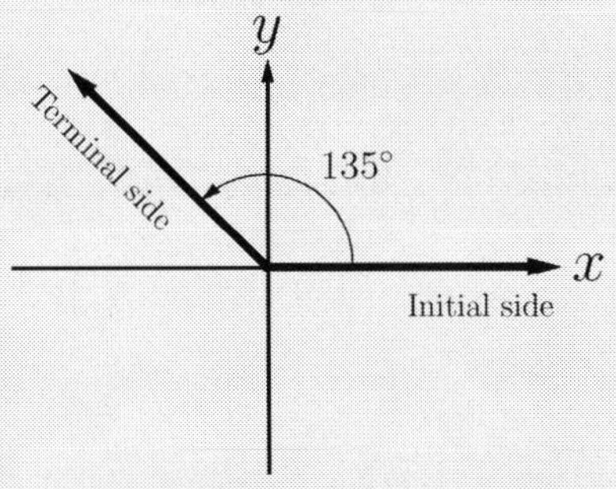

Fig. 2: Positive angle

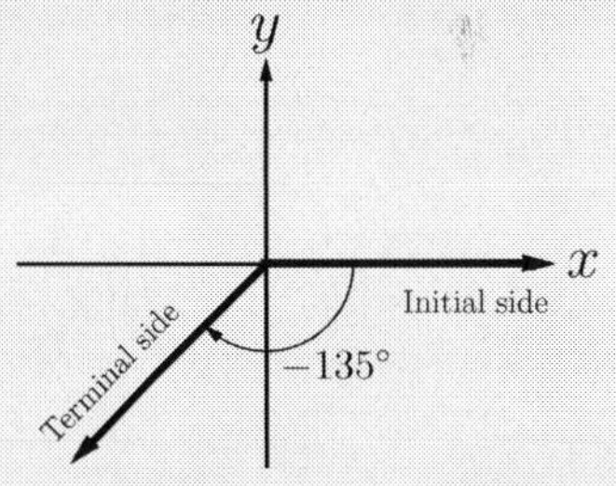

Fig. 3: Negative angle

The angle shows the direction and amount of rotation from the initial side to the terminal side. If the rotation is in a counterclockwise direction, the angle is **positive** shown in Figure 2. Whereas, if the rotation is in a clockwise direction, the angle is **negative** shown in Figure 3.

Coterminal angle are angles in standard position that have a common terminal side. For instance, angles $135°$ and $-225°$, shown in Figure 4, are coterminal angles.

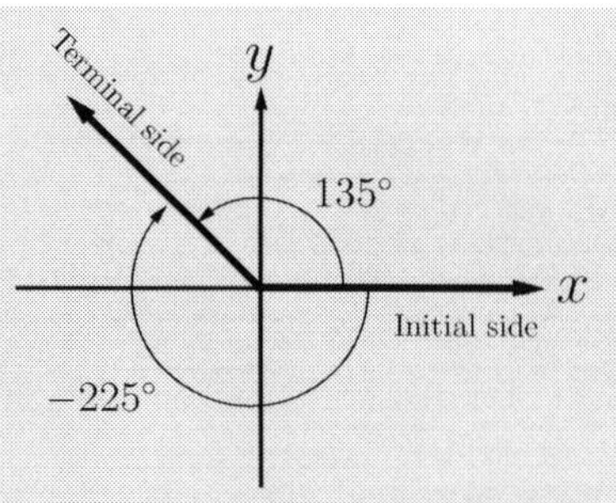

Fig. 4: Coterminal angles

Reference angle, β, is a positive acute angle formed by the terminal side and the closest x-axis, not the y-axis. If the terminal side lies in the first quadrant, reference angle β is the same as angle θ as shown in Figure 5. However, if the terminal side lies in other quadrants, reference angle β is different from the angle θ as shown in Figures 6, 7, and 8.

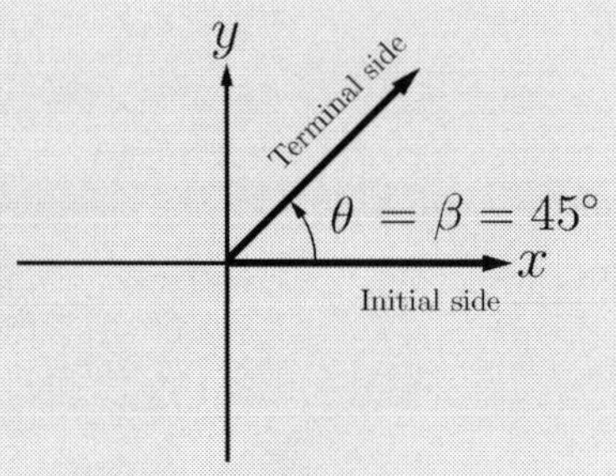

Fig. 5: When θ in the 1st quadrant

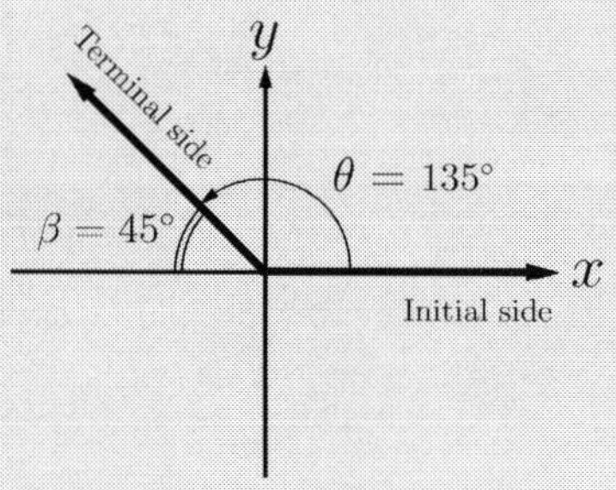

Fig. 6: When θ in the 2nd quadrant

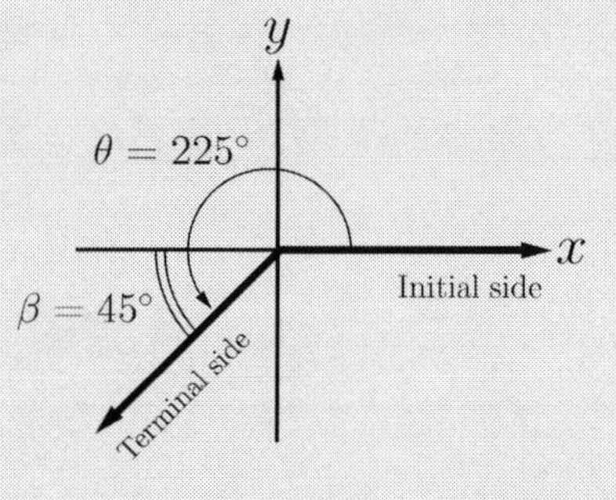

Fig. 7: When θ in the 3rd quadrant

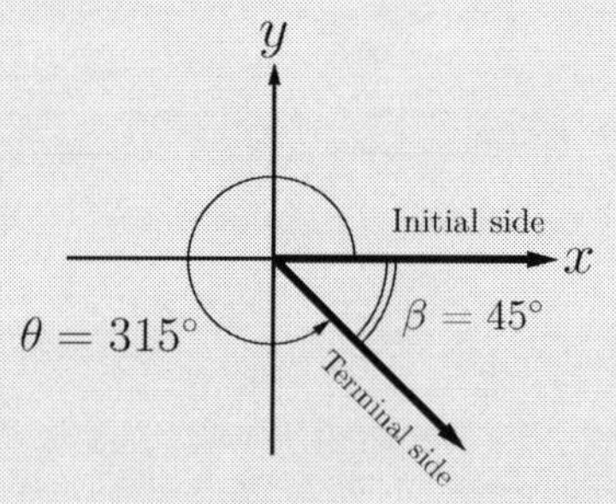

Fig. 8: When θ in the 4th quadrant

Radians

The radian is a very useful angular measure used in mathematics. Mathematicians prefer the radian to the degree (°) because it is a number that does not need an unit symbol. Although the radian can be denoted by the symbol "rad", it is usually omitted.

A **radian** is the measure of an angle θ at which the arc length is equal to the radius of the circle as shown in Figure 9.

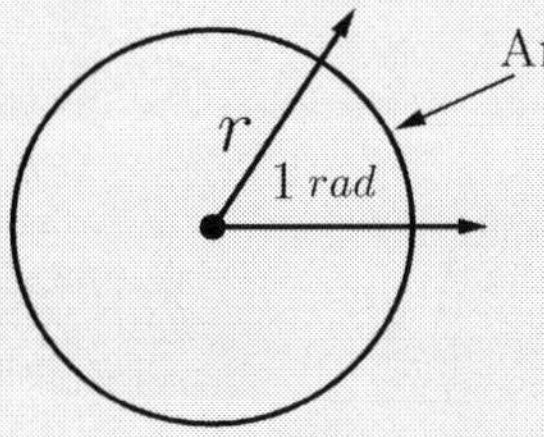

Fig. 9: At 1 radian, arc length = radius

Measuring one radian with a protractor, it is approximately 57.3°. Thus,

$1\,rad \approx 57.3°$ — Multiply each side by $\pi = 3.141592\cdots$

$\pi\,rad = 180°$

Since $\pi\,rad = 180°$, $2\pi\,rad = 360°$.

5.2 Arc length and Area of a sector

Arc length and Area of a sector

An arc, shown in Figure 10, is a part of the circumference of a circle. A part can be expressed as the ratio of the central angle to 360° or 2π.

When θ (°) is given: Arc length $= 2\pi r \times \dfrac{\theta}{360°}$

When θ (rad) is given: Arc length $= \cancel{2\pi} r \times \dfrac{\theta}{\cancel{2\pi}} = r\theta\ (rad)$

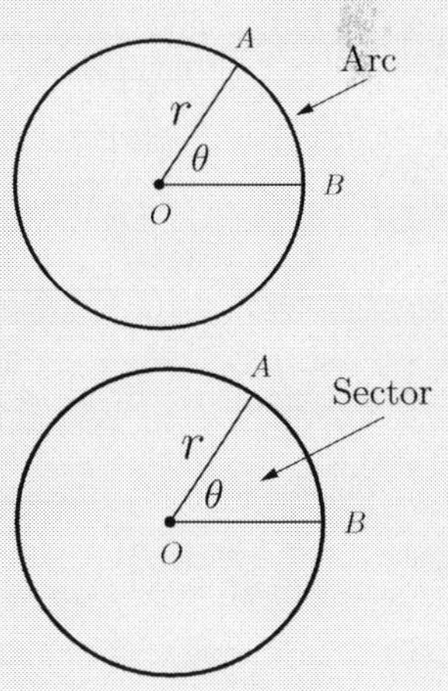

Figure 10

A sector, shown in Figure 10, is a part of the area of a circle. A part can be expressed as the ratio of the central angle to 360° or 2π.

When θ (°) is given: Area of a sector $= \pi r^2 \times \dfrac{\theta}{360°}$

When θ (rad) is given: Area of a sector $= \cancel{\pi} r^2 \times \dfrac{\theta}{2\cancel{\pi}} = \dfrac{1}{2}r^2\theta\ (rad)$

Conversion of Angles Between Degrees and Radians

The table below shows the conversion of angles between degrees and radians.

Degrees	30°	45°	60°	90°	120°	135°	150°	180°
Radians	$\frac{\pi}{6}$	$\frac{\pi}{4}$	$\frac{\pi}{3}$	$\frac{\pi}{2}$	$\frac{2\pi}{3}$	$\frac{3\pi}{4}$	$\frac{5\pi}{6}$	π

Degrees	210°	225°	240°	270°	300°	315°	330°	360°
Radians	$\frac{7\pi}{6}$	$\frac{5\pi}{4}$	$\frac{4\pi}{3}$	$\frac{3\pi}{2}$	$\frac{5\pi}{3}$	$\frac{7\pi}{4}$	$\frac{11\pi}{6}$	2π

Tips

1. To convert degrees to radians, multiply degrees by $\frac{\pi}{180°}$.
2. To convert radians to degrees, multiply radians by $\frac{180°}{\pi}$.

5.3 Definitions of Six Trigonometric Functions

Definitions of Six Trigonometric Functions

The six trigonometric functions are defined as ratios of sides in a right triangle. In the right triangle, shown to the right, the definitions of the six trigonometric functions are as follows:

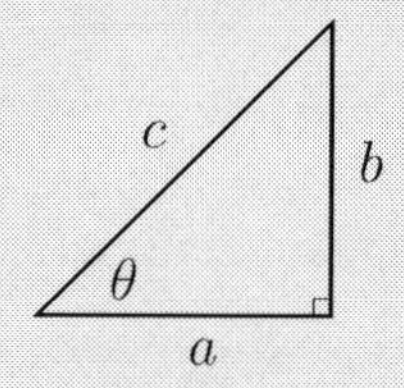

$$\sin\theta = \frac{\text{opposite}}{\text{hypotenuse}} = \frac{b}{c} \qquad \cos\theta = \frac{\text{adjacent}}{\text{hypotenuse}} = \frac{a}{c} \qquad \tan\theta = \frac{\text{opposite}}{\text{adjacent}} = \frac{b}{a}$$

$$\csc\theta = \frac{1}{\sin\theta} = \frac{c}{b} \qquad \sec\theta = \frac{1}{\cos\theta} = \frac{c}{a} \qquad \cot\theta = \frac{1}{\tan\theta} = \frac{a}{b}$$

Tips Note that $\tan\theta = \frac{\sin\theta}{\cos\theta}$ and $\cot\theta = \frac{\cos\theta}{\sin\theta}$.

5.4 Finding the Exact Value of Trigonometric Functions

Finding the Exact Value of Trigonometric Functions

The table below shows the exact value of $\sin\theta$, $\cos\theta$, and $\tan\theta$ at reference angle, β.

	Reference angle, β		
	$30^\circ\ (\frac{\pi}{6})$	$45^\circ\ (\frac{\pi}{4})$	$60^\circ\ (\frac{\pi}{3})$
$\sin\theta$	$\frac{1}{2}$	$\frac{\sqrt{2}}{2}$	$\frac{\sqrt{3}}{2}$
$\cos\theta$	$\frac{\sqrt{3}}{2}$	$\frac{\sqrt{2}}{2}$	$\frac{\sqrt{1}}{2}$
$\tan\theta$	$\frac{\sqrt{3}}{3}$	1	$\sqrt{3}$

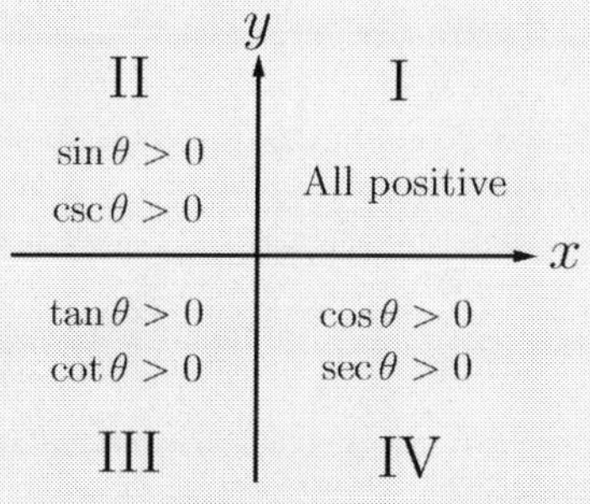

The sign of a trigonometric function is determined by the quadrant the terminal side of the angle (or simply the angle) lies in. The chart above shows which quadrants the six trigonometric functions are positive. For instance, $\sin\theta$ and $\csc\theta$ are positive in the 1st and 2nd quadrants, $\cos\theta$ and $\sec\theta$ are positive in the 1st and 4th quadrants, and $\tan\theta$ and $\cot\theta$ are positive in the 1st and 3rd quadrants.

Evaluating trigonometric functions using the reference angle

When the angle θ lies in the either 2nd, or 3rd, or 4th quadrant, use the following formulas to evaluate the trigonometric functions.

$$\sin\theta = \pm\sin\beta \qquad \cos\theta = \pm\cos\beta \qquad \tan\theta = \pm\tan\beta$$

where β is the reference angle. Note that the sign of a trigonometric function, either $+$ or $-$, is determined by the quadrant the terminal side of the angle lies in.

Let's evaluate $\cos 225^\circ$. As shown in the figure below, the angle $\theta = 225^\circ$ lies in the third quadrant.

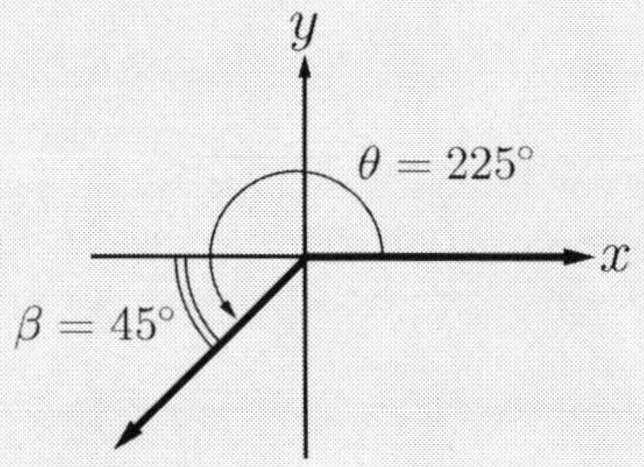

The reference angle β, an angle formed by the terminal side and the closest x-axis, is 45°. Since the angle θ lies in the 3rd quadrant, the sign of the cosine function is negative. Thus,

$$\begin{aligned} \cos 225^\circ &= \pm\cos 45^\circ && \text{Since cosine is negative in the } 3^{\text{rd}} \text{ quadrant} \\ &= -\cos 45^\circ && \text{Since } \cos 45^\circ = \frac{\sqrt{2}}{2} \\ &= -\frac{\sqrt{2}}{2} \end{aligned}$$

Therefore, the exact value of $\cos 225^\circ$ is $-\frac{\sqrt{2}}{2}$.

Example Finding the quadrant where an angle θ lies

Find the quadrant where each of the following angles θ lies.

(a) If $\sin\theta < 0$ and $\cos\theta > 0$

(b) If $\tan\theta < 0$ and $\cos\theta < 0$

(c) If $\cot\theta > 0$ and $\csc\theta < 0$

Solution

(a) $\sin\theta < 0$ indicates that θ lies in the 3rd quadrant or 4th quadrant. Furthermore, $\cos\theta > 0$ indicates that θ lies in the 1st quadrant or 4th quadrant. Thus, θ must be in the 4th quadrant.

(b) $\tan\theta < 0$ indicates that θ lies in the 2nd quadrant or 4th quadrant. Furthermore, $\cos\theta < 0$ indicates that θ lies in the 2nd quadrant or 3rd quadrant. Thus, θ must be in the 2nd quadrant.

(c) $\cot\theta > 0$ indicates that θ lies in the 1st quadrant or 3rd quadrant. Furthermore, $\csc\theta < 0$ indicates that θ lies in the 3rd quadrant or 4th quadrant. Thus, θ must be in the 3rd quadrant.

Example Finding exact values of trigonometric functions

If $\cos\theta = -\frac{3}{5}$ and $\sin\theta > 0$, find the exact value of each of the remaining trigonometric functions.

Solution $\cos\theta$ is negative in the 2nd and 3rd quadrants, and $\sin\theta$ is positive in the 1st and 2nd quadrants. Thus, θ must be in the 2nd quadrant. Since $\cos\theta = -\frac{3}{5}$, the length of the hypotenuse of a right triangle is 5 and the length of the adjacent side of θ is 3 as shown below. Thus, the length of the opposite side of θ is 4 using the Pythagorean theorem: $c^2 = a^2 + b^2$.

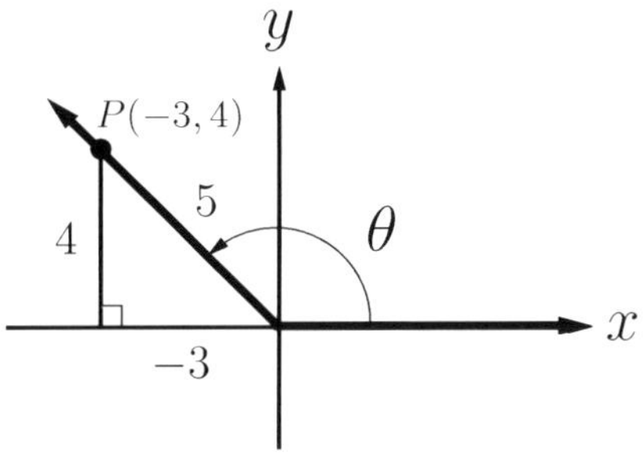

Suppose point $P(x, y)$ is on the terminal side of θ. Since θ lies in the 2nd quadrant, the x and y coordinates of point P is $(-3, 4)$. Use the definition of the trigonometric functions to find the exact values of the remaining trigonometric functions.

$$\sin\theta = \frac{\text{opposite}}{\text{hypotenuse}} = \frac{4}{5} \qquad \cos\theta = \frac{\text{adjacent}}{\text{hypotenuse}} = -\frac{3}{5} \qquad \tan\theta = \frac{\text{opposite}}{\text{adjacent}} = -\frac{4}{3}$$

$$\csc\theta = \frac{1}{\sin\theta} = \frac{5}{4} \qquad \sec\theta = \frac{1}{\cos\theta} = -\frac{5}{3} \qquad \cot\theta = \frac{1}{\tan\theta} = -\frac{3}{4}$$

5.5 Pythagorean Identities

Pythagorean Identities

$$\sin^2\theta + \cos^2\theta = 1 \qquad 1 + \tan^2\theta = \sec^2\theta \qquad 1 + \cot^2\theta = \csc^2\theta$$

Tips

1. Note that $\sin^2\theta = (\sin\theta)^2$ and $\cos^2\theta = (\cos\theta)^2$.
2. The following variations of the Pythagorean identities are often used.

$$\sin^2\theta = 1 - \cos^2\theta, \qquad \cos^2\theta = 1 - \sin^2\theta$$

5.6 Even-Odd Properties

Even-Odd Properties

Knowing whether a trigonometric function is odd or even is useful when evaluating the trigonometric function of a negative angle. $\sin\theta$, $\csc\theta$, $\tan\theta$, and $\cot\theta$ are odd functions that satisfy $f(-\theta) = -f(\theta)$ for all θ. Whereas, $\cos\theta$ and $\sec\theta$ are even functions that satisfy $f(-\theta) = f(\theta)$ for all θ. Below is a summary of the even-odd properties for the six trigonometric functions.

$$\sin(-\theta) = -\sin\theta \qquad \csc(-\theta) = -\csc\theta$$
$$\cos(-\theta) = \cos\theta \qquad \sec(-\theta) = \sec\theta$$
$$\tan(-\theta) = -\tan\theta \qquad \cot(-\theta) = -\cot\theta$$

Example **Finding exact values using even-odd properties**

Find the exact value of the following expressions.

(a) $\sin(-30°)$

(b) $\cos(-\frac{\pi}{6})$

Solution

(a) Since $\sin(-\theta) = -\sin\theta$, $\sin(-30°) = -\sin(30°) = -\frac{1}{2}$.

(b) Since $\cos(-\theta) = \cos\theta$, $\cos(-\frac{\pi}{6}) = \cos(\frac{\pi}{6}) = \frac{\sqrt{3}}{2}$.

5.7 Cofunctions Identities

Cofunctions Identities

Two angles are **complementary** if their sum is equal to 90°. The following cofunction identities show relationships between sine and cosine, tangent and cotangent, and secant and cosecant. The value of a trigonometric function of an angle is equal to the value of the cofunction of the complementary of the angle.

$$\sin(90° - \theta) = \cos\theta \qquad \tan(90° - \theta) = \cot\theta \qquad \sec(90° - \theta) = \csc\theta$$

For instance, 50° and 40° are complementary angles. Thus,

$$\sin 50° = \cos 40° \qquad \tan 50° = \cot 40° \qquad \sec 50° = \csc 40°$$

Tips

Since $180° = \pi$ radians, $90° = \frac{\pi}{2}$ radians. Thus, the cofunction identities can be expressed in radians.

$$\sin\left(\frac{\pi}{2} - \theta\right) = \cos\theta \qquad \tan\left(\frac{\pi}{2} - \theta\right) = \cot\theta \qquad \sec\left(\frac{\pi}{2} - \theta\right) = \csc\theta$$

5.8 Graphs of Six Trigonometric Functions

Graphs of Six Trigonometric Functions

Below are the graphs of the six trigonometric functions: sine, cosine, tangent, cosecant, secant, and cotangent.

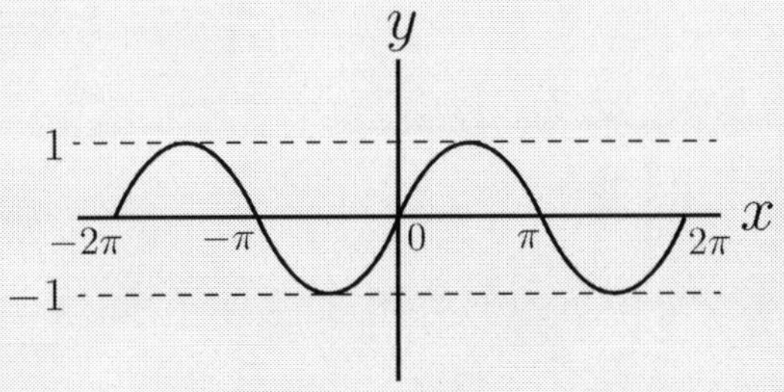

$y = \sin x$

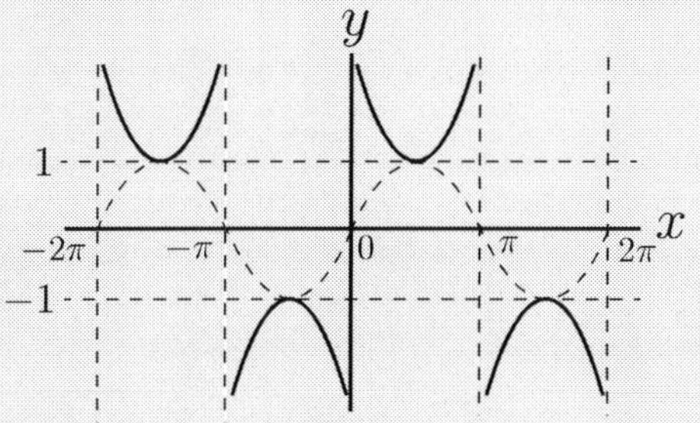

$y = \csc x$

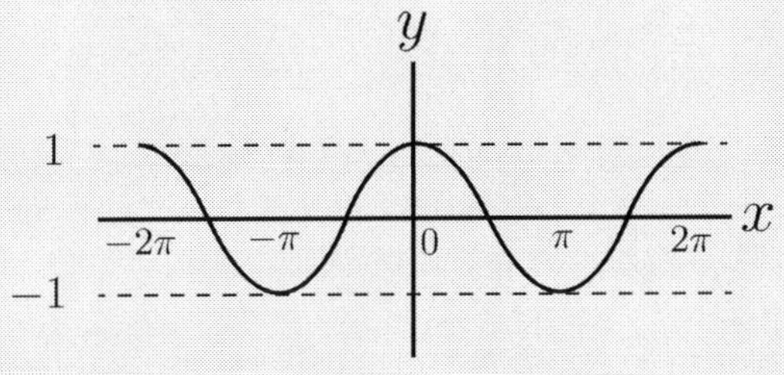

$y = \cos x$

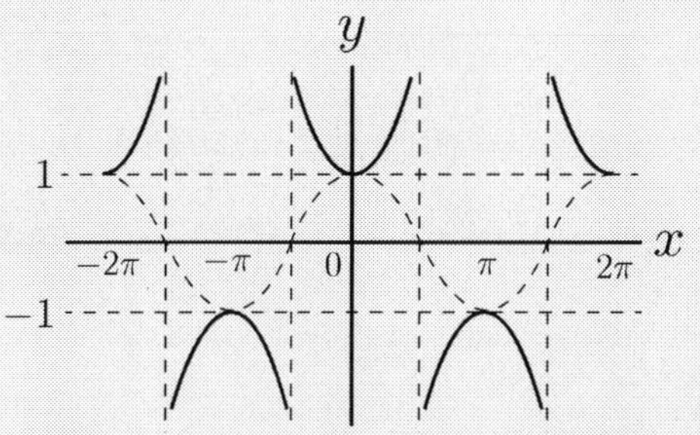

$y = \sec x$

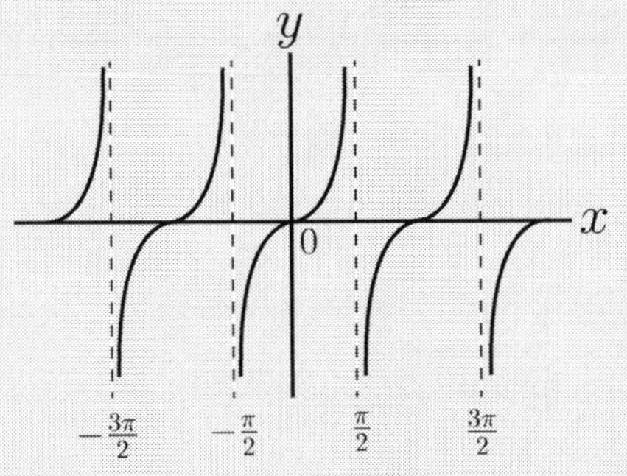

$y = \tan x$

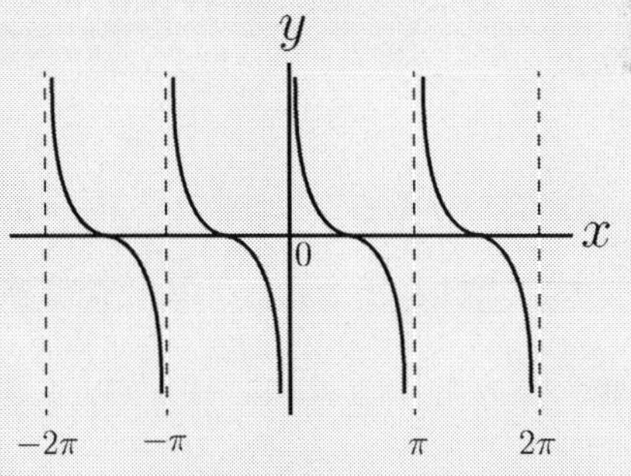

$y = \cot x$

5.9 Finding amplitude, period, horizontal translation, and vertical translation

Graphing the Sine and Cosine Functions

The general forms of the sine function and cosine function are as follows:

$$y = A\sin\left(B(x-C)\right)+D \qquad \text{or} \qquad y = A\cos\left(B(x-C)\right)+D$$

where A, B, C and D affect the amplitude, period, horizontal translation(horizontal shift), and vertical translation(vertical shift) of the graphs of the sine and cosine functions.

- A affects the amplitude. The amplitude is half the distance between the maximum and minimum values of the function. Since distance is always positive, the amplitude is $|A|$. For instance, both $y = 2\sin x$ and $y = -2\cos x$ have an amplitude of 2.

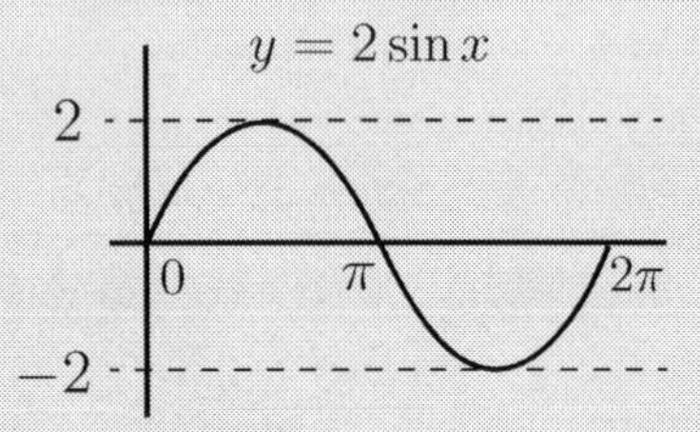

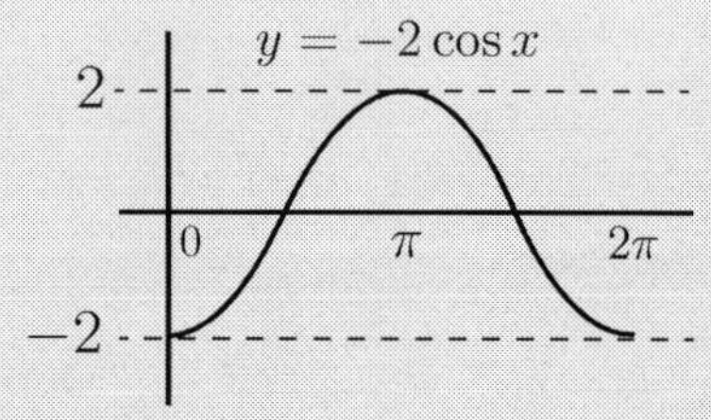

- B affects the period. The period, P, is the horizontal length of one complete cycle obtained by $P = \frac{2\pi}{B}$. For instance, the period of $y = \sin(2x)$ is $\frac{2\pi}{2} = \pi$, and the period of $y = \cos(\frac{1}{3}x)$ is $\frac{2\pi}{\frac{1}{3}} = 6\pi$.

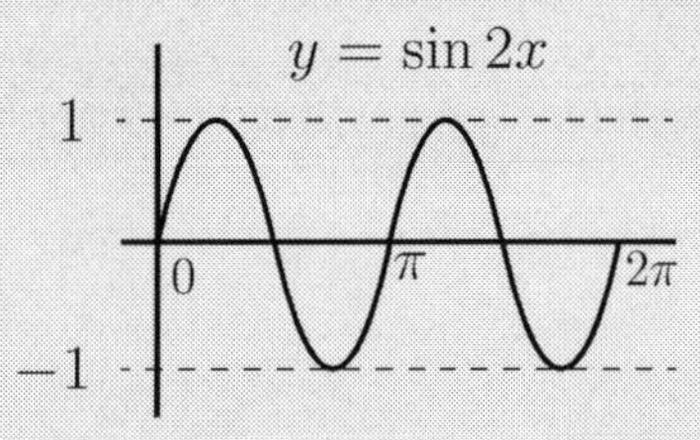

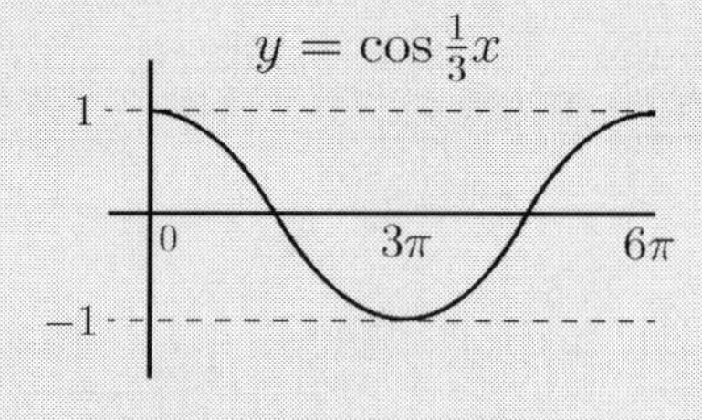

- C affects the horizontal translation. The horizontal translation is the measure of how far the graph has shifted horizontally. For instance, $y = \sin(x - \frac{\pi}{4})$ means a horizontal shift of $\frac{\pi}{4}$ to the right. Whereas, $y = \cos(x + \frac{\pi}{2})$ means a horizontal shift of $\frac{\pi}{2}$ to the left.

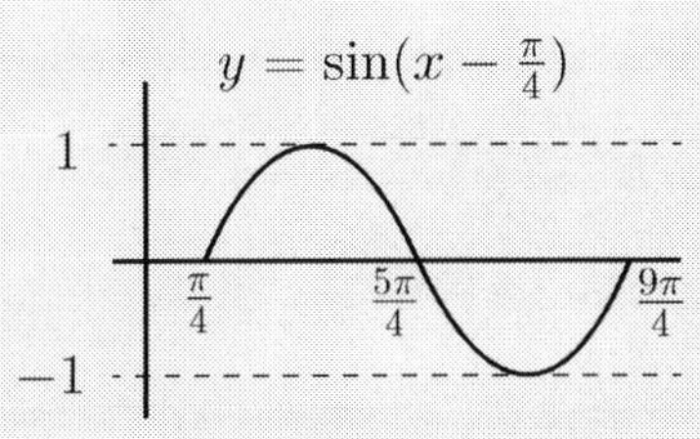

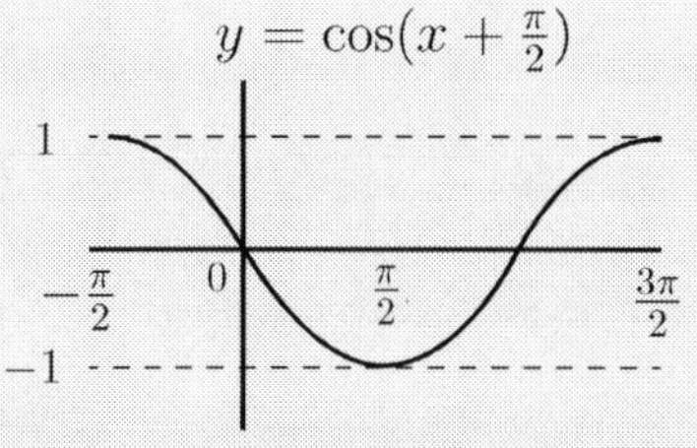

- D affects the vertical translation. The vertical translation is the measure of how far the graph has shifted vertically. For instance, $y = \sin x + 1$ means a vertical shift of 1 up. Whereas, $y = \cos x - 2$ means a vertical shift of 2 down.

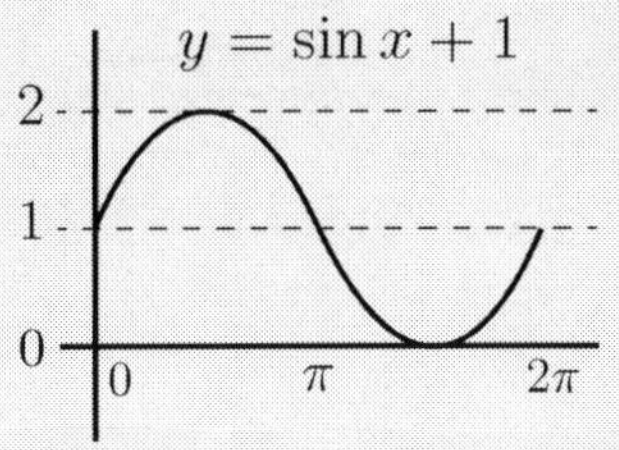

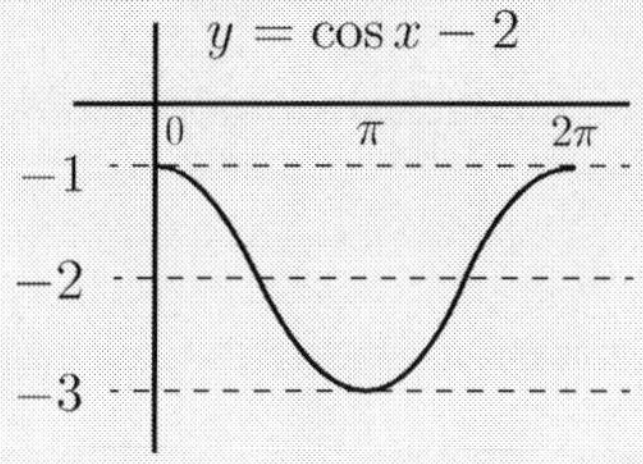

Graphing the Tangent Functions

The general form of the tangent functions is as follows:

$$y = A\tan\left(B(x - C)\right) + D$$

where B, C and D affect the period, horizontal translation(horizontal shift), and vertical translation(vertical shift) of the graphs of the tangent functions.

- The tangent function does not have an amplitude because it has no maximum or minimum value. If $|A| > 1$, the graph of the tangent function is vertically stretched. Whereas, if $0 < |A| < 1$, the graph of the tangent function is vertically compressed.
- B affects the period. The tangent function has the period of $\frac{\pi}{B}$ as opposed to the sine and cosine functions which have the period of $\frac{2\pi}{B}$. For instance, the period of $y = \tan(2x)$ is $\frac{\pi}{2}$. The graph of $y = \tan(2x)$ is shown in Figure 1.
- C affects the horizontal translation. For instance, $y = \tan(x - \frac{\pi}{2})$ means a horizontal translation of $\frac{\pi}{2}$ to the right. The graph of $y = \tan(x - \frac{\pi}{2})$ is shown in Figure 2.
- D affects the vertical translation. For instance, $y = \tan x + 3$ means a vertical translation of 3 up. The graph of $y = \tan x + 3$ is shown in Figure 3.

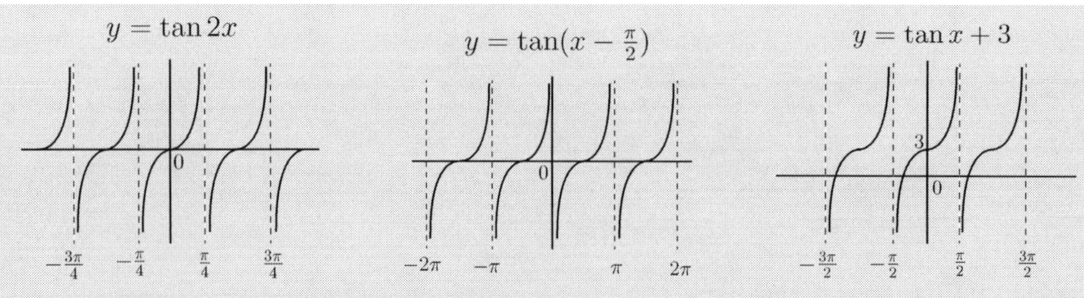

Figure 1 Figure 2 Figure 3

Example Finding amplitude, period, horizontal and vertical translation

Find the amplitude, period, horizontal and vertical translations of the following trigonometric functions.

(a) $y = 2\cos(x - \frac{\pi}{6}) + 1$

(b) $y = -3\sin(2x + \frac{\pi}{2}) - 2$

(c) $y = \tan(\frac{1}{2}x - \frac{\pi}{4}) + 3$

Solution

(a) Comparing $y = 2\cos(x - \frac{\pi}{6}) + 1$ to the general form of $y = A\cos\big(B(x - C)\big) + D$, we found that $A = 2$, $B = 1$, $C = \frac{\pi}{6}$, and $D = 1$. Thus, the amplitude is 2. The period, P, is $P = \frac{2\pi}{B} = \frac{2\pi}{1} = 2\pi$. The horizontal translation is $\frac{\pi}{6}$ to the right, and the vertical translation is 1 up.

(b) Change $y = -3\sin(2x + \frac{\pi}{2}) - 2$ to $y = -3\sin\big(2(x - (-\frac{\pi}{4}))\big) - 2$. Then, compare $y = -3\sin\big(2(x - (-\frac{\pi}{4}))\big) - 2$ to $y = A\sin\big(B(x - C)\big) + D$. We found that $A = -3$, $B = 2$, $C = -\frac{\pi}{4}$, and $D = -2$. Thus, the amplitude is $|-3| = 3$. The period, P, is $P = \frac{2\pi}{B} = \frac{2\pi}{2} = \pi$. The horizontal translation is $\frac{\pi}{4}$ to the left, and the vertical translation is 2 down.

(c) Change $y = \tan(\frac{1}{2}x - \frac{\pi}{4}) + 3$ to $y = \tan(\frac{1}{2}(x - \frac{\pi}{2})) + 3$. Then compare $y = \tan(\frac{1}{2}(x - \frac{\pi}{2})) + 3$ to $y = A\tan\big(B(x - C)\big) + D$. We found that $A = 1$, $B = \frac{1}{2}$, $C = \frac{\pi}{2}$, and $D = 3$. The tangent function does not have an amplitude because it has no maximum or minimum value. The period, P, is $P = \frac{\pi}{B} = \frac{\pi}{\frac{1}{2}} = 2\pi$. The horizontal translation is $\frac{\pi}{2}$ to the right, and the vertical translation is 3 up.

Example Finding range of a trigonometric function

Find the range of the following trigonometric functions.

(a) $y = 2\sin(2x - 1) + 1$

(b) $y = -3\cos(x + \frac{\pi}{2}) - 2$

Solution

(a) For any angle x, the range of a sine function is $[-1, 1]$. For instance, both sine functions, $\sin x$ and $\sin(2x-1)$ have the range of $[-1, 1]$.

$$
\begin{aligned}
-1 &\le \sin(2x-1) \le 1 && \text{Multiply each side of inequality by 2}\\
-2 &\le 2\sin(2x-1) \le 2 && \text{Add 1 to each side of inequality}\\
-1 &\le 2\sin(2x-1)+1 \le 3
\end{aligned}
$$

Thus, the range of $y = 2\sin(2x-1)+1$ is $[-1, 3]$.

(b) For any angle x, the range of a cosine function is $[-1, 1]$.

$$
\begin{aligned}
-1 &\le \cos\left(x+\frac{\pi}{2}\right) \le 1 && \text{Multiply each side of inequality by } -3\\
-3 &\le -3\cos\left(x+\frac{\pi}{2}\right) \le 3 && \text{Subtract 2 from each side of inequality}\\
-5 &\le -3\cos\left(x+\frac{\pi}{2}\right)-2 \le 1
\end{aligned}
$$

Thus, the range of $y = -3\cos(x+\frac{\pi}{2})-2$ is $[-5, 1]$.

Example Finding period from the graph of a trigonometric function

Graph $y = |\sin 2x|$, $0 \le x \le 2\pi$ and find the period of $|\sin 2x|$.

Solution The period, P, of $y = \sin 2x$ is $P = \frac{2\pi}{2} = \pi$, which indicates that there are two complete cycles in the interval $[0, 2\pi]$ as shown in Figure 4.

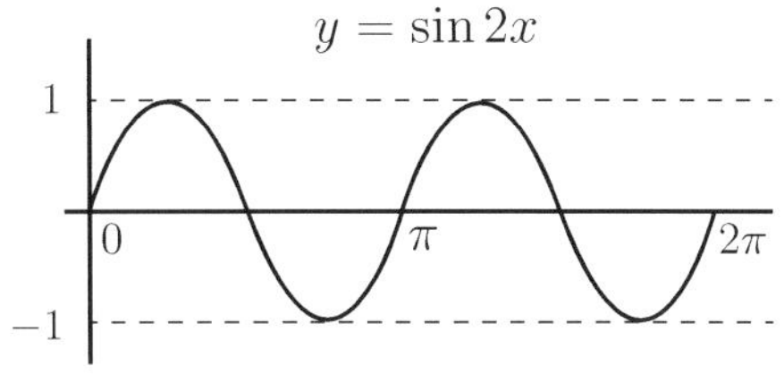

Figure 4

In order to graph $y = |\sin 2x|$, determine the part of the graph of $y = \sin 2x$ that lies below the x-axis as shown in Figure 5.

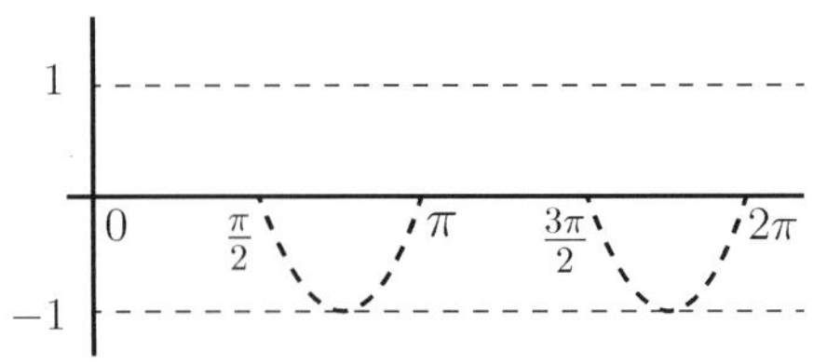

Figure 5

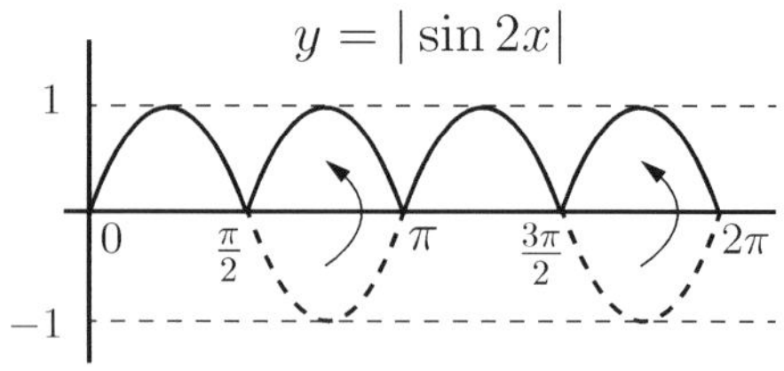

Figure 6

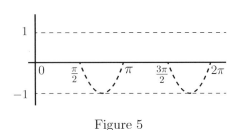

Lastly, reflect the part of the graph that lies below the x-axis about the x-axis as shown in Figure 6. Since the graph of $y = |\sin 2x|$ completes its cycle every $\frac{\pi}{2}$, the period $y = |\sin 2x|$ is $\frac{\pi}{2}$.

5.10 Angle Formulas

Angle Formulas

- Sum and difference Formulas

$$\sin(\alpha + \beta) = \sin\alpha\cos\beta + \cos\alpha\sin\beta \qquad \sin(\alpha - \beta) = \sin\alpha\cos\beta - \cos\alpha\sin\beta$$
$$\cos(\alpha + \beta) = \cos\alpha\cos\beta - \sin\alpha\sin\beta \qquad \cos(\alpha - \beta) = \cos\alpha\cos\beta + \sin\alpha\sin\beta$$
$$\tan(\alpha + \beta) = \frac{\tan\alpha + \tan\beta}{1 - \tan\alpha\tan\beta} \qquad \tan(\alpha - \beta) = \frac{\tan\alpha - \tan\beta}{1 + \tan\alpha\tan\beta}$$

- Double-Angle Formulas

$$\sin 2\theta = 2\sin\theta\cos\theta$$
$$\begin{aligned}\cos 2\theta &= \cos^2\theta - \sin^2\theta \\ &= 2\cos^2\theta - 1 \\ &= 1 - 2\sin^2\theta\end{aligned}$$

- Half-Angle Formulas

$$\begin{aligned}\sin\frac{\theta}{2} &= \pm\sqrt{\frac{1-\cos\theta}{2}} \\ \cos\frac{\theta}{2} &= \pm\sqrt{\frac{1+\cos\theta}{2}} \\ \tan\frac{\theta}{2} &= \pm\sqrt{\frac{1-\cos\theta}{1+\cos\theta}} = \frac{1-\cos\theta}{\sin\theta} = \frac{\sin\theta}{1+\cos\theta}\end{aligned}$$

Tips

1. Using the sum formula for cosine, the double-angle formula for cosine can be derived as follows:

$$\begin{aligned}\cos 2\theta &= \cos(\theta+\theta)\\ &= \cos\theta\cdot\cos\theta - \sin\theta\cdot\sin\theta\\ &= \cos^2\theta - \sin^2\theta\end{aligned}$$

2. Using the half-angle formulas, $\sin\theta$ and $\sin 2\theta$ can be derived as follows:

$$\sin\theta = \pm\sqrt{\frac{1-\cos 2\theta}{2}}$$
$$\sin 2\theta = \pm\sqrt{\frac{1-\cos 4\theta}{2}}$$

Compound Angles

The following compound angles are obtained by adding or subtracting $30°(=\frac{\pi}{6})$, $45°(=\frac{\pi}{4})$, and $60°(=\frac{\pi}{3})$.

$$15° = 60° - 45° \qquad 75° = 30° + 45° \qquad 105° = 60° + 45°$$

$$\frac{\pi}{12} = \frac{\pi}{3} - \frac{\pi}{4} \qquad \frac{5\pi}{12} = \frac{\pi}{6} + \frac{\pi}{4} \qquad \frac{7\pi}{12} = \frac{\pi}{3} + \frac{\pi}{4}$$

Tips When you make compound angles, make sure you include $45°$ or $\frac{\pi}{4}$.

Example **Finding exact values using sum formula**

Find the exact value of $\cos\dfrac{5\pi}{12}$.

Solution

$$\begin{aligned}\cos\frac{5\pi}{12} &= \cos\left(\frac{\pi}{6}+\frac{\pi}{4}\right)\\ &= \cos\frac{\pi}{6}\cos\frac{\pi}{4}-\sin\frac{\pi}{6}\sin\frac{\pi}{4}\\ &= \frac{\sqrt{3}}{2}\cdot\frac{\sqrt{2}}{2}-\frac{1}{2}\cdot\frac{\sqrt{2}}{2}\\ &= \frac{\sqrt{6}}{4}-\frac{\sqrt{2}}{4}\\ &= \frac{\sqrt{6}-\sqrt{2}}{4}\end{aligned}$$

Example Finding exact values using double-angle formula

If $\sin\theta = -\frac{12}{13}$, $\pi < \theta < \frac{3\pi}{2}$, find the exact values of $\sin 2\theta$ and $\cos 2\theta$.

Solution $\pi < \theta < \frac{3\pi}{2}$ indicates that θ lies in the 3rd quadrant. Since $\sin\theta = -\frac{12}{13}$, the length of the hypotenuse of a right triangle is 13 and the length of the opposite side of θ is 12 as shown below. Thus, the length of the adjacent side of θ is 5 using the Pythagorean theorem.

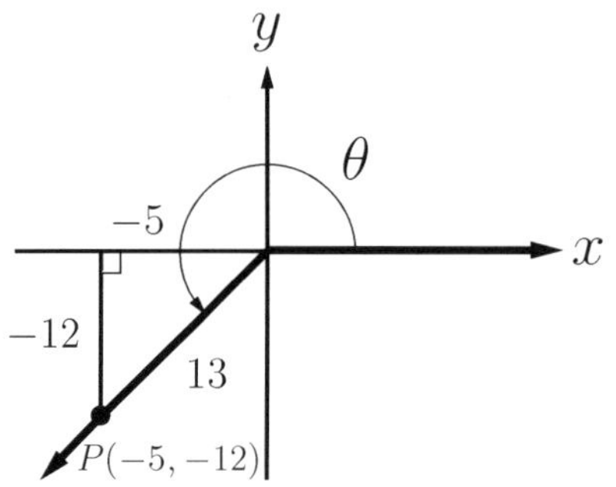

Suppose point $P(x, y)$ is on the terminal side of θ. Since θ lies in the 3rd quadrant, the x and y coordinates of point P is $(-5, -12)$ and $\cos\theta = -\frac{5}{13}$. Thus,

$$\sin 2\theta = 2\sin\theta\cos\theta = 2\left(-\frac{12}{13}\right)\left(-\frac{5}{13}\right) = \frac{120}{169}$$

$$\cos 2\theta = 1-2\sin^2\theta = 1-2\left(-\frac{12}{13}\right)^2 = 1-2\left(\frac{144}{169}\right) = -\frac{119}{169}$$

5.11 The Inverse Trigonometric Functions

The Restricted Domains of Trigonometric Functions

A function that passes the horizontal line test to have an inverse is **one-to-one**. Since all trigonometric functions are periodic, none of them are one-to-one. This means that none of them have inverse functions unless the domain of each is restricted.

Restricted Domain		
Function	Domain	Range
$\sin x$	$[\frac{-\pi}{2}, \frac{\pi}{2}]$	$[-1, 1]$
$\cos x$	$[0, \pi]$	$[-1, 1]$
$\tan x$	$(\frac{-\pi}{2}, \frac{\pi}{2})$	$(-\infty, \infty)$
$\csc x$	$[-\frac{\pi}{2}, 0) \cup (0, \frac{\pi}{2}]$	$(-\infty, -1] \cup [1, \infty)$
$\sec x$	$[0, \frac{\pi}{2}) \cup (\frac{\pi}{2}, \pi]$	$(-\infty, -1] \cup [1, \infty)$
$\cot x$	$(0, \pi)$	$(-\infty, \infty)$

The Inverse Trigonometric Functions

When the trigonometric functions have restricted domains, they become one-to-one functions so that they have their inverse functions. For the inverse sine function, we use the notation $\sin^{-1}(x)$ or $\arcsin(x)$.

The following table summarizes the domain and range of the inverse trigonometric functions. Note that for each inverse trig function, we have simply swapped the domain and range for the corresponding trigonometric function.

Domain and Range of Inverse Trig. Functions		
Inverse Function	Domain	Range
$\sin^{-1} x$	$[-1, 1]$	$[\frac{-\pi}{2}, \frac{\pi}{2}]$
$\cos^{-1} x$	$[-1, 1]$	$[0, \pi]$
$\tan^{-1} x$	$(-\infty, \infty)$	$(\frac{-\pi}{2}, \frac{\pi}{2})$
$\cot^{-1} x$	$(-\infty, \infty)$	$(0, \pi)$
$\sec^{-1} x$	$(-\infty, -1] \cup [1, \infty)$	$[0, \frac{\pi}{2}) \cup (\frac{\pi}{2}, \pi]$
$\csc^{-1} x$	$(-\infty, -1] \cup [1, \infty)$	$[-\frac{\pi}{2}, 0) \cup (0, \frac{\pi}{2}]$

Tips

1. Note that $\sin^{-1} x \neq \frac{1}{\sin x}$.
2. $\sin\theta = \text{value} \Longrightarrow \theta = \sin^{-1}(\text{value})$.

Example Finding the exact value of the inverse trig. function

Find the exact value of $\sin^{-1}\big(-\frac{1}{2}\big)$.

Solution Let $\theta = \sin^{-1}\big(-\frac{1}{2}\big)$.

$$\theta = \sin^{-1}\Big(-\frac{1}{2}\Big)$$
$$\sin\theta = -\frac{1}{2}$$

When $\theta = \frac{7\pi}{6}$ or $\theta = -\frac{\pi}{6}$, $\sin\theta = -\frac{1}{2}$. The only angle within the interval $-\frac{\pi}{2} \leq \theta \leq \frac{\pi}{2}$ is $-\frac{\pi}{6}$. Therefore, $\sin^{-1}\big(-\frac{1}{2}\big) = -\frac{\pi}{6}$.

Example Finding the exact value of the inverse trig. function

Find the exact value of $\tan\Big(\cos^{-1}\big(-\frac{3}{5}\big)\Big)$.

Solution Let $\theta = \cos^{-1}\big(-\frac{3}{5}\big)$.

$$\theta = \cos^{-1}\Big(-\frac{3}{5}\Big)$$
$$\cos\theta = -\frac{3}{5}$$

When θ is in either Quadrant II or Quadrant III, $\cos\theta$ is negative. The only angle within the interval $0 \le \theta \le \pi$ is in Quadrant II as shown below.

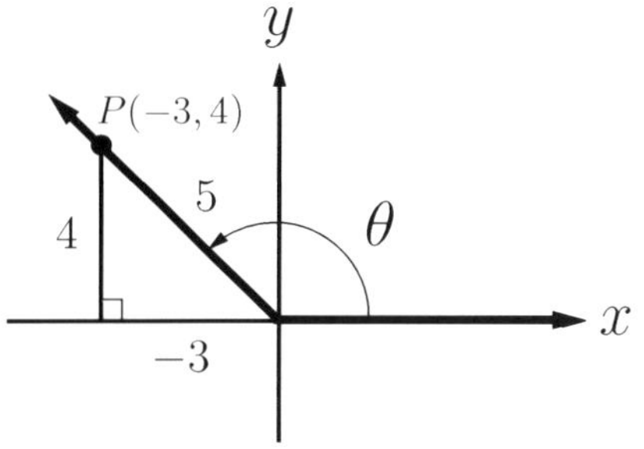

Therefore, $\tan\left(\cos^{-1}\left(-\frac{3}{5}\right)\right) = \tan\theta = -\frac{4}{3}$.

5.12 Solving Trigonometric Equations

Solving Trigonometric Equations

A trigonometric equation is an equation that involves trigonometric functions. The solutions of the trigonometric equation are the angles that satisfy the equation. In most cases, the Pythagorean Identities, factoring, the distributive property, or other algebraic skills are used to find the solutions of the equation.

Let's solve the trigonometric equation: $\sin\theta = -\frac{\sqrt{2}}{2}$, $0 \le \theta < 2\pi$.

First, find the reference angle β for which $\sin\beta = \frac{\sqrt{2}}{2}$. The reference angle is $\beta = 45°$. Since the sine function is negative, the angle θ lies in either 3rd quadrant or 4th quadrant as shown below.

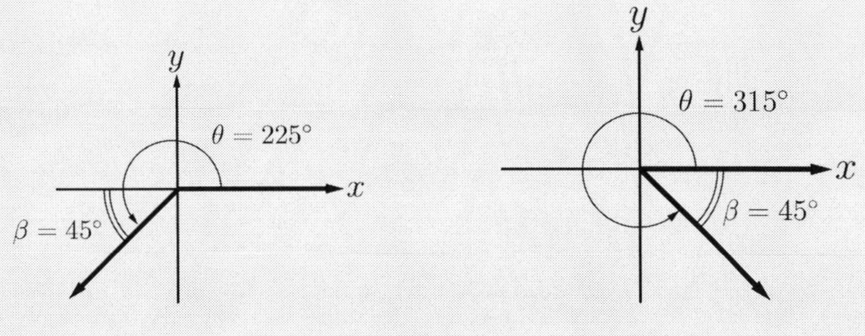

Therefore, the solutions of the equation are $225°$ (or $\frac{5\pi}{4}$) or $315°$ (or $\frac{7\pi}{4}$).

Example Solving a trigonometric equation

Solve the equation: $2\sin^2\theta - 5\sin\theta + 2 = 0,\ \ 0 \le \theta < 2\pi$.

Solution Factor the expression $2\sin^2\theta - 5\sin\theta + 2$ and solve for θ.

$$2\sin^2\theta - 5\sin\theta + 2 = 0 \qquad \text{Factor}$$
$$(\sin\theta - 2)(2\sin\theta - 1) = 0 \qquad \text{Solve}$$
$$\sin\theta = 2 \quad \text{or} \quad \sin\theta = \frac{1}{2}$$

Since $-1 \le \sin\theta \le 1$ for any angle θ, the equation $\sin\theta = 2$ has no solution. The solutions to $\sin\theta = \frac{1}{2}$, where $0 \le \theta < 2\pi$ are $\frac{\pi}{6}$ and $\frac{5\pi}{6}$ or 30° and 150°.

Example Solving a trigonometric equation

Solve the equation: $\sin\theta + \cos\theta = 1,\ \ 0 \le \theta < 2\pi$.

Solution Square each side of the equation.

$$\sin\theta + \cos\theta = 1$$
$$(\sin\theta + \cos\theta)^2 = 1$$
$$\sin^2\theta + 2\sin\theta\cos\theta + \cos^2\theta = 1 \qquad \sin^2\theta + \cos^2\theta = 1$$
$$2\sin\theta\cos\theta = 0$$

Thus, $\sin\theta = 0$ or $\cos\theta = 0$. Therefore, solutions to $\sin\theta + \cos\theta = 1$ are 0, π, $\frac{\pi}{2}$, and $\frac{3\pi}{2}$.

Example Solving a trigonometric equation

Solve the equation: $\cos 2\theta = \cos\theta,\ \ 0 \le \theta < 2\pi$.

Solution Use $\cos 2\theta = 2\cos^2\theta - 1$.

$$\cos 2\theta = \cos\theta$$
$$2\cos^2\theta - 1 = \cos\theta$$
$$2\cos^2\theta - \cos\theta - 1 = 0$$
$$(2\cos\theta + 1)(\cos\theta - 1) = 0$$

Thus, $\cos\theta = -\frac{1}{2}$ or $\cos\theta = 1$. Therefore, solutions to $\cos 2\theta = \cos\theta$ are $\frac{2\pi}{3}$, $\frac{4\pi}{3}$ and 0.

5.13 The Area of a SAS Triangle

The Area of a SAS Triangle

If triangle ABC shown at the right is a SAS triangle (a, b, and $m\angle C$ are known), the area of triangle ABC is as follows:

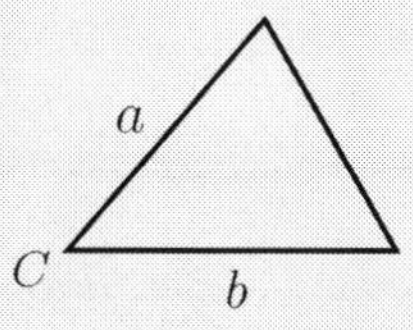

$$A = \frac{1}{2}ab\sin C$$

For instance, if triangle ABC shown at the right is a SAS triangle with $a = 5$, $b = 8$, and $m\angle C = 50°$, the area of triangle ABC is shown below.

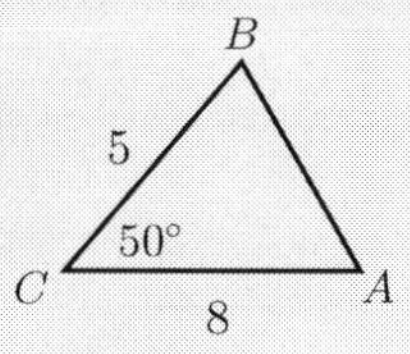

$$A = \frac{1}{2}(5)(8)\sin 50° \approx 15.32$$

5.14 Solving Triangles

Solving Triangles

Solving a triangle means finding the missing lengths of its sides and the measures of its angles. In general, solving a triangle can be classified as either solving a right triangle or solving a non-right triangle. The general rules for solving triangles are as follows:

- To solve a right triangle, use the definition of the six trigonometric functions or the Pythagorean theorem.
- To solve a non-right triangle, use the Law of Sines or Law of Cosines.

Solving Non-Right Triangles

Classifying non-right triangles

Depending on the information about the sides and angles given, non-right triangles can be classified as follows:

- ASA triangle: Two angles and the included side are known.
- SAA triangle: One side and two angles are known.
- SAS triangle: Two sides and the included angle are known.
- SSS triangle: Three sides are known.

The general rules for solving non-right triangles are as follows:

- To solve ASA and SAA triangles, use the Law of Sines.
- To solve SAS and SSS triangles, use the Law of Cosines.

Tips

1. If none of the angles of a triangle is a right angle, the triangle is called either a non-right triangle or an oblique triangle.
2. SSA (Two sides and one angle opposite one of them) triangle is referred to as the **ambiguous case** because the given information may result in one triangle, two triangles, or no triangle.

5.15 The Law of Sines

The Law of Sines (ASA and SAA)

If a, b, and c are the lengths of the sides of a triangle, and A, B, and C are the opposite angles, then

$$\frac{a}{\sin A} = \frac{b}{\sin B} = \frac{c}{\sin C}$$

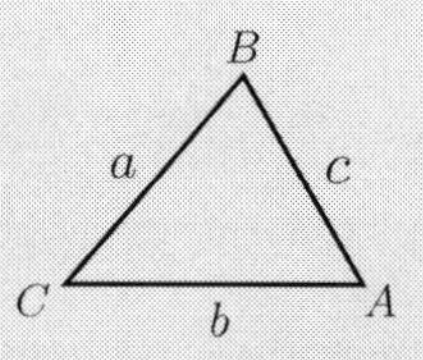

The Law of Sines implies that the largest angle is opposite the longest side and the smallest angle is opposite the shortest side. For instance, let a and c be the sides opposite the angles A and C of the triangle above, respectively. The Law of Sines satisfies the following:

$$\text{If } m\angle C < m\angle A \implies c < a$$
$$\text{If } c < a \implies m\angle C < m\angle A$$

Let's solve a non-right triangle ABC shown at the right. If $a = 8$, $m\angle A = 60°$ and $m\angle C = 40°$, find $m\angle B$, b, and c.

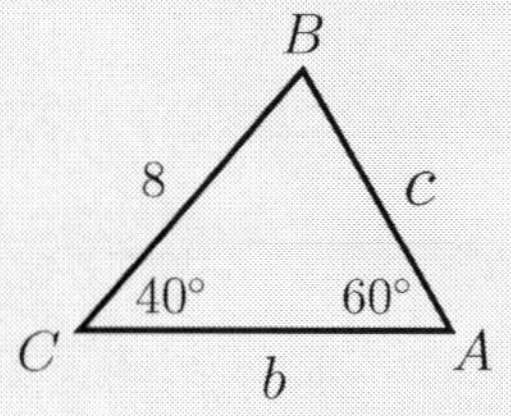

Since $m\angle A + m\angle B + m\angle C = 180°$, $m\angle B = 80$. Triangle ABC is a SAA triangle. Use the Law of Sines to find the sides b and c.

$$\frac{8}{\sin 60°} = \frac{b}{\sin 80°} \implies b = \frac{8\sin 80°}{\sin 60°} \approx 9.1$$

$$\frac{8}{\sin 60°} = \frac{c}{\sin 40°} \implies c = \frac{8\sin 40°}{\sin 60°} \approx 5.94$$

5.16 The Law of Cosines

The Law of Cosines (SAS and SSS)

- If triangle ABC shown at the right is a SAS triangle (a, b, and $m\angle C$ are known), side c can be calculated by the Law of Cosines.

$$c^2 = a^2 + b^2 - 2ab\cos C$$

  Note that side c is opposite angle C.

- If triangle ABC shown at the right is a SSS triangle (a, b, and c are known), the measure of angle A can be calculated by the Law of Cosines.

$$m\angle A = \cos^{-1}\left(\frac{a^2 - b^2 - c^2}{-2bc}\right)$$

  Note that side a is opposite angle A.

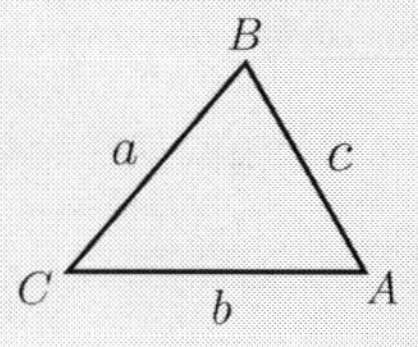

Let's find the side c and $m\angle B$ of a non-right triangle ABC shown at the right when $a = 4$, $b = 5$, and $m\angle C = 70°$.

Since triangle ABC is a SAS triangle, use the Law of Cosines to find the side c.

$$c^2 = 4^2 + 5^2 - 2(4)(5)\cos 70° \implies c \approx 5.23$$

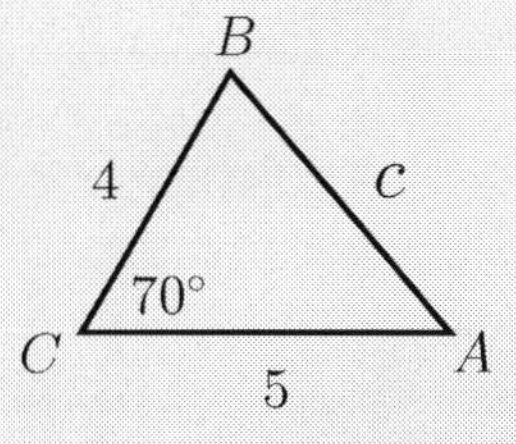

To find the measure of angle B, use the Law of Cosines. Since side b is opposite angle B,

$$m\angle B = \cos^{-1}\left(\frac{b^2 - a^2 - c^2}{-2ac}\right) = \cos^{-1}\left(\frac{5^2 - 4^2 - 5.23^2}{-2(4)(5.23)}\right) \approx 63.98°$$

5.17 Polar Coordinates

Polar Coordinates

In rectangular coordinates shown in Figure 1, a point is determined by (x, y), where x, and y represent where the point is x units horizontally and y units vertically from the origin, respectively.

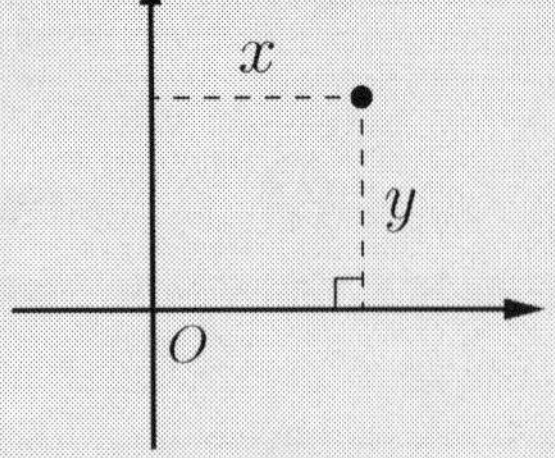

Fig. 1: Rectangular Coordinates

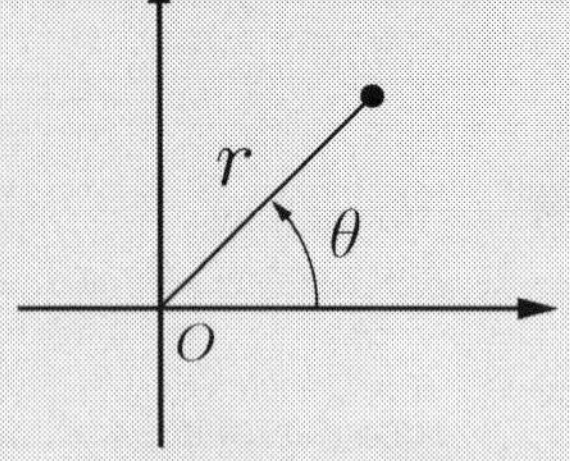

Fig. 2: Polar Coordinates

Whereas, in polar coordinates shown in Figure 2, a point is determined by (r, θ), where r represents the distance between the point and the origin, and θ represents the counterclockwise angle formed by the positive x-axis and the terminal side.

Identical Points in Polar Coordinates

In polar coordinates, two points are considered the same in the following two cases.

- Case 1: $(r, \theta) = (r, \theta + 2\pi k)$, where k is an integer.

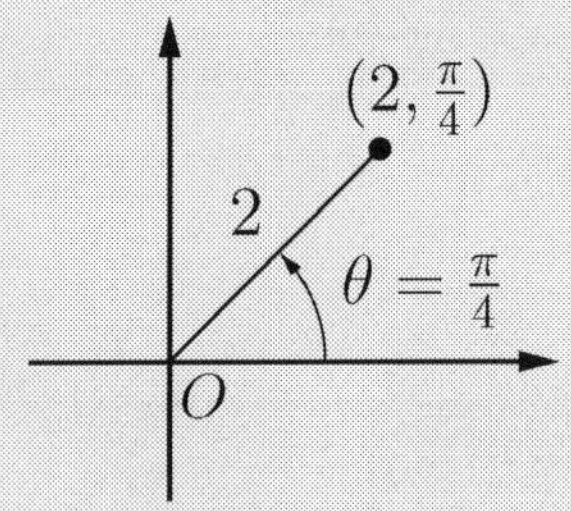

Figure 3: $(2, \frac{\pi}{4})$

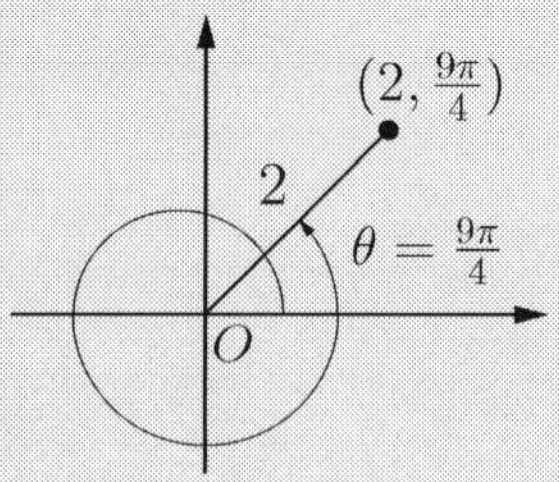

Figure 4: $(2, \frac{9\pi}{4})$

For instance, point $(2, \frac{\pi}{4})$ is plotted in the polar coordinates shown in Figure 3. Point $(2, \frac{9\pi}{4})$ is the same point as $(2, \frac{\pi}{4})$, and is plotted in Figure 4.

- Case 2: $(-r, \theta) = (r, \theta \pm \pi)$ Note: If $\theta + \pi > 2\pi$, use $\theta - \pi$ instead.

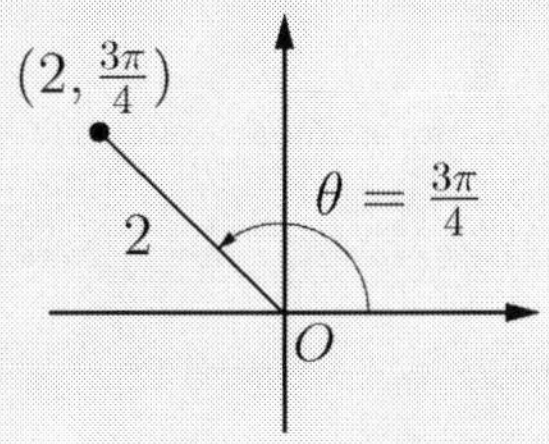

Figure 5: $(2, \frac{3\pi}{4})$

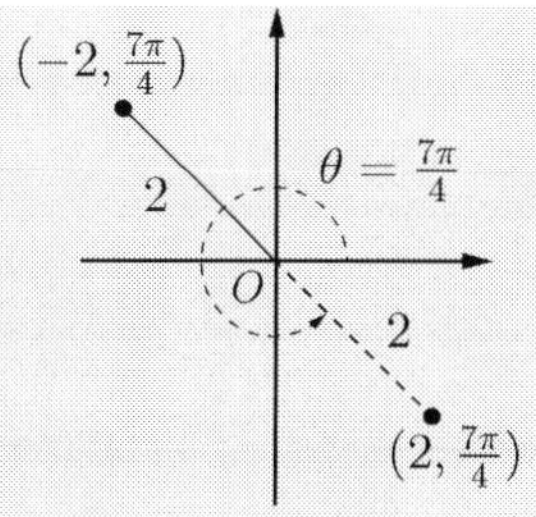

Figure 6: $(-2, \frac{7\pi}{4})$

For instance, points $(2, \frac{3\pi}{4})$ and $(2, \frac{7\pi}{4})$ are plotted in the polar coordinates shown in Figure 5 and 6. To plot $(-2, \frac{7\pi}{4})$, go to the direction $\frac{7\pi}{4}$ and then move a distance 2 in the opposite direction.

$$\left(-2, \frac{7\pi}{4}\right) = \left(2, \frac{7\pi}{4} - \pi\right) = \left(2, \frac{3\pi}{4}\right)$$

Thus, point $(-2, \frac{7\pi}{4})$ is the same point as $(2, \frac{3\pi}{4})$, and is plotted in Figure 6.

5.18 Converting from Polar Coordinates to Rectangular Coordinates

Converting from Polar Coordinates to Rectangular Coordinates

If the polar coordinates of a point is (r, θ), the rectangular coordinates of the point (x, y) are given by

$$x = r\cos\theta, \qquad y = r\sin\theta$$

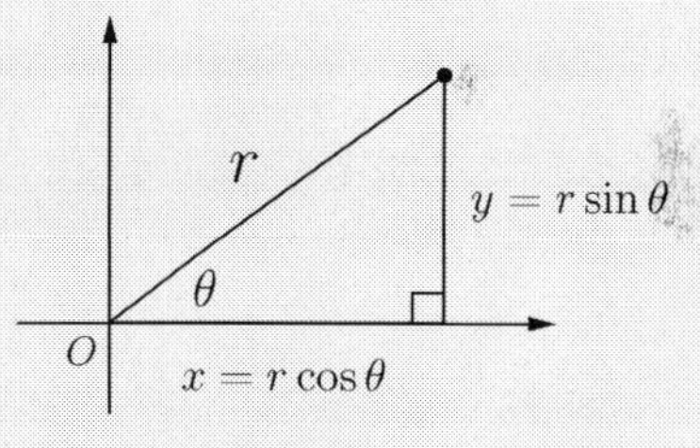

For instance, if the polar coordinates of a point is $(2, \frac{3\pi}{4})$, the rectangular coordinates of the point are as follows:

$$x = r\cos\theta \implies x = 2\cos\frac{3\pi}{4} = 2\left(-\frac{\sqrt{2}}{2}\right) = -\sqrt{2}$$

$$y = r\sin\theta \implies y = 2\sin\frac{3\pi}{4} = 2\left(\frac{\sqrt{2}}{2}\right) = \sqrt{2}$$

Thus, the rectangular coordinates of the point is $(-\sqrt{2}, \sqrt{2})$.

5.19 Converting from Rectangular Coordinates to Polar Coordinates

Converting from Rectangular Coordinates to Polar Coordinates

To convert from the rectangular coordinates (x, y) to the polar coordinates (r, θ), do the following three steps:

- Step 1: Plot the point (x, y) to determine the quadrant the angle θ lies in.
- Step 2: Find the distance between the point (x, y) and the origin, r, and the reference angle, β, formed by the positive x-axis and the terminal side.

$$r = \sqrt{x^2 + y^2}, \qquad \beta = \left| \tan^{-1} \frac{y}{x} \right|$$

  Note that the reference angle β is the **absolute value** of the inverse tangent function of $\frac{y}{x}$.
- Step 3: Find θ using the reference angle based on the quadrant that θ lies in.

Example **Converting from rectangular coordinates to polar coordinates**

Find the polar coordinates of a point with the rectangular coordinates $(-1, -\sqrt{3})$.

Solution To convert from the rectangular coordinates $(-1, -\sqrt{3})$ to the polar coordinates (r, θ), do the following three steps:

- Step 1: Plot the point $(-1, -\sqrt{3})$ as shown in Figure 7. Since the point $(-1, -\sqrt{3})$ is in the third quadrant, $\pi < \theta < \frac{3\pi}{2}$.
- Step 2: Find the distance between the point $(-1, -\sqrt{3})$ and the origin, r, and the reference angle, β, formed by the positive x-axis and the terminal side as shown in Figure 8.

$$r = \sqrt{x^2 + y^2} = \sqrt{(-1)^2 + (-\sqrt{3})^2} = 2$$
$$\beta = \left| \tan^{-1} \frac{y}{x} \right| = \left| \tan^{-1} \left(\frac{-\sqrt{3}}{-1} \right) \right| = \frac{\pi}{3}$$

- Step 3: Find θ using the reference angle based on the quadrant that θ lies in as shown in Figure 9. Since $\beta = \frac{\pi}{3}$ and θ lies in the third quadrant, $\theta = \pi + \beta = \pi + \frac{\pi}{3} = \frac{4\pi}{3}$.

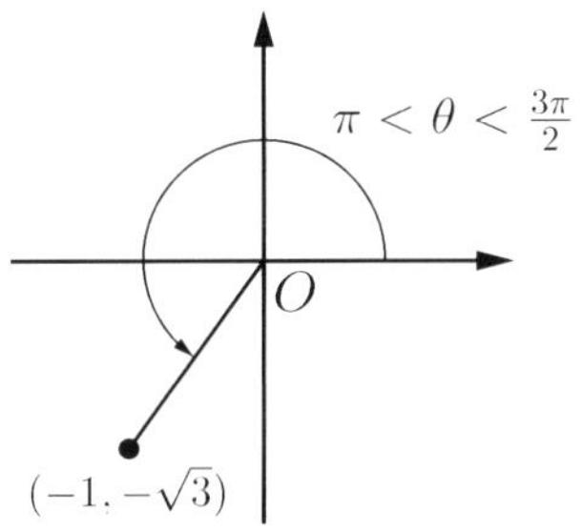

Figure 7

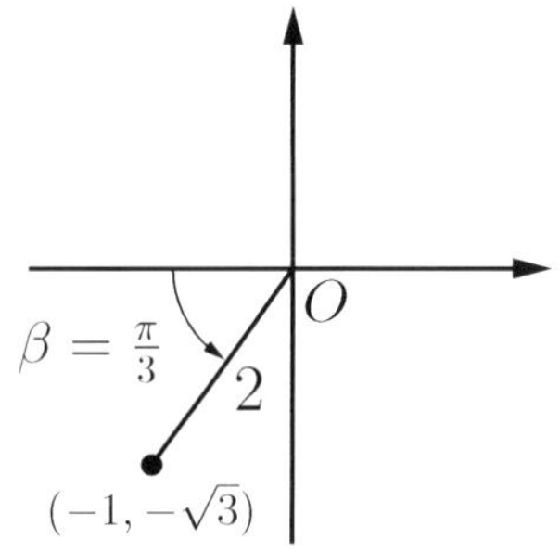

Figure 8

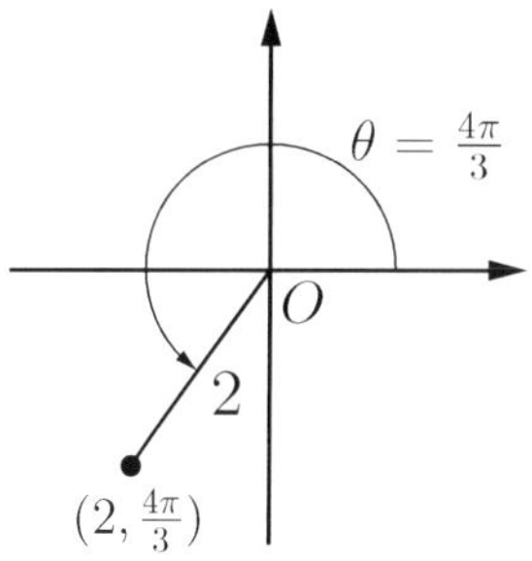

Figure 9

Therefore, the polar coordinates of a point with the rectangular coordinates $(-1, -\sqrt{3})$ are $(2, \frac{4\pi}{3})$.

5.20 Converting between Polar and Rectangular Equations

Converting between Polar and Rectangular Equations

To convert from a polar equation to a rectangular equation, or vice versa, use the following conversion formulas:

$$r^2 = x^2 + y^2, \qquad x = r\cos\theta, \qquad y = r\sin\theta, \qquad \tan\theta = \frac{y}{x}$$

Example **Converting a polar equation to a rectangular equation**

Write the polar equation $r = 2\sin\theta$ in rectangular form.

Solution To use $r^2 = x^2 + y^2$ and $y = r\sin\theta$, multiply each side of the polar equation by r.

$r = 2\sin\theta$	Multiply each side by r
$r^2 = 2r\sin\theta$	Replace r^2 with $x^2 + y^2$, and $r\sin\theta$ with y
$x^2 + y^2 = 2y$	

Example **Converting a rectangular equation to a polar equation**

Write the rectangular equation $(x-2)^2+y^2=4$ in polar form.

Solution To use $r^2=x^2+y^2$ and $x=r\cos\theta$, expand $(x-2)^2$ and simplify the equation.

$(x-2)^2+y^2=4$	Expand $(x-2)^2$
$x^2-4x+4+y^2=4$	Simplify
$x^2+y^2-4x=0$	Replace x^2+y^2 with r^2, and x with $r\cos\theta$
$r^2-4r\cos\theta=0$	Add $4r\cos\theta$ to each side
$r^2=4r\cos\theta$	Divide each side by r
$r=4\cos\theta$	

5.21 Cartesian and Polar Form of Complex Numbers

Cartesian and Polar Form of Complex Numbers

Cartesian form of z
Suppose the complex number $z=a+bi$ is represented by a point in the figure at the right. $a+bi$ is the **Cartesian form** of z. The angle θ is the **argument** of z, or simply arg z.

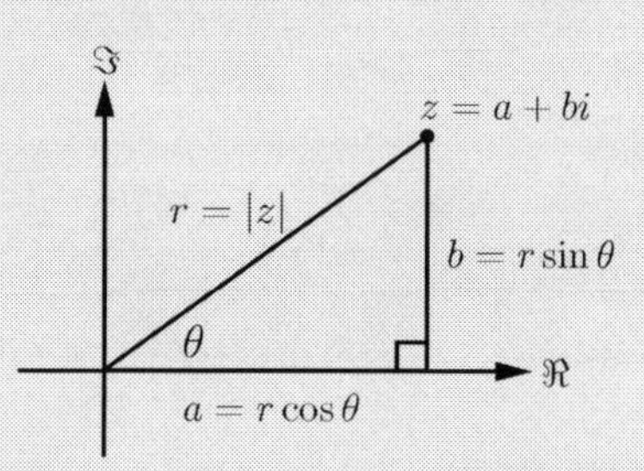

Polar form of z
Let $r=|z|$. $a=r\cos\theta$ and $b=r\sin\theta$. Thus, the Cartesian form of z can be converted into

$$a+bi=r\cos\theta+i(r\sin\theta)=r(\cos\theta+i\sin\theta)=\text{r cis }\theta$$

$rcis\ \theta$ is the **polar form** of z.

Euler form of z
$z=re^{i\theta}$ is the Euler form of z, where $r=|z|$ and $\theta=\arg z$

Tips The conjugate of z is $z^*=r\text{ cis }(-\theta)$.

5.22 Converting Cartesian Forms to Polar Forms

Converting Cartesian Forms to Polar Forms

To convert Cartesian form $x + yi$ to polar form r cis θ, do the following five steps:

- Step 1: Convert $x + yi$ to a point (x, y) in Cartesian plane.
- Step 2: Plot the point (x, y) to determine the quadrant the angle θ lies in.
- Step 3: Find the distance between the point (x, y) and the origin, r, and the reference angle, β, formed by the positive x-axis and the terminal side.

$$r = \sqrt{x^2 + y^2}, \qquad \beta = \left|\tan^{-1}\frac{y}{x}\right|$$

  Note that the reference angle β is the modulus(absolute value) of the inverse tangent function of $\frac{y}{x}$.
- Step 4: Find θ using the reference angle based on the quadrant that θ lies in.
- Step 5: Write the complex number z as r cis θ.

Example Writing the complex number in polar form

Find the polar form of the complex number $-1 - i\sqrt{3}$.

Solution To convert $-1 - i\sqrt{3}$ to polar form r cis θ, do the following five steps:

- Step 1: Convert $-1 - i\sqrt{3}$ to a point $(-1, -\sqrt{3})$ in Cartesian plane.
- Step 2: Plot the point $(-1, -\sqrt{3})$ as shown in Figure 1. Since the point $(-1, -\sqrt{3})$ is in the third quadrant, $\pi < \theta < \frac{3\pi}{2}$.
- Step 3: Find the distance between the point $(-1, -\sqrt{3})$ and the origin, r, and the reference angle, β, formed by the positive x-axis and the terminal side as shown in Figure 2.

$$r = \sqrt{x^2 + y^2} = \sqrt{(-1)^2 + (-\sqrt{3})^2} = 2$$
$$\beta = \left|\tan^{-1}\frac{y}{x}\right| = \left|\tan^{-1}\left(\frac{-\sqrt{3}}{-1}\right)\right| = \frac{\pi}{3}$$

- Step 4: Find θ using the reference angle based on the quadrant that θ lies in as shown in Figure 3. Since $\beta = \frac{\pi}{3}$ and θ lies in the third quadrant, $\theta = \pi + \beta = \pi + \frac{\pi}{3} = \frac{4\pi}{3}$.

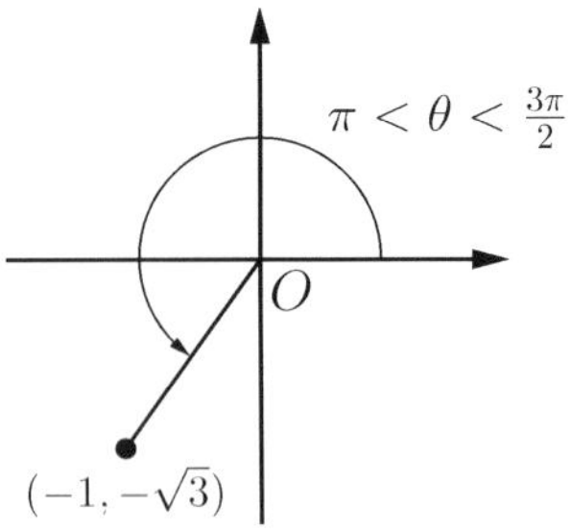

Figure 1

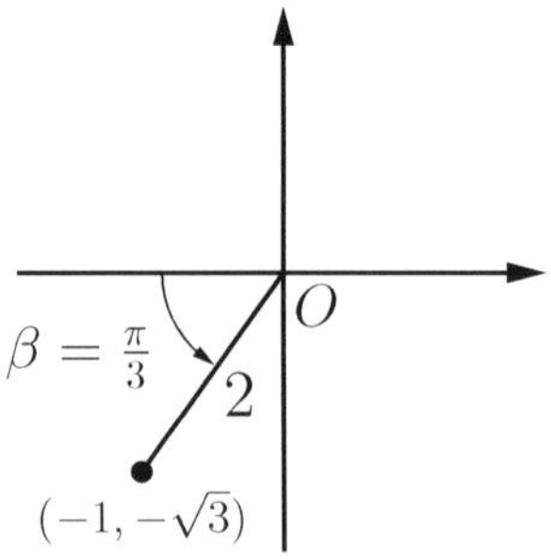

Figure 2

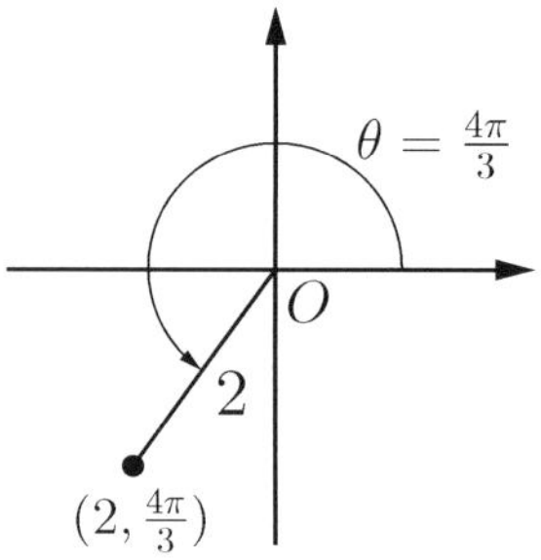

Figure 3

- Step 5: Since $r = 2$ and $\theta = \dfrac{4\pi}{3}$, the complex number $-1 - i\sqrt{3} = 2$ cis $\dfrac{4\pi}{3}$.

5.23 Multiplying and Dividing in Polar Form

Multiplying and Dividing in Polar Form

cis θ has three useful properties.

- cis $\theta \times$ cis $\phi =$ cis $(\theta + \phi)$
- $\dfrac{\text{cis } \theta}{\text{cis } \phi} = \text{cis } (\theta - \phi)$
- cis $(\theta + 2\pi k) =$ cis θ for all integers k.

5.24 De Moivre's Theorem

De Moivre's Theorem

If $z = r$ cis θ, then

$$z^n = r^n \text{ cis } n\theta \quad \text{for all rational } n.$$

Example **Using De Moivre's theorem**

Use De Moivre's theorem to find the exact value of $(-1-i\sqrt{3})^7$.

Solution From the previous example, we found that $-1-i\sqrt{3}=2\text{ cis }\dfrac{4\pi}{3}$.

$$\begin{aligned}(-1-i\sqrt{3})^7 &= \left(2\text{ cis }\frac{4\pi}{3}\right)^7 = 2^7\text{ cis }\frac{28\pi}{3} \\ &= 128\text{ cis }\frac{4\pi}{3} = 64\left(2\text{ cis }\frac{4\pi}{3}\right) \\ &= 64(-1-i\sqrt{3}) \\ &= -64-64i\sqrt{3}\end{aligned}$$

Since $\text{cis }\dfrac{28\pi}{3}=\text{cis }\left(\dfrac{4\pi}{3}+8\pi\right)=2\text{ cis }\dfrac{4\pi}{3}$

5.25 Finding nth Roots of Complex Numbers

Finding nth Roots of Complex Numbers

Let c be a given complex number. Any complex number z that satisfies the equation $z^n=c$ is called a **complex nth root** of c.

Two methods to find nth roots of complex number

- Factorization
- Using the nth root method of complex numbers.

Since factorization can be very difficult or impossible, the nth root method is preferable.

The nth root method

Let c be a complex number in polar form $r\text{ cis }\theta$. The general solutions to $z^n = r\text{ cis }\theta$ are as follows:

$$z_k=\sqrt[n]{r}\text{ cis }\left(\frac{\theta}{n}+\frac{2k\pi}{n}\right),\qquad \text{where } k=0,1,2,\cdots,n-1$$

Tips The nth foots of unity are the solutions of $z^n=1=\text{cis }(0+2k\pi)$

Example Finding the fourth roots

Find the fourth roots of $-1-i\sqrt{3}$ and draw them on an Argand diagram.

Solution We need to find the solutions to $z^4=-1-i\sqrt{3}$. We found that $-1-i\sqrt{3}=2\text{ cis }\frac{4\pi}{3}$ in the previous example. $z^4=-1-i\sqrt{3}$ can be converted to $z^4=2\text{ cis }\frac{4\pi}{3}$. The fourth roots of $z^4=2$ cis $\frac{4\pi}{3}$ are as follows:

$$z_k=\sqrt[4]{2}\text{ cis }\left(\frac{\frac{4\pi}{3}}{4}+\frac{2k\pi}{4}\right),\qquad \text{where } k=0,1,2,3$$

- When $k=0$: $z_0=\sqrt[4]{2}\text{ cis }\left(\frac{\pi}{3}\right)=\sqrt[4]{2}\left(\cos\frac{\pi}{3}+i\sin\frac{\pi}{3}\right)=\sqrt[4]{2}\left(\frac{1}{2}+i\frac{\sqrt{3}}{2}\right)$
- When $k=1$: $z_1=\sqrt[4]{2}\text{ cis }\left(\frac{\pi}{3}+\frac{\pi}{2}\right)=\sqrt[4]{2}\text{ cis }\left(\frac{5\pi}{6}\right)=\sqrt[4]{2}\left(-\frac{\sqrt{3}}{2}+i\frac{\sqrt{1}}{2}\right)$
- When $k=2$: $z_2=\sqrt[4]{2}\text{ cis }\left(\frac{\pi}{3}+\pi\right)=\sqrt[4]{2}\text{ cis }\left(\frac{4\pi}{3}\right)=\sqrt[4]{2}\left(-\frac{1}{2}-i\frac{\sqrt{3}}{2}\right)$
- When $k=3$: $z_3=\sqrt[4]{2}\text{ cis }\left(\frac{\pi}{3}+\frac{3\pi}{2}\right)=\sqrt[4]{2}\text{ cis }\left(\frac{11\pi}{6}\right)=\sqrt[4]{2}\left(\frac{\sqrt{3}}{2}-i\frac{\sqrt{1}}{2}\right)$

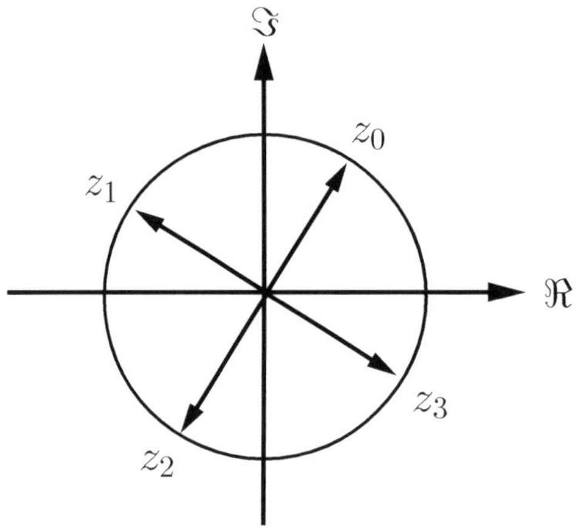

The fourths roots z_0, z_1, z_2, and z_3 are shown on the Argand diagram above.

5.26 Vectors

Vectors

A vector is a quantity that has a magnitude and a direction. In 2-dimension, if point $A(x_1, y_1)$ is the initial point and point $B(x_2, y_2)$ is the terminal point, a vector, denoted by either $\overrightarrow{AB}$ or **AB**, is defined as

$$\text{In 2-dimension:} \qquad \mathbf{AB} = \begin{bmatrix} x_2 - x_1 \\ y_2 - y_1 \end{bmatrix}$$

and the magnitude of the vector, denoted by either $|\overrightarrow{AB}|$ or $|\mathbf{AB}|$, is defined as

$$|\mathbf{AB}| = \sqrt{(x_2 - x_1)^2 + (y_2 - y_1)^2}$$

Similarly, in 3-dimension, if point $A(x_1, y_1, z_1)$ is the initial point and point $B(x_2, y_2, z_2)$ is the terminal point, a vector, denoted by either $\overrightarrow{AB}$ or **AB**, is defined as

$$\text{In 3-dimension:} \qquad \mathbf{AB} = \begin{bmatrix} x_2 - x_1 \\ y_2 - y_1 \\ z_2 - z_1 \end{bmatrix}$$

and the magnitude of the vector, denoted by either $|\overrightarrow{AB}|$ or $|\mathbf{AB}|$, is defined as

$$|\mathbf{AB}| = \sqrt{(x_2 - x_1)^2 + (y_2 - y_1)^2 + (z_2 - z_1)^2}$$

Tips

1. The unit vector in the direction of positive x-axis is $\mathbf{i} = \begin{bmatrix} 1 \\ 0 \end{bmatrix}$. The unit vector in the direction of positive y-axis is $\mathbf{j} = \begin{bmatrix} 0 \\ 1 \end{bmatrix}$.

2. Let $\mathbf{v} = \begin{bmatrix} a \\ b \end{bmatrix}$, where a and b are the horizontal and vertical components of $\mathbf{v}$. $\mathbf{v} = \begin{bmatrix} a \\ b \end{bmatrix}$ is called the **component form** of vector $\mathbf{v}$. Another way to define vector $\mathbf{v}$ using the unit vectors $\mathbf{i}$ and $\mathbf{j}$ is as follows:

$$\mathbf{v} = \begin{bmatrix} a \\ b \end{bmatrix} = a \begin{bmatrix} 1 \\ 0 \end{bmatrix} + b \begin{bmatrix} 0 \\ 1 \end{bmatrix} = a\mathbf{i} + b\mathbf{j}$$

5.27 Algebraic Operations on Vectors

Algebraic Operations on Vectors

If $\mathbf{u} = \begin{bmatrix} a \\ b \end{bmatrix}$, $\mathbf{v} = \begin{bmatrix} c \\ d \end{bmatrix}$, and c is a scalar (Constant), then

Addition: $\mathbf{u} + \mathbf{v} = \begin{bmatrix} a+c \\ b+d \end{bmatrix} = (a+c)\mathbf{i} + (b+d)\mathbf{j}$

Subtraction: $\mathbf{u} - \mathbf{v} = \begin{bmatrix} a-c \\ b-d \end{bmatrix} = (a-c)\mathbf{i} + (b-d)\mathbf{j}$

Scalar multiplication: $c\mathbf{u} = \begin{bmatrix} ca \\ cb \end{bmatrix} = ca\mathbf{i} + cb\mathbf{j}$

Example **Algebraic operations on vectors**

If $\mathbf{v} = \begin{bmatrix} 3 \\ 4 \end{bmatrix}$, $\mathbf{w} = \begin{bmatrix} 2 \\ 8 \end{bmatrix}$, find $\mathbf{v} + \mathbf{w}$, $\mathbf{w} - \mathbf{v}$, $5\mathbf{v}$, and $|\mathbf{v} + \mathbf{w}|$.

Solution

$$\mathbf{v} + \mathbf{w} = \begin{bmatrix} 3 \\ 4 \end{bmatrix} + \begin{bmatrix} 2 \\ 8 \end{bmatrix} = \begin{bmatrix} 5 \\ 12 \end{bmatrix}$$

$$\mathbf{w} - \mathbf{v} = \begin{bmatrix} 2 \\ 8 \end{bmatrix} - \begin{bmatrix} 3 \\ 4 \end{bmatrix} = \begin{bmatrix} -1 \\ 4 \end{bmatrix}$$

$$5\mathbf{v} = 5\begin{bmatrix} 3 \\ 4 \end{bmatrix} = \begin{bmatrix} 15 \\ 20 \end{bmatrix}$$

$$|\mathbf{v} + \mathbf{w}| = \sqrt{5^2 + 12^2} = 13$$

5.28 Drawing the resultant vectors

Graphing Vectors

Vector equality
Two vectors **u** and **v** are equal if they have the same magnitude and the same direction. In Figure 1 below, three vectors **u**, **v**, and **w** are drawn. Although the three vectors have different initial points and different terminal points, they are equal because they have the same magnitude and the same direction.

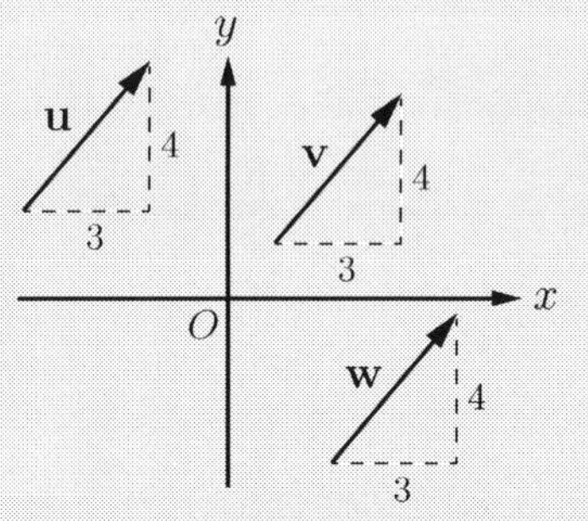

Figure 1

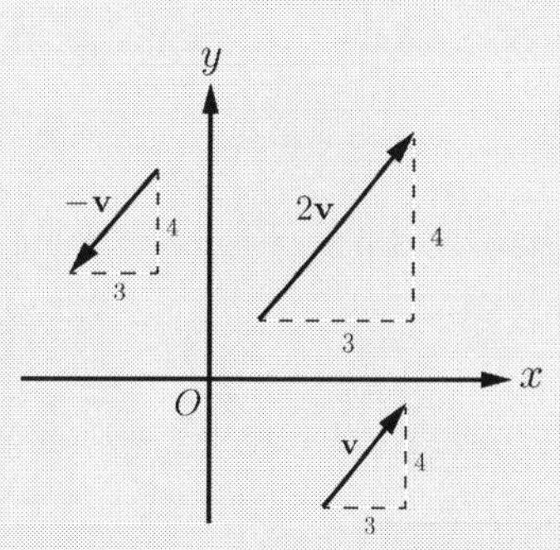

Figure 2

If **v** is a vector drawn in Figure 2, −**v** is a vector whose magnitude is the same as **v**, but whose direction is opposite to **v**. Whereas, 2**v** is a vector whose magnitude is twice the magnitude of **v**, but whose direction is the same as **v**.

Drawing the resultant vectors

The sum of two vectors is called the resultant vector. The resultant vector can be drawn in the following steps:

- Step 1: Draw the first vector **u** as shown in Figure 3.
- Step 2: Draw the second vector, **v**, so that the initial point of the second vector coincides with the terminal point of the first vector **u** as shown in Figure 3.
- Step 3: Draw the resultant vector, **u** + **v**, from the initial point of the first vector **u** to the terminal point of the second vector **v** as shown in Figure 4.

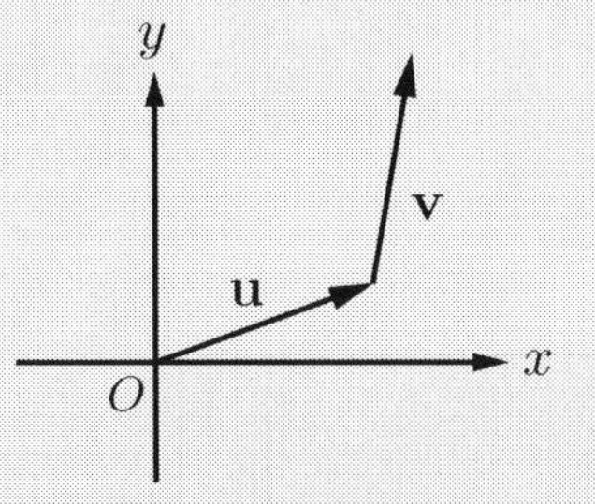

Figure 3

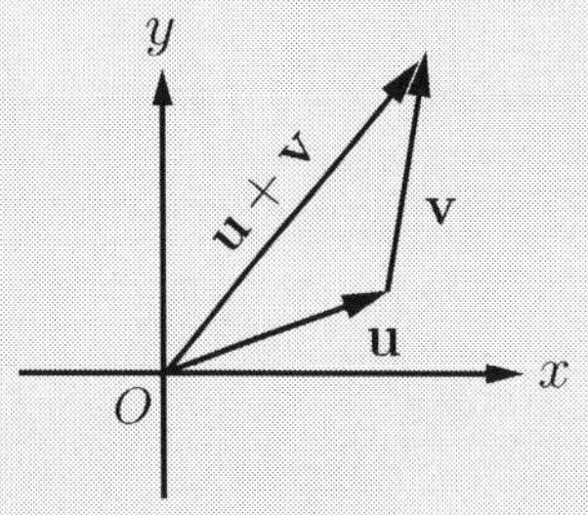

Figure 4

Chapter 6

Calculus

6.1 Definition of Limit

Definition of Limit

Let f be a function defined on some open interval that contains the number a, except possibly at a itself. Then we say that the limit of $f(x)$ as x approaches a is L, and we write

$$\lim_{x \to a} f(x) = L$$

if for every number $\varepsilon > 0$ there is a corresponding number $\delta > 0$ such that $|f(x) - L| < \varepsilon$ whenever $0 < |x - a| < \delta$

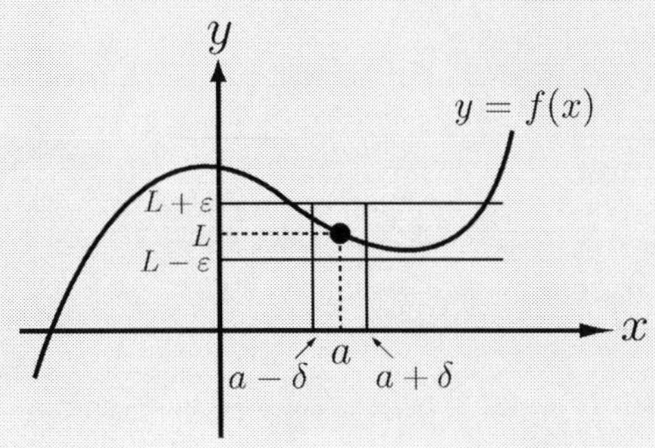

6.2 One-Sided Limits

One-Sided Limits

We write

$$\lim_{x \to a^-} f(x) = L$$

and say the **left-hand limit** of $f(x)$ as x approaches a from the left is equal to L as shown in figure 1. Similarly, the **right-hand limit** of $f(x)$ as x approaches a from the right is equal to L as shown in figure 2 and we write

$$\lim_{x \to a^+} f(x) = L$$

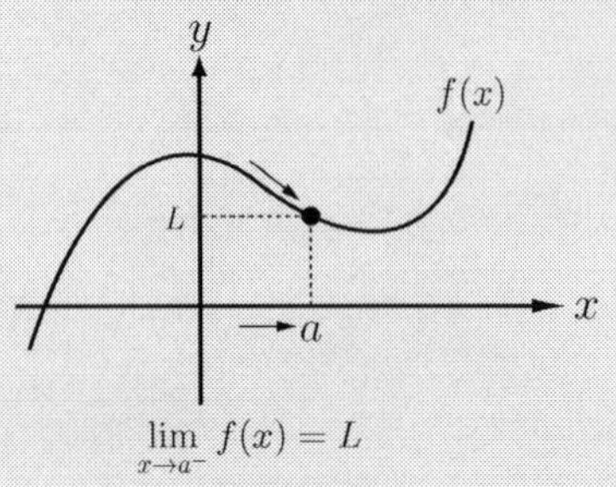

Figure 1

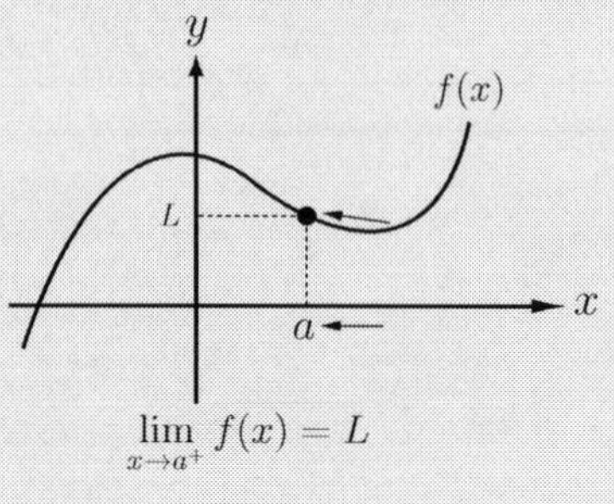

Figure 2

When does the Limit Exist?

The limit exists when the left-hand limit and the right-hand limit are the same.

$$\lim_{x \to a} f(x) = L \quad \text{if and only if} \quad \lim_{x \to a^-} f(x) = L \quad \text{and} \quad \lim_{x \to a^+} f(x) = L$$

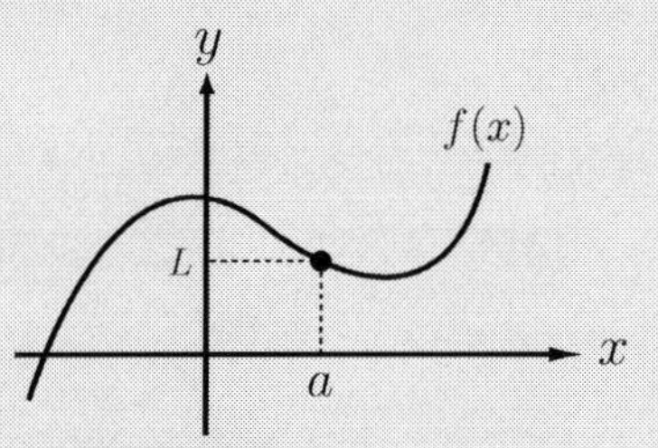

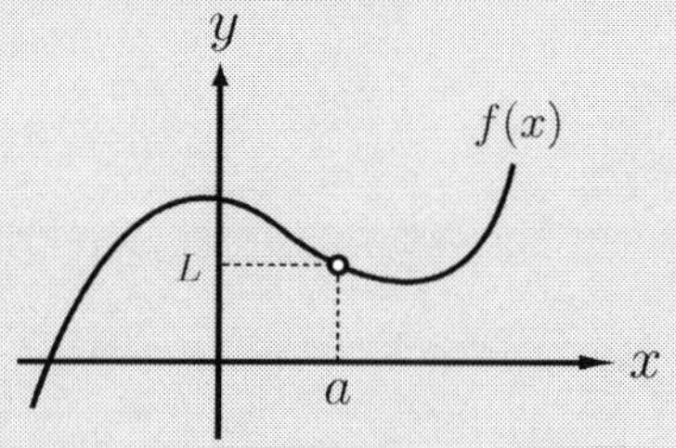

Both graphs above show that the limit exists and $\lim_{x \to a} f(x) = L$.

Tips

The limit of a function does not exist for one of three reasons:

1. The one-sided limits are not the same.
2. The function does not approach a finite value.
3. The function oscillates as x approaches a.

Example Having different One-sided limits

Find $\lim_{x \to 3} \frac{|x-3|}{x-3}$

Solution The left-hand limit is -1 and the right-hand limit is 1 as shown below.

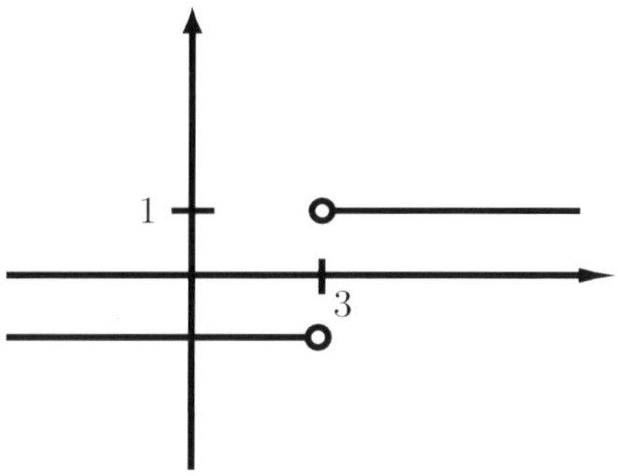

Since the left-hand limit and the right-hand limit are different, the limit does not exist at $x = 3$.

Example Finding the limit of an oscillating function

Find $\lim_{x \to 0} \sin \frac{\pi}{x}$.

Solution The value of $\sin \frac{\pi}{x}$ oscillates between 1 and -1 infinite often as x approaches 0 as shown below.

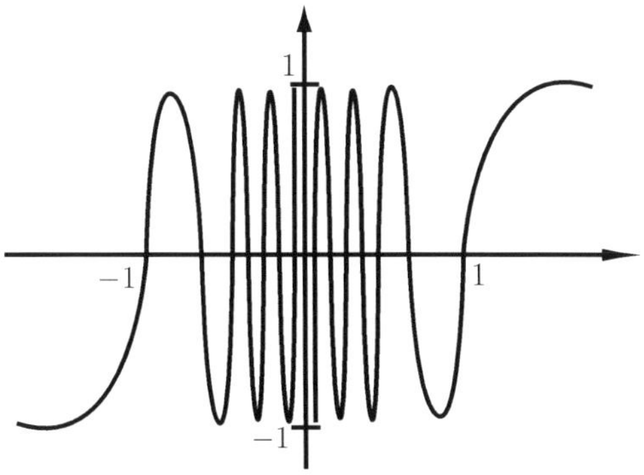

Therefore, $\lim_{x \to 0} \sin \frac{\pi}{x}$ does not exist.

6.3 Properties of Limits

Properties of Limits

Suppose that c is a constant and the limits

$$\lim_{x\to a} f(x) \qquad \text{and} \qquad \lim_{x\to a} g(x)$$

exist. Then use the following properties of limits to calculate limits.

1. $\lim_{x\to a}[f(x) \pm g(x)] = \lim_{x\to a} f(x) \pm \lim_{x\to a} g(x)$
2. $\lim_{x\to a} cf(x) = c\lim_{x\to a} f(x)$
3. $\lim_{x\to a}[f(x)\cdot g(x)] = \lim_{x\to a} f(x) \cdot \lim_{x\to a} g(x)$
4. $\lim_{x\to a} \dfrac{f(x)}{g(x)} = \dfrac{\lim_{x\to a} f(x)}{\lim_{x\to a} g(x)}$
5. $\lim_{x\to a}[f(x)]^n = \left[\lim_{x\to a} f(x)\right]^n$
6. $\lim_{x\to a} c = c$
7. $\lim_{x\to a} x^n = a^n$
8. $\lim_{x\to a} \sqrt[n]{x} = \sqrt[n]{a}$
9. $\lim_{x\to a} \sqrt[n]{f(x)} = \sqrt[n]{\lim_{x\to a} f(x)}$

Tips

1. $\lim_{x\to a} = L$ if and only if $\lim_{x\to a^-} = L$ and $\lim_{x\to a^+} = L$
2. If f is a polynomial or rational function and a is in the domain of f, then

$$\lim_{x\to a} f(x) = f(a)$$

6.4 Limit of a Rational Function

Limit of a Rational Function

In order to find the limit of a rational function $f(x) = \frac{p(x)}{q(x)}$ at $x = a$, plug in $x = a$ to both the numerator and denominator. That is,

$$\lim_{x\to a} \frac{p(x)}{q(x)} = \frac{p(a)}{q(a)}$$

The value of $\frac{p(a)}{q(a)}$ determines the limit of f. Consider the following four cases.

- Case 1: If $\frac{p(a)}{q(a)} = \frac{\text{constant}}{\text{constant}}$, the limit is $\frac{\text{constant}}{\text{constant}}$. For instance, let $f(x) = \frac{x-1}{x+1}$.

$$\lim_{x\to 2} \frac{x-1}{x+1} = \frac{2-1}{2+1} = \frac{1}{3} \implies \text{Limit of } f \text{ is } \frac{1}{3}$$

- Case 2: If $\frac{p(a)}{q(a)} = \frac{0}{\text{constant}}$, the limit is 0. For instance, let $f(x) = \frac{x-3}{x^2-1}$.

$$\lim_{x\to 3} \frac{x-3}{x^2-1} = \frac{3-3}{3^2-1} = 0 \implies \text{Limit of } f \text{ is } 0.$$

- Case 3: If $\frac{p(a)}{q(a)} = \frac{\text{constant}}{0}$, the limit does not exist. For instance, let $f(x) = \frac{1}{(x+1)^2}$.

$$\lim_{x\to -1} \frac{1}{(x+1)^2} = \frac{1}{(-1+1)^2} = \frac{1}{0} \implies \text{Limit of } f \text{ does not exist.}$$

- Case 4: If $\frac{p(a)}{q(a)} = \frac{0}{0}$, do the following three extra steps.
  - Step 1: Factor both the numerator and denominator.
  - Step 2: Cancel out a common factor.
  - Step 3: Plug-in $x = a$.

For instance, let $f(x) = \frac{x^2-1}{x-1}$. Since $\lim_{x\to 1} \frac{x^2-1}{x-1} = \frac{0}{0}$, do the following steps.

$$\begin{aligned}
\lim_{x\to 1} \frac{x^2-1}{x-1} &= \lim_{x\to 1} \frac{(x+1)(x-1)}{x-1} && \text{Factor the numerator} \\
&= \lim_{x\to 1} \frac{(x+1)\cancel{(x-1)}}{\cancel{x-1}} && \text{Cancel out } x-1 \\
&= \lim_{x\to 1} (x+1) && \text{Plug-in } x = 1 \\
&= 2
\end{aligned}$$

Tips: $\frac{0}{0}$ or $\frac{\infty}{\infty}$ are called an **indeterminate form**. The limit of the indeterminate form may or may not exist. The limit of the indeterminate form can be easily found using the **L'Hospital's Rule**.

Example **Finding the limit of a rational function**

Find $\lim\limits_{x\to 0} \dfrac{\sqrt{x+2}-\sqrt{2}}{x}$

Solution

$$\begin{aligned}
\lim_{x\to 0} \frac{\sqrt{x+2}-\sqrt{2}}{x} &= \lim_{x\to 0} \frac{\sqrt{x+2}-\sqrt{2}}{x} \cdot \frac{\sqrt{x+2}+\sqrt{2}}{\sqrt{x+2}+\sqrt{2}} \\
&= \lim_{x\to 0} \frac{x+2-2}{x(\sqrt{x+2}+\sqrt{2})} \\
&= \lim_{x\to 0} \frac{x}{x(\sqrt{x+2}+\sqrt{2})} \\
&= \lim_{x\to 0} \frac{1}{(\sqrt{x+2}+\sqrt{2})} \\
&= \frac{1}{\sqrt{0+2}+\sqrt{2}} \\
&= \frac{1}{2\sqrt{2}}
\end{aligned}$$

6.5 Special Limits

Special Limits

The limits of the three functions shown below involve the indeterminate form of $\frac{0}{0}$. Finding the limit of these functions are extremely hard unless you use **L'Hospital's Rule**. Memorize these limits until you learn it.

$$\lim_{x\to 0} \frac{\sin ax}{bx} = \frac{a}{b}, \qquad \lim_{x\to 0} \frac{1-\cos ax}{bx} = 0 \qquad \lim_{x\to 0} \frac{\tan ax}{bx} = \frac{a}{b}$$

Tips: When you evaluate these limits using a calculator, Make sure to change the Mode to radian. Substitute $x = 0.001$ into the numerator and the denominator to evaluate these limits.

6.6 Limits at Infinity

Limits at Infinity

Let f be a function defined on some interval (a, ∞). Then

$$\lim_{x \to \infty} f(x) = L$$

means that the value of $f(x)$ is close to L as x becomes increasing large as shown in Figure 1. Similarly, Let f be a function defined on some interval $(-\infty, a)$. Then

$$\lim_{x \to -\infty} f(x) = L$$

means that the value of $f(x)$ is close to L as x becomes increasing large negative as shown in Figure 2. The line $y = L$ is called a **horizontal asymptote**.

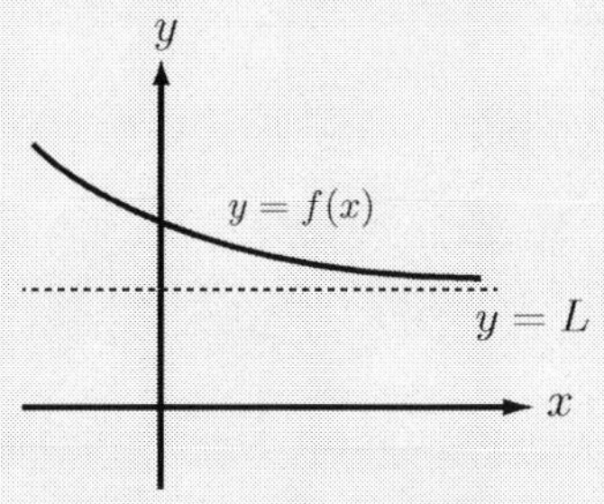

Figure 1

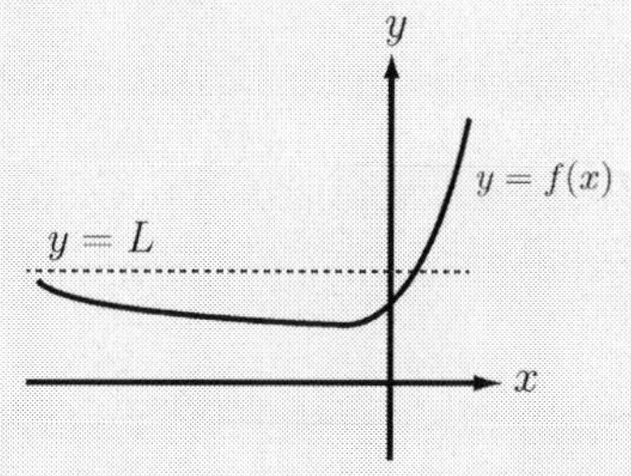

Figure 2

Example **Finding the horizontal asymptotes**

Find $\lim_{x \to \infty} \tan^{-1} x$ and $\lim_{x \to -\infty} \tan^{-1} x$

Solution

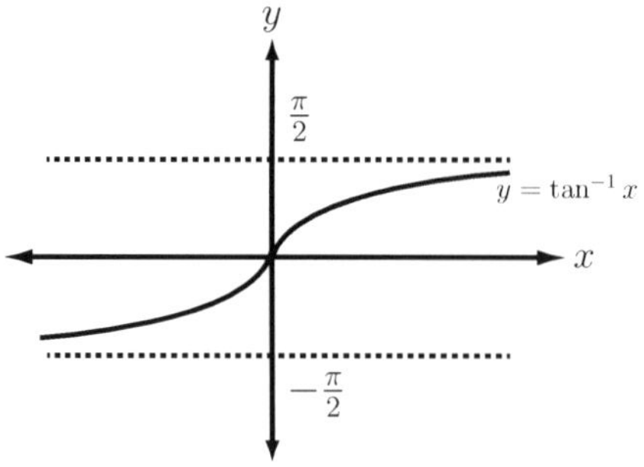

The value of y is close to the line $y = \frac{\pi}{2}$ as x approaches ∞. Whereas, the value of y is close to the line $y = -\frac{\pi}{2}$ as x approaches $-\infty$. Therefore, $\lim_{x\to\infty} \tan^{-1} x = \frac{\pi}{2}$ and $\lim_{x\to-\infty} \tan^{-1} x = -\frac{\pi}{2}$.

6.7 Finding Horizontal Asymptote of a Rational Function

$\lim_{x\to\infty} \frac{p(x)}{q(x)}$: Finding Horizontal Asymptote of a Rational Function

For the rational function

$$f(x) = \frac{p(x)}{q(x)} = \frac{ax^m + \cdots}{bx^n + \cdots}$$

where m is the degree of the numerator and n is the degree of the denominator, a horizontal asymptote can be determined by the following three cases.

- Case 1: If $n < m$, there is no horizontal asymptote. In other words, the value of $f(x)$ approaches ∞ or $-\infty$ as x approaches ∞.
- Case 2: If $n = m$, f has a horizontal asymptote of $y = \frac{a}{b}$, where a and b are the leading coefficients of the numerator and denominator.
- Case 3: If $n > m$, f has a horizontal asymptote of $y = 0$.

For instance, for the rational function $f(x) = \frac{1}{x} = \frac{1 \cdot x^0}{x^1}$ whose graph is shown below,

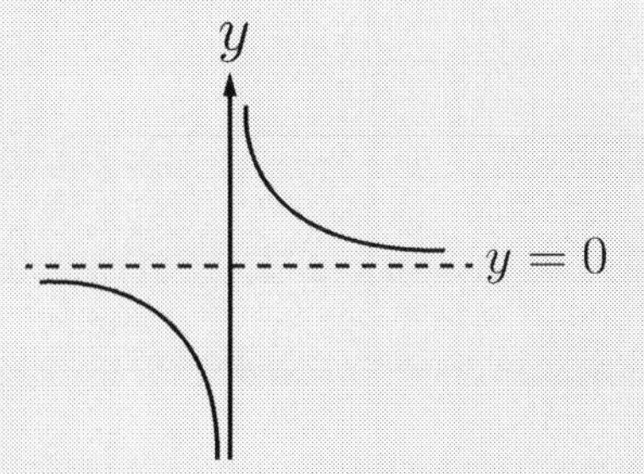

the degree of numerator is 0 and the degree of the denominator is 1. Thus, the rational function has the horizontal asymptote of $y = 0$, which can be denoted by $\lim_{x\to\infty} \frac{1}{x} = 0$ and $\lim_{x\to-\infty} \frac{1}{x} = 0$.

Example   Finding horizontal asymptotes

Find the horizontal asymptotes of each rational function.

(a) $\lim_{x\to\infty} \frac{1-3x}{2x^2+3x}$

(b) $\lim_{x\to\infty} \frac{-x^3+1}{x^2-2x+2}$

(c) $\lim_{x\to\infty} \frac{2x^2-2x+3}{2-4x+3x^2}$

Solution

(a) The numerator is a first degree polynomial ($m = 1$) and the denominator is a second degree polynomial ($n = 2$). Since $n > m$, the horizontal asymptote of f is $y = 0$. Thus, $\lim_{x\to\infty} \frac{1-3x}{2x^2+3x} = 0$.

(b) The numerator is a third degree polynomial ($m = 3$) and the denominator is a second degree polynomial ($n = 2$). Since $n < m$, the value of $f(x)$ approaches $-\infty$ as x approaches ∞. Thus, $\lim_{x\to\infty} \frac{-x^3+1}{x^2-2x+2} = -\infty$

(c) $f(x) = \frac{2x^2-2x+3}{2-4x+3x^2} = \frac{2x^2-2x+3}{3x^2-4x+2}$. Both the numerator and the denominator are 2nd degree polynomials. Thus, the horizontal asymptote of f is the ratio of the leading coefficients, or $y = \frac{2}{3}$. Thus, $\lim_{x\to\infty} \frac{2x^2-2x+3}{2-4x+3x^2} = \frac{2}{3}$.

6.8 Continuity

Definition of Continuity

A function can be either continuous or discontinuous. The easiest way to test of continuity of a function is to see whether the graph of a function can be traced with a pen without lifting the pen from the paper. In general, mathematical proof of continuity of a function can be done using the concepts of limits.

A function f is continuous at $x = a$ if

$$\lim_{x \to a} f(x) = f(a)$$

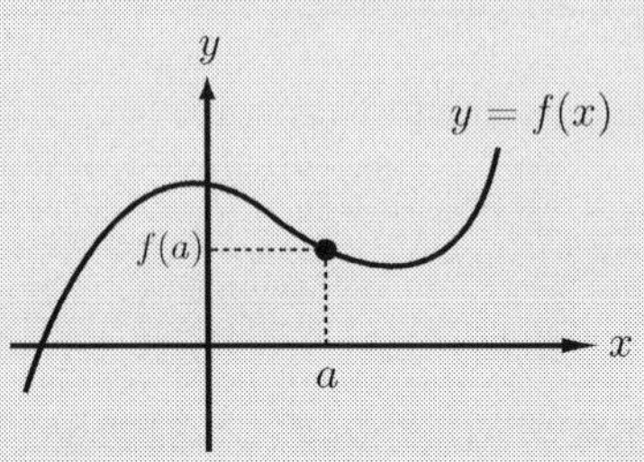

Figure 1

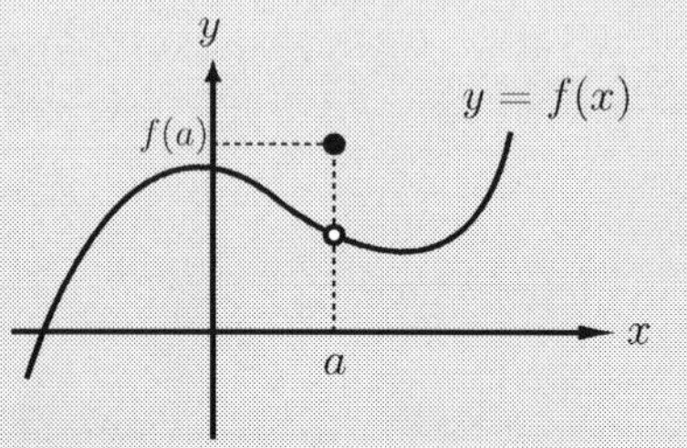

Figure 2

In Figure 1, $\lim_{x \to a} f(x)$ exists and $f(a)$ is defined. Since $\lim_{x \to a} f(x) = f(a)$, the function f is continuous at $x = a$. Whereas, the function f in Figure 2 is discontinuous at $x = a$ because $\lim_{x \to a} f(x) \neq f(a)$.

Tips

Testing continuity of a function at $x = a$ requires three steps.

1. Check whether $\lim_{x \to a} f(x)$ exists.
2. Check whether $f(a)$ is defined.
3. Check whether $\lim_{x \to a} f(x) = f(a)$.

6.9 Types of Discontinuities

Types of Discontinuities

A function f is discontinuous at $x = a$ if f has either a hole, a jump, or vertical asymptote at $x = a$ on its graph.

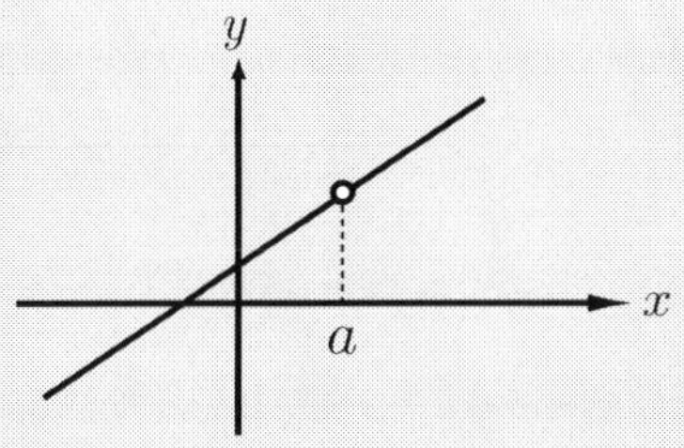

Figure 1:Hole

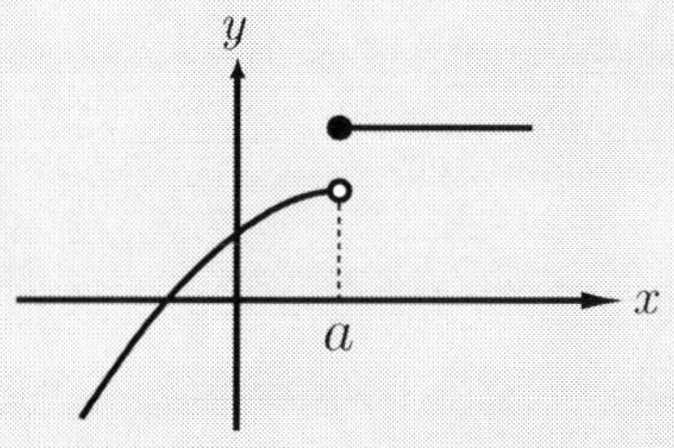

Figure 2:Jump

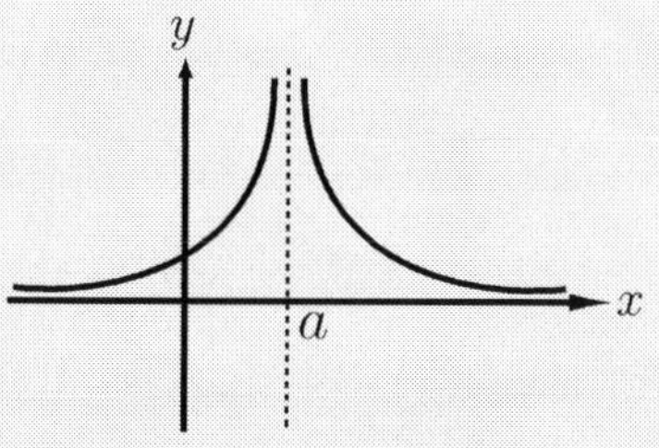

Figure 3:Vertical asymptote

First discontinuity illustrated in Figure 1 is called **removable discontinuity** because we can remove the discontinuity by redefining f. In other words, a removable discontinuity is a point at which the graph is not connected but can be connected by filling in a single point. Second discontinuity illustrated in Figure 2 is called **jump discontinuity** because the function jumps from one value to another. Third discontinuity illustrated in Figure 3 is called **infinite discontinuity** because the function has a vertical asymptote. The jump and infinite discontinuities are called **non-removable discontinuity** because the graph can not be connected by filling in a single point.

6.10 The Intermediate Value Theorem

The Intermediate Value Theorem

An important characteristic of continuous functions is shown in the following theorem. Suppose that

f is continuous on the closed interval $[a, b]$ and let N be any number between $f(a)$ and $f(b)$. Then there exists a number c in (a, b) such that $f(c) = N$.

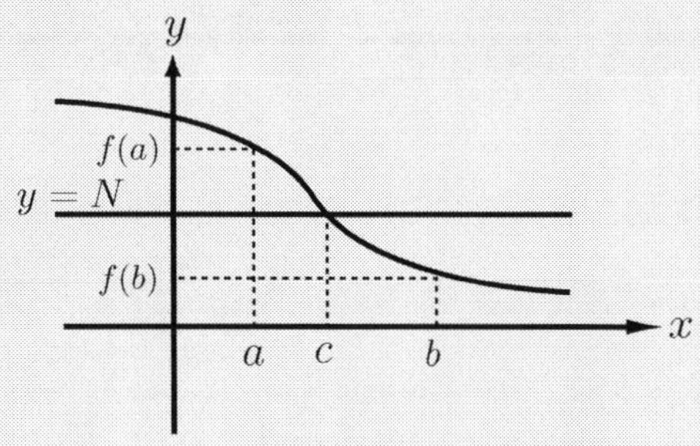

Tips

1. Intermediate value theorem is true for any continuous functions.
2. The use of the Intermediate value theorem is to find a zero of a continuous function: If $f(a)$ and $f(b)$ are of opposite signs, there must be at least one zero between a and b.

Example Finding a zero using the Intermediate value theorem

Show that $f(x) = 2x^3 + 7x^2 - 3x - 18$ has a zero between 1 and 2.

Solution

$$f(1) = 2(1)^3 + 7(1)^2 - 3(1) - 18 = -12$$
$$f(2) = 2(2)^3 + 7(2)^2 - 3(2) - 18 = 20$$

Since $f(1)$ and $f(2)$ are of opposite signs, there must be a zero between 1 and 2.

6.11 Rate of Change and Instantaneous Rate of Change

Rate of Change

Average rate change measures how much f changes over an interval from $x = a$ to $x = a + h$. Thus, average rate of change is defined as

$$\text{Average rate of change} = \frac{\Delta f}{\Delta x} = \frac{f(a+h) - f(a)}{h}$$

Notice that the average rate of change is the slope of the secant line in Figure 1. Whereas, **instantaneous rate of change** measures how much f changes over a very short interval($h \approx 0$). Thus, instantaneous rate of change is defined as

$$\text{Instantaneous rate of change} = \lim_{h\to 0} \frac{\Delta f}{\Delta x} = \lim_{h\to 0} \frac{f(a+h) - f(a)}{h}$$

Notice that the instantaneous rate of change is the slope of the tangent line in Figure 2.

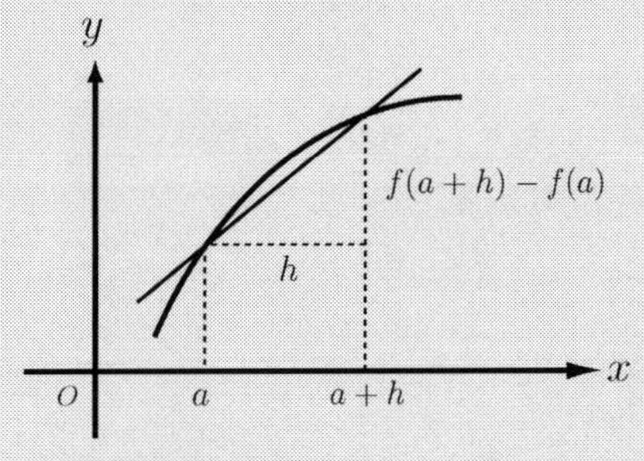

Figure 1

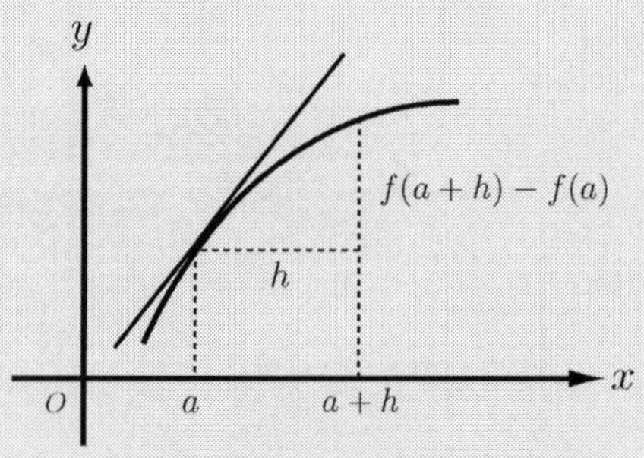

Figure 2

Tips Instantaneous rate of change can be expressed by one of the two forms shown below.

$$\lim_{h\to 0} \frac{f(a+h) - f(a)}{h} \quad \text{or} \quad \lim_{x\to a} \frac{f(x) - f(a)}{x - a}$$

6.12 Writing an Equation of the Tangent line

Tangent Line

The tangent line to the curve $y = f(x)$ at the point $(a, f(a))$ is the line with slope m where

$$m = \lim_{h \to 0} \frac{f(a+h) - f(a)}{h}$$

Thus, the equation of the tangent line at the point $(a, f(a))$ is as follows:

$$y - f(a) = m(x - a), \qquad \text{where} \quad m = \lim_{h \to 0} \frac{f(a+h) - f(a)}{h}$$

Tips

Point-slope form of a line through the point (x_0, y_0) with slope m is as follows:

$$y - y_0 = m(x - x_0)$$

6.13 Definition of the Derivative Function

Definition of the Derivative Function

The definition of the **derivative of** f is defined as

$$f'(x) = \lim_{h \to 0} \frac{f(x+h) - f(x)}{h}$$

and $f'(x)$ is read as f prime of x. The derivative of f is a function that determines the slope of the tangent lines to a graph of f. Similarly, $f(a)$ is defined as

$$f'(a) = \lim_{h \to 0} \frac{f(a+h) - f(a)}{h}$$

and $f'(a)$ determines the slope of the tangent to the graph of f at $x = a$.

Tips

The common notations for the derivative are $f'(x)$, $\frac{dy}{dx}$, y', $\frac{d}{dx}f(x)$.

6.14 Differentiability

Differentiability

A function f is differentiable at $x = a$ if $f'(a)$ exists. It is differentiable on an open interval (a, b) if it is differentiable at every point in the interval. A graph of a differentiable function on the interval (a, b) looks like a continuous smooth curve as shown below.

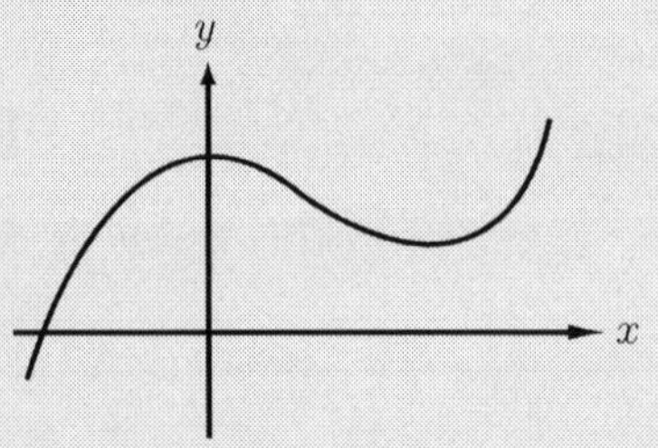

Tips

1. If f is differentiable at $x = a$, then f is continuous at $x = a$.
2. Although f is continuous at $x = a$, it does not mean that f is differentiable at $x = a$.

Non Differentiable Functions

Some functions are not differentiable at $x = a$. f is said to be a non differentiable function at $x = a$ if it has a hole, jump, sharp corner, vertical asymptote, and cusp at $x = a$ as shown below.

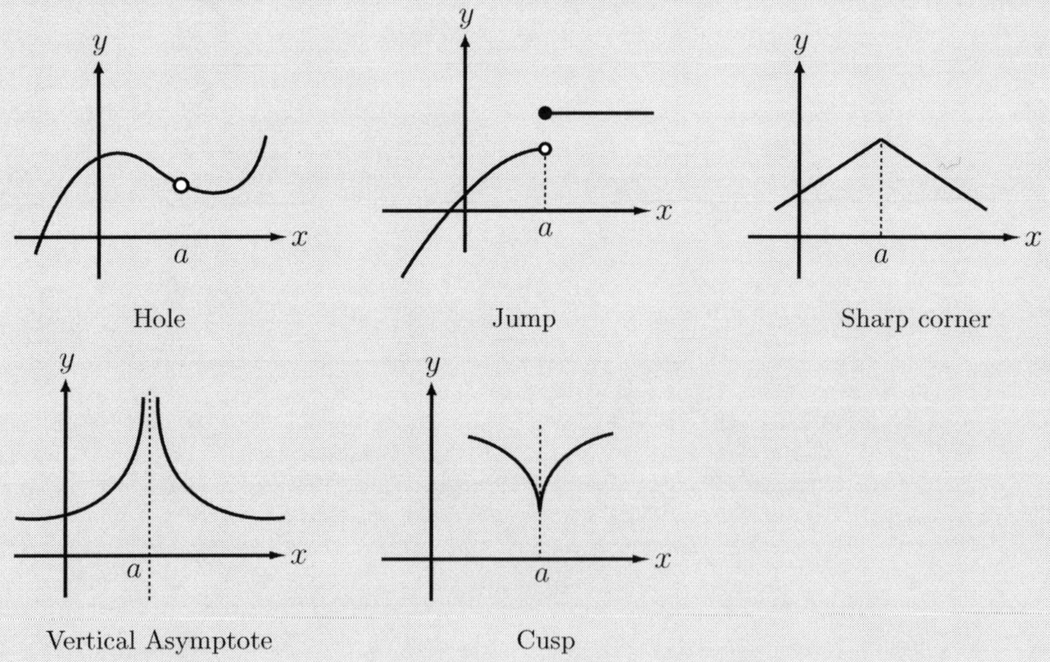

Tips

Cusp shown above has a vertical tangent at $x = a$. Since the slope of the vertical tangent is undefined, cusp is not differentiable at $x = a$.

6.15 The Graph of the Derivative Function

How to Sketch the Graph of the Derivative Function?

Draw many tangent lines to a curve $y = f(x)$ and estimate the slope of each tangent line as shown in Figure 1 . For instance, we draw the tangent line to the curve at $x = -3$ and estimate its slope to be about 2. So, $f'(-3) = 2$.

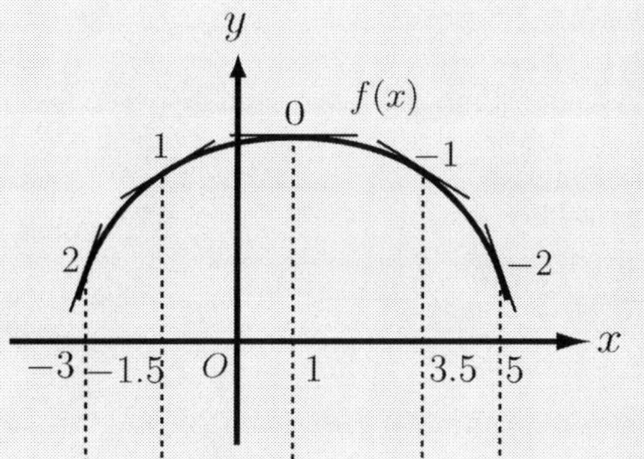

Figure 1

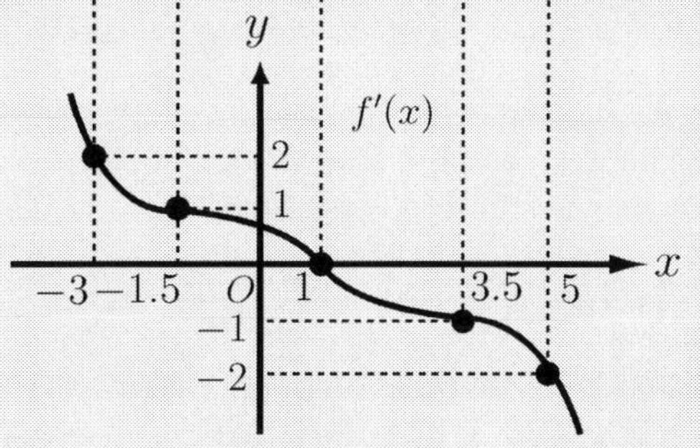

Figure 2

Plot the point $(-3, 2)$ in Figure 2. Repeat this procedure at several points. Since $f'(-1.5) = 1$, $f'(1) = 0$, $f'(3.5) = -1$, and $f'(5) = -2$, plot the points $(-1.5, 1)$, $(1, 0)$, $(3.5, -1)$, and $(5, -2)$ in Figure 2. Finally, connect the points to sketch the graph of $f'(x)$.

6.16 Differentiation Rules

Differentiation Rules

Differentiation means finding the derivative function. In general, finding the derivative function using the definition of the derivative is very tedious and takes long time. In this lesson, you will learn about the differentiation rules without using the definition of the derivative so that you can find the derivative function with ease.

The table below summarizes the differentiation rules.

Differentiation rules	Example
1. $\frac{d}{dx}(c) = 0$	1. $\frac{d}{dx}(2) = 0$
2. $\frac{d}{dx}cf(x) = c \cdot \frac{d}{dx}f(x)$	2. $\frac{d}{dx}2x^2 = 2 \cdot \frac{d}{dx}x^2$
3. $\frac{d}{dx}x^n = nx^{n-1}$	3. $\frac{d}{dx}x^3 = 3x^{3-1} = 3x^2$
4. $\frac{d}{dx}[f(x) \pm g(x)] = \frac{d}{dx}f(x) \pm \frac{d}{dx}g(x)$	4. $\frac{d}{dx}(x^3 + x) = \frac{d}{dx}x^3 + \frac{d}{dx}x = 3x^2 + 1$
5. $\frac{d}{dx}a^x = a^x \cdot \ln a$	5. $\frac{d}{dx}e^x = e^x \cdot \ln e = e^x$
6. $\frac{d}{dx}\log_a x = \frac{1}{x} \cdot \ln a$	6. $\frac{d}{dx}\ln x = \frac{1}{x} \cdot \ln e = \frac{1}{x}$

Tips

1. Note that $\frac{d}{dx}cf(x) \neq \frac{d}{dx}c \cdot \frac{d}{dx}f(x)$. For instance,

$$\frac{d}{dx}2x^2 \neq \frac{d}{dx}2 \cdot \frac{d}{dx}x^2$$

2. The 3rd differentiation rule shown above is called the **Power Rule**. You can apply the power rule to any power function $f(x) = x^n$, where the base is variable and exponent is constant.. The derivative function of the following power functions are worth memorizing.

$$\frac{d}{dx}x = 1, \quad \frac{d}{dx}x^2 = 2x, \quad \frac{d}{dx}x^3 = 3x^2, \quad \frac{d}{dx}\sqrt{x} = \frac{1}{2\sqrt{x}}, \quad \frac{d}{dx}\frac{1}{x} = -\frac{1}{x^2}$$

6.17 Product Rule and Quotient Rule

Product Rule and Quotient Rule

Product rule and quotient rule are the differentiation rules that enable us to find the derivative of product function and quotient function.

- The Product Rule: If f and g are both differentiable, then
$$(f \cdot g)' = f' \cdot g + f \cdot g'$$
- The Quotient Rule: If If f and g are both differentiable, then
$$\left(\frac{f}{g}\right)' = \frac{f' \cdot g - f \cdot g'}{g^2}$$

Tips

1. Note that the derivative of a product of two functions is **NOT** the product of derivatives as shown below.
$$(f \cdot g)' \neq f' \cdot g'$$
2. The derivative of a product of three functions is as follows:
$$(f \cdot g \cdot h)' = f' \cdot g \cdot h + f \cdot g' \cdot h + f \cdot g \cdot h'$$
3. Note that the derivative of a quotient of two functions is **NOT** the quotient of derivatives as shown below.
$$\left(\frac{f}{g}\right)' \neq \frac{f'}{g'}$$

6.18 Derivatives of Six Trigonometric Functions

Derivatives of Six Trigonometric Functions

$$\frac{d}{dx}(\sin x) = \cos x \qquad \frac{d}{dx}(\cos x) = -\sin x$$
$$\frac{d}{dx}(\tan x) = \sec^2 x \qquad \frac{d}{dx}(\cot x) = -\csc^2 x$$
$$\frac{d}{dx}(\sec x) = \sec x \tan x \qquad \frac{d}{dx}(\csc x) = -\csc x \cot x$$

Example Applying the Quotient rule

Differentiate $y = \tan x$ using the Quotient rule.

Solution Since $\tan x = \frac{\sin x}{\cos x}$,

$$\begin{aligned}
y' = (\tan x)' &= \left(\frac{\sin x}{\cos x}\right)' && \text{Apply the quotient rule} \\
&= \frac{(\sin x)' \cdot \cos x - \sin x \cdot (\cos x)'}{\cos^2 x} \\
&= \frac{\cos x \cos x - \sin x \cdot (-\sin x)}{\cos^2 x} \\
&= \frac{\cos^2 x + \sin^2 x}{\cos^2 x} && \text{Use } \cos^2 x + \sin^2 x = 1 \\
&= \frac{1}{\cos^2 x} \\
&= \sec^2 x
\end{aligned}$$

Example Applying the Product rule

Find the derivative function of $y = e^x \sin x$.

Solution Since $e^x \sin x$ is a product of two functions, apply the Product rule to the function.

$$\begin{aligned}
y' &= (e^x \sin x)' \\
&= (e^x)' \cdot \sin x + e^x \cdot (\sin x)' && \text{Since } (e^x)' = e^x \\
&= e^x \sin x + e^x \cos x
\end{aligned}$$

6.19 The Chain Rule

The Chain Rule

If you want to differentiate the function $f(x) = (x+1)^3$ using the differentiation rules that you have learned so far, you need to expand $(x+1)^3$ and apply the sum rule and power rule to each term of the function. Since $(x+1)^3 = x^3 + 3x^2 + 3x + 1$, the derivative function is

$$\frac{d}{dx}(x+1)^3 = (x^3 + 3x^2 + 3x + 1)' = 3x^2 + 6x + 3$$

However, a serious problem arises when you want to differentiate the function $(x+1)^{100}$. According to the Binomial theorem, $(x+1)^{100}$ can be written as

$$(x+1)^{100} = \sum_{k=0}^{100} \binom{100}{k} x^{100-k} 1^k$$

which indicates that the function $(x+1)^{100}$ has 101 terms. So, if you want to differentiate the function $f(x) = (x+1)^{100}$, you need to expand the function and differentiate 101 terms of the function. In this lesson, you will learn about the new differentiation rule called the **Chain Rule** which will help you differentiate a composition function like $f(x) = (x+1)^{100}$ with ease.

- The Chain Rule

  If f and g are both differentiable and F is the composition function defined by $F(x) = f(g(x))$, then F' is given by the product

  $$F'(x) = f'(g(x))g'(x)$$

  In Leibniz notion, if $y = f(u)$ and $y = g(x)$ are both differentiable function, then

  $$\frac{dy}{dx} = \frac{dy}{du} \cdot \frac{du}{dx}$$

Tips: The Chain Rule is the one of the most important differentiation rules that you are going to use a lot throughout the AP Calculus AB and AP Calculus BC courses. Many students tend to make mistake by forgetting the Chain rule when they differentiate a composition function.

Example Applying the Chain rule

Differentiate $y = (x+1)^{100}$ using the Chain rule.

Solution Let $y = u^{100}$ and $u = x + 1$. If you substitute u for $x+1$, then $y = (x+1)^{100}$. Since $(x+1)^{100}$ is a composition function, apply the Chain rule to the function.

$y = u^{100}$ $\dfrac{dy}{du} = 100u^{99}$ $= 100(x+1)^{99}$	$u = x+1$ $\dfrac{du}{dx} = 1$

Thus,

$$\begin{aligned}\frac{dy}{dx} &= \frac{dy}{du} \cdot \frac{du}{dx} \\ &= 100(x+1)^{99} \cdot 1 \\ &= 100(x+1)^{99}\end{aligned}$$

Therefore, the derivative function of $y = (x+1)^{100}$ is $100(x+1)^{99}$.

Example Applying the Chain rule

Differentiate $y = \sqrt{1-x^2}$.

Solution Let $y = \sqrt{u}$ and $u = 1 - x^2$. If you substitute u for $1 - x^2$, then $y = \sqrt{1-x^2}$. Since $y = \sqrt{1-x^2}$ is a composition function, apply the Chain rule to the function.

$y = \sqrt{u}$ $\dfrac{dy}{du} = \dfrac{1}{2\sqrt{u}}$ $= \dfrac{1}{2\sqrt{1-x^2}}$	$u = 1 - x^2$ $\dfrac{du}{dx} = -2x$

Thus,

$$\begin{aligned}\frac{dy}{dx} &= \frac{dy}{du} \cdot \frac{du}{dx} \\ &= \frac{1}{2\sqrt{1-x^2}} \cdot -2x \\ &= \frac{-x}{\sqrt{1-x^2}}\end{aligned}$$

Therefore, the derivative function of $y = \sqrt{1-x^2}$ is $\dfrac{-x}{\sqrt{1-x^2}}$.

6.20 Implicit Differentiation

Implicit Differentiation

We have learned many differentiation rules so far. These rule can be applied to a function, $y = f(x)$, defined explicitly. In case you want to differentiate some functions defined implicitly as shown below,

$$x^2 + y^2 = 25 \quad \text{(Implicit function)} \quad \Longrightarrow \quad y = \pm\sqrt{25 - x^2} \quad \text{(Explicit function)}$$

you need to redefine the functions explicitly as shown above and use the differentiation rules. However, some implicit functions like one shown below

$$x^4 + 2x^2y^2 + y^5 = 7$$

are impossible to define explicitly so that you are not able to use any one of the differentiation rules to find the derivative functions. Fortunately, the **Implicit differentiation** help you find the derivative function directly from the implicit equation without solve an equation for y in terms of x.

How to do implicit differentiation

1. Consider y as a function of x.
2. Differentiate both sides of an implicit equation with respect to x.
3. Whenever differentiating y, multiply the result by $\frac{dy}{dx}$.
4. Solve the resulting equation for $\frac{dy}{dx}$.

Tips

1. Consider y as a function of x. In other words, $y = f(x)$. So, $y^2 = [f(x)]^2$. Since $y^2 = [f(x)]^2$ is a composition function, use the Chain rule to differentiate y^2 with respect to x.

$$\begin{aligned} (y^2)' &= ([f(x)]^2)' \\ &= 2f(x) \cdot f'(x) && \text{Use the Chain rule} \\ &= 2y\frac{dy}{dx} && \text{Since } y = f(x) \text{ and } f'(x) = \frac{dy}{dx} \end{aligned}$$

2. In order to differentiate xy, use the Chain rule and the Product rule.

$$\begin{aligned} (xy)' &= (x)' \cdot y + x(y)' \\ &= y + x\frac{dy}{dx} \end{aligned}$$

Example Applying Implicit differentiation

If $x^2 + y^2 = 25$, find $\dfrac{dy}{dx}$.

Solution Differentiate both sides of an implicit equation with respect to x.

$$\begin{aligned} x^2 + y^2 &= 25 \\ 2x + 2y\frac{dy}{dx} &= 0 \\ 2y\frac{dy}{dx} &= -2x \\ \frac{dy}{dx} &= -\frac{x}{y} \end{aligned}$$

Therefore, $\dfrac{dy}{dx} = -\dfrac{x}{y}$.

Example Applying Implicit differentiation

If $x^3 + y^3 = 6xy$, find $\dfrac{dy}{dx}$.

Solution Differentiate both sides of an implicit equation with respect to x.

$$\begin{aligned} x^3 + y^3 &= 6xy && \text{Use the Product rule to differentiate } xy \\ 3x^2 + 3y^2\frac{dy}{dx} &= 6\left(y + x\frac{dy}{dx}\right) && \text{Since } (xy)' = y + x\frac{dy}{dx} \\ 3x^2 + 3y^2\frac{dy}{dx} &= 6y + 6x\frac{dy}{dx} \\ (3y^2 - 6x)\frac{dy}{dx} &= 6y - 3x^2 && \text{Divide both sides by } (3y^2 - 6x) \\ \frac{dy}{dx} &= \frac{6y - 3x^2}{3y^2 - 6x} \\ \frac{dy}{dx} &= \frac{2y - x^2}{y^2 - 2x} \end{aligned}$$

Therefore, $\dfrac{dy}{dx} = \dfrac{2y - x^2}{y^2 - 2x}$.

6.21 Higher Derivatives

Higher Derivatives

If f is a differentiable function, the derivative of f is called the **first derivative**. The notations of the first derivative are

$$f' = y' = \frac{dy}{dx}$$

The derivative of the first derivative is called **second derivative** which is denoted by

$$f'' = y'' = \frac{d^2y}{dx^2}$$

The **third derivative** is the derivative of second derivative and is denoted by

$$f''' = y''' = \frac{d^3y}{dx^3}$$

In general, the nth derivative of f is obtained by differentiating f n times and is denoted by

$$f^{(n)}(x) = y^{(n)} = \frac{d^ny}{dx^n}$$

6.22 Velocity and Acceleration

Velocity and Acceleration

If $f(t)$ is the position function of a particle, the first derivative of $f(t)$ represents **velocity** and is denoted by $v(t) = f'(t)$. The second derivative of the position function is called **acceleration** and is the derivative of the velocity. The acceleration is denoted by $a(t) = v'(t) = f''(t)$.

The following guidelines will help you solve a problem regarding velocity and acceleration.

1. Time at which a particle is at rest: Let v(t)=0 and solve for t.
2. Time at which a particle about to change its direction: Let v(t)=0 and solve for t.
3. When the particle speed up or slow down:
    - The particle speed up: when the velocity and acceleration have the same sign.
    - The particle slow down: when the velocity and acceleration have the opposite signs.

Example Finding the velocity and acceleration

If the position function $f(t)$ is defined by $f(t) = t^3 - 3t^2 - 9t$, where t measured in seconds and f in meters.

(a) Find the velocity at $t = 3$.

(b) Find the acceleration at $t = 2$

Solution

(a) Since the velocity function is the first derivative of position function,

$$v(t) = f'(t) = 3t^2 - 6t - 9$$

Thus, the velocity at $t = 3$ is $v(3) = 3(3)^2 - 6(3) - 9 = 0$, which indicates that the particle is at rest or is about to change its direction.

(b) Since the acceleration function is the first derivative of velocity function,

$$a(t) = v'(t) = 6t - 6$$

Thus, the acceleration at $t = 2$ is $a(2) = 6\ m/s^2$.

Example Finding the first and second derivatives

If $f(x) = xe^x$, find $f'(x)$ and $f''(x)$.

Solution Since xe^x is the product of two function, use the Product rule to differentiate xe^x with respect to x.

$$f'(x) = (x \cdot e^x)' = e^x + xe^x$$

Since $f''(x)$ is the derivative of $f'(x)$, differentiate $f'(x)$ with respect to x again.

$$\begin{aligned} f''(x) &= (e^x + xe^x)' \\ &= (e^x)' + (xe^x)' \\ &= e^x + e^x + xe^x \\ &= 2e^x + xe^x \end{aligned}$$

6.23 L'Hospital's Rule

L'Hospital's Rule

Let f and g are differentiable and $g'(x) \neq 0$ near a. Suppose you have one of the following cases

$$\lim_{x \to a} \frac{f(x)}{g(x)} = \frac{0}{0} \qquad \text{or} \qquad \lim_{x \to a} \frac{f(x)}{g(x)} = \frac{\pm\infty}{\pm\infty}$$

where a can be any real number, infinity, or negative infinity. Then,

$$\lim_{x \to a} \frac{f(x)}{g(x)} = \lim_{x \to a} \frac{f'(x)}{g'(x)}$$

Tips

1. L'Hospital's Rule says that the limit of a quotient of functions is equal to the limit of the quotient of their derivatives.
2. L'Hospital's Rule is also valid for one-sided limits: that is, $x \to a$ can be replaced by any of the followings: $x \to a^+$, $x \to a^-$.

Example **Finding the limit**

Find $\lim\limits_{x \to 0} \dfrac{\sin x}{x}$.

Solution Substitute x for 0 in the numerator and the denominator. Then, you will get an indeterminate form of $\dfrac{0}{0}$. Use the L'Hospital's rule to find the limit.

$$\begin{aligned} \lim_{x \to 0} \frac{\sin x}{x} &= \lim_{x \to 0} \frac{(\sin x)'}{(x)'} \\ &= \lim_{x \to 0} \frac{\cos x}{1} && \text{Substitute } x \text{ for } 0 \\ &= 1 \end{aligned}$$

Therefore, $\lim\limits_{x \to 0} \dfrac{\sin x}{x} = 1$.

Example Finding the limit

Find $\lim_{x\to 2} \frac{x-2}{\ln(x-1)}$.

Solution Substitute x for 2 in the numerator and the denominator. Then, you will get an indeterminate form of $\frac{0}{0}$. Use the L'Hospital's rule to find the limit.

$$\begin{aligned}
\lim_{x\to 2} \frac{x-2}{\ln(x-1)} &= \lim_{x\to 2} \frac{(x-2)'}{(\ln(x-1))'} \\
&= \lim_{x\to 2} \frac{1}{\frac{1}{x-1}} && \text{Use the Chain rule to differentiate } \ln(x-1) \\
&= \lim_{x\to 2} (x-1) \\
&= 1
\end{aligned}$$

Therefore, $\lim_{x\to 2} \frac{x-2}{\ln(x-1)} = 1$.

Example Finding the limit

Find $\lim_{x\to\infty} \frac{e^x}{x^2}$.

Solution Substitute x for ∞ in the numerator and the denominator. Then, you will get an indeterminate form of $\frac{\infty}{\infty}$. Use the L'Hospital's rule to find the limit.

$$\begin{aligned}
\lim_{x\to\infty} \frac{e^x}{x^2} &= \lim_{x\to\infty} \frac{(e^x)'}{(x^2)'} \\
&= \lim_{x\to\infty} \frac{e^x}{2x} && \text{Substitute } x \text{ for } \infty\text{, you get a } \frac{\infty}{\infty} \\
&= \lim_{x\to\infty} \frac{(e^x)'}{(2x)'} && \text{Use the L'Hospital rule again} \\
&= \lim_{x\to\infty} \frac{e^x}{2} && \text{Substitute } x \text{ for } \infty \text{ again} \\
&= \frac{\infty}{2} \\
&= \infty
\end{aligned}$$

Therefore, $\lim_{x\to\infty} \frac{e^x}{x^2} = \infty$.

6.24 Related Rates

Related Rates

In a related rates problem, we are trying to find the rate of change of one quantity in terms of the rate of change of another quantity that is already measured. Related rates is an application of an implicit differentiation. The quantities that you are about to see in a related rate problem are functions of time t.

How to do related rates problems

1. Read a problem and draw a diagram.
2. Identify all quantities that are function of time t.
3. Assign variables to all quantities that are function of time t.
4. Write down all information and given rates in terms of derivatives.
5. Set up an equation that relates the quantities.
6. Use the Chain rule to differentiate both sides of the equation with respect to t.
7. Solve for the unknown rate.

Tips

Suppose x is a quantity that is a function of time t in a related rates problem: $x = f(t)$. Below shows you how to differentiate x^2 with respect to t using the Chain rule.

$$\begin{aligned}(x^2)' &= \frac{d}{dt}(f(t))^2 && \text{Since } x = f(t)\text{, Use the Chain rule}\\ &= 2f(t)\cdot f'(t) && \text{Since } f(t) = x \text{ and } f'(t) = \frac{dx}{dt}\\ &= 2x\frac{dx}{dt}\end{aligned}$$

Example Solving a related rates problem

A ladder 10 ft long leans against a building. If the bottom of the ladder slides away from the wall at a rate of 2 ft/sec, how fast is the top of the ladder sliding down the wall when the bottom of the ladder is 6 ft from the wall?

Solution Let x be the distance from the bottom of the ladder to the wall and y be the distance from the top of the ladder to the ground as shown in figures below. Since the top of the ladder slides down, y decreases as time increases. However, the bottom of the lader slides away. So, x increases as time increases. Thus, x and y are functions of time t.

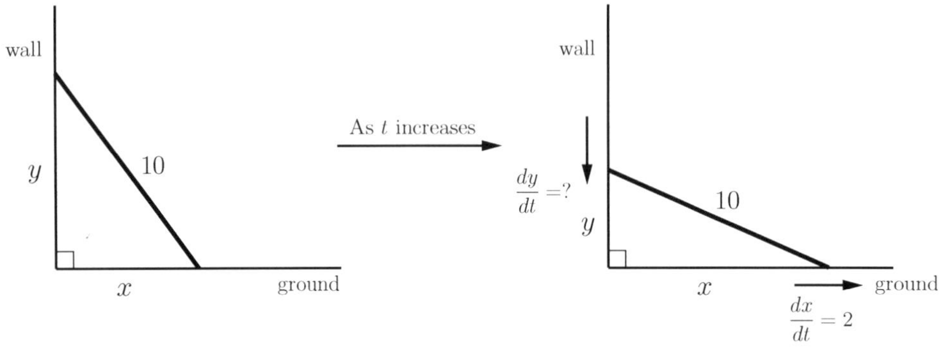

We are given that $\frac{dx}{dt} = 2$ ft/sec and try to find $\frac{dy}{dt}$ when $x = 6$ ft. Let's set up an equation that relates x and y using the Pythagorean theorem.

$$x^2 + y^2 = 10^2$$

Differentiate both sides with respect to t using the Chain rule and solve for $\frac{dy}{dt}$.

$$\begin{aligned} 2x\frac{dx}{dt} + 2y\frac{dy}{dt} &= 0 \\ 2y\frac{dy}{dt} &= -2x\frac{dx}{dt} \\ \frac{dy}{dt} &= -\frac{x}{y}\frac{dx}{dt} \end{aligned}$$

From the equation $x^2 + y^2 = 10^2$, $y = 8$ when $x = 6$. Substituting $x = 6$, $y = 8$ and $\frac{dx}{dt} = 2$,

$$\frac{dy}{dt} = -\frac{x}{y}\frac{dx}{dt} = -\frac{6}{8}(2) = -\frac{3}{2}$$

Therefore, the top of the ladder is sliding down the wall at a rate of $-\frac{3}{2}$ ft/sec.

Example Solving a related rates problem

If a spherical snowball melts so that its volume decreases at a rate of 1 cm^3/min, find the rate at which the radius decreases when the radius is 10 cm.

Solution Let V be the volume of the sphere and r be the radius of the sphere. As shown in the figures below, both the volume and radius decrease as time t increases. So, the volume and the radius are the functions of t.

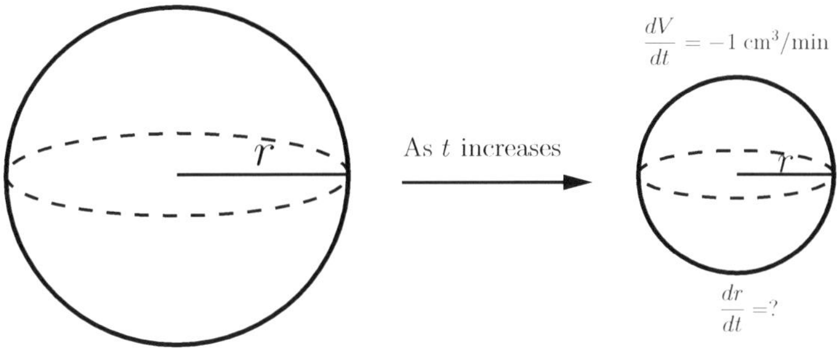

We are given that $\frac{dV}{dt} = -1 \text{ cm}^3/\text{min}$ and try to find $\frac{dr}{dt}$ when $r = 10$ cm. Let's set up an equation that relates V and r.

$$V = \frac{4}{3}\pi r^3$$

Differentiate both sides with respect to t using the Chain rule and solve for $\frac{dr}{dt}$.

$$\begin{aligned}\frac{dV}{dt} &= 4\pi r^2 \frac{dr}{dt}\\ \frac{dr}{dt} &= \frac{1}{4\pi r^2}\frac{dV}{dt}\end{aligned}$$

Substituting $r = 10$, $\frac{dV}{dt} = -1$

$$\begin{aligned}\frac{dr}{dt} &= \frac{1}{4\pi r^2}\frac{dV}{dt}\\ &= \frac{1}{4\pi(10)^2}(-1)\\ &\approx -0.000796\end{aligned}$$

Therefore, the rate at which the radius decreases when the radius is 10 cm is 0.000796 cm/min.

6.25 The Mean Value Theorem

The Mean Value Theorem

Let f be a function that satisfies the following hypotheses:

1. f is continuous on the closed interval $[a, b]$.
2. f is differentiable on the open interval (a, b).

Then there is a c in (a, b) such that $f'(c) = \dfrac{f(b) - f(a)}{b - a}$.

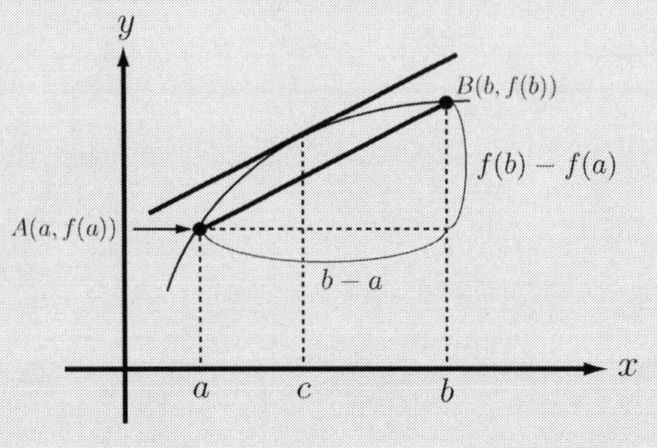

The Mean Value theorem can be stated in terms of slopes. $\dfrac{f(b) - f(a)}{b - a}$ represents the slope of the line that passes through the points A and B, and $f'(c)$ represents the slope of the tangent line at $x = c$ as shown in the figure above. Thus, the conclusion of the Mean Value theorem is that there is c in (a, b) such that the tangent line at $x = c$ is parallel to the line that passes through the points A and B.

Example Mean Value theorem

If $f(x) = -x^2 + 8x - 6$ on the closed interval $[1, 4]$, find all numbers c that satisfy the conclusion of the Mean Value theorem.

Solution $f(x)$ is a polynomial function. So, f is continuous on $[1, 4]$ and is differentiable on $(1, 4)$. Since $f'(x) = -2x + 8$ and the slope of line that passes through $(1, 1)$ and $(4, 10)$ is $\frac{10-1}{4-1} = 3$,

$$
\begin{aligned}
f'(c) &= \frac{f(b) - f(a)}{b - a} \\
-2c + 8 &= 3 \\
c &= \frac{5}{2}
\end{aligned}
$$

Therefore, the number c that satisfy the conclusion of the Mean Value theorem and in the interval $[1, 4]$ is 2.5.

6.26 Increasing and Decreasing Test

Increasing and Decreasing Test

Increasing and Decreasing Test

1. If $f'(x) > 0$ for all x on an interval, then f is increasing on that interval.
2. If $f'(x) < 0$ for all x on an interval, then f is decreasing on that interval.

Example **Finding where a function is increasing or decreasing**

Find where the function $f(x) = x^3 - 9x^2 + 24x + 1$ is increasing and where it is decreasing.

Solution $f'(x) = 3x^2 - 18x + 24 = 3(x-2)(x-4)$.

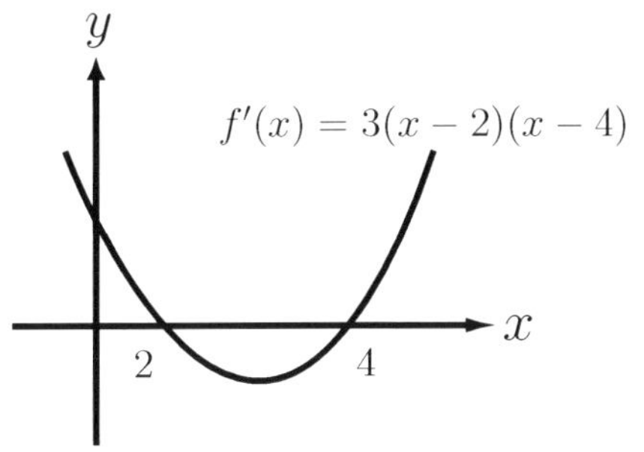

As shown in the figure above, $f'(x) > 0$ for $x < 2$ and also for $x > 4$. Whereas, $f'(x) < 0$ for $2 < x < 4$. Therefore, f is increasing for $x < 2$ and $x > 4$, and f is decreasing for $2 < x < 4$.

6.27 Concavity Test

Concavity Test

Concavity Test

1. If $f''(x) > 0$ for all x on an interval, then the graph of f is concave upward on that interval.
2. If $f''(x) < 0$ for all x on an interval, then the graph of f is concave downward on that interval.

Tips

1. $f''(x) > 0$ means that $f'(x)$ is increasing. Thus the graph of f is concave upward.
2. $f''(x) < 0$ means that $f'(x)$ is decreasing. Thus the graph of f is concave downward.

Inflection Point

A point P on the curve is called an **inflection point** if the curve changes from concave upward to concave downward or from concave downward to concave upward at P.

If there is an inflection point on the curve at $x = a$, $f''(a) = 0$.

Example **Finding the intervals of concavity and the inflection point**

If $f(x) = x^3 - 9x^2 + 24x + 1$, find the intervals of concavity and the inflection point.

Solution $f'(x) = 3x^2 - 18x + 24 = 3(x-2)(x-4)$ and $f''(x) = 6x - 18$. Since $f''(x) = 0$ when $x = 3$, $(3, 19)$ is the inflection point. Using the Concavity test,

$$\begin{array}{llll} f''(x) > 0 & \text{for } x > 3 & \Longrightarrow & f \text{ is concave upward} \\ f''(x) < 0 & \text{for } x < 3 & \Longrightarrow & f \text{ is concave downward} \end{array}$$

Therefore, f is concave upward for $x > 3$, and f is concave downward for $x < 3$.

6.28 Finding a Local Maximum and a Local Minimum

Finding a Local Maximum and a Local Minimum

There are two ways to find a local maximum and a local minimum: **The first derivative test** and **the second derivative test**.

The First Derivative Test: Suppose that c is a critical number of a continuous function f.

1. If f' changes from positive to negative at c, then f has a local maximum at c.
2. If f' changes from negative to positive at c, then f has a local minimum at c.

The Second Derivative Test: Suppose f'' is continuous near c.

1. If $f'(c) = 0$ and $f''(c) > 0$, then f has a local minimum at c.
2. If $f'(c) = 0$ and $f''(c) < 0$, then f has a local maximum at c.

Example **Finding the local maximum and local minimum**

If $f(x) = x^3 - 9x^2 + 24x + 1$, find the local maximum and local minimum values of f.

Solution $f'(x) = 3x^2 - 18x + 24 = 3(x-2)(x-4)$ and $f''(x) = 6x - 18$. $f'(x) = 0$ for $x = 2$ and $x = 4$. So, the critical numbers are 2 and 4. Let's find the local maximum and local minimum values of f using both the First Derivative test and Second Derivative test.

- Using the First Derivative Test:
  As shown in the figure below, f' changes positive to negative at $x = 2$. Thus, f has a local maximum at $x = 2$. The local maximum of value of f is $f(2) = 21$.

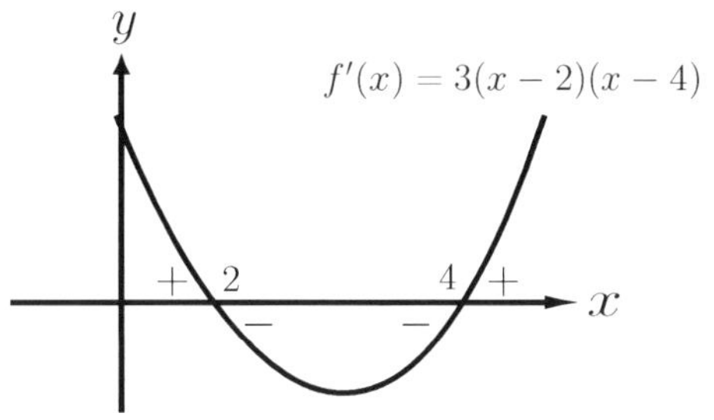

  However, f' changes negative to positive at $x = 4$. Thus, f has a local minimum at $x = 4$. The local minimum of value of f is $f(4) = 17$.

- Using the Second Derivative Test:
  Since the critical numbers are 2 and 4, substituting these values into the second derivative $f''(x) = 6x - 18$ will determine the local maximum and local minimum value of f.

$$f''(2) = 6(2) - 18 < 0 \quad \Longrightarrow \quad f \text{ has the local maximum at } x = 2$$
$$f''(4) = 6(4) - 18 > 0 \quad \Longrightarrow \quad f \text{ has the local minimum at } x = 4$$

  Therefore, the local maximum of value of f is $f(2) = 21$, and the local minimum of value of f is $f(4) = 17$.

6.29 Optimization Problems

Optimization Problems

Optimization is one of the most important applications of the first derivative because it has many applications in real life. In general, optimization consists of maximizing or minimizing a function with a constraint. The following guidelines will help you solve optimization problems.

1. Read the problem and draw a diagram.
2. Define variables and label your diagram with these variables. It will help you set up mathematical equations.
3. Set up two equations that are related to the diagram. One equation is an optimization equation and the other is a constraint equation. The constraint equation is used to solve for one of the variables.
4. Set up the optimization equation as a function of only one variable using the constraint equation.
5. Differentiate the optimization equation and find the critical numbers.
6. Find the local maximum and minimum using the first or second derivative tests.

Example Solving optimization problems

A farmer has 1000 m of fencing and wants to fence off a rectangular field that borders a straight river. He does not need any fence along the river. Find the dimensions of the field that has the largest area.

Solution As shown in the figure below, let x and y be the width and length of the rectangular field, respectively.

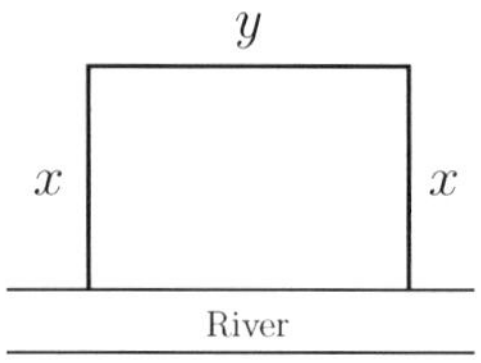

So, the area A and constraint can be defined as

$$\text{Maximization equation:} \quad A(x, y) = xy$$
$$\text{Constraint equation:} \quad 2x + y = 1000$$

From the constraint equation, we get $y = 1000 - 2x$. Substituting this into the maximization equation,

$$A(x) = x(1000 - 2x) = 1000x - 2x^2$$

Differentiate $A(x)$ with respect to x and find the critical numbers.

$$A'(x) = 1000 - 4x$$

Since $A'(x) = 0$ when $x = 250$, the critical number is 250. Note that $A''(x) = -4$ for all x. Using the Second Derivative test, $A''(250) < 0$ which indicates that the function $A(x)$ has the local maximum at $x = 250$. Thus, $y = 1000 - 2x = 1000 - 2(250) = 500$. Therefore, the dimensions of the field that has the largest area are width of 250 m and length of 500 m.

6.30 Basic Indefinite Integrals

Basic Indefinite Integrals

1. $\int cf(x)\,dx = c\int f(x)\,dx$
2. $\int [f(x) \pm g(x)]\,dx = \int f(x)\,dx \pm \int g(x)\,dx$
3. $\int k\,dx = kx + C$
4. $\int x^n\,dx = \frac{1}{n+1}x^{n+1} + C \quad (n \neq -1)$
5. $\int \frac{1}{x}\,dx = \ln|x| + C$
6. $\int a^x\,dx = \frac{a^x}{\ln a} + C$
7. $\int e^x\,dx = e^x + C$
8. $\int \sin x\,dx = -\cos x + C$
9. $\int \cos x\,dx = \sin x + C$
10. $\int \sec^2 x\,dx = \tan x + C$
11. $\int \csc^2 x\,dx = -\cot x + C$
12. $\int \sec x \tan x\,dx = \sec x + C$
13. $\int \csc x \cot x\,dx = -\csc x + C$
14. $\int \frac{1}{x^2+1}\,dx = \tan^{-1} x + C$
15. $\int \frac{1}{\sqrt{1-x^2}}\,dx = \sin^{-1} x + C$
16. $\int \tan x\,dx = \ln|\sec x| + C$
17. $\int \cot x\,dx = \ln|\sin x| + C$

Tips

1. We need to use the Substitution rule to find the indefinite integrals of $\tan x$ and $\cot x$. However, consider these indefinite integrals as basic integrals and memorize them for now.
2. Note that $\int f(x)\cdot g(x)dx \neq \int f(x)dx \cdot \int g(x)dx$

Example Finding the indefinite integral

Find the indefinite integral of $f(x) = \dfrac{x^2+x+1}{x}$.

Solution

$$\begin{aligned}\int \frac{x^2+x+1}{x}dx &= \int \frac{x^2}{x} + \frac{x}{x} + \frac{1}{x}dx \\ &= \int x + 1 + \frac{1}{x}dx \\ &= \frac{1}{2}x^2 + x + \ln|x| + C\end{aligned}$$

6.31 Numerical Approximations of a Definite Integral

Left Endpoint Approximation and Right Endpoint Approximation

Suppose we divide $[a, b]$ into n subintervals of equal length $\Delta x = \frac{b-a}{n}$. Then,

$$\int_a^b f(x)\,dx \approx \sum_{i=1}^{n} f(x_i^*)\Delta x$$

where x_i^* is any point in the ith subinterval $[x_{i-1}, x_i]$. If x_{i-1} is chosen to be the left endpoint of the interval as shown in Figure 1, then $x_i^* = x_{i-1}$. Thus,

$$\int_a^b f(x)\,dx \approx L_n = \sum_{i=1}^{n} f(x_{i-1})\Delta x$$

L_n is called the **Left endpoint approximation**.

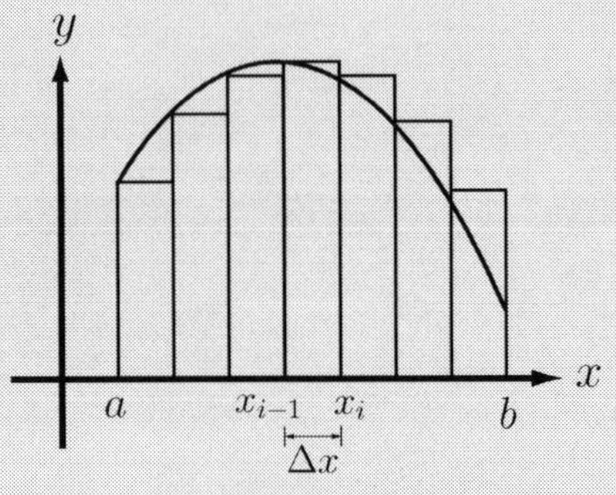

Figure 1

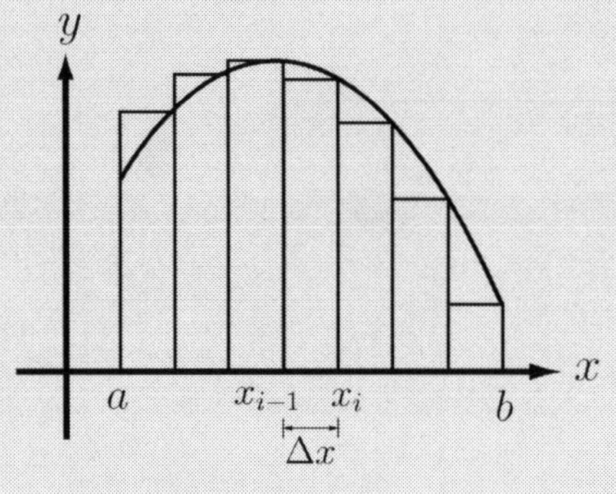

Figure 2

Whereas, if x_i is chosen to be the right endpoint of the interval as shown in Figure 2, then $x_i^* = x_i$. Thus,

$$\int_a^b f(x)\,dx \approx R_n = \sum_{i=1}^{n} f(x_i)\Delta x$$

R_n is called the **Right endpoint approximation**.

Tips

1. If f is increasing on $[a, b]$, $\quad L_n < \int_a^b f(x)\,dx < R_n$
2. If f is decreasing on $[a, b]$, $\quad R_n < \int_a^b f(x)\,dx < L_n$

Midpoint Approximation and Trapezoidal Approximation

Suppose we divide $[a, b]$ into n subintervals of equal length $\Delta x = \frac{b-a}{n}$. Then,

$$\int_a^b f(x)\,dx \approx \sum_{i=1}^{n} f(x_i^*)\Delta x$$

where x_i^* is any point in the ith subinterval $[x_{i-1}, x_i]$. If $\dfrac{x_{i-1}+x_i}{2}$ is chosen to be the midpoint of the interval as shown in Figure 3, then $x_i^* = \dfrac{x_{i-1}+x_i}{2}$. Thus,

$$\int_a^b f(x)\,dx \approx M_n = \sum_{i=1}^{n} f\left(\frac{x_{i-1}+x_i}{2}\right)\Delta x$$

M_n is called the **Midpoint Rule** or **Midpoint approximation**.

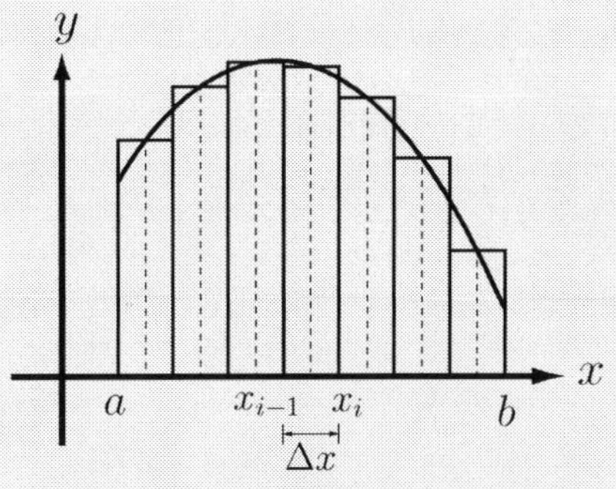

Figure 3

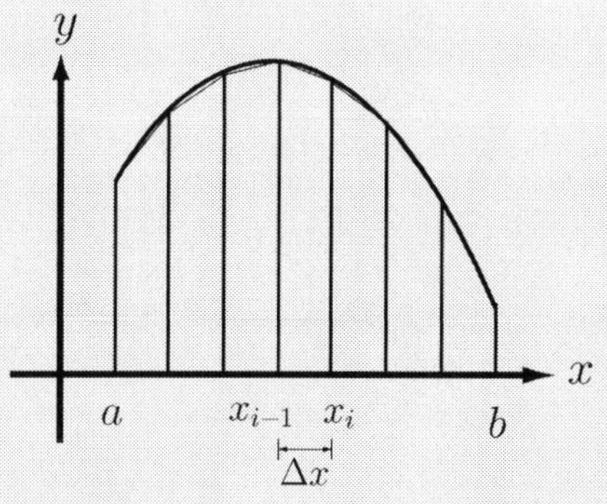

Figure 4

In general, the sum of areas of trapezoids gives you a better approximation of a definite integral than the sum of areas of rectangles over n subintervals. As shown in Figure 4, the area of trapezoid that lies above the ith subinterval can be written as

$$\frac{1}{2}\Big(f(x_{i-1}) + f(x_i)\Big)\Delta x$$

Thus,

$$\begin{aligned}\int_a^b f(x)\,dx \approx T_n &= \sum_{i=1}^{n} \frac{1}{2}\Big(f(x_{i-1}) + f(x_i)\Big)\Delta x \\ &= \frac{\Delta x}{2}[f(x_0) + 2f(x_1) + 2f(x_2) + \cdots + 2f(x_{n-1}) + f(x_n)]\end{aligned}$$

where $x_0 = a$ and $x_n = b$. T_n is called **Trapezoidal Rule** or **Trapezoidal approximation**.

Tips

1. If f is concave up on $[a, b]$, $\quad M_n < \int_a^b f(x)\,dx < T_n$
2. If f is concave down on $[a, b]$, $\quad T_n < \int_a^b f(x)\,dx < M_n$

Example Approximating a definite integral

Use the left endpoint approximation with $n = 4$ to approximate the integral $\int_1^7 x^2\,dx$.

Solution Interval width Δx is $\Delta x = \frac{b-a}{n} = \frac{7-1}{4} = 1.5$ and the left endpoints are 1, 2.5, 4, and 5.5.

$$\begin{aligned}
\int_1^7 x^2\,dx \approx L_4 &= \sum_{i=1}^{4} f(x_{i-1})\Delta x \\
&= f(1)\Delta x + f(2.5)\Delta x + f(4)\Delta x + f(5.5)\Delta x \\
&= \Delta x\Big(f(1) + f(2.5) + f(4) + f(5.5)\Big) \\
&= 1.5(1 + 6.25 + 16 + 30.25) \\
&= 80.25
\end{aligned}$$

Example Approximating a definite integral

Use the Trapezoidal Rule with $n = 5$ to approximate the integral $\int_1^3 \frac{1}{x}\,dx$.

Solution Interval width Δx is $\Delta x = \frac{b-a}{n} = \frac{3-1}{5} = 0.4$. So, the Trapezoidal Rule gives

$$\begin{aligned}
\int_1^3 \frac{1}{x}\,dx \approx T_5 &= \sum_{i=1}^{5} \frac{1}{2}\Big(f(x_{i-1}) + f(x_i)\Big)\Delta x \\
&= \frac{\Delta x}{2}[f(x_0) + 2f(x_1) + 2f(x_2) + \cdots + 2f(x_{n-1}) + f(x_n)] \\
&= \frac{0.4}{2}[f(1) + 2f(1.4) + 2f(1.8) + 2f(2.2) + 2f(2.6) + f(3)] \\
&= 0.2\Big(\frac{1}{1} + \frac{2}{1.4} + \frac{2}{1.8} + \frac{2}{2.2} + \frac{2}{2.6} + \frac{1}{3}\Big) \\
&\approx 1.1103
\end{aligned}$$

6.32 The Fundamental Theorem of Calculus

The Fundamental Theorem of Calculus, Part I

If f is continuous on $[a, b]$, then the function g defined by

$$g(x) = \int_a^x f(t)\,dt \qquad a \leq x \leq b$$

is continuous on $[a, b]$ and differentiable on (a, b), and

$$g'(x) = \frac{d}{dx}\int_a^x f(t)\,dt \quad \Longrightarrow \quad g'(x) = f(x)$$

Tips

1. The Fundamental Theorem of Calculus, Part I is important because it guarantees that the existence of antiderivatives for continuous functions.
2. You can choose any arbitrary number for the lower limit a because $g'(x)$ is not affected by a. For instance,

$$g(x) = \int_2^x f(t)\,dt, \quad \Longrightarrow \quad g'(x) = \frac{d}{dx}\int_2^x f(t)\,dt = f(x)$$
$$g(x) = \int_0^x f(t)\,dt, \quad \Longrightarrow \quad g'(x) = \frac{d}{dx}\int_0^x f(t)\,dt = f(x)$$

3. In case the upper limit is $p(x)$, then $g'(x)$ is

$$g'(x) = \frac{d}{dx}\int_a^{p(x)} f(t)\,dt \quad \Longrightarrow \quad g'(x) = f(p(x)) \cdot (p(x))'$$

For instance, if $g(x) = \displaystyle\int_0^{x^2} \sin t\,dt$, then $g'(x)$ is

$$g'(x) = \frac{d}{dx}\int_0^{x^2} \sin t\,dt \quad \Longrightarrow \quad g'(x) = \sin(x^2) \cdot (2x)$$

4. In case the lower limit is $q(x)$ and upper limit is $p(x)$, then $g'(x)$ is

$$g'(x) = \frac{d}{dx}\int_{q(x)}^{p(x)} f(t)\,dt \quad \Longrightarrow \quad g'(x) = f(p(x)) \cdot (p(x))' - f(q(x)) \cdot (q(x))'$$

The Fundamental Theorem of Calculus, Part II

If f is continuous on $[a,b]$, then

$$\int_a^b f(x)\,dx = F(x)\Big]_a^b = F(b) - F(a)$$

Where F is any antiderivative of f such that $F' = f$.

Example Finding the derivative using the Fundamental Theorem of Calculus, Part I

If $g(x) = \displaystyle\int_1^{2x} \sqrt{3t+1}\,dt$, find $g'(x)$.

Solution

$$g'(x) = \frac{d}{dx}\int_1^{2x} \sqrt{3t+1}\,dt = \sqrt{3(2x)+1}\cdot(2x)' = 2\sqrt{6x+1}$$

The Total Change Theorem

Let $F'(x)$ be a rate of change. Then, the integral of a rate of change given by $\displaystyle\int_a^b F'(x)\,dx$ is

$$\int_a^b F'(x)\,dx = F(x)\Big]_a^b = F(b) - F(a)$$

and is the total change such that $F(b) - F(a)$.

Tips

1. If $F'(x)$ is the rate of growth of a population, $\displaystyle\int_{t_1}^{t_2} F'(x)\,dx$ is the total change in population from time period $t = t_1$ to $t = t_2$.
2. If $F'(x)$ is the velocity of an object, $\displaystyle\int_{t_1}^{t_2} F'(x)\,dx$ is the total change in position, or **displacement** of the particle from time period $t = t_1$ to $t = t_2$.

6.33 U-Substitution Rule

U-Substitution Rule

Suppose f is continuous on $[a, b]$ and $u = g(x)$ is a differentiable function on $[a, b]$. Then, $du = g'(x)dx$. Thus,

$$\int f\big(g(x)\big)g'(x)\,dx = \int f(u)\,du$$

Tips

1. The most important part of the U-Substitution Rule is to change from the variable x to a new variable u, and change from dx to du. The new integral $\int f(u)\,du$ after the U-Substitution becomes one of the basic indefinite integrals so that you can evaluate the new integral at ease.
2. du is the differential. For instance, if $u = x^2$, then $du = 2x\,dx$.

Example **Evaluating an indefinite integral using the U-Substitution rule**

Evaluate $\int \frac{\ln x}{x}\,dx$.

Solution Let $u = \ln x$. Then $du = \frac{1}{x}\,dx$. Thus,

$$\begin{aligned}\int \frac{\ln x}{x}\,dx &= \int \ln x\,\frac{1}{x}\,dx = \int u\,du \\ &= \frac{1}{2}u^2 + C = \frac{1}{2}\ln^2 x + C\end{aligned}$$

Example **Evaluating an definite integral using the U-Substitution rule**

Evaluate $\int_1^5 \sqrt{x-1}\,dx$.

Solution Let $u = x - 1$. Then $du = dx$. Let's find the new lower limit and upper limit for the integration.

When $x = 1$, $u = x - 1 = 0$, When $x = 5$, $u = x - 1 = 4$

Thus, the new lower limit and upper limit for the integration are 0 and 4, respectively.

$$\int_1^5 \sqrt{x-1}\,dx = \int_0^4 \sqrt{u}\,du = \frac{2}{3}u^{\frac{3}{2}}\Big]_0^4 = \frac{16}{3}$$

6.34 Integration by parts

Integration by parts

$$\int u\,dv = uv - \int v\,du$$

Applying integration by parts transforms a difficult integral (on the left side) into the difference of the product of two functions (in the middle) and a easy integral (on the right side)

Guidelines for choosing u and dv

$$\ln x \qquad (\sin^{-1} x, \tan^{-1} x) \qquad (x^n, 1) \qquad (\sin x, \cos x) \qquad e^x$$

$u \leftarrow$ easier to differentiate | easier to integrate $\rightarrow dv$

A list above shows five different types of functions: a logarithmic function, an inverse trigonometric function, power function including 1, trigonometric function, and exponential function. If the integrand is a product of two functions from the list, choose one function as u if it is closer to the left side and then choose another function as dv. For instance, in $\int xe^x\,dx$, the integrand is xe^x, which is the product of a power function and an exponential function. Choose x as u and $e^x\,dx$ as dv since the power function is closer to the left side than the exponential function.

Tips In general, use the integration by parts if the integrand is a product of two functions from the list shown above.

Example Evaluating the integral using integration by parts

Evaluate $\int \ln x\,dx$.

Solution $\int \ln x\,dx = \int \ln x \cdot 1\,dx$. According to the list below,

$$\ln x \qquad (\sin^{-1} x, \tan^{-1} x) \qquad (x^n, 1) \qquad (\sin x, \cos x) \qquad e^x$$

$u \leftarrow$ easier to differentiate | easier to integrate $\rightarrow dv$

$\ln x$ is closer to the left side than 1. Let $u = \ln x$ and $dv = 1\,dx$. So, $\int \ln x\,dx = \int u\,dv$. Then

$$u = \ln x \qquad v = x$$
$$du = \frac{1}{x}\,dx \qquad dv = dx$$

Thus,

$$\begin{aligned}\int u\,dv &= uv - \int v\,du \\ &= x\ln x - \int x \cdot \frac{1}{x}\,dx \\ &= x\ln x - \int 1\,dx \\ &= x\ln x - x + C\end{aligned}$$

Example Evaluating the definite integral using integration by parts

Evaluate $\int_1^e \ln x\,dx$.

Solution As you obtained in Example 1, $\int \ln x\,dx = x\ln x - \int 1\,dx$. Thus,

$$\begin{aligned}\int_1^e \ln x\,dx &= x\ln x\Big]_1^e - \int_1^e 1\,dx \\ &= x\ln x\Big]_1^e - x\Big]_1^e \\ &= e - (e-1) \\ &= 1\end{aligned}$$

6.35 Area Between Curves

Finding Area between Curves Using ith Vertical Rectangle

Suppose $y = f_T$ and $y = f_B$ are continuous functions in $[a, b]$ and $f_T(x) \geq f_B(x)$ for all x in $[a, b]$ as shown below. f_T and f_B represent the top curve and bottom curve, respectively.

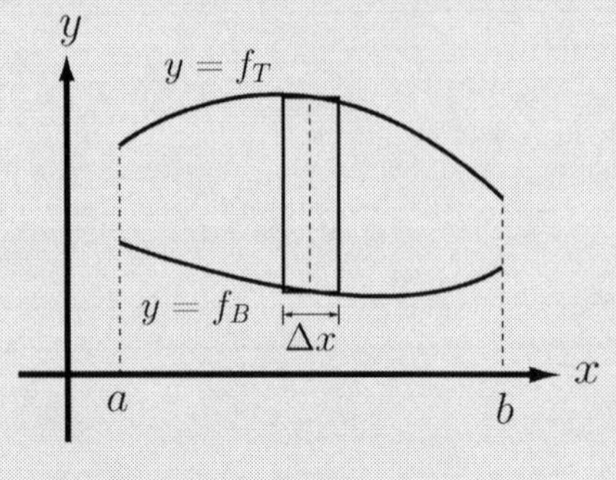

The area of ith vertical rectangle is $(f_T - f_B)\Delta x$. Thus, the area A enclosed by region enclosed by two curves f_T and f_B, and two vertical lines $x = a$ and $x = b$ is

$$A = \int_a^b [f_T - f_B]\, dx$$

Finding Area between Curves Using ith Horizontal Rectangle

Suppose $x = f_R$ and $x = f_L$ are continuous functions and $f_R \geq f_L$ for $c \leq y \leq d$ as shown below. f_R and f_L represent the right curve and left curve, respectively.

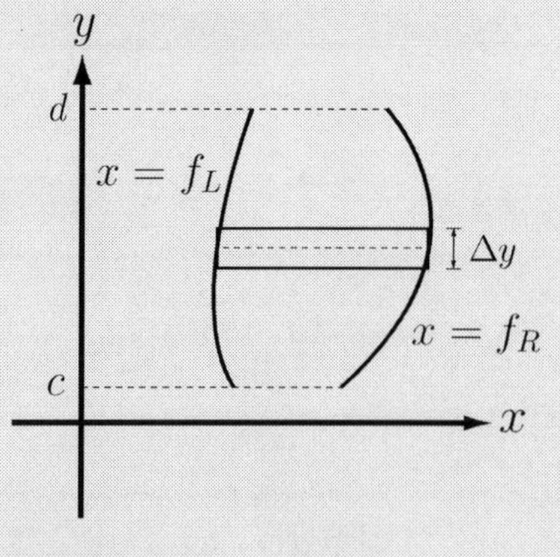

The area of ith horizontal rectangle is $(f_R - f_L)\Delta y$. Thus, the area A enclosed by region enclosed by two curves f_R and f_L, and two horizontal lines $y = c$ and $y = d$ is

$$A = \int_c^d [f_R - f_L]\, dy$$

Example Finding the area between curves

Find the area of the region enclosed by $y = x^2 - 3x$ and $y = 2x$.

Solution Sketch the graphs of $y = 2x$ and $y = x^2 - 3x$ as shown below.

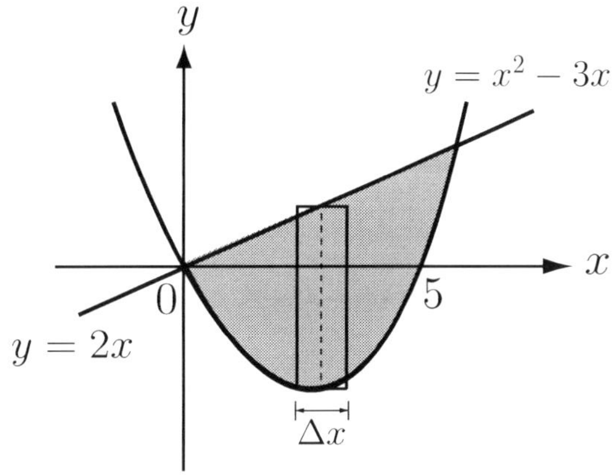

Set $x^2 - 3x = 2x$ and and solve for x to find the intersection points. This gives $x^2 - 5x = 0$ or $x(x-5) = 0$. Thus, $x = 0$ or $x = 5$. Draw ith rectangle to determine the top curve f_T and the bottom curve f_B. So, $f_T = 2x$ and $f_B = x^2 - 3x$. The area of ith rectangle is $(f_T - f_B)\Delta x$ and the total area of region enclosed by $y = x^2 - 3x$ and $y = 2x$ from $x = 0$ and $x = 5$ is

$$\begin{aligned}
A &= \int_a^b [f_T - f_B]\,dx \\
&= \int_0^5 [2x - (x^2 - 3x)]\,dx \\
&= \int_0^5 (-x^2 + 5x)\,dx \\
&= -\frac{1}{3}x^3 + \frac{5}{2}x^2\Big]_0^5 \\
&= -\frac{1}{3}5^3 + \frac{5}{2}5^2 \\
&= \frac{125}{6}
\end{aligned}$$

6.36 Average Value of a Function

Average Value of a Function

If f is continuous on $[a, b]$, then there exists a number called **average value of** f in $[a, b]$ such that

$$f_{ave} = \frac{1}{b-a}\int_a^b f(x)\,dx$$

In Figure 1, $\int_a^b f(x)\,dx$ represents the area under curve. In Figure 2, there is a rectangle whose length is $(b-a)$. Finding the average value of f is to find the width of the rectangle f_{ave} such that the area of the rectangle equals the area under curve.

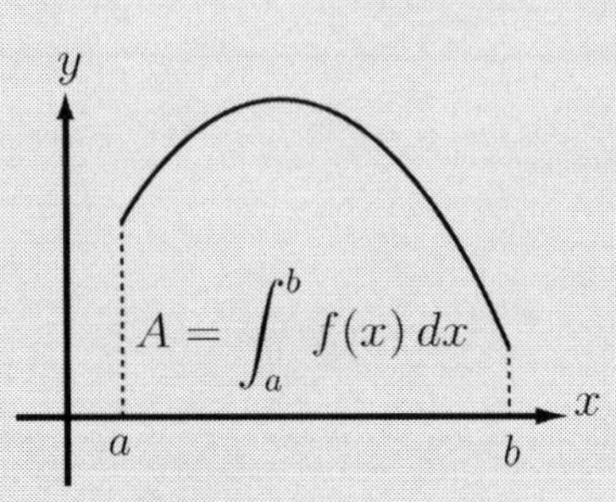

Figure 1

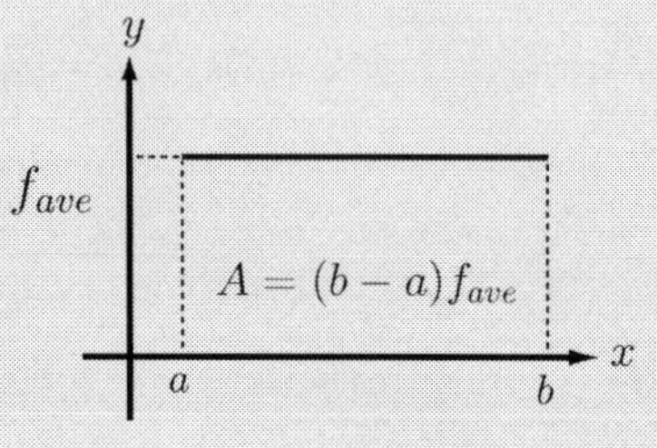

Figure 2

Example Finding the average value of the function

Find the average value of the function $f(x) = \dfrac{1}{x}$ on the interval $[1, 2]$.

Solution With $a = 1$ and $b = 2$,

$$\begin{aligned} f_{ave} &= \frac{1}{b-a}\int_a^b f(x)\,dx = \frac{1}{2-1}\int_1^2 \frac{1}{x}\,dx \\ &= \ln|x|\Big]_1^2 = \ln 2 - \ln 1 \\ &= \ln 2 \end{aligned}$$

Therefore, the average value of the function $f(x) = \dfrac{1}{x}$ on the interval $[1, 2]$ is $\ln 2$.

6.37 Volume by the Disk Method

Volume by the Disk Method

The region shown in Figure 1 is enclosed by $y = f(x)$ and vertical lines $x = a$ and $x = b$. If the region is rotated about the x-axis, then we get the solid shown in Figure 2.

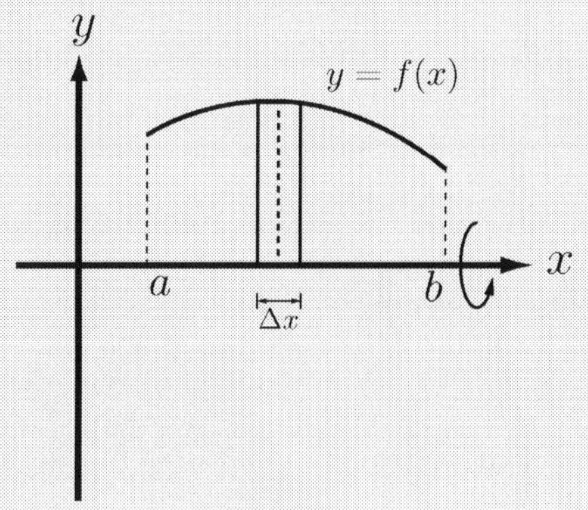

Figure 1

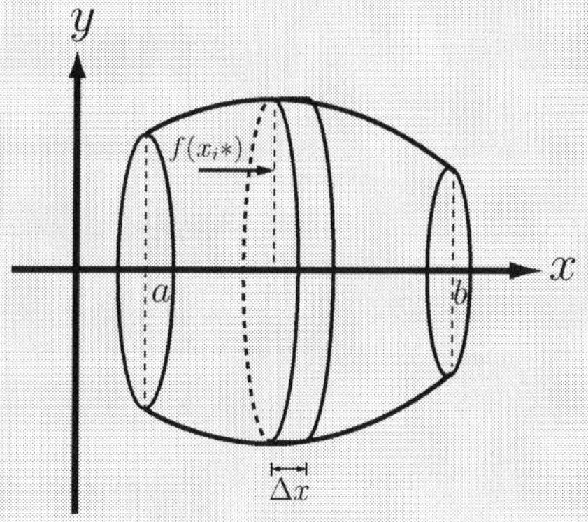

Figure 2

When we slice the solid in $[x_{i-1}, x_i]$, we get a disk with radius $f(x_i*)$ and with Δx. The volume of ith disk is

$$\pi(f(x_i*))^2\Delta x$$

The volume V of the solid equals the sum of volumes of infinitely many disks. Thus,

$$V = \lim_{n\to\infty}\sum_{i=1}^{n}\pi[f(x_i^*)]^2\Delta x = \pi\int_a^b [f(x)]^2\,dx$$

Tips

1. In order to find the volume of the solid by the Disk method, draw an ith rectangle **perpendicular** to the line of rotation.

   For a vertical ith rectangle: $\Longrightarrow$ $\displaystyle\int_a^b dx$

   For a horizontal ith rectangle: $\Longrightarrow$ $\displaystyle\int_c^d dy$

2. If $\int dx$ is set up, then the integrand must be a function of x; that is, $\displaystyle\int_a^b \boldsymbol{f(x)}\,dx$.

   Whereas, if $\int dy$ is set up, the integrand must be a function of y; that is $\displaystyle\int_c^d \boldsymbol{g(y)}\,dy$.

Volume of a Solid of Revolution: Rotating about the x- or y-axis

If the region enclosed by $y = f(x)$, $x = a$, and $x = b$ as shown in Figure 3 is rotated about the x-axis, the volume of a solid is given by

$$V = \pi \int_a^b [f(x)]^2\, dx$$

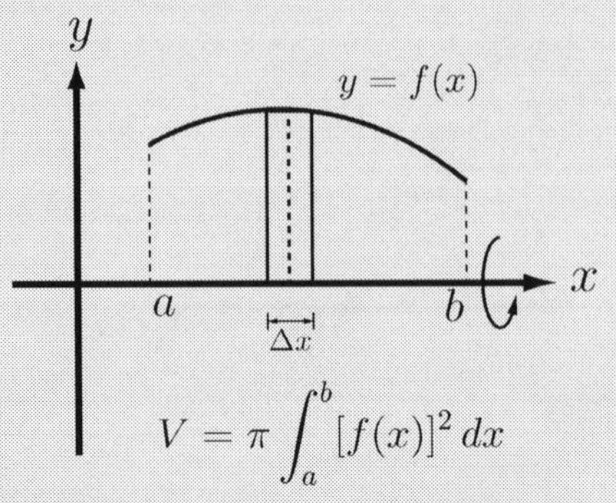

Figure 3: Rotating about the x-axis

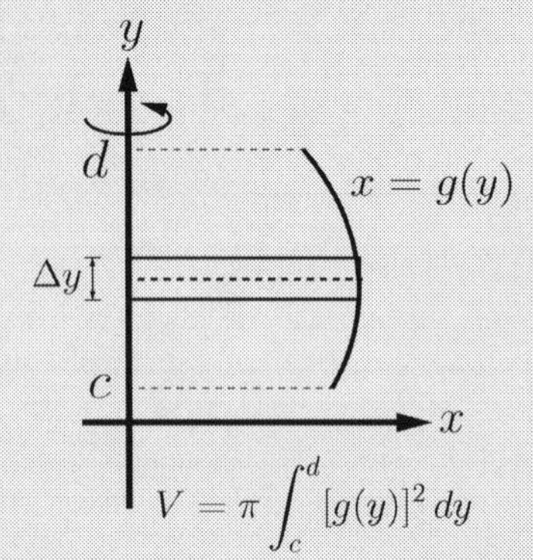

Figure 4: Rotating about the y-axis

If the region enclosed by $x = g(y)$, $y = c$, and $y = d$ as shown in Figure 4 is rotated about the y-axis, the volume of a solid is given by

$$V = \pi \int_c^d [g(y)]^2\, dy$$

Tips: Before using the Disk method, draw an ith rectangle **perpendicular** to the line of rotation, either x- or y- axis.

Example — Finding the volume by the Disk method

Find the volume of the solid obtained by rotating the region bounded by $y = \sqrt{x}$ and the x-axis from 0 to 4 about the x-axis.

Solution The line of rotation is the x-axis. So, draw an ith rectangle perpendicular to the x-axis as shown below.

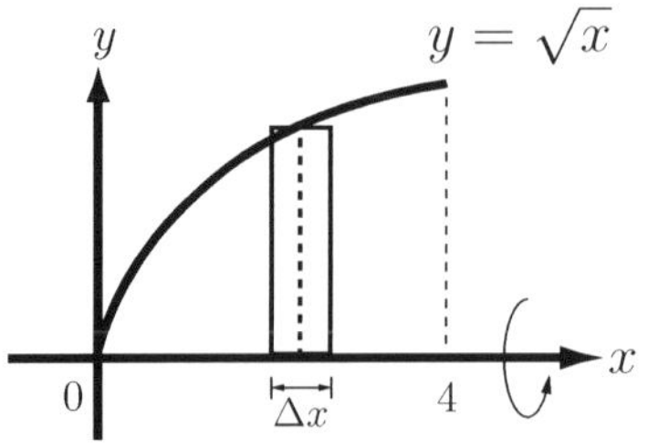

The volume of ith disk is $\pi(\sqrt{x}))^2\Delta x$ and the volume V of the solid is

$$\begin{aligned} V &= \pi\int_a^b [f(x)]^2\,dx = \pi\int_0^4 (\sqrt{x})^2\,dx \\ &= \pi\int_0^4 x\,dx = \pi\,\frac{1}{2}x^2\Big]_0^4 \\ &= 8\pi \end{aligned}$$

6.38 Volume by the Washer Method

Volume by the Washer Method

The region shown in Figure 5 is enclosed by $y = f(x)$ and $y = g(x)$. Draw a vertical ith rectangle and rotate it about the x-axis as shown in Figure 6. Then we get an ith washer (a ring) with outer radius r_{out} of $f(x)$ and inner radius r_{out} of $g(x)$. The volume of the ith washer is

$$\pi\Big((r_{out})^2 - (r_{in})^2\Big)\Delta x$$

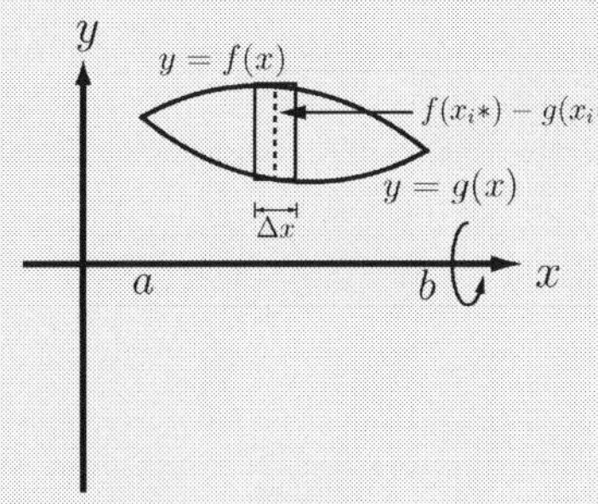

Figure 5

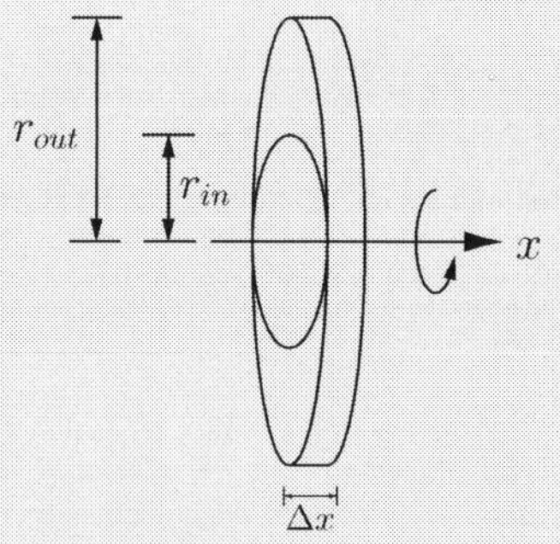

Figure 6

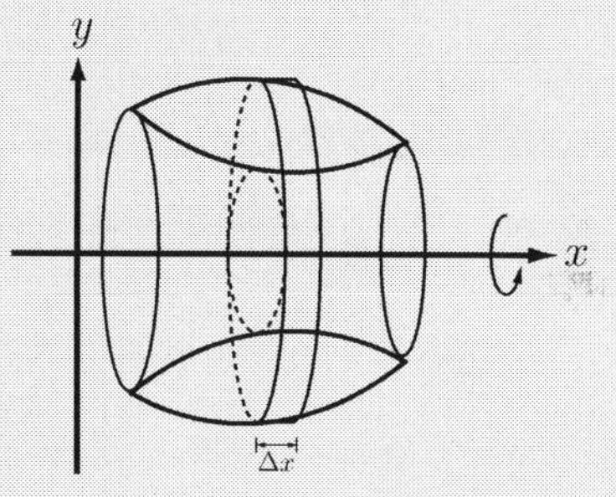

Figure 7

and the volume V of a solid shown in Figure 7 is

$$V = \pi\int_a^b \Big((r_{out})^2 - (r_{in})^2\Big)\,dx = \pi\int_a^b \Big((f(x))^2 - (g(x))^2\Big)\,dx$$

Tips

Use the Washer method when there is an open space between the enclosed region and the line of rotation. Similar to the Disk method, draw an ith rectangle **perpendicular** to the line of rotation.

6.39 The Limit of a Sequence

Sequences

A sequence is a list of numbers in order. The numbers in the list are called **terms** of the sequence and are denoted with subscripted letters: a_1 for the first term, a_2 for the second term, a_n for the nth term.

For every positive integer n, there is a corresponding number a_n. So, a sequence can be defined as a function whose domain is the set of positive integers.

The following sequence $\left\{\frac{1}{2}, \frac{2}{3}, \frac{3}{4}, \frac{4}{5}, \cdots\right\}$ can also be defined by

$$\left\{\frac{n}{n+1}\right\}_{n=1}^{\infty} \qquad \text{or} \qquad a_n = \frac{n}{n+1}$$

The Limit of a Sequence

A sequence a_n has the limit L if $\lim_{n\to\infty} a_n = L$. If $\lim_{n\to\infty} a_n$ exits, we say that the sequence converges. Otherwise, the sequence diverges.

Example Determining whether the sequence converges or diverges

Determine whether the sequence $\left\{\frac{n^2+n-1}{2n^2-3n+4}\right\}_1^{\infty}$ converges or diverges.

Solution In order to determine whether the sequence converges or diverges, take the limit of the function at infinity. Notice that $\lim_{n\to\infty} \frac{n^2+n-1}{2n^2-3n+4}$ is identical to finding the horizontal asymptote of the rational function $\frac{n^2+n-1}{2n^2-3n+4}$. Since the degree of the numerator and the denominator of the rational function are the same, the horizontal asymptote of the rational function is the ratio of leading coefficients. Thus,

$$\lim_{n\to\infty} \frac{n^2+n-1}{2n^2-3n+4} = \frac{1}{2}$$

Therefore, the sequence $\left\{\frac{n^2+n-1}{2n^2-3n+4}\right\}_1^{\infty}$ converges.

6.40 Convergence of Series

Definition of Convergent and Divergent Series

The nth partial sum of the series $\sum_{n=1}^{\infty} a_n$ is given by $S_n = a_1 + a_2 + a_3 + \cdots + a_n$.

$$\begin{aligned} S_1 &= a_1 \\ S_2 &= a_1 + a_2 \\ S_3 &= a_1 + a_2 + a_3 \\ \vdots \quad & \quad \vdots \\ S_n &= a_1 + a_2 + a_3 + \cdots + a_n = \sum_{i=1}^{n} a_i \end{aligned}$$

If the sequence of these partial sum $\{S_n\}$ shown above converges to S, then the $\sum_{n=1}^{\infty} a_n$ is called **convergent**. Otherwise the series is called **divergent**. The real number S is called the **sum** of the series.

Determining whether a series converges or diverges is not an easy task. With the following convergence tests, you will be able to evaluate some series for its convergence.

Test for Divergence

If $\lim_{n\to\infty} a_n \neq 0$, then the series $\sum_{n=1}^{\infty} a_n$ is divergent.

Tips

1. The contrapositive of the Test for Divergence is also true.
   $\sum_{n=1}^{\infty} a_n$ is convergent, then $\lim_{n\to\infty} a_n = 0$.
2. Note that the following statement is **NOT** true in general.
   If $\lim_{n\to\infty} a_n = 0$, then $\sum_{n=1}^{\infty} a_n$ is convergent.

Geometric Series Test

Given the geometric series $\sum_{n=1}^{\infty} ar^{n-1} = a + ar + ar^2 + \cdots$, it is convergent if $|r| < 1$, and its sum is $\frac{a}{1-r}$. Otherwise, the geometric series is divergent if $|r| \geq 1$.

$$\sum_{n=1}^{\infty} ar^{n-1} = \begin{cases} \frac{a}{1-r}, & |r| < 1 \\ \infty, & |r| \geq 1 \end{cases}$$

P-Series Test

The p-series $\sum_{n=1}^{\infty} \frac{1}{n^p}$ is convergent if $p > 1$ and divergent if $p \leq 1$.

Tips

The p-series with $p = 1$ is called the **harmonic series** and is divergent.

$$\sum_{n=1}^{\infty} \frac{1}{n} = 1 + \frac{1}{2} + \frac{1}{3} + \frac{1}{4} + \cdots = \infty$$

Alternating Series Test

If the alternating series

$$\sum_{n=1}^{\infty} (-1)^n a_n = -a_1 + a_2 - a_3 + \cdots \quad \text{or} \quad \sum_{n=1}^{\infty} (-1)^{n-1} a_n = a_1 - a_2 + a_3 + \cdots$$

satisfies the following two conditions

1. $a_{n+1} \leq a_n$ for all n
2. $\lim_{n \to \infty} a_n = 0$.

then the series converges.

Tips

When considering the two conditions, ignore $(-1)^n$ or $(-1)^{n-1}$ in the series.

Example Determining whether the series is convergent or divergent

Determine whether the series $\sum_{n=1}^{\infty} \frac{n+1}{\sqrt{2n^2+n+3}}$ is convergent or divergent.

Solution

$$\begin{aligned}\lim_{n\to\infty} \frac{n+1}{\sqrt{2n^2+n+3}} &= \lim_{n\to\infty} \frac{n+1}{\sqrt{2n^2+n+3}} \cdot \frac{\frac{1}{n}}{\frac{1}{n}} \\ &= \lim_{n\to\infty} \frac{1+\frac{1}{n}}{\sqrt{\frac{2n^2+n+3}{n^2}}} \\ &= \lim_{n\to\infty} \frac{1+\frac{1}{n}}{\sqrt{2+\frac{1}{n}+\frac{3}{n^2}}} \\ &= \frac{1}{\sqrt{2}}\end{aligned}$$

Since $\lim_{n\to\infty} \frac{n+1}{\sqrt{2n^2+n+3}} \neq 0$, the series $\sum_{n=1}^{\infty} \frac{n+1}{\sqrt{2n^2+n+3}}$ is divergent by the Test for Divergence.

Example Determining whether the series is convergent or divergent

Determine whether the series $\sum_{n=1}^{\infty} \frac{\cos n\pi}{n}$ is convergent or divergent.

Solution $\left\{\cos n\pi\right\}_1^{\infty} = \left\{(-1)^n\right\}_1^{\infty}$. Thus, $\sum_{n=1}^{\infty} \frac{\cos n\pi}{n} = \sum_{n=1}^{\infty} (-1)^n \frac{1}{n}$. Let's check the two conditions for the alternating series.

1. $a_{n+1} = \frac{1}{n+1} \leq a_n = \frac{1}{n}$ for all n
2. $\lim_{n\to\infty} \frac{1}{n} = 0$.

Since the series satisfies the two condition, the series $\sum_{n=1}^{\infty} \frac{\cos n\pi}{n}$ is convergent by the Alternating Series Test.

Chapter 7

Geometry

7.1 Angles

Angles

An angle is formed by two rays and is measured in degrees (°). The angle A is expressed as $\angle A$ and the measure of the angle A is expressed as $m\angle A$.
Two angles, A and B, that have the same measure are called **congruent angles**. They are expressed as $\angle A \cong \angle B$.
Angles are classified by their measures.

- Acute angle is less than 90°.
- Right angle is 90°.
- Obtuse angle is greater than 90°.
- Straight angle is 180°.
- Vertical angles are formed by intersecting two lines. Vertical angles are congruent. In the figure below, $\angle 1$ and $\angle 3$, and $\angle 2$ and $\angle 4$ are vertical angles.
- Complementary angles are two angles whose sum of their measures is 90°. In the figure below, $\angle 5$ and $\angle 6$ are complementary angles.
- Supplementary angles are two angles whose sum of their measures is 180°. In the figure below, $\angle 7$ and $\angle 8$ are supplementary angles.

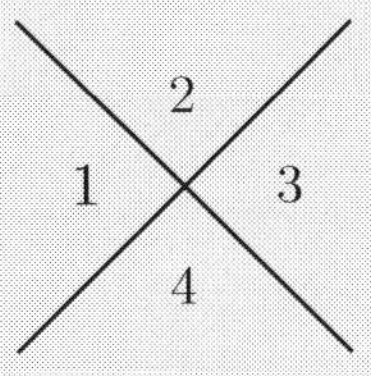

Vertical angles

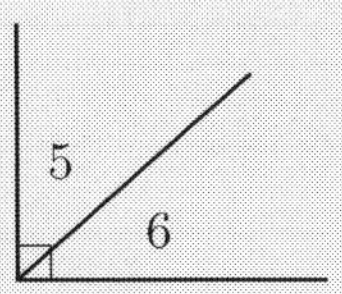

Complementary angles

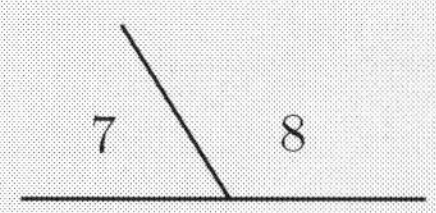

Supplementary angles

7.2 Parallel Lines and Transversals

Parallel Lines

When two parallel lines are cut by a third line called the transversal, the following angles are formed.

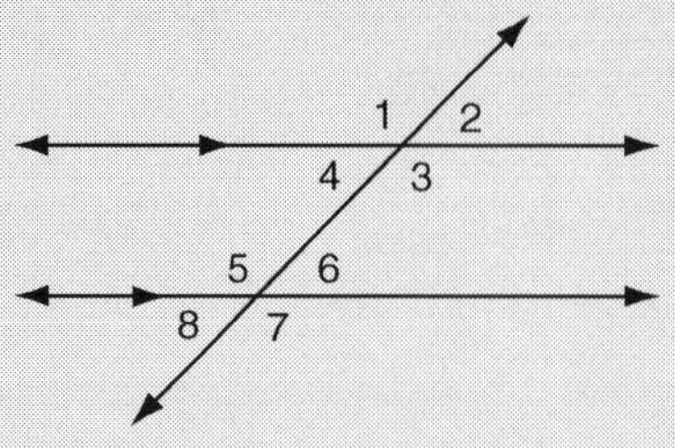

- Corresponding angles are congruent: $\angle 1 \cong \angle 5$, $\angle 4 \cong \angle 8$, $\angle 2 \cong \angle 6$, and $\angle 3 \cong \angle 7$.
- Alternate interior angles are congruent: $\angle 4 \cong \angle 6$, and $\angle 3 \cong \angle 5$.
- Alternate exterior angles are congruent: $\angle 1 \cong \angle 7$, and $\angle 2 \cong \angle 8$.
- Consecutive angles are supplementary: $\angle 4$ and $\angle 5$, and $\angle 3$ and $\angle 6$ are supplementary. In other words, $m\angle 4 + m\angle 5 = 180°$, and $m\angle 3 + m\angle 6 = 180°$.

Example **Parallel lines and angles**

If the two lines are parallel in the figure below, what is the value of $x + y$?

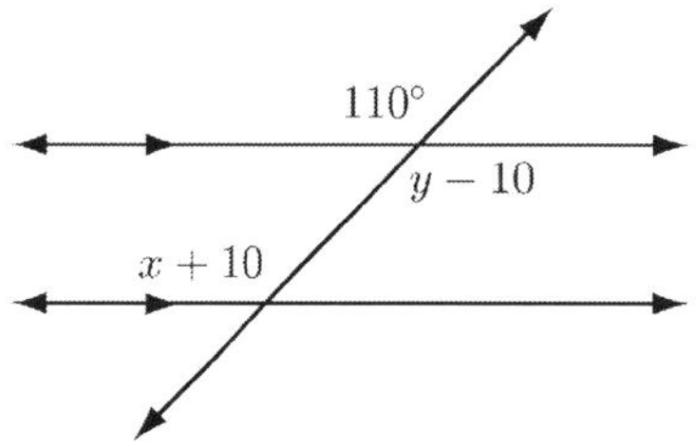

Solution The angles 110° and $y - 10$ are vertical angles and congruent. Thus,

$$\begin{aligned} y - 10 &= 110 \\ y &= 120 \end{aligned}$$

Additionally, angles 110° and $x + 10$ are corresponding angles and congruent. Thus,

$$\begin{aligned} x + 10 &= 110 \\ x &= 100 \end{aligned}$$

Therefore, the value of $x + y = 220$.

7.3 Names of Triangles

Names of Triangles

A triangle is a figure formed by three segments joining three points called **vertices**. A triangle ABC is expressed as $\triangle ABC$. A triangle can be classified according to its sides or its angles.

Classification by Sides

- Equilateral triangle: All sides are equal in length. The measure of each angle is $60°$.
- Isosceles triangle: Two sides are equal in length. If two sides of a triangle are congruent, then the angles (**base angles**) opposite them are congruent as shown in the figure below.
- Scalene triangle: All sides are unequal in length.

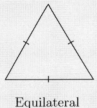

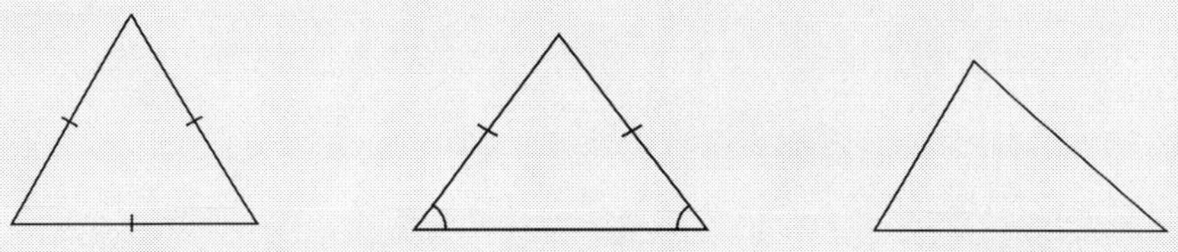

Equilateral　　Isosceles　　Scalene

Classification by Angles

- Acute triangle: All interior angles measure less than $90°$.
- Right triangle: One of the interior angles measures $90°$.
- Obtuse triangle: One of the interior angles measures more than $90°$.

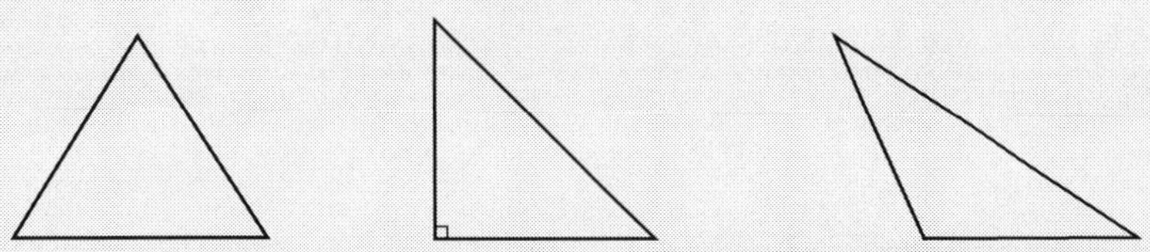

Acute　　Right　　Obtuse

Area of a Triangle

- The area of a triangle is $A = \frac{1}{2}bh$, where b is base and h is height.
- The area of an equilateral triangle with side length of s is $A = \frac{\sqrt{3}}{4}s^2$.
- The areas of two triangles are equal if the bases and heights of the two triangles are the same.

7.4 Theorems of Triangles

Theorems of Triangles

- **Triangle sum theorem**: The sum of the measures of interior angles of a triangle is 180°.

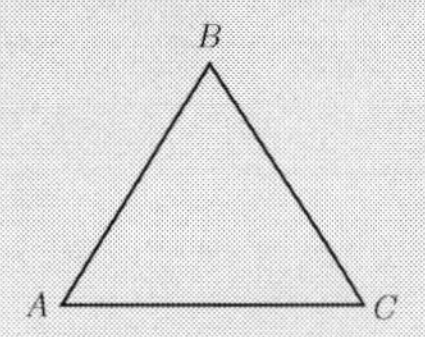

$$m\angle A + m\angle B + m\angle C = 180^\circ$$

- **Exterior angle theorem**: The measure of an exterior angle of a triangle is equal to the sum of the measures of the two non-adjacent interior angles.

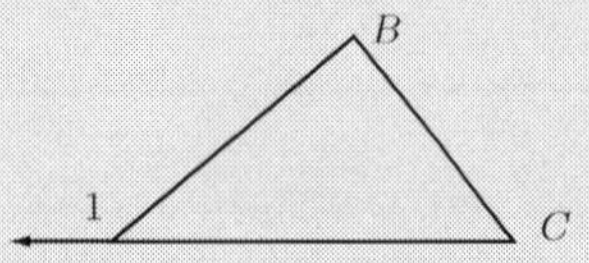

$$m\angle 1 = m\angle B + m\angle C$$

- **Triangle inequality theorem**: The length of a side of a triangle is always less than the sum of the lengths of the other two sides, but always greater than the difference of the lengths of the other two sides. For instance, let a, b, and c be the lengths of the three sides of a triangle, where $a < b < c$. Then, the triangle inequality satisfies the following.

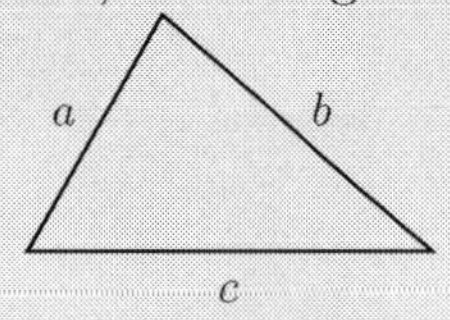

$$c - b < a < c + b$$
$$c - a < b < c + a$$
$$b - a < c < b + a$$

- **Midsegment theorem**: The segment connecting the midpoints of two sides of a triangle is called midsegment. It is parallel to the third side and is half as long.

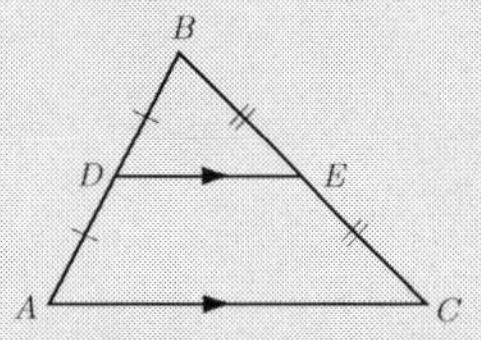

$$\overline{DE} \parallel \overline{AC}$$
$$DE = \frac{1}{2}AC$$

- **Law of Sines**: The largest angle is opposite the longest side and the smallest angle is opposite the shortest side. For instance, let a and b be the sides opposite the angles A and B, respectively. The law of sines satisfies the following.

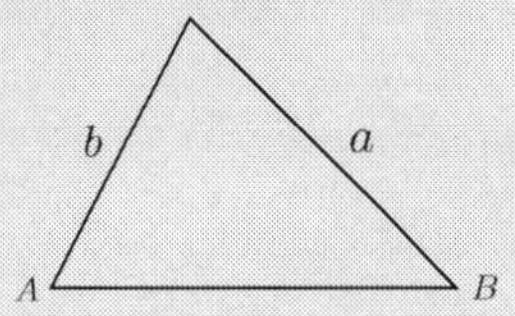

$$\text{If } m\angle B < m\angle A \implies b < a$$
$$\text{If } b < a \implies m\angle B < m\angle A$$

7.5 Proving Triangles are Congruent

Congruent Triangles

When triangle ABC and triangle DEF are congruent, denoted by $\triangle ABC \cong \triangle DEF$, there is a correspondence between their angles and sides such that corresponding angles are congruent and corresponding sides are congruent.

To prove two triangles are congruent, use one of the following postulates and theorems.

1. **SSS** (Side-Side-Side) congruence postulate: If three sides of one triangle are congruent to three sides of a second triangle, then the two triangles are congruent.
2. **SAS** (Side-Angle-Side) congruence postulate: If two sides and the included angle of one triangle are congruent to two sides and the included angle of a second triangle, then the two triangles are congruent.
3. **ASA** (Angle-Side-Angle) congruence postulate: If two angles and the included side of one triangle are congruent to two angles and the included side of a second triangle, then the two triangles are congruent.
4. **AAS** (Angle-Angle-Side) congruence theorem: If two angles and a nonincluded side of one triangle are congruent to two angles and the corresponding nonincluded side of a second triangle, then the two triangles are congruent.
5. **HL** (Hypotenuse-Leg) congruence theorem: If the hypotenuse and a leg of a right triangle are congruent to the hypotenuse and a leg of a second right triangle, then the two triangles are congruent.

Tips: **SSA** (Side-Side-Angle) and **AAA** (Angle-Angle-Angle) **CANNOT** be used to prove that two triangles are congruent.

7.6 Perpendicular Bisector Theorem and Angle Bisector Theorem

Bisector Theorems

- **Perpendicular Bisector Theorem**: If a point on the perpendicular bisector of a segment, then it is equidistant from the endpoints of the segment.

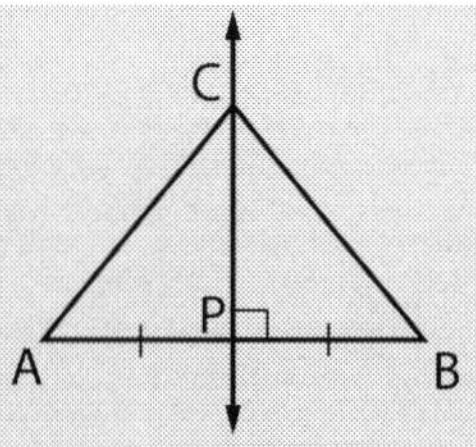

If $\overleftrightarrow{CP}$ is the perpendicular bisector of $\overline{AB}$, then $CA = CB$.

- **Angle Bisector Theorem**: If a point is on the bisector of an angle, then it is equidistant from the two sides of the angle.

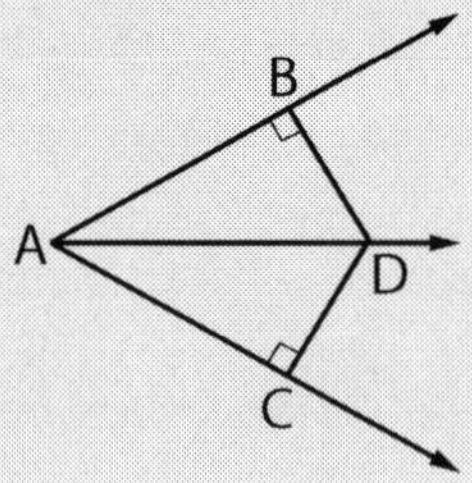

If $m\angle BAD = m\angle CAD$, then $DB = DC$.

7.7 Bisectors of a Triangle

Perpendicular Bisectors of a Triangle

The perpendicular bisectors of a triangle intersect at point P that is equidistant from the vertices of the triangle. So $PA = PB = PC$.

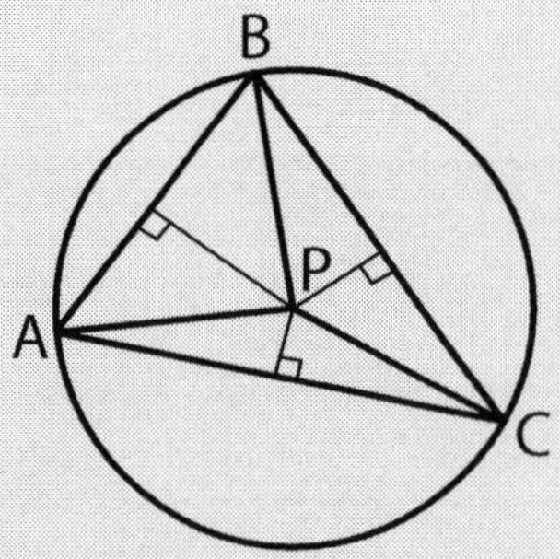

The point of concurrency of the perpendicular bisectors of a triangle, P, is called the **circumcenter** of the triangle.

Angle Bisectors of a Triangle

The angle bisectors of a triangle intersect at point P that is equidistant from the sides of the triangle. So $PD = PE = PF$.

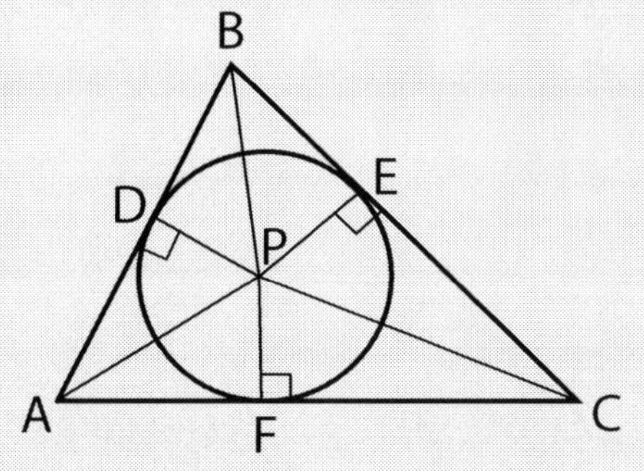

The point of concurrency of the angle bisectors of a triangle, P, is called the **incenter** of the triangle.

Medians of a Triangle

A **median** of a triangle is a line segment whose endpoints are a vertex of the triangle and the midpoint of the opposite side.

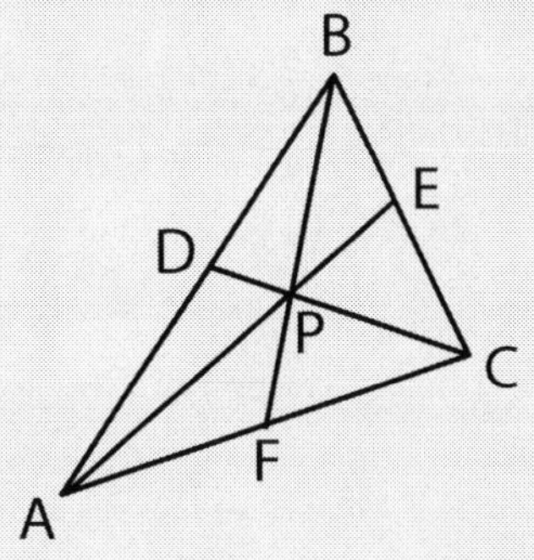

The medians of a triangle intersect at point P that is two thirds of the distance from each vertex to the midpoint of the opposite side.

$$AP = \frac{2}{3}AE, \quad BP = \frac{2}{3}BF, \quad CP = \frac{2}{3}CD$$

The point of concurrency of the medians of a triangle, P, is called the **centroid** of the triangle.

7.8 Properties of Regular Polygons

Regular Polygons

A **polygon** is a plane figure that has at least three straight sides and angles. A polygon is **convex** if all of the interior angles are less than 180°. A polygon that is not convex is called **concave**. A polygon is **regular** if it is equilateral and equiangular. The table below summarizes the properties of regular polygons.

Sides	Name	Each Exterior Angle	Each Interior angle	Sum of Interior angles	Diagonals
3	Triangle	120°	60°	180°	0
4	Square	90°	90°	360°	2
5	Pentagon	72°	108°	540°	5
6	Hexagon	60°	120°	720°	9
8	Octagon	45°	135°	1080°	20
9	Nonagon	40°	140°	1260°	27
10	Decagon	36°	144°	1440°	35
n	**n-gon**	$\frac{360}{n}$	**180 − Exterior angle**	$180(n-2)$	$\frac{n(n-3)}{2}$

Tips

- A heptagon is a regular polygon with 7 sides.
- The sum of the interior angle and the exterior angle is 180°.

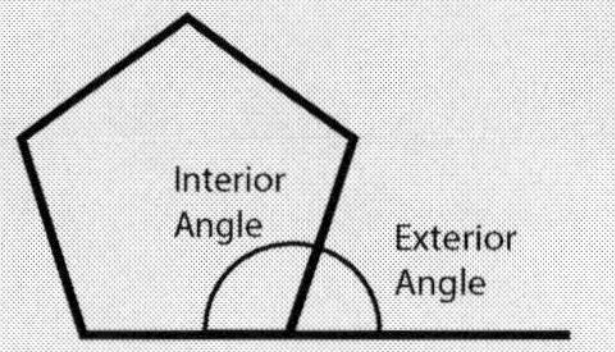

7.9 Pythagorean Theorem and Special Right Triangles

Pythagorean Theorem and Special Right Triangles

In the right triangle, shown at the right, the longest side opposite the right angle is called the **hypotenuse** and the other two sides are called **legs** of the triangle. There is a special relationship between the length of the hypotenuse and the lengths of the legs. It is known as the Pythagorean theorem.

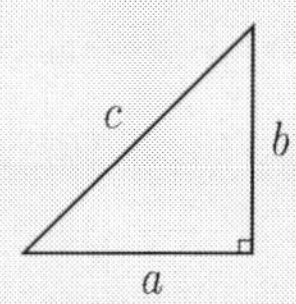

Pythagorean Theorem

In the right triangle above, the square of the length of the hypotenuse is equal to the sum of the squares of the lengths of the legs.

$$c^2 = a^2 + b^2$$

The Pythagorean theorem is very useful because it helps you find the length of the third side of a right triangle when the lengths of two sides of the right triangle are known.

Pythagorean Triples

A Pythagorean triple consists of three positive integers, $a - b - c$. It represents integer lengths of the sides of a right triangle such that $c^2 = a^2 + b^2$. The most well-known Pythagorean triple is $3 - 4 - 5$. Below is a list of the Pythagorean triples that are required for solving math problems.

$3 - 4 - 5$ $\qquad$ $5 - 12 - 13$ $\qquad$ $7 - 24 - 25$ $\qquad$ $8 - 15 - 17$

Any multiple of a Pythagorean triple is also a Pythagorean triple. For instance, $6 - 8 - 10$ is a Pythagorean triple because it is a multiple of $3 - 4 - 5$. In other words, $(3 - 4 - 5) \times 2 = 6 - 8 - 10$.

$45° - 45° - 90°$ Special Right Triangles

In a $45° - 45° - 90°$ right triangle, the sides of the triangle are in the ratio $1 : 1 : \sqrt{2}$, respectively. In other words, the length of the hypotenuse is $\sqrt{2}$ times the length of each leg.

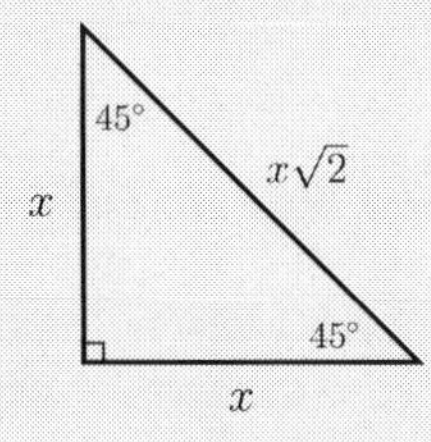

$$\text{Hypotenuse} = \text{Leg} \times \sqrt{2} \quad \Longleftrightarrow \quad \text{Leg} = \frac{\text{Hypotenuse}}{\sqrt{2}}$$

$30° - 60° - 90°$ Special Right Triangles

In a $30° - 60° - 90°$ triangle, the sides of the triangle are in the ratio $1 : \sqrt{3} : 2$, respectively. In other words, the length of the hypotenuse is twice the length of the shorter leg, and the length of the longer leg is $\sqrt{3}$ times the length of the shorter leg.

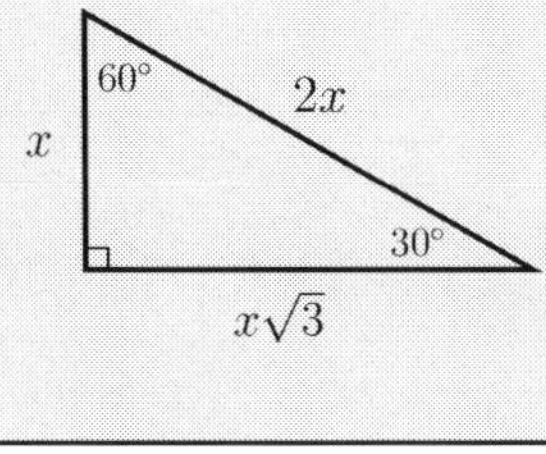

$$\text{Hypotenuse} = \text{Shorter leg} \times 2$$

$$\text{Longer leg} = \text{Shorter leg} \times \sqrt{3}$$

7.10 Properties of Quadrilaterals

Properties of Quadrilaterals

A **quadrilateral** is a four-sided closed figure. It has four straight sides and four vertices. The sum of the measures of interior angles is 360°.
There are special types of quadrilaterals: parallelogram, rectangle, rhombus, square, and trapezoid. Some quadrilaterals can be other types of the quadrilaterals. For instance, a square can be a rectangle as well as a parallelogram. Below shows the properties and areas of the special types of the quadrilaterals.

Parallelogram

- Opposite sides are parallel. $\overline{AB} \parallel \overline{DC}$, $\overline{BC} \parallel \overline{AD}$
- Opposite sides are congruent. $\overline{AB} \cong \overline{DC}$, $\overline{BC} \cong \overline{AD}$
- Opposite angles are congruent. $\angle A \cong \angle C$, $\angle B \cong \angle D$
- Consecutive angles are supplementary.
  $m\angle A + m\angle D = 180°$, $m\angle A + m\angle B = 180°$
- Diagonals bisect each other. $\overline{AE} \cong \overline{CE}$, $\overline{BE} \cong \overline{DE}$
- Area $= bh$, where b is the base and h is the height.

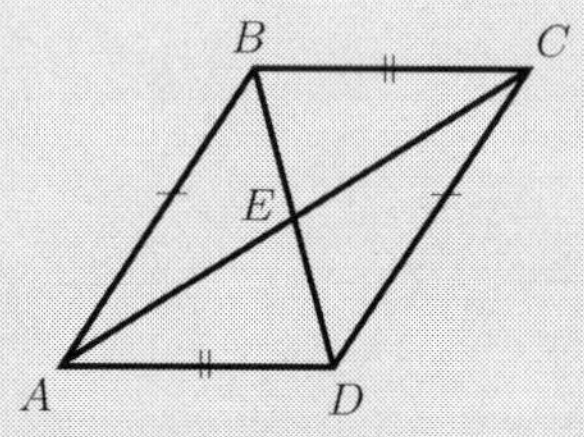

Rhombus

- A parallelogram with four congruent sides. Thus, a rhombus has all the properties of a parallelogram.
- Diagonals are perpendicular to each other.
- Diagonals bisect a pair of opposite angles.
  $\angle 1 \cong \angle 5$, $\angle 8 \cong \angle 4$, $\angle 2 \cong \angle 6$, $\angle 3 \cong \angle 7$
- Area $= \frac{1}{2}d_1d_2$, where d_1 and d_2 are the lengths of the diagonals.

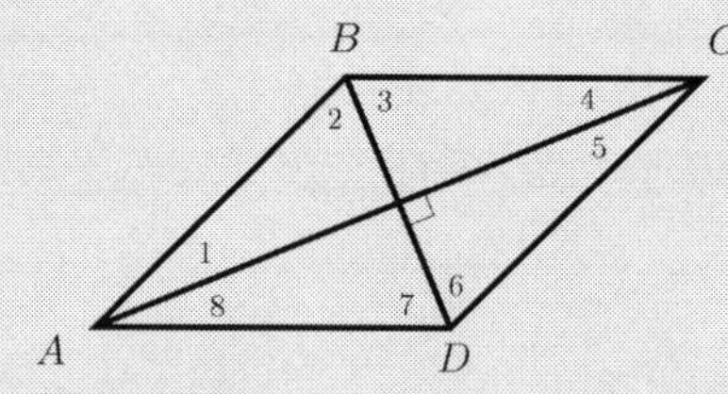

Rectangle

- A parallelogram with four right angles. Thus, a rectangle has all the properties of a parallelogram.
- Diagonals are equal in length.
- Area $= lw$, where l is the length and w is the width.

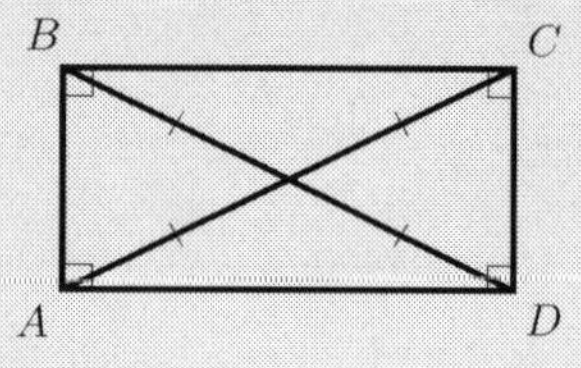

Square

- A square is a rhombus and a rectangle. Thus, a square has all the properties of a rhombus and a rectangle.
- Diagonals are equal in length.
- Area $= S^2$, where S is the length of the side. Or, Area $= \frac{1}{2}d^2$, where d is the length of the diagonal.

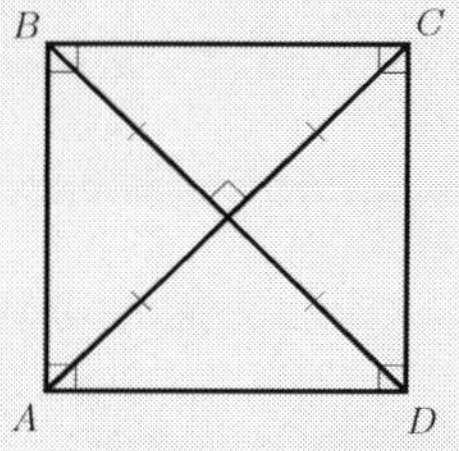

Trapezoid

- A quadrilateral with exactly one pair of parallel sides. $\overline{BC} \parallel \overline{AD}$
- Area $= \frac{1}{2}(b_1 + b_2)h$, where b_1 is the length of the top side, b_2 is the length of the bottom side, and h is the height.

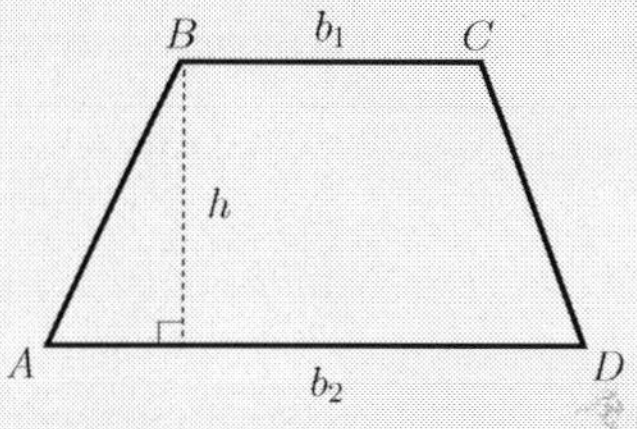

Isosceles Trapezoid

- A trapezoid with congruent nonparallel sides (Legs).
- The base angles are congruent.
- Diagonals are congruent.
- Area $= \frac{1}{2}(b_1 + b_2)h$, where b_1 is the length of the top side, b_2 is the length of the bottom side, and h is the height.

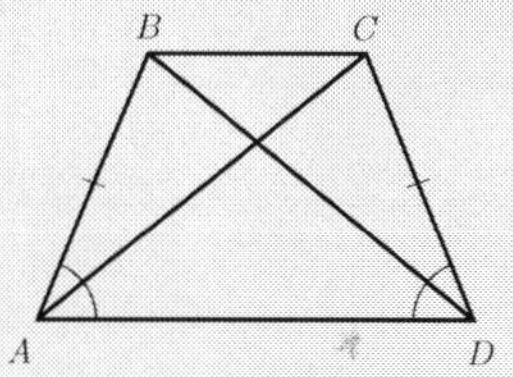

Example **The sum of the measures of the interior angles of a quadrilateral**

If the measures of the interior angles of a quadrilateral are $40°$, $x + 30$, $2x$, and $3x - 10$, what is the value of x ?

Solution The sum of the measures of the interior angles of a quadrilateral is $360°$. Thus,

$$\begin{aligned} 40 + x + 30 + 2x + 3x - 10 &= 360 \\ 6x + 60 &= 360 \\ 6x &= 300 \\ x &= 50 \end{aligned}$$

Therefore, the value of x is $50°$.

7.11 Similar Polygons

Two polygons are **similar** if their corresponding angles are congruent and the ratios of their corresponding sides are equal. The symbol $\sim$ is used to indicate that two polygons are similar.

In the figures shown at right, $\triangle ABC \sim \triangle DEF$. Therefore,

$$\angle A \cong \angle D,\ \angle B \cong \angle E,\ \angle C \cong \angle F$$

$$\frac{AB}{DE} = \frac{BC}{EF} = \frac{AC}{DF}$$

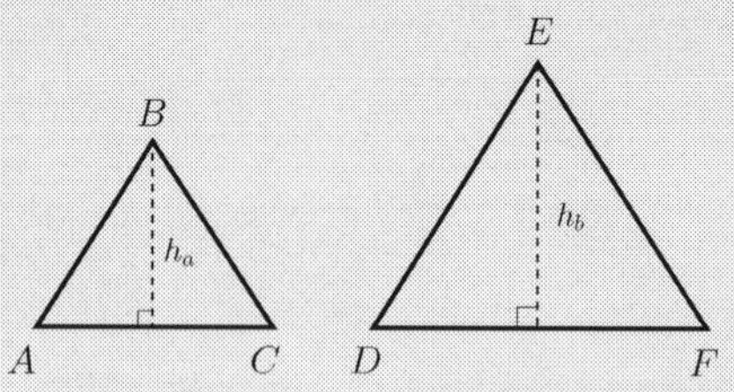

Theorems

- If two polygons are similar, the ratio of any pair of corresponding segments (heights or medians) is equal to the ratio of any pair of corresponding sides. If $\triangle ABC \sim \triangle DEF$ shown above, the ratio of heights is equal to

$$\frac{h_a}{h_b} = \frac{AB}{DE} = \frac{BC}{EF} = \frac{AC}{DF}$$

- If two polygons are similar, the ratio of their perimeters is equal to the ratio of any pair of corresponding sides. If $\triangle ABC \sim \triangle DEF$, the ratio of perimeters is equal to

$$\frac{\text{Perimeter of } \triangle ABC}{\text{Perimeter of } \triangle DEF} = \frac{AB}{DE} = \frac{BC}{EF} = \frac{AC}{DF}$$

- If two polygons are similar, the ratio of their areas is equal to the square of the ratio of any pair of corresponding sides. If $\triangle ABC \sim \triangle DEF$, the ratio of areas is equal to

$$\frac{\text{Area of } \triangle ABC}{\text{Area of } \triangle DEF} = \left(\frac{AB}{DE}\right)^2 = \left(\frac{BC}{EF}\right)^2 = \left(\frac{AC}{DF}\right)^2$$

Example — Finding the ratio of the perimeters of two equilateral triangles

If there are two equilateral triangles with side lengths of 2 and 3 respectively, what is the ratio of the perimeter of the smaller equilateral triangle to that of the larger equilateral triangle?

Solution Although you may find the perimeter of each equilateral triangle and the ratio of the perimeters, use the theorem such that if the two polygons are similar, the ratio of their perimeters is equal to the ratio of any pair of corresponding sides. Since two equilateral triangles are similar and have side lengths of 2 and 3, the ratio of the perimeter of the smaller equilateral triangle to that of the larger equilateral triangle is 2 : 3.

7.12 Reflection, Rotation, Translation, and Dilation

Rigid Transformations

Figures in a plane can be reflected, rotated, or translated to produce new figures. The original figure is called the **preimage**, and the new figure is called the **image**. The operation that maps the preimage onto the image is called a **transformation**. For each of the four transformations below, ABC is the preimage, and $A'B'C'$ is the image.

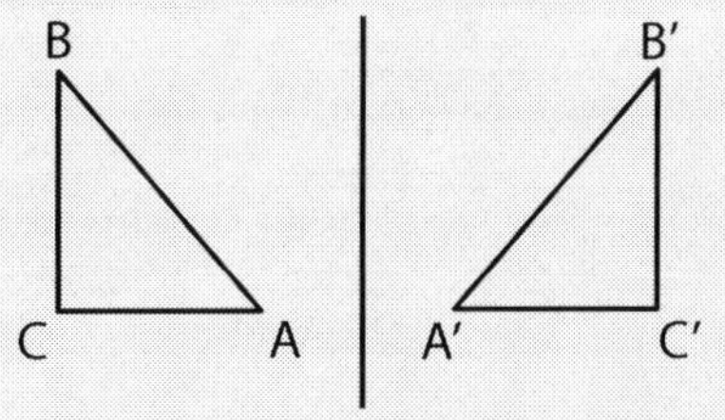

Reflection in a line

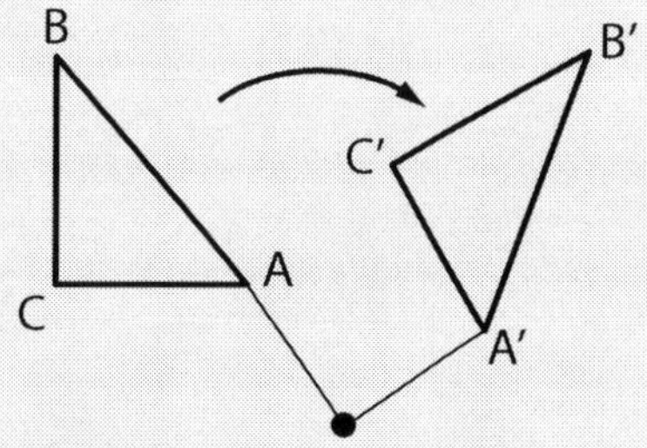

Rotation about a point

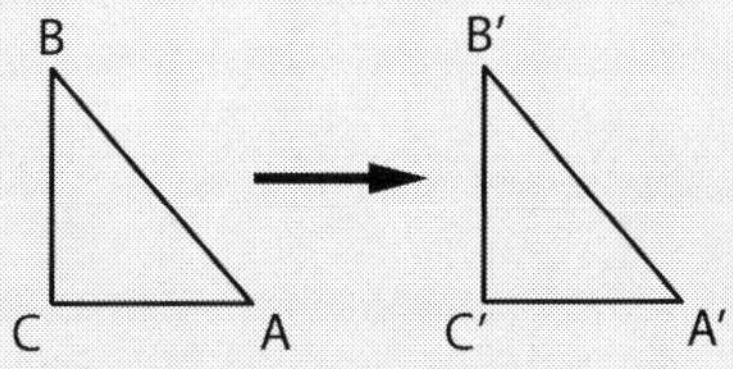

Translation

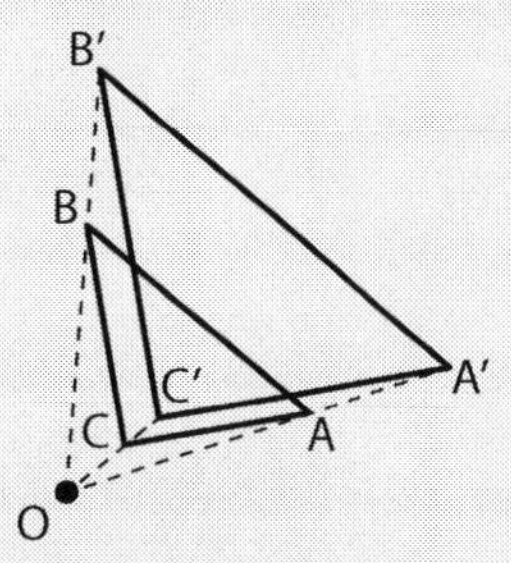

Dilation

An **isometry** is a transformation that preserves length, angle measures, parallel lines, and distance between points. Reflection, rotation, and translation are isometries. Transformations that are isometries are called **rigid transformations**.

Dilation

A dilation is a transformation that produces an image that is the same shape as the original, but is a different size. Thus, a dilation is **NOT** an isometry.

- A dilation that creates a larger image is called an enlargement (Scale factor > 1).
- A dilation that creates a smaller image is called a reduction (Scale factor < 1).

7.13 Symmetry

Symmetry

- A figure in the plane has a **line of symmetry** if the figure can be mapped onto itself by a reflection in the line.

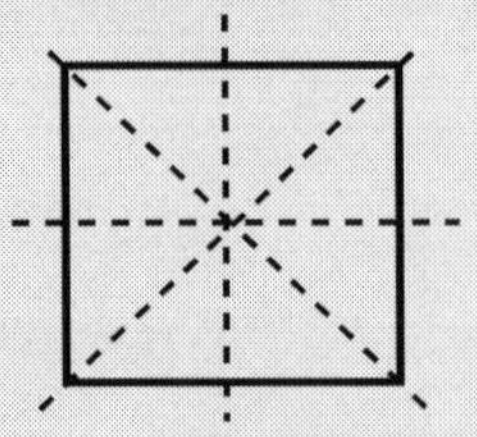
Four lines of symmetry

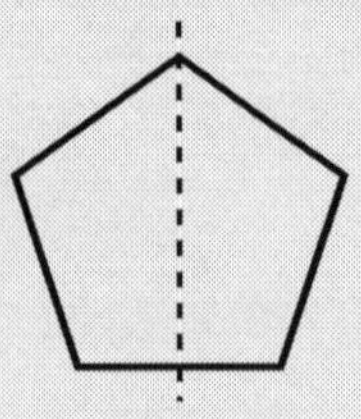
One line of symmetry

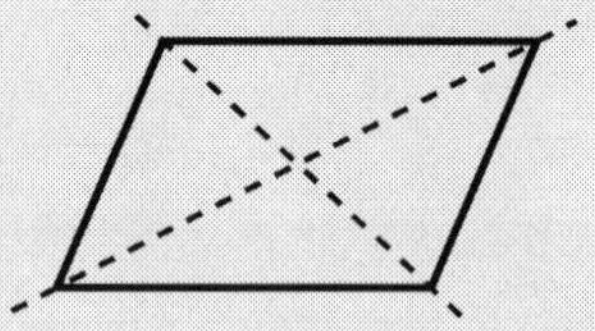
Two lines of symmetry

- A figure in the plane has **rotational symmetry** if the figure can be mapped onto itself by a rotation of 180° or less.

0° rotation

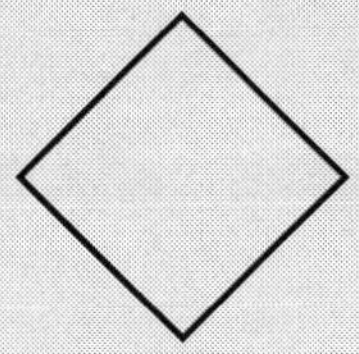
45° rotation

90° rotation

For instance, a square has rotational symmetry because it maps onto itself by a rotation of 90°.

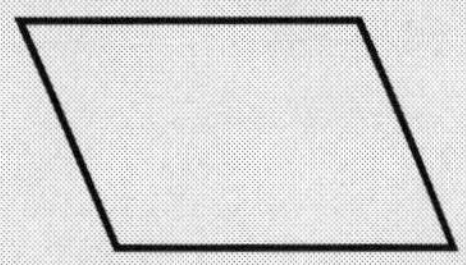
Parallelogram

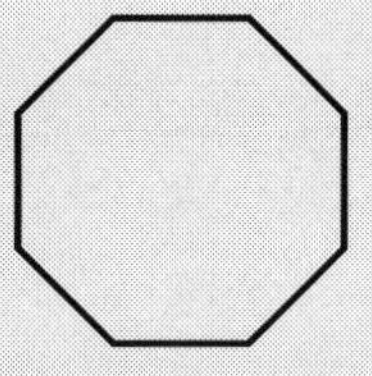
Regular Octagon

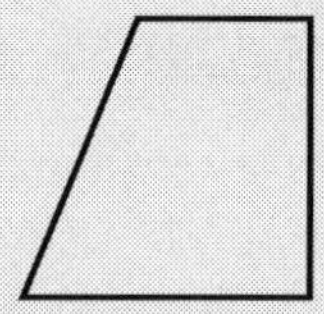
Trapezoid

- The parallelogram above has rotational symmetry. It can be mapped onto itself by a clockwise or counterclockwise rotation of 180° about its center.
- The regular octagon above has rotational symmetry. It can be mapped onto itself by a clockwise or counterclockwise rotation of 45°, 90°, 135°, or 180° about its center.
- The trapezoid above does not have rotational symmetry.

7.14 Properties and Theorems of Circles

Properties and Theorems of Circles

Circles

A **circle** is a set of all points that are equidistant from a fixed point called the **center** of the circle. The distance from the center to a point on the circle is the **radius** of the circle. If the radius of a circle, r, is given, the circumference, C, and the area, A, are as follows:

$$C = 2\pi r, \qquad A = \pi r^2$$

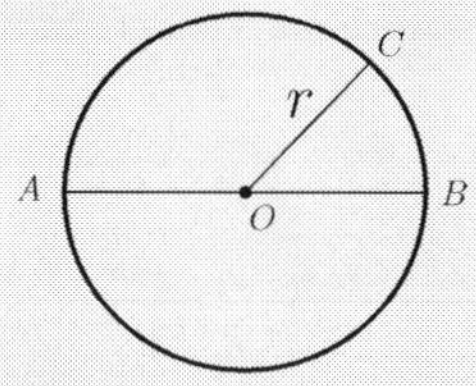

Figure 1

A **chord** is a line segment whose endpoints are on the circle. A **diameter** is a chord that passes through the center of the circle. A diameter is the longest chord and is twice the length of the radius.
In figure 1, O is the center, $\overline{OC}$ is the radius, and $\overline{AB}$ is a chord and a diameter.

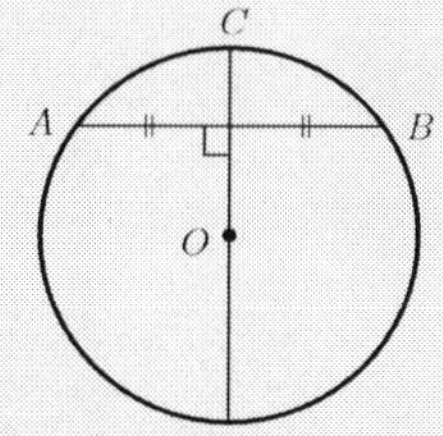

Figure 2

The diameter or the radius of the circle is a perpendicular bisector of a chord. In figure 2, the radius $\overline{OC}$ is a perpendicular bisector of chord $\overline{AB}$. $\overline{OC}$ divides $\overline{AB}$ into two equal smaller segments and $\overline{OC} \perp \overline{AB}$.

Tangent lines to a circle

A **tangent line** is a line that is drawn from outside of the circle and touches the circle at exactly one point. The point at which a tangent line touches the circle is the **point of tangency**.

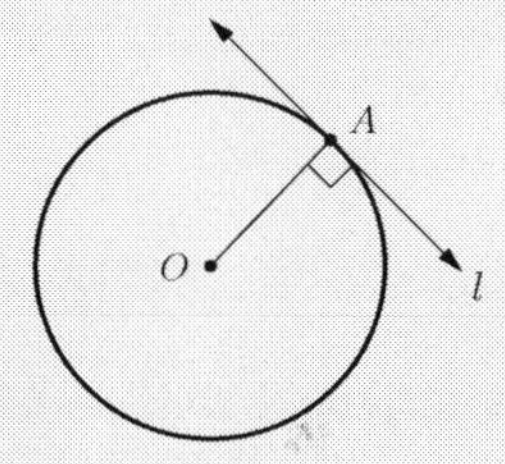

Figure 3

A tangent line is **perpendicular** to the radius drawn to the point of tangency. In figure 3, A is the point of tangency and l is the tangent line to the circle. $\overline{OA} \perp l$.

Central angles and Inscribed angles

A **central angle** is an angle whose vertex is on the center of the circle and whose sides are the radii. An **inscribed angle** is an angle whose vertex is on the circle and whose sides are the chords of the circle. In figure 4, $\angle AOB$ is the central angle and $\angle ACB$ is the inscribed angle.

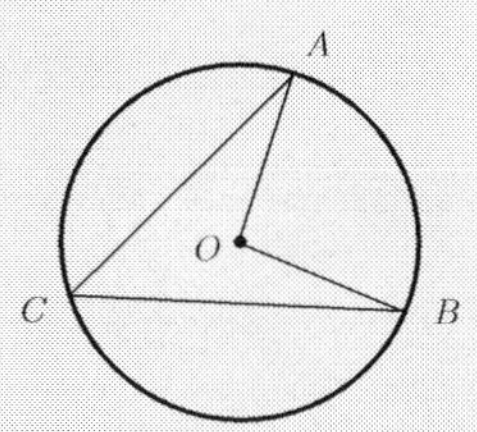

Figure 4

If the central angle and the inscribed angle contains the same part of the circumference of the circle, the measure of the inscribed angle is half the measure of the central angle. In figure 4,

$$m\angle ACB = \frac{1}{2} m\angle AOB$$

Inscribed Triangles

A triangle inscribed in a semicircle is a right triangle. The hypotenuse of a right triangle inscribed in a semicircle is the diameter of the semicircle. In figure 5, the central angle is 180° and $\angle C$ is the inscribed angle. Since the measure of the inscribed angle is half the measure of the central angle,

$$m\angle C = \frac{1}{2}\text{central angle} = \frac{1}{2}(180°) = 90°$$

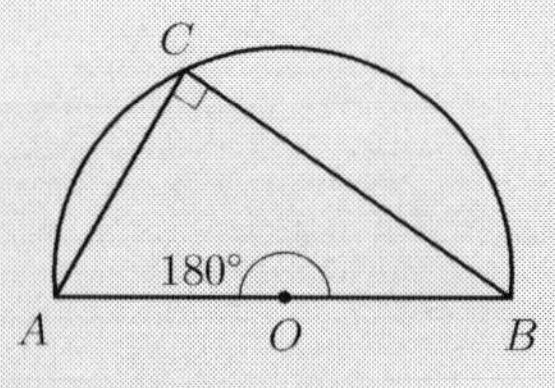

Figure 5

Inscribed Circles and Circumscribed Circles

An **inscribed circle** is a circle that lies in a polygon and touches all sides of the polygon. In figure 6, a circle is inscribed in the square.

$$\text{Radius of inscribed circle} = \frac{1}{2} \times \text{Length of square}$$

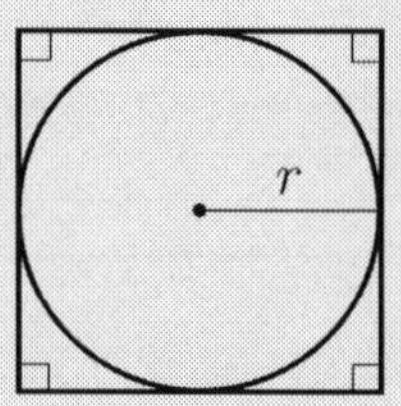

Figure 6

A **circumscribed circle** is a circle that passes through all the vertices of the polygon. In general, a circle is circumscribed about a polygon means exactly the same as a polygon is inscribed in the circle.

In figure 7, a square is inscribed in the circle. The diagonal of the square is the diameter of the circle. Triangle ABC is a 45°-45°-90° special right triangle. There are relationships between the length of the square and the radius of the circumscribed circle.

$$\text{Length of square} = \text{Radius} \times \sqrt{2}$$

$$\text{Radius} = \text{Length of square} \times \frac{\sqrt{2}}{2}$$

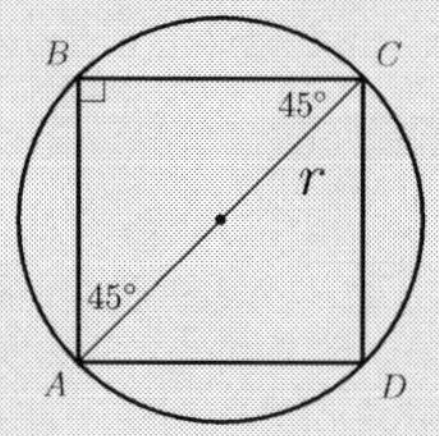

Figure 7

Arc length and Area of a sector

An arc is a part of the circumference of a circle. A part can be expressed as the ratio of the central angle to 360°. An arc is shown in figure 8.

$$\text{Arc length} = 2\pi r \times \frac{\theta}{360°}, \quad \text{where } \theta \text{ is the central angle}$$

A sector is a part of the area of a circle. A part can be expressed as the ratio of the central angle to 360°. A sector is shown in figure 8.

$$\text{Area of a sector} = \pi r^2 \times \frac{\theta}{360°}, \quad \text{where } \theta \text{ is the central angle}$$

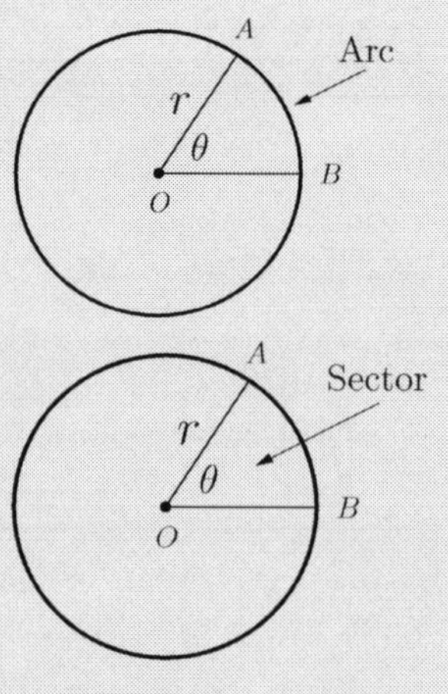

Figure 8

7.15 Perimeter, Area, and Volume

Perimeter, Area, and Volume

Rectangular box

The volume V, surface area A, and longest diagonal AB of a rectangular box with side lengths a, b, and c are defined as follows:

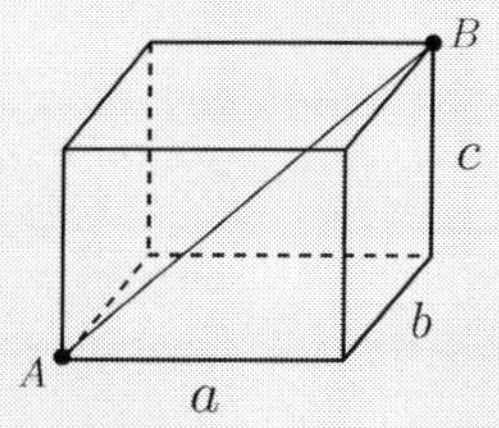

Volume: $V = abc$

Surface area: $A = 2(ab + bc + ca)$

Longest diagonal: $AB = \sqrt{a^2 + b^2 + c^2}$

Cube

The volume V, surface area A, and longest diagonal AB of a cube with side lengths x are defined as follows:

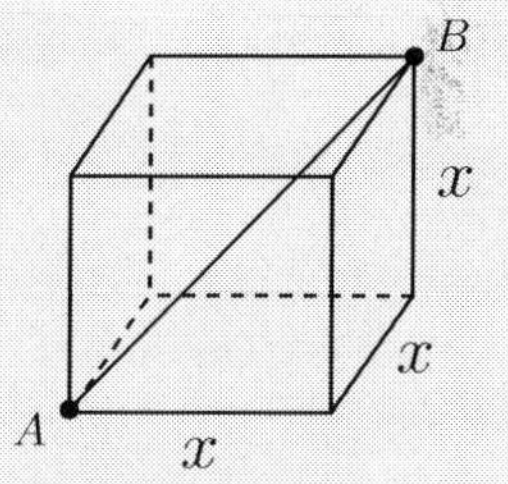

Volume: $V = x^3$

Surface area: $A = 6x^2$

Longest diagonal: $AB = \sqrt{x^2 + x^2 + x^2} = x\sqrt{3}$

Rectangular pyramid

The volume V of a rectangular pyramid is one-third of the area of the base B times the height h.

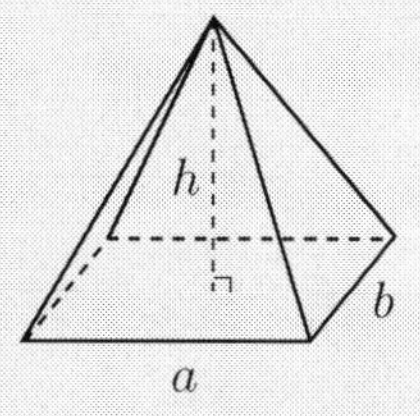

Volume: $V = \frac{1}{3}Bh = \frac{1}{3}abh$

Surface area: Base area and sum of areas of triangular faces

Cylinder

The volume V of a cylinder with radius r is the area of the base B times the height h.

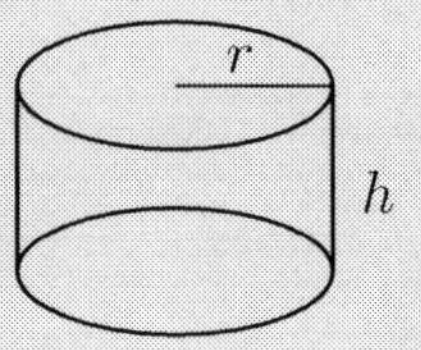

Volume: $V = Bh = \pi r^2 h$

Surface area: $A = 2\pi rh + 2\pi r^2$

Right circular cone

The volume V of a right circular cone with radius r is one-third of the area of the base B times the height h. The lateral area A of a right circular cone with circumference of the base c and slant height l is half times the product of the circumference of the base and the slant height.

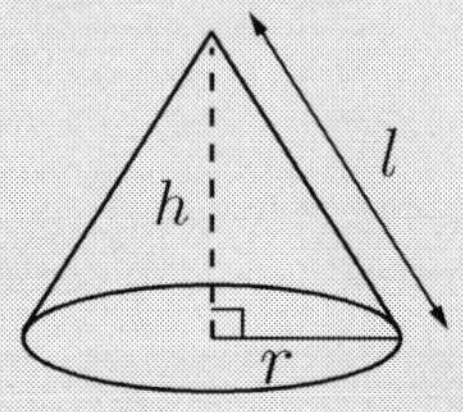

Volume: $V = \frac{1}{3}Bh = \frac{1}{3}\pi r^2 h$

Lateral area: $A = \frac{1}{2}cl = \pi rl$

Surface area: $A = \pi rl + \pi r^2$

Sphere

The general equation of a sphere with center (x_0, y_0, z_0) and radius r is $(x - x_0)^2 + (y - y_0)^2 + (z - z_0)^2 = r^2$. The volume V and surface area A of a sphere with radius r are as follows:

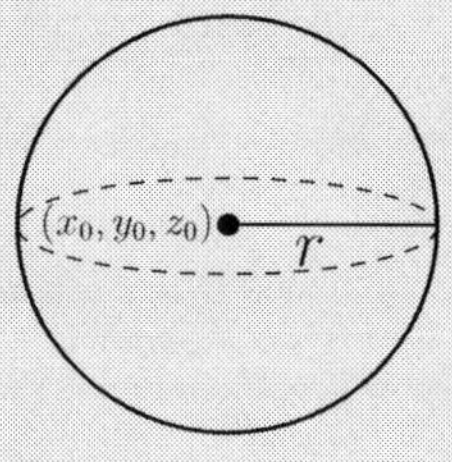

Volume: $V = \frac{4}{3}\pi r^3$

Surface area: $A = 4\pi r^2$

7.16 Identifying Conic Sections

Identifying Conic Sections

Conic sections, or conics, consist of circles, parabolas, ellipses, and hyperbolas. The following guidelines summarize how to identify the conics from the equations given.

- When the equation contains $Ax^2 + By^2$ (Squared terms for both x and y):
  - If $A = B$, the equation defines a circle.
  - If $A \neq B$, the equation defines an ellipse.
- When the equation contains $Ax^2 - By^2$ (Squared terms have a negative sign in between them):
  - If $A = B$, the equation defines a hyperbola.
  - If $A \neq B$, the equation defines a hyperbola.
- When the equation contains $Ax + By^2$ or $Ax^2 + By$ (Squared term for only x or y):

  The equation defines a parabola when it contains the squared term for only the x or y variable.

Example Identifying conic sections

Identify the conic section that each equation represents.

(a) $3x^2 + 6x + y^2 + 4y - 6 = 0$

(b) $x^2 - 2y^2 - 4x + 2y + 1 = 0$

(c) $2x^2 - 4x + 2y^2 - 8y - 2 = 0$

(d) $4y^2 + 4y + 2x + 4 = 0$

Solution

(a) The equation has squared terms $3x^2 + y^2$, where $A = 3$ and $B = 1$. Thus, the equation represents an ellipse.

(b) Since the squared terms, $x^2 - 2y^2$, have a negative sign in between them, the equation represents a hyperbola.

(c) The equation has squared terms $2x^2 + 2y^2$, where $A = 2$ and $B = 2$. Thus, the equation represents a circle.

(d) Since the equation contains the squared term for only y, the equation represents a parabola.

7.17 Circles

Circles

A circle is the set of all points that are equidistant from a fixed point called the center. The general equation of a circle is given by

$$(x-h)^2+(y-k)^2=r^2$$

where the point (h,k) is the center of the circle, and r is the radius of the circle.

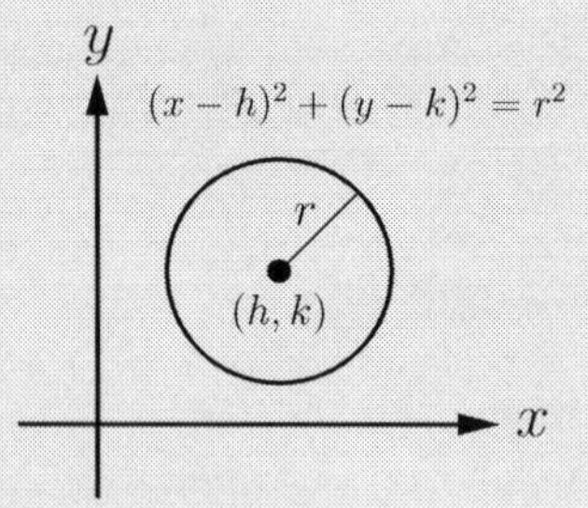

7.18 Ellipses

Ellipses

An ellipse is the set of all points in a plane such that the sum of the distances from two fixed points, called the **foci**, is a constant. The longer side of the ellipse is called the **major axis**, the shorter side of the ellipse is called the **minor axis**. The two endpoints along the major axis are the **vertices**. The other two endpoints along the minor axis are the **co-vertices**. The general equation of an ellipse is given by

$$\frac{(x-h)^2}{a^2}+\frac{(y-k)^2}{b^2}=1$$

where the point (h,k) is the center of the ellipse. The lengths of the major axis and minor axis can be determined by the following rules.

- If $a>b$, the length of the major axis is $2a$, and the length of the minor axis is $2b$ as shown in Figure 1.
- If $a<b$, the length of the major axis is $2b$, and the length of the minor axis is $2a$ as shown in Figure 2.

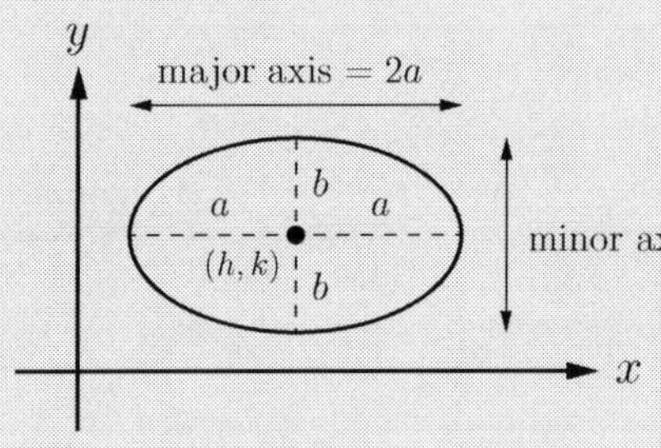

Fig. 1: $\frac{(x-h)^2}{a^2}+\frac{(y-k)^2}{b^2}=1$, if $a>b$

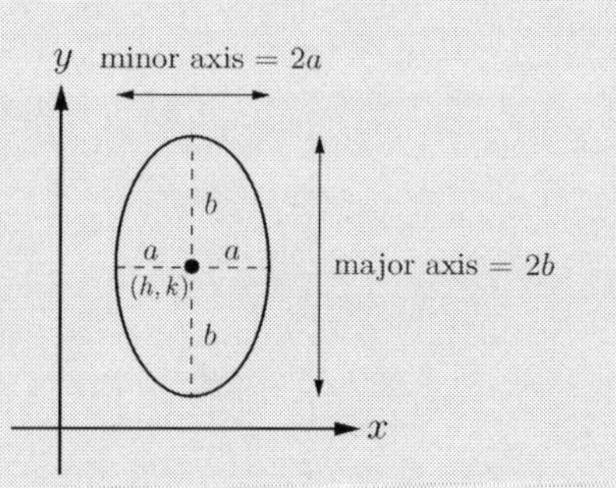

Fig. 2: $\frac{(x-h)^2}{a^2}+\frac{(y-k)^2}{b^2}=1$, if $a<b$

Tips: Let c be the distance between the center and foci of an ellipse. c can be determined by either $c^2=a^2-b^2$ (if $a>b$) or $c^2=b^2-a^2$ if (if $a<b$).

Example Finding the center of a circle

Find the center and radius of the circle $(x-1)^2+(y+2)^2=9$.

Solution In order to find the center of the circle, set $x-1=0$ and $y+2=0$ and solve for x and y. Thus, the center of the circle is $(1,-2)$. Since $9=3^2$, the radius of the circle is 3, not 9.

Example Finding the center and the length of the major axis of an ellipse

Find the center, vertices, and the lengths of the major and minor axis of the ellipse shown below.

$$4x^2+y^2+16x-6y+21=0$$

Solution In order to write a general equation of the ellipse $\frac{(x-h)^2}{a^2}+\frac{(y-k)^2}{b^2}=1$, proceed to complete the squares in x and in y.

$$4x^2+y^2+16x-6y+21=0$$

$4x^2+y^2+16x-6y=-21$	Subtract 21 from each side
$4(x^2+4x)+(y^2-6y)=-21$	Rearrange the terms
$4(x^2+4x+4)+(y^2-6y)=-5$	Add 16 to each side to complete squares in x
$4(x+2)^2+(y^2-6y+9)=4$	Add 9 to each side to complete squares in y
$4(x+2)^2+(y-3)^2=4$	Divide each side by 4
$\frac{(x+2)^2}{1^2}+\frac{(y-3)^2}{2^2}=1$	

In order to find the center of the ellipse, set $x+2=0$ and $y-3=0$ and solve for x and y. Thus, the center of the ellipse is $(-2,3)$.

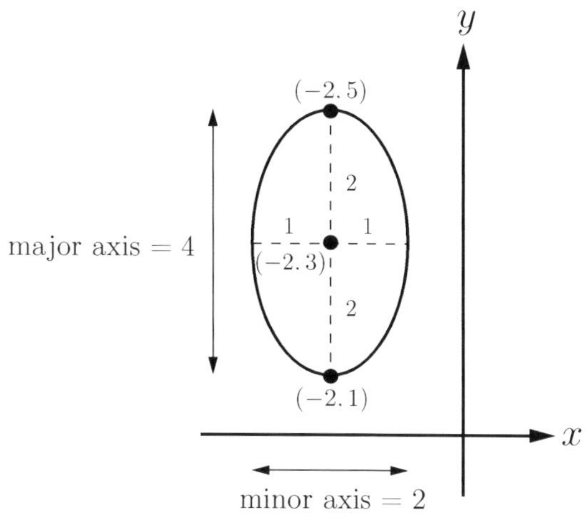

The lengths of the major axis and minor axis are 4 and 2, respectively. Since the vertices are vertically 2 units from the center, vertices are at $(-2,5)$, and $(-2,1)$.

7.19 Parabolas

Parabolas

A parabola is the set of all points in the plane that are same distance from a fixed point F as they are from a fixed line D. The point F is called **focus** and the line D is its **directrix**. The general forms of parabola and its graphs are shown in Figure 3 through Figure 6.

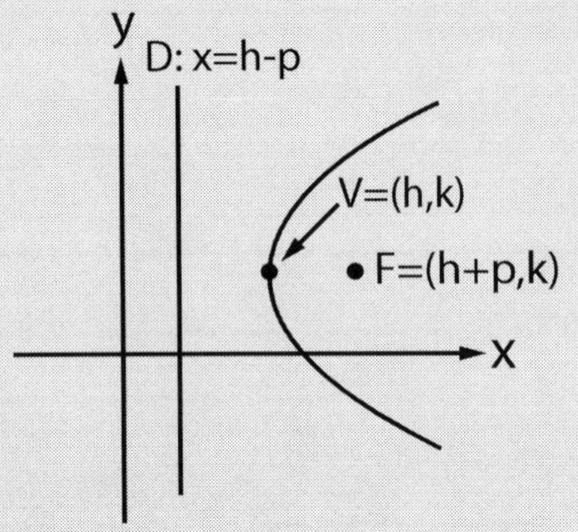

Fig. 3: $4p(x-h)=(y-k)^2$, where $p>0$

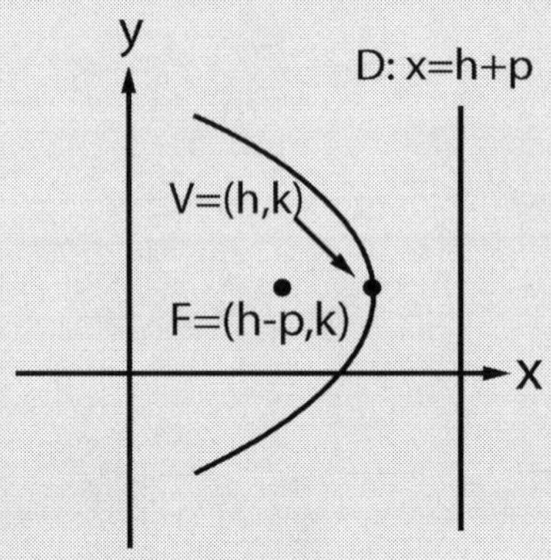

Fig. 4: $4p(x-h)=(y-k)^2$, where $p<0$

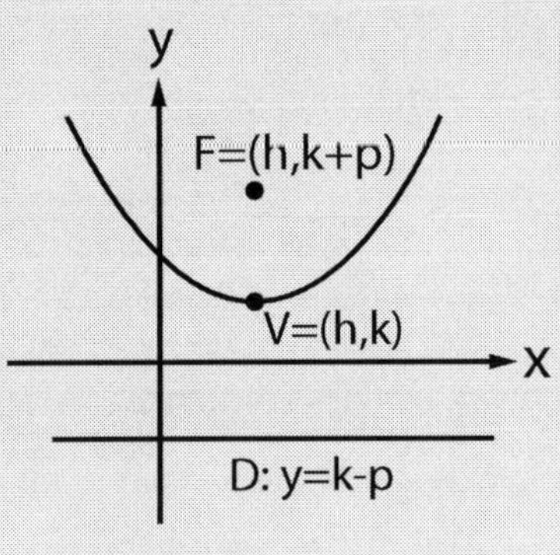

Fig. 5: $4p(y-k)=(x-h)^2$, where $p>0$

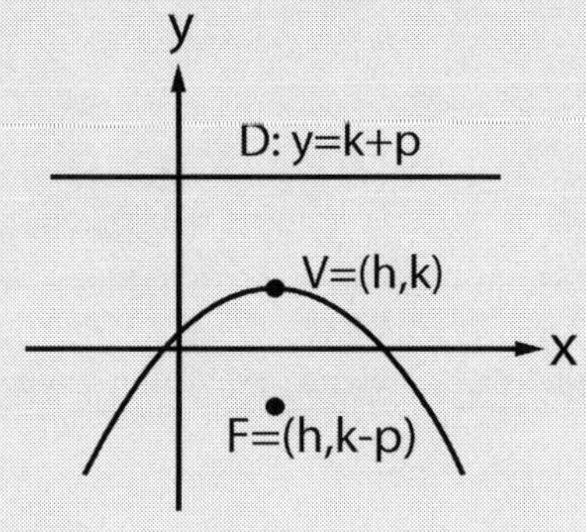

Fig. 6: $4p(y-k)=(x-h)^2$, where $p<0$

7.20 Hyperbolas

Hyperbolas

Hyperbola is the set of all points in a plane such that the difference of the distances from two fixed points, called the foci, is a constant. The two endpoints on the hyperbola are the vertices. The midpoint of the line segment joining the vertices is called the **center** of the hyperbola. The line passes through the vertices and the center is called the **transverse axis**. The line through the center and perpendicular to the transverse axis is called the conjugate axis.

There are two types of equations of a hyperbola based on a horizontal transverse axis or a vertical transverse axis.

- An equation of a hyperbola with a horizontal transverse axis: $\dfrac{(x-h)^2}{a^2} - \dfrac{(y-k)^2}{b^2} = 1$

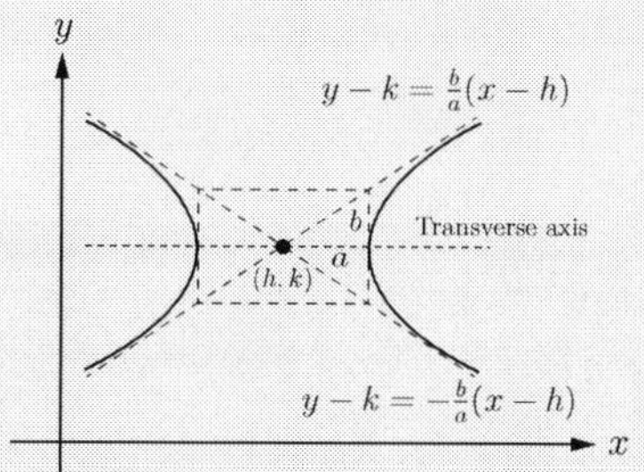

Figure 7: $\frac{(x-h)^2}{a^2} - \frac{(y-k)^2}{b^2} = 1$

where the center of the hyperbola is (h, k). The equations of asymptotes are $y-k = \pm\frac{b}{a}(x-h)$ as shown in Figure 7.

- An equation of a hyperbola with a vertical transverse axis: $\dfrac{(y-k)^2}{a^2} - \dfrac{(x-h)^2}{b^2} = 1$

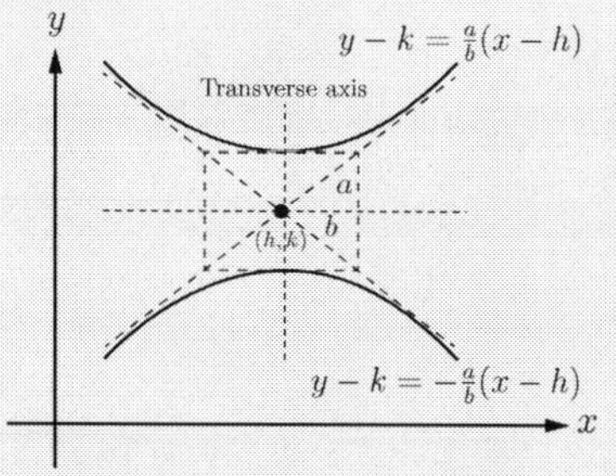

Figure 8: $\frac{(y-k)^2}{a^2} - \frac{(x-h)^2}{b^2} = 1$

where the center of the hyperbola is (h, k). The equations of asymptotes are $y-k = \pm\frac{a}{b}(x-h)$ as shown in Figure 8.

Tips: Let c be the distance between the center and foci of a hyperbola. c can be determined by $c^2 = a^2 + b^2$.

Example Finding the equation of a parabola

Find the equation of the parabola with vertex at $(2, 4)$ and focus at $(5, 4)$.

Solution Since the vertex is at $(2, 4)$ and the focus is at $(5, 4)$, the parabola opens right as shown in the figure below. The general form of the parabola is $4p(x - h) = (y - k)^2$, where $p > 0$. The distance between the vertex $(2, 4)$ to the focus $(5, 4)$ is 3. Thus, $p = 3$. Thus, the equation of the parabolas is $4(3)(x - 2) = (y - 4)^2$ or $12(x - 2) = (y - 4)^2$ and the equation of the directrix is $x = 2 - 3 = -1$.

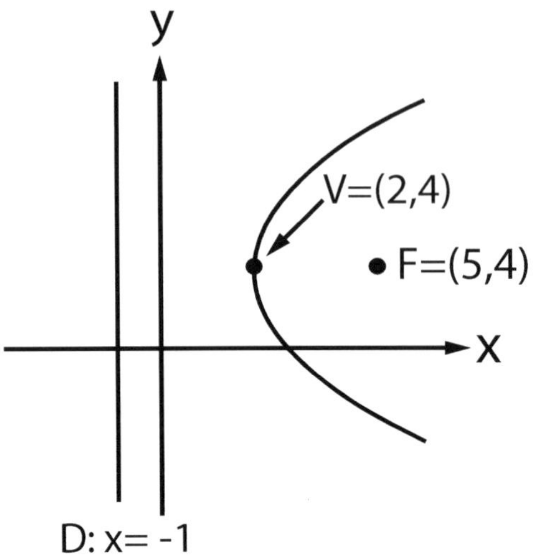

Example Finding the center and asymptotes of a hyperbola

Find the center, vertices, and asymptotes of the hyperbola shown below.

$$x^2 - 4y^2 - 6x + 5 = 0$$

Solution In order to write a general equation of the hyperbola $\frac{(x-h)^2}{a^2} - \frac{(y-k)^2}{b^2} = 1$, proceed to complete the squares in x and in y.

$x^2 - 4y^2 - 6x + 5 = 0$	
$x^2 - 4y^2 - 6x = -5$	Subtract 5 from each side
$(x^2 - 6x) - 4y^2 = -5$	Rearrange the terms
$(x^2 - 6x + 9) - 4y^2 = 4$	Add 9 to each side to complete squares in x
$(x-3)^2 - 4y^2 = 4$	Divide each side by 4
$\frac{(x-3)^2}{2^2} - \frac{(y)^2}{1^2} = 1$	

In order to find the center of the hyperbola, set $x - 3 = 0$ and $y = 0$ and solve for x and y. Thus, the center of the hyperbola is $(3, 0)$.

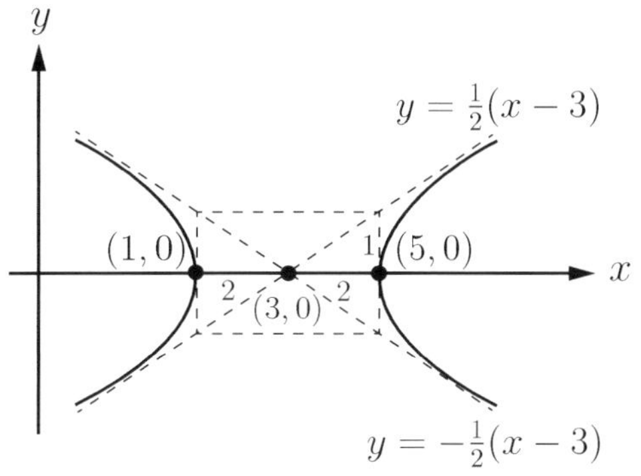

Since the vertices are horizontally 2 units from the center, the vertices are at $(1, 0)$ and $(5, 0)$. The slopes of the asymptotes are $\pm\frac{1}{2}$ and the asymptotes pass through the center $(3, 0)$. Thus, the equations of the asymptotes are $y = \frac{1}{2}(x-3)$ and $y = -\frac{1}{2}(x-3)$.

7.21 Solving Systems of Nonlinear Equations

Solving Systems of Nonlinear Equations

A nonlinear equation represents a curve, not a straight line. Usually, the curve is one of the four conic sections: a circle, a parabola, an ellipse, and a hyperbola. A system means more than one. Thus, a **system of nonlinear equations** contains at least one curve. Below is an example of a system of nonlinear equations.

$$x^2 + y^2 = 41$$
$$y = x - 1$$

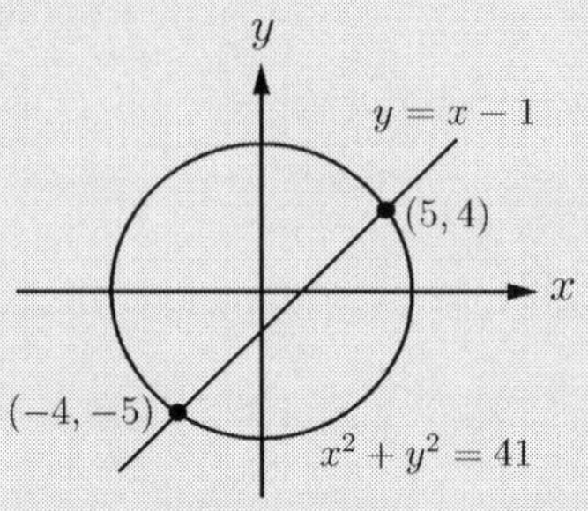

Solutions to a system of nonlinear equations are ordered pairs (x, y) that satisfy all equations in the system. In other words, solutions to a system of nonlinear equations are intersection points that lie on all graphs. In the figure above, $(5, 4)$ and $(-4, -5)$ are ordered pairs that satisfy all equations,

$$x^2 + y^2 = 41 \implies 5^2 + 4^2 = 41 \qquad x^2 + y^2 = 41 \implies (-4)^2 + (-5)^2 = 41$$
$$y = x - 1 \implies 4 = 5 - 1 \qquad y = x - 1 \implies -5 = -4 - 1$$

and are the intersection points of both graphs.

Solving a system of nonlinear equations means finding the x and y coordinates of the intersection points of both graphs. There are two methods to solve a system of nonlinear equations: **substitution** and **elimination**.

Let's solve the nonlinear equations shown below using the substitution method.

$$x^2 + y^2 = 41$$
$$y = x - 1$$

Substitute $x - 1$ for y in the first equation $x^2 + y^2 = 41$.

$x^2 + y^2 = 41$	Substitute $x - 1$ for y
$x^2 + (x-1)^2 = 41$	Simplify
$2x^2 - 2x - 40 = 0$	Divide each side by 2
$x^2 - x - 20 = 0$	Factor
$(x+4)(x-5) = 0$	Solve for x
$x = -4$ or $x = 5$	

In order to find the values of y, substitute $x = 5$ and $x = -4$ into $y = x - 1$. Thus, $y = 4$ and $y = -5$, respectively. Therefore, the solutions to the system of nonlinear equations are $(5, 4)$ and $(-4, -5)$.

Example Solving a system of nonlinear equations

Solve the following system of nonlinear equations.

$$2x^2 - y^2 = 14$$
$$x^2 + y^2 = 13$$

Solution $2x^2 - y^2 = 14$ represents a hyperbola and $x^2 + y^2 = 13$ represents a circle as shown below.

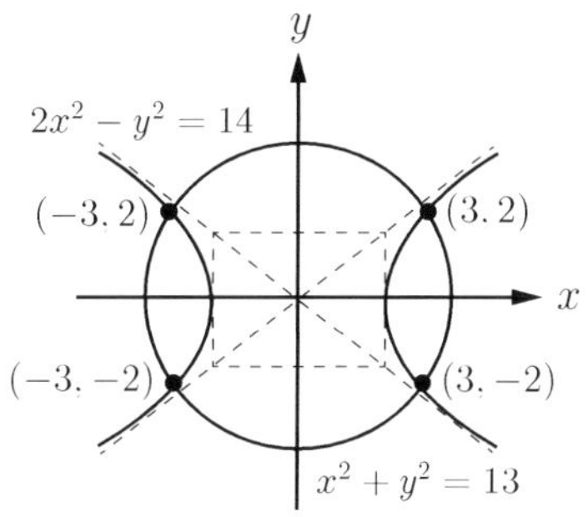

Both graphs intersect four times. In order to find the intersection points of both graphs, use the elimination method since the coefficients of y^2 are opposite.

$$\begin{aligned} 2x^2 - y^2 &= 14 \\ x^2 + y^2 &= 13 && \text{Add two equations} \\ \hline 3x^2 \quad &= 27 && \text{Divide each side by 3} \\ x^2 \quad &= 9 && \text{Solve for } x \\ x &= \pm 3 \end{aligned}$$

Substitute 3 and -3 for x in $x^2 + y^2 = 13$, respectively and solve for y. Thus, $y = \pm 2$ when $x = 3$, and $y = \pm 2$ when $x = -3$. Therefore, the solutions to the system of nonlinear equations are $(3, 2)$, $(3, -2)$, $(-3, 2)$, and $(-3, -2)$.

Chapter 8

Probability and Statistics

8.1 Probability

Probability

The definition of probability of an event, E, is as follows:

$$\text{Probability(E)} = \frac{\text{The number of outcomes event } E \text{ that can happen}}{\text{The total number of possible outcomes}}$$

where the total number of possible outcomes is the **sample space**.

Probability is a measure of how likely an event will happen. Probability can be expressed as a fraction, a decimal, and a percent, and is measured on scale from 0 to 1. Probability can not be less than 0 nor greater than 1. In other words, $0 \leq P(E) \leq 1$.

- Probability equals 0 means an event will never happen.
- Probability equals 1 means an event will always happen.
- Higher the probability, higher chance an event will happen.

For instance, what is the probability of selecting a prime number at random from 1 to 5? In this problem, the event E is selecting a prime number from three possible prime numbers: 2, 3, and 5. The total possible outcomes are numbers from 1 to 5. Thus, the probability of selecting a prime number is $P(E) = \frac{\{2,3,5\}}{\{1,2,3,4,5\}} = \frac{3}{5}$.

Venn Diagram

A venn diagram is very useful in probability.

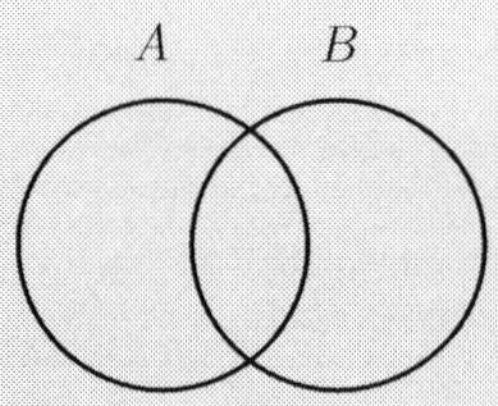

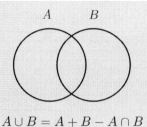

$$A \cup B = A + B - A \cap B$$

In the figure above, $A \cup B$ represents the combined area of two circles A and B. $A \cap B$ represents the common area where the two circles overlap. The venn diagram suggests that the combined area $(A \cup B)$ equals the sum of areas of circles $(A + B)$ minus the common area $(A \cap B)$.

$P(A \cup B)$ using the venn diagram can be calculated as follows:

$$P(A \cup B) = P(A) + P(B) - P(A \cap B)$$

8.2 Complementary and Independent Events

Complementary and Independent Events

- **Complementary events**: Two events are **complementary** if exactly one of the events must occur. If A is an event, then A' is the complementary event of A, or 'not A'.

$$P(A) + P(A') = 1$$

- **Independent events**: If A and B are **independent events**, then

$$P(A \textbf{ and } B) = P(A) \times P(B)$$

Tips

If A and B are NOT independent events or **dependent events**, then

$$P(A \text{ and } B) \neq P(A) \times P(B)$$

8.3 Laws of Probability

Laws of Probability

- **Addition law**

$$P(A \cup B) = P(A) + P(B) - P(A \cap B), \quad \text{or} \quad P(A \text{ or } B) \ = P(A) + P(B) - P(\text{both } A \text{ and } B)$$

- **Mutually exclusive or Disjoint events**: If A and B are **mutually exclusive** events, then $P(A \cap B) = 0$. Thus, the addition law becomes

$$P(A \cup B) = P(A) + P(B)$$

- **Conditional probability**: If A and B are two events, then

$$P(A|B) = \frac{P(A \cap B)}{P(B)}$$

where $A|B$ represents that "A occurs knowing that B has occurred" and is read as "A given B.

Tips

1. If A and B are independent events, then $P(A|B) = P(A)$ and $P(B|A) = P(B)$.

$$P(A|B) = \frac{P(A \cap B)}{P(B)} = \frac{P(A) \times P(B)}{P(B)} = P(A)$$
$$P(B|A) = \frac{P(B \cap A)}{P(A)} = \frac{P(A) \times P(B)}{P(A)} = P(B)$$

2. In $P(A|B)$, the sample space is B.
3. It two events A and B are dependent events, $P(A \cap B) = P(A)P(B|A)$.

Example Finding probabilities

Use the table below to find the following probabilities.

	Junior	Senior	Total
Music	30	60	90
Physics	40	50	90
Total	70	110	180

(a) Find the probability that a student selected at random is a junior?

(b) Find the probability that a student selected at random is taking music.

(c) Are taking music and physics independent events?

(d) Find the probability that a student selected at random is taking physics given that s/he is a senior.

(e) Find the probability that a student selected at random is a junior given that s/he is taking music.

Solution

(a) The sample space is 180 students. The probability that a student selected at random is a junior is $\frac{70}{180} = \frac{7}{18}$.

(b) The sample space is 180 students. The probability that a student selected at random is taking music is $\frac{90}{180} = \frac{1}{2}$.

(c) $P(\text{music}) = \frac{1}{2}$, $P(\text{physics}) = \frac{1}{2}$, and $P(\text{music and physics}) = 0$. Since $P(\text{music and physics}) \neq P(\text{music}) \times P(\text{physics})$, taking music and physics are NOT independent events.

(d) The sample space is 110 seniors. Out of 110 seniors, the number of students taking physics is 50. Thus, the probability that a student selected at random is taking physics given that s/he is a senior is $\frac{50}{110} = \frac{5}{11}$.

(e) The sample space is 90 students taking music. Out of 90 students taking music, the number of junior students is 30. Thus, the probability that a student selected at random is a junior given that s/he is taking music is $\frac{30}{90} = \frac{1}{3}$.

8.4 Key Statistical Concepts

Key Statistical Concepts

Statistics is a mathematic branch that deals with collecting, organizing, and analyzing data. The list below shows the words that are commonly used in statistics.

- **Population:** A collection of individuals about which we want to draw conclusions.
- **Census:** A collection of information from every individual in the population.
- **Sample:** A subset of the population. It is important to choose an SRS(simple random sample) to avoid bias in the results.
- **Data:** Information about individuals in a population.
- **Categorical variable:** places an individual into one of categories. For instance, color and gender.
- **Numerical variable:** takes numerical values. For instance, height and weight.
  - A **discrete numerical variable**: takes exact number values. For instance, the number of students in a class.
  - A **continuous numerical variable**: takes numerical values within a certain continuous rage. For instance, the weight of a student.
- **Parameter:** A numerical quantity measuring some aspect of a population.

- **Statistic:** A quantity calculated from data gathered from a sample. It is usually used to estimate a population parameter.
- **Distribution:** The pattern of variation of data. The distribution may be described as symmetrical, positively skewed(Right skewed), or negatively skewed(Left skewed).
- **Outliers:** Data values are either much larger or much smaller than the general body of data. They should be included in an analysis unless they are result of human or other error.

8.5 Display of Numerical Data

Display of Numerical Data

There are five way to examine the distribution of a numerical variable.

1. Pie Graph (table below shows class breakdown in a high school)

Freshmen	Sophomore	Junior	Senior
22%	28%	27%	23%

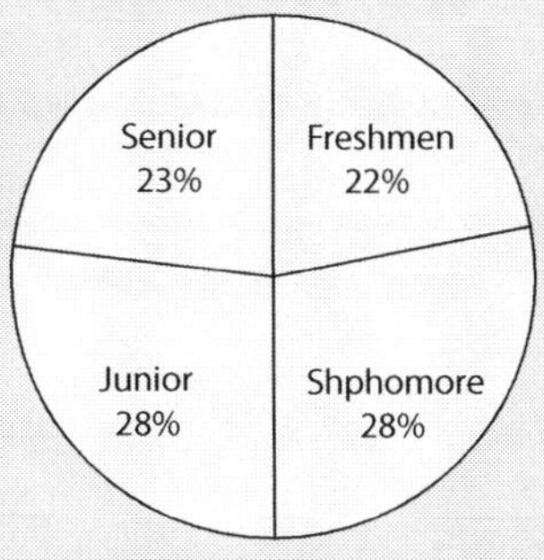

2. Dot plot (table below shows minutes to brush teeth)

4	3	5	4	2	5	5	1	2	6	4	2

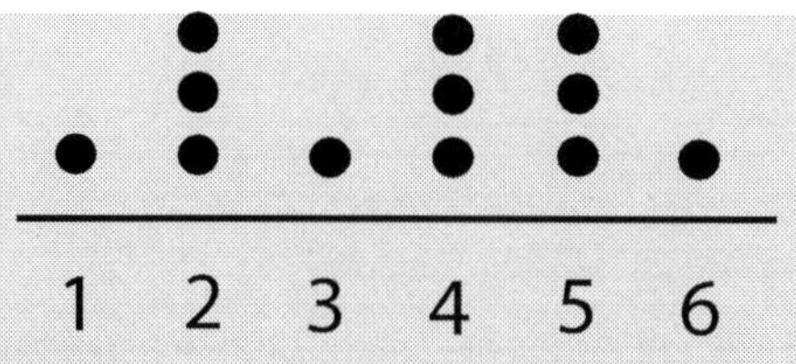

3. Step-and-leaf plot (table below shows weight of 11th grade students)

142	153	177	163	183	131
146	155	143	148	159	162

13	1
14	2 3 6 8
15	3 5 9
16	2 3
17	7
18	3

13 | **1** represents 131

4. Histogram (table below shows test scores of 30 students)

69	73	80	63	78	82	67	77	83	94
78	88	90	72	61	83	74	83	69	71
89	76	63	84	97	73	79	52	74	59

Score range	Frequency
50-60	2
60-70	6
70-80	11
80-90	8
90-100	3

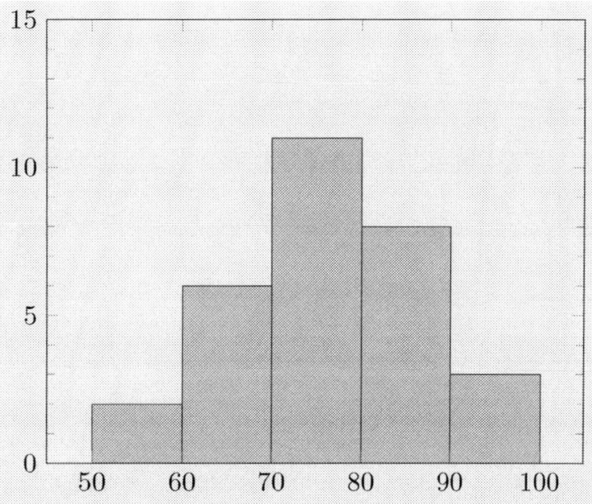

5. Box plot (table below shows the weights of eleven 3rd grade students)

24	30	31	33	34	36	39	40	44	45	49

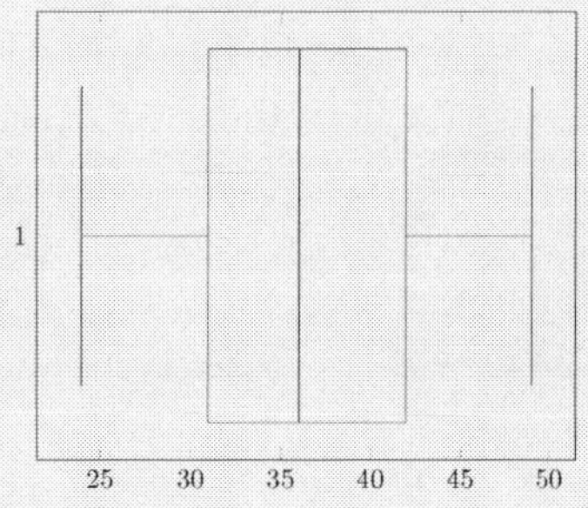

- Five number summary: Min, Q1(25%), Median(50%) ,Q3(75%), Max
- Range = Max − Min
- Interquartile range(IQR) = Q3 − Q1
- Outliers: $1.5 \times$ IQR from Min or Max
- Box plot does not show two things:
  - Mean
  - The number of observations

8.6 Measuring the Center of Data

Measuring the Center of Data

The three statistics that are used to measure the center of a data set are the mean, the median, and the mode.

1. **Mean**: Arithmetic average of the data set.

$$\overline{x} = \frac{1}{n}\sum_{i=1}^{n} x_i$$

   where $\overline{x}$ represents the mean, x_i represents the ith data value, n represents the number of data values.

   - Most popular measure of center
   - **Sensitive** to outliers
   - The mean is pulled toward its skewness

2. **Median**: The middle value of an ordered data set.

   - **Robust** to outliers
   - When the number of observation is
     - **odd**: the median is $\left(\frac{n+1}{2}\right)$th data value.
     - **even**: the median is the mean of $\left(\frac{n}{2}\right)$th and $\left(\frac{n}{2}+1\right)$th data values.

3. **Mode**: The number that is frequently occurring value in the data set.

8.7 Comparing the Mean and Median of a Distribution

Comparing the Mean and Median of a Distribution

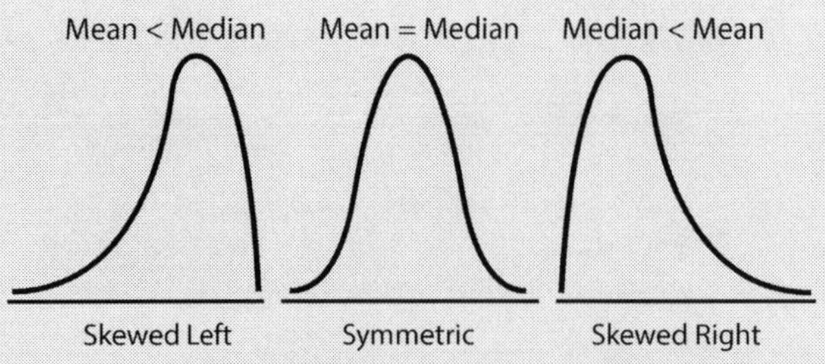

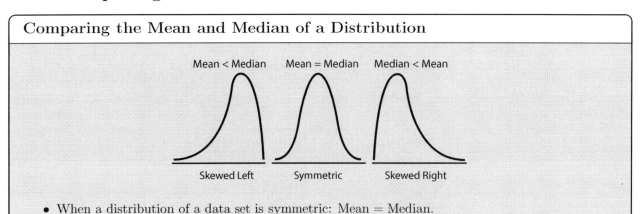

- When a distribution of a data set is symmetric: Mean = Median.

- When a distribution of a data set is skewed left: Mean < Median.
- When a distribution of a data set is skewed right: Mean > Median.

8.8 Measuring the Spread of Data

Measuring the Spread of Data

Four different measures of spread(dispersion) of a distribution are range, interquartile range, variance, and standard deviation.

1. **Range** = Max − Min
2. **Interquartile range(IQR)** = Q3(75th percentile) − Q1(25th percentile).
3. **Variance** s_n^2 measures the average of the squared deviation of each data value from the mean.

$$s_n^2 = \frac{\sum_{i=1}^{n}(x_i - \overline{x})^2}{n}$$

   where $(x_i - \overline{x})$ represents the deviation from the mean.

4. **Standard deviation** s_n is the square root of variance.

$$s_n = \sqrt{\frac{\sum_{i=1}^{n}(x_i - \overline{x})^2}{n}}$$

   - Measure of spread most common used.
   - Close link with mean.
   - **Sensitive** to outliers.
   - The greater the spread, the greater the standard deviation.
   - All values of data are the same, the standard deviation is zero.

8.9 Properties of the Standard Deviation

Properties of the Standard Deviation

1. The standard deviation is always positive.
2. The standard deviation is zero if all the numbers in the data set are the same. For instance, If a data set is $\{3, 3, 3, 3, 3\}$, the standard deviation of the data set is zero.
3. If all numbers in the data set are added by the same number, k, the standard deviation does not change. For instance, let $A = \{2, 5, 8, 9, 15\}$ and $\sigma_A = 4.35$. If each element in set $B = \{4, 7, 10, 11, 17\}$ is 2 more than each element in set A, the standard deviation of set B, σ_B, is $\sigma_B = \sigma_A = 4.35$.
4. If all numbers in the data set are subtracted by the same number, k, the standard deviation does not change. For instance, let $A = \{2, 5, 8, 9, 15\}$ and $\sigma_A = 4.35$. If each element in set $B = \{-1, 2, 5, 6, 12\}$ is 3 less than each element in set A, the standard deviation of set B is $\sigma_B = \sigma_A = 4.35$.
5. If all numbers in the data set are multiplied by the same number, k, the standard deviation is multiplied by k. For instance, let $A = \{2, 5, 8, 9, 15\}$ and $\sigma_A = 4.35$. If each element in set $B = \{6, 15, 24, 27, 45\}$ is three times each element in set A, the standard deviation of set B is $\sigma_B = 3\sigma_A = 3(4.35) = 13.05$.
6. If all numbers in the data set are divided by the same number, k, the standard deviation is divided by k. For instance, let $A = \{2, 5, 8, 9, 15\}$ and $\sigma_A = 4.35$. If each element in set $B = \{1, 2.5, 4, 4.5, 7.5\}$ is one-half each element in set A, the standard deviation of set B is $\sigma_B = \frac{\sigma_A}{2} = \frac{4.35}{2} = 2.175$.

Example Finding mean, median and standard deviation

Let the mean, median, and standard deviation of set A is 10, 8, and 6.72, respectively. If 5 is added to each element in set A, find the new mean, new median, and new standard deviation.

Solution Let $A = \{1, 6, 8, 15, 20\}$ so that the mean is 10, the median is 8, and the standard deviation is 6.72. Let $B = \{6, 11, 13, 20, 25\}$ so that each element in set B is 5 more than each element in set A. Therefore, the mean of set B is 15, the median of set B is 13, and the standard deviation of set B is the same as standard deviation of set A, which is 6.72. That is, both the new mean and median are 5 more than the old mean and old median. However, the new standard deviation is the same as the old standard deviation.

8.10 Random Variables

Random Variables

A **Random variable** is a variable whose value is a numerical outcome of a random phenomenon. For instance, the number of heads in 3 tosses of a coin.

- A **discrete random variable** X has a countable number of possible values. For instance, the number of students in a class.
- A **continuous random variable** X takes numerical values within a certain continuous rage. For instance, the weight of a student.

Discrete Probability Distributions

A discrete random variable X has a countable number of possible values as shown in the table below.

Value of X	x_1	x_2	x_3	$\cdots$	x_n
Prob	p_1	p_2	p_3	$\cdots$	p_n

The probability p_i of any given outcome x_i must follow two conditions:

- p_i lies between 0 and 1.
- $\sum_{i=1}^{n} p_i = p_1 + p_2 + p_3 + \cdots + p_n = 1$

Expected Value of Discrete Random Variables

Expected value(Expectation) $E(X)$ of a discrete random variable are as follows:

Expected value: $E(X) = \mu = \sum_{i=1}^{n} x_i p_i$

Tips $E(X) = 0$ represents that the trial or game is fair.

Example Finding E(X)

Let X be the number of heads in 3 tosses of a coin.

(a) Fill the table below.

Value of X				
Prob				

(b) Find $E(X)$.

Solution

(a)

Value of X	0	1	2	3
Prob	$\frac{1}{8}$	$\frac{3}{8}$	$\frac{3}{8}$	$\frac{1}{8}$

(b)

$$E(X) = \mu = \sum_{i=1}^{4} x_i p_i = 0 \times \frac{1}{8} + 1 \times \frac{3}{8} + 2 \times \frac{3}{8} + 3 \times \frac{1}{8} = \frac{12}{8} = 1.5$$

8.11 Normal Distributions

Normal Distributions

A function that is used to specify the probability distribution for a continuous random variable is called the **probability density function**. A bell-shaped probability density function for a continuous random variable is called the **normal distribution**. It is the most important distribution for the continuous random variable.

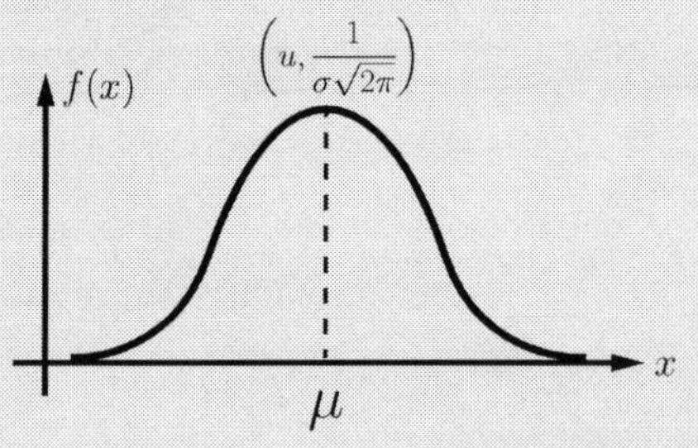

The normal distributions have following characteristics:

- Symmetric about the vertical line $x = \mu$.
- Area under the normal distribution is 1.

$68 - 99 - 99.7$ Rule (Empirical Rule)

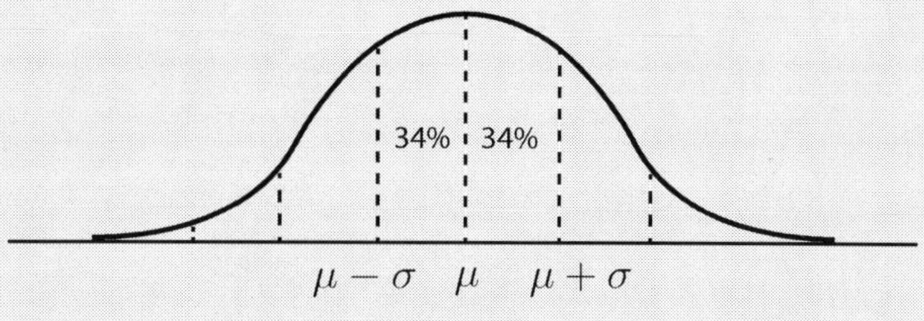

- Approximately **68%** of the population will measure between 1 standard deviation either side of the mean.
- Approximately **95%** of the population will measure between 2 standard deviations either side of the mean.
- Approximately **99.7%** of the population will measure between 3 standard deviations either side of the mean.

8.12 The Standard Normal Distribution(Z-distribution)

The Standard Normal Distribution(Z-distribution)

Every normal distribution can be transformed into the **standard normal distribution** or **Z-distribution** using the transformation $z = \dfrac{x-\mu}{\sigma}$. Z-distribution has the mean 0 and standard deviation 1, which is denoted by $z \sim N(0,1)$.

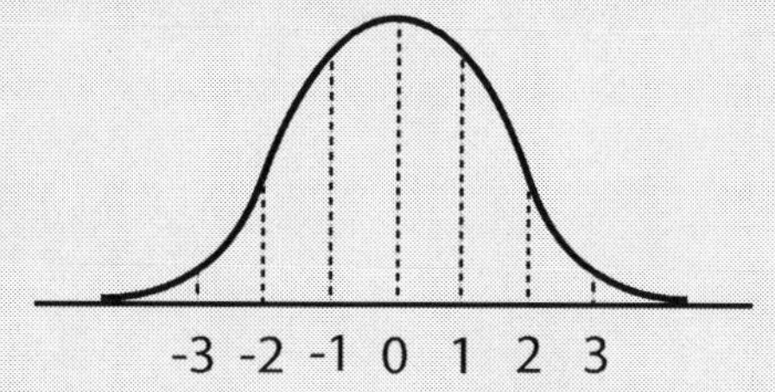

The standard normal distribution with mean 0 and standard deviation 1 also follows **$68 - 99 - 99.7$** Rule.

- Approximately **68%** of the population will measure between 1 standard deviation either side of the mean.
- Approximately **95%** of the population will measure between 2 standard deviations either side of the mean.
- Approximately **99.7%** of the population will measure between 3 standard deviations either side of the mean.

Example Finding percents using 68 – 95 – 99.7 Rule

The distribution of heights of high school senor students is normal with mean 65 inches and standard deviation 3 inches.

(a) What percent of students are taller than 68 inches?

(b) What percent of students are shorter than 59 inches?

(c) Between what heights do the middle 95% of students fall?

Solution

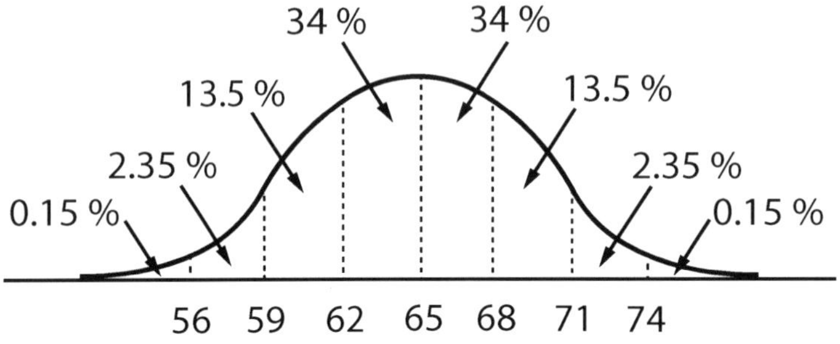

(a)

$$P(\text{Height} > 68) = 13.5\% + 2.35\% + 0.15\% = 15.87\%$$

(b)

$$P(\text{Height} < 59) = 2.35\% + 0.15\% = 2.5\%$$

(c) Approximately 95% of the heights will measure between 2 standard deviations either side of the mean. Thus, the heights should be between 59 inches and 71 inches.

Example Comparing z-scores

Joshua scored 740 on the SAT math test. The distribution of SAT math scores are normal with mean 540 and standard deviation 80. Jason scored 30 on ACT math test. The distribution of ACT math scores are normal with mean 18 and standard deviation 5. Who did relatively better?

Solution z-scores is $z = \dfrac{x-\mu}{\sigma}$. Let's calculate z-scores for the SAT math test and the ACT math test.

$$z_{SAT} = \frac{740-540}{80} = 2.5, \qquad z_{ACT} = \frac{30-18}{5} = 2.4$$

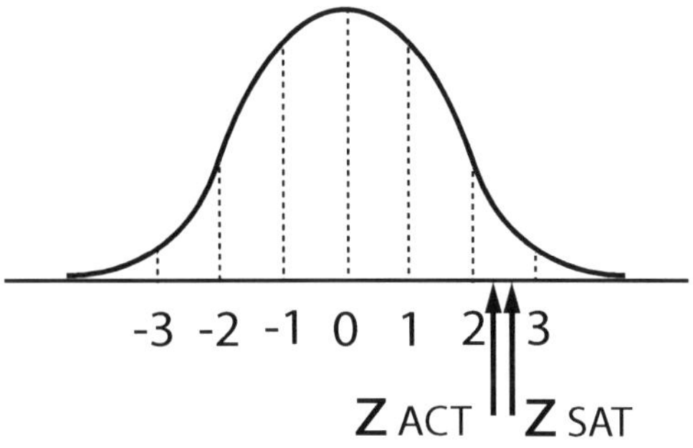

Since z_{SAT} is greater than z_{ACT}, Joshua did better.

8.13 Determining whether two variables are related

Scatter Plots and Correlation

There are two ways of determining whether two variables are related or not.

1. Graphical approach: **Scatter plots**.
2. Numerical approach: **Correlation** .

A scatter plot shows the relationship between two quantitative variables measured on the same individuals. A **response variable** measures the outcome of a study. An **explanatory variable** helps explain change in a response variable. The values of the explanatory variable appear on the horizontal axis, and the values of the response variable appear on the vertical axis.

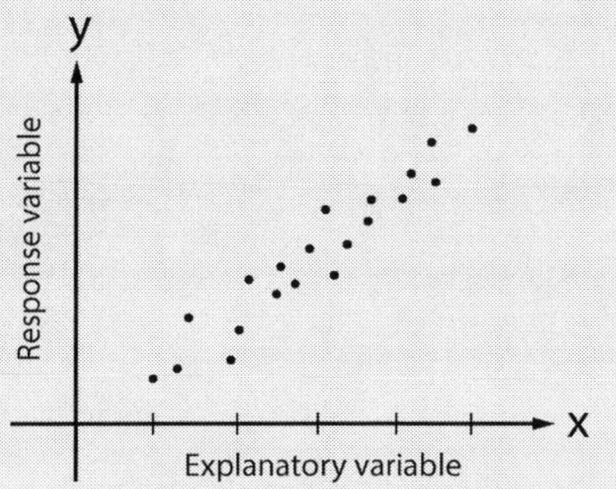

The correlation, r, measures the strength and direction of the **linear relationship** between two quantitative variable. The figures below show scatter plots and their corresponding correlation.

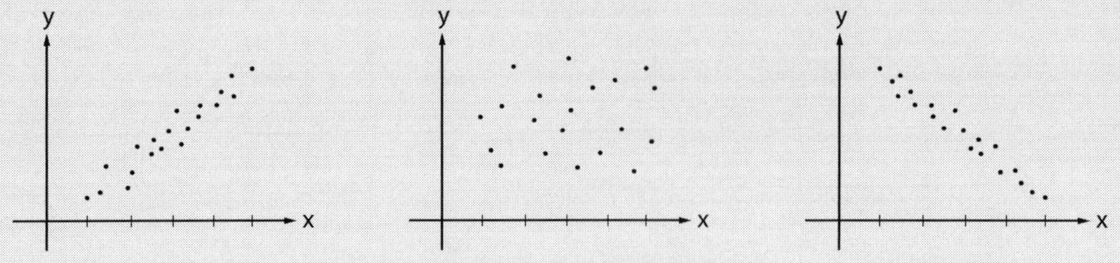

Correlation $r = 0.8$ Correlation $r = 0$ Correlation $r = -0.9$

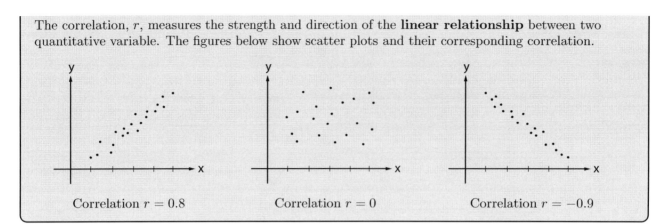

8.14 Facts about Correlation, r

Facts about Correlation, r

1. Positive r means when x increases, y increases.
2. Negative r means when x increases, y decreases.
3. Correlation must be between -1 and 1.
4. $r = 1$ or $r = -1$ indicates that x and y have a perfect linear relationship.
5. $r = 0$ indicates that x and y have a very weak linear relationship.
6. Correlation remains unchanged when switching x and y variables.
7. Correlation does not have units. Changing the units on your data will not affect the correlation.
8. Correlation is sensitive to outliers like mean and standard deviation.
9. Correlation implies association, not causation.
10. Correlation requires that both variables must be quantitative.

8.15 Least Squares Regression Line

Least Squares Regression Line

Least square regression line or **line of best fit** is a straight line that describes how a response variable y changes as an explanatory variable x changes. The least square regression line is used to predict what the value of y will be based on the value of x.

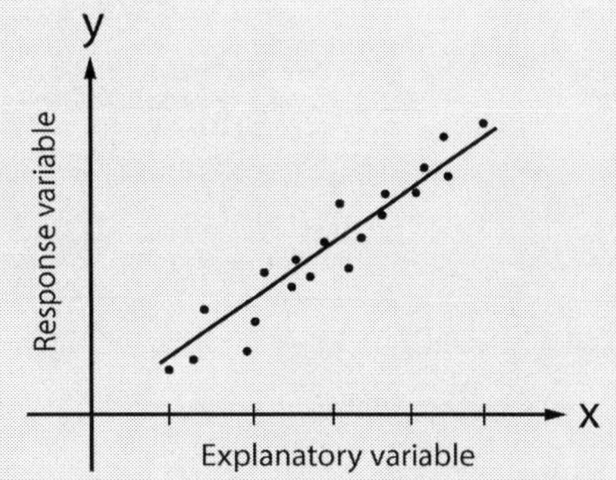

The least square regression line has the form $\hat{y} = ax + b$, where a is the slope of the line, and b is the y-intercept.

The following table shows the amount of time, in hours, that nine students spend for a Statistics test and scores on the test.

Score y	76	75	81	88	92	91	97	89	93
Time x	0.7	0.9	1.4	1.6	1.8	2.2	2.7	3.1	3.2

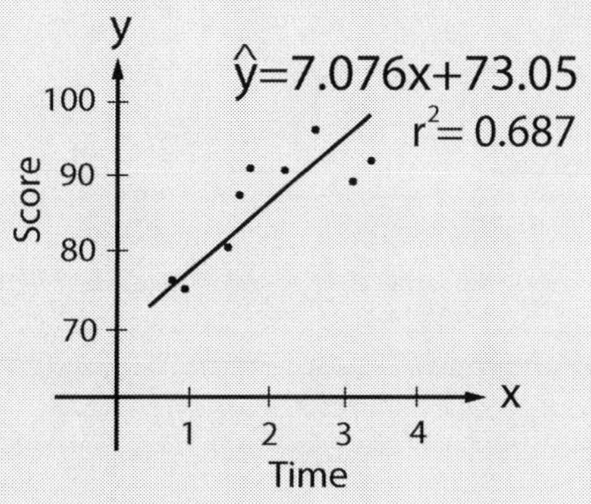

The least square regression line is $\hat{y} = 7.076x + 73.05$.

Interpretations

- The slope 7.076 means that the test score increases by 7.076 points as the amount of time increases by 1 hour.
- The y-intercept 73.05 means that when a student studies 0 hour, the test score s/he will get is 73.05 points.

The coefficient of determination r^2

The coefficient of determination, r^2, is the proportion of the variation in y that is predictable from x. Larger the r^2, better the least square regression model is. $r^2 = 0.687$ means that 68.7% of test score variation is explained by the amount of time spent studying.

Predictions

The least square regression line $\hat{y} = 7.076x + 73.05$ enables us to make predictions about the test score based on the amount of time spent studying. If a student studies 2.5 hours, s/he will get $7.067(2.5) + 73.05 = 90.74$ points.

Extrapolation

Extrapolation is the use of the least square regression line for prediction outside the domain of the explanatory variable x which is used to obtain the line. Such predictions cannot be trusted.

8.16 How Good is our Least Square Regression Line?

How Good is our Least Square Regression Line?

Residuals

A Residual e is the difference between the observed value of the response variable y, and the predicted value $\hat{y}$; that is, $e = y - \hat{y}$. Each data point has one residual.

Residual Plots

A residual plot is a graph that shows the residuals on the vertical axis and the explanatory variable x on the horizontal axis. If the points in a residual plot are randomly dispersed around the horizontal axis as shown in the figure below, a linear regression model is appropriate for the data.

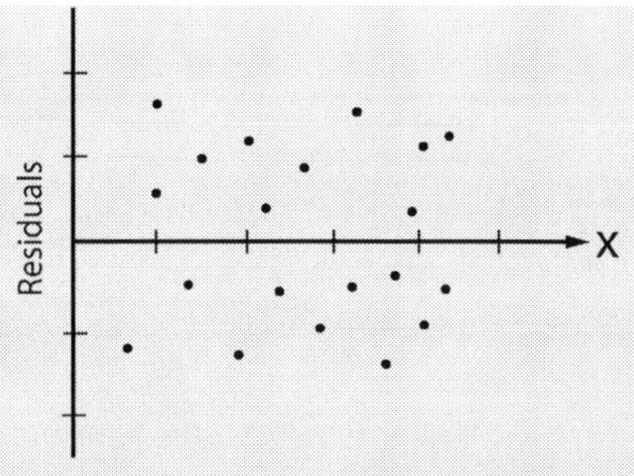

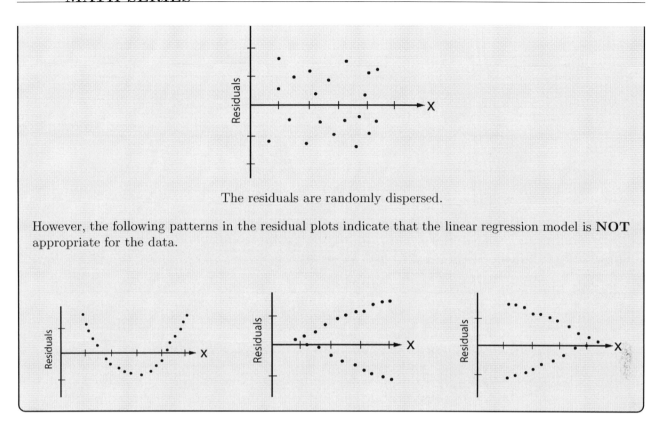

The residuals are randomly dispersed.

However, the following patterns in the residual plots indicate that the linear regression model is **NOT** appropriate for the data.

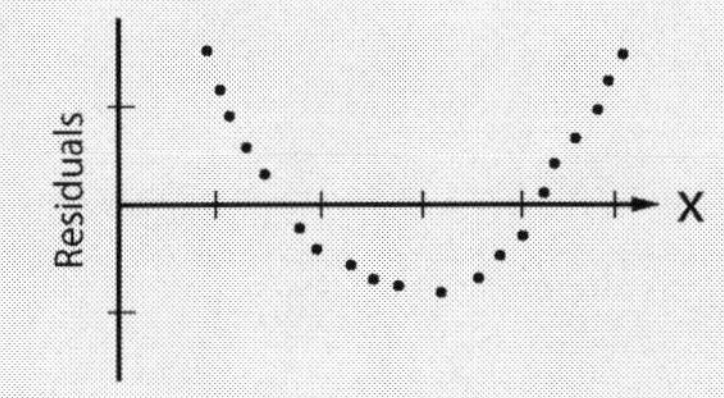

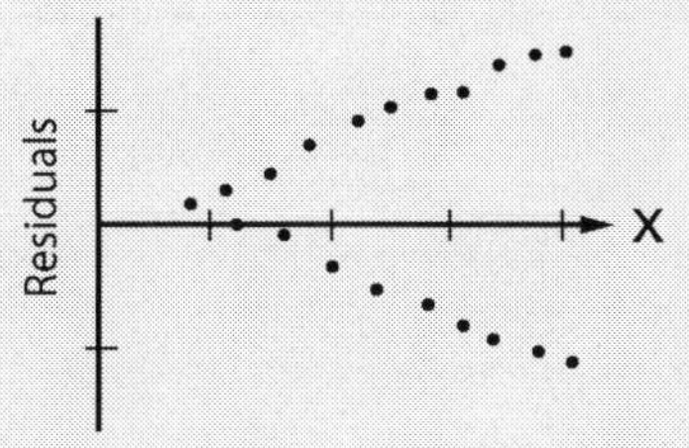

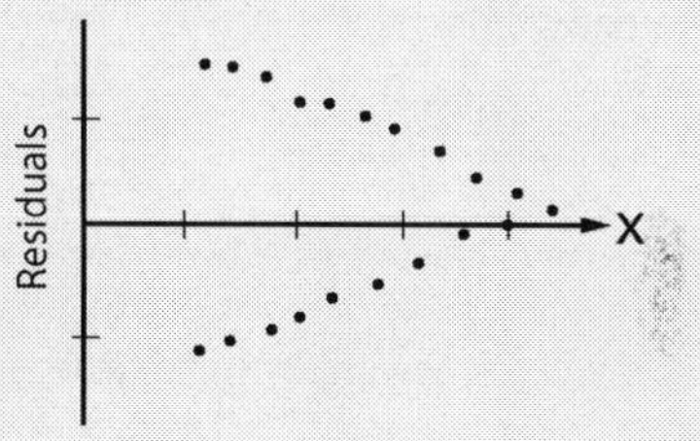

8.17 Observational studies and Experiments

Observational studies and Experiments

- In an **observational study**, researchers observe subjects(people) and measure variables of interest without assigning treatments to the subjects. Researchers should not interfere with the subjects or variables in any way.
- In an **experiment**, researchers apply treatments to subjects and then proceed the observed the effect of treatments on the subjects. The three principles of designing an experiment are as follows:
    1. Control: Two or more treatments should be compared.
    2. Randomization: The subjects should be randomly divided into groups in order to avoid selection bias.
    3. Replication: Having enough subjects will decrease the experimental error and increase precision.

8.18 Sampling from a Population

Sampling from a Population

An simple random sample(SRS) of size n is taken from the population to reflect the characteristics of the population. The sample must be sufficiently large so that the results are unbiased.
In order to distinguish between a sample and the whole population, different notations are used for the mean, variance, and the standard deviation.

	Mean	Variance	Standard deviation
Population	μ	σ^2	σ
Sample	$\overline{x}$	s_n^2	s_n

When a sample size of n is used to draw inference about a population

- The mean of the sample $\overline{x}$ is an unbiased estimate of population mean μ.
- The standard deviation of a sample s_n is an estimate of the standard deviation of population σ.

Tips: A simple random sample is a subset of a statistical population in which each member of the subset has an equal probability of being chosen. An example of a simple random sample of 100 would be the names of 100 students being chosen out of a hat from a college of 1000 students. In this case, the population is all 1000 students.

8.19 Sampling Distribution of a Sample Mean

Sampling Distribution of a Sample Mean

Draw an simple random sample of size n from a population that has a normal distribution with mean μ and standard deviation σ. Then the sample mean $\overline{x}$ has a normal distribution with mean μ and standard deviation $\sigma_{\overline{x}} = \dfrac{\sigma}{n}$. In other words,

$$\overline{x} \sim N\left(\mu, \frac{\sigma}{n}\right)$$

Chapter 9

Discrete Mathematics

9.1 Sequences

Sequences

A sequence (or progression) is a list of numbers in order. The numbers in the list are called **terms** of the sequence and are denoted with subscripted letters: a_1 for the first term, a_2 for the second term, a_n for the nth term.

To evaluate the value of a_n, there are two types of formulas: the **explicit formula** and the **recursive formula**. The explicit formula evaluates a_n directly by substituting a value into the formula. Whereas, the recursive formula involves all previous terms to evaluate a_n. For instance, to evaluate the 10th term using the recursive formula, we need to evaluate the first nine terms.

Example **Evaluating the nth term using an explicit formula**

If the sequence is defined by $a_n = 2n + 5$, evaluate the 5th term and the 11th term.

Solution In order to evaluate the 5th term and the 11th term, substitute $n = 5$ and $n = 11$ into $a_n = 2n + 5$, respectively.

$$a_n = 2n + 5 \quad \Longrightarrow \quad a_5 = 2(5) + 5 = 15$$
$$a_n = 2n + 5 \quad \Longrightarrow \quad a_{11} = 2(11) + 5 = 27$$

Therefore, the value of a_5 is 15 and the value of a_{11} is 27.

Example **Evaluating the nth term using a recursive formula**

If the sequence is defined by $a_n = 2a_{n-1} + 3$, $a_1 = 4$, evaluate the 5th term.

Solution In order to evaluate the 5th term, we need to find the previous four terms as shown below.

$a_n = 2a_{n-1} + 3,\ a_1 = 4$	Recursive formula with $a_1 = 4$
$a_2 = 2a_1 + 3 = 2(4) + 3 = 11$	Substitute 2 for n to find a_2
$a_3 = 2a_2 + 3 = 2(11) + 3 = 25$	Substitute 3 for n to find a_3
$a_4 = 2a_3 + 3 = 2(25) + 3 = 53$	Substitute 4 for n to find a_4
$a_5 = 2a_4 + 3 = 2(53) + 3 = 109$	Substitute 5 for n to find a_5

Therefore, the value of a_5 is 109.

9.2 Arithmetic Sequences and Geometric Sequences

Arithmetic Sequences and Geometric Sequences

There are two most common sequences: Arithmetic sequences and geometric sequences.

- In an **arithmetic sequence**, add or subtract the same number (common difference) to one term to get the next term.
- In a **geometric sequence**, multiply or divide one term by the same number (common ratio) to get the next term.

Type	Definition	Example	nth term
Arithmetic sequence	The common difference between any consecutive terms is constant.	$1, 3, 5, 7, \ldots$	$a_n = a_1 + (n-1)d$ where d is the common difference.
Geometric sequence	The common ratio between any consecutive terms is constant	$2, 4, 8, 16, \ldots$	$a_n = a_1 \times r^{n-1}$ where r is the common ratio.

Example **Writing the nth term of an arithmetic sequence**

In the arithmetic sequence, if $a_9 = 51$ and $a_{17} = 99$, write an explicit formula for a_n.

Solution Write the 9th term and 17th term of the arithmetic sequence in terms of a_1 and d using the nth term formula: $a_n = a_1 + (n-1)d$.

$$a_{17} = a_1 + 16d = 99$$
$$a_9 = a_1 + 8d = 51$$

Use the linear combinations method to solve for d and a_1.

$$a_1 + 16d = 99$$
$$a_1 + 8d = 51 \qquad \text{Subtract the two equations}$$
$$8d = 48 \qquad \text{Divide both sides by 8}$$
$$d = 6$$

Substitute $d = 6$ into $a_9 = a_1 + 8d = 51$ and solve for a_1. Thus, $a_1 = 3$. Therefore, the nth term of the arithmetic sequence is $a_n = a_1 + (n-1)d = 3 + (n-1)6 = 6n - 3$.

9.3 Series

Series

A **series** is the sum of a sequence. A series can be either a finite series, S_n or infinite series, S. The finite series S_n is the sum of a finite number of terms. Whereas, the infinite series is the sum of an infinite number of terms. Often, the finite series S_n is called the ***n*th partial sum** and the infinite series is called an **infinite sum**.

A series can be represented in a compact form, called summation notation or sigma notation $\sum$. Using the summation notation, the nth partial sum S_n and infinite sum S can be expressed as follows:

$$S_n = a_1 + a_2 + \cdots + a_n = \sum_{k=1}^{n} a_k,$$
$$S = a_1 + a_2 + a_3 \cdots = \sum_{k=1}^{\infty} a_k$$

where k is called the **index** of the sum. $k = 1$ indicates where to start the sum and $k = n$ indicates where to end the sum. For instance,

$$\sum_{k=1}^{5} k^2 = 1^2 + 2^2 + 3^2 + 4^2 + 5^2$$

9.4 Arithmetic Series and Geometric Series

Arithmetic Series and Geometric Series

An arithmetic series is the sum of an arithmetic sequence. A geometric series is the sum of a geometric sequence. For instance, $1+3+5+7+\cdots$ is an arithmetic series and $\frac{1}{2}+\frac{1}{4}+\frac{1}{8}+\frac{1}{16}+\cdots$ is a geometric series.

Below summarizes the nth partial sum and infinite sum for an arithmetic series and a geometric series.

Type	Arithmetic Series	Geometric Series
nth Partial Sum	$S_n = \frac{n}{2}(a_1 + a_n)$	$S_n = \frac{a_1(1-r^n)}{1-r}$
Infinite Sum	$S = \infty$	$S = \begin{cases} \dfrac{a_1}{1-r}, & \lvert r\rvert < 1 \\ \infty, & \lvert r\rvert \geq 1 \end{cases}$

Tips: Note that the infinite sum S of a geometric series converges to $\frac{a_1}{1-r}$ if $|r| < 1$, where r is the common ratio of a geometric sequence.

Example — Finding the sum of an arithmetic series

Find the sum of the arithmetic series shown below.

$$3+7+11+\cdots+83$$

Solution $3, 7, 11, \cdots, 83$ is the arithmetic sequence with a common difference of 4. Using the nth term formula $a_n = a_1 + (n-1)d$,

$$\begin{aligned}
a_n &= a_1 + (n-1)d && \text{Substitute 83 for } a_n,\ 3 \text{ for } a_1, \text{ and 4 for } d \\
83 &= 3 + (n-1)4 && \text{Subtract 3 from each side} \\
4(n-1) &= 80 && \text{Divide each side by 4} \\
n-1 &= 20 && \text{Add 1 to each side} \\
n &= 21
\end{aligned}$$

we found that 83 is the 21st term of the arithmetic sequence. Thus, $3+7+11+\cdots+83$ is the sum of the first 21 terms of the arithmetic sequence.

$$S_n = \frac{n}{2}(a_1 + a_n) \qquad \text{Substitute 21 for } n$$

$$S_{21} = \frac{21}{2}(a_1 + a_{21}) \qquad \text{Substitute 3 for } a_1 \text{ and 83 for } a_{21}$$

$$= \frac{21}{2}(3 + 83) = 903$$

Therefore, $3 + 7 + 11 + \cdots + 83 = 903$.

Example **Finding the sum of a geometric series**

Find the sum of each geometric series.

(a) $\frac{1}{2} + \frac{3}{4} + \frac{9}{8} + \cdots$

(b) $1 - \frac{1}{2} + \frac{1}{4} - \frac{1}{8} + \cdots$

(c) $\displaystyle\sum_{k=1}^{\infty} 4\left(-\frac{2}{3}\right)^{k-1}$

Solution

(a) The common ratio is

$$r = \frac{\frac{3}{4}}{\frac{1}{2}} = \frac{3}{2}$$

Since $|r| > 1$, the infinite sum S of the geometric series diverges. In other words, $S = \infty$.

(b) The common ratio is $-\frac{1}{2}$. Since $|r| < 1$,

$$S = \frac{a_1}{1-r} = \frac{1}{1-(-\frac{1}{2})} = \frac{1}{\frac{3}{2}} = \frac{2}{3}$$

Therefore, the infinite sum S of the geometric series is $\frac{2}{3}$.

(c) Substitute $k = 1$, $k = 2$, and $k = 3$ to write out the sum.

$$\sum_{k=1}^{\infty} 4\left(-\frac{2}{3}\right)^{k-1} = 4 - \frac{8}{3} + \frac{16}{9} + \cdots$$

The common ratio is $-\frac{2}{3}$. Since $|r| < 1$,

$$S = \frac{a_1}{1-r} = \frac{4}{1-(-\frac{2}{3})} = \frac{4}{\frac{5}{3}} = \frac{12}{5}$$

Therefore, the infinite sum S of the geometric series is $\frac{12}{5}$.

9.5 Properties of Sigma Notation

Properties of Sigma Notation

1. $\displaystyle\sum_{k=1}^{n}(a_k \pm b_k) = \sum_{k=1}^{n} a_k \pm \sum_{k=1}^{n} b_k$
2. $\displaystyle\sum_{k=1}^{n} c \cdot a_k = c \cdot \sum_{k=1}^{n} a_k$, where c is a constant.
3. $\displaystyle\sum_{k=1}^{n} c = cn$, where c is a constant.
4. $\displaystyle\sum_{k=1}^{n} k = 1 + 2 + \cdots + n = \frac{n(n+1)}{2}$
5. $\displaystyle\sum_{k=1}^{n} k^2 = 1^2 + 2^2 + \cdots + n^2 = \frac{n(n+1)(2n+1)}{6}$
6. $\displaystyle\sum_{k=1}^{n} k^3 = 1^3 + 2^3 + \cdots + k^3 = \left(\frac{n(n+1)}{2}\right)^2$

Tips $\displaystyle\sum_{k=1}^{n}(a_k \cdot b_k) \neq \sum_{k=1}^{n} a_k \cdot \sum_{k=1}^{n} b_k$

Example Finding the sum using the properties of sigma notation

Find the sum of the following series using the properties of sigma notation.

(a) $\displaystyle\sum_{k=1}^{20}(2k+3)$

(b) $\displaystyle\sum_{k=1}^{50}k(k-1)$

Solution

(a) Using the properties of sigma notation,

$$\begin{aligned}\sum_{k=1}^{20}(2k+3) &= 2\cdot\sum_{k=1}^{20}k+\sum_{k=1}^{20}3 = 2\left(\frac{20(21)}{2}\right)+3(20)\\ &= 480\end{aligned}$$

(b) Using the properties of sigma notation,

$$\begin{aligned}\sum_{k=1}^{50}k(k-1) &= \sum_{k=1}^{50}(k^2-k) = \sum_{k=1}^{50}k^2-\sum_{k=1}^{50}k\\ &= \frac{50(51)(101)}{6}-\frac{50(51)}{2}\\ &= 41650\end{aligned}$$

9.6 Converse, Inverse, and Contrapositive

Converse, Inverse, and Contrapositive

A conditional statement consists of two parts, a hypothesis in the if clause and a conclusion in the then clause. Let P and Q be the hypothesis and conclusion, respectively.

Conditional statement	If P, then Q
Converse	If Q, then P
Inverse	If Not P, then Not Q
Contrapositive	If Not Q, then Not P

Tips A conditional statement and its contrapositive are logically equivalent.

9.7 Equivalence Relations

Equivalence Relations

A relation $\Re$ on a set S

reflexive if $x \Re x$ for all $x \in S$

symmetric if $x \Re y \Rightarrow y \Re x$ for all $x,\, y \in S$

transitive if $(x \Re y$ and $y \Re z) \Rightarrow x \Re z$ for all $x,\, y,\, z \in S$

antisymmetric if $(x \Re y$ and $y \Re x) \Rightarrow x = y$ for all $x,\, y \in S$

An equivalence relation is a reflexive, symmetric, and transitive relation.

The following are all equivalence relations:

- "Is equal to " on the set of numbers. For instance, $\frac{1}{2}$ is equal to $\frac{2}{4}$.
- "Has the same image under a function" on the elements of the domain of the function.
- " Has the same cosine" on the set of all angles

9.8 Counting

Counting

Counting integers

How many positive integers are there between 42 and 97 inclusive? Are there 54, 55, or 56 integers? Even in this simple counting problem, many students are not sure what the right answer is. A rule for counting integers is as follows:

$$\text{The number of integers} = \text{Greatest integer} - \text{Least integer} + 1$$

According to this rule, the number of integers between 42 and 97 inclusive is $97 - 42 + 1 = 56$ integers.

Venn Diagram

A venn diagram is very useful in counting. It helps you count numbers correctly.

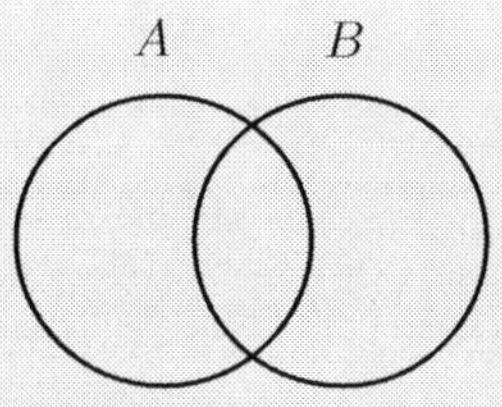

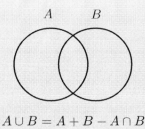

$$A \cup B = A + B - A \cap B$$

In the figure above, $A \cup B$ represents the combined area of two circles A and B. $A \cap B$ represents the common area where the two circles overlap. The venn diagram suggests that the combined area ($A \cup B$) equals the sum of areas of circles ($A + B$) minus the common area ($A \cap B$).
In counting, each circle A and B represents a set of numbers. $n(A)$ and $n(B)$ represent the number of elements in set A and B, respectively. For instance, $A = \{2, 4, 6, 8, 10\}$ and $n(A) = 5$. Thus, the total number of elements that belong to either set A or set B, $n(A \cup B)$, can be counted as follows:

$$n(A \cup B) = n(A) + n(B) - n(A \cap B)$$

Let's find out how many positive integers less than or equal to 20 are divisible by 2 or 3. Define A as the set of numbers divisible by 2 and B as the set of numbers divisible by 3.

$$\begin{aligned} A &= \{2, 4, 6, \cdots, 18, 20\}, & n(A) &= 10 \\ B &= \{3, 6, 9, 12, 15, 18\}, & n(B) &= 6 \\ A \cap B &= \{6, 12, 18\}, & n(A \cap B) &= 3 \end{aligned}$$

Notice that $A \cap B = \{6, 12, 18\}$ are multiples of 2 and multiples of 3. They are counted twice so they must be excluded in counting. Thus,

$$\begin{aligned} n(A \cup B) &= n(A) + n(B) - n(A \cap B) \\ &= 10 + 6 - 3 \\ &= 13 \end{aligned}$$

Therefore, the total number of positive integers less than or equal to 20 that are divisible by 2 or 3 is 13.

9.9 The Fundamental Counting Principle

The Fundamental Counting Principle(The Multiplication Principle)

If one event can occur in m ways and another event can occur in n ways, then the number of ways both events can occur is $m \times n$. For instance, Jason has three shirts and four pairs of jeans. He can dress up in $3 \times 4 = 12$ different ways.

9.10 Permutation and Combination

Permutation and Combination

Factorial notation

n factorial, denoted by $n!$, is defined as $n! = n(n-1)(n-2)\cdots 3\cdot 2\cdot 1$. In other words, n factorial is the product of all positive integers less than or equal to n. For instance, $3! = 3\cdot 2\cdot 1 = 6$. Below are the properties of factorials.

1. $0! = 1$ and $1! = 1$.
2. $n! = n \times (n-1)!$ or $n! = n \cdot (n-1) \cdot (n-2)!$.
   For instance, $5! = 5 \cdot 4!$, or $5! = 5 \cdot 4 \cdot 3!$.

Permutations without repetition

A permutation, denoted by ${}_nP_r$, represents a number of ways to select r objects from the total number of objects n where the order is important. The permutation ${}_nP_r$ is given by

$${}_nP_r = \frac{n!}{(n-r)!}, \qquad \text{where } r \le n$$

For instance, how many words can be formed using all the letters in the word ABCDE?

Since all the letters A, B, C, D, and E are distinguishable, the order is important. Thus, this is a permutation problem.

$${}_5P_5 = \frac{5!}{(5-5)!} = \frac{5!}{0!} = 120$$

Therefore, the number of different words can be formed using the letters in word ABCDE is 120.

Permutations with repetition

The number of permutations of n objects, where there are n_1 indistinguishable objects of one kind, and n_2 indistinguishable objects of a second kind, is given by

$$\text{Permutations with repetition} = \frac{n!}{n_1! \cdot n_2!}$$

For instance, how many words can be formed using all the letters in the word AABBB?

Since letters A and B are distinguishable, the order is important. However, there are 2 A's and 3 B's out of 5 letters.

$$\text{Permutations with repetition} = \frac{5!}{2!\cdot 3!} = \frac{5\cdot 4\cdot \cancel{3!}}{2!\cdot \cancel{3!}} = 10$$

Therefore, the number of different words can be formed using the letters in word AABBB is 10.

Combinations

A combination, denoted by ${}_nC_r$ or $\binom{n}{r}$, represents a number of ways to select r objects from the total number of objects n where the order is NOT important. The combination $\binom{n}{r}$ is given by

$$\binom{n}{r} = \frac{n!}{(n-r)! \cdot r!}, \qquad \text{where } r \leq n$$

For instance, how many 2 different books can be selected from a list of 10 books?

Since 2 books are indistinguishable, the order is not important. Thus, this is a combination problem.

$$\binom{10}{2} = \frac{10!}{8! \cdot 2!} = \frac{10 \cdot 9 \cdot \cancel{8!}}{\cancel{8!} \cdot 2!} = 45$$

Therefore, the number of selecting 2 different books from a list of 10 books is 45.

Example **Permutations and Combinations**

(a) How many ways can a group of 10 people elect a president and a vice president?

(b) How many different committees of 2 officers can be formed from a group of 10 people?

Solution

(a) Since a president and a vice president are distinguishable, the order is important. Thus, this is a permutation problem.

$$_{10}P_2 = \frac{10!}{8!} = \frac{10 \cdot 9 \cdot \cancel{8!}}{\cancel{8!}} = 90$$

Therefore, the number of ways to elect a president and a vice present from a group of 10 people is 90.

(b) Since 2 officers are indistinguishable, the order is not important. Thus, this is a combination problem.

$$\binom{10}{2} = \frac{10!}{8! \cdot 2!} = \frac{10 \cdot 9 \cdot \cancel{8!}}{\cancel{8!} \cdot 2!} = 45$$

Therefore, the number of different committees of 2 officers can be formed from a group of 10 people is 45.

9.11 The Binomial Theorem

Binomial Expansions

$a+b$ is called a **binomial** as it contains two terms. Any expression of the term $(a+b)^n$ is called a **power of a binomial**. Let's consider the following algebraic expansions of the binomial $(a+b)^n$.

$$\begin{aligned}
(a+b)^1 &= a+b \\
(a+b)^2 &= a^2+2ab+b^2 \\
(a+b)^3 &= (a+b)(a+b)^2 = a^3+3a^2b+3ab^2+b^3 \\
(a+b)^4 &= (a+b)(a+b)^3 = a^4+4a^3b+6a^2b^2+4ab^3+b^4
\end{aligned}$$

The algebraic expansions of $(a+b)^n$ get longer and longer as n increases. However, these algebraic expansions show some kind of pattern. The pattern is summed up by the **Binomial Theorem**.

The Binomial Theorem

$$(a+b)^n = \sum_{k=0}^{n} \binom{n}{k} a^{n-k} b^k$$

where $\binom{n}{k} = \dfrac{n!}{(n-k)! \cdot k!}$ is the binomial coefficient which represents the number of combinations of n objects when k objects are taken at a time.

In general,

1. The number of terms of $(a+b)^n$ is $n+1$.
2. As the powers of a decreases by 1, the powers of b increases by 1.
3. The sum of the powers of a and b in each term of the expansion is n.
4. The general term, or $(r+1)$th term is $T_{r+1} = \binom{n}{r} a^{n-r} b^r$.

Example Expand using the Binomial Theorem

Use the Binomial Theorem to expand $(x+2)^5$.

Solution

$$\begin{aligned}(x+2)^5 &= \sum_{k=0}^{5}\binom{5}{k}x^{5-k}2^k \\ &= \binom{5}{0}x^5(2^0)+\binom{5}{1}x^4(2^1)+\binom{5}{2}x^3(2^2)+\binom{5}{3}x^2(2^3)+\binom{5}{4}x^1(2^4)+\binom{5}{5}x^0(2^5) \\ &= x^5+5(2)x^4+10(4)x^3+10(8)x^2+5(16)x+32 \\ &= x^5+10x^4+40x^3+80x^2+80x+32\end{aligned}$$

Example Finding the coefficient in a Binomial expansion

Find the coefficient of x^6 in the expansion of $(x^2-3)^4$.

Solution

$$(x^2-3)^4 = \sum_{k=0}^{4}\binom{4}{k}(x^2)^{4-k}(-3)^k$$

When $k=1$, the term containing x^6 is $\binom{4}{1}(x^2)^3(-3)^1$ or $-12x^6$. Therefore, the coefficient of x^6 is -12.

PRAXIS II 5161 PRACTICE TEST 1

Time — 150 minutes
Number of questions — 60

Directions: Solve each of the following problems using the available space for scratch work. Choose the best answer among the answer choices given and fill in the corresponding circle on the answer sheet.

1. If the diameter of a circle is 14, what is the ratio of the area of the circle to the circumference of the circle?

   (A) $7:2$

   (B) $5:2$

   (C) $4:3$

   (D) $3:7$

2. A water cooler was filled with water and then $\frac{7}{8}$ gallon of water was used. If $1\frac{7}{8}$ gallons of water is still remaining in the cooler, what is the capacity of the cooler?

   (A) $2\dfrac{1}{2}$ gallons

   (B) $2\dfrac{5}{8}$ gallons

   (C) $2\dfrac{3}{4}$ gallons

   (D) $2\dfrac{7}{8}$ gallons

3. Which of the following quadratic function is decreasing over the entire interval $(2, 4)$?

   (A) $y = (x-4)^2$

   (B) $y = (x-3)^2$

   (C) $y = (x-2)^2$

   (D) $y = (x-1)^2$

4. If both n and k are prime numbers, which of the following statement must be true?

   (A) $n + k$ is an even number.

   (B) If $n > 2$ and $k > 2$, $n + k$ is an even number.

   (C) nk is an odd number.

   (D) If $n < k$, $k - n$ is divisible by 3.

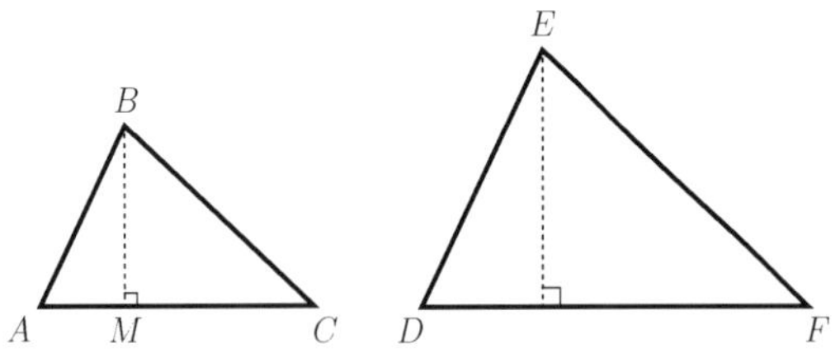

5. $\triangle ABC$ and $\triangle DEF$ are similar triangles. If $AC = 5$, $BM = 4$, and $DF = 15$, what is the area of $\triangle DEF$?

(A) 90

(B) 100

(C) 110

(D) 120

6. Joshua can wash 5 cars in one hour and Jason can wash 3 cars in one hour. At this rate, how long will it take Joshua and Jason to wash 26 cars if they work together?

(A) 4 hours and 15 minutes

(B) 3 hours and 45 minutes

(C) 3 hours and 30 minutes

(D) 3 hours and 15 minutes

7. The graph of the hyperbola $\frac{x^2}{9} - \frac{y^2}{4} = 1$ intersects the x-axis. What are the x-intercepts?

(A) 9 and -9

(B) 6 and -6

(C) 4 and -4

(D) 3 and -3

8. A is a 2×4 matrix and B is a 4×3 matrix. What are the dimensions of the product of the two matrices, AB ?

(A) 2×2

(B) 2×3

(C) 3×2

(D) Undefined

9. If $5^x = 14$, which of the following **CANNOT** be the solution of the equation?

(A) $\log_5 14$

(B) $\ln\left(\frac{14}{5}\right)$

(C) $\frac{\ln 14}{\ln 5}$

(D) $\frac{\log 14}{\log 5}$

10. What are the rectangular coordinates (x, y) that correspond with the polar coordinates $(2, \frac{\pi}{3})$?

(A) $(\sqrt{3}, 1)$

(B) $(1, \sqrt{3})$

(C) $(2, 2\sqrt{3})$

(D) $(-\sqrt{3}, 1)$

11. If $f(x) = x^2$, $x \leq 0$, what is the inverse function of f ?

(A) $\frac{1}{x^2}$

(B) $\sqrt{x}$

(C) $-x^2$

(D) $-\sqrt{x}$

12. Two standard dice are rolled. What is the probability that the sum of the two numbers on top of each die is 7?

(A) $\frac{1}{6}$

(B) $\frac{1}{4}$

(C) $\frac{1}{3}$

(D) $\frac{5}{12}$

13. If $f(x) = \frac{1}{1-x}$, then $f'(x) =$

(A) $-\frac{1}{(1-x)^2}$

(B) $\frac{1}{(1-x)^2}$

(C) $-\ln|1-x|$

(D) $\ln|1-x|$

14. If $f(x) = 2x^3 + 7x^2 + kx - 3$ has a factor of $x + 3$, what is the value of k ?

(A) 2

(B) 3

(C) 5

(D) 7

15. Joshua has taken three tests in math class. The three test scores are 91, 86, and 87. In order for him to get an A in the class, he needs to get an average of at least 90 on the 4 tests. Which of the following score, s, must he receive to get an A ? (Let s be the score on his 4th test.)

(A) $s < 96$

(B) $s \geq 96$

(C) $s \leq 94$

(D) $s > 94$

16. In a lake, a wildlife biologist captured 10 fish on the first day. He put a tag on each fish's tail fin and released all fish back to the lake. On the second day, the biologist returned and recaptured 100 fish. Of these, 2 fish had tags. How many fish are there in the lake?

(A) 500

(B) 1000

(C) 1500

(D) 2500

17. What is the equation of the perpendicular bisector of a segment whose endpoints are $(-2, 0)$ and $(0, 4)$?

(A) $x - 2y = 3$

(B) $x + 2y = -3$

(C) $x + 2y = 3$

(D) $2x - y = 4$

$$2x + 6y = 5$$
$$x + ay = 1$$

18. For the system of linear equations above, what must be the value of a so that the system has no solution?

(A) -3

(B) -1

(C) 3

(D) 6

19. For $0 \le \theta < 2\pi$, solve the inequality $\cos\theta < 0$.

(A) $0 \le \theta < \pi$

(B) $\frac{\pi}{2} < \theta < \frac{3\pi}{2}$

(C) $\frac{\pi}{4} < \theta < \frac{7\pi}{4}$

(D) $\frac{4\pi}{3} < \theta < \frac{5\pi}{3}$

20. How many perfect squares are there between 101 and 1025?

(A) 20

(B) 21

(C) 22

(D) 23

21. If a triangle with vertices $(1, 2)$, $(3, 4)$, and $(5, 6)$ is reflected about the x-axis, which of the following product of two matrices best represents a reflection image of the triangle?

(A) $\begin{bmatrix} -1 & 0 \\ 0 & 1 \end{bmatrix} \begin{bmatrix} 1 & 2 \\ 3 & 4 \\ 5 & 6 \end{bmatrix}$

(B) $\begin{bmatrix} -1 & 0 \\ 0 & 1 \end{bmatrix} \begin{bmatrix} 1 & 3 & 5 \\ 2 & 4 & 6 \end{bmatrix}$

(C) $\begin{bmatrix} 1 & 0 \\ 0 & -1 \end{bmatrix} \begin{bmatrix} 1 & 2 \\ 3 & 4 \\ 5 & 6 \end{bmatrix}$

(D) $\begin{bmatrix} 1 & 0 \\ 0 & -1 \end{bmatrix} \begin{bmatrix} 1 & 3 & 5 \\ 2 & 4 & 6 \end{bmatrix}$

22. You purchased a car for \$20,000. If the value of the car depreciates at a rate of 15% per year, how much is the car worth after 5 years?

(A) \$13,862.92

(B) \$12,474.58

(C) \$10,440.10

(D) \$8,874.11

E(Energy)	C(Energy Conversion)
$1 \times 10^4 \le E < 1 \times 10^5$	4
$1 \times 10^5 \le E < 1 \times 10^6$	5
$1 \times 10^6 \le E < 1 \times 10^7$	6
$1 \times 10^7 \le E < 1 \times 10^8$	7

23. In the equation $R = \frac{2}{3}C + 1.5$, R is the Richter scale, a number that determines the strength of earthquakes and C is an energy conversion shown on the table above. If the energy, $E = 1,000,000$, what is the value of the Richter scale, R ?

(A) 3.5

(B) 4.2

(C) 4.8

(D) 5.5

24. Let $f(x) = |x|$. If $g(x)$ is obtained by translating $f(x)$ 3 units to the left and 2 units down, what is the value of $g(-4)$?

(A) -1

(B) 3

(C) 5

(D) 9

25. If $\int_1^3 g(x)\,dx = 4$, then which of the following is the value of $\int_1^3 2x + 3g(x)\,dx$?

(A) 8

(B) 12

(C) 20

(D) 24

For the following question, enter your answer in the answer box.

26. There are nine points on a circle. A chord is a line segment that connects two points on the circle. How many chords can be drawn?

[ ]

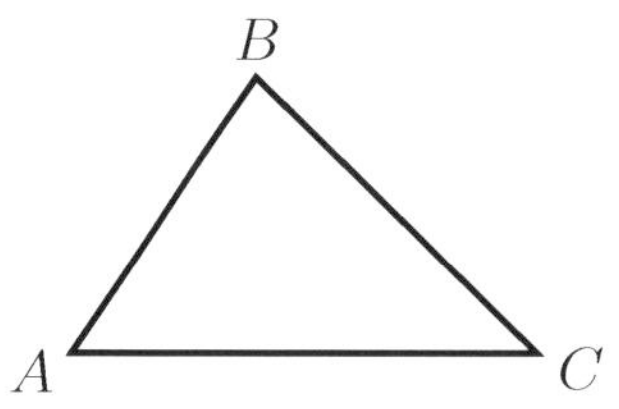

27. In $\triangle ABC$ above, $m\angle C = 40°$, $m\angle A = 60°$, and $AB = 6$. What is the length of $\overline{AC}$?

(A) 7.39

(B) 8.07

(C) 9.19

(D) 10.95

For the following question, enter your answer in the answer box.

$$ab = 3, \qquad a + b = 5$$

28. If a and b are the real numbers that satisfy the equations above, what is the value of $\frac{1}{a} + \frac{1}{b}$?

Give your answer as a fraction.

$$\frac{1}{a} + \frac{1}{b} = \frac{\square}{\square}$$

29. The graphs below show the distributions of scores. Which of the following distributions has the largest standard deviation ?

(A)

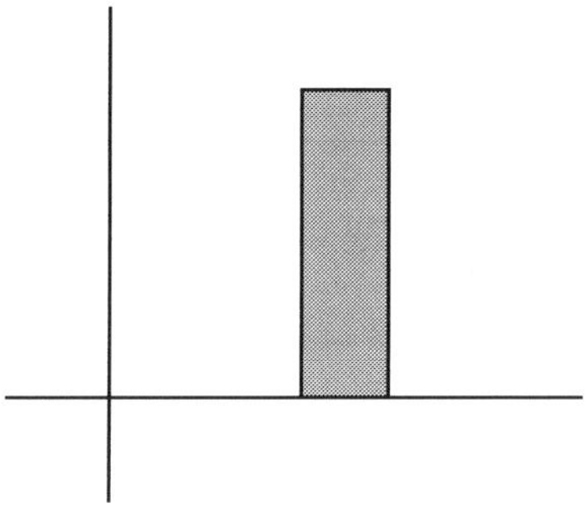

(B)

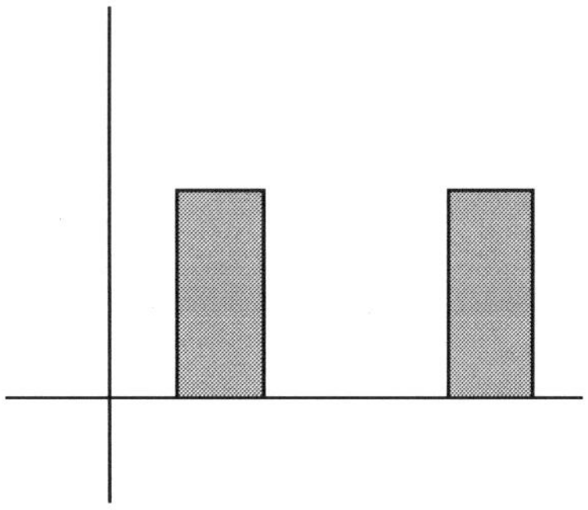

(C)

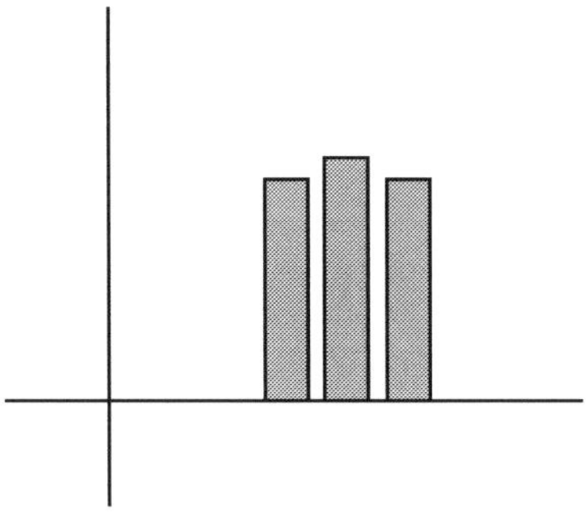

(D)

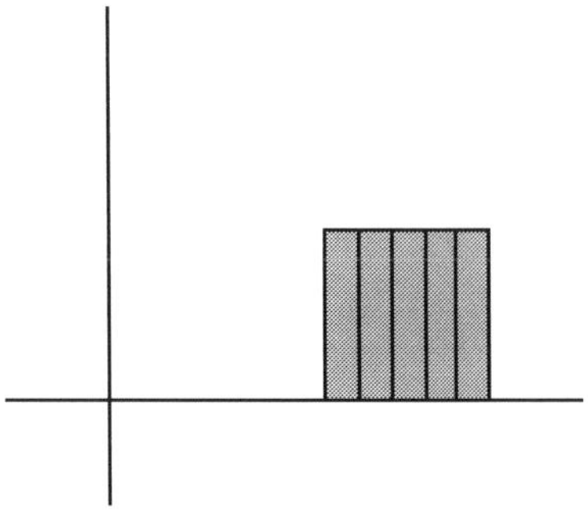

x	1	2	4
f	2	1	-3
g	-1	-3	4
f'	3	2	-1
g'	-2	3	1

30. The table above shows values of f, g, f', and g' for selected values of x. If the function h is defined by $h(x) = f(x) \cdot g(x)$, which of the following is the value of $h'(2)$?

(A) -3

(B) 4

(C) 9

(D) 10

31. Of the 43 students in a group, each student plays Tennis, Soccer, both or neither. 25 students play Tennis, 28 students play soccer and 5 students play neither. If 15 students play both Tennis and Soccer, what is the sum of the number of students who play only Tennis or only Soccer?

(A) 16

(B) 23

(C) 33

(D) 38

32. The initial number of cell is N_0. If the number of cells doubles every 12 minutes, which of the following best represents the number of cell, $N(t)$, after t hours?

(A) $N(t) = N_0(32)^t$

(B) $N(t) = N_0(32)^{\frac{t}{5}}$

(C) $N(t) = N_0(2)^{12t}$

(D) $N(t) = N_0(2)^{\frac{12t}{5}}$

33. The length of cube A is 4 inches. If the length of cube A is increased by 75% to form cube B, how much greater, in square inches, is the surface area of cube B than the surface area of cube A ?

(A) 96 square inches

(B) 132 square inches

(C) 198 square inches

(D) 279 square inches

$$g(x) = \int_1^{x^2} 2t - 1 \, dt$$

34. Let g be the function defined above. What is the slope of the tangent line to the graph of g at $x = 2$?

(A) 6

(B) 15

(C) 21

(D) 28

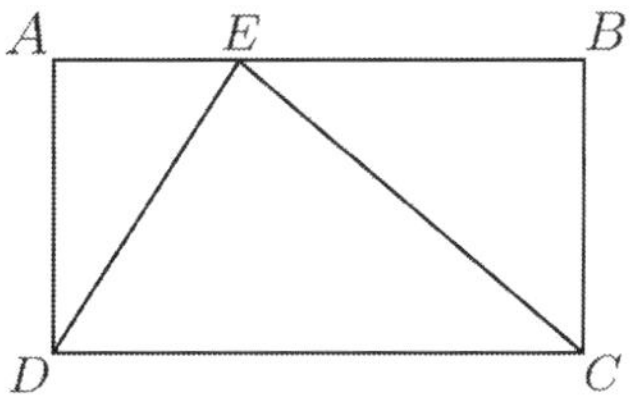

35. In the figure above, $ABCD$ is a rectangle whose area is 72 and $AD = 6$. If the ratio of three areas of $\triangle AED$, $\triangle EBC$, and $\triangle DEC$ is $1:2:3$ respectively, which of the following is $AE : BE : DC$?

(A) $2:3:4$

(B) $1:3:4$

(C) $1:2:4$

(D) $1:2:3$

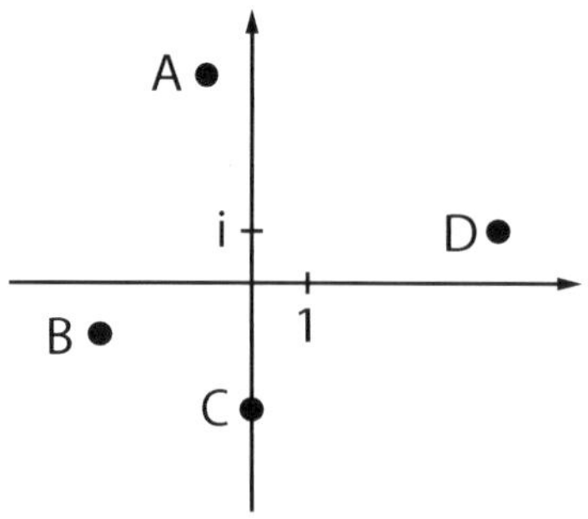

36. If $z_1 = 2 + i$ and $z_2 = 1 + 3i$, which of the following letter in the complex plane above represents the product of the two complex numbers, $z_1 z_2$?

(A) A

(B) B

(C) C

(D) D

37. Which of the following measure is the most robust to outliers in the data set?

(A) Range

(B) Median

(C) Mean

(D) Standard deviation

38. Students walked into the Auditorium with rows of two. Jason noticed that his row is the 11th row from the front and the 10th row from the back. How many students went to the Auditorium?

(A) 22

(B) 40

(C) 42

(D) 80

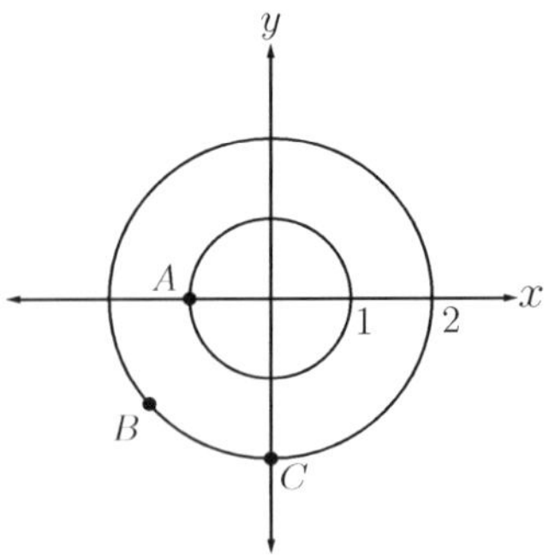

39. In the polar coordinate plane above, which of the following could **NOT** be the polar coordinates of points A, B, or C ?

(A) $(1, \pi)$

(B) $\left(-2, \frac{\pi}{2}\right)$

(C) $\left(2, -\frac{5\pi}{4}\right)$

(D) $\left(2, \frac{5\pi}{4}\right)$

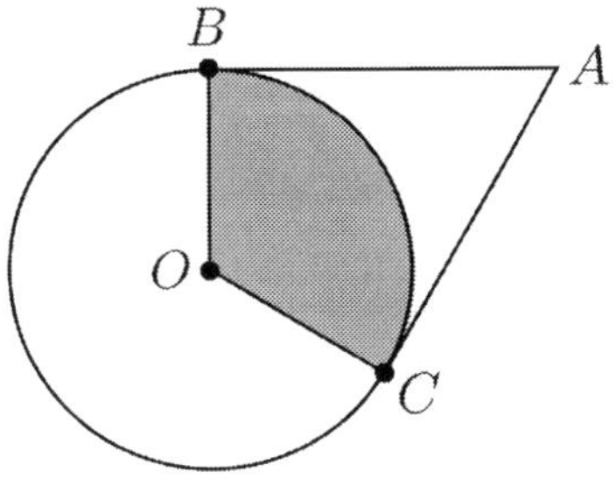

40. In the figure above, the radius of the circle is 6. Two segments drawn from point A touch the circle at two points B and C. If $m\angle A = 60°$, what is the area of the shaded region?

(A) 12π

(B) 15π

(C) 18π

(D) 21π

41. If p and q are positive integers and $pq = 99$, how many ordered pairs (p, q) are possible?

(A) 3

(B) 4

(C) 5

(D) 6

42. Which of the following statement is **NOT** true about the radian measure?

(A) 1 radian $\approx 57.3°$

(B) 2π radian $= 360°$

(C) $\frac{7\pi}{12}$ radian $= 125°$

(D) $\frac{7\pi}{6}$ radian $= 210°$

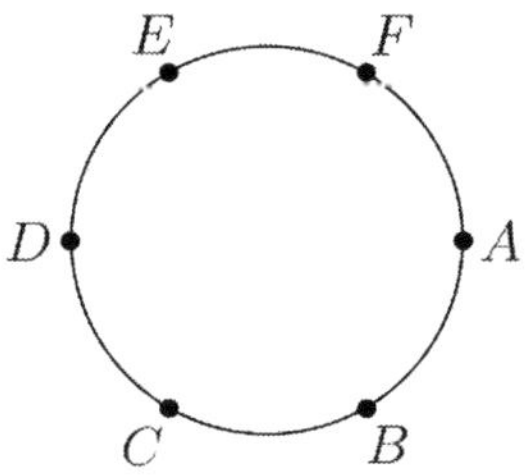

43. In the circular track whose circumference is 120 meters shown above, Joshua and Jason are running in opposite directions from the starting position, A. Joshua is running at 4 meters per second clockwise and Jason is running at 2 meters per second counterclockwise. Which of the following lettered position represents the second time Joshua and Jason meet after they begin running? (Assume that all the lettered positions are equally spaced.)

(A) C

(B) D

(C) E

(D) F

44. Which of the following conic section does the equation $3x^2-6x+4y^2+4y-6=0$ represent?

(A) Parabola

(B) Circle

(C) Ellipse

(D) Hyperbola

For the following question, select all the answer choices that apply.

$$a_n = \frac{2n-4}{n^2+1}, \quad \text{where } n \text{ is positive integers}$$

45. If the sequence is defined above, which of the following statement is true about the sequence?

Select all that apply.

(A) All terms of the sequence is positive.

(B) The sequence a_n is a function.

(C) If n is indefinitely large, a_n approaches 0

(D) The smallest value of the sequence is -2

46. If $z = 2\left(\cos\frac{\pi}{4} + i\sin\frac{\pi}{4}\right)$, what is the value of z^4 ?

(A) $\sqrt[4]{2}(\cos\pi + i\sin\pi)$

(B) $\sqrt[4]{2}\left(\cos\frac{\pi}{2} + i\sin\frac{\pi}{2}\right)$

(C) $16\left(\cos\frac{\pi}{2} + i\sin\frac{\pi}{2}\right)$

(D) $16(\cos\pi + i\sin\pi)$

47. The maximum height H of a projectile is given by

$$H = \frac{v_0^2\sin^2\theta}{2g}$$

where v_0 is an initial velocity in feet per second, θ is an angle to the horizontal in degrees, and g is the acceleration due to gravity and is 32. If the projectile is launched at an angle of 25° to the horizontal with an initial velocity of 100 feet per second, what is the maximum height of the projectile?

(A) 27.91 feet

(B) 34.25 feet

(C) 47.28 feet

(D) 54.33 feet

For the following question, enter your answer in the answer box.

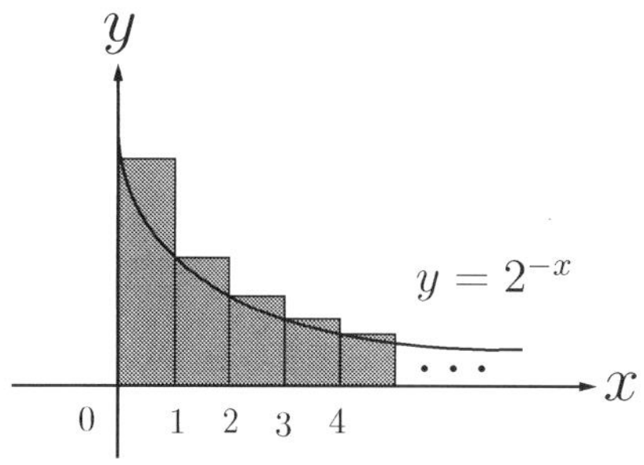

Note: Figure not drawn to scale.

48. A portion of the graph of $y = 2^{-x}$ is shown in the figure above. Let the area of the shaded region S equal the sum of the areas of an infinite number of rectangles, of which only five rectangles are shown in the figure. What is the value of S ?

$S =$ [ ]

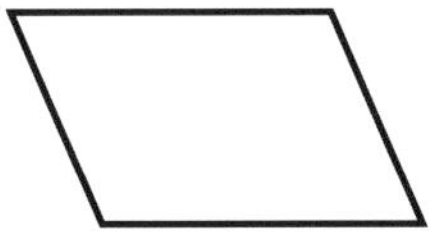

49. By what degrees of clockwise rotation about its center, the parallelogram above can be mapped onto itself?

(A) 60°

(B) 90°

(C) 120°

(D) 180°

50. A three-digit number ABC is called an increasing number if $A < B < C$. Three numbers are selected at random from the set $\{1, 2, 3, 4\}$ without replacement to form an increasing number. What is the probability that the three-digit number formed is an increasing number?

(A) $\frac{2}{3}$

(B) $\frac{1}{2}$

(C) $\frac{1}{3}$

(D) $\frac{1}{6}$

51. What is the local maximum value of the function $f(x) = x^3 - 3x^2 - 9x + 2$?

(A) -25

(B) -1

(C) 7

(D) 25

For the following question, select all the answer choices that apply.

52. Which of the following statements are true about correlation?

Select all that apply.

(A) Correlation must be between 0 and 1

(B) Correlation remains unchanged when switching x and y variables.

(C) Correlation implies causation.

(D) Changing the units on your data will not affect the correlation.

53. Using the substitution $u = x - 1$, which of the following is equivalent to $\int_1^2 x\sqrt{x-1}\,dx$?

(A) $\int_0^1 u^{\frac{3}{2}} + u^{\frac{1}{2}}\,du$

(B) $\frac{1}{2}\int_0^1 u^{\frac{3}{2}} + u^{\frac{1}{2}}\,du$

(C) $\int_2^3 u^{\frac{3}{2}}\,du$

(D) $2\int_2^3 u^{\frac{3}{2}}\,du$

$$S_1 = \{1, 3, 7\}, \quad S_2 = \{2, 3, 5\}, \quad S_3 = \{2, 4, 7\}$$

54. Sets S_1, S_2, and S_3 are defined above. If S_{ij} denotes an element that belongs to both S_i and S_j, which of the following sets has S_{12}, S_{13}, and S_{23} ?

(A) $\{1, 3, 5\}$

(B) $\{2, 3, 5\}$

(C) $\{2, 4, 5\}$

(D) $\{2, 3, 7\}$

For the following question, enter your answer in the answer box.

$$f(n) = f(n-1) - f(n-2)$$

55. A function f above is defined recursively for all integers $n \geq 3$. If $f(1) = f(2) = 1$, what is the value of $f(8)$?

$f(8) =$ ☐

56. A palindrome is a number that is read the same backward and forward. For instance, 5335 is a four-digit palindrome. How many 4-digit palindromes contain the digits either 2, 3, or 5?

(A) 3

(B) 6

(C) 7

(D) 9

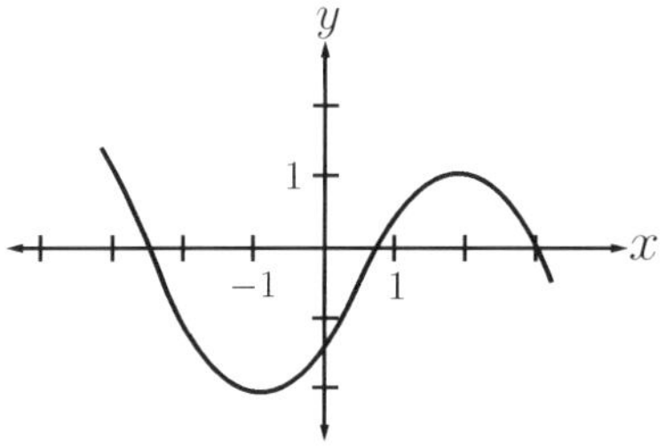

Graph of f'

57. The figure above shows the graph of f', the first derivative function of f. At which of the following value of x does f have an inflection point?

(A) $x = -1$ and $x = 2$

(B) $x = -2.5$, $x = 0.6$ and $x = 3$

(C) $x = 0.5$ only

(D) $x = 0$ only

58. Two events A and B are mutually exclusive. If $P(A) = 0.4$ and $P(B) = 0.5$, what is $P(A \cup B)$?

(A) 0.2

(B) 0.4

(C) 0.7

(D) 0.9

$$f(x) = \begin{cases} 3x + 2, & x < 0 \\ e^x, & x \geq 0 \end{cases}$$

59. Which of the following is the range of the function f above?

(A) All real numbers

(B) $y \geq 0$

(C) $y < 0$

(D) Integers

60. $i + i^2 + i^3 + \cdots + i^{11} + i^{12} =$

(A) -1

(B) $-i$

(C) 0

(D) i

STOP

Answers and Solutions

PRAXIS II 5161 PRACTICE TEST 1

Answers

1. A	11. D	21. D	31. B	41. D	51. C
2. C	12. A	22. D	32. A	42. C	52. B,D
3. A	13. B	23. D	33. C	43. A	53. A
4. B	14. A	24. A	34. D	44. C	54. D
5. A	15. B	25. C	35. D	45. B,C	55. 1
6. D	16. A	26. 36	36. A	46. D	56. D
7. D	17. C	27. C	37. B	47. A	57. A
8. B	18. C	28. $\frac{5}{3}$	38. B	48. 2	58. D
9. B	19. B	29. B	39. C	49. D	59. A
10. B	20. C	30. A	40. A	50. D	60. C

Solutions

1. (A) **Geometry**

   If the diameter of a circle is 14, the radius of the circle is 7. Thus, the area of the circle is $\pi(7)^2 = 49\pi$, and the circumference of the circle is $2\pi(7) = 14\pi$. Therefore, the ratio of the area of the circle to the circumference of the circle is $49\pi : 14\pi$ or $7 : 2$.

2. (C) **Number and Quantity**

   After $\frac{7}{8}$ gallon of water was used, $1\frac{7}{8}$ gallon of water is still remaining in the cooler. Therefore, the capacity of the cooler is $\frac{7}{8} + 1\frac{7}{8} = 1\frac{14}{8} = 2\frac{3}{4}$ gallons.

3. (A) **Algebra**

The vertex of a quadratic function written in vertex form $y = (x - h)^2 + k$ is (h, k). For instance, the vertex of a quadratic function $y = (x - 4)^2$ is $(4, 0)$. The graphs below show the quadratic functions given in the answer choices.

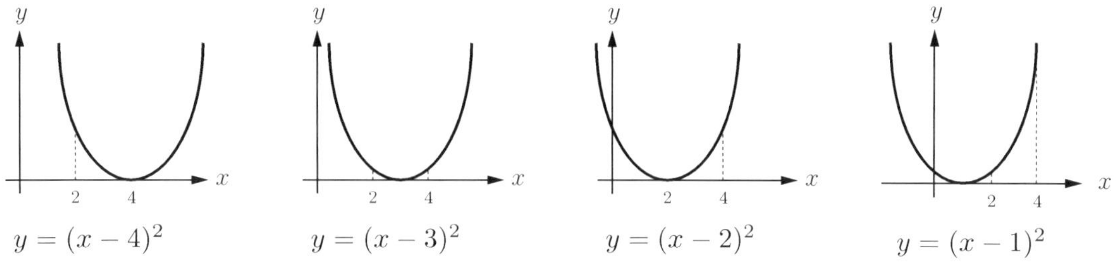

Only $y = (x - 4)^2$ is the quadratic function that is decreasing over the entire interval $2 < x < 4$. Therefore, (A) is the correct answer.

4. (B) **Number and Quantity**

List prime numbers: $2, 3, 5, 7, 11, \cdots$. It is worth noting that 2 is the smallest and the first prime number, and the only even prime number. Other than 2, all the prime numbers are odd numbers. If $n = 2$ and $k = 3$, $n + k = 5$ and $nk = 6$. Thus, eliminate answer choices (A) and (C). If $k = 7$ and $n = 5$, $k - n = 2$, which is not divisible by 3. Eliminate answer choice (D). If $n > 2$ and $k > 2$, n and k are odd numbers. Thus, $n + k$ is an even number. Therefore, (B) is the correct answer.

5. (A) **Geometry**

Since the two triangles are similar triangles, set up a proportion to determine the height of triangle DEF. First, let's define x as the height of triangle DEF.

$$\frac{4}{x} = \frac{5}{15}$$
$$5x = 60$$
$$x = 12$$

Thus, the height of triangle DEF is 12.

$$\text{Area of } \triangle\text{DEF} = \frac{1}{2}bh = \frac{1}{2}(15)(12) = 90$$

Therefore, the area of $\triangle DEF$ is 90.

6. (D) **Number and Quantity**

Joshua can wash 5 cars in one hour and Jason can wash 3 cars in one hour. This means that Joshua and Jason can wash 8 cars in one hour if they work together. Since $\frac{26 \text{ cars}}{8 \text{ cars per hour}} = 3.25$ hours, it will take Joshua and Jason 3.25 hours or 3 hours and 15 minutes to wash 26 cars.

7. (D) **Geometry**

In order to find the x-intercepts, substitute 0 for y and solve for x.

$$
\begin{aligned}
\frac{x^2}{9} - \frac{y^2}{4} &= 1 && \text{Substitute 0 for } y \\
\frac{x^2}{9} &= 1 && \text{Multiply each side by 9} \\
x^2 &= 9 && \text{Take the square root of both sides} \\
x = 3 \quad \text{or} \quad x &= -3
\end{aligned}
$$

Therefore, the x-intercepts are 3 and -3.

8. (B) **Number and Quantity**

> Tips: Let A be a $m \times n$ matrix and B be a $n \times p$ matrix. The product of the two matrices, AB, is defined if the number of columns in matrix A is equal to the number of rows in matrix B, and is a $m \times p$ matrix.

Since the number of columns in matrix A is the same as the number of rows in matrix B, the product of two matrices, AB, is defined and is a 2×3 matrix.

9. (B) **Functions**

> Tips: Change-of-base formula: $\log_a b = \dfrac{\log_c b}{\log_c a} = \dfrac{\log_{10} b}{\log_{10} a} = \dfrac{\ln b}{\ln a}$

Since each side of the equation has a different base (the left side has a base of 5 and the right side has a base of 14), convert the exponential equation to a logarithmic equation.

$$
\begin{aligned}
5^x &= 14 && \text{Convert the equation to a logarithmic equation} \\
x &= \log_5 14
\end{aligned}
$$

According to the Change-of-base formula,

$$\log_5 14 = \frac{\log 14}{\log 5} = \frac{\ln 14}{\ln 5}$$

Therefore, (B) is the correct answer.

10. (B) **Trigonometry**

> Tips: If the polar coordinates of a point are (r, θ), the rectangular coordinates of the point (x, y) are given by $x = r\cos\theta$ and $y = r\sin\theta$.

The polar coordinates of the point are $\left(2, \frac{\pi}{3}\right)$. Thus, $r = 2$ and $\theta = \frac{\pi}{3}$. Since $\cos\frac{\pi}{3} = \frac{1}{2}$ and $\sin\frac{\pi}{3} = \frac{\sqrt{3}}{2}$,

$$x = 2\cos\frac{\pi}{3} = 2\cdot\frac{1}{2} = 1$$
$$y = 2\sin\frac{\pi}{3} = 2\cdot\frac{\sqrt{3}}{2} = \sqrt{3}$$

Therefore, the rectangular coordinates that correspond with the polar coordinates $\left(2, \frac{\pi}{3}\right)$ are $(1, \sqrt{3})$.

11. (D) **Functions**

The domain of $f(x) = x^2,\ x \le 0$ is $x \le 0$. Since the domain of f is the range of the inverse function, the range of the inverse function is $y \le 0$. In order to find the inverse function algebraically, switch the x and y variables and solve for y.

$y = x^2$	Switch the x and y variables
$x = y^2$	Take the square root of both sides
$y = \pm\sqrt{x}$	Select the inverse function
$y = -\sqrt{x}$	Since the range of the inverse function is $y \le 0$

Therefore, the inverse function of $f(x) = x^2,\ x \le 0$ is $f^{-1}(x) = -\sqrt{x}$.

12. (A) **Probability and Statistics**

The first and the second die have 6 possible outcomes each: 1, 2, 3, 4, 5, and 6, which are shown in the second row and the second column of the table below. There are total number of $6 \times 6 = 36$ possible outcomes. Each of the 36 outcomes represents the sum of the two numbers on the top of the first and the second die. For instance, when 2 is on the first die and 5 is on the second die, expressed as $(2, 5)$, the sum of the two numbers is 7.

		1st die					
		1	2	3	4	5	6
2nd die	1						7
	2					7	
	3				7		
	4			7			
	5		7				
	6	7					

There are 6 outcomes for which the sum of the two numbers is 7: $(1, 6)$, $(2, 5)$, $(3, 4)$, $(4, 3)$, $(5, 2)$, and $(6, 1)$. Therefore, the probability that the sum of the two numbers on the top of each die is 7 is $\frac{6}{36}$ or $\frac{1}{6}$.

13. (B) **Calculus**

> Tips — The Quotient rule
> $$\left(\frac{f}{g}\right)' = \frac{f'g - fg'}{g^2}$$

Let's differentiate $f(x) = \dfrac{1}{1-x}$ using the Quotient rule.

$$\begin{aligned}\left(\frac{1}{1-x}\right)' &= \frac{(1)'(1-x) - 1(1-x)'}{(1-x)^2} \\ &= \frac{0(1-x) - 1(-1)}{(1-x)^2} \\ &= \frac{1}{(1-x)^2}\end{aligned}$$

Therefore, $f'(x) = \frac{1}{(1-x)^2}$.

14. (A) **Algebra**

> Tips — Factor Theorem: If $x - k$ is a factor of $f(x)$, then the remainder $r = f(k) = 0$.

Since $x + 3$ is the factor of f, the remainder $r = f(-3) = 0$.

$$\begin{aligned} f(x) &= 2x^3 + 7x^2 + kx - 3 && \text{Substitute } -3 \text{ for } x \\ f(-3) &= 2(-3)^3 + 7(-3)^2 + k(-3) - 3 && \text{Simplify} \\ &= 6 - 3k \end{aligned}$$

Since $f(-3) = 0$, set $6 - 3k = 0$ and solve for k. Therefore, the value of k is 2.

15. (B) **Number and Quantity**

Joshua has taken three out of four tests and received the scores: 91, 86, and 87. In order to get an A for the math class, which is an average of 90 or more, the sum of the four tests must be at least $90 \times 4 = 360$. Set up the inequality and solve for s which represents the score needed on the 4th test.

$$\begin{aligned} 91 + 86 + 87 + s &\geq 360 \\ s &\geq 96 \end{aligned}$$

Joshua must obtain a score that is greater than or equal to 96 in order to receive an A for the math class.

16. (A) **Probability and Statistics**

Tips

The assumption behind tag-recapture method is that the proportion of tagged individuals recaptured in the second sample represent the proportion of tagged individuals in the population as a whole. In other words,

$$\frac{R}{S} = \frac{T}{N}$$

where

- R is the number of fish recaptured on the second day
- S is the number of sample on the second day
- T is the number of fish captured and tagged on the first day
- N is the fish population

In this problem, $R = 2$, $S = 100$, $T = 10$. Set up the proportion and solve for N.

$$\frac{R}{S} = \frac{T}{N} \implies \frac{2}{100} = \frac{10}{N} \implies N = 500$$

Therefore, the number of fish in the lake is 500.

17. (C) **Algebra**

Tips

1. The midpoint between two points (x_1, y_1) and (x_2, y_2) is given by
$$\left(\frac{x_1 + x_2}{2}, \frac{y_1 + y_2}{2}\right)$$
2. Perpendicular lines have negative reciprocal slopes. In other words, the product of the slopes equals -1.

The slope of the line segment connected by $(-2, 0)$ and $(0, 4)$ is $\frac{4-0}{0-(-2)} = 2$. The midpoint between $(-2, 0)$ and $(0, 4)$ is $\left(\frac{-2+0}{2}, \frac{0+4}{2}\right) = (-1, 2)$. The slope of the perpendicular bisector is the negative reciprocal of 2 or $-\frac{1}{2}$. Thus, the equation of the perpendicular bisector in slope-intercept form is $y = -\frac{1}{2}x + b$. The perpendicular bisector passes through the midpoint of the line segment which means that $(-1, 2)$ is on the perpendicular bisector. In other words, $(-1, 2)$ is the solution to the equation $y = -\frac{1}{2}x + b$.

$$y = -\frac{1}{2}x + b \qquad \text{Substitute } -1 \text{ for } x \text{ and } 2 \text{ for } y$$
$$2 = -\frac{1}{2}(-1) + b \qquad \text{Solve for } b$$
$$b = \frac{3}{2}$$

Thus, the equation of the perpendicular bisector is $y = -\frac{1}{2}x + \frac{3}{2}$, which is equivalent to $x + 2y = 3$ in standard form. Therefore, the equation of the perpendicular bisector of a segment whose endpoints are $(-2, 0)$ and $(0, 4)$ is $x + 2y = 3$.

18. (C) **Algebra**

> Tips
> In the system of linear equations given below,
> $$ax + by = c$$
> $$dx + ey = f$$
> the number of solutions to the system is zero if $\frac{a}{d} = \frac{b}{e} \neq \frac{c}{f}$.

The number of solutions to the system of linear equations below is zero if

$$\frac{2}{1} = \frac{6}{a}$$
$$2a = 6$$
$$a = 3$$

Therefore, the value of a so that the system has no solution is 3.

19. (B) **Trigonometry**

Solving $\cos\theta < 0$ means finding the angle θ for which the cosine function lies below the x-axis.

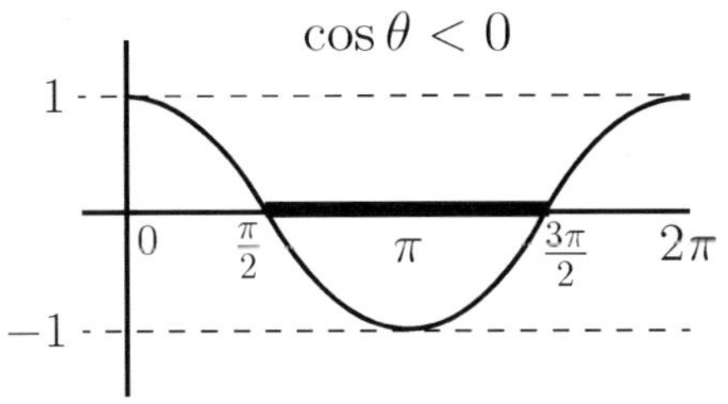

As shown in the figure above, the cosine function lies below the x-axis when $\frac{\pi}{2} < \theta < \frac{3\pi}{2}$. Therefore, the solution to $\cos\theta < 0$ is $\frac{\pi}{2} < \theta < \frac{3\pi}{2}$.

20. (C) **Number and Quantity**

> Tips Number of integers = Largest integer − Smallest integer + 1.

The first perfect square greater than 100 is $11^2 = 121$.

$$11^2 = 121$$
$$12^2 = 144$$
$$\vdots$$
$$31^2 = 961$$
$$32^2 = 1024$$

Therefore, there are $32 - 11 + 1 = 22$ the perfect squares between 101 and 1025.

21. (D) **Number and Quantity**

A vertex matrix for the triangle is $\begin{bmatrix} 1 & 3 & 5 \\ 2 & 4 & 6 \end{bmatrix}$. The standard matrix for the reflection about the x-axis is $\begin{bmatrix} 1 & 0 \\ 0 & -1 \end{bmatrix}$. Therefore, the product of two matrices $\begin{bmatrix} 1 & 0 \\ 0 & -1 \end{bmatrix}\begin{bmatrix} 1 & 3 & 5 \\ 2 & 4 & 6 \end{bmatrix}$ creates a reflection image of the triangle.

22. (D) **Functions**

The value of the car depreciates 15% per year. The value of the car for the first five years is shown below.

The value of the car after 1 year: $\$20,000(1-0.15) = \$17,000$
The value of the car after 2 year: $\$20,000(1-0.15)^2 = \$14,450$
The value of the car after 3 year: $\$20,000(1-0.15)^3 = \$12,282.50$
The value of the car after 4 year: $\$20,000(1-0.15)^4 = \$10,440.10$
The value of the car after 5 year: $\$20,000(1-0.15)^5 = \$8,874.11$

Therefore, the value of the car after 5 years is $\$8,874.11$.

23. (D) **Number and Quantity**

Convert $1,000,000$ to scientific notation as 1×10^6. According to the table below, when the energy, $E = 1\times10^6$, the energy conversion, $C = 6$.

E(Energy)	C(Energy Conversion)
$1\times10^4 \le E < 1\times10^5$	4
$1\times10^5 \le E < 1\times10^6$	5
$1\times10^6 \le E < 1\times10^7$	6
$1\times10^7 \le E < 1\times10^8$	7

To find the Richter scale, R, substitute 6 for C in the equation $R = \frac{2}{3}C + 1.5$.

$$\begin{aligned} R &= \frac{2}{3}C + 1.5 && \text{Substitute 6 for } C \\ &= \frac{2}{3}(6) + 1.5 \\ &= 5.5 \end{aligned}$$

Therefore, the value of the Richter scale, R, when $E = 1,000,000$ is 5.5

24. (A) **Functions**

Since $g(x)$ is obtained by translating $f(x)$ 3 units to the left and 2 units down, $g(x) = f(x+3) - 2$ or $g(x) = |x+3| - 2$. In order to evaluate $g(-4)$, substitute -4 for x in $g(x)$.

$$g(x) = |x+3| - 2 \qquad \text{Substitute } -4 \text{ for } x$$
$$g(-4) = |-4+3| - 2 = -1$$

Therefore, the value of $g(-4)$ is -1.

25. (C) **Calculus**

Tips

The Fundamental Theorem of Calculus, Part II

$$\int_a^b f(x)\,dx = F(x)\Big]_a^b = F(b) - F(a)$$

Where F is any antiderivative of f such that $F' = f$.

$\int_1^3 g(x)\,dx = 4.$

$$\begin{aligned}\int_1^3 2x + 3g(x)\,dx &= \int_1^3 2x\,dx + 3\int_1^3 g(x)\,dx \\ &= x^2\Big]_1^3 + 3(4) \\ &= (3^2 - 1^2) + 12 \\ &= 20\end{aligned}$$

Therefore, the value of $\int_1^3 2x + 3g(x)\,dx$ is 20.

26. (36) **Discrete Mathematics**

Tips

The combination $\binom{n}{r}$ is given by

$$\binom{n}{r} = \frac{n!}{(n-r)! \times r!}$$

Out of 9 points, choose 2 points to draw a chord. Therefore, the total number of chords is $\binom{9}{2} = \dfrac{9!}{7! \times 2!} = 36.$

27. (C) **Trigonometry**

The sum of the measures of interior angles is 180°. Thus, $m\angle B = 80°$ as shown below.

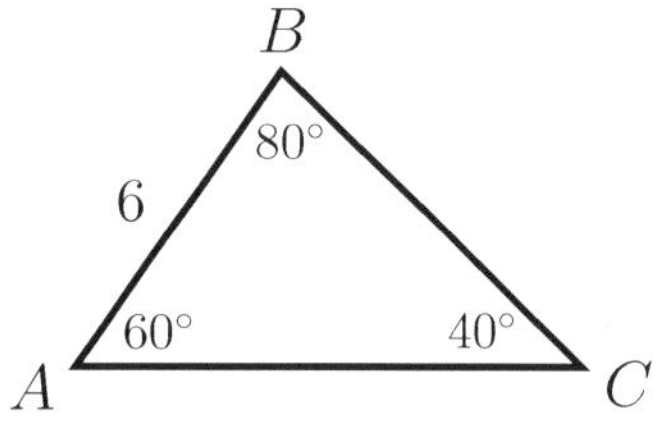

Use the Law of Sines to find AC.

$$\frac{6}{\sin 40°} = \frac{AC}{\sin 80°} \implies AC = \frac{6\sin 80°}{\sin 40°} = 9.19$$

Therefore, the length of $\overline{AC}$ is 9.19.

28. ($\frac{5}{3}$) **Algebra**

$ab = 3$ and $a + b = 5$.

$$\frac{1}{a} + \frac{1}{b} = \frac{b}{ab} + \frac{a}{ab} = \frac{a+b}{ab} = \frac{5}{3}$$

Therefore, the value of $\frac{1}{a} + \frac{1}{b}$ is $\frac{5}{3}$.

29. (B) **Probability and Statistics**

The distribution that are more spread out have a greater standard deviation. Therefore, (B) is the correct answer.

30. (A) **Calculus**

Tips The product rule

$$(f \cdot g)' = f' \cdot g + f \cdot g'$$

x	1	2	4
f	2	1	-3
g	-1	-3	4
f'	3	2	-1
g'	-2	3	1

$$h'(x) = f'(x) \cdot g(x) + f(x) \cdot g'(x)$$

Since $f'(2) = 2$, $g(2) = -3$, $f(2) = 1$, and $g'(2) = 3$,

$$h'(2) = f'(2) \cdot g(2) + f(2) \cdot g'(2) = -3$$

Therefore, the value of $h'(2)$ is -3.

31. (B) **Discrete Mathematics**

The venn diagram below shows the complete breakdown of the given information.

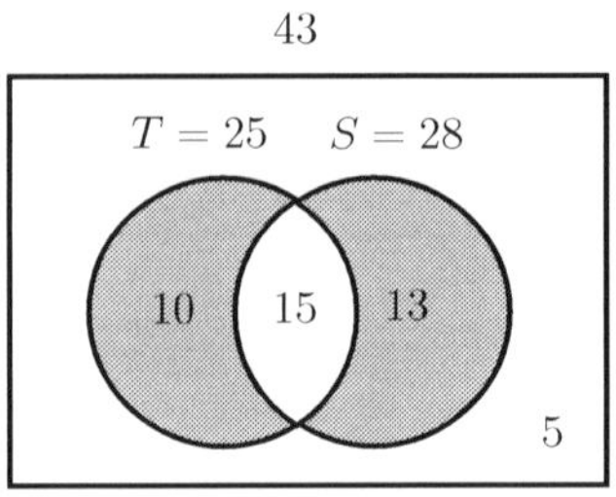

The shaded region in the venn diagram represents the sum of the number of students who play only Tennis or only Soccer, which is $10 + 13 = 23$.

32. (A) **Functions**

The number of cells doubles every 12 minutes or $\frac{1}{5}$ hour.

hour, t	0	$\frac{1}{5}$	$\frac{2}{5}$	$\frac{3}{5}$	$\frac{4}{5}$	1
Number of cell, $N(t)$	N_0	$2N_0$	$4N_0$	$8N_0$	$16N_0$	$32N_0$

The number of cells in 1 hour is $32N_0$. Therefore, the number of cell, $N(t)$, after t hours can be expressed as $N(t) = N_0(32)^t$.

33. (C) **Geometry**

The length of cube A is increased by 75%, which means that it becomes 1.75 times longer than the original length. Since the length of cube A is 4, the length of cube B is $4 \times 1.75 = 7$. Use the surface area of a cube formula: $A = 6s^2$, where s is the length of a cube.

$$\begin{aligned}\text{Difference of surface areas} &= \text{Surface area of cube } B - \text{Surface area of cube } A \\ &= 6(7)^2 - 6(4)^2 \\ &= 198\end{aligned}$$

Therefore, the surface area of cube B is 198 square inches greater than that of cube A.

34. (D) **Calculus**

Tips

The Fundamental Theorem of Calculus, Part I

$$g'(x) = \frac{d}{dx}\int_a^{p(x)} f(t)\,dt \quad\Longrightarrow\quad g'(x) = f(p(x)) \cdot (p(x))'$$

$$g'(x) = \frac{d}{dx}\int_1^{x^2} 2t - 1\,dt \quad\Longrightarrow\quad g'(x) = \big(2(x^2) - 1\big) \cdot (x^2)' = (2x^2 - 1)(2x)$$

Therefore, the slope of the tangent line to the graph of g at $x = 2$ is $g'(2) = 7(4) = 28$.

35. (D) **Geometry**

In the figure below, $\triangle AED$, $\triangle EBC$, and $\triangle DEC$ have the same height of 6. Since the area of a triangle is $\frac{1}{2}bh$, the areas of $\triangle AED$, $\triangle EBC$, and $\triangle DEC$ can be written as $\frac{1}{2}AE(6)$, $\frac{1}{2}BE(6)$, and $\frac{1}{2}DC(6)$, respectively.

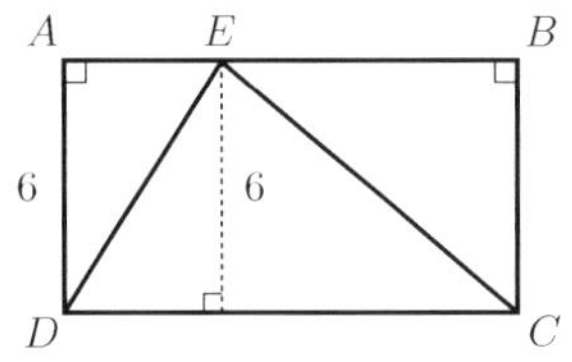

The ratio of the areas of $\triangle AED$, $\triangle EBC$, and $\triangle DEC$ is $1:2:3$. Thus,

$$\frac{1}{2}AE(6) : \frac{1}{2}BE(6) : \frac{1}{2}DC(6) = 1:2:3 \qquad \text{Multiply left side by 2}$$
$$6AE : 6BE : 6DC = 1:2:3 \qquad \text{Divide left side by 6}$$
$$AE : BE : DC = 1:2:3$$

Therefore, $AE : BE : DC = 1 : 2 : 3$. In general, if triangles have the same height but have different bases, the ratio of their areas is the same as the ratio of their bases.

36. (A) **Number and Quantity**

Tips $\quad i^2 = -1.$

$$\begin{aligned} z_1z_2 &= (2+i)(1+3i) \\ &= 2+6i+i+3i^2 \\ &= 2-3+6i+i \\ &= -1+7i \end{aligned}$$

Therefore, point A best represents the product of two complex numbers, z_1z_2.

37. (B) **Probability and Statistics**

An outlier is extreme value. it can be either the minimum or maximum value. The range, mean, and standard deviation is very sensitive to outliers. Since the median is the middle value of an ordered data set, it is robust to outliers. Therefore, (B) is the correct answer.

38. (B) **Number and Quantity**

Since Jason's row is the 11th row from the front, there are 10 rows in front of Jason. Since Jason's row is the 10th row from the back, there are 9 rows behind Jason. Thus, there are $10+1+9=20$ rows in the Auditorium. Since each row is occupied by 2 students, there are $20 \times 2 = 40$ students who went to the Auditorium.

39. (C) **Trigonometry**

> Tips: In polar coordinates,
> $$(-r,\theta)=(r,\theta\pm\pi) \qquad \text{Note: If } \theta+\pi>2\pi \text{, use } \theta-\pi \text{ instead.}$$

$(1,\pi)$ is the polar coordinates of point A, $\left(-2,\frac{\pi}{2}\right)$ is the polar coordinates of point C, and $\left(2,\frac{5\pi}{4}\right)$ is the polar coordinates of point B. Therefore, (C) is the correct answer.

40. (A) **Geometry**

In the figure below, the radius of the circle is 6. Segments $\overline{AB}$ and $\overline{AC}$ are tangent to the circle at points B and C and are perpendicular to the radii drawn to points B and C. Thus, $m\angle OBA = m\angle OCA = 90°$.

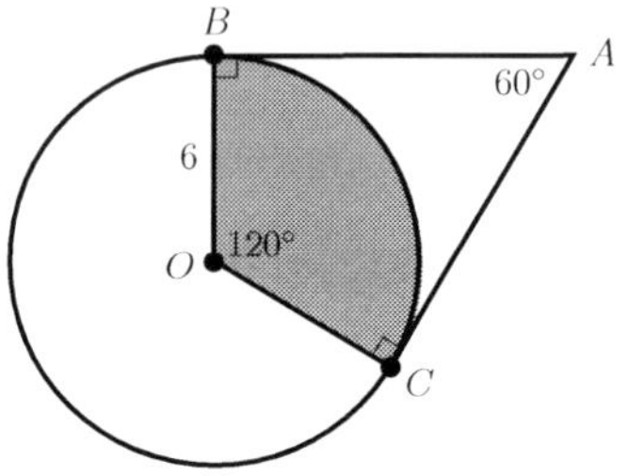

The area of the shaded region equals the area of the sector. To find the area of the sector, it is necessary to find the measure of the central angle of the sector. Points A, B, O, and C form a quadrilateral whose sum of the measures of interior angles is 360°. Since $m\angle A = 60°$, the measure of the central angle, $m\angle BOC$, can be determined by $360° - 90° - 90° - 60°$ or 120°. Thus,

$$\begin{aligned}\text{Area of sector} &= \pi r^2 \times \frac{\theta}{360°}, \qquad \text{where } \theta \text{ is the central angle}\\ &= \pi(6)^2 \times \frac{120°}{360°}\\ &= 12\pi\end{aligned}$$

Therefore, the area of the shaded region is 12π.

41. (D) **Number and Quantity**

Since p and q are positive integers and $pq = 99$, p and q must be the factors of 99.

p	q
1	99
3	33
9	11
11	9
33	3
99	1

Therefore, the number of ordered pairs (p,q) is 6.

42. (C) **Trigonometry**

Tips π radian $= 180°$, 1 radian $= \dfrac{180°}{\pi} \approx 57.3°$

$$\frac{7\pi}{12} = \frac{7}{12} \cdot 180° = 105°$$

Therefore, (C) is the correct answer.

43. (A) **Algebra**

A circular track whose circumference is 120 meters has 6 different labeled positions: A, B, C, D, E, and F. There are $\frac{120}{6} = 20$ meters in between each different labeled position. Joshua and Jason run in opposite directions from position A at a rate of 4 meters per second clockwise and 2 meters per second counterclockwise, respectively. Let t be the time when Joshua and Jason meet for the first time. Then, the distances that Joshua and Jason run for time t are $4t$ and $2t$, respectively. When Joshua and Jason meet for the first time, the sum of the distances they run is equal to the circumference of the circular track, 120 meters. Set up an equation in terms of the sum of distances and solve for t.

$$4t + 2t = 120 \qquad \Longrightarrow \qquad t = 20$$

$t = 20$ implies that Joshua and Jason meet each other every 20 seconds. Joshua and Jason meet for the first time at $t = 20$ and second time at $t = 40$. At $t = 40$, Joshua runs $4 \times 40 = 160$ meters and Jason runs $2 \times 40 = 80$ meters. Therefore, Joshua and Jason meet each other for the second time at position C.

44. (C) **Geometry**

Tips When the equation contains $Ax^2 + By^2$ (Squared terms for both x and y):

- If $A = B$, the equation defines a circle.
- If $A \neq B$, the equation defines an ellipse.

The equation $3x^2 + 4y^2 - 6x + 4y - 6 = 0$ contains squared terms for both x and y, and $A \neq B$. Therefore, the equation represents an ellipse.

45. (B, C) **Discrete Mathematics**

Tips

For the sequence

$$a_n = \frac{a \cdot n^p + \cdots}{b \cdot n^q + \cdots}$$

where p is the degree of the numerator, and q is the degree of the denominator. The convergence of the sequence can be determined by the following three cases.

Case 1: If $p > q$, $\lim_{n\to\infty} an = \infty$.

Case 2: If $p = q$, $\lim_{n\to\infty} an = \frac{a}{b}$.

Case 3: If $p < q$, $\lim_{n\to\infty} an = 0$.

$$a_1 = \frac{2(1)-4}{(1)^2+1} = -1, \qquad a_2 = \frac{2(2)-4}{(2)^2+1} = 0, \qquad a_3 = \frac{2(3)-4}{(3)^2+1} = \frac{1}{5}$$

$a_1 = -1$, $a_2 = 0$, and $a_3 = \frac{1}{5}$. So eliminate answer choices (A) and (D). A sequence is a function whose domain is positive integers. When n is indefinitely large, a_n approaches 0 (Case 3: $p = 1$ and $q = 2$) as shown below.

$$\lim_{n\to\infty} \frac{2n-4}{n^2+1} = 0$$

Therefore, the correct answers are (B) and (C).

46. (D) **Trigonometry**

Tips

De Moivre's Theorem

If $z = r \text{ cis } \theta$, $\quad z^n = r^n \text{ cis } n\theta$ for all rational n.

$z = 2\left(\cos\frac{\pi}{4} + i\sin\frac{\pi}{4}\right)$. Thus,

$$z^4 = 2^4\left(\cos 4\cdot\frac{\pi}{4} + i\sin 4\cdot\frac{\pi}{4}\right) = 16(\cos\pi + i\sin\pi)$$

Therefore, the value of z^4 is $16(\cos\pi + i\sin\pi)$.

47. (A) **Trigonometry**

In order to find the maximum height of the projectile, substitute $v_0 = 100$, $\theta = 25°$, and $g = 32$.

$$H = \frac{v_0^2 \sin^2\theta}{2g} = \frac{100^2 \cdot (\sin 25°)^2}{2(32)} = 27.91$$

Therefore, the maximum height of the projectile is 27.91 feet.

48. (2) **Discrete Mathematics**

Tips Infinite sum S of geometric series: $S = \dfrac{a_1}{1-r}$, if $|r| < 1$

In order to find the heights of the first five rectangles, substitute $x = 0$, $x = 1$, $x = 2$, $x = 3$, and $x = 4$ into 2^{-x}. Thus, the heights of the first five rectangles are 1, $\frac{1}{2}$, $\frac{1}{4}$, $\frac{1}{8}$, and $\frac{1}{16}$ as shown below.

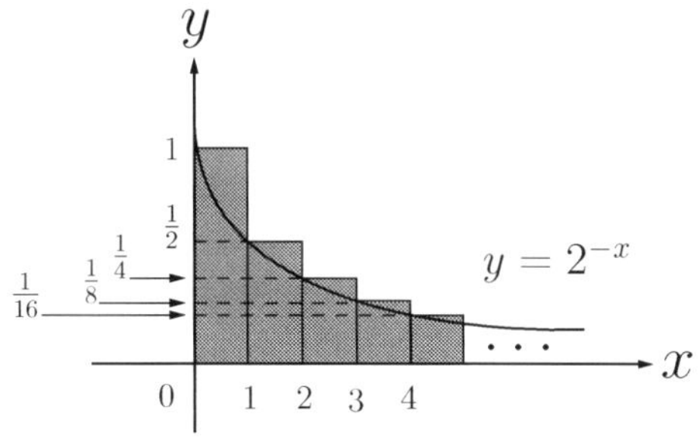

Since the length of each rectangle is 1, the sum of the areas S of the infinite number of rectangles is the geometric series with the common ration $r = \frac{1}{2}$.

$$S = 1 + \frac{1}{2} + \frac{1}{4} + \frac{1}{8} + \frac{1}{16} + \cdots = \frac{1}{1 - \frac{1}{2}} = 2$$

Therefore, the area of the shaded region S which is equal to the sum of the areas of the infinite number of rectangles is 2.

49. (D) **Geometry**

Tips A parallelogram has rotational symmetry. It can be mapped onto itself by a clockwise or counterclockwise rotation of 180° about its center.

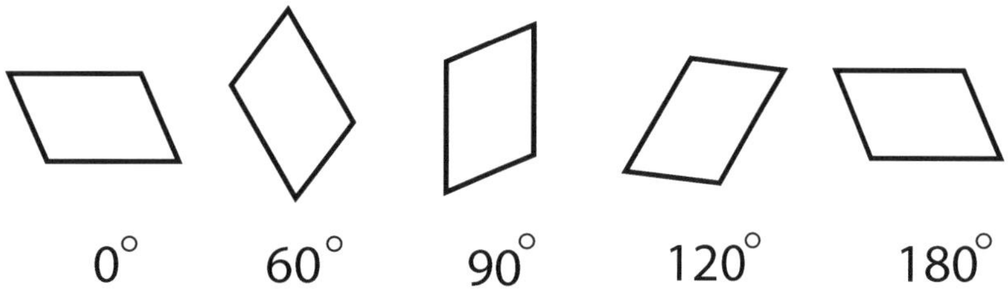

The parallelogram above can be mapped onto itself by a clockwise rotation of 180° about its center.

50. (D) **Probability and Statistics**

Three numbers are selected at random without replacement from the set $\{1, 2, 3, 4\}$ to form a three-digit number. To find the total number of three-digit numbers, use the fundamental counting principle. Define event 1, event 2, and event 3 as selecting a digit for the hundreds' place, tens' place, and ones' place, respectively. Event 1 has 4 ways to select a digit out of 4 digits. After one digit is taken, event 2 has 3 ways, and event 3 has 2 ways to select a digit. Thus, there are $4 \times 3 \times 2 = 24$ possible three-digit numbers using 1, 2, 3, and 4. Out of 24 possible three-digit numbers, there are four three-digit numbers that satisfy $A < B < C$: 123, 124, 134, and 234. Therefore, the probability that the three-digit number formed is an increasing number is $\frac{4}{24}$ or $\frac{1}{6}$.

51. (C) **Calculus**

If $f(x) = x^3 - 3x^2 - 9x + 2$, $f'(x) = 3x^2 - 6x - 9 = 3(x+1)(x-3)$ and $f''(x) = 6x - 6$. $f'(x) = 0$ for $x = -1$ and $x = 3$. So the critical numbers are -1 and 3. Let's find the local maximum and local minimum values of f using both the First Derivative test and Second Derivative test.

- Using the First Derivative Test: As shown in the figure below, f' changes positive to negative at $x = -1$. Thus, f has a local maximum at $x = -1$. The local maximum value of f is $f(-1) = 7$.

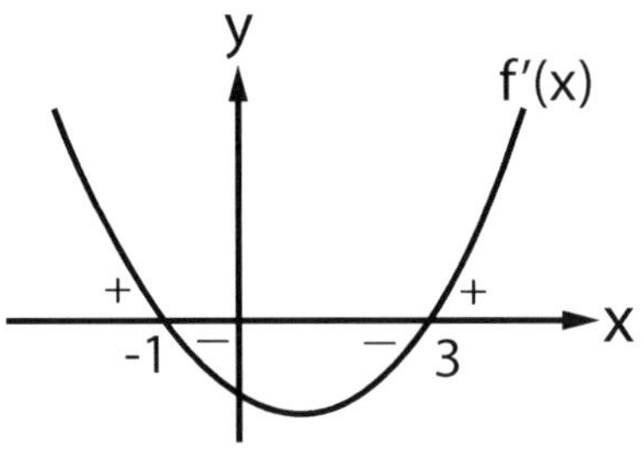

  However, f' changes negative to positive at $x = 3$. Thus, f has a local minimum at $x = 3$. The local minimum value of f is $f(4) = -25$.

- Using the Second Derivative Test: Since the critical numbers are -1 and 3, substituting these values into the second derivative $f''(x) = 6x - 6$ will determine the local maximum and local minimum values of f.

$$f''(-1) = 6(-1) - 6 < 0 \implies f \text{ has the local maximum at } x = -1$$
$$f''(3) = 6(3) - 6 > 0 \implies f \text{ has the local minimum at } x = 3$$

  Thus, the local maximum value of f is $f(-1) = 7$, and the local minimum value of f is $f(3) = -25$. Therefore, (C) is the correct answer.

52. (B, D) **Probability and Statistics**

Tips

Facts about correlation:

1. Correlation must be between -1 and 1.
2. Correlation remains unchanged when switching x and y variables.
3. Correlation does not have units. Changing the units on your data will not affect the correlation.
4. Correlation implies association, not causation.

Therefore, (B) and (D) are correct answers.

53. (A) **Calculus**

Let $u = x - 1$. Then $du = dx$, and $x = u + 1$. Let's find the new lower limit and upper limit for the integration.

When $x = 1$, $u = x - 1 = 0$, When $x = 2$, $u = x - 1 = 1$

Thus, the new lower limit and upper limit for the integration are 0 and 1, respectively.

$$\int_1^2 x\sqrt{x-1}\,dx = \int_0^1 (u+1)\sqrt{u}\,du = \int_0^1 (u+1)u^{\frac{1}{2}}\,du = \int_0^1 u^{\frac{3}{2}} + u^{\frac{1}{2}}\,du$$

Therefore, $\int_1^2 x\sqrt{x-1}\,dx$ is equivalent to $\int_0^1 u^{\frac{3}{2}} + u^{\frac{1}{2}}\,du$.

54. (D) **Discrete Mathematics**

$S_1 = \{1, 3, 7\}$, $S_2 = \{2, 3, 5\}$, $S_3 = \{2, 4, 7\}$.

$S_{12} = S_1 \cap S_2 = \{3\}$, $S_{13} = S_1 \cap S_3 = \{7\}$, $S_{23} = S_2 \cap S_3 = \{2\}$

Therefore, a set that has S_{12}, S_{13}, and S_{23} is $\{2, 3, 7\}$.

55. (1) **Discrete Mathematics**

n	1	2	3	4	5	6	7	8
$f(n)$	1	1	0	-1	-1	0	1	1

Therefore, the value of $f(8)$ is 1.

56. (D) **Discrete Mathematics**

Tips

The fundamental counting principle: If one event can occur in m ways and another event can occur in n ways, then the number of ways both events can occur is $m \times n$.

Event 1 is selecting a digit for the thousands and units digit, and event 2 is selecting a digit for the hundreds and tens digit. Event 1 has 3 ways$(2, 3, 5)$, and event 2 has 3 ways$(2, 3, 5)$. According to the fundamental counting principle, there are $3 \times 3 = 9$ 4-digit palindromes that contain the digits either 2, 3, or 5.

57. (A) **Calculus**

Tips If there is an inflection point on the curve at $x = a$, $f''(a) = 0$.

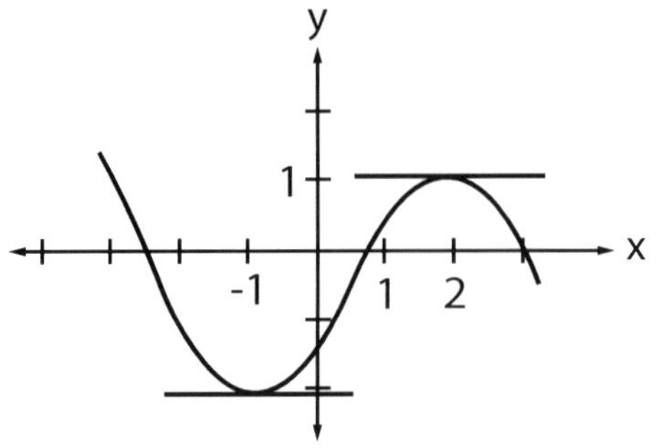

Graph of f'

The derivative function of $f'(x)$ is $f''(x)$. At $x = -1$, and $x = 2$, $f''(x) = 0$. Therefore, there are two inflection points at $x = -1$ and $x = 2$.

58. (D) **Probability and Statistics**

Tips If A and B are **mutually exclusive** events, then $P(A \cap B) = 0$. Thus, the addition law becomes

$$P(A \cup B) = P(A) + P(B)$$

$P(A) = 0.4$ and $P(B) = 0.5$. Since two events A and B are mutually exclusive,

$$P(A \cup B) = P(A) + P(B) = 0.4 + 0.5 = 0.9$$

Therefore, (D) is the correct answer.

59. (A) **Functions**

The graph of the piecewise function f is shown below.

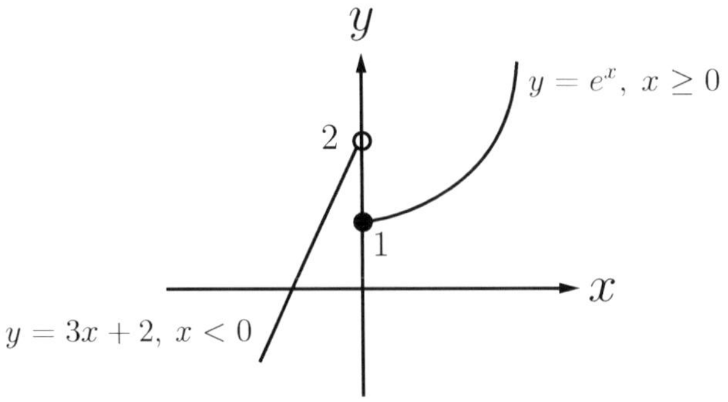

Therefore, the range of the piecewise function is all real numbers.

60. (C) **Number and Quantity**

Tips

The table below shows the powers of i.

Powers of i	i	i^2	i^3	i^4	i^5	i^6	i^7	i^8	i^9	i^{10}	i^{11}	i^{12}
Value	i	-1	$-i$	1	i	-1	$-i$	1	i	-1	$-i$	1

The powers of i repeat in a pattern: i, -1, $-i$, and 1. Thus, $i+i^2+i^3+i^4=0$, $i^5+i^6+i^7+i^8=0$, and $i^9+i^{10}+i^{11}+i^{12}=0$. Therefore, $i+i^2+i^3+\cdots+i^{11}+i^{12}=0$.

PRAXIS II 5161 PRACTICE TEST 2

Time — 150 minutes

Number of questions — 60

Directions: Solve each of the following problems using the available space for scratch work. Choose the best answer among the answer choices given and fill in the corresponding circle on the answer sheet.

1. Joshua bought 2 oranges at \$1.19 each and 2 mangoes at \$1.89 each at the store yesterday. The store goes on sales today. The new price of each orange and mango are \$0.99 and \$1.59, respectively. How much would Joshua have saved if he bought the same number of fruits at the store today?

   (A) \$0.60

   (B) \$0.80

   (C) \$0.90

   (D) \$1.00

$$0 \leq x^2 \leq 9$$

2. Set S consists of integers that satisfy the inequality above. How many elements does set S have?

   (A) 4

   (B) 5

   (C) 6

   (D) 7

For the following question, enter your answer in the answer box.

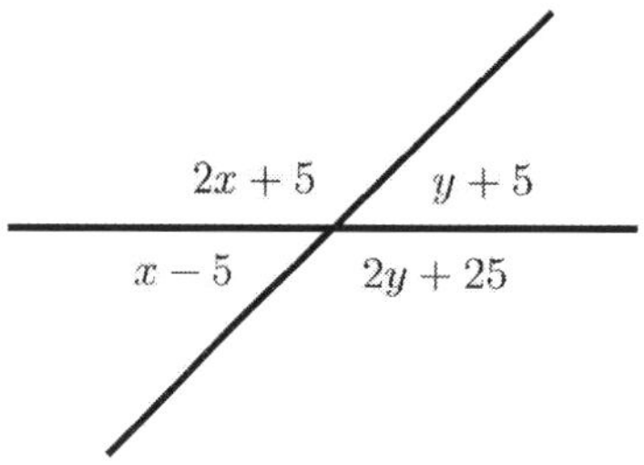

3. Two lines intersect and form two pairs of vertical angles. What is the value of $x + y$?

   $x + y =$ [ ]

$$f(x) = -2(x - 7)^2 + 16$$

4. The function $f(x)$ above has a maximum value at $x = 7$. At what value of x does $f(x + 10)$ have the maximum value?

   (A) -3

   (B) -1

   (C) 6

   (D) 10

5. There are three books on a bookshelf: two math books and a history book. If you arrange these three books, how many different arrangements are possible?

(A) 1

(B) 3

(C) 6

(D) 9

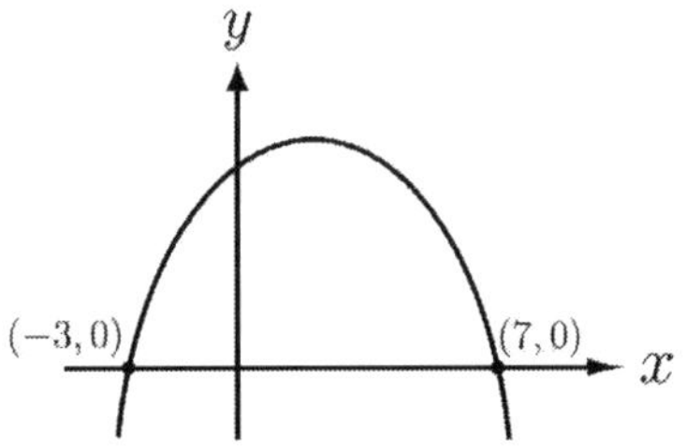

6. The graph above shows the graph of a quadratic function. Which of the following is the equation of the axis of symmetry, a line that passes through the vertex and divides the graph into two perfect halves, of the quadratic function?

(A) $x = 2$

(B) $y = 2$

(C) $x = 4$

(D) $y = 4$

7. If $\sqrt{x} \cdot \sqrt[3]{x} = x^n$, what is the value of n ?

(A) $\frac{7}{2}$

(B) $\frac{7}{6}$

(C) $\frac{5}{6}$

(D) $\frac{2}{5}$

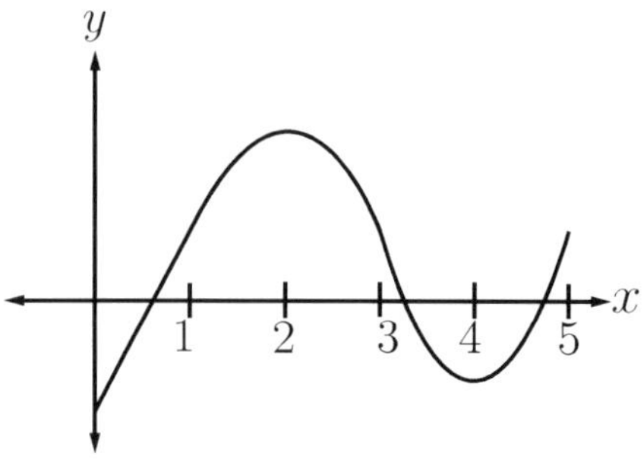

Graph of f

8. Let f be a twice differentiable function whose graph is shown above. Which of the following statement must be true?

(A) $f'(2) < f'(3) < f'(1)$

(B) $f'(1) < f'(2) < f'(3)$

(C) $f''(2) < f''(3) < f''(4)$

(D) $f''(4) < f''(3) < f''(2)$

9. If vector **V** has a terminal point of $(-2, 3)$ and an initial point of $(3, -4)$, what is the position vector **V** ?

(A) $\langle 5, -7 \rangle$

(B) $\langle 1, -1 \rangle$

(C) $\langle -1, 1 \rangle$

(D) $\langle -5, 7 \rangle$

10. If $10^{\log_{10} x} < 10$, what is the largest possible positive integer value of x ?

(A) 7

(B) 8

(C) 9

(D) 10

11. If $x = -6$ is a solution to $x^2 + bx - 30 = 0$, what is the other solution?

(A) 4

(B) 5

(C) 6

(D) 8

12. A proportion of all U.S. retail sales that involves the internet is modeled by

$$P(t) = \frac{0.7}{1 + 3e^{-0.28t}}$$

where t represents years after 2010. For example, $t = 0$ represents 2010, $t = 1$ represents 2011, and so on. What proportion of U.S. retail sales involve the internet in 2020 ?

(A) 0.56

(B) 0.59

(C) 0.62

(D) 0.65

For the following question, enter your answer in the answer box.

13. Three points A, B, and C lie on the same number line, not necessarily in that order. Point A and point B are 50 units apart and point C and point A are 17 units apart. What is the maximum distance that point C and point B are apart?

Year	2012	2013	2014	2015	2016
User	20	28	40	56	83

14. The table above shows the number of smart phone users (in millions) from 2012 to 2016. Which of the following scatter plot best represents the table?

(A)

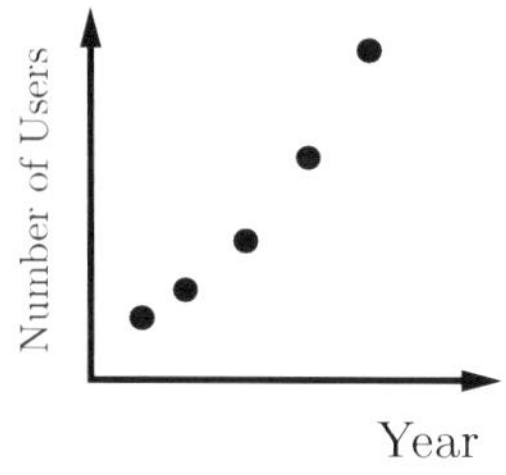

(B)

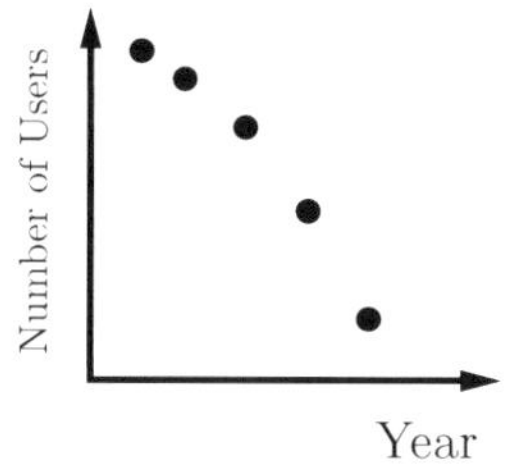

(C)

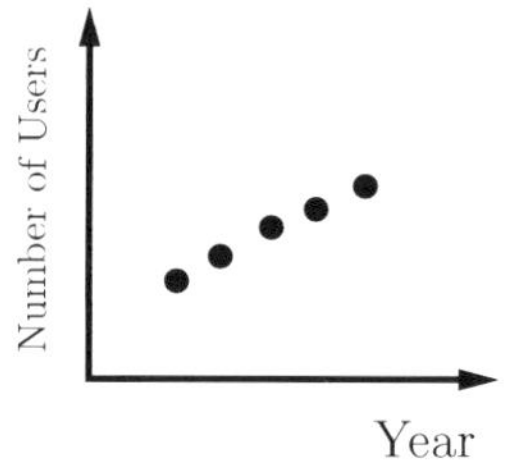

(D)

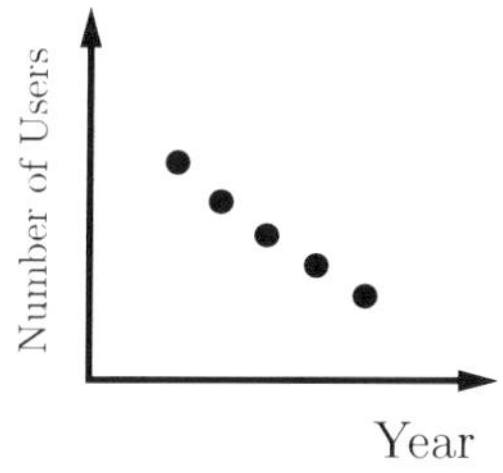

15. $\sin\frac{\pi}{3} + \sin\frac{2\pi}{3} + \sin\frac{4\pi}{3} + \sin\frac{5\pi}{3} =$

(A) 0

(B) $\frac{\sqrt{3}}{2}$

(C) $\sqrt{3}$

(D) $2\sqrt{3}$

For the following question, select all the answer choices that apply.

16. Which of the following statements are true about the inverse function?

Select all that apply.

(A) The graph of the inverse function is obtained by reflecting the graph of $f(x)$ about the line $y = x$.

(B) The domain of the inverse function is the range of $f(x)$.

(C) The inverse function of $f(x)$ is $\frac{1}{f(x)}$.

(D) The inverse function of $f(x) = e^x$ is $f^{-1}(x) = \sqrt{x}$.

17. If $x^2 = 2$, what is the value of $\left(x + \frac{1}{x}\right)^2$?

(A) $\frac{5}{2}$

(B) $\frac{7}{2}$

(C) $\frac{9}{2}$

(D) $\frac{11}{2}$

18. What is the value of $\lim_{x \to 0} \frac{e^x - 1}{\sin x}$?

(A) -1

(B) 0

(C) 1

(D) Does not exist.

19. Car A is 80 miles west of a train station. Car B is 35 miles south of the same train station. At noon, car B begins traveling 55 mph due north of the station. Two hours later, car A begins traveling 50 mph due east of the station. At 5 pm, how far apart are these two cars?

(A) 250 miles

(B) 300 miles

(C) 350 miles

(D) 400 miles

20. On which of he following interval does the equation $2x^3 - x + 2 = 0$ have at least one solution?

(A) $(-3, -2)$

(B) $(-2, -1)$

(C) $(0, 1)$

(D) $(2, 3)$

	Calculus	Chemistry	
Junior			55
Senior			45
	60	40	100

21. According to the table shown above, there are 55 juniors and 45 seniors in a high school. The number of students who are taking Calculus is 60, and the number of students who are taking Chemistry is 40, and the number of juniors who are taking Calculus is 25. If a student is randomly selected, what is the probability that the selected student is a senior who is taking Chemistry?

(A) 0.1

(B) 0.3

(C) 0.35

(D) 0.4

22. Which of the following is the range of $y = -6\sin\left(3t + \frac{3\pi}{4}\right) - 5$?

(A) $-11 \le y \le 1$

(B) $-9 \le y \le -1$

(C) $-6 \le y \le -1$

(D) $-5 \le y \le 1$

23. If a car factory produces x cars in y months, how many cars does the car factory produce in z years?

(A) $\frac{xy}{z}$

(B) $\frac{12yz}{x}$

(C) $\frac{12xz}{y}$

(D) $\frac{12xy}{z}$

24. Which of the following is the value of x for which $\frac{1}{2}x^3 - 1 = 0.6$?

(A) 0.21

(B) 0.89

(C) 1.13

(D) 1.47

25. If a sequence is defined by $a_{n+2} = a_{n+1} \cdot a_n$ for $n \ge 1$, $a_1 = 2$, and $a_2 = 3$, which of the following is **NOT** a factor of the fifth term?

(A) 6

(B) 12

(C) 18

(D) 24

For the following question, select all the answer choices that apply.

a	$\lim_{x\to a^-} f(x)$	$\lim_{x\to a^+} f(x)$	$f(a)$
1	2	2	3
2	$-\infty$	∞	undefined
3	1	1	1
4	∞	∞	undefined

26. According to the table shown above, Which of the following statements are true about the function f ?

Select all that apply.

(A) f has a hole at $x = 1$.

(B) f has vertical asymptotes at $x = 2$ and $x = 4$.

(C) f has a horizontal asymptote at $y = 1$.

(D) f is continuous at $x = 3$.

$$\frac{4x-1}{(x-1)(2x-1)} = \frac{A}{x-1} - \frac{2}{2x-1}$$

27. An identity equation is an equation that is true no matter what value is substituted for x. For the identity equation above, what is the value of A ?

(A) 1

(B) 2

(C) 3

(D) 4

$$y > x^2$$
$$y < x + 2$$

28. Which of the following point (x, y) satisfies the system of inequalities shown above?

(A) $(-1, -2)$

(B) $(-1, -1)$

(C) $(0, 3)$

(D) $(1, 2)$

Score	Frequency
81	6
84	5
88	4
92	5
96	2

29. The table above shows math scores of students in a class. What is the median of the math scores in the class?

(A) 84

(B) 86

(C) 88

(D) 90

30. The price of a jacket in January was n dollars. In February, the price of the jacket was increased by 25 percent. In March, the price of the jacket was reduced by 20 percent. How much would you pay if you buy the jacket in March, including 8% sales tax?

(A) $1.08n$ dollars

(B) $1.13n$ dollars

(C) $1.18n$ dollars

(D) $1.23n$ dollars

For the following question, enter your answer in the answer box.

31. Two standard dice are rolled. What is the probability that the product of the two numbers shown on top of the two dice is even?

Give your answer as a fraction.

32. Which of the following best represents the set of points equidistant from two points in the xy-plane?

(A) A line

(B) A triangle

(C) A square

(D) A circle

33. Which of the following is an equation of the line tangent to the graph of $y = \sqrt[3]{x-2}$ at the point $(1, -1)$?

(A) $y = \frac{1}{3}x - \frac{2}{3}$

(B) $y = \frac{1}{3}x - \frac{4}{3}$

(C) $y = -\frac{1}{3}x + \frac{1}{3}$

(D) $y = -\frac{1}{3}x + \frac{5}{3}$

$$f(x) = \cos 2x, \qquad g(x) = \frac{x}{x^2+1}$$

34. If f and g are defined as shown above, what is the value of $g\left(f\left(\frac{\pi}{6}\right)\right)$?

(A) 0.30

(B) 0.35

(C) 0.40

(D) 0.45

35. A lamp post casts a shadow of 25 feet when the sun makes a 35° angle of elevation. What is the height of the lamp post?

(A) 12.3 feet

(B) 14.1 feet

(C) 15.6 feet

(D) 17.5 feet

36. Point A and point B are located on the xy coordinate plane. A line that passes through the two points, A and B, has a slope of $\frac{3}{2}$. Point A and point B are reflected about the y-axis so that they become A' and B'. What is the slope of a new line that passes through point A' and point B' ?

(A) $\frac{3}{2}$

(B) $\frac{1}{2}$

(C) $-\frac{2}{3}$

(D) $-\frac{3}{2}$

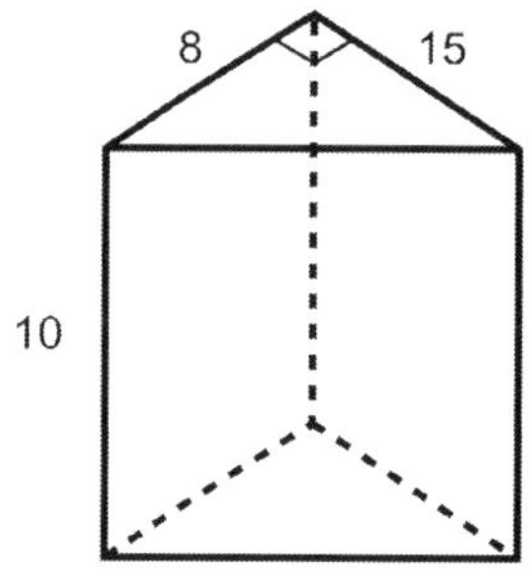

Note: Figure not drawn to scale.

37. In the right triangular prism above, the top face and the bottom face are identical right triangles. What is the surface area of the triangular prism including the top and bottom faces?

(A) 680

(B) 600

(C) 520

(D) 440

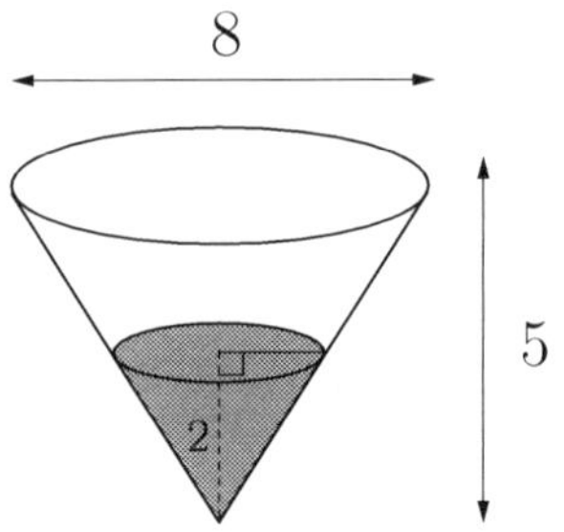

38. A water tank has the shape of an inverted cone with a diameter of 8 feet and a height of 5 feet as shown in Figure 2. The water is being pumped into the tank so that the water level is rising. If the height of the water is 2 feet, what is the radius of the surface of the water?

(A) $\frac{2}{5}$ feet

(B) $\frac{3}{5}$ feet

(C) $\frac{6}{5}$ feet

(D) $\frac{8}{5}$ feet

39. y varies directly with the cube of x and inversely with the square root of z. When $x = 2$ and $z = 16$, $y = 6$. What is the value of y when $x = \frac{1}{3}$ and $z = \frac{1}{4}$?

(A) $\frac{9}{2}$

(B) $\frac{5}{9}$

(C) $\frac{2}{5}$

(D) $\frac{2}{9}$

40. A manufacturing company that produces light bulbs found out that 3% of their production is defective. If you have purchased five light bulbs from the company, what is the probability that none of them are defective?

(A) 0.97

(B) 0.92

(C) 0.86

(D) 0.15

For the following question, select all the answer choices that apply.

41. An isometry is a transformation that preserves length, angle measures, parallel lines, and distance between points. Which of the following transformations are isometries?

Select all that apply.

(A) Reflection

(B) rotation

(C) translation

(D) Dilation

42. Which of the following expression is a factor of $f(x) = x^3 - 3x^2 + 4x - 4$?

(A) $x + 2$

(B) $x + 1$

(C) $x - 2$

(D) $x - 3$

43. $\dfrac{3-4i}{2-3i}=$

(A) $-\dfrac{18}{13}-\dfrac{i}{13}$

(B) $-\dfrac{6}{13}-\dfrac{i}{13}$

(C) $\dfrac{6}{13}+\dfrac{i}{13}$

(D) $\dfrac{18}{13}+\dfrac{i}{13}$

44. If $\log_2 3 = m$ and $\log_2 5 = n$, what is $\log_2 30$ in terms of m and n ?

(A) $m+n$

(B) $m+n+1$

(C) mn

(D) $mn+1$

For the following question, enter your answer in the answer box.

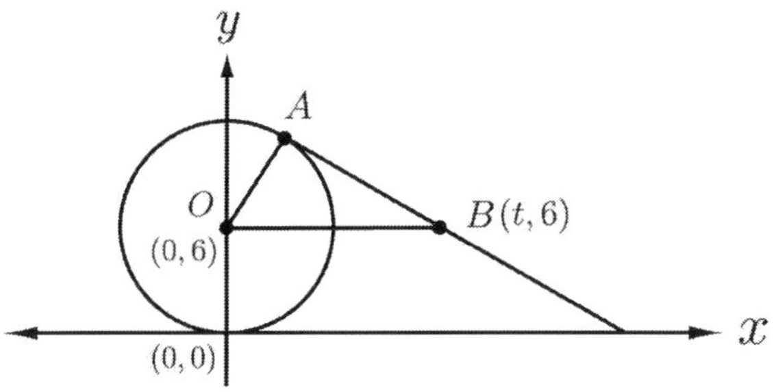

Note: Figure not drawn to scale.

45. In the figure above, a line that passes through point B is tangent to a circle at point A. The center of the circle, O, is along the y axis. If $AB = 8$, what is the value of t ?

$t =$ [ ]

46. Joshua has m liters of a 10% acid solution, and n liters of a 30% acid solution. If he mixes these solutions up, he will make 100 liters of a 15% acid solution. Which of the following is the value of $m-n$?

(A) 5

(B) 20

(C) 35

(D) 50

47. What is the units digit of $7^{1002}-2^{1002}$?

(A) 2

(B) 3

(C) 4

(D) 5

48. If $\lim_{h\to 0}\dfrac{\arctan(a+h)-\arctan(a)}{h}=\dfrac{1}{4}$, then what could be the value of a ?

(A) $\dfrac{\sqrt{2}}{2}$

(B) $\dfrac{\sqrt{3}}{2}$

(C) $\sqrt{2}$

(D) $\sqrt{3}$

For the following question, enter your answer in the answer box.

49. A pitcher had won 60% of the games he pitched. For the next five games, the pitcher won 2 games and lost 3, to finish the season having won 56% of his games. How many games did the pitcher play in all?

50. What are the equations of the asymptotes of $16x^2 - 9y^2 = 144$?

(A) $y = \pm\frac{16}{9}x$

(B) $y = \pm\frac{4}{3}x$

(C) $y = \pm\frac{3}{4}x$

(D) $y = \pm\frac{9}{16}x$

51. A half full water tank has a square base with side length 200 cm and a height of 400 cm. If a cube with side length 50 cm is placed inside the water tank, how many meters does the water rise?

(A) $\frac{1}{32}$ meter

(B) $\frac{1}{16}$ meter

(C) $\frac{1}{8}$ meter

(D) $\frac{1}{4}$ meter

52. Which of the following is the average value of $\tan^2 x$ over the interval $\left[0, \frac{\pi}{4}\right]$?

(A) $1 - \frac{\pi}{4}$

(B) $1 + \frac{\pi}{4}$

(C) $\frac{4}{\pi} - 1$

(D) $\frac{4}{\pi} + 1$

53. If $x^a = y^b$, and $y^c = x^d$, where a, b, c, and d are real numbers that are not equal to 0, which of the following statements must be true?

(A) $a = \frac{bd}{c}$

(B) $a = \frac{bc}{d}$

(C) $b = \frac{cd}{a}$

(D) $b - \frac{c}{ad}$

54. A local telephone company provides wireless communication services to residential customers for a monthly charge of \$13.50 plus 1.5 cents per minute for the first 800 minutes used, and 2.5 cents thereafter in one month. If the company charged a customer \$26.75 for October, how many minutes did the customer use in October?

(A) 700 minutes

(B) 750 minutes

(C) 800 minutes

(D) 850 minutes

55. If $\dfrac{7p+2q}{p+q} = 4$, what is the value of $\dfrac{p}{q}$?

(A) $\dfrac{7}{2}$

(B) $\dfrac{5}{3}$

(C) $\dfrac{2}{3}$

(D) $\dfrac{3}{5}$

56. If $f(x) = -|x-1| - 3$, what is the x-intercept of f ?

(A) $x = 2$ only

(B) $x = -2$ only

(C) $x = 4$ or $x = -2$

(D) There is no x-intercept.

For the following question, enter your answer in the answer box.

57. If $\sin 2\theta = \dfrac{2}{3}$, which of the following is the value of $(\sin\theta + \cos\theta)^2$?

Give your answer as a fraction.

$$(\sin\theta + \cos\theta)^2 = \frac{\square}{\square}$$

58. $\csc^2 x(1 - \cos^2 x) =$

(A) $\sec^2 x$

(B) $\tan^2 x$

(C) $\cot^2 x$

(D) 1

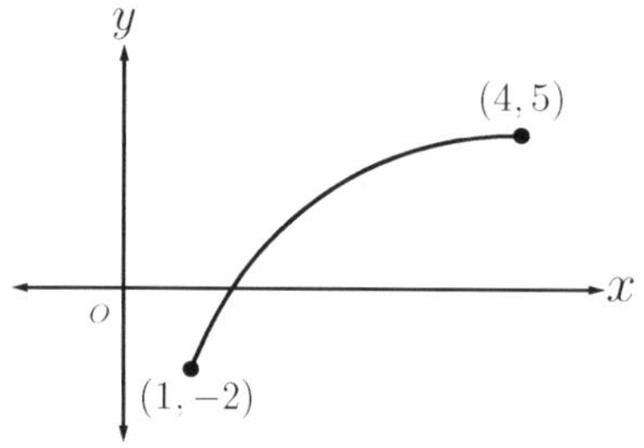

Graph of f

59. A portion of the graph of a differentiable function f is shown above. If c is the value that satisfies the conclusion of the Mean Value Theorem, which of the following must be the slope of the tangent line to the graph of f at $x = c$?

(A) $-\dfrac{3}{5}$

(B) $-\dfrac{3}{7}$

(C) $\dfrac{5}{3}$

(D) $\dfrac{7}{3}$

60. How many arrangements can be formed using all the letters in the word SOLOMON?

(A) 720

(B) 840

(C) 1680

(D) 2520

STOP

Answers and Solutions

PRAXIS II 5161 PRACTICE TEST 2

Answers

1. D	11. B	21. A	31. $\frac{3}{4}$	41. A,B,C	51. A
2. D	12. B	22. A	32. A	42. C	52. C
3. 110	13. 67	23. C	33. B	43. D	53. A
4. A	14. A	24. D	34. C	44. B	54. D
5. B	15. A	25. D	35. D	45. 10	55. C
6. A	16. A,B	26. A,B,D	36. D	46. D	56. D
7. C	17. C	27. C	37. C	47. D	57. $\frac{5}{3}$
8. C	18. C	28. D	38. D	48. D	58. D
9. D	19. A	29. B	39. D	49. 25	59. D
10. C	20. B	30. A	40. C	50. B	60. B

Solutions

1. (D) **Number and Quantity**

   Joshua would have saved \$0.20 per orange and \$0.30 per mango if he went to the store today.

$$\begin{aligned} \text{Savings} &= 2(1.19 - 0.99) + 2(1.89 - 1.59) \\ &= 2(0.2) + 2(0.3) \\ &= \$1.00 \end{aligned}$$

   Therefore, Joshua would have saved \$1.00 if he went to the store today.

2. (D) **Algebra**

   The solution to the inequality $0 \le x^2 \le 9$ is $-3 \le x \le 3$. Since the values of x are integers,

$$-3 \le x \le 3 \quad \Longrightarrow \quad x = \{-3, -2, -1, 0, 1, 2, 3\}$$

   Therefore, there are seven elements in set S.

3. (110) **Geometry**

$2x+5$ and $x-5$ are supplementary angles. Thus, the sum of their measures is $180°$.

$$\begin{aligned} 2x+5+x-5 &= 180 \\ 3x &= 180 \\ x &= 60 \end{aligned}$$

Additionally, $y+5$ and $2y+25$ are supplementary angles.

$$\begin{aligned} y+5+2y+25 &= 180 \\ 3y+30 &= 180 \\ y &= 50 \end{aligned}$$

Therefore, $x+y=60+50=110$.

4. (A) **Functions**

To evaluate $f(x+10)$, substitute $x+10$ for x in $f(x)$.

$$\begin{aligned} f(x) &= -2(x-7)^2+16 && \text{Substitute } x+10 \text{ for } x \\ f(x+10) &= -2(x+10-7)^2+16 \\ &= -2(x+3)^2+16 && \text{Vertex is } (-3,16) \end{aligned}$$

Since $f(x+10)$ is expressed in the vertex form, the x-coordinate of the vertex of $f(x+10)$ is -3. Therefore, $f(x+10)$ has the maximum value at $x=-3$.

5. (B) **Discrete Mathematics**

The list below shows the possible arrangements for the two math books and the history book (M and H are used for the math book and the history book, respectively).

$$\begin{matrix} M & M & H \\ M & H & M \\ H & M & M \end{matrix}$$

Therefore, there are three possible arrangements for the two math books and the history book.

6. (A) **Functions**

Both the axis of symmetry and the x-coordinate of the vertex are the mean of the x-intercepts of the quadratic function. Since the x-intercepts are -3 and 7, the axis of symmetry is $\frac{-3+7}{2}=2$. Therefore, the equation of the axis of symmetry is $x=2$.

7. (C) **Number and Quantity**

Tips	
	1. $\sqrt[n]{a}=a^{\frac{1}{n}}$
	2. $a^m \cdot a^n = a^{m+n}$

$$\sqrt{x}\cdot\sqrt[3]{x} = x^{\frac{1}{2}}\cdot x^{\frac{1}{3}} = x^{\frac{1}{2}+\frac{1}{3}} = x^{\frac{5}{6}}$$

Therefore, the value of n is $\dfrac{5}{6}$.

8. (C) **Calculus**

Tips

Increasing and Decreasing Test

- If $f'(x) > 0$ for all x on an interval, then f is increasing on that interval.
- If $f'(x) < 0$ for all x on an interval, then f is decreasing on that interval.

Concavity Test

- If $f''(x) > 0$ for all x on an interval, then the graph of f is concave upward on that interval.
- If $f''(x) < 0$ for all x on an interval, then the graph of f is concave downward on that interval.

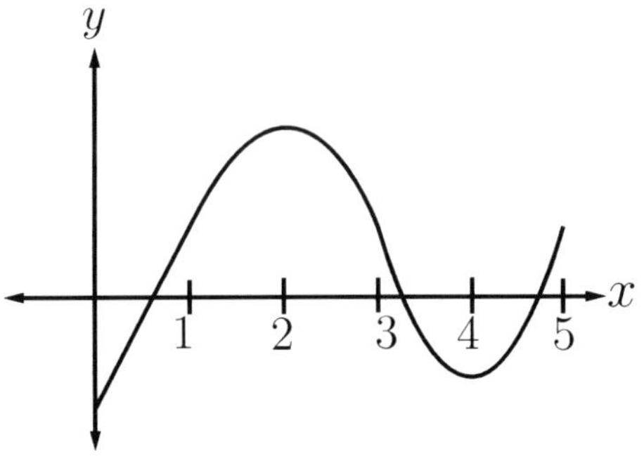

Graph of f

	1	2	3	4
$f'(x)$	$+$	0	$-$	0
$f''(x)$	$-$	$-$	0	$+$

At $x = 1$, the graph of f is increasing, and is concave down. So $f'(1) > 0$ and $f''(1) < 0$. At $x = 2$, f has a local maximum, and is concave down. So $f'(2) = 0$ and $f''(2) < 0$. At $x = 3$, the graph of f is decreasing, and has an inflection point because the graph changes from concave down to concave up. So $f'(3) < 0$ and $f''(3) = 0$. At $x = 4$, f has a local minimum, and is concave up. So $f'(4) = 0$ and $f''(4) > 0$. Therefore, (C) is the correct answer.

9. (D) **Trigonometry**

Tips

If point $A(x_1, y_1)$ is the initial point and point $B(x_2, y_2)$ is the terminal point, a vector, **AB**, is defined as

$$\mathbf{AB} = \langle x_2 - x_1, y_2 - y_1 \rangle$$

Since the initial point is $(3, -4)$ and the terminal point is $(-2, 3)$, vector **V** is defined as follows:

$$\mathbf{V} = \langle x_2 - x_1, y_2 - y_1 \rangle = \langle -2 - 3, 3 - (-4) \rangle = \langle -5, 7 \rangle$$

Therefore, the position vector **V** is $\langle -5, 7 \rangle$.

10. (C) **Functions**

Tips $a^{\log_a x} = x^{\log_a a} = x$

Since $10^{\log_{10} x} = x$, $10^{\log_{10} x} < 10$ simplifies to $x < 10$. Therefore, the largest possible positive integer value of x for which $x < 10$ is 9.

11. (B) **Functions**

Since -6 is a solution to the quadratic equation, substitute -6 for x in the equation and solve for b.

$$\begin{aligned} x^2+bx-30&=0 && \text{Substitute } -6 \text{ for } x\\ (-6)^2+b(-6)-30&=0\\ -6b&=-6\\ b&=1 \end{aligned}$$

$x^2+bx-30=0$ becomes $x^2+x-30=0$. Use the factoring method to solve for other solution.

$$\begin{aligned} x^2+x-30&=0 && \text{Use the factoring method}\\ (x-5)(x+6)&=0 && \text{Use the zero product property}\\ x=5 \quad \text{or} \quad x&=-6 \end{aligned}$$

Therefore, the other solution to the quadratic equation is 5.

12. (B) **Functions**

$t=10$ represents 2010. In order to find the proportion of U.S. retail sales involving the internet in 2020, substitute $t=10$ into $P(t)$.

$$P(t)=\frac{0.7}{1+3e^{-0.28t}} \implies P(10)=\frac{0.7}{1+3e^{-0.28(10)}}=0.59$$

Therefore, the proportion of U.S. retail sales involving the internet in 2020 is 0.59.

13. (67) **Geometry**

Place point A in the middle on the number line as shown in figure 1. Since points A, B and C lie on the same number line, not necessarily in that order, place point B 50 units left of point A or 50 units right of point A.

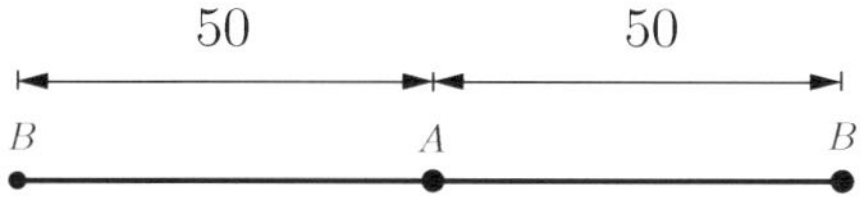

Figure 1

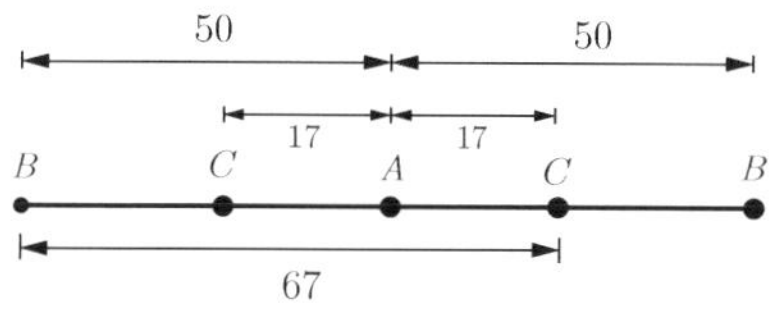

Figure 2

Point C and point A are 17 units apart. So, place point C 17 units left of point A or 17 units right of point A as shown in figure 2. Therefore, the maximum distance that point C and point B are apart is 67 units.

14. (A) **Probability and Statistics**

The number of smart phone users increases exponentially from 2012 to 2016. Therefore, the scatter plot in (A) best represents the table.

15. (A) **Trigonometry**

$\sin\frac{2\pi}{3} = \sin\frac{\pi}{3}$. $\sin\frac{4\pi}{3} = \sin\frac{5\pi}{3} = -\sin\frac{\pi}{3}$. Thus,

$$\sin\frac{\pi}{3} + \sin\frac{2\pi}{3} + \sin\frac{4\pi}{3} + \sin\frac{5\pi}{3} = \sin\frac{\pi}{3} + \sin\frac{\pi}{3} - \sin\frac{\pi}{3} - \sin\frac{\pi}{3} = 0$$

Therefore, (A) is the correct answer.

16. (A, B) **Functions**

Tips

1. The graph of the inverse function $f^{-1}(x)$ is obtained by reflecting the graph of $f(x)$ about the line $y = x$.
2. The domain of $f(x)$ is the range of $f^{-1}(x)$. Whereas, the range of $f(x)$ is the domain of $f^{-1}(x)$.
3. $f^{-1}(x) \neq \dfrac{1}{f(x)}$.

The inverse function of $f(x) = e^x$ is $f^{-1}(x) = \ln x$. Therefore, (A) and (B) are correct answers.

17. (C) **Algebra**

Tips

The binomial expansion

$$(x+y)^2 = x^2 + 2xy + y^2$$

$$\begin{aligned}
\left(x + \frac{1}{x}\right)^2 &= x^2 + 2(x)\left(\frac{1}{x}\right) + \left(\frac{1}{x}\right)^2 \\
&= x^2 + 2 + \frac{1}{x^2} && \text{Substitute 2 for } x^2 \\
&= 2 + 2 + \frac{1}{2} \\
&= \frac{9}{2}
\end{aligned}$$

Therefore, $\left(x + \frac{1}{x}\right)^2 = \frac{9}{2}$.

18. (C) **Calculus**

Tips

L'Hospital's Rule: Let f and g are differentiable and $g'(x) \neq 0$ near a. Suppose you have one of the following cases

$$\lim_{x \to a} \frac{f(x)}{g(x)} = \frac{0}{0} \quad \text{or} \quad \lim_{x \to a} \frac{f(x)}{g(x)} = \frac{\pm\infty}{\pm\infty}$$

where a can be any real number, infinity, or negative infinity. Then,

$$\lim_{x \to a} \frac{f(x)}{g(x)} = \lim_{x \to a} \frac{f'(x)}{g'(x)}$$

Substitute x for 0 in the numerator and the denominator. Then, you will get an indeterminate form of $\frac{0}{0}$. Use the L'Hospital's rule to find the limit.

$$\lim_{x \to 0} \frac{e^x - 1}{\sin x} = \lim_{x \to 0} \frac{(e^x - 1)'}{(\sin x)'} = \lim_{x \to 0} \frac{e^x}{\cos x} = \frac{e^0}{\cos 0} = 1$$

Therefore, the value of $\lim_{x \to 0} \frac{e^x - 1}{\sin x}$ is 1.

19. (A) **Geometry**

In figure 1, car A is 80 miles west of a train station and car B is 35 miles south of the same train station at noon. Car B begins traveling 55 mph due north of the station at noon for two hours. Thus, car B is 75 miles north of the station at 2pm as shown in figure 2.

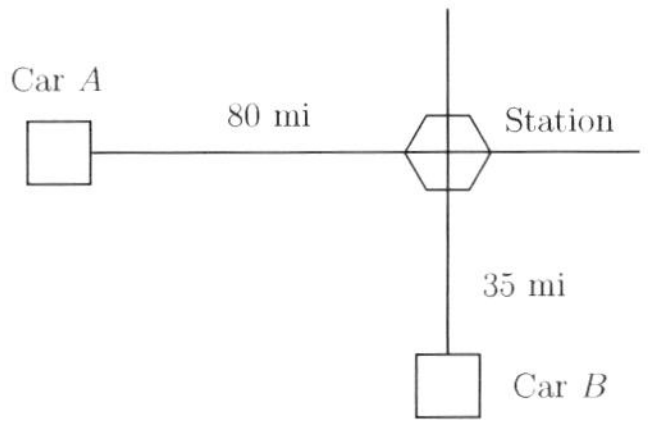

Figure 1: At noon

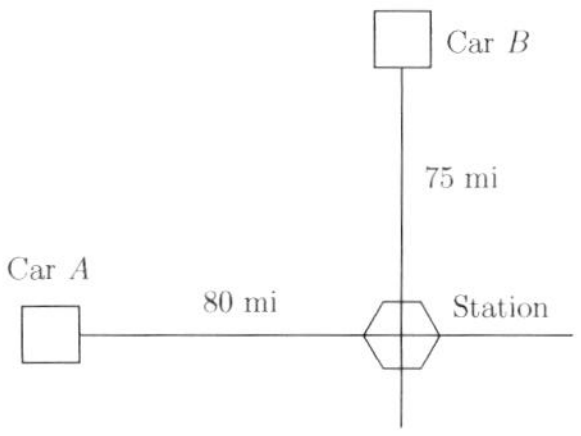

Figure 2: At 2pm

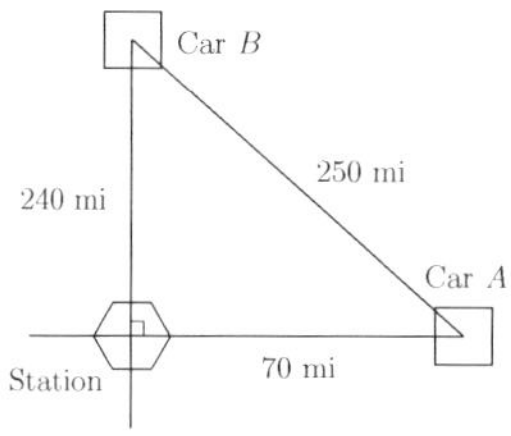

Figure 3: At 5pm

Additionally, car A begins traveling 50 mph due east of the station at 2pm for three hours. Thus, car A is 70 miles east of the station and car B is 240 miles north of the station at 5pm as shown in figure 3. To find the distance between car A and car B, use the Pythagorean theorem: $C^2 = 70^2 + 240^2$, or use a multiple of the Pythagorean triple: $(7 - 24 - 25) \times 10 = 70 - 240 - 250$. Therefore, car A and car B are 250 miles apart at 5pm.

20. (B) **Calculus**

Tips

The Intermediate Value Theorem: If f is continuous on the closed interval $[a, b]$, and $f(a)$ and $f(b)$ are of opposite signs, there must be at least one zero on the closed interval $[a, b]$.

Let $f(x) = 2x^3 - x + 2$. According to the Intermediate value theorem, $f(-2) = -12$ and $f(-1) = 1$, which are of opposite signs. Therefore, there must be at least one zero on the closed interval $[-2, -1]$

21. (A) **Probability and Statistics**

There are 55 juniors, and the number of juniors taking Calculus is 25. So the number of juniors who are taking chemistry is $55 - 25 = 30$ as shown below.

	Calculus	Chemistry	
Junior	25	30	55
Senior		**10**	45
	60	40	100

Since there are 40 students who are taking Chemistry, and the number of juniors who are taking Chemistry is 30, the number of seniors who are taking Chemistry is $40 - 30 = 10$. Therefore, the probability that the selected student is a senior who is taking Chemistry is $\frac{10}{100} = 0.1$.

22. (A) **Trigonometry**

$y = -6\sin\left(3t + \frac{3\pi}{4}\right) - 5$. Let $\theta = 3t + \frac{3\pi}{4}$. For any angle θ, the range of the sine function is all real numbers from -1 to 1, inclusive. Thus,

$$\begin{aligned} -1 &\le \sin\theta \le 1 \\ -6 &\le -6\sin\theta \le 6 && \text{Multiply each side of the inequality by } -6 \\ -11 &\le -6\sin\theta - 5 \le 1 && \text{Subtract 5 from each side of the inequality} \\ -11 &\le y \le 1 \end{aligned}$$

Therefore, the range of $y = -6\sin\left(3t + \frac{3\pi}{4}\right) - 5$ is $-11 \le y \le 1$.

23. (C) **Number and Quantity**

There are 12 months in 1 year. Convert z years to $12z$ months. Define p as the number of cars that the car factory produce in $12z$ months. Set up a proportion in terms of cars and months.

$$\begin{aligned} x_{\text{cars}} : y_{\text{months}} &= p_{\text{cars}} : 12z_{\text{months}} \\ \frac{x}{y} &= \frac{p}{12z} && \text{Use cross product property} \\ py &= 12xz \\ p &= \frac{12xz}{y} \end{aligned}$$

Therefore, the number of cars that the car factory produce in z years is $\frac{12xz}{y}$.

24. (D) **Algebra**

$$\frac{1}{2}x^3 - 1 = 0.6 \qquad \text{Add 1 to each side}$$
$$\frac{1}{2}x^3 = 1.6 \qquad \text{Multiply each side 2}$$
$$x^3 = 3.2 \qquad \text{Take the cube root of both sides}$$
$$x = \sqrt[3]{3.2} = 1.47$$

Therefore, the value of x for which $\frac{1}{2}x^3 - 1 = 0.6$ is 1.47.

25. (D) **Discrete Mathematics**

In order to evaluate the fifth term, we need to find the previous four terms as shown below.

$$a_{n+2} = a_{n+1} \cdot a_n,\ a_1 = 2, a_2 = 3 \qquad \text{Recursive formula with } a_1 = 2 \text{ and } a_2 = 3$$
$$a_3 = a_2 \cdot a_1 = 3(2) = 6 \qquad \text{Substitute 1 for } n \text{ to find } a_3$$
$$a_4 = a_3 \cdot a_2 = 6(3) = 18 \qquad \text{Substitute 2 for } n \text{ to find } a_4$$
$$a_5 = a_4 \cdot a_3 = 18(6) = 108 \qquad \text{Substitute 3 for } n \text{ to find } a_5$$

Since the fifth term of the sequence is 108, the factors of 108 are 1, 2, 3, 4, 6, 9, 12, 18, 27, 36, 54, and 108. Therefore, (D) is the correct answer.

26. (A, B, D) **Calculus**

a	$\lim_{x\to a^-} f(x)$	$\lim_{x\to a^+} f(x)$	$f(a)$
1	2	2	3
2	$-\infty$	∞	undefined
3	1	1	1
4	∞	∞	undefined

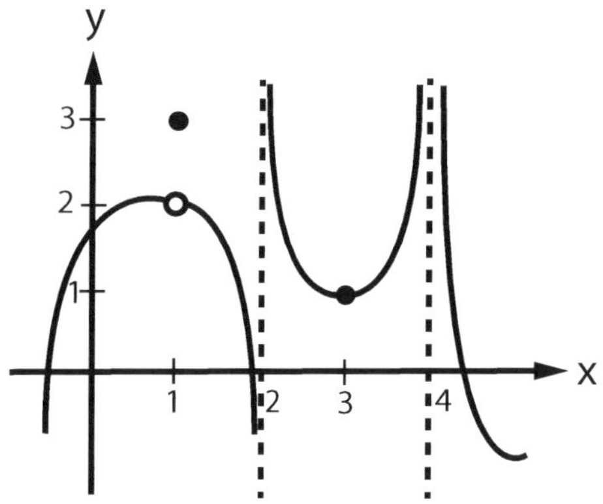

The graph of f is shown above. The function f has a hole at $x = 1$, and has vertical asymptotes at $x = 2$ and $x = 4$. f is continuous at $x = 3$. Therefore, (A), (B), and (D) are correct answers.

27. (C) **Algebra**

Multiply each side by $(x-1)(2x-1)$, and find the value for A.

$$(x-1)(2x-1)\cdot\frac{4x-1}{(x-1)(2x-1)}=\left(\frac{A}{x-1}-\frac{2}{2x-1}\right)(x-1)(2x-1)$$
$$4x-1=A(2x-1)-2(x-1)$$
$$4x-1=2Ax-A-2x+2$$
$$4x-1=(2A-2)x-A+2$$

Since the equation $4x-1=(2A-2)x-A+2$ is an identity equation, the coefficients of x on each side of the equation must be the same; that is, $4=2A-2$. Therefore, the value of A is 3.

28. (D) **Algebra**

The point $(1,2)$ satisfies the system of inequalities shown below.

$$y>x^2 \implies 2>1^2 \quad \checkmark\text{(True)}$$
$$y<x+2 \implies 2<1+2 \quad \checkmark\text{(True)}$$

Therefore, (D) is the correct answer.

29. (B) **Probability and Statistics**

Tips

Median: The middle value of an ordered data set.

When the number of observation is

- **odd**: the median is $\left(\frac{n+1}{2}\right)$th data value.
- **even**: the median is the mean of $\left(\frac{n}{2}\right)$th and $\left(\frac{n}{2}+1\right)$th data values.

The number of math scores is 22. The 11th score is 84, and the 12th score is 88. The median is the mean of the 11th and 12th scores. Therefore, the median of the math scores in the class is $\frac{84+88}{2}=86$.

30. (A) **Number and Quantity**

	Jan.	Feb.	Mar.	With 8% tax
Price	$\$n$	$\$1.25n$	$\$1.25(0.8)n=\$n$	$1.08n$

Therefore, the amount that you would pay for the jacket in March, including 8% sales tax is $1.08n$ dollars.

31. ($\frac{3}{4}$) **Probability and Statistics**

Tips **Complement rule for Probability**: Two events are **complementary** if exactly one of the events must occur. If A is an event, then A' is the complementary event of A, or 'not A'.

$$P(A') = 1 - P(A)$$

Use the complement rule for probability. Define event 1 and event 2 as selecting a number from the first and second die, respectively. There are six outcomes from each event. Thus, the total number of outcomes for event 1 and event 2 is $6 \times 6 = 36$. Define event 3 and event 4 as selecting an odd number from the first and second die, respectively. There are three outcomes from each event: 1, 3, and 5. Thus, the total number of outcomes for event 3 and event 4 is $3 \times 3 = 9$. Thus,

$$\begin{aligned}\text{Probability that the product is even} &= 1 - \text{Probability that the product is odd}\\ &= 1 - \frac{9}{36}\\ &= \frac{3}{4}\end{aligned}$$

Therefore, the probability that the product of the two numbers is even is $\frac{3}{4}$.

32. (A) **Geometry**

Tips The perpendicular bisector of a line segment is the set of all points that are equidistant from its endpoints.

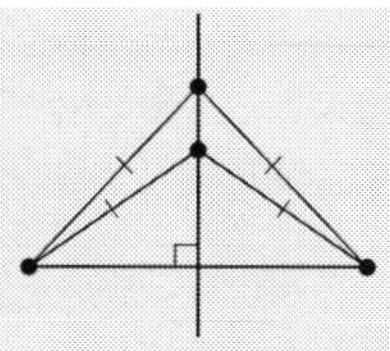

Draw a line segment that connects the two points in the xy-plane. The set of all points that are equidistant from the two points is the perpendicular bisector of the line segment. Since the perpendicular bisector of the line segment is a line, (A) is the correct answer.

33. (B) **Calculus**

Tips If the slope of the tangent line is $f'(a)$, and the point of tangency is $(a, f(a))$, the equation of the tangent line is given by

$$y - f(a) = f'(a)(x - a)$$

$f(x) = \sqrt[3]{x-2} = (x-2)^{\frac{1}{3}}$.

$$\begin{aligned}f'(x) &= \frac{1}{3}(x-2)^{-\frac{2}{3}} = \frac{1}{3\sqrt[3]{(x-2)^2}}\\ f'(1) &= \frac{1}{3\sqrt[3]{(1-2)^2}} = \frac{1}{3}\end{aligned}$$

Therefore, the equation of the line tangent to the graph of $y = \sqrt[3]{x-2}$ at the point $(1, -1)$ is $y - (-1) = \frac{1}{3}(x-1)$ or $y = \frac{1}{3}x - \frac{4}{3}$.

34. (C) **Trigonometry**

$f(x) = \cos 2x$, and $g(x) = \dfrac{x}{x^2+1}$. $f\left(\dfrac{\pi}{6}\right) = \cos 2\left(\dfrac{\pi}{6}\right) = \cos\dfrac{\pi}{3} = 0.5.$

$$g\left(f\left(\frac{\pi}{6}\right)\right) = g(0.5) = \frac{0.5}{(0.5)^2+1} = 0.4$$

35. (D) **Trigonometry**

Let x be the height of the lamp post as shown below.

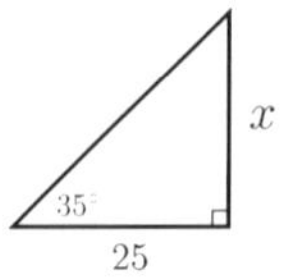

Since the lamp casts a shadow of 25 feet when the sun makes a 35° angle of elevation, use the definition of the tangent function to find the height of the lamp post.

$$\tan 35^\circ = \frac{x}{25} \quad \Longrightarrow \quad x = 25\tan 35^\circ = 17.5$$

Therefore, the height of the lamp post is 17.5 feet.

36. (D) **Geometry**

For simplicity, let's choose two points, A and B, in the first quadrant: $A(1,1)$ and $B(3,4)$. Thus, the slope of the line that passes through point A and point B is $\frac{3}{2}$. If points A and B are reflected about the y-axis, they become A' and B' and their x- and y- coordinates are $A'(-1,1)$ and $B'(-3,4)$, respectively.

$$\text{Slope of new line} = \frac{4-1}{-3-(-1)} = \frac{3}{-2} = -\frac{3}{2}$$

Therefore, the slope of the new line that passes through points A' and B' is $-\frac{3}{2}$.

37. (C) **Geometry**

The surface area of the prism equals the sum of the areas of the five faces: top, bottom, front, right and left.

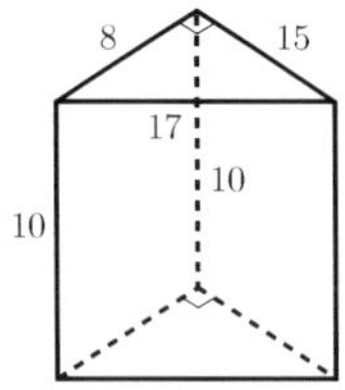

To find the length of the missing side of the triangle on the top and bottom face of the prism, use the Pythagorean theorem: $C^2 - 8^2 + 15^2$ or the Pythagorean triple: $8 - 15 - 17$. Thus, the length of the missing side of the triangle is 17.

$$\text{Surface Area} = \text{top}+\text{bottom}+\text{front}+\text{right}+\text{left} = 60 + 60 + 170 + 150 + 80 = 520$$

Therefore, the surface area of the triangular prism is 520.

38. (D) **Geometry**

$\triangle ABC$ and $\triangle ADE$ are similar triangle as shown below.

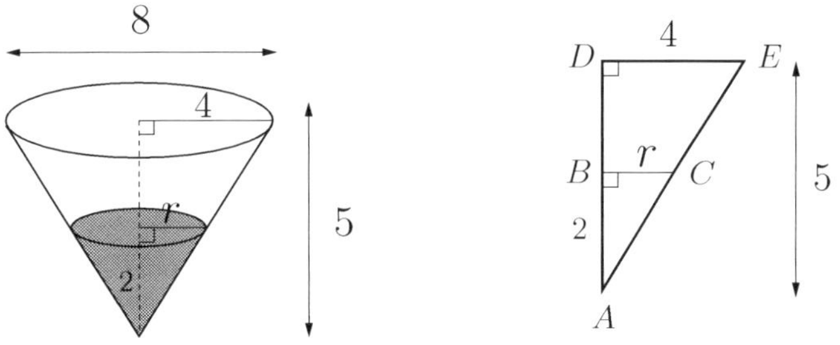

Set up a proportion to find the radius of the surface of the water.

$$\frac{r}{2} = \frac{4}{5} \quad \Longrightarrow \quad r = \frac{8}{5}$$

Therefore, the radius of the surface of the water is $\frac{8}{5}$ feet.

39. (D) **Algebra**

Since y varies directly with the cube of x and inversely with the square root of z, start with $y = \frac{kx^3}{\sqrt{z}}$. Substitute 2 for x, 16 for z, and 6 for y to find the value of k.

$$y = \frac{kx^3}{\sqrt{z}} \qquad \text{Substitute 2 for } x\text{, 16 for } z\text{, and 6 for } y$$

$$6 = \frac{8k}{4} \qquad \text{Solve for } k$$

$$k = 3$$

Thus, the equation that relates x, y, and z is $y = \frac{3x^3}{\sqrt{z}}$. Substitute $\frac{1}{3}$ for x, and $\frac{1}{4}$ for z to find the value of y.

$$y = \frac{3x^3}{\sqrt{z}} \qquad \text{Substitute } \frac{1}{3} \text{ for } x \text{ and } \frac{1}{4} \text{ for } z$$

$$y = \frac{3\left(\frac{1}{3}\right)^3}{\sqrt{\frac{1}{4}}} \qquad \text{Solve for } y$$

$$y = \frac{\frac{1}{9}}{\frac{1}{2}}$$

$$y = \frac{2}{9}$$

Therefore, the value of y when $x = \frac{1}{3}$ and $z = \frac{1}{4}$ is $\frac{2}{9}$.

40. (C) **Probability and Statistics**

A manufacturing company found out that 3% of their production was defective, which means that the probability that each light bulb you have purchased is NOT defective is $1 - 0.03$ or 0.97. Since you have purchased five light bulbs, the probability that none of them are defective is $(0.97)^5 = 0.86$.

41. (A, B, C) **Geometry**

An isometry is a transformation that preserves length, angle measures, parallel lines, and distance between points. Only reflection, rotation, and translation are isometries. Therefore, (A), (B), and (C) are correct answers.

42. (C) **Algebra**

Tips: Factor Theorem: If $x - k$ is a factor of $f(x)$, then the remainder $r = f(k) = 0$.

Since $f(2) = (2)^3 - 3(2)^2 + 4(2) - 4 = 0$, $x - 2$ is a factor of $f(x) = x^3 - 3x^2 + 4x - 4$. Therefore, (C) is the correct answer.

43. (D) **Number and Quantity**

Tips:

1. $i^2 = -1$
2. $(a + bi)(a - bi) = a^2 - bi^2 = a^2 + b^2$
3. In order to rationalize the denominator, multiply the numerator and the denominator by the denominator's conjugate. For instance,

$$\frac{1}{a+bi} = \frac{1}{(a+bi)} \cdot \frac{(a-bi)}{(a-bi)} = \frac{a-bi}{a^2+b^2}$$

$$\frac{3-4i}{2-3i} = \frac{(3-4i)}{(2-3i)} \cdot \frac{(2+3i)}{(2+3i)} = \frac{18+i}{13} = \frac{18}{13} + \frac{i}{13}$$

Therefore, (D) is the correct answer.

44. (B) **Functions**

Tips:

1. $\log_a a = 1$
2. $\log_a xy = \log_a x + \log_a y$

$$\begin{aligned} \log_2 30 &= \log_2(2 \cdot 3 \cdot 5) \\ &= \log_2 2 + \log_2 3 + \log_2 5 \\ &= 1 + m + n \end{aligned}$$

Therefore, $\log_2 30$ in terms of m and n is $m + n + 1$.

45. (10) **Geometry**
In the figure below, the circle whose center is $(0, 6)$ touches the x-axis. This means that the radius of the circle is 6. Since $\overline{AO}$ is the radius, $AO = 6$.

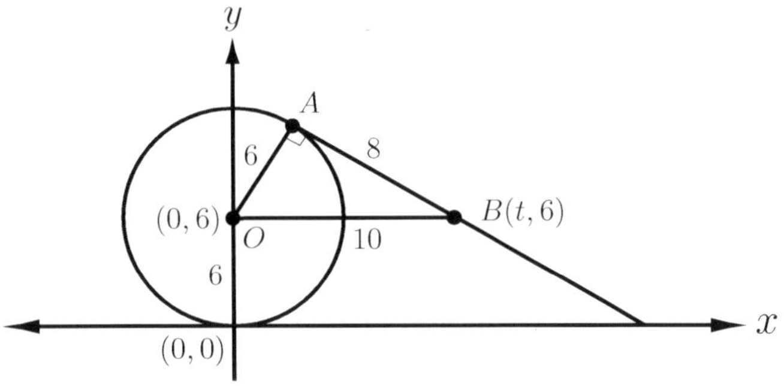

$\overline{BA}$ is tangent to the circle at A. Since a tangent line is perpendicular to the radius drawn to the point of tangency, $\overline{BA} \perp \overline{AO}$. Thus, $\triangle BAO$ is a right triangle with $AO = 6$ and $AB = 8$. To find the length of the hypotenuse of the right triangle, BO, use the Pythagorean theorem: $C^2 = 6^2 + 8^2$ or a multiple of the Pythagorean triple: $(3 - 4 - 5) \times 2 = 6 - 8 - 10$. Thus, $BO = 10$. Point B is 10 units from the point O horizontally. Therefore, the x-coordinate of point B, or t is 10.

46. (D) **Number and Quantity**

Joshua has m liters of a 10% acid solution, and n liters of a 30% acid solution. If he mixes these solutions up, he will make 100 liters of a 15% acid solution. Thus, $m + n = 100$ or $n = 100 - m$.

	Liters	Amount of acid
10% solution	m	$0.1m$
30% solution	$100 - m$	$0.3(100 - m)$
15% solution	100	$0.15(100) = 15$

Let's set up an equation in terms of amount of acid and solve for m.

$$\begin{aligned} 0.1m + 0.3(100 - m) &= 0.15(100) \\ 0.1m + 30 - 0.3m &= 15 \\ -0.2m &= -15 \\ m &= 75 \end{aligned}$$

Since $m = 75$, $n = 100 - m = 25$. Therefore, the value of $m - n$ is $75 - 25 = 50$.

47. (D) **Number and Quantity**

The units digits of powers of 7, and powers of 2 are shown below.

$$\begin{array}{ll} 7^1 = 7, & 2^1 = 2 \\ 7^2 = 9, & 2^2 = 4 \\ 7^3 = 3, & 2^3 = 8 \\ 7^4 = 1, & 2^4 = 6 \\ 7^5 = 7, & 2^5 = 2 \\ \vdots & \vdots \end{array}$$

The units digits of powers of 7 are 7, 9, 3, and 1, and they are repeating. The units digits of powers of 2 are 2, 4, 8, and 6, and they are repeating. Thus,

$$\begin{aligned} \text{Units digit of } 7^{1002} &= \text{units digit of } 7^2 = 9 \\ \text{Units digit of } 2^{1002} &= \text{units digit of } 2^2 = 4 \end{aligned}$$

Therefore, the units digit of $7^{1002} - 2^{1002}$ is $9 - 4 = 5$.

48. (D) **Calculus**

Tips

1. $\arctan x = \tan^{-1} x$.
2. If $f(x) = \tan^{-1} x$, $f'(x) = \dfrac{1}{1+x^2}$.
3. $f'(a) = \lim\limits_{h\to 0} \dfrac{f(a+h) - f(a)}{h}$.

The expression $\lim\limits_{h\to 0} \dfrac{\arctan(a+h) - \arctan(a)}{h}$ means that the slope of the tangent line to the graph of $\tan^{-1} x$ at $x = a$. Thus,

$$\begin{aligned} \lim_{h\to 0} \frac{\arctan(a+h) - \arctan(a)}{h} &= \frac{1}{4} \\ (\tan^{-1} x)'(a) &= \frac{1}{4} \\ \frac{1}{1+a^2} &= \frac{1}{4} \\ 1 + a^2 &= 4 \\ a = -\sqrt{3} \text{ or } a &= \sqrt{3} \end{aligned}$$

Therefore, (D) is the correct answer.

49. (25) **Number and Quantity**

Define x as the number of games the pitcher played before the next five games. Since the pitcher has won 60% of the games he pitched, the number of games he has won can be expressed as $0.6x$. For the next five games, the pitcher won 2 games. Thus, the total number of games he has won can be expressed as $0.6x+2$. Furthermore, the pitcher won 2 games and lost 3 so that he finished the season having won 56% of his games. Thus, the total number of games he has won also can be expressed as $0.56(x+5)$. Set $0.6x+2$ and $0.56(x+5)$ equal to each other and solve for x.

$$\begin{aligned} 0.6x+2 &= 0.56(x+5) \\ 0.6x+2 &= 0.56x+2.8 \\ 0.04x &= 0.8 \\ x &= 20 \end{aligned}$$

Therefore, the total number of games that the pitcher played in all is $x+5=25$.

50. (B) **Geometry**

In order to have a general equation of a hyperbola $\frac{(x-h)^2}{a^2}-\frac{(y-k)^2}{b^2}=1$, divide each side of the equation $16x^2-9y^2=144$ by 144. Thus, $\dfrac{x^2}{3^2}-\dfrac{y^2}{4^2}=1$. The graph of the hyperbola is shown below.

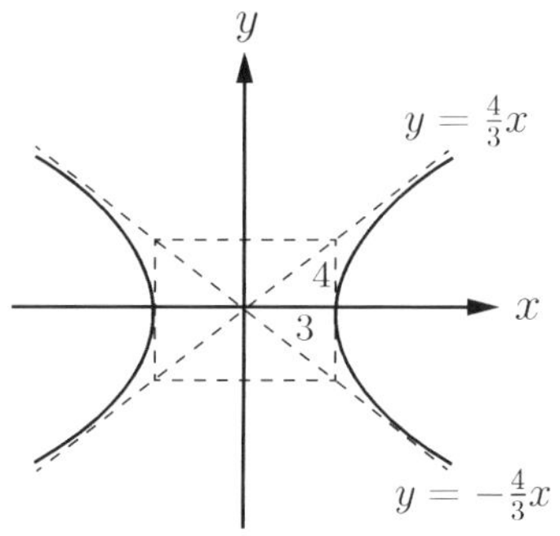

Since the slopes of the asymptotes are $\pm\frac{4}{3}$ and the asymptotes pass through the center $(0,0)$, the equations of the asymptotes are $y=\pm\frac{4}{3}x$.

51. (A) **Geometry**

50 cm is $\frac{1}{2}$ meter. If a cube is placed inside the tank, the water level of the tank will rise by the volume of the cube. Let h be the number of meters that the water level rises. Thus,

$$\begin{aligned} 2\times 2\times h &= \frac{1}{2}\times\frac{1}{2}\times\frac{1}{2} \\ h &= \frac{\frac{1}{8}}{4} \\ &= \frac{1}{32} \end{aligned}$$

Therefore, the water level rises $\frac{1}{32}$ meter.

52. (C) **Calculus**

Tips

1. Average Value of a Function: If f is continuous on $[a, b]$, then there exists a number called **average value of f** in $[a, b]$ such that

$$f_{ave} = \frac{1}{b-a}\int_a^b f(x)\,dx$$

2. $1 + \tan^2 x = \sec^2 x$ or $\tan^2 x = \sec^2 x - 1$.

$$\int_a^b \tan^2 x\,dx = \int_a^b \sec^2 x - 1\,dx = \tan x - x + c$$

With $a = 0$ and $b = \frac{\pi}{4}$,

$$\begin{aligned} f_{ave} &= \frac{1}{b-a}\int_a^b f(x)\,dx = \frac{1}{\frac{\pi}{4}-0}\int_0^{\frac{\pi}{4}} \tan^2 x\,dx \\ &= \frac{4}{\pi}\int_0^{\frac{\pi}{4}} \sec^2 x - 1\,dx = \frac{4}{\pi}\Big[\tan x - x\Big]_0^{\frac{\pi}{4}} \\ &= \frac{4}{\pi}\left(\tan\frac{\pi}{4} - \frac{\pi}{4}\right) = \frac{4}{\pi}\left(1 - \frac{\pi}{4}\right) = \frac{4}{\pi} - 1 \end{aligned}$$

Therefore, the average value of $\tan^2 x$ over the interval $\left[0, \dfrac{\pi}{4}\right]$ is $\frac{4}{\pi} - 1$.

53. (A) **Number and Quantity**

Tips

1. $(a^m)^n = a^{mn}$
2. If $a^x = a^y$, then $x = y$

$x^a = y^b$, and $y^c = x^d$. Let's solve for y from each equation.

$$\begin{aligned} x^a &= y^b, \\ (x^a)^{\frac{1}{b}} &= (y^b)^{\frac{1}{b}}, \\ x^{\frac{a}{b}} &= y, \end{aligned} \qquad\qquad \begin{aligned} y^c &= x^d \\ (y^c)^{\frac{1}{c}} &= (x^d)^{\frac{1}{c}} \\ y &= x^{\frac{d}{c}} \end{aligned}$$

$x^{\frac{a}{b}} = y = x^{\frac{d}{c}}$. So $x^{\frac{a}{b}} = x^{\frac{d}{c}}$, which implies that $\frac{a}{b} = \frac{d}{c}$ or $a = \frac{bd}{c}$. Therefore, (A) is the correct answer.

54. (D) **Number and Quantity**

The amount of money that the company charged a customer who used 800 minutes in October would be $\$13.5 + \$0.015(800) = \$25.5$. The company charged the customer \$26.75, which means that the customer used more than 800 minutes. Since the company charges 2.5 cents per minute after the first 800 minutes used, the customer used $\dfrac{26.75 - 25.5}{0.025} = 50$ minutes after 800 minutes. Therefore, the total number of minutes that the customer used was $800 + 50 = 850$ minutes.

55. (C) **Number and Quantity**

$$\frac{7p+2q}{p+q} = 4 \qquad \text{Multiply each side by } p+q$$
$$7p + 2q = 4p + 4q \qquad \text{Subtract } 2q \text{ and } 4p \text{ from each side}$$
$$3p = 2q$$
$$\frac{p}{q} = \frac{2}{3}$$

Therefore, the value of $\frac{p}{q}$ is $\frac{2}{3}$.

56. (D) **Functions**

The vertex of the absolute value function $f(x) = -|x-1| - 3$ is $(1, -3)$ as shown below.

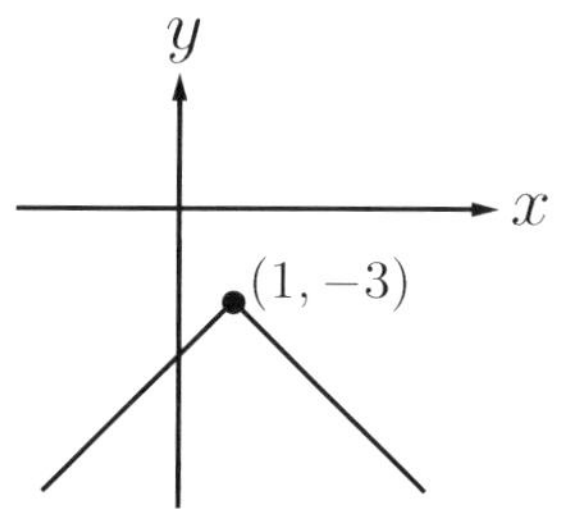

Since the graph of f never touches or crosses the x-axis, there is no x-intercept.

57. $(\frac{5}{3})$ **Trigonometry**

Tips

1. $(a+b)^2 = a^2 + 2ab + b^2$
2. $\cos^2\theta + \sin^2\theta = 1$
3. $\sin 2\theta = 2\sin\theta\cos\theta$

$$\begin{aligned}(\sin\theta + \cos\theta)^2 &= \sin^2\theta + 2\sin\theta\cos\theta + \cos^2\theta \\ &= 1 + 2\sin\theta\cos\theta \\ &= 1 + \sin 2\theta \\ &= 1 + \frac{2}{3} \\ &= \frac{5}{3}\end{aligned}$$

58. (D) **Trigonometry**

Tips

1. $\csc^2 x = \dfrac{1}{\sin^2 x}$
2. $\sin^2 x + \cos^2 x = 1 \implies \sin^2 x = 1 - \cos^2 x$

$$\csc^2 x(1 - \cos^2 x) = \frac{1}{\sin^2 x} \cdot \sin^2 x = 1$$

Therefore, (D) is the correct answer.

59. (D) **Calculus**

Tips

The Mean Value Theorem

Let f be a function that satisfies the following hypotheses:

- f is continuous on the closed interval $[a, b]$.
- f is differentiable on the open interval (a, b).

Then there is a c in (a, b) such that $f'(c) = \dfrac{f(b) - f(a)}{b - a}$.

The function f is continuous on the closed interval $[1, 4]$, and is differential on the open interval $(1, 4)$. According to the Mean value theorem,

$$f'(c) = \frac{f(b) - f(a)}{b - a} = \frac{5 - (-2)}{4 - 1} = \frac{7}{3}$$

Therefore, the slope of the tangent line to the graph of f at $x = c$ is $f'(c) = \frac{7}{3}$.

60. (B) **Discrete Mathematics**

Tips

The number of permutations of n objects, where there are n_1 indistinguishable objects of one kind, and n_2 indistinguishable objects of a second kind, is given by

$$\text{Permutations with repetition} = \frac{n!}{n_1! \cdot n_2!}$$

The word SOLOMON has 7 letters. Since the letters S, O, L, M, and N are distinguishable, the order is important. However, there are 3 O's out of 7 letters. Thus,

$$\text{Permutations with repetition} = \frac{7!}{3!} = \frac{7 \cdot 6 \cdot 5 \cdot 4 \cdot \cancel{3!}}{\cancel{3!}} = 840$$

Therefore, the number of different arrangements that can be formed using the letters in word SOLOMON is 840.

PRAXIS II 5161 PRACTICE TEST 3

Time — 150 minutes
Number of questions — 60

Directions: Solve each of the following problems using the available space for scratch work. Choose the best answer among the answer choices given and fill in the corresponding circle on the answer sheet.

1. What is the sum of the two x-intercepts of the quadratic function $f(x) = (2x-3)(2x+1)$?

   (A) -2

   (B) -1

   (C) $-\frac{1}{2}$

   (D) 1

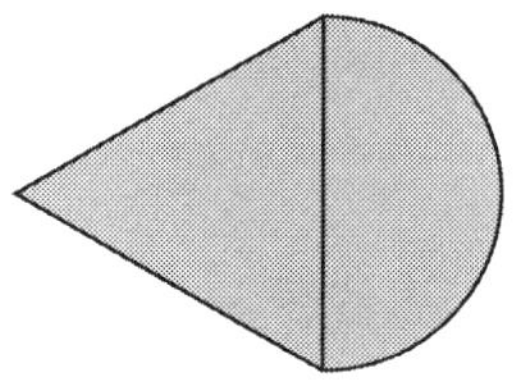

2. The figure above consists of an equilateral triangle and a semicircle. If the diameter of the semicircle is 8, what is the perimeter of the shaded area?

   (A) $8+4\pi$

   (B) $12+8\pi$

   (C) $16+4\pi$

   (D) $16+8\pi$

Time	Average Speed
9 am to 10 am	50 miles per hour
10 am to 11:30 am	60 miles per hour
11:30 am to 12:00pm	Break
12:00 pm to 4:00 pm	55 miles per hour

3. According to the chart above, what is the total distance that Mr. Rhee traveled between 9 am to 4 pm?

   (A) 240 miles

   (B) 280 miles

   (C) 320 miles

   (D) 360 miles

4. There are two red marbles and a certain number of green and blue marbles in a bag. If the probability of selecting a red marble is $\frac{1}{6}$, how many non-red marbles are in the bag?

   (A) 8

   (B) 10

   (C) 12

   (D) 14

5. If $5^{y+1} = \left(\frac{1}{5}\right)^{2y-2}$, what is the value of y ?

(A) $\frac{1}{3}$

(B) $\frac{1}{2}$

(C) $\frac{2}{3}$

(D) $\frac{3}{4}$

For the following question, enter your answer in the answer box.

6. If you toss a coin three times, what is the probability that two heads will be shown?

Give your answer as a fraction.

7. Which of the following measures in radians is equal to $105°$?

(A) $\frac{2\pi}{3}$

(B) $\frac{5\pi}{12}$

(C) $\frac{3\pi}{4}$

(D) $\frac{7\pi}{12}$

For the following question, select all the answer choices that apply.

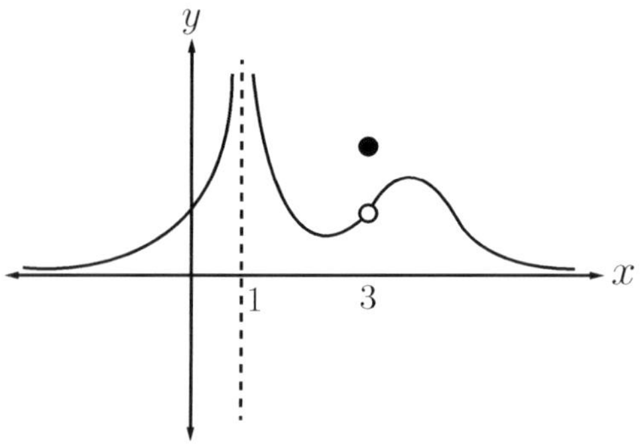

Graph of f

8. The graph of the function f is shown above. Which of the following statements are true?

Select all that apply.

(A) $\lim_{x\to 1} f(x)$ exists

(B) $\lim_{x\to 3^-} f(x) = \lim_{x\to 3^+} f(x) = f(3)$

(C) $\lim_{x\to \infty} f(x) = 0$

9. If $f(x) = x\sqrt{x} - 3x^{-1} + 5$, what is the value of $f'(1)$?

(A) $\frac{3}{2}$

(B) $\frac{5}{2}$

(C) $\frac{7}{2}$

(D) $\frac{9}{2}$

10. The equation $x^2 + y^2 + 4x - 2y - 3 = 0$ represents a circle. What is the center of the circle?

(A) $(-2, -1)$

(B) $(-2, 1)$

(C) $(2, -1)$

(D) $(2, 1)$

11. A number is selected at random from the first ten positive integers. What is the probability that the selected number is a prime, given that the selected number is an odd number?

(A) $\frac{1}{3}$

(B) $\frac{2}{5}$

(C) $\frac{3}{5}$

(D) $\frac{2}{3}$

12. A statistician asked a random sample of 187 U.S. adults whether they own a tablet computer. Of the respondents, 79 said "Yes." The statistician used the sample to estimate the total number of U.S. adults who own a tablet computer. If the population of U.S. adults is 192 million, which of the following best approximates the total number of U.S. adults who own a tablet computer?

(A) 75 million

(B) 77 million

(C) 79 million

(D) 81 million

13. $\int \frac{x^3 + 2x + 1}{x}\, dx =$

(A) $\frac{1}{3}x^3 + 2\ln|x+1| + C$

(B) $\frac{1}{3}x^3 + 2x + \ln|x| + C$

(C) $\frac{1}{4}x^4 + x^2 + x + C$

(D) $\frac{1}{4}x^4 + x^2 + \ln|x-1| + C$

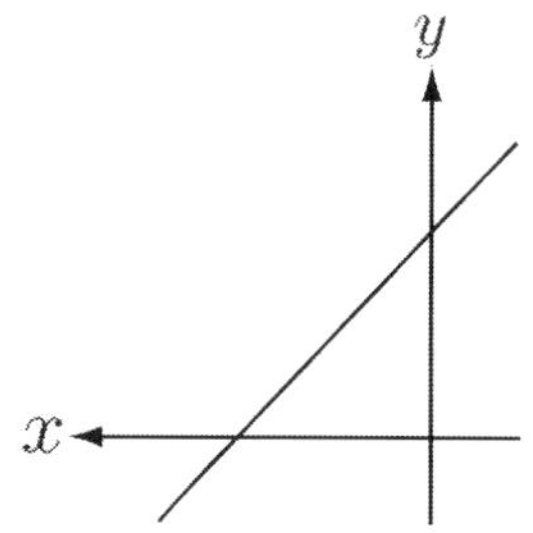

14. The graph above shows the graph of $y = 5x + 6$. If the line is shifted right 2 units and down 1 unit, what is the equation of the new line?

(A) $y = 3x + 5$

(B) $y = 3x - 5$

(C) $y = 5x + 1$

(D) $y = 5x - 5$

For the following question, enter your answer in the answer box.

$$xz + yz - 12z = 0$$

15. If $z > 0$, what is the value of $x + y$?

$x + y =$ [ ]

16. The lengths of the three sides of a triangle are 4, 5, and n. What is the largest possible integer value of n ?

(A) 7

(B) 8

(C) 9

(D) 10

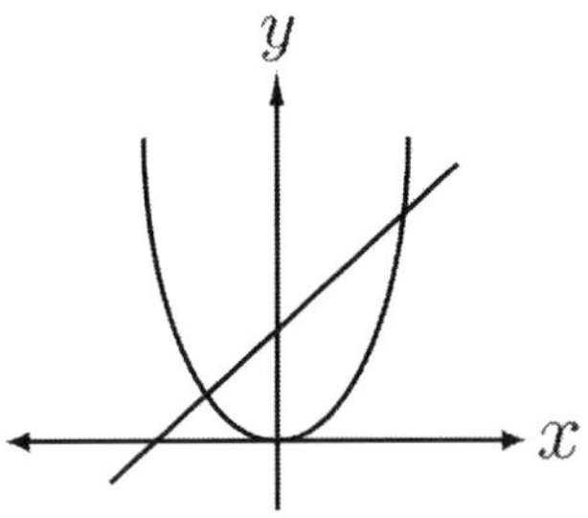

Note: Figure not drawn to scale.

17. In the graph above, a line $y = 3x + 4$ intersects a parabola $y = x^2$. What are the x-coordinates of the two intersection points?

(A) $x = -2$ or $x = 3$

(B) $x = -2$ or $x = 4$

(C) $x = -1$ or $x = 3$

(D) $x = -1$ or $x = 4$

18. Which of the following is the slope of the tangent line to the graph of $y = \sin x \cos x$ at $x = \dfrac{\pi}{12}$?

(A) $\dfrac{\sqrt{3}}{2}$

(B) $\dfrac{\sqrt{2}}{2}$

(C) $\dfrac{1}{2}$

(D) 0

19. If $f(x) = -x^2 + 1$, which of the following expression is equal to $f(x + h) - f(x)$?

(A) $-2xh - h^2$

(B) $-2xh + h^2$

(C) $2xh - h^2$

(D) $2xh + h^2$

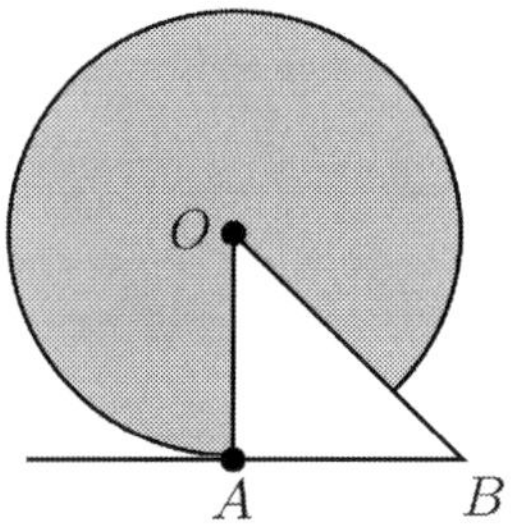

20. In the figure above, circle O is tangent to a line at point A and $\triangle OAB$ is an isosceles right triangle. If $AB = 4$, what is the area of the shaded region?

(A) 10π

(B) 12π

(C) 14π

(D) 16π

For the following question, enter your answer in the answer box.

21. Ten cards, each labeled with a number from 1 through 10, are in a bag. What is the smallest number of cards you need to select so that at least one prime number is guaranteed among the selected cards?

22. A number N of bacteria is defined by the function $N(t) = N_0 e^{0.35t}$, where N_0 is the initial number of bacteria, and t is a time in hours. If the initial number of bacteria is 100, what is the number of bacteria after 90 minutes?

(A) 135

(B) 142

(C) 169

(D) 197

23. A Statistic professor announced a review session to be held the day before a test. He listed the students who attended the session and compared their scores to the remaining student's scores. This is an example of which of the following study?

(A) Observational

(B) Experimental

(C) Explanatory

(D) Dependent

24. Which of the following quadratic function has a zero of $2 - \sqrt{3}$?

(A) $x^2 - 2x - 1$

(B) $x^2 + 2x - 3$

(C) $x^2 + 4x + 3$

(D) $x^2 - 4x + 1$

For the following question, select all the answer choices that apply.

25. Which of the following lines are the asymptotes of the rational function $y = \dfrac{x-2}{x^2-4}$?

Select all that apply.

(A) $x = -2$

(B) $x = 2$

(C) $y = -2$

(D) $y = 0$

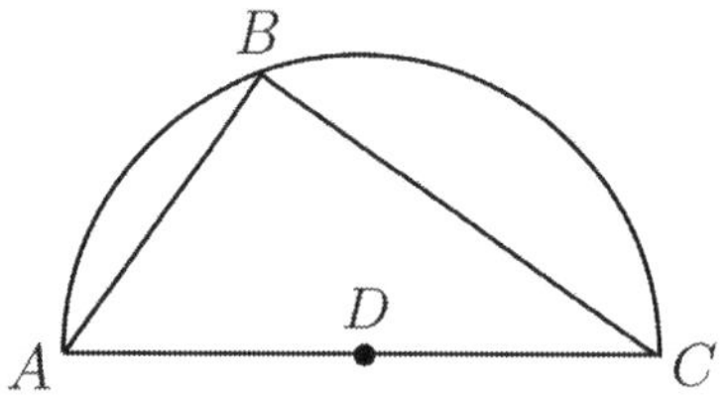

26. In the figure above, $\triangle ABC$ is inscribed in a semicircle whose center is D. The measure of $\angle A$ is twice the measure of $\angle C$. If $BC = 10\sqrt{3}$, what is $AB + AC$?

(A) 20

(B) $20 + 5\sqrt{2}$

(C) $20 + 5\sqrt{3}$

(D) 30

27. $\tan x + \cot x =$

(A) $\csc x \sec x$

(B) $\csc x \cos x$

(C) $\sin x \sec x$

(D) $\sin x \cos x$

28. Which of the following equation is perpendicular to the line that passes through the points $(-1, 1)$ and $(2, -5)$?

(A) $x + 2y = 6$

(B) $x - 2y = 6$

(C) $2x + y = -6$

(D) $2x - y = -6$

29. If f is the function with $f'(x) = x\sqrt{x-1}$, at what value of x does f have an inflection point?

(A) $\frac{1}{2}$

(B) $\frac{1}{3}$

(C) $\frac{2}{3}$

(D) Nonexistent

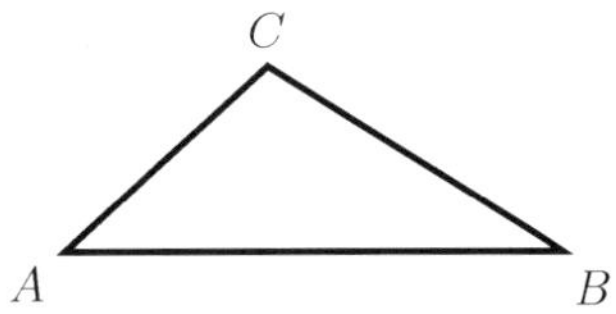

30. In $\triangle ABC$ above, $m\angle A = 64°$ and $m\angle B = 32°$. If $AC = 1$, what is BC ?

(A) 1.38

(B) 1.52

(C) 1.70

(D) 1.87

31. The weights of adult males are normally distributed with a mean of 172 pounds and a standard deviation of 15 pounds. Approximately what percent of weights of adult males is between 142 pounds and 187 pounds?

(A) 68%

(B) 81.5%

(C) 89.5%

(D) 95%

For the following question, enter your answer in the answer box.

32. If a sphere is inscribed in a cube, the ratio of the volume of the sphere to that of the cube is $\frac{\pi}{n}$. What is the value of n ?

$n =$ [ ]

33. Joshua can type m words in a seconds. Jason can type n words in b minutes. If both Joshua and Jason type together, how many words can they type in t minutes?

(A) $t(ma + bn)$

(B) $t\left(\frac{a}{60m} + \frac{b}{n}\right)$

(C) $t\left(\frac{m}{a} + \frac{n}{b}\right)$

(D) $t\left(\frac{60m}{a} + \frac{n}{b}\right)$

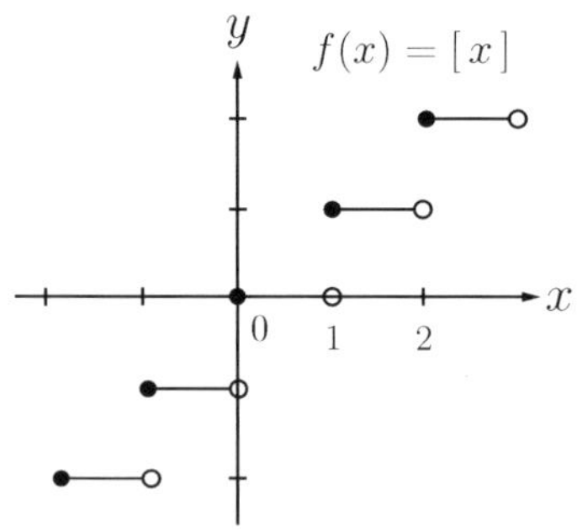

34. The greatest integer function $f(x) = [x]$ is the function that assigns each number to the greatest integer less than or equal to that number. If a part of the graph of f is shown above, what is the domain of f ?

(A) Integers

(B) Rational numbers

(C) Irrational numbers

(D) All real numbers

35. There are twenty nine questions on a math exam worth a total of one hundred points. Each question is worth either three points or four points. How many questions on the math exam are worth four points?

(A) 12

(B) 13

(C) 14

(D) 15

For the following question, enter your answer in the answer box.

36. What is the value of $\log_2 \sqrt{2} - \log_4 2 + \log_8 2$?

Give your answer as a fraction.

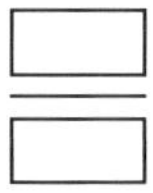

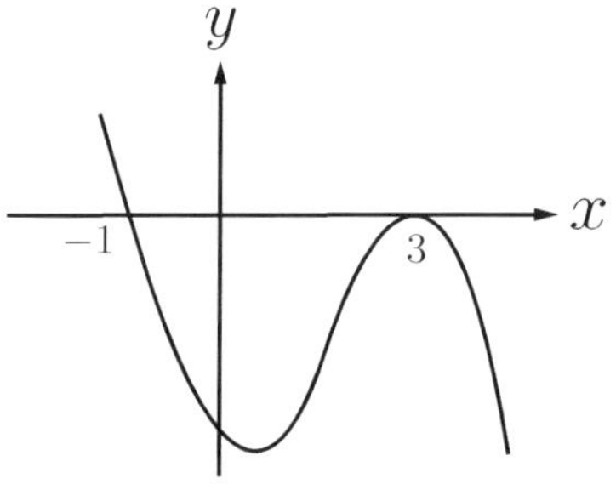

37. The graph above shows a cubic function whose zeros are −1 and 3. Which of the following cubic function best represents the graph?

(A) $(x+1)(x-1)(x-3)$

(B) $(x+1)^2(x-3)$

(C) $-(x+1)^2(x-3)$

(D) $-(x+1)(x-3)^2$

x	1	2	3	4	5	6	7
$f(x)$	42	38	35	36	40	42	45

38. The table above shows the selected values of a continuous function f on the closed interval $[1, 7]$. Which of the following could be the value of $\int_1^7 f(x)\,dx$ using a midpoint sum with three subintervals of equal length?

(A) 228

(B) 232

(C) 234

(D) 240

39. Which of the following set of numbers has the smallest standard deviation?

(A) $2, 6, 10, 14, 18$

(B) $4, 7, 10, 13, 16$

(C) $6, 8, 10, 12, 14$

(D) $8, 9, 10, 11, 12$

40. If $\sin\theta = \frac{3}{5}$, $\frac{\pi}{2} < \theta < \pi$, what is the value of $\cos 2\theta$?

(A) $-\frac{24}{25}$

(B) $-\frac{16}{25}$

(C) $\frac{7}{25}$

(D) $\frac{16}{25}$

41. The digits 1 through 4 are randomly arranged to make a four-digit number. What is the probability that the four-digit number is divisible by 4?

(A) $\frac{1}{6}$

(B) $\frac{1}{4}$

(C) $\frac{1}{3}$

(D) $\frac{2}{5}$

42. The region R is enclosed by the line $2x + 3y = 6$, the x-axis, and the y-axis. If the region R is rotated about the y-axis, what is the volume of the resulting solid?

(A) 4π

(B) 6π

(C) 8π

(D) 12π

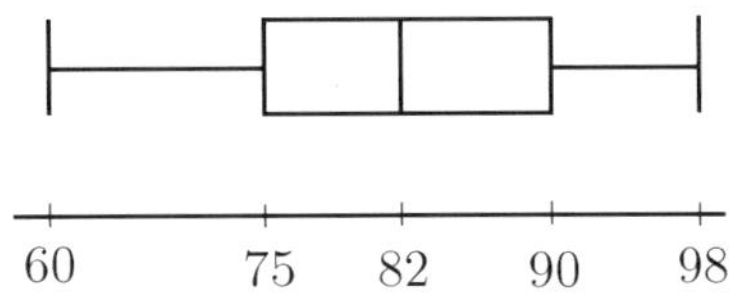

43. The box-and-whisker plot above shows the distribution of math scores in a class. The interquartile range (IQR) is upper quartile minus lower quartile. what is the interquartile range of the class?

(A) 38

(B) 26

(C) 15

(D) 12

For the following question, enter your answer in the answer box.

44. If the ratio of the three sides of a triangle is $5 : 5 : 8$, what is the largest angle of the triangle? (Round your answer to the nearest integer)

[ ] $^\circ$

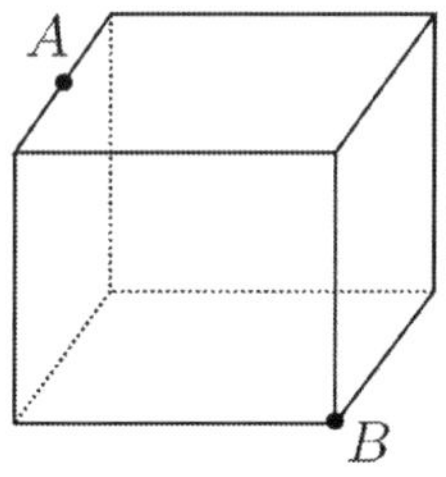

45. The cube shown above has a side length of 2. Point A is the midpoint of one side of the cube and point B is located at one vertex of the cube. If a segment is drawn from point A to point B, what is the length of $\overline{AB}$?

(A) 2

(B) 3

(C) $2\sqrt{2}$

(D) $2\sqrt{3}$

46. $\lim_{x \to 2^+} \frac{2x - 4}{|4 - 2x|} =$

(A) -1

(B) 0

(C) 1

(D) Nonexistent

47. Which of the following equation is equivalent to $\log_{3.72} x = 1.5$?

(A) $x = (3.72)^{1.5}$

(B) $x = (1.5)^{3.72}$

(C) $x = (10)^{3.72}$

(D) $x = (10)^{1.5}$

48. The two complex numbers $z_1 = 2y + (x+6)i$ and $z_2 = (3-x)+yi$ are equal. If $z_3 = x+yi$, what is the value of z_3 ?

(A) $6+3i$

(B) $3-3i$

(C) $-3+3i$

(D) $-3-3i$

49. Jason rolls two dice to form a two-digit integer. If the number on the first die represents the tens digit and the number on the second die represents the units digit, what is the probability that the integer formed is divisible by 8?

(A) $\frac{2}{9}$

(B) $\frac{7}{36}$

(C) $\frac{1}{6}$

(D) $\frac{5}{36}$

50. What is the period of $y = |\sin 2x|$?

(A) $\frac{\pi}{4}$

(B) $\frac{\pi}{2}$

(C) π

(D) 2π

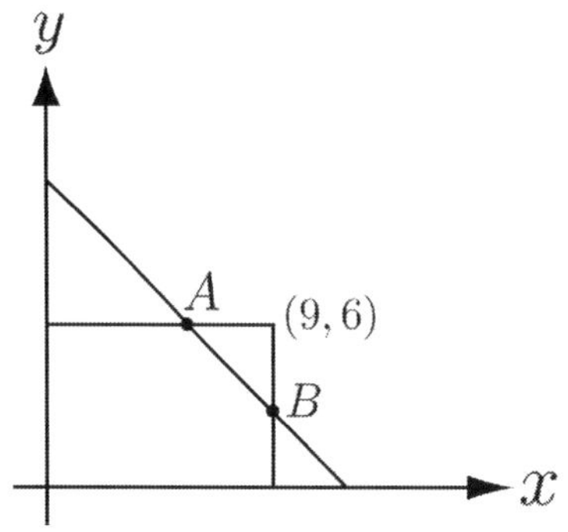

Note: Figure not drawn to scale.

51. In the figure above, two vertices of the rectangle are on the x-axis and the right upper corner of the rectangle is located at $(9,6)$. If the line $y = -\frac{4}{3}x+14$ intersects the rectangle at A and B, what is the length of $\overline{AB}$?

(A) $\sqrt{11}$

(B) $\sqrt{15}$

(C) 4

(D) 5

For the following question, enter your answer in the answer box.

52. What is the value of $\sum_{n=1}^{10}(-1)^n 2n$?

$\sum_{n=1}^{10}(-1)^n 2n =$ [ ]

53. $\dfrac{1}{x-3} - \dfrac{6}{x^2-9} =$

(A) $\dfrac{3-x}{x^2-9}$

(B) $\dfrac{x+9}{x^2-9}$

(C) $\dfrac{1}{x-3}$

(D) $\dfrac{1}{x+3}$

54. Which of the following rectangular equation is equivalent to $r = 3\csc\theta$?

(A) $y = 3$

(B) $x = 3$

(C) $x^2 + y^2 = 3$

(D) $x^2 + y^2 = 3x$

55. What is the area of a triangle with vertices $(2, 3)$, $(5, 7)$, and $(6, 5)$?

(A) 5

(B) 5.5

(C) 6

(D) 6.5

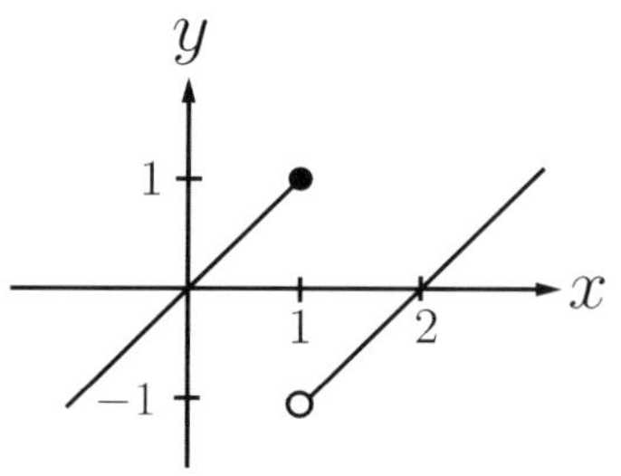

56. The graph of f is shown above. Which of the following graph represents $|f(x)|$?

(A)

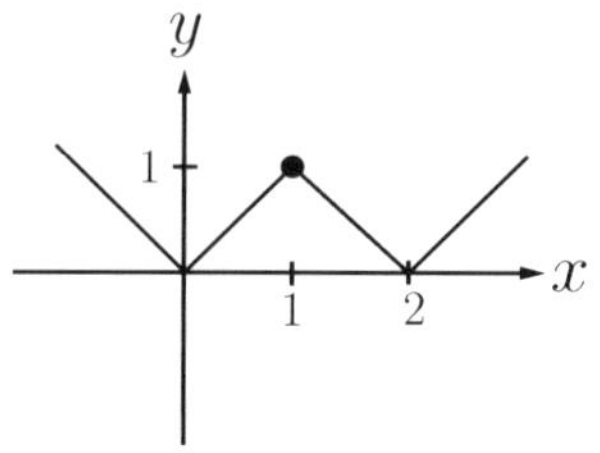

(B)

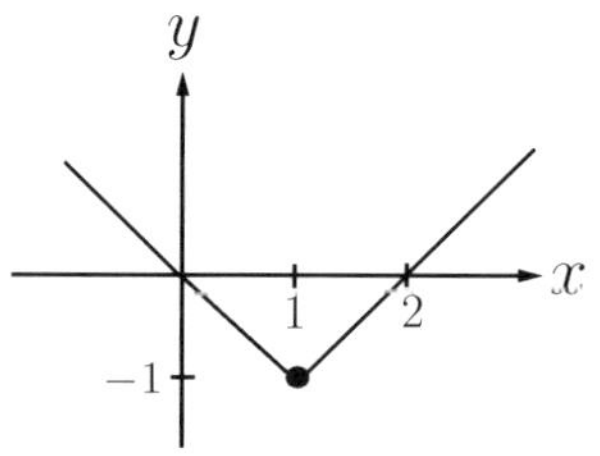

(C)

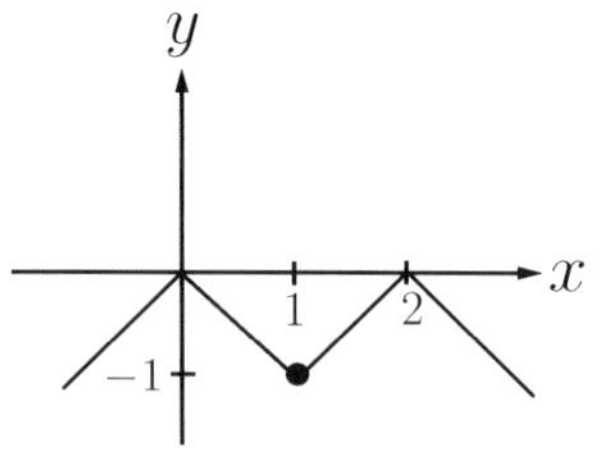

(D)

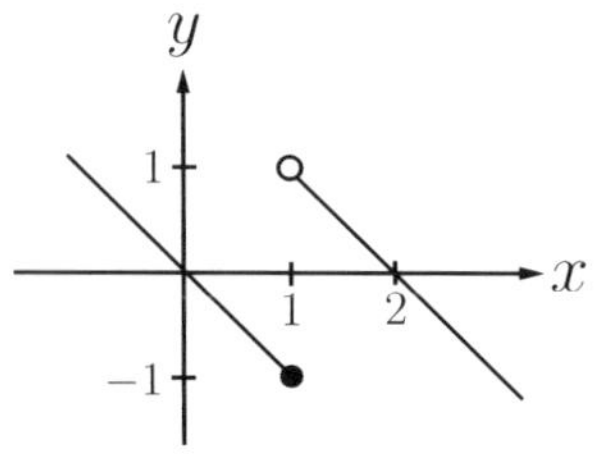

57. Let f be a differential function with $f'(x) > 0$ for all real numbers x. If g is the function defined by $g(x) = f(x^2 + 4x)$, on which of the following intervals is g decreasing?

(A) $(-\infty, -2)$

(B) $(-3, 2)$

(C) $(1, 4)$

(D) $(-1, 1)$ and $(2, \infty)$

58. From the equation of the ellipse $\frac{x^2}{a^2} + \frac{y^2}{b^2} = 1$, the area A of the ellipse can be determined by $A = \pi ab$. If an ellipse is defined by $16x^2 + 9y^2 = 144$, what is the area of the ellipse?

(A) 6π

(B) 12π

(C) 24π

(D) 48π

59. Solve: $x - 3 = \sqrt{2x - 3}$

(A) $x = -2$ only

(B) $x = 6$ only

(C) $x = -2$ and $x = 6$

(D) $x = 2$ and $x = -6$

60. An airplane flying horizontally at 600 mph at an altitude of 2 miles passes directly over a radar station. What is the rate at which the distance from the airplane and the station is increasing when it is 4 miles away from the station?

(A) $200\sqrt{2}$ mph

(B) $200\sqrt{3}$ mph

(C) $300\sqrt{2}$ mph

(D) $300\sqrt{3}$ mph

STOP

Answers and Solutions

PRAXIS II 5161 PRACTICE TEST 3

Answers

1. D	11. C	21. 7	31. B	41. B	51. D
2. C	12. D	22. C	32. 6	42. B	52. 10
3. D	13. B	23. A	33. D	43. C	53. D
4. B	14. D	24. D	34. D	44. 106	54. A
5. A	15. 12	25. A,D	35. B	45. B	55. A
6. $\frac{3}{8}$	16. B	26. D	36. $\frac{1}{3}$	46. C	56. A
7. D	17. D	27. A	37. D	47. A	57. A
8. C	18. A	28. B	38. B	48. C	58. B
9. D	19. A	29. C	39. D	49. D	59. B
10. B	20. C	30. C	40. C	50. B	60. D

Solutions

1. (D) **Algebra**

Substitute 0 for y, and solve for x.

$$y = (2x-3)(2x+1)$$
$$(2x-3)(2x+1) = 0$$
$$x = \frac{3}{2} \quad \text{or} \quad x = -\frac{1}{2}$$

Therefore, the sum of the x-intercepts of the quadratic function is $\frac{3}{2} + (-\frac{1}{2}) = 1$.

2. (C) **Geometry**

In the figure below, the diameter of the semicircle is 8. This means that the length of the side of the equilateral triangle is 8 and the radius of the semicircle is 4.

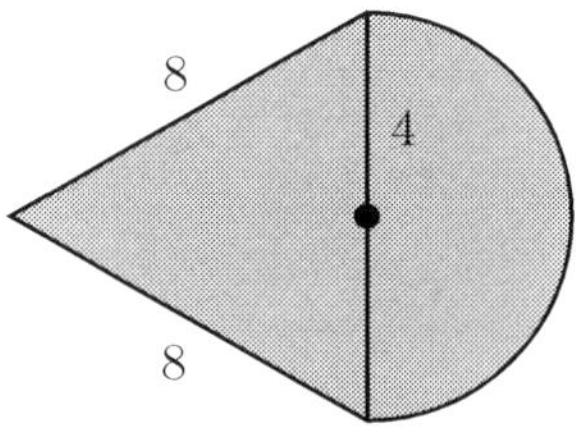

The perimeter is the distance around the figure. Since the diameter of the semicircle is inside the shaded region, it should be excluded from the perimeter of the shaded region. Thus, the perimeter of the shaded region equals the sum of the lengths of two sides of the equilateral triangle and half the circumference of the circle with a radius of 4. Therefore, the perimeter of the shaded region is $8 + 8 + \frac{1}{2}(2\pi(4)) = 16 + 4\pi$.

3. (D) **Number and Quantity**

Tips

$$\text{Distance} = \text{Speed} \times \text{Time}$$

The table below shows the distance that Mr. Rhee traveled during the different time intervals.

Time	Average Speed	Distance traveled
9 am to 10 am	50 miles per hour	50 mph × 1 hour = 50 miles
10 am to 11:30 am	60 miles per hour	60 mph × 1.5 hour = 90 miles
11:30 am to 12:00pm	Break	0 mile
12:00 pm to 4:00 pm	55 miles per hour	55 mph × 4 hour = 220 miles

Therefore, the total distance that Mr. Rhee traveled between 9 am to 4 pm is $50 + 90 + 220 = 360$ miles.

4. (B) **Probability and Statistics**

Define x as the total number of marbles in the bag. There are two red marbles and the probability of selecting a red marble is $\frac{1}{6}$.

$$\text{Probability of selecting a red marble} = \frac{\text{Number of red marbles}}{\text{Total number of marbles}}$$

$$\frac{1}{6} = \frac{2}{x} \qquad \text{Cross multiply}$$

$$x = 12$$

Thus, the total number of marbles in the bag is 12. Therefore, there are $12 - 2 = 10$ non-red marbles in the bag.

5. (A) **Functions**

$$\begin{aligned} 5^{y+1} &= \left(\frac{1}{5}\right)^{2y-2} \\ 5^{y+1} &= (5^{-1})^{2y-2} \\ 5^{y+1} &= 5^{-2y+2} \end{aligned}$$

Since the expressions on both sides of the equation have the same base, the exponents on both sides must be the same. Thus,

$$\begin{aligned} y+1 &= -2y+2 \\ 3y &= 1 \\ y &= \frac{1}{3} \end{aligned}$$

Therefore, the value of y for which $5^{y+1} = \left(\frac{1}{5}\right)^{2y-2}$ is $\frac{1}{3}$.

6. ($\frac{3}{8}$) **Probability and Statistics**

When a coin is tossed, there are two possible outcomes: head or tail. If you toss a coin three times, according to the fundamental counting principle, the total number of the possible outcomes is $2 \times 2 \times 2 = 8$. The table below shows the 8 possible outcomes.

H	H	H	
H	H	T	✓
H	T	H	✓
H	T	T	
T	H	H	✓
T	H	T	
T	T	H	
T	T	T	

Out of 8 possible outcomes, there are 3 outcomes that have two heads: $H\ H\ T$, $H\ T\ H$, and $T\ H\ H$. Therefore, the probability that two heads will be shown is $\frac{3}{8}$.

7. (D) **Trigonometry**

Tips In order to convert degrees to radians, multiply degrees by $\frac{\pi}{180°}$.

$$105° \times \frac{\pi}{180°} = \frac{105°}{180°}\pi = \frac{7\pi}{12}$$

Therefore, (D) is the correct answer.

8. (C) **Calculus**

Tips: A function f is continuous at $x = a$ if

$$\lim_{x \to a} f(x) = f(a)$$

The vertical asymptote of f is $x = 1$ which means that $\lim_{x \to 1} f(x)$ does not exist. The limit $\lim_{x \to 3} f(x)$ exists because $\lim_{x \to 3^-} f(x) = \lim_{x \to 3^+} f(x)$. Since there is a hole at $x = 3$, f is not continuous at $x = 3$. Thus, $\lim_{x \to 3^-} f(x) = \lim_{x \to 3^+} f(x) \neq f(3)$. The horizontal asymptote of f is $y = 0$ which means that $\lim_{x \to \infty} f(x) = 0$. Therefore, (C) is the correct answer.

9. (D) **Calculus**

Tips:
1. $x\sqrt{x} = x^1 \cdot x^{\frac{1}{2}} = x^{1+\frac{1}{2}} = x^{\frac{3}{2}}$.
2. $(x^n)' = nx^{n-1}$

$f(x) = x\sqrt{x} - 3x^{-1} + 5 = x^{\frac{3}{2}} - 3x^{-1} + 5$.

$$f'(x) = \frac{3}{2}x^{\frac{1}{2}} + 3x^{-2} \qquad \Longrightarrow \qquad f'(1) = \frac{3}{2} + 3 = \frac{9}{2}$$

Therefore, the value of $f'(1)$ is $\frac{9}{2}$.

10. (B) **Geometry**

Tips: The general equation of a circle: $(x - h)^2 + (y - k)^2 = r^2$.

In order to write the general equation of the circle $x^2 + y^2 + 4x - 2y - 3 = 0$, complete the squares in x and y.

$$\begin{aligned} x^2 + y^2 + 4x - 2y - 3 &= 0 && \\ x^2 + y^2 + 4x - 2y &= 3 && \text{Add 3 to each side} \\ x^2 + 4x + y^2 - 2y &= 3 && \text{Rearrange the terms} \\ (x+2)^2 + y^2 - 2y &= 7 && \text{Add 4 to each side to complete squares in } x \\ (x+2)^2 + (y-1)^2 &= 8 && \text{Add 1 to each side to complete squares in } y \end{aligned}$$

Therefore, the center of the circle is $(-2, 1)$.

11. (C) **Probability and Statistics**

There are five odd numbers from the first ten positive integers: 1, 3, 5, 7, and 9. Out of 5 odd numbers, there are three prime numbers: 3, 5, and 7. Thus,

$$\text{Prob (prime} \mid \text{odd)} = \frac{\{3, 5, 7\}}{\{1, 3, 5, 7, 9\}} = \frac{3}{5}$$

Therefore, the probability that the selected number is a prime, given that the selected number is an odd number is $\frac{3}{5}$.

12. (D) **Probability and Statistics**

Of 187 adults, 79 said "Yes". This implies that $\frac{79}{187}$ or about 42.2% of the sample of 187 adults have a tablet computer. Therefore, the total number of U.S. adults who own a tablet computer is 192 million $\times$ 0.422 = 81 million.

13. (B) **Calculus**

Tips 1. $\int x^n\,dx = \frac{1}{n+1}x^{n+1} + C \quad (n \neq -1)$ 2. $\int \frac{1}{x}\,dx = \ln|x| + C$

$$\begin{aligned}\int \frac{x^3 + 2x + 1}{x}\,dx &= \int x^2 + 2 + \frac{1}{x}\,dx \\ &= \frac{1}{3}x^3 + 2x + \ln|x| + C\end{aligned}$$

Therefore, (B) is the correct answer.

14. (D) **Functions**

The graph of $y = 5x + 6$ is shown below. The slope of the line is 5 and the x and y coordinates of the y-intercept of the line is $(0, 6)$. When the line is shifted right 2 units and down 1 unit, the slope of the line remains the same. However, the y-intercept of the line, $(0, 6)$, is shifted to $(2, 5)$.

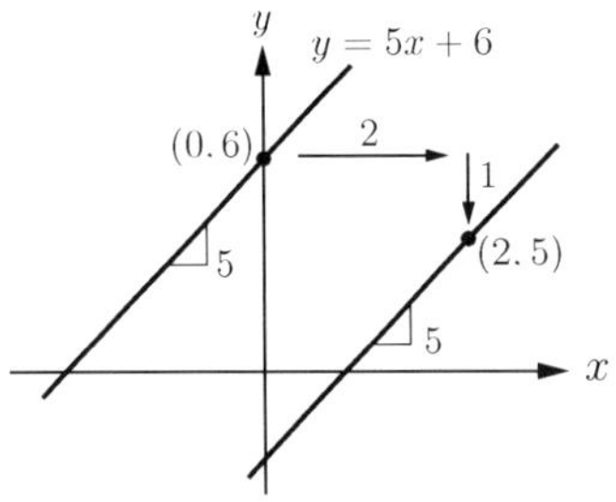

To write the equation of the new line, let's start with $y = mx + b$, where m is the slope and b is the y-intercept. The slope of the new line is 5 because the slope of the line remains the same after the shift. Thus, $m = 5$. Since the new line passes through $(2, 5)$, substitute 2 for x and 5 for y to solve for b.

$y = 5x + b$	Substitute 2 for x and 5 for y
$5 = 5(2) + b$	Solve for b
$b = -5$	

Therefore, the equation of the new line is $y = 5x - 5$.

15. (12) **Algebra**

Since $z > 0$, divide each side of the equation $xz + yz - 12z = 0$ by z and solve for $x + y$.

$$\frac{xz + yz - 12z}{z} = \frac{0}{z} \qquad \text{Divide each side by } z$$

$$\frac{xz}{z} + \frac{yz}{z} - \frac{12z}{z} = 0 \qquad \text{Simplify}$$

$$x + y - 12 = 0 \qquad \text{Add 12 to each side}$$

$$x + y = 12$$

Therefore, the value of $x + y$ is 12.

16. (B) **Geometry**

> **The Triangle inequality theorem**
>
> Tips — The length of a side of a triangle is always less than the sum of the lengths of the other two sides, but always greater than the difference of the lengths of the other two sides.

The lengths of the three sides of a triangle is 4, 5, and n. Use the Triangle inequality theorem to find the largest possible integer value of n.

$$5 - 4 < n < 5 + 4 \qquad \text{Use the triangle inequality theorem}$$

$$1 < n < 9 \qquad n \text{ is a positive integer}$$

$$n = 2, 3, \cdots, 8$$

Therefore, the largest possible value of n is 8.

17. (D) **Algebra**

A line $y = 3x + 4$ intersects a parabola $y = x^2$ as shown below.

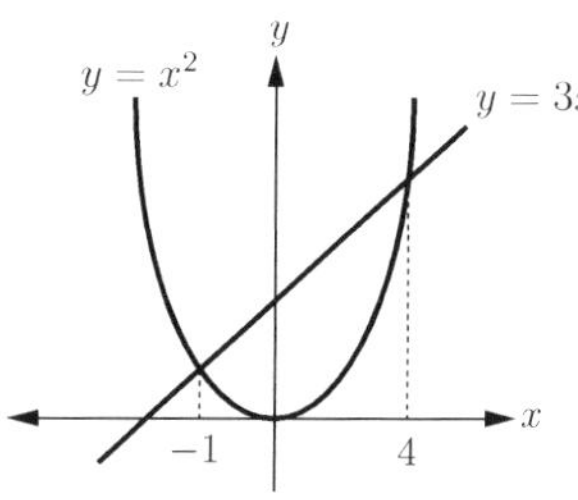

Set the two equations equal to each other and solve for x.

$$x^2 = 3x + 4 \qquad \text{Subtract } 3x + 4 \text{ from each side}$$

$$x^2 - 3x - 4 = 0 \qquad \text{Use the Factoring method}$$

$$(x + 1)(x - 4) = 0 \qquad \text{Use the zero-product property}$$

$$x = -1 \quad \text{or} \quad x = 4$$

Therefore, the x-coordinates of the two intersection points are -1 or 4.

18. (A) **Calculus**

Tips
1. The Product Rule: $(f \cdot g)' = f' \cdot g + f \cdot g'$
2. $\cos^2 x - \sin^2 x = \cos 2x$

$f(x) = \sin x \cos x$.

$$\begin{aligned} f'(x) &= (\sin x)' \cdot \cos x + \sin x(\cos x) \\ &= \cos^2 x - \sin^2 x \\ &= \cos 2x \end{aligned}$$

Therefore, $f'\left(\frac{\pi}{12}\right) = \cos\left(2 \cdot \frac{\pi}{12}\right) = \cos\frac{\pi}{6} = \frac{\sqrt{3}}{2}$.

19. (A) **Functions**

In order to evaluate $f(x+h)$, substitute $x+h$ for x in $f(x) = -x^2+1$. We found that $f(x+h) = -(x+h)^2+1 = -x^2 - 2xh - h^2 + 1$. Thus,

$$\begin{aligned} f(x+h) - f(x) &= -(x+h)^2 + 1 - (-x^2+1) \\ &= -x^2 - 2xh - h^2 + 1 + x^2 - 1 \\ &= -2xh - h^2 \end{aligned}$$

Therefore, $f(x+h) - f(x) = -2xh - h^2$.

20. (C) **Geometry**

Tips
The area of a sector is given by

$$\text{Area of a sector} = \pi r^2 \times \frac{\theta^\circ}{360^\circ}$$

In the figure below, $\triangle OAB$ is an isosceles right triangle. This means that $AB = OA = 4$ and $m\angle AOB = m\angle OBA = 45^\circ$. Thus, the radius of the circle, $\overline{OA}$, is 4.

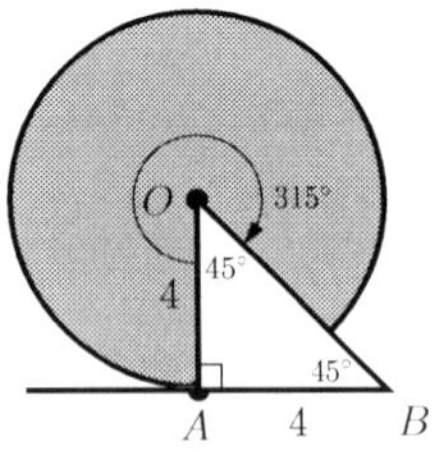

The area of the shaded region equals the area of a sector whose central angle is 315°.

$$\text{Area of shaded region} = \pi(4)^2 \times \frac{315^\circ}{360^\circ} = 16\pi \times \frac{7}{8} = 14\pi$$

Therefore, the area of the shaded region is 14π.

21. (7) **Discrete Mathematics**

There are six non-prime numbers from 1 to 10: 1, 4, 6, 8, 9, and 10. There are four prime numbers: 2, 3, 5, and 7. If all six non-prime numbers are selected, the next number will be a prime number. Therefore, seven cards must be selected to guarantee that at least one prime number is selected.

22. (C) **Functions**

Since t is a time in hours, change 90 minutes to 1.5 hours. In order to find the number of bacteria after 90 minutes, substitute 100 for N_0 and 1.5 for t.

$$N(t) = N_0 e^{0.35t} \qquad \text{Substitute 100 for } N_0 \text{ and 1.5 for } t$$
$$N(1.5) = 100e^{0.35\times 1.5} = 169$$

Therefore, the number of bacteria after 90 minutes is 169.

23. (A) **Probability and Statistics**

Tips

- In an **observational study**, researchers observe subject and measure variables of interest without assigning treatments to the subjects(people). Researchers should not interfere with the subjects or variables in any way.
- In an **experiment**, researchers apply treatments to subjects and then proceed the observed the effect of treatments on the subjects. The three principles of designing an experiment are control, randomization, and replication.

A Statistics professor listed the students who attended the session and compared their scores to the remaining student's scores. He didn't attempt to intervene his study at all. Therefore, this is an example of an observational study.

24. (D) **Algebra**

Tips

1. The conjugate pairs theorem states that complex zeros and irrational zeros always occur in conjugate pairs.
2. Vieta's formulas relate the coefficients of a polynomial to the sum and product of its zeros and are described below. For a quadratic function $f(x) = x^2 + bx + c$, let z_1 and z_2 be the zeros of f.

$$z_1 + z_2 = -b \quad \text{Sum of zeros equals the opposite of the coefficient of } x$$
$$z_1 z_2 = c \quad \text{Product of zeros equals the constant term}$$

According to the conjugate pairs theorem, $2+\sqrt{3}$ is also a zero of the quadratic function. Thus, $2+\sqrt{3}$ and $2-\sqrt{3}$ are zeros of the quadratic function. Since the irrational zeros are given, use Vieta's formulas to write a quadratic function with leading coefficient 1.

$$\text{Sum of zeros: } (2+\sqrt{3}) + (2-\sqrt{3}) = 4 \xrightarrow{\text{Opposite}} -4 \text{ (Coefficient of } x)$$
$$\text{Product of zeros: } (2+\sqrt{3})(2-\sqrt{3}) = 1 \xrightarrow{\text{Same}} 1 \text{ (Constant term)}$$

Therefore, the quadratic function whose zeros are $2+\sqrt{3}$ and $2-\sqrt{3}$ is $x^2 - 4x + 1$.

25. (A, D) **Functions**

Tips: Cancelling out a common factor $x - c$ from both the numerator and the denominator of a rational function produces a hole in the graph of the rational function.

The rational function $f(x) = \dfrac{x-2}{x^2-4}$ has a common factor of $x - 2$ in both the numerator and the denominator.

$$f(x) = \frac{x-2}{x^2-4} = \frac{\cancel{(x-2)}}{(x+2)\cancel{(x-2)}} = \frac{1}{x+2}$$

Thus, cancelling out $x - 2$ produces a hole in the graph of f at $x = 2$ and does not create a vertical asymptote at $x = 2$. Since f simplifies to $\frac{1}{x+2}$, f has a vertical asymptote at $x = -2$. Furthermore, the numerator of $\frac{1}{x+2}$ is a constant (degree $= 0$) and the denominator of $\frac{1}{x+2}$ is a first degree polynomial ($n = 1$), the horizontal asymptote of $\frac{1}{x+2}$ is $y = 0$. Therefore, $f(x) = \frac{x-2}{x^2-4}$ has a vertical asymptote at $x = -2$ and a horizontal asymptote at $y = 0$.

26. (D) **Geometry**

Tips: Any triangle inscribed in a semicircle is a right triangle.

In the figure below, $\triangle ABC$ is inscribed in the semicircle. Thus, it is a right triangle where $m\angle B = 90°$. Define x and $2x$ as the measure of angle C and the measure of angle A, respectively. Since $\angle A$ and $\angle C$ are complementary angles whose sum of their measures is $90°$, $x + 2x = 90$ or $x = 30$. Thus, $m\angle C = 30°$ and $m\angle A = 60°$.

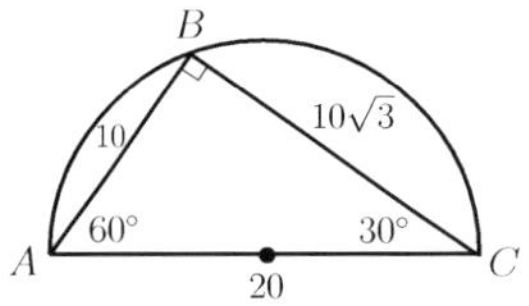

$\triangle ABC$ is a $30°$-$60°$-$90°$ special right triangle whose sides are in the ratio $1 : \sqrt{3} : 2$. $\overline{BC}$ is the longer leg, the side opposite the angle $60°$, and $BC = 10\sqrt{3}$ is given. $\overline{AB}$ is the shorter leg, the side opposite the angle $30°$, and $AB = \frac{10\sqrt{3}}{\sqrt{3}} = 10$. The length of the hypotenuse, AC, is twice the length of the shorter leg, AB. Thus, $AC = 2 \times AB = 2 \times 10 = 20$. Therefore, $AB + AC = 10 + 20 = 30$.

27. (A) **Trigonometry**

Tips: $\cos^2 x + \sin^2 x = 1$

$$\tan x + \cot x = \frac{\sin x}{\cos x} + \frac{\cos x}{\sin x} = \frac{\sin^2 x}{\sin x \cos x} + \frac{\cos^2 x}{\sin x \cos x}$$
$$= \frac{1}{\sin x \cos x} = \frac{1}{\sin x} \cdot \frac{1}{\cos x} = \csc x \sec x$$

28. (B) **Algebra**

The slope of the line that passes through the points $(-1,1)$ and $(2,-5)$ is as follows:

$$\text{Slope} = \frac{-5-1}{2-(-1)} = -2$$

The slope of the perpendicular line is the negative reciprocal of -2 or $\frac{1}{2}$. Since the slope of the line $x-2y=6$ is $\frac{1}{2}$, (B) is the correct answer.

29. (C) **Calculus**

Tips

1. An inflection point is a point on the graph of a function at which the concavity changes. Inflection points can occur where the second derivative is zero.
2. The Product Rule: $(f\cdot g)' = f'\cdot g + f\cdot g'$
3. If $f(x)=\sqrt{x-1}$, then $f'(x)=\dfrac{1}{2\sqrt{x-1}}$

$f'(x)=x\sqrt{x-1}$. Use the Product rule to differentiate $f'(x)$.

$$\begin{aligned} f''(x) &= (x)'\cdot\sqrt{x-1} + x\cdot(\sqrt{x-1})' = \sqrt{x-1} + \frac{x}{2\sqrt{x-1}} \\ &= \frac{2(x-1)+x}{2\sqrt{x-1}} = \frac{3x-2}{2\sqrt{x-1}} \end{aligned}$$

Solving for $f''(x)=0$ gives $x=\frac{2}{3}$. Therefore, f has an inflection point at $x=\frac{2}{3}$.

30. (C) **Trigonometry**

Tips

The Law of Sines: If a, b, and c are the lengths of the sides of a triangle, and A, B, and C are the opposite angles, then

$$\frac{a}{\sin A} = \frac{b}{\sin B} = \frac{c}{\sin C}$$

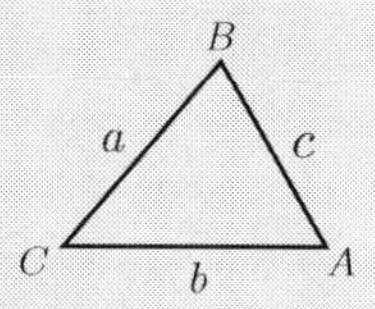

Since $AC=1$, $m\angle A = 64°$, and $m\angle B = 32°$, $\triangle ABC$ is a SAA triangle as shown below.

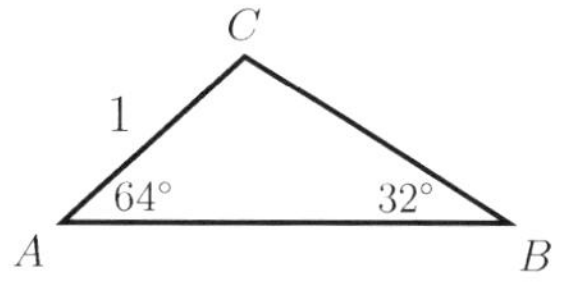

In order to find BC, use the Law of Sines.

$$\frac{BC}{\sin 64°} = \frac{1}{\sin 32°} \implies BC = \frac{\sin 64°}{\sin 32°} = 1.70$$

Therefore, $BC = 1.70$.

31. (B) **Probability and Statistics**

Tips

68 – 99 – 99.7 Rule (Empirical Rule):

- Approximately **68%** of the population will measure between 1 standard deviation either side of the mean.
- Approximately **95%** of the population will measure between 2 standard deviations either side of the mean.
- Approximately **99.7%** of the population will measure between 3 standard deviations either side of the mean.

The weights of adult males are normally distributed with a mean of 172 pounds and a standard deviation of 15 pounds. The distribution of the weights is shown below.

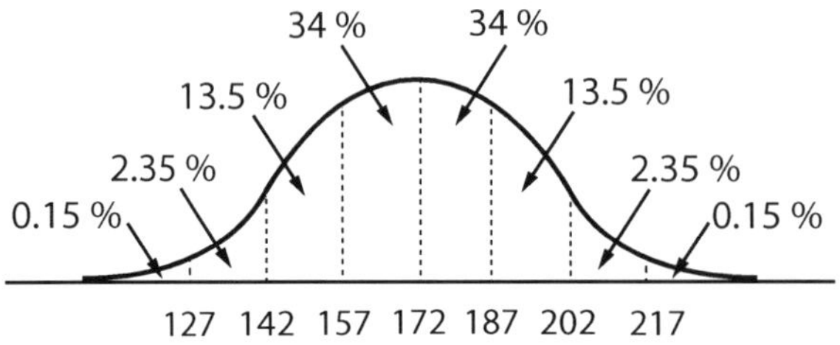

Using the Empirical rule, the percent of the weights of adult males between 142 pounds and 187 pounds is $13.5\% + 34\% + 34\% = 81.5\%$.

32. (6) **Geometry**

In the figure below, the diameter of a sphere is the same as the length of a cube since the sphere is inscribed in the cube. Define $2x$ as the length of the cube. Then, the diameter of the sphere is $2x$ and the radius is x.

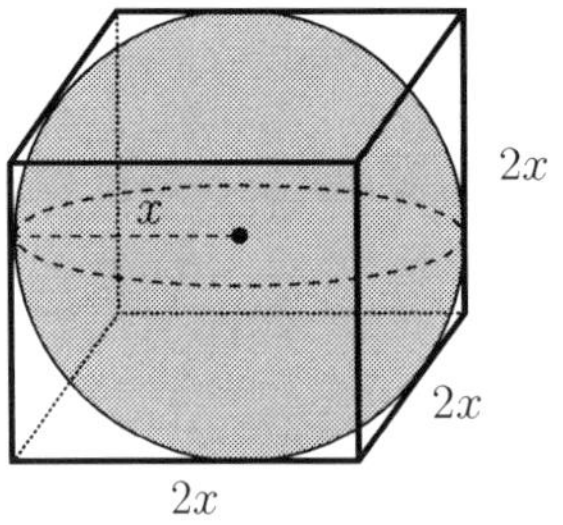

The volume of the cube can be expressed as $(2x)^3 = 8x^3$ and the volume of the sphere can be expressed as $\frac{4}{3}\pi x^3$. Thus,

$$\frac{\text{Volume of sphere}}{\text{Volume of cube}} = \frac{\frac{4}{3}\pi x^3}{8x^3} = \frac{\pi}{6}$$

Since the ratio of the volume of the sphere to that of the cube is $\frac{\pi}{6}$, the value of n is 6.

33. (D) **Number and Quantity**

Joshua can type m words in a seconds. That implies that Joshua can type $\frac{m}{a}$ words in 1 second, $60\left(\frac{m}{a}\right)$ words in 60 seconds, or $60t\left(\frac{m}{a}\right)$ words in t minutes. In addition, Jason can type n words in b minutes. This implies that Jason can type $\frac{n}{b}$ words in 1 minute, or $t\left(\frac{n}{b}\right)$ words in t minutes. Since both Joshua and Jason type together, the total number of words that they can type in t minutes is as follows:

$$60t\left(\frac{m}{a}\right) + t\left(\frac{n}{b}\right) = t\left(\frac{60m}{a} + \frac{n}{b}\right)$$

Therefore, (D) is the correct answer.

34. (D) **Functions**

The domain of a function is the set of the x-values. The graph shows that the domain of f is all real numbers.

35. (B) **Algebra**

There are two different type of questions on the math exam. One is worth 4 points and another is worth 3 points. Define x as the number of questions worth 4 points. Since there are 29 questions on the math exam, $29 - x$ is the number of questions worth 3 points. Below shows how to obtain the sum of points for each type of questions.

	A question worth 4 points	A question worth 3 points	Total
Number of questions	x	$29 - x$	29
Sum of points	$4x$	$3(29 - x)$	100

Since the math exam is worth a total of 100 points, set up an equation in terms of the sum of points shown on the table above.

$$4x + 3(29 - x) = 100 \quad \text{Expand } 3(29 - x)$$
$$4x - 3x + 87 = 100 \quad \text{Solve for } x$$
$$x = 13$$

Therefore, the number of questions that are worth 4 points is 13.

36. ($\frac{1}{3}$) **Number and Quantity**

Tips $\log_a a = 1, \quad \log_a x^n = n \log_a x, \quad \log_{a^n} x = \frac{1}{n} \log_a x$

$$\log_2 \sqrt{2} = \log_2 2^{\frac{1}{2}} = \frac{1}{2}, \qquad \log_4 2 = \log_{2^2} 2 = \frac{1}{2}, \qquad \log_8 2 = \log_{2^3} 2 = \frac{1}{3}$$

Therefore, $\log_2 \sqrt{2} - \log_4 2 + \log_8 2 = \frac{1}{2} - \frac{1}{2} + \frac{1}{3} = \frac{1}{3}$.

37. (D) **Functions**

Tips

Let $(x-c)^m$ be a factor of a polynomial function f.

If $m=$ odd $\Longrightarrow$ graph of f crosses the x-axis at $x=c$.

If $m=$ even $\Longrightarrow$ graph of f touches the x-axis at $x=c$.

The graph of the cubic function touches the x-axis at $x=3$. This implies that 3 is a zero of multiplicity 2, and $(x-3)^2$ is a factor of the cubic function. Additionally, the graph of the cubic function crosses the x-axis at $x=-1$. This implies that -1 is a zero of multiplicity 1 and $(x+1)$ is a factor of the cubic function. Furthermore, the graph of the cubic function goes down as x increases and goes up as x decreases, which means that the leading coefficient is negative. Therefore, the cubic function $-(x+1)(x-3)^2$ best represents the graph.

38. (B) **Calculus**

x	1	**2**	3	**4**	5	**6**	7
$f(x)$	42	38	35	36	40	42	45

The midpoints of each subinterval are highlighted above. $\int_1^7 f(x)\,dx$ can be approximated by the sum of three midpoint rectangles shown below.

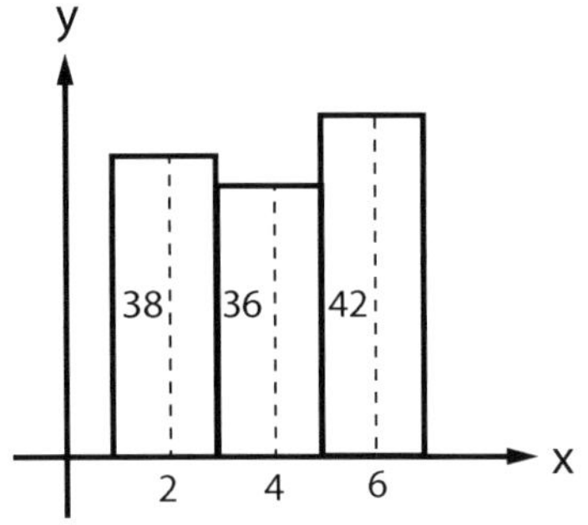

Therefore, $\int_1^7 f(x)\,dx \approx 2(38)+2(36)+2(42)=232$.

39. (D) **Probability and Statistics**

Tips

The standard deviation measures the amount of variation or dispersion from the mean. In other words, it is a measure of how spread out the numbers are. A small standard deviation indicates that the numbers tend to be very close to the mean.

The mean of each set of numbers in all of the answer choices is 10. Since the numbers in answer choice (D) are closest to the mean, the set of numbers in answer choice (D) has the smallest standard deviation.

40. (C) **Trigonometry**

Tips $\cos 2\theta = 1 - 2\sin^2\theta$

$$\begin{aligned}\cos 2\theta &= 1 - 2\sin^2\theta \\ &= 1 - 2\left(\frac{3}{5}\right)^2 \\ &= \frac{7}{25}\end{aligned}$$

Therefore, (C) is the correct answer.

41. (B) **Probability and Statistics**

The digits 1 through 4 are randomly arranged to make a four-digit number. To count the total number of possible four-digit numbers, use permutation: ${}_4P_4 = 4! = 4 \times 3 \times 2 \times 1 = 24$, or use the fundamental counting principle. Define event 1, event 2, event 3, and event 4 as selecting a digit for the thousands' place, hundreds' place, tens' place, and ones' place, respectively. Event 1 has 4 ways to select a digit out of 4 digits. After one digit is taken, event 2 has 3 ways to select a digit out of the three remaining digits. Event 3 has 2 ways and event 4 has 1 way. Thus, there are $4 \times 3 \times 2 \times 1 = 24$ possible four-digit numbers using 1, 2, 3, and 4.

In order for a number to be divisible by 4, the last two digits of the number must be divisible by 4. Thus, the last two digits of the numbers should be either 12, 24, and 32. Let's consider three cases:

Case 1: The last two digits of the number is 12. There are two possible four-digit numbers as shown below.

3 4 1 2   4 3 1 2

Case 2: The last two digits of the number is 24. There are two possible four-digit numbers as shown below.

1 3 2 4   3 1 2 4

Case 3: The last two digits of the number is 32. There are two possible four-digit numbers as shown below.

1 4 3 2   4 1 3 2

Thus, there are 6 four-digit numbers that are divisible by 4. Therefore, the probability that the four-digit number that is divisible by 4 is $\frac{6}{24} = \frac{1}{4}$.

42. (B) **Geometry**

Tips The volume V of a cone: $V = \frac{1}{3}\pi r^2 h$.

The x-intercept and the y-intercept of the line $2x + 3y = 6$ are 3 and 2, respectively. The shaded area in the first figure shows the region R enclosed by the line $2x + 3y = 6$, the x-axis, and the y-axis. The second figure shows the resulting solid after the region R is rotated about the y-axis.

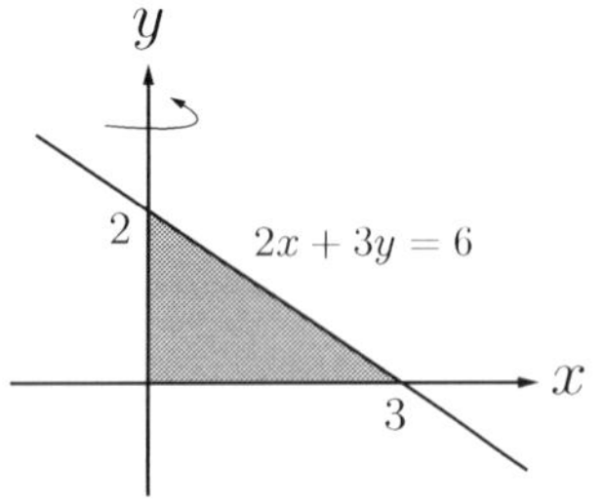

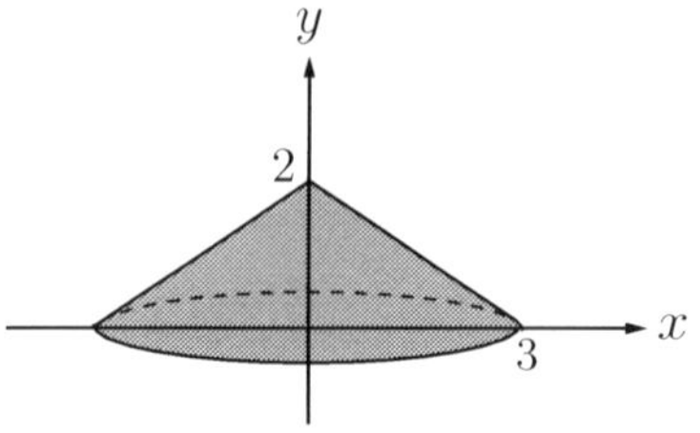

The resulting solid is a cone with a radius of 3 and a height of 2. Therefore, the volume of the cone is $V = \frac{1}{3}\pi r^2 h = \frac{1}{3}\pi(3)^2(2) = 6\pi$.

43. (C) **Probability and Statistics**

IQR $= Q3 - Q1 = 90 - 75 = 15$.

44. (106) **Trigonometry**

Tips If triangle ABC shown at the right is a SSS triangle (a, b, and c are known), the measure of angle A can be calculated by the Law of Cosines.

$$m\angle A = \cos^{-1}\left(\frac{a^2 - b^2 - c^2}{-2bc}\right)$$

Note that side a is opposite angle A.

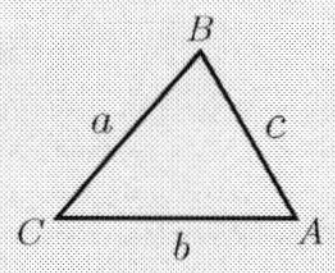

In the figure below, let the three sides b, c and a be 5, 5, and 8, respectively, since the ratio of the three sides is $5 : 5 : 8$. The Law of Sines implies that the largest angle is opposite the longest side. Thus, $\angle A$ is the largest angle since side a is the longest side.

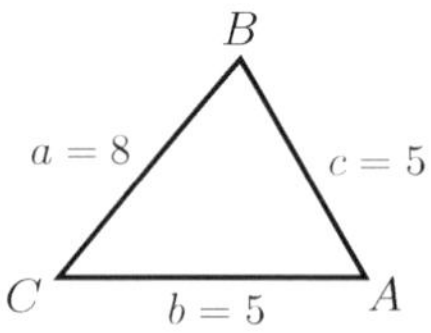

In order to find the measure of angle A, use the Law of Cosines. Since side a is opposite angle A,

$$m\angle A = \cos^{-1}\left(\frac{a^2 - b^2 - c^2}{-2bc}\right) = \cos^{-1}\left(\frac{8^2 - 5^2 - 5^2}{-2(5)(5)}\right) = 106.26^\circ$$

Therefore, the largest angle of the triangle is 106°.

45. (B) **Geometry**

In the figure below, the cube has a side length of 2 and point A is the midpoint of one side of the cube. Point C is directly below point A so that it is also the midpoint of another side of the cube. Thus, $CD = 1$. Draw a segment from point C to point B to form a triangle CBD. $\triangle CBD$ is a right triangle with $CD = 1$ and $DB = 2$. To find CB, use the Pythagorean theorem: $CB^2 = 1^2 + 2^2$. Thus, $CB = \sqrt{5}$.

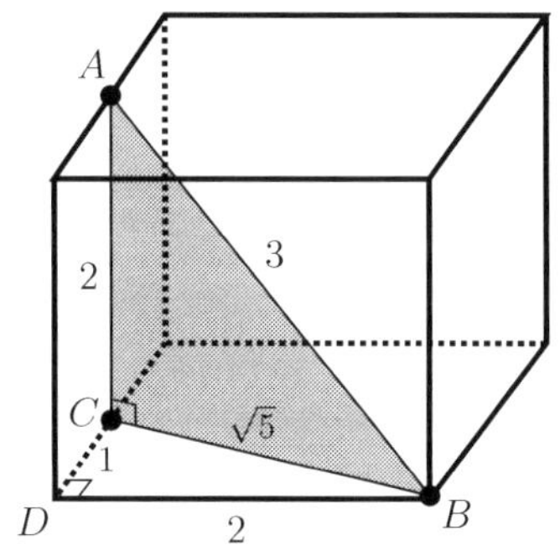

Draw a segments from point A to point C and draw another segment from point A to B to form triangle ABC. $\triangle ABC$ is a right triangle with $AC = 2$ and $CB = \sqrt{5}$. To find AB, use the Pythagorean theorem: $AB^2 = 2^2 + (\sqrt{5})^2$. Thus, $AB = 3$. Therefore, the length of $\overline{AB}$ is 3.

46. (C) **Calculus**

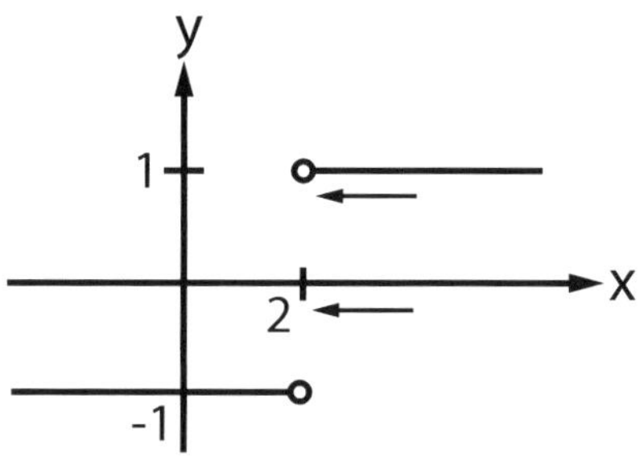

The graph of the function $f(x) = \dfrac{2x-4}{|4-2x|}$ is shown above. As x approaches 2 from right, the right-hand limit of $f(x)$ is equal to 1. Therefore, (C) is the correct answer.

47. (A) **Functions**

> **Tips** Two equations below are equivalent.
>
> $$a^n = b \quad \Longleftrightarrow \quad n = \log_a b$$

$$\log_{3.72} x = 1.5 \quad \Longleftrightarrow \quad x = (3.72)^{1.5}$$

Therefore, (A) is the correct answer.

48. (C) **Number and Quantity**

Tips: Two complex numbers are equal if and only if their real parts are equal and their imaginary parts are equal.

Since $z_1 = 2y + (x+6)i$ and $z_2 = (3-x) + yi$ are equal, $2y = 3 - x$, and $x + 6 = y$. Since $2y = 3 - x$ is equivalent to $x + 2y = 3$, and $x + 6 = y$ is equivalent to $x - y = -6$, use the linear combination method to find the values of x and y.

$$\begin{aligned} x + 2y &= 3 \\ x - y &= -6 \quad \text{Subtract the two equations} \\ \hline 3y &= 9 \\ y &= 3 \end{aligned}$$

Since $y = 3$ and $x - y = -6$, $x = -3$. Therefore, the value of $z_3 = x + yi = -3 + 3i$.

49. (D) **Probability and Statistics**

Jason rolls two dice to form a two-digit integer. Since the number on the first die represents the tens digit and the number on the second die represents the units digit, there are a total number of $6 \times 6 = 36$ possible two-digit integers. Out of these 36 integers, there are only 5 integers that are divisible by 8: 16, 24, 32, 56, 64. Note that 40 and 48 can not be formed because a die has numbers 1 through 6. Therefore, the probability that the integer formed is divisible by 8 is $\frac{5}{36}$.

50. (B) **Trigonometry**

As shown in Figure A, the period of $\sin 2x$ is $\dfrac{2\pi}{2} = \pi$.

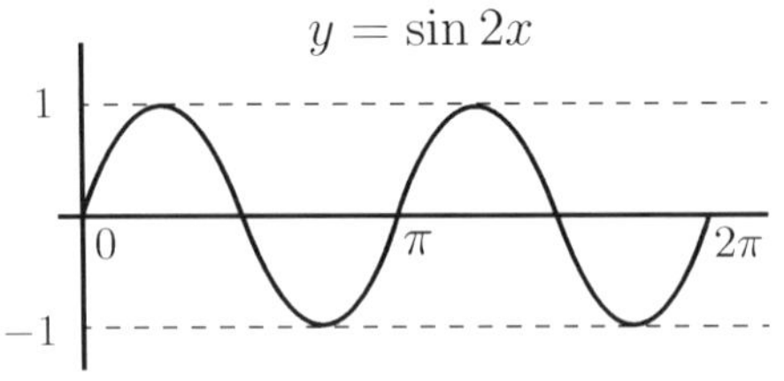

Figure A

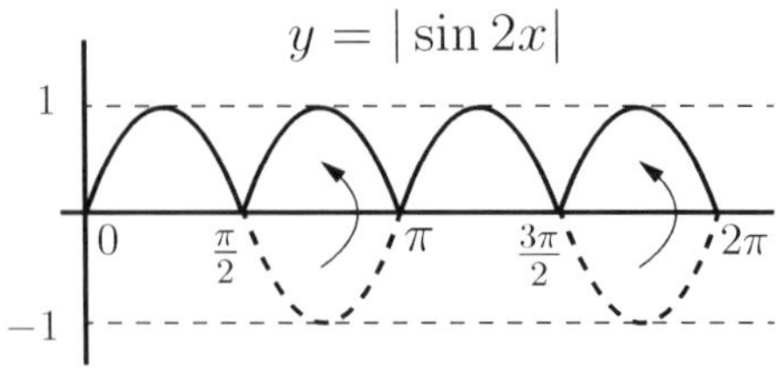

Figure B

However, the graph of $y = |\sin 2x|$ completes its cycle every $\dfrac{\pi}{2}$ as shown in Figure B, the period of $y = |\sin 2x|$ is $\dfrac{\pi}{2}$.

51. (D) **Geometry**

Since point A lies on the line $y = 6$, the x and y coordinates of point A is $(6, 6)$. Additionally, to find the y-coordinate of point B, substitute 9 for x in $y = -\frac{3}{4}x + 14$ and solve for y.

$$y = -\frac{4}{3}x + 14 \qquad \text{Substitute 9 for } x$$

$$y = -\frac{4}{3}(9) + 14 \qquad \text{Solve for } x$$

$$y = 2$$

Since point B lies on the line $x = 9$, the x and y coordinates of point B is $(9, 2)$. Finally, use the distance formula to find out the length of $\overline{AB}$.

$$\begin{aligned} AB &= \sqrt{(x_2 - x_1)^2 + (y_2 - y_1)^2} && \text{Since } A(6,6) \text{ and } B(9,2) \\ &= \sqrt{(9-6)^2 + (2-6)^2} \\ &= \sqrt{(3)^2 + (-4)^2} \\ &= 5 \end{aligned}$$

Therefore, the length of $\overline{AB}$ is 5.

52. (10) **Discrete Mathematics**

$$\begin{aligned} \sum_{n=1}^{10}(-1)^n 2n &= -2 + 4 - 6 + 8 - 10 + 12 - 14 + 16 - 18 + 20 \\ &= (-2+4) + (-6+8) + (-10+12) + (-14+16) + (-18+20) \\ &= 2 + 2 + 2 + 2 + 2 \\ &= 10 \end{aligned}$$

Therefore, $\sum_{n=1}^{10}(-1)^n 2n = 10$.

53. (D) **Algebra**

The least common denominators of the rational expressions is $x^2 - 9$ or $(x+3)(x-3)$.

$$\begin{aligned} \frac{1}{x-3} - \frac{6}{x^2-9} &= \frac{x+3}{(x+3)(x-3)} - \frac{6}{(x+3)(x-3)} \\ &= \frac{x-3}{(x+3)(x-3)} \\ &= \frac{1}{x+3} \end{aligned}$$

Therefore, $\frac{1}{x-3} - \frac{6}{x^2-9} = \frac{1}{x+3}$.

54. (A) **Trigonometry**

> Tips
>
> To convert from a polar equation to a rectangular equation,
>
> $$x = r\cos\theta, \qquad y = r\sin\theta$$

Since $\csc\theta = \dfrac{1}{\sin\theta}$, $r = 3\csc\theta$ is equivalent to $r = \dfrac{3}{\sin\theta}$.

$$r = \frac{3}{\sin\theta} \qquad \text{Multiply each side by } \sin\theta$$

$$r\sin\theta = 3$$

$$y = 3$$

Therefore, the rectangular equation $y = 3$ is equivalent to $r = 3\csc\theta$.

55. (A) **Number and Quantity**

> Tips
>
> The area of a triangle with vertices (a, b), (c, d), and (e, f) is given by
>
> $$\text{Area} = \pm\frac{1}{2}\begin{vmatrix} a & b & 1 \\ c & d & 1 \\ e & f & 1 \end{vmatrix}$$
>
> 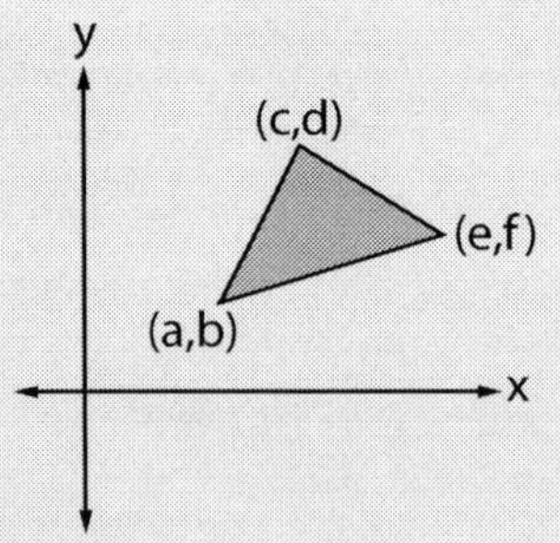
>
>
> where the symbol $\pm$ indicates that the appropriate sign should be chosen to yield a positive value.

The vertices of a triangle are $(2, 3)$, $(5, 7)$, and $(6, 5)$.

$$\begin{vmatrix} 2 & 3 & 1 \\ 5 & 7 & 1 \\ 6 & 5 & 1 \end{vmatrix} = 2\begin{vmatrix} 7 & 1 \\ 5 & 1 \end{vmatrix} - 3\begin{vmatrix} 5 & 1 \\ 6 & 1 \end{vmatrix} + 1\begin{vmatrix} 5 & 7 \\ 6 & 5 \end{vmatrix} = 2(7-5) - 3(5-6) + 1(25-42) = -10$$

Therefore, the area of a triangle with vertices $(2, 3)$, $(5, 7)$, and $(6, 5)$ is $-\frac{1}{2}(-10) = 5$.

56. (A) **Functions**

In order to graph $|f(x)|$, start with the graph shown in Figure 4A.

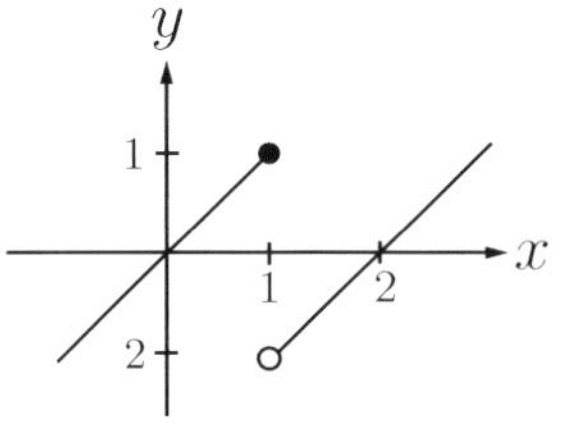

Fig 4A: $f(x)$

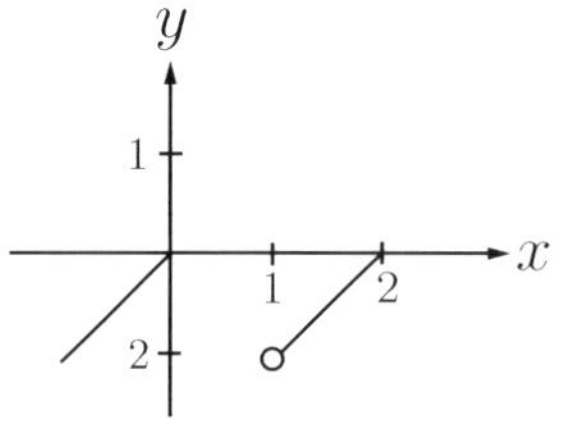

Fig 4B: Part below the x-axis

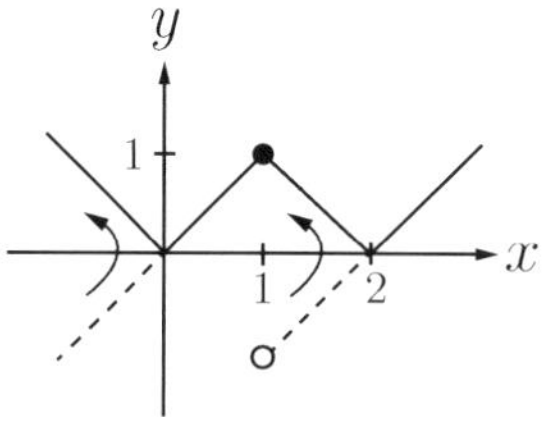

Fig 4C: $y = |f(x)|$

Determine the part of the graph that lies below the x-axis as shown in Figure 4B. Lastly, reflect the part of the graph that lies below the x-axis as shown in Figure 4C.

57. (A) **Calculus**

Tips
1. If $f'(x) > 0$, then f is increasing.
2. If $f'(x) < 0$, then f is decreasing.
3. The Chain Rule: $f(g(x))' = f'(g(x)) \cdot g'(x)$

f is a differential function with $f'(x) > 0$ for all real numbers x. $g(x) = f(x^2 + 4x)$. Let's differentiate $g(x)$ using the Chain rule.

$$\begin{aligned} g'(x) &= f'(x^2 + 4x) \cdot (x^2 + 4x)' \\ &= f'(x^2 + 4x) \cdot (2x + 4) \end{aligned}$$

In order to find the interval where $g(x)$ is decreasing, we need to solve the inequality $g'(x) < 0$.

$$\begin{aligned} g'(x) &< 0 \\ f'(x^2 + 4x) \cdot (2x + 4) &< 0 \qquad \text{Divide each side by } f'(x) \text{ since } f'(x) > 0 \\ (2x + 4) &< 0 \\ x &< -2 \end{aligned}$$

Therefore, $g(x)$ is decreasing on the interval $(-\infty, -2)$.

58. (B) **Geometry**

Divide each side of the equation $16x^2 + 9y^2 = 144$ by 144. Thus, $\dfrac{x^2}{3^2} + \dfrac{y^2}{4^2} = 1$. Therefore, the area of the ellipse is $A = \pi(3)(4) = 12\pi$.

59. (B) **Algebra**

$x-3=\sqrt{2x-3}$	Square both sides
$(x-3)^2=2x-3$	Use the binomial expansion formula
$x^2-8x+12=0$	Factor the quadratic expression
$(x-2)(x-6)=0$	Use the zero product property: If $ab=0$, then $a=0$ or $b=0$.
$x=2$ or $x=6$	

Substitute 2 and 6 for x in the original equation to check the solutions.

$$2-3=\sqrt{4-3}$$
$$-1\neq 1 \quad \text{(Not a solution)}$$

$$6-3=\sqrt{12-3}$$
$$3=3 \quad \checkmark \text{ (Solution)}$$

Therefore, the only solution to $x-3=\sqrt{2x-3}$ is $x=6$.

60. (D) **Calculus**

In the figure below, let x be the distance between the airplane and the point directly over the radar station, and let y be the distance between the airplane and the radar station. As time increases, both x and y increase.

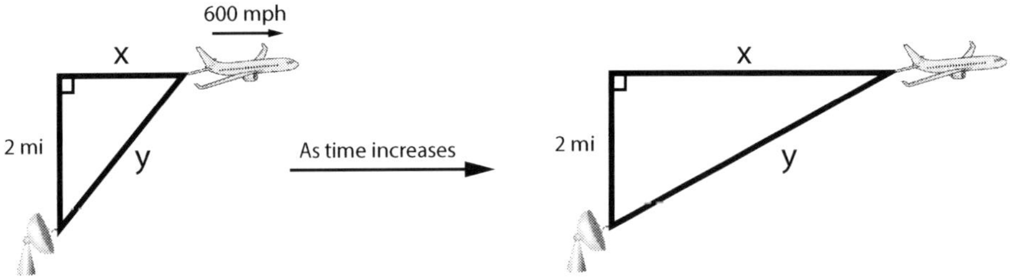

We are given that $\frac{dx}{dt}=600$ mph, and try to find $\frac{dy}{dt}$ when $y=4$ miles. Let's set up an equation that relates x and y.

$$y^2=x^2+2^2$$

Differentiate both sides with respect to t using the Chain rule, and solve for $\frac{dy}{dt}$.

$$2y\frac{dy}{dt}=2x\frac{dx}{dt}$$
$$\frac{dy}{dt}=\frac{x}{y}\frac{dx}{dt}$$

Using the Pythagorean theorem, we find that $x=2\sqrt{3}$ when $y=4$. Thus,

$$\frac{dy}{dt}=\frac{x}{y}\frac{dx}{dt}=\frac{2\sqrt{3}}{4}(600 \text{ mph})=300\sqrt{3} \text{ mph}$$

Therefore, the rate at which the distance from the airplane and the station is increasing when it is 4 miles away from the station is $300\sqrt{3}$ mph.

PRAXIS II 5161 PRACTICE TEST 4

Time — 150 minutes
Number of questions — 60

Directions: Solve each of the following problems using the available space for scratch work. Choose the best answer among the answer choices given and fill in the corresponding circle on the answer sheet.

1. A tulip grows $\frac{1}{2}$ of an inch for a week. At this rate, how many weeks will it take the tulip to grow 1 foot?

   (A) 12 weeks

   (B) 16 weeks

   (C) 20 weeks

   (D) 24 weeks

2. The Pythagorean theorem states that in a right triangle, the square of the length of the hypotenuse is equal to the sum of the squares of the lengths of the legs. Which of the following is a set of three positive integers that satisfies the Pythagorean theorem?

   (A) $1, 1, \sqrt{2}$

   (B) $5, 12, 15$

   (C) $7, 23, 25$

   (D) $8, 15, 17$

For the following question, enter your answer in the answer box.

3. Mr. Rhee is 5 ft 9 inches tall. His son, Joshua, is $\dfrac{2}{3}$ of Mr. Rhee's height. What is the difference of their heights in inches?

   [ ] inches

For the following question, select all the answer choices that apply.

4. Which of the following statements are true?

   Select all that apply.

   (A) The solutions to $x^2 = 81$ are 9 or -9.

   (B) The values of $\sqrt{4}$ are 2 or -2.

   (C) The value of $\dfrac{1}{0}$ is undefined.

   (D) If $x < 0$, $|x| = x$.

5. The probability that it will rain on Monday is $\frac{7}{10}$. The probability that it will snow on Tuesday is $\frac{1}{5}$. What is the probability that it will not rain on Monday and it will snow on Tuesday? (Assume that rain on Monday and snow on Tuesday are independent events.)

(A) $\frac{1}{50}$

(B) $\frac{3}{50}$

(C) $\frac{7}{50}$

(D) $\frac{7}{25}$

6. What are the rectangular coordinates (x, y) that correspond with the polar coordinates $(10, 135°)$?

(A) $(-5, -5)$

(B) $(-5, 8.66)$

(C) $(-7.07, 7.07)$

(D) $(7.07, -7.07)$

7. If $a = 2^x$ and $b = 3^x$, what is 6^x in terms of a and b ?

(A) $a + b$

(B) $a^2 - b^2$

(C) ab

(D) $\frac{b}{a}$

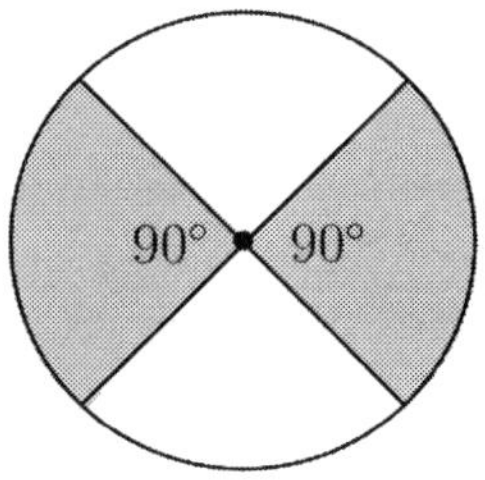

Note: Figure not drawn to scale.

8. In the figure above, the radius of the circle is 2. What is the area of the shaded region?

(A) $\frac{\pi}{2}$

(B) π

(C) 2π

(D) 4π

9. $\lim_{x \to 4} \frac{\sqrt{x} - 2}{x - 4} =$

(A) $\frac{1}{6}$

(B) $\frac{1}{4}$

(C) $\frac{1}{3}$

(D) $\frac{1}{2}$

10. What is the amplitude of the trigonometric function $y = -4\cos(\pi x + 1) - 2$?

(A) -4

(B) -2

(C) 1

(D) 4

11. What is the sum of the units digit of the first seven positive perfect squares?

(A) 25

(B) 30

(C) 35

(D) 40

12. Solve: $5x^2 + 7 = -3$

(A) $x = i$ or $x = -i$

(B) $x = i\sqrt{2}$ or $x = -i\sqrt{2}$

(C) $x = 2i$ or $x = -2i$

(D) $x = \sqrt{2}$ or $x = -\sqrt{2}$

For the following question, enter your answer in the answer box.

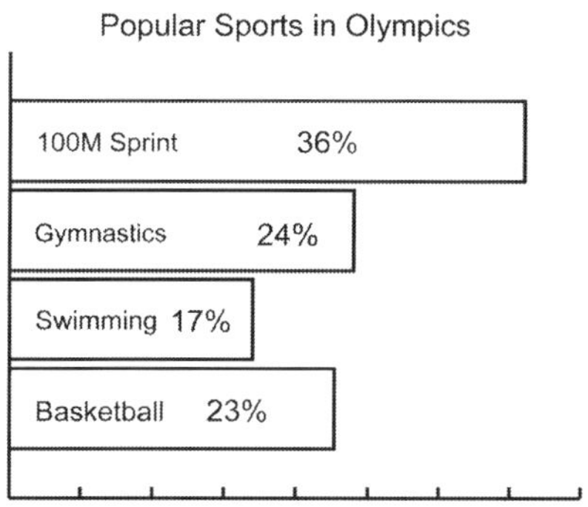

13. A survey asks people in the US which sport they are going to watch in the upcoming Olympics. The chart above shows the results of the survey. If the US population is 300 million, how many more people, in million, are going to watch the most popular sport compared to the least popular sport in the chart?

[ ] milion

14. The equation $x^2 + y^2 + 4x - 6y = 3$ represents a circle. What is the radius of the circle?

(A) 4

(B) 6

(C) 8

(D) 12

15. Which of the following rational function has a slant asymptote?

(A) $y = \frac{1}{x}$

(B) $y = \frac{1}{x^2}$

(C) $y = \frac{x^2 - x - 2}{x + 3}$

(D) $y = \frac{x^2 - 3x - 1}{x^2 + 1}$

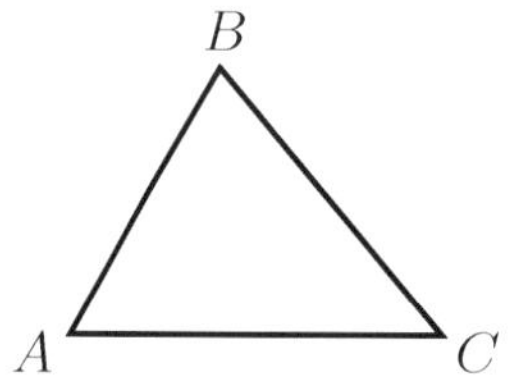

16. In the figure above, $BC = 5$, $AC = 6$, and $m\angle C = 55°$. What is the area of $\triangle ABC$?

(A) 6.15

(B) 8.36

(C) 12.29

(D) 18.82

17. What is the coefficient of x in the expansion of $(x+\frac{1}{x})^5$?

(A) 1

(B) 5

(C) 8

(D) 10

18. What is the probability that a randomly selected positive factor of 180 is odd?

(A) $\frac{1}{6}$

(B) $\frac{1}{5}$

(C) $\frac{1}{4}$

(D) $\frac{1}{3}$

x	-3	-2	-1	0	1	2	3	4
$f'(x)$	-2	-1	3	2	1	3	-2	-1

19. Let f be a continuous function. If the table above shows values of the derivative of f, f', for selected values of x, which of the following intervals is f increasing?

(A) $(-3,-1)$

(B) $(-2,1)$

(C) $(-1,2)$

(D) $(0,4)$

20. Two six-sided fair dice are rolled. What is the probability that the sum of the two numbers on the dice is greater than the product of the two numbers on the dice?

(A) $\frac{1}{6}$

(B) $\frac{5}{36}$

(C) $\frac{1}{4}$

(D) $\frac{11}{36}$

$$x^2-y^2=27$$
$$x-y=3$$

21. From the equations above, what is the value of x^2+y^2 ?

(A) 18

(B) 27

(C) 36

(D) 45

22. If $f(x)=2x^3-x^2-8x+4$, what are the real zeros of f ?

(A) $-1,\ \frac{1}{4},\ 2$

(B) $-2,\ \frac{1}{2},\ 2$

(C) $\frac{1}{2},\ 1,\ 2$

(D) $\frac{1}{4},\ \frac{1}{2},\ 2$

For the following question, enter your answer in the answer box.

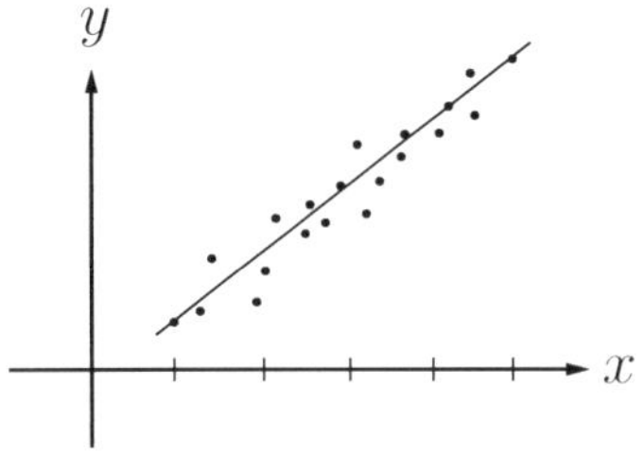

23. A scatter plot in the figure above displays the weight in pounds (y) versus the height in inches (x) of 20 students. The equation of the linear regression line is $y = 4.88x - 185$. Using the regression line, what would be the weight of a student who is 6 feet tall? (Round your answer to the nearest integer.)

[ ] pounds

24. If h approaches 0, which of the following best approximates the value of $\dfrac{(2+h)^2 - 2^2}{h}$?

(A) 1

(B) 2

(C) 3

(D) 4

25. What is the minimum value of the trigonometric function $y = -5\sin(2\pi x + 4) + 3$ for $-3 < x < 3$?

(A) -6

(B) -5

(C) -3

(D) -2

26. For all numbers a and b, a linear function, $f(x)$, satisfies $f(a) > f(b)$ if $a < b$. Which of the following statement must be true about the graph of the linear function $f(x)$ on the xy-coordinate plane?

(A) A line with undefined slope.

(B) A line with positive slope.

(C) A line with negative slope.

(D) A line that passes through the origin.

27. Solve: $\sqrt{x+1} - \sqrt{x-1} = 1$

(A) $\frac{1}{4}$

(B) $\frac{1}{2}$

(C) $\frac{3}{4}$

(D) $\frac{5}{4}$

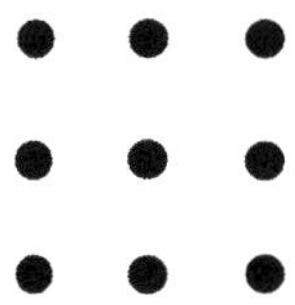

28. Each point in the grid above has the same probability of being selected. If three distinct points are randomly selected, what is the probability that the three points are on the same line?

(A) $\frac{2}{21}$

(B) $\frac{5}{42}$

(C) $\frac{1}{6}$

(D) $\frac{1}{5}$

x	1	2	4	5	10
y	10	5	2.5	2	1

29. The table above shows five points on the graph of a function. Which of the following functions best represents the table above?

(A) $y = 10x$

(B) $y = |x + 10|$

(C) $\frac{10}{x}$

(D) $\frac{x}{10}$

30. Which of the following trigonometric function has an amplitude of 4, a period of π, and a vertical shift of 1 down ?

(A) $y = -2\cos 2x + 1$

(B) $y = 2\cos\left(\frac{1}{2}x\right) + 1$

(C) $y = -4\sin 2x - 1$

(D) $y = 4\sin\left(\frac{1}{2}x\right) - 1$

31. Solve: $-(x-1)(x-2)(x-3) < 0$

(A) $x < 1$ or $x > 3$

(B) $1 < x < 3$

(C) $x < 1$ or $2 < x < 3$

(D) $1 < x < 2$ or $x > 3$

32. If $f(x) = \frac{x+1}{x-2}$ and $g(x) = \frac{1}{x}$, what is $f(g(x))$?

(A) $\frac{1-2x}{1+x}$

(B) $\frac{1+x}{1-2x}$

(C) $\frac{2x-1}{x+1}$

(D) $\frac{x+1}{2x-1}$

For the following question, enter your answer in the answer box.

33. In a store, Jason paid \$39 for one book and two DVDs. If he buys two books and one DVD, he would pay \$27. What is the average price, in dollars, of the book and the DVD?

[ ] dollars

Stem	Leaf
3	1 4
4	2 7 8
5	3 4 9
6	5

34. In stem-and-leaf plot above, which of the following is the median of the data?

(A) 47

(B) 48

(C) 53

(D) 54

$$2x^2 + y^2 = 9$$
$$x^2 + y^2 = 5$$

35. What is the number of solutions to the following system of nonlinear equations?

(A) 0

(B) 1

(C) 2

(D) 4

36. If $y = \dfrac{\sin x - 1}{\cos x}$, then $\dfrac{dy}{dx} =$

(A) $\dfrac{\cos x - 1}{\cos^2 x}$

(B) $\dfrac{\cos x + 1}{\cos^2 x}$

(C) $\dfrac{1 + \sin x}{\cos^2 x}$

(D) $\dfrac{1 - \sin x}{\cos^2 x}$

$$9, 27, 81, 243, \cdots$$

37. In the geometric sequence above, the first term is 9, the second term is 27, and so on. What is the ratio of the 19th term to the 17th term?

(A) $\dfrac{1}{9}$

(B) $\dfrac{1}{3}$

(C) 3

(D) 9

38. If $f(x) = 2\log_7 x$, what is the value of $f^{-1}(0.3)$?

(A) 1.34

(B) 2.11

(C) 3.08

(D) 4.52

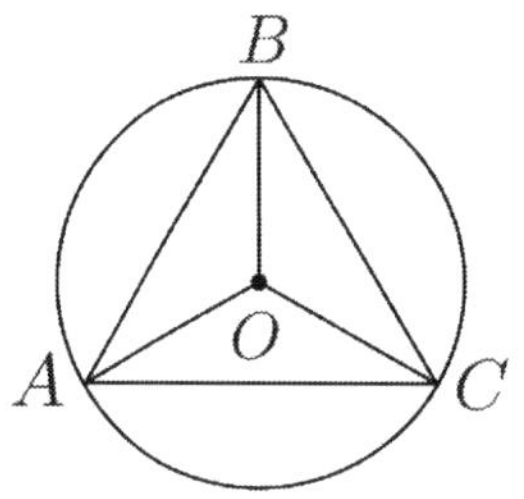

Note: Figure not drawn to scale.

39. In the figure above, the radius of the circle is 10. If the measure of $\angle OAC$ is $30°$, what is the height of the $\triangle ABC$?

(A) 10

(B) $10\sqrt{3}$

(C) 15

(D) $15\sqrt{3}$

For the following question, enter your answer in the answer box.

40. If $\dfrac{\sqrt{2} \cdot \sqrt[3]{4}}{\sqrt[4]{8}} = 2^k$, what is the value of k ?

Give your answer as a fraction.

$k = \dfrac{\square}{\square}$

41. In a set of five distinct positive integers, the average of the two smallest integers is 2, the average of the three smallest integers is 3, the average of the four smallest is 4, and the average of all five integers is 5. What is the largest integer in the set?

(A) 9

(B) 10

(C) 11

(D) 12

42. The acceleration of a particle moving in the y-axis at any time $t \geq 0$ is given by $a(t) = \dfrac{1}{1+t^2}$. If the velocity of the particle at time $t = 0$ is $v(0) = \dfrac{\pi}{2}$, which of the following is $v(1)$?

(A) $\dfrac{\pi}{3}$

(B) $\dfrac{2\pi}{3}$

(C) $\dfrac{3\pi}{4}$

(D) $\dfrac{11\pi}{12}$

$$x^2 - 6x + a = (x+b)^2$$

43. The equation above shows that the expression on the left side is equal to the expression on the right side. What is the value of $a + b$?

(A) -12

(B) -6

(C) 6

(D) 9

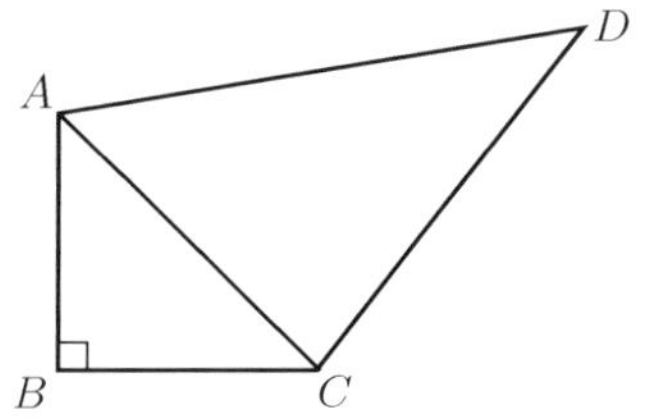

44. In quadrilateral ABCD above, $AB = BC = \sqrt{2}$, $m\angle BCD = 110°$, and $CD = 3$. What is AD ?

(A) 2.45

(B) 2.82

(C) 3.19

(D) 3.67

45. Suppose vector $\mathbf{V} = \langle a, b\rangle$, where a and b are the horizontal and vertical components of $\mathbf{V}$. If the horizontal component of $\mathbf{V}$ is three times the vertical component of $\mathbf{V}$, and the magnitude of $\mathbf{V}$ is $\sqrt{40}$, which of the following vector can be vector $\mathbf{V}$?

(A) $\langle -6, -2\rangle$

(B) $\langle -3, -1\rangle$

(C) $\langle 2, -6\rangle$

(D) $\langle 3, -1\rangle$

46. For $x > 1$, what is the value of x for which $e^x - 3 = \ln x$?

(A) 1.14

(B) 1.73

(C) 2.12

(D) 2.78

$$\mathbf{A} = \begin{bmatrix} 1 & 0 & -1 \\ 2 & 1 & 0 \end{bmatrix}, \quad \mathbf{B} = \begin{bmatrix} 2 & 1 \\ -1 & -2 \\ 0 & -1 \end{bmatrix}$$

47. Two matrices **A** and **B** are defined above. Which of the following is the product of the two matrices **AB** ?

(A) $\mathbf{AB} = \begin{bmatrix} 2 & 3 \\ 2 & 0 \end{bmatrix}$

(B) $\mathbf{AB} = \begin{bmatrix} 2 & 2 \\ 3 & 0 \end{bmatrix}$

(C) $\mathbf{AB} = \begin{bmatrix} 0 & 1 & -2 \\ -1 & 1 & -1 \\ -2 & 1 & 0 \end{bmatrix}$

(D) $\mathbf{AB} = \begin{bmatrix} 0 & -1 & -2 \\ 1 & 1 & 1 \\ -2 & -1 & 0 \end{bmatrix}$

48. A licence plate in a certain state consists of three digits and three letters, not necessarily distinct. If three digits must appear next to each other, how many different license plates are possible?

(A) 9×26^3

(B) 26×10^3

(C) $10^3 \times 26^3$

(D) $4 \times 10^3 \times 26^3$

For the following question, enter your answer in the answer box.

49. A big water bottle on the cooler was full on Monday. Students drank one-fourth the water on Tuesday, one-third of the remaining on Wednesday, one-half of the remaining on Thursday. What fractional part of the water would be remaining in the water bottle?

Give your answer as a fraction.

$$\frac{\square}{\square}$$

50. A population is normally distributed with a mean of 125 and a standard deviation of 15 which is denoted by $N(125, 15)$. If an simple random sample of 100 is drawn from the population, which of the following best represents the sampling distribution?

(A) $N(12.5, 1.5)$

(B) $N(12.5, 15)$

(C) $N(125, 1.5)$

(D) $N(125, 15)$

51. The area of an equilateral triangle is increasing at a rate of $2\sqrt{3}$ cm^2/sec. Which of the following is the rate at which each side of the equilateral triangle is increasing when the side length of the equilateral triangle is 3 cm?

(A) $\frac{1}{4}$ cm/sec

(B) $\frac{3}{5}$ cm/sec

(C) $\frac{2}{3}$ cm/sec

(D) $\frac{4}{3}$ cm/sec

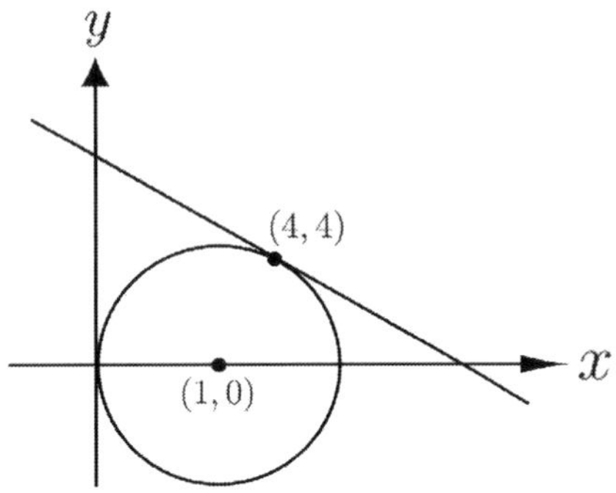

Note: Figure not drawn to scale.

52. In the figure above, the center of a circle is located at $(1, 0)$ and a line is tangent to the circle at $(4, 4)$. What is the equation of the tangent line?

(A) $4x + 3y = 28$

(B) $4x - 3y = 4$

(C) $3x - 4y = -4$

(D) $3x + 4y = 28$

53. If $\sec\theta + \tan\theta = \frac{1}{2}$, what is the value of $\sec\theta - \tan\theta$?

(A) 1

(B) 2

(C) 4

(D) 6

54. The equation $x^2 - 4y^2 - 8x + 8y + 8 = 0$ represents a hyperbola. Which of the following equation can be the asymptote of the hyperbola?

(A) $y + 1 = \frac{1}{2}(x + 4)$

(B) $y - 1 = \frac{1}{2}(x - 4)$

(C) $y + 1 = 2(x + 4)$

(D) $y - 1 = 2(x - 4)$

55. Joshua is riding his bicycle to visit Alex's house. He averages x miles per hour on the way to Alex's house and averages y miles per hour on the way home. What is the average speed of the entire trip in terms of x and y ?

(A) $\frac{xy}{2}$

(B) $\frac{2xy}{x+y}$

(C) $\frac{x+y}{2}$

(D) $\frac{x+y}{xy}$

56. Which of the following is the equation of the tangent line to the graph of $y = \ln(e - x)$ at the point $(e - 1, 0)$?

(A) $y = x - e + 1$

(B) $y = x + e - 1$

(C) $y = -x - e + 1$

(D) $y = -x + e - 1$

$$\frac{1}{2} + \frac{1}{2^2} + \frac{1}{2^3} + \cdots + \frac{1}{2^9}$$

57. What is the sum of the series above?

(A) $\frac{255}{256}$

(B) $\frac{511}{512}$

(C) $\frac{1023}{1024}$

(D) 1

58. If the function f is given by $f(x) = e^{x^2}$, on which of the following intervals is the graph of f concave up?

(A) $(-\infty, \infty)$

(B) $(-\infty, e)$

(C) $(-e, e)$

(D) (e, ∞)

$$a_n = \frac{a_{n-1} \cdot a_{n-2}}{2},\ a_1 = 1, a_2 = 2,\ \text{for } n \geq 3$$

59. If the sequence is defined above, what is the 8th term?

(A) $\frac{1}{128}$

(B) $\frac{1}{64}$

(C) $\frac{1}{32}$

(D) $\frac{1}{16}$

60. Jason is about to make a sandwich. He has three types of breads: wheat, rye, and sourdough. He has four types of deli meats: ham, chicken, turkey, and pastrami. If Jason chooses one type of bread and any collection of deli meats(no meat is possible), how many different sandwiches can Jason make?

(A) 24

(B) 36

(C) 48

(D) 64

STOP

Answers and Solutions

PRAXIS II 5161 PRACTICE TEST 4

Answers

1. D	11. D	21. D	31. D	41. A	51. D
2. D	12. B	22. B	32. B	42. C	52. D
3. 23	13. 57	23. 166	33. 11	43. C	53. B
4. A,C	14. A	24. D	34. B	44. B	54. B
5. B	15. C	25. D	35. D	45. A	55. B
6. D	16. C	26. C	36. D	46. A	56. D
7. C	17. D	27. D	37. D	47. B	57. B
8. C	18. D	28. A	38. A	48. D	58. A
9. B	19. C	29. C	39. C	49. $\frac{1}{4}$	59. A
10. D	20. D	30. C	40. $\frac{5}{12}$	50. C	60. C

Solutions

1. (D) **Number and Quantity**

   There are 12 inches in one foot. Define x as the number of weeks that the tulip needs to grow 12 inches. Set up a proportion in terms of inches and weeks.

$$\frac{1}{2}_{\text{ inch}} : 1_{\text{ week}} = 12_{\text{ inches}} : x_{\text{ weeks}}$$

$$\frac{\frac{1}{2}}{1} = \frac{12}{x} \qquad \text{Use cross product property}$$

$$\frac{1}{2}x = 12$$

$$x = 24$$

   Therefore, it will take 24 weeks for the tulip to grow one foot.

2. (D) **Geometry**

   Answer choice (A) and (D) satisfy the Pythagorean theorem: $c^2 = a^2 + b^2$. However, $\sqrt{2}$ in answer choice (A) is not a positive integer. Thus, eliminate answer choice (A). Therefore, (D) is the correct answer.

3. (23) **Number and Quantity**

   There are 12 inches in one foot. Convert Mr. Rhee's height to inches. Mr. Rhee is $5 \times 12 + 9 = 69$ inches tall. Joshua is $\frac{2}{3} \times 69 = 46$ inches tall. Therefore, the difference in their heights in inches is $69 - 46 = 23$.

4. (A,C) **Number and Quantity**

The value of $\sqrt{4}$ is 2, not -2. If $x < 0$, $|x| = -x$, not x. The statements in (A) and (C) are correct.

5. (B) **Probability and Statistics**

> Tips: Two events, A and B, are said to be independent if the outcome of A does not affect the outcome of B. If two events, A and B, are independent, the probability of both occurring is as follows:
>
> $$\text{P}(A \text{ and } B) = P(A) \times P(B)$$

The probability that it will rain on Monday is $\frac{7}{10}$. Thus, the probability that it will not rain on Monday is $1 - \frac{7}{10} = \frac{3}{10}$. The probability that it will snow on Tuesday is $\frac{1}{5}$. Since rain on Monday and snow on Tuesday are independent events, the probability that it will not rain on Monday and it will snow on Tuesday is $\frac{3}{10} \times \frac{1}{5} = \frac{3}{50}$.

6. (D) **Trigonometry**

> Tips: If the polar coordinates of a point is (r, θ), the rectangular coordinates of the point (x, y) are given by
>
> $$x = r\cos\theta, \qquad y = r\sin\theta$$

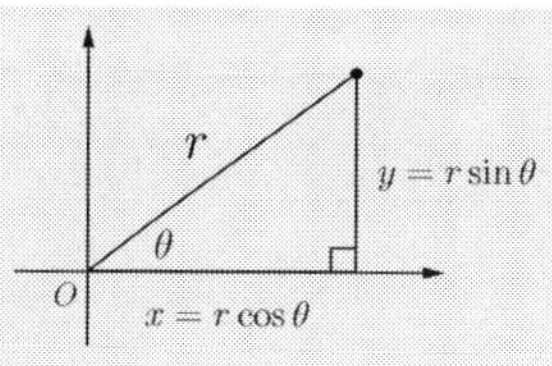

$$x = r\cos\theta \quad \Longrightarrow \quad x = 10\cos 135^\circ = 10\left(-\frac{\sqrt{2}}{2}\right) = -7.07$$

$$y = r\sin\theta \quad \Longrightarrow \quad y = 10\sin 135^\circ = 10\left(\frac{\sqrt{2}}{2}\right) = 7.07$$

Therefore, the rectangular coordinates (x, y) that correspond with the polar coordinates $(10, 135^\circ)$ are $(-7.07, 7.07)$.

7. (C) **Number and Quantity**

> Tips: $(ab)^n = a^n b^n$

$$\begin{aligned} 6^x &= (2 \times 3)^x \\ &= 2^x \times 3^x && \text{Substitute } a \text{ for } 2^x \text{ and } b \text{ for } 3^x \\ &= ab \end{aligned}$$

Therefore, 6^x in terms of a and b is ab.

8. (C) **Geometry**

In the figure below, the area of each sector is the area of a quarter circle with a radius of 2 because its central angle is 90°.

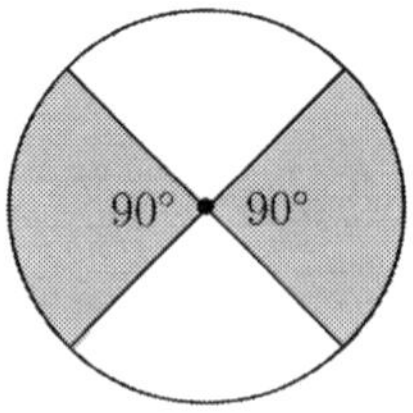

Thus, the sum of the area of the two sectors equals the area of half of the circle. Therefore, the area of the shaded region is $\frac{1}{2}\pi(2)^2 = 2\pi$.

9. (B) **Calculus**

Tips

L'Hospital's Rule

Let f and g are differentiable and $g'(x) \neq 0$ near a. Suppose you have one of the following cases

$$\lim_{x\to a}\frac{f(x)}{g(x)} = \frac{0}{0} \quad \text{or} \quad \lim_{x\to a}\frac{f(x)}{g(x)} = \frac{\pm\infty}{\pm\infty}$$

where a can be any real number, infinity, or negative infinity. Then,

$$\lim_{x\to a}\frac{f(x)}{g(x)} = \lim_{x\to a}\frac{f'(x)}{g'(x)}$$

Since $\lim\limits_{x\to 4}\frac{\sqrt{x}-2}{x-4} = \frac{\sqrt{4}-2}{4-4} = \frac{0}{0}$, use the L'Hospital's rule to find the limit.

$$\lim_{x\to 4}\frac{\sqrt{x}-2}{x-4} = \lim_{x\to 4}\frac{\frac{1}{2\sqrt{x}}}{1} = \frac{\frac{1}{2\sqrt{4}}}{1} = \frac{1}{4}$$

Therefore, $\lim\limits_{x\to 4}\frac{\sqrt{x}-2}{x-4} = \frac{1}{4}$.

10. (D) **Trigonometry**

Tips

For the general form of the cosine function $y = A\cos\big(B(x-C)\big) + D$, A affects the amplitude. The amplitude is half the distance between the maximum and minimum values of the function and is $|A|$.

The amplitude of the trigonometric function $y = -4\cos(\pi x + 1) - 2$ is $|-4| = 4$. Therefore, (D) is the correct answer.

11. (D) **Number and Quantity**

The units digit also means ones digit. The first seven positive squares are 1, 4, 9, 16, 25, 36, and 49. Thus, the units digit of the first seven positive squares are 1, 4, 9, 6, 5, 6, and 9, respectively.

$$\text{Sum of units digits} = 1 + 4 + 9 + 6 + 5 + 6 + 9 = 40$$

Therefore, the sum of the units digits of the first seven positive squares is 40.

12. (B) **Number and Quantity**

Tips $i^2 = -1$

$5x^2 + 7 = -3$	Subtract 7 from each side
$5x^2 = -10$	Divide each side by 5
$x^2 = -2$	Convert -2 to $2i^2$
$x^2 = 2i^2$	Take the square root of both sides
$x = \pm i\sqrt{2}$	

Therefore, the solutions to $5x^2 + 7 = -3$ are $i\sqrt{2}$ or $-i\sqrt{2}$.

13. (57) **Number and Quantity**

According to the survey, the most popular sport is the 100 meter sprint and the least popular sport is swimming.

$$\text{100 meter sprint} = 300 \times 0.36 = 108$$
$$\text{Swimming} = 300 \times 0.17 = 51$$

Therefore, $108 - 51 = 57$ million more people are going to watch the 100 meter sprint compared to swimming.

14. (A) **Geometry**

Tips The general equation of a circle is given by $(x - h)^2 + (y - k)^2 = r^2$, where (h, k) is the center of the circle and r is the radius of the circle.

$x^2 + y^2 + 4x - 6y = 3$	Rearrange the terms
$x^2 + 4x + y^2 - 6y = 3$	Add 4 to each side to complete squares in x
$(x + 2)^2 + y^2 - 6y = 7$	Add 9 to each side to complete squares in y
$(x + 2)^2 + (y - 3)^2 = 4^2$	

Therefore, the radius of the circle $x^2 + y^2 + 4x - 6y = 3$ is 4.

15. (C) **Functions**

Tips

For the rational function

$$f(x) = \frac{p(x)}{q(x)} = \frac{ax^m + \cdots}{bx^n + \cdots}$$

where m is the degree of the numerator and n is the degree of the denominator, f has a slant asymptote if $n < m$.

For the rational function $y = \dfrac{x^2 - x - 2}{x + 3}$ in answer choice (C), the numerator is a second degree polynomial ($m = 2$) and the denominator is a first degree polynomial ($n = 1$). Since $n < m$, the rational function $y = \dfrac{x^2 - x - 2}{x + 3}$ has a slant asymptote. Therefore, (C) is the correct answer.

16. (C) **Trigonometry**

Tips

If a triangle shown at the right is a SAS triangle (a, b, and $m\angle C$ are known), the area of the triangle is as follows:

$$A = \frac{1}{2}ab\sin C$$

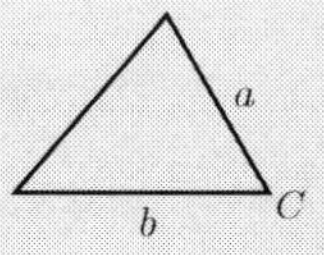

In $\triangle ABC$, $BC = 5$, $AC = 6$, and $m\angle C = 55°$ as shown in the figure below.

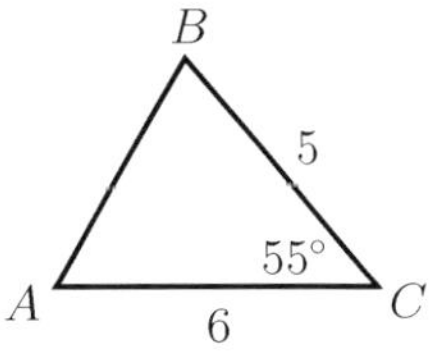

Therefore, the area A of $\triangle ABC$ is $A = \frac{1}{2}ab\sin C = \frac{1}{2}(5)(6)\sin 55° = 12.29$.

17. (D) **Discrete Mathematics**

$$\text{The Binomial Theorem:} \quad \left(x + \frac{1}{x}\right)^5 = \sum_{k=0}^{5} \binom{5}{k} (x)^{5-k} \left(\frac{1}{x}\right)^k$$

When $k = 2$, the term containing x is $\dbinom{5}{2}(x)^3\left(\dfrac{1}{x}\right)^2$ or $10x$. Therefore, the coefficient of x is 10.

18. (D) **Probability and Statistics**

Tips

If a prime factorization of a number, n, is $n = 2^a \times 3^b \times 5^c$, the total number of factors of n is $(a+1) \times (b+1) \times (c+1)$.

The prime factorization of 180 is $2^2 \cdot 3^2 \cdot 5$. Thus, the number of factors of 180 is $3 \cdot 3 \cdot 2 = 18$. Out of 18 factors, there are 6 odd factors: 1, 3, 5, 9, 15, and 45. Therefore, the probability that a randomly selected positive factor of 180 is odd is $\frac{6}{18} = \frac{1}{3}$.

19. (C) **Calculus**

Tips: If $f'(x) > 0$, then f is increasing.

x	-3	-2	-1	0	1	2	3	4
$f'(x)$	-2	-1	3	2	1	3	-2	-1

According to the table, $f'(x) > 0$ on the interval $(-1, 2)$. Therefore, f is increasing on the interval $(-1, 2)$.

20. (D) **Probability and Statistics**

		2nd die					
		1	2	3	4	5	6
1st die	1	○	○	○	○	○	○
	2	○					
	3	○					
	4	○					
	5	○					
	6	○					

There are 11 outcomes for which the sum of the two numbers is greater than the product of the two numbers. They are represented by circles in the table above. Therefore, the probability that the sum of the two numbers on the dice is greater than the product of the two numbers on the dice is $\frac{11}{36}$.

21. (D) **Algebra**

Tips: The difference of two squares pattern: $x^2 - y^2 = (x+y)(x-y)$

Use the difference of two squares pattern..

$$\begin{aligned} x^2 - y^2 &= 27 && \text{Factor} \\ (x+y)(x-y) &= 27 && \text{Substitute 3 for } x-y \\ 3(x+y) &= 27 \\ x+y &= 9 \end{aligned}$$

Set up a system of equations: $x + y = 9$ and $x - y = 3$. Use the linear combinations method to solve for x and y.

$$\begin{aligned} x+y &= 9 \\ x-y &= 3 && \text{Add two equations} \\ \hline 2x \quad &= 12 \\ x &= 6 \end{aligned}$$

$x = 6$ and $x + y = 9$ gives $y = 3$. Therefore, $x^2 + y^2 = (6)^2 + (3)^2 = 45$.

22. (B) **Algebra**

Substitute 0 for y and solve for x.

$$\begin{aligned}
2x^3 - x^2 - 8x + 4 &= 0 && \text{Group the first two terms and last two terms}\\
(2x^3 - x^2) + (-8x + 4) &= 0 && \text{Factor}\\
x^2(2x-1) - 4(2x-1) &= 0\\
(2x-1)(x^2-4) &= 0\\
(2x-1)(x+2)(x-2) &= 0\\
x &= -2,\ \frac{1}{2},\ 2
\end{aligned}$$

Therefore, the real zeros of $f(x) = 2x^3 - x^2 - 8x + 4$ are -2, $\frac{1}{2}$, and 2.

23. (166) **Probability and Statistics**

6 feet is equal to $6 \times 12 = 72$ inches. Substitute 72 for x in $y = 4.88x - 185$. Thus,

$$y = 4.88(72) - 185 = 166.36 \approx 166$$

Therefore, the weight of a student who is 6 feet tall would be 166 pounds.

24. (D) **Calculus**

$$\begin{aligned}
\lim_{h\to 0} \frac{(2+h)^2 - 2^2}{h} &= \lim_{h\to 0} \frac{4 + 4h + h^2 - 4}{h} = \lim_{h\to 0} \frac{h(4+h)}{h}\\
&= \lim_{h\to 0}(4+h) = 4
\end{aligned}$$

Therefore, the value of $\frac{(2+h)^2 - 2^2}{h}$ when h approaches 0 is 4.

25. (D) **Trigonometry**

For any angle x, the range of a sine function is $[-1, 1]$. For instance, both sine functions, $\sin x$ and $\sin(2x - 1)$ have the range of $[-1, 1]$.

$$\begin{aligned}
&-1 \le \sin(2\pi x + 4) \le 1 && \text{Multiply each side of inequality by } -5\\
&-5 \le -5\sin(2\pi x + 4) \le 5 && \text{Add 3 to each side of inequality}\\
&-2 \le -5\sin(2\pi x + 4) + 3 \le 8
\end{aligned}$$

Since the range of $y = -5\sin(2\pi x + 4) + 3$ is $[-2, 8]$, the minimum value of $y = -5\sin(2\pi x + 4) + 3$ is -2.

26. (C) **Algebra**

In the figure below, the linear function $f(x)$ represents a line.

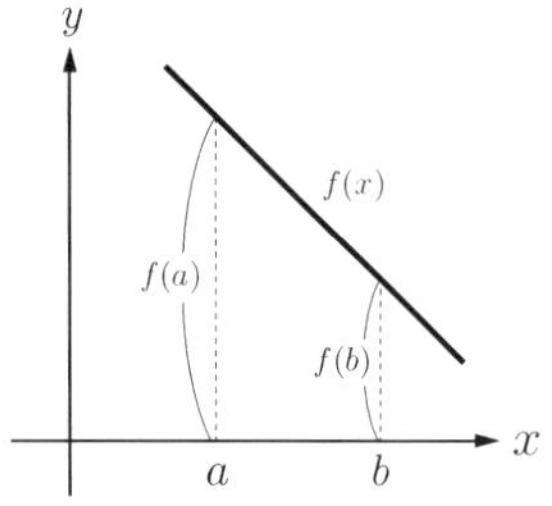

Thus, $f(a)$ and $f(b)$ represent the function's values at $x = a$ and $x = b$, respectively. Since $a < b$ and $f(a) > f(b)$, the linear function $f(x)$ must have a negative slope. Therefore, (C) is the correct answer.

27. (D) **Algebra**

Tips $(a-b)^2 = a^2 - 2ab + b^2$

$$\begin{aligned} \sqrt{x+1} - \sqrt{x-1} &= 1 && \text{Add } \sqrt{x+1} \text{ to each side} \\ \sqrt{x+1} &= 1 + \sqrt{x-1} && \text{Square both sides} \\ x+1 &= 1 + 2\sqrt{x-1} + x - 1 && \text{Subtract } x \text{ from each side} \\ 1 &= 2\sqrt{x-1} \\ x &= \frac{5}{4} \end{aligned}$$

Since $x = \frac{5}{4}$ satisfies the original equation, the solution to $\sqrt{x+1} - \sqrt{x-1} = 1$ is $x = \frac{5}{4}$.

28. (A) **Probability and Statistics**

Out of 9 points, the 3 points are randomly selected. So there are $\binom{9}{3} = 84$ ways of selecting the three points.

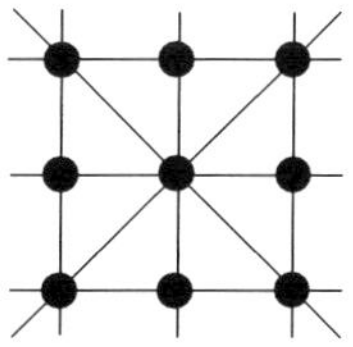

There are 8 ways to draw a line that contains the three points as shown above. Therefore, the probability that the three points are on the same line is $\frac{8}{84} = \frac{2}{21}$.

29. (C) **Functions**

From the table, notice that as the x value increases, the y value decreases. Among the answer choices, a rational function, $y = \frac{10}{x}$ best represents the table. Therefore, (C) is the correct answer.

30. (C) **Trigonometry**

Compare $y = -4\sin 2x - 1$ in answer choice (C) to $y = A\sin\big(B(x - C)\big) + D$. We found that $A = -4$, $B = 2$, $C = 0$, and $D = -1$. Thus, the amplitude is $|-4| = 4$. The period P is $P = \frac{2\pi}{B} = \frac{2\pi}{2} = \pi$. The vertical shift is 1 down. Therefore, (C) is the correct answer.

31. (D) **Algebra**

Tips: Solving $-(x-1)(x-2)(x-3) < 0$ means finding the x-values for which the graph of $f(x) = -(x-1)(x-2)(x-3)$ lies below the x-axis.

First, graph the polynomial function $f(x) = -(x-1)(x-2)(x-3)$ with the leading coefficient 1. Since 1, 2, and 3 are zeros of multiplicity 1, the graph of f crosses the x-axis at $x = 1$, $x = 2$, and $x = 3$ as shown in Figure A.

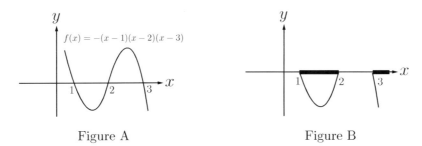

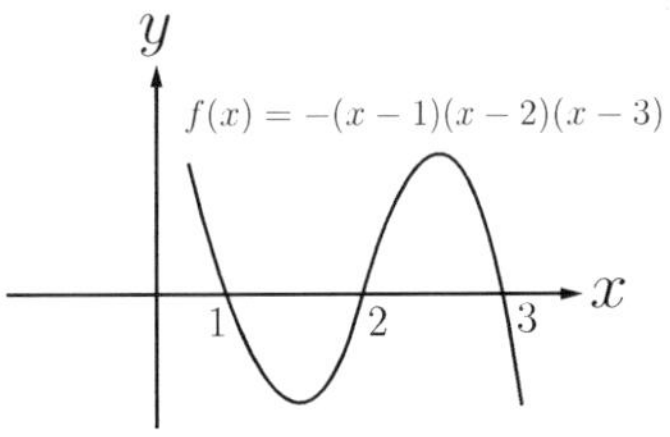

Figure A

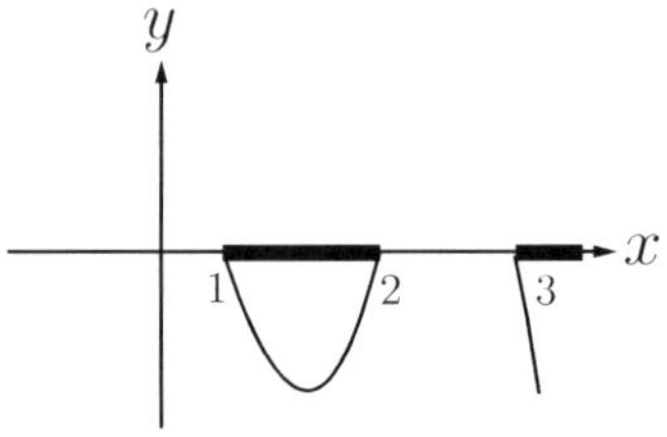

Figure B

As shown in Figure B, the graph of f lies below the x-axis when $1 < x < 2$ or $x > 3$. Therefore, the solution to $(x-1)(x-2)(x-3) > 0$ is $1 < x < 2$ or $x > 3$.

32. (B) **Functions**

$$f(g(x)) = f\left(\frac{1}{x}\right) = \frac{\frac{1}{x} + 1}{\frac{1}{x} - 2} = \frac{\frac{1+x}{x}}{\frac{1-2x}{x}} = \frac{1+x}{1-2x}$$

Therefore, $f(g(x)) = \dfrac{1+x}{1-2x}$.

33. (11) **Algebra**

Define x as the price of one book and y as the price of one DVD. Set up a system of linear equations in terms of x and y. The cost of one book and two DVDs is \$39. This can be expressed as $x + 2y = 39$. Additionally, the cost of two books and one DVD is \$27. This can be expressed as $2x + y = 27$.

$$\begin{aligned} x + 2y &= 39 \\ 2x + y &= 27 && \text{Add two equations} \\ \hline 3x + 3y &= 66 && \text{Divide each side by 3} \\ x + y &= 22 \end{aligned}$$

Thus, $x + y = 22$. This means that the price of one book and one DVD is \$22. Therefore, the average price of the book and the DVD is $\frac{x+y}{2} = 11$.

34. (B) **Probability and Statistics**

There are 9 numbers in the data. Thus, the fifth largest number in the data is the median. Therefore, the median of the data is 48.

35. (D) **Algebra**

Subtract the second equation $x^2 + y^2 = 5$ from the first equation $2x^2 + y^2 = 9$ as shown below.

$$\begin{aligned} 2x^2 + y^2 &= 9 \\ x^2 + y^2 &= 5 \qquad \text{Subtract the two equations} \\ \hline x^2 \qquad &= 4 \\ x \qquad &= \pm 2 \end{aligned}$$

In order to find the y-values, substitute $x = 2$ and $x = -2$ into the second equation $x^2 + y^2 = 5$. When $x = 2$, $y = \pm 1$. When $x = -2$, $y = \pm 1$. Thus, the solutions to the system of nonlinear equations are $(2, 1)$, $(2, -1)$, $(-2, 1)$, and $(-2, -1)$. Therefore, there are 4 solutions to the system of nonlinear equations.

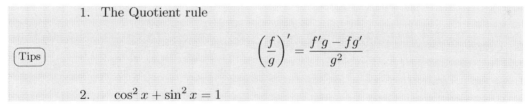

36. (D) **Calculus**

Tips

1. The Quotient rule

$$\left(\frac{f}{g}\right)' = \frac{f'g - fg'}{g^2}$$

2. $\cos^2 x + \sin^2 x = 1$

Let's differentiate $y = \dfrac{\sin x - 1}{\cos x}$ using the Quotient rule.

$$\begin{aligned} \left(\frac{\sin x - 1}{\cos x}\right)' &= \frac{(\sin x - 1)'(\cos x) - (\sin x - 1)(\cos x)'}{(\cos x)^2} \\ &= \frac{\cos x \cos x - (\sin x - 1)(-\sin x)}{\cos^2 x} \\ &= \frac{\cos^2 x + \sin^2 x - \sin x}{\cos^2 x} \\ &= \frac{1 - \sin x}{\cos^2 x} \end{aligned}$$

Therefore, $\dfrac{dy}{dx} = \dfrac{1 - \sin x}{\cos^2 x}$.

37. (D) **Discrete Mathematics**

> Tips: The nth term of a geometric sequence: $a_n = a_1 \times r^{n-1}$, where r is the common ratio.

In the geometric sequence, the first term is 9 and the second term is 27. This means that the common ratio (a number that you multiply or divide one term by to get the next term), $r = 3$. Use the nth term formula to find the ratio of the 19th term to the 17th term.

$$\begin{aligned} \frac{a_{19}}{a_{17}} &= \frac{a_1 \times r^{18}}{a_1 \times r^{16}} \\ &= r^2 && \text{Since } r = 3 \\ &= 9 \end{aligned}$$

Therefore, the ratio of the 19th term to the 17th term is 9.

38. (A) **Functions**

> Tips: $\log_a y = x \iff y = a^x$

In order to find the inverse function of $y = 2\log_7 x$, switch the x and y variables and solve for y.

$$\begin{aligned} y &= 2\log_7 x && \text{Switch the } x \text{ and } y \text{ variables} \\ x &= 2\log_7 y && \text{Divide each side by 2} \\ \log_7 y &= \frac{x}{2} && \text{Convert the equation to an exponential equation} \\ y &= 7^{\frac{x}{2}} \end{aligned}$$

Thus, the inverse function is $f^{-1}(x) = 7^{\frac{x}{2}}$. Therefore, the value of $f^{-1}(0.3) = 7^{\frac{0.3}{2}} = 1.34$.

39. (C) **Geometry**

In the figure below, $\overline{AO}$, $\overline{BO}$, and $\overline{CO}$ are radii of the circle. Thus, $AO = BO = CO = 10$. $\triangle AOC$ is an isosceles triangle so the base angles $\angle OAC$ and $\angle OCA$ are congruent. In other words, $m\angle OAC = m\angle OCA = 30°$. Since the sum of measures of the interior angles of $\triangle AOC$ is $180°$, $m\angle AOC = 120°$.

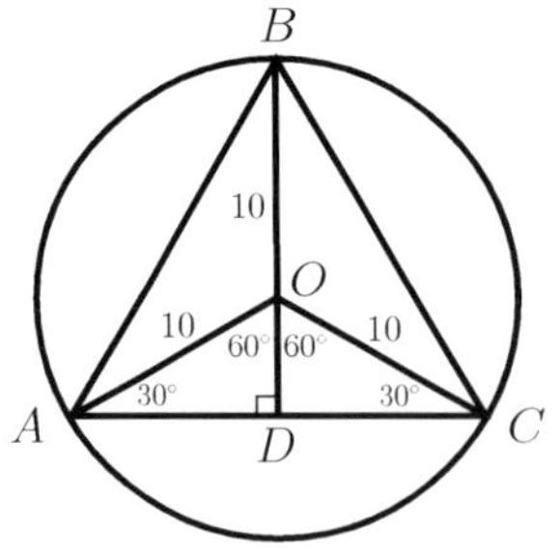

$\overline{OD}$, the height of $\triangle AOC$, is drawn from vertex O to $\overline{AC}$, the base of $\triangle AOC$. Thus, $\overline{OD} \perp \overline{AC}$. $\triangle AOD$ is a 30°-60°-90° special right triangle with $AO = 10$. Since $\overline{OD}$ is the shorter leg of $\triangle AOD$, OD is half AO, which is 5. The height of $\triangle ABC$ is BD and $BD = BO + OD = 15$. Therefore, the height of $\triangle ABC$ is 15.

40. ($\frac{5}{12}$) **Number and Quantity**

Tips
1. $a^m \cdot a^n = a^{m+n}$
2. $\frac{a^m}{a^n} = a^{m-n}$
3. $\sqrt[n]{a^m} = a^{\frac{m}{n}}$

Change $\sqrt{2}$ to $2^{\frac{1}{2}}$, $\sqrt[3]{4} = \sqrt[3]{2^2} = 2^{\frac{2}{3}}$, and $\sqrt[4]{8} = \sqrt[4]{2^3} = 2^{\frac{3}{4}}$.

$$\frac{\sqrt{2} \cdot \sqrt[3]{4}}{\sqrt[4]{8}} = \frac{2^{\frac{1}{2}} \cdot 2^{\frac{2}{3}}}{2^{\frac{3}{4}}} = 2^{\frac{1}{2}+\frac{2}{3}-\frac{3}{4}} = 2^{\frac{5}{12}}$$

Therefore, the value of k is $\dfrac{5}{12}$.

41. (A) **Number and Quantity**

Distinct means different. There are five different positive integers in the set. It is necessary to solve this problem in terms of the sum: the sum is the average of the elements in the set times the number of the elements in the set. The average of the two smallest integers in the set is 2. This means that the sum of the two smallest integers is 4. Since the five integers in the set are positive and different, the two smallest positive integers in the set must be 1 and 3, neither 2 and 2, nor 0 and 4. Additionally, the averages of the three smallest integers, four smallest integers, and five integers in the set are 3, 4, and 5, respectively. Thus, the sums of the three smallest integers, four smallest integers and five integers in the set are 9, 16, and 25, respectively. Below shows how to obtain the five positive integers in the set.

Sum of two smallest integers $= 1 + 3 = 4$
Sum of three smallest integers $= 1 + 3 + 5 = 9$
Sum of four smallest integers $= 1 + 3 + 5 + 7 = 16$
Sum of five integers in the set $= 1 + 3 + 5 + 7 + 9 = 25$

Thus, there are 1, 3, 5, 7, and 9 in the set. Therefore, the largest integer in the set is 9.

42. (C) **Calculus**

Tips
1. If $a(t)$ is the acceleration of an object, $\displaystyle\int_{t_1}^{t_2} a(t)\,dt$ is the total change in velocity from time period $t = t_1$ to $t = t_2$.
2. $v(1) = v(0) + \displaystyle\int_0^1 a(t)\,dt$
3. $\displaystyle\int_0^1 \frac{1}{1+t^2}\,dt = \tan^{-1} t\Big]_0^1 = \tan^{-1}(1) - \tan^{-1}(0) = \frac{\pi}{4}$

$$v(1) = v(0) + \int_0^1 \frac{1}{1+t^2}\,dt = \frac{\pi}{2} + \tan^{-1} t\Big]_0^1 = \frac{\pi}{2} + \frac{\pi}{4} = \frac{3\pi}{4}$$

Therefore, the value of $v(1)$ is $\frac{3\pi}{4}$.

43. (C) **Algebra**

Tips The binomial expansion formula: $(x + y)^2 = x^2 + 2xy + y^2$.

Expand $(x + b)^2$ using the binomial expansion formula. Thus, $(x + b)^2 = x^2 + 2bx + b^2$.

$$
\begin{aligned}
x^2 - 6x + a &= (x + b)^2 \\
x^2 - 6x + a &= x^2 + 2bx + b^2 \qquad \text{Subtract } x^2 \text{ from each side} \\
-6x + a &= 2bx + b^2
\end{aligned}
$$

The expression on the left side is equal to the expression on the right side. It means that the coefficients of x and constants on both expressions are the same: $-6 = 2b$ and $a = b^2$. Thus, $b = -3$ and $a = b^2 = (-3)^2 = 9$. Therefore, the value of $a + b = 9 - 3 = 6$.

44. (B) **Geometry**

Tips If triangle ABC shown to the right is a SAS triangle (a, b, and $m\angle C$ are known), side c can be calculated by the Law of Cosines.

$$c^2 = a^2 + b^2 - 2ab\cos C$$

Note that side c is opposite angle C.

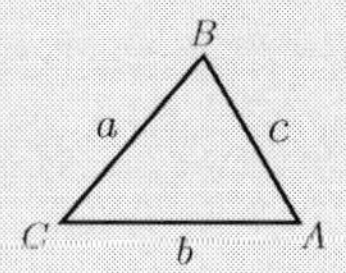

$\triangle ABC$ is a 45°-45°-90° right triangle with $AB = BC = \sqrt{2}$ as shown in the figure below. Use the Phygorean theorem: $AB^2 = (\sqrt{2})^2 + (\sqrt{2})^2$ or use the ratio $1 : 1 : \sqrt{2}$ such that the length of the hypotenuse is $\sqrt{2}$ times the length of each leg. Thus, $AB = 2$. Since $m\angle BCD = 110°$ and $m\angle BCA = 45°$, $m\angle ACD = 65°$.

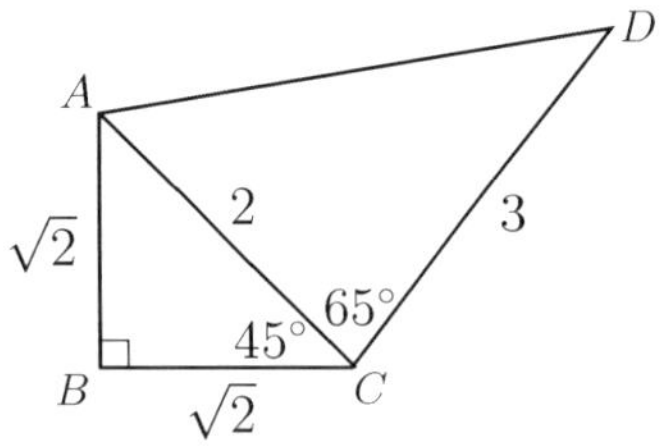

Since $\triangle ACD$ is a SAS triangle (AC, CD, and $m\angle ACD$ are known), use the Law of Cosines to find AD.

$$
\begin{aligned}
AD^2 &= AC^2 + CD^2 - 2(AC)(CD)\cos 65° \\
AD^2 &= 2^2 + 3^2 - 2(2)(3)\cos 65° = 7.929 \\
AD &= 2.82
\end{aligned}
$$

Therefore, $AD = 2.82$.

45. (A) **Trigonometry**

Tips If vector $\mathbf{V} = \langle a, b \rangle$, the magnitude of the vector $\mathbf{V}$ is $|\mathbf{V}| = \sqrt{a^2 + b^2}$

Vector $\mathbf{V}$ is given as $\langle a, b \rangle$. The horizontal component of $\mathbf{V}$ is three times the vertical component of $\mathbf{V}$. Thus, $a = 3b$. Since the magnitude of $\mathbf{V}$ is $\sqrt{40}$,

$$
\begin{aligned}
|\mathbf{V}| &= \sqrt{a^2 + b^2} && \text{Substitute } 3b \text{ for } a \text{ and } \sqrt{40} \text{ for } |\mathbf{V}| \\
\sqrt{40} &= \sqrt{(3b)^2 + b^2} && \text{Square both sides} \\
10b^2 &= 40 && \text{Divide each side by 10} \\
b^2 &= 4 && \text{Solve for } b \\
b &= \pm 2
\end{aligned}
$$

When $b = 2$, $a = 3b = 6$. When $b = -2$, $a = -6$. Thus, vector $\mathbf{V}$ can be either $\langle 6, 2 \rangle$ or $\langle -6, -2 \rangle$. Therefore, (A) is the correct answer.

46. (A) **Functions**

Graph the two functions $y = e^x - 3$ and $y = \ln x$ in your graphing calculator and find the intersection point for $x > 1$ as shown below in the figure below.

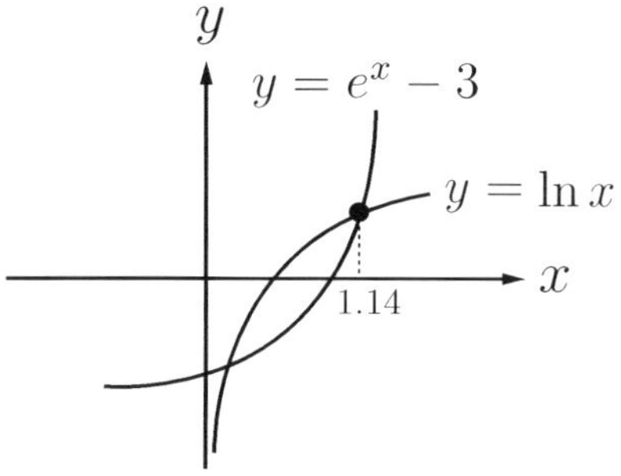

Since the graph of $y = e^x - 3$ intersects the graph of $y = \ln x$ at $x = 1.14$, the value of x for which $e^x - 3 = \ln x$ is 1.14.

47. (B) **Number and Quantity**

Tips The product of an $m \times n$ matrix $\mathbf{A}$ with an $n \times p$ matrix $\mathbf{B}$ is the $m \times p$ $\mathbf{AB}$ matrix.

The product of an 2×3 matrix $\mathbf{A}$ with an 3×2 matrix $\mathbf{A}$ is the 2×2 $\mathbf{AB}$ matrix.

$$
\mathbf{AB} = \begin{bmatrix} 1 & 0 & -1 \\ 2 & 1 & 0 \end{bmatrix} \begin{bmatrix} 2 & 1 \\ -1 & -2 \\ 0 & -1 \end{bmatrix} = \begin{bmatrix} 1(2) + 0(-1) - 1(0) & 1(1) + 0(-2) - 1(-1) \\ 2(2) + 1(-1) + 0(0) & 2(1) + 1(-2) + 0(-1) \end{bmatrix} = \begin{bmatrix} 2 & 2 \\ 3 & 0 \end{bmatrix}
$$

Therefore, (B) is the correct answer.

48. (D) **Discrete Mathematics**

There are 10^3 ways to choose three digits and 26^3 ways to choose three letters. Since the three digits must appear next to each other, there are 4 possible locations for the three digits out of 6 blanks. Therefore, the number of different possible license plates is $4 \times 10^3 \times 26^3$.

49. ($\frac{1}{4}$) **Number and Quantity**

On Tuesday, students drank $\frac{1}{4}$ of the water. Thus, $\frac{3}{4}$ of the water would be remaining on Tuesday. Students drank $\frac{1}{3}$ of the remaining water on Wednesday. Thus, $\frac{2}{3}$ of the remaining water would be remaining on Wednesday. This means that $\frac{2}{3} \times \frac{3}{4} = \frac{1}{2}$ of the water would be remaining on Wednesday. Students drank $\frac{1}{2}$ of the remaining water on Thursday. Thus, $\frac{1}{2}$ of the remaining water would be remaining. Therefore, $\frac{1}{2} \times \frac{1}{2} = \frac{1}{4}$ of the water would be remaining on Thursday.

50. (C) **Probability and Statistics**

Tips

Draw an simple random sample of size n from a population that has a normal distribution with mean μ and standard deviation σ. Then the sample mean $\overline{x}$ has a normal distribution with mean μ and standard deviation $\sigma_{\overline{x}} = \dfrac{\sigma}{n}$. In other words,

$$\overline{x} \sim N\left(\mu, \frac{\sigma}{n}\right)$$

A population is normally distributed with a mean of 125 and a standard deviation of 15 which is denoted by $N(125, 15)$. An simple random sample of 100 is taken from the population. Thus, the standard deviation of the sample is $\sigma_{\overline{x}} = \frac{15}{\sqrt{100}} = 1.5$. Therefore, the sampling distribution is $N(125, 1.5)$.

51. (D) **Calculus**

Tips

The area A of an equilateral triangle with a side length S is $A = \dfrac{\sqrt{3}}{4}S^2$.

We are given that $\dfrac{dA}{dt} = 2\sqrt{3}\ \text{cm}^2/\text{sec}$, and try to find $\frac{dS}{dt}$ when $S = 3$ cm. Differentiate $A = \dfrac{\sqrt{3}}{4}S^2$ with respect to t using the Chain rule and solve for $\dfrac{dS}{dt}$.

$$\frac{dA}{dt} = \frac{\sqrt{3}}{4} \cdot 2S \cdot \frac{dS}{dt}$$
$$\frac{dS}{dt} = \frac{2}{\sqrt{3}S}\frac{dA}{dt}$$

Substituting $S = 3$, and $\dfrac{dA}{dt} = 2\sqrt{3}\ \text{cm}^2/\text{sec}$ gives

$$\frac{dS}{dt} = \frac{2}{\sqrt{3}(3)} \cdot 2\sqrt{3} = \frac{4}{3}$$

Therefore, the rate at which each side of the equilateral triangle is increasing when the side length of the equilateral triangle is 3 cm is $\dfrac{4}{3}$ cm/sec.

52. (D) **Geometry**

In the figure below, the tangent line is perpendicular to the radius drawn from the center $(1, 0)$ to the point of tangency $(4, 4)$. Since the slope of the radius is $\frac{4-0}{4-1} = \frac{4}{3}$, the slope of the tangent line is the negative reciprocal, or $-\frac{3}{4}$.

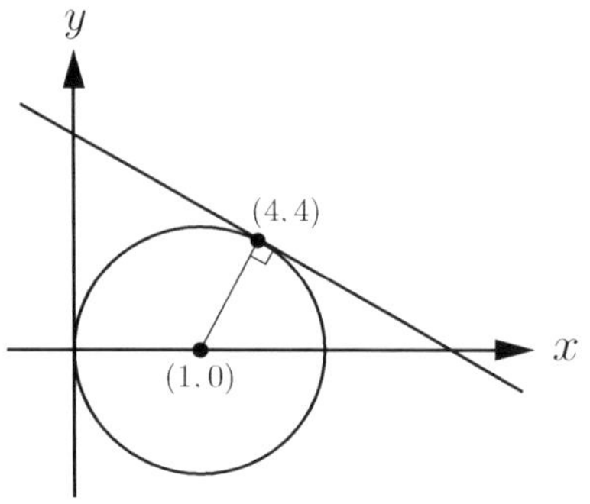

The equation of the tangent line is $y = -\frac{3}{4}x + b$, where b is the y-intercept. Since the tangent line passes through the point $(4, 4)$, substitute 4 for x and 4 for y to find the y-intercept.

$$y = -\frac{3}{4}x + b \qquad \text{Substitute 4 for } x \text{ and 4 for } y$$
$$4 = -\frac{3}{4}(4) + b \qquad \text{Solve for } b$$
$$b = 7$$

Thus, the equation of the tangent line is $y = -\frac{3}{4}x + 7$. Multiply each side of the equation of the tangent line by 4 to write the equation in standard form. Therefore, the equation of the tangent line is $3x + 4y = 28$.

53. (B) **Trigonometry**

Tips
1. $\sec^2\theta - \tan^2\theta = 1$
2. $\sec^2\theta - \tan^2\theta = (\sec\theta + \tan\theta)(\sec\theta - \tan\theta)$

$$\sec^2\theta - \tan^2\theta = 1 \qquad \text{Factor}$$
$$(\sec\theta + \tan\theta)(\sec\theta - \tan\theta) = 1 \qquad \text{Substitute } \frac{1}{2} \text{ for } \sec\theta + \tan\theta$$
$$\frac{1}{2}(\sec\theta - \tan\theta) = 1 \qquad \text{Multiply each side by 2}$$
$$\sec\theta - \tan\theta = 2$$

Therefore, the value of $\sec\theta - \tan\theta$ is 2.

54. (B) **Geometry**

Tips: The general equation of a hyperbola with a horizontal transverse axis is $\frac{(x-h)^2}{a^2} - \frac{(y-k)^2}{b^2} = 1$, where the center of the hyperbola is (h,k). The equations of asymptotes are $y - k = \pm\frac{b}{a}(x-h)$

In order to write a general equation of the hyperbola $\frac{(x-h)^2}{a^2} - \frac{(y-k)^2}{b^2} = 1$, complete the squares in x and in y.

$x^2 - 4y^2 - 8x + 8y + 8 = 0$	Subtract 8 from each side
$x^2 - 4y^2 - 8x + 8y = -8$	Rearrange the terms
$(x^2 - 8x) - 4(y^2 - 2y) = -8$	Add 16 to each side to complete the squares in x
$(x^2 - 8x + 16) - 4(y^2 - 2y) = 8$	Subtract 4 from each side to complete the squares in y
$(x-4)^2 - 4(y^2 - 2y + 1) = 4$	Divide each side by 4
$\frac{(x-4)^2}{2^2} - \frac{(y-1)^2}{1^2} = 1$	

In order to find the center of the hyperbola, set $x - 4 = 0$ and $y - 1 = 0$ and solve for x and y. Thus, the center of the hyperbola is $(4,1)$ as shown in the figure below.

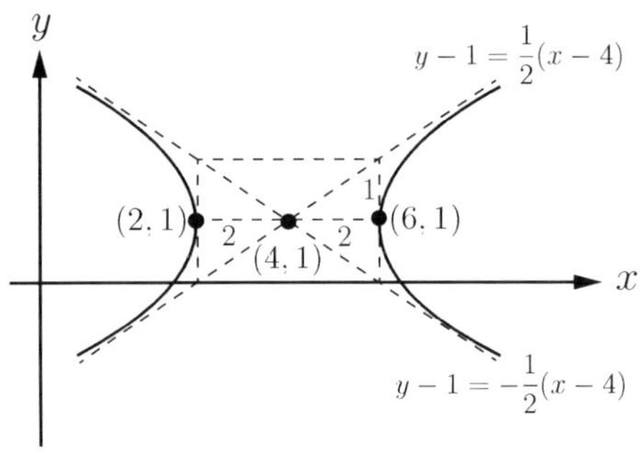

Since the vertices are horizontally 2 units from the center, the vertices are at $(6,1)$ and $(2,1)$. The slopes of the asymptotes are $\pm\frac{1}{2}$ and the asymptotes pass through the center $(4,1)$. Thus, the equations of the asymptotes are $y - 1 = \frac{1}{2}(x-4)$ and $y - 1 = -\frac{1}{2}(x-4)$. Therefore, (B) is the correct answer.

55. (B) **Number and Quantity**

Define z as the distance between Joshua's home and Alex's house. Additionally, define T_{JA} and T_{AJ} as the times Joshua needed to travel from his home to Alex's house and Alex's house to his home, respectively. Use the time formula, time $= \frac{\text{distance}}{\text{rate}}$. Since Joshua averages x miles per hour on the way to Alex's house and averages y miles per hour on the way home, $T_{JA} = \frac{z}{x}$ and $T_{AJ} = \frac{z}{y}$.

$$\begin{aligned}\text{Average speed of entire trip} &= \frac{\text{total distance}}{\text{total time}} = \frac{z+z}{T_{JA}+T_{AJ}} \\ &= \frac{2z}{\frac{z}{x}+\frac{z}{y}} = \frac{2z}{\frac{xz+yz}{xy}} \\ &= \frac{2z}{\frac{z(x+y)}{xy}} = \frac{2xyz}{z(x+y)} \\ &= \frac{2xy}{x+y}\end{aligned}$$

Therefore, the average speed of the entire trip in terms of x and y is $\frac{2xy}{x+y}$.

56. (D) **Calculus**

Tips The Chain rule: If $y = \ln h(x)$, $\dfrac{dy}{dx} = \dfrac{h'(x)}{h(x)}$.

Differentiate $f(x) = \ln(e - x)$ using the Chain rule.

$$f'(x) = \frac{-1}{e-x} \quad \Longrightarrow \quad f'(e-1) = \frac{-1}{e-(e-1)} = -1$$

Therefore, the equation of the tangent line to the graph of $y = \ln(e - x)$ at the point $(e - 1, 0)$ is $y = -1(x - (e - 1))$ or $y = -x + e - 1$.

57. (B) **Discrete Mathematics**

Tips The nth partial sum of a geometric series: $S_n = \dfrac{a_1(1-r^n)}{1-r}$

$\dfrac{1}{2} + \dfrac{1}{2^2} + \dfrac{1}{2^3} + \cdots + \dfrac{1}{2^9}$ is the 9th partial sum S_9 of a geometric series with $r = \dfrac{1}{2}$.

$$S_9 = \frac{\frac{1}{2}\left(1-\left(\frac{1}{2}\right)^9\right)}{1-\frac{1}{2}} = 1 - \left(\frac{1}{2}\right)^9 = 1 - \frac{1}{512} = \frac{511}{512}$$

Therefore, $\dfrac{1}{2} + \dfrac{1}{2^2} + \dfrac{1}{2^3} + \cdots + \dfrac{1}{2^9} = \dfrac{511}{512}$.

58. (A) **Calculus**

> Tips
> 1. If $f''(x) > 0$, then f is concave up.
> 2. The Product rule: $(f \cdot g)' = f' \cdot g + f \cdot g'$

$$f(x) = e^{x^2}$$
$$f'(x) = 2xe^{x^2}$$
$$f''(x) = 2e^{x^2} + 2x \cdot 2xe^{x^2} = e^{x^2}(2 + 4x^2)$$

Since $e^{x^2} > 0$ for all real numbers, and $2 + 4x^2 > 0$ for all real numbers, $f''(x) > 0$ for all real numbers. Thus, f is concave up for all real numbers. Therefore, (A) is the correct answer.

59. (A) **Discrete Mathematics**

In order to evaluate the 8th term, we need to find the previous seven terms as shown below.

$a_n = \dfrac{a_{n-1} \cdot a_{n-2}}{2}$, $a_1 = 1, a_2 = 2,$	Recursive formula with $a_1 = 1$ and $a_2 = 2$
$a_3 = \dfrac{a_2 \cdot a_1}{2} = \dfrac{2 \cdot 1}{2} = 1$	Substitute 3 for n to find a_3
$a_4 = \dfrac{a_3 \cdot a_2}{2} = \dfrac{1 \cdot 2}{2} = 1$	Substitute 4 for n to find a_4
$a_5 = \dfrac{a_4 \cdot a_3}{2} = \dfrac{1 \cdot 1}{2} = \dfrac{1}{2}$	Substitute 5 for n to find a_5
$a_6 = \dfrac{a_5 \cdot a_4}{2} = \dfrac{\frac{1}{2} \cdot 1}{2} = \dfrac{1}{4}$	Substitute 6 for n to find a_6
$a_7 = \dfrac{a_6 \cdot a_5}{2} = \dfrac{\frac{1}{4} \cdot \frac{1}{2}}{2} = \dfrac{1}{16}$	Substitute 7 for n to find a_7
$a_8 = \dfrac{a_7 \cdot a_6}{2} = \dfrac{\frac{1}{16} \cdot \frac{1}{4}}{2} = \dfrac{1}{128}$	Substitute 8 for n to find a_8

Therefore, the value of the 8th term is $\dfrac{1}{128}$.

60. (C) **Discrete Mathematics**

Tips

1. The fundamental counting principle: If one event can occur in m ways and another event can occur in n ways, then the number of ways both events can occur is $m \times n$.

2. The sum of the entries in the nth row of Pascal's triangle is 2^n.

$$\binom{n}{0} + \binom{n}{1} + \binom{n}{2} + \cdots + \binom{n}{n} = 2^n$$

Let event 1 be selecting the type of bread, and event 2 be selecting any collection of deli meats. For event 1, there are $\binom{3}{1} =$ ways to select the type of bread. For event 2, Jason can select either 0, 1, 2, 3, or 4 deli meats. This can be calculated as follows:

$$\binom{4}{0} + \binom{4}{1} + \binom{4}{2} + \binom{4}{3} + \binom{4}{4} = 2^4 = 16$$

Thus, event 1 has 3 outcomes, and event 2 has 16 outcomes. According to the fundamental counting principle, Jason can make $3 \times 16 = 48$ different sandwiches.

PRAXIS II 5161 PRACTICE TEST 5

Time — 150 minutes
Number of questions — 60

Directions: Solve each of the following problems using the available space for scratch work. Choose the best answer among the answer choices given and fill in the corresponding circle on the answer sheet.

1. Joshua traveled 220 miles at 55 miles per hour. How many minutes longer would the return trip take if he travels at 50 miles per hour?

   (A) 12 minutes

   (B) 18 minutes

   (C) 24 minutes

   (D) 30 minutes

$$B = \{9, 6, 11, 5, 12, 15\}$$

2. Set B above has six positive integers. What is the median of set B ?

   (A) 6

   (B) 9

   (C) 10

   (D) 11

3. What is the slope of a line that passes through the points $(1, 2)$ and $(1, 8)$?

   (A) 0

   (B) 2

   (C) 5

   (D) Undefined

4. There are 12 parallelograms. Each parallelogram is either a rectangle, a rhombus, or both. If there are 7 rhombuses and 8 rectangles, how many parallelograms are squares among the 12 parallelograms?

   (A) 1

   (B) 2

   (C) 3

   (D) 4

5. $f(x) = -x^2 + 4x + 5$. If $f(k) = f(0)$, which of the following can be the value of k ?

   (A) 1

   (B) 2

   (C) 3

   (D) 4

For the following question, enter your answer in the answer box.

6. If the length of the diagonal of a square is 10, what is the area of the square?

   Area = [ ]

7. Scores on a math test are normally distributed with a mean of 82 and a standard deviation of 6. What is the z-score for a student who received a 94 on the test?

   (A) 1.5

   (B) 2

   (C) 2.5

   (D) 3

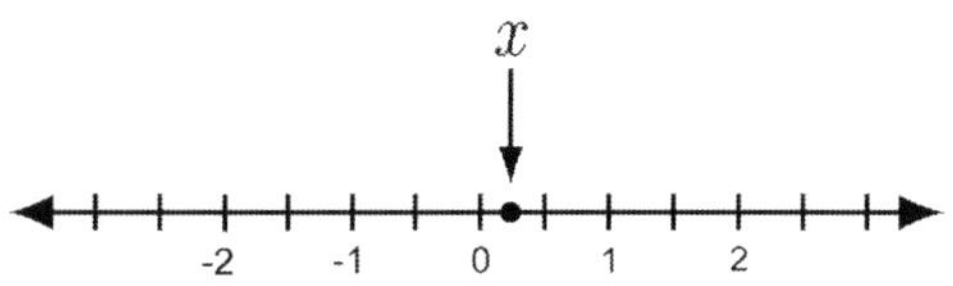

8. As shown above, x is on the number line. Which of the following expression has the largest value?

   (A) x

   (B) x^2

   (C) $\dfrac{1}{x}$

   (D) $\dfrac{1}{x^2}$

9. If $a < 0$, solve the inequality: $ax - 2a > 5a$

   (A) $x > -3$

   (B) $x < 3$

   (C) $x > 7$

   (D) $x < 7$

10. $\displaystyle\int_{\frac{\pi}{4}}^{\frac{3\pi}{4}} \cos x \, dx =$

   (A) 0

   (B) $\dfrac{\sqrt{2}}{2}$

   (C) $\sqrt{2}$

   (D) 2

For the following question, select all the answer choices that apply.

11. A bag contains \$2.70 in nickels and dimes. There are 3 more nickels than dimes. Which of the following equations correctly represents this information?

Select all that apply.

(A) $5(d+3)+10d=270$

(B) $5n+10(n-3)=270$

(C) $5x+10(x+3)=270$

12. The numbers 1 through 10 inclusive are in a hat. If a number is selected at random, what is the probability that the number is neither divisible by 3 nor 4?

(A) $\frac{1}{4}$

(B) $\frac{1}{3}$

(C) $\frac{1}{2}$

(D) $\frac{3}{5}$

$$|2x+4|<6$$

13. Which of the following is the solution to the inequality above?

(A) $x>1$

(B) $1<x<5$

(C) $-7<x<1$

(D) $-5<x<1$

14. If f is an odd function, which of the following graph best represents f ?

(A)

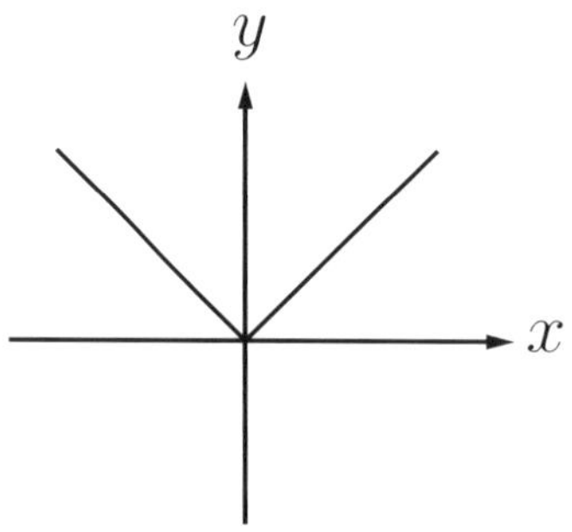

(B)

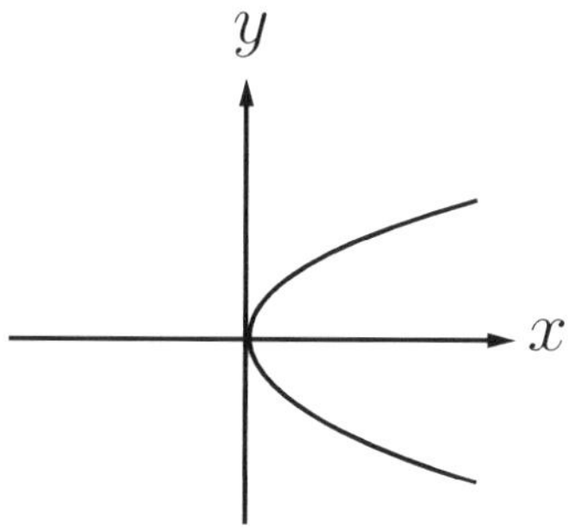

(C)

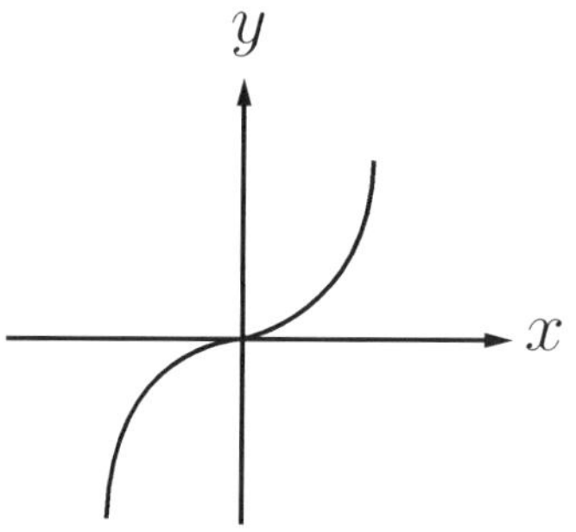

(D)

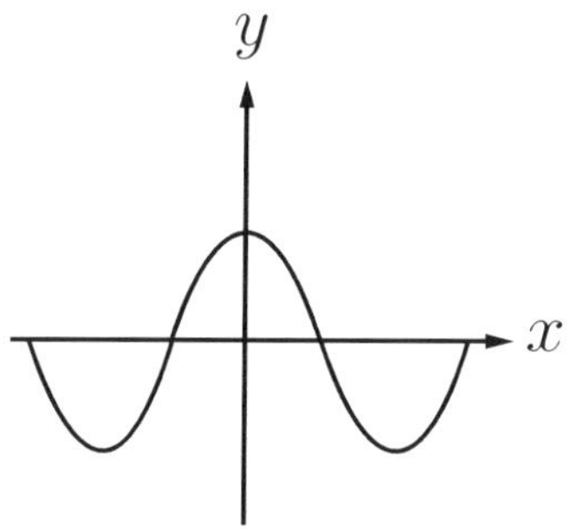

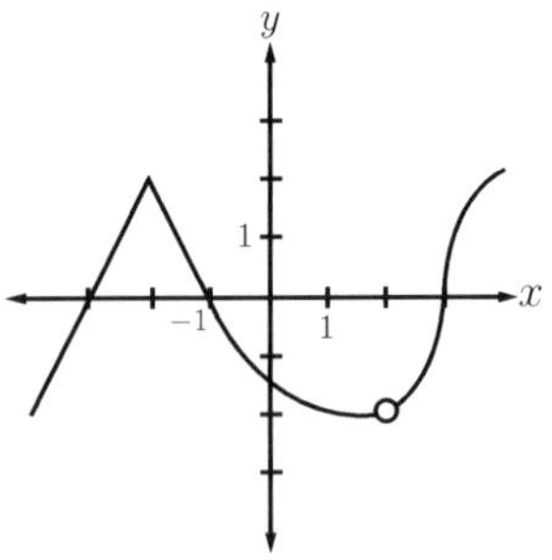

Graph of f

15. The figure above shows the graph of the function f. Which of the following statement must be true?

    (A) f is differentiable at $x = -2$.

    (B) f is differentiable at $x = -1$.

    (C) f is differentiable at $x = 2$.

    (D) f is differentiable at $x = 3$.

16. If $\sin\theta = -\dfrac{12}{13}$ and $\cos\theta > 0$, what is the value of $\tan\theta$?

    (A) $-\dfrac{13}{5}$

    (B) $-\dfrac{13}{12}$

    (C) $-\dfrac{12}{5}$

    (D) $-\dfrac{5}{12}$

17. Joshua walks x feet in y seconds. How many feet will Joshua walk in z minutes?

    (A) $\dfrac{xy}{z}$

    (B) $\dfrac{60xy}{z}$

    (C) $\dfrac{xz}{y}$

    (D) $\dfrac{60xz}{y}$

18. If $f(x) = \dfrac{-x+3}{x-1}$ and $g(x) = f(x-1) + 2$, what are the vertical and horizontal asymptotes of $g(x)$?

    (A) $x = 2$ and $y = 1$

    (B) $x = 2$ and $y = -1$

    (C) $x = 1$ and $y = 2$

    (D) $x = 1$ and $y = -1$

19. A number is selected at random from the first 20 nonnegative integers. What is the probability that the number selected is an even number?

    (A) $\dfrac{2}{5}$

    (B) $\dfrac{9}{20}$

    (C) $\dfrac{1}{2}$

    (D) $\dfrac{11}{20}$

20. Solve: $\sqrt[3]{1-x} + 0.4 = 1$

    (A) 0.91

    (B) 0.86

    (C) 0.82

    (D) 0.78

21. Which of the following logarithmic expression is equivalent to $\ln(x^2 + x - 2) - \ln(x - 1)$?

(A) $\ln x + 2$

(B) $\ln(x + 2)$

(C) $\ln x^2 - 1$

(D) $\ln(x^2 - 1)$

For the following question, enter your answer in the answer box.

22. 6 people who work at the same rate can paint a house in 4 days. What fractional part of the house can 3 people paint the house is 6 days?

Give your answer as a fraction.

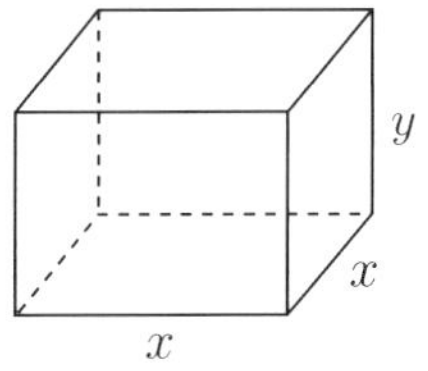

23. The figure above shows a rectangular box with a square base that has a volume of 1000 cubic inches. What is the surface area of the box in terms of x ?

(A) $2x^2 + \dfrac{8000}{x}$

(B) $2x^2 + \dfrac{4000}{x}$

(C) $2x^2 + 2000x$

(D) $2x^2 + 1000x$

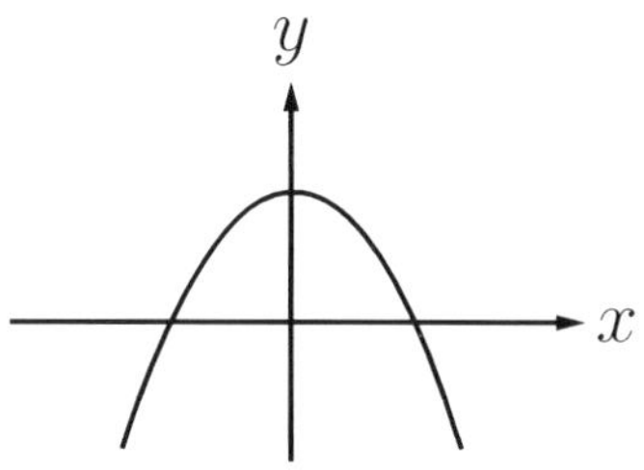

24. The figure above shows the graph of a quadratic function $y = ax^2 + bx + c$, which is symmetric with respect to the y-axis. Which of the following statement is true about a, b, and c ?

(A) $a < 0,\ b < 0,\ c < 0$

(B) $a < 0,\ b = 0,\ c > 0$

(C) $a > 0,\ b > 0,\ c < 0$

(D) $a > 0,\ b = 0,\ c > 0$

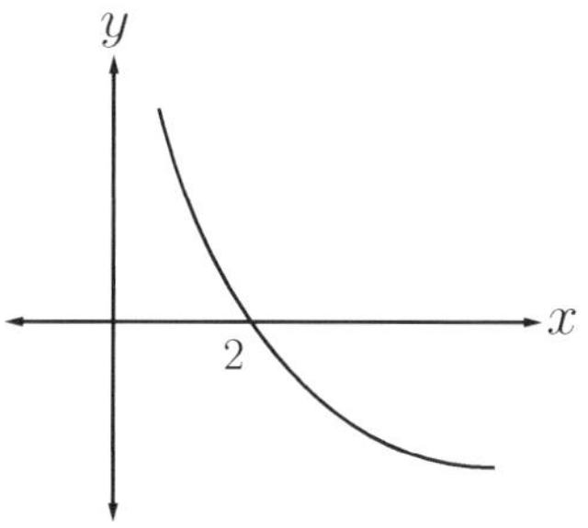

25. A portion of the graph of the function f is shown above. Which of the following statement must be true?

(A) $f(2) < f''(2) < f'(2)$

(B) $f''(2) < f'(2) < f(2)$

(C) $f'(2) < f(2) < f''(2)$

(D) $f(2) < f'(2) < f''(2)$

26. A set T has five numbers. The five numbers in set T form an arithmetic sequence with the third term being 10. If 5 is added to each number in set T, what is the sum of the new mean and median of set T ?

(A) 25

(B) 30

(C) 35

(D) 40

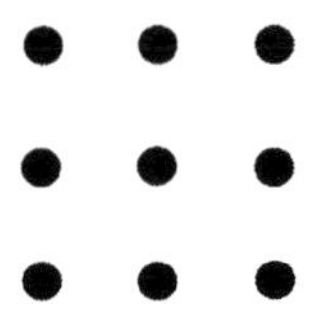

For the following question, enter your answer in the answer box.

27. In the figure above, all the nine points are equally spaced. How many different lines can be drawn that connect at least two points?

28. Let f be a differentiable function. If the function g is given by $g(x) = e^{f(x)}$, which of the following is the second derivative of g ?

(A) $e^{f(x)}\left[\left(f'(x)\right)^2 + \left(f''(x)\right)^2\right]$

(B) $e^{f(x)}\left[\left(f'(x)\right)^2 + f''(x)\right]$

(C) $e^{f(x)}\left[f'(x) + \left(f''(x)\right)^2\right]$

(D) $e^{f(x)}\left(f'(x) + f''(x)\right)$

29. Vector $\mathbf{V}$ has an initial point of $(-2, -3)$. Which of the following ordered pair represents the terminal point of vector $\mathbf{V}$ such that $|\mathbf{V}| = 10$?

(A) $(-8, -9)$

(B) $(-2, 11)$

(C) $(4, 6)$

(D) $(6, 3)$

30. If two solutions to $ax^4 + bx^3 + cx^2 + dx + e = 0$ are $2 + \sqrt{2}$ and $1 - 3i$, what are the other solutions?

(A) $2 + \sqrt{2}$ and $3 - i$

(B) $2 + \sqrt{2}$ and $1 + 3i$

(C) $2 - \sqrt{2}$ and $3 - i$

(D) $2 - \sqrt{2}$ and $1 + 3i$

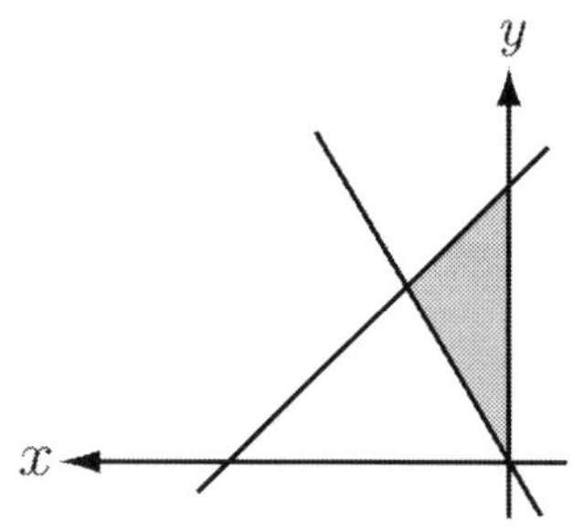

31. If $y = 2x + 8$ intersects $y = -3x$ as shown above, what is the area of the shaded region?

(A) 4.6

(B) 6.4

(C) 8.2

(D) 10.6

$$\text{If } x = 3, \text{ then } x^2 = 9.$$

32. If a conditional statement is given above, which of the following is the contrapositive of the statement?

(A) If $x^2 = 9$, then $x = 3$.

(B) If $x^2 \neq 9$, then $x \neq 3$.

(C) If $x \neq 3$, then $x^2 \neq 9$.

(D) $x^2 = 9$ if and only if $x = 3$.

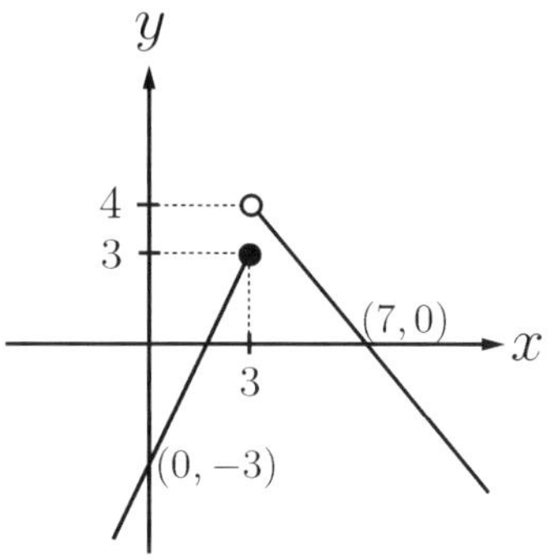

33. Which of the following piecewise function best represents the graph above?

(A)

$$f(x) = \begin{cases} 2x - 3, & x \leq 3 \\ -2x + 5, & x > 3 \end{cases}$$

(B)

$$f(x) = \begin{cases} 2x - 3, & x \leq 3 \\ -x + 7, & x > 3 \end{cases}$$

(C)

$$f(x) = \begin{cases} x + 3, & x \leq 3 \\ -2x + 10, & x > 3 \end{cases}$$

(D)

$$f(x) = \begin{cases} x + 3, & x < 3 \\ -x + 5, & x \geq 3 \end{cases}$$

For the following question, enter your answer in the answer box.

34. Two numbers are selected at random without replacement from the set $\{1, 2, 3, 4\}$ to form a two-digit number. What is the probability that the two-digit number selected is a prime number?

Give your answer as a fraction.

$$\frac{\square}{\square}$$

35. Solve: $x - 1 = \sqrt{2x + 22}$

(A) $x = 3$ or $x = -7$

(B) $x = -3$ or $x = 7$

(C) $x = 3$ only

(D) $x = 7$ only

$$\binom{n}{r} = \frac{n!}{(n-r)! \times r!}$$

36. If the combination notation $\binom{n}{r}$ is defined as above, which of the following statement must be true?

(A) $\binom{10}{0} = \binom{10}{1}$

(B) $\binom{10}{2} = \binom{10}{9}$

(C) $\binom{10}{3} = \binom{10}{8}$

(D) $\binom{10}{4} = \binom{10}{6}$

37. x, y, and z are positive integers. If $x = 3y$ and $x^2 + y^2 = z$, which of the following cannot be equal to z ?

(A) 30

(B) 36

(C) 40

(D) 60

x	-2	-1	0	2	3	5
y	56	0	-20	0	16	0

38. A polynomial function f contains a set of ordered pairs as shown in the table above. Which of the following function best represents f ?

(A) $y = 10(x-1)(x+2)$

(B) $y = -10(x+1)(x-2)$

(C) $y = 2(x-1)(x+2)(x+5)$

(D) $y = -2(x+1)(x-2)(x-5)$

39. For $0 < \theta < \frac{\pi}{2}$, solve the trigonometric equation: $2\cos\theta + 0.36 = 1$.

(A) 1.25

(B) 1.48

(C) 1.73

(D) 1.96

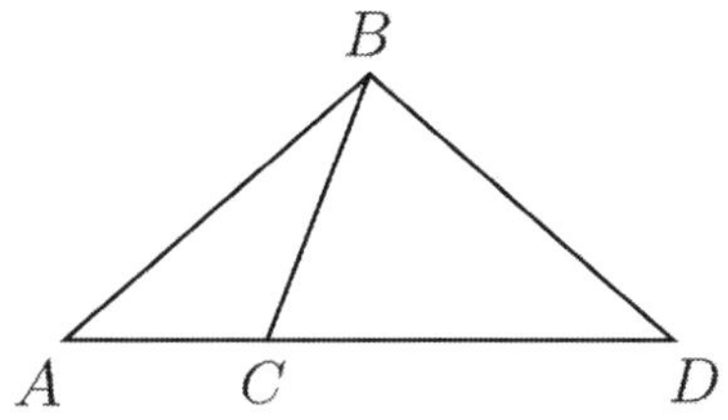

40. In the figure above, points A, C, and D are on the same line. If $AC : CD = 1 : 2$, what is the ratio of the area of $\triangle ABC$ to that of $\triangle CBD$?

(A) $\frac{1}{3}$

(B) $\frac{2}{5}$

(C) $\frac{1}{2}$

(D) $\frac{3}{5}$

41. Jason bought a stock for \$312. If the value of the stock increases 20% every year, how much is the stock worth in three years?

(A) \$493.62

(B) \$504.79

(C) \$517.32

(D) \$539.14

$$(x+y)^{\frac{1}{2}} = 4$$
$$(x-y)^{\frac{3}{2}} = 8$$

42. In the equations above, what is the value of $x^2 - y^2$?

(A) 24

(B) 36

(C) 48

(D) 64

43. The sum of the ages of Mr. Rhee and Joshua is 47. The sum of the ages of Joshua and Vivian is 46. The sum of the ages of Vivian and Mr. Rhee is 79. What is the sum of all the ages of Mr. Rhee, Joshua, and Vivian?

(A) 83

(B) 84

(C) 85

(D) 86

For the following question, select all the answer choices that apply.

44. Which of the following statements are true?

Select all that apply.

(A) All squares are parallelograms.

(B) All rectangles are rhombuses.

(C) Al rhombuses are squares.

(D) All squares are rhombuses.

45. A pizza baked at $450°F$ is removed from the oven and is allowed to cool in a room with a temperature of $72°F$. The temperature of the pizza after t minutes is given by $P(t) = 72 + (450 - 72)e^{-0.4t}$. At what time does the temperature of the pizza reach $85°F$?

(A) 9.18 minutes

(B) 8.42 minutes

(C) 7.31 minutes

(D) 6.56 minutes

46. The eccentricity of an ellipse is a measure of how circular the ellipse is. At $e \approx 0$, an ellipse is nearly a circle. From the equation of the ellipse $\dfrac{x^2}{a^2} + \dfrac{y^2}{b^2} = 1$, the eccentricity e is defined by $e = \sqrt{1 - \dfrac{b^2}{a^2}}$. What is the eccentricity of the ellipse $x^2 + 4y^2 = 4$?

(A) 0.52

(B) 0.75

(C) 0.87

(D) 1.15

$$(x-2)^2 + (y-2)^2 = 4$$
$$y = -x - 1$$

47. What are the solutions to the system of nonlinear equations above?

(A) $(2, 2)$ only

(B) $(1, 1)$ and $(3, 2)$

(C) $(2, 0)$ and $(-3, 2)$

(D) No solutions

For the following question, enter your answer in the answer box.

48. If $5^{\log_5 3} + 7^{\log_7 6} = 2^{\log_2 x}$, what is the value of x ?

$x =$ [answer box]

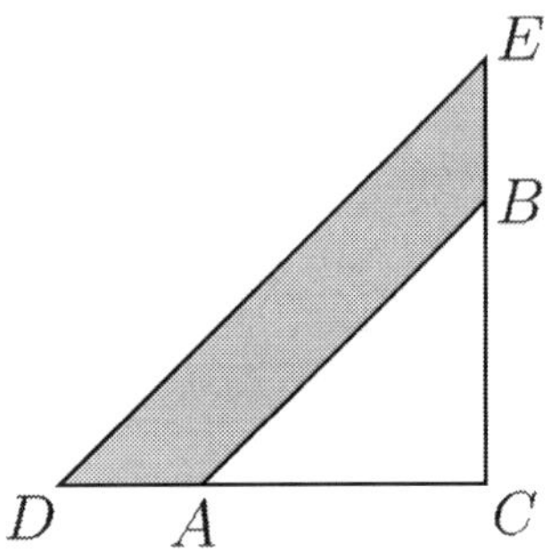

49. In the figure above, $\triangle ABC$ and $\triangle DEC$ are isosceles right triangles. If $AC = 4$ and $DC = 6$, what is the perimeter of the shaded region ABED ?

(A) $6\sqrt{2} + 4$

(B) $10\sqrt{2}$

(C) $10\sqrt{2} + 4$

(D) $16\sqrt{2}$

50. $(\sin\theta + \cos\theta)^2 - (\sin\theta - \cos\theta)^2 =$

(A) 0

(B) 2

(C) $4(\sin\theta - \cos\theta)$

(D) $4\sin\theta\cos\theta$

For the following question, select <u>all</u> the answer choices that apply.

51. The frequency f of a vibrating guitar string is given by

$$f = \frac{1}{2L}\sqrt{\frac{T}{\mu}}$$

where L is the length of the string, T is the tension, and μ is the linear density. Which of the following statements are true?

Select <u>all</u> that apply.

(A) The larger the linear density, the higher the frequency.

(B) The shorter the length of the sting, the higher the frequency.

(C) The higher the tension of the string, the higher the frequency.

(D) If the length of the string is doubled, the frequency is reduced by half.

52. Which of the following complex number is farthest away from the origin?

(A) $3i$

(B) $\sqrt{3} + i$

(C) $-\sqrt{3} - 2i$

(D) $-2 + \sqrt{2}i$

Move	Direction	Distance
1st	South	1 foot
2nd	West	2 feet
3rd	North	3 feet
4th	East	4 feet
5th	South	5 feet
6th	West	6 feet
7th	North	7 feet
8th	East	8 feet

53. Mr. Rhee starts walking according to the directions above. For instance, on the first move, he walks 1 foot due south from the starting position. He then walks 2 feet due west on the second move, walks 3 feet due north on the third move, and so on and so forth. When Mr. Rhee finishes the 8th move, how far is he from the starting position?

(A) $4\sqrt{2}$

(B) $6\sqrt{2}$

(C) $8\sqrt{2}$

(D) $10\sqrt{2}$

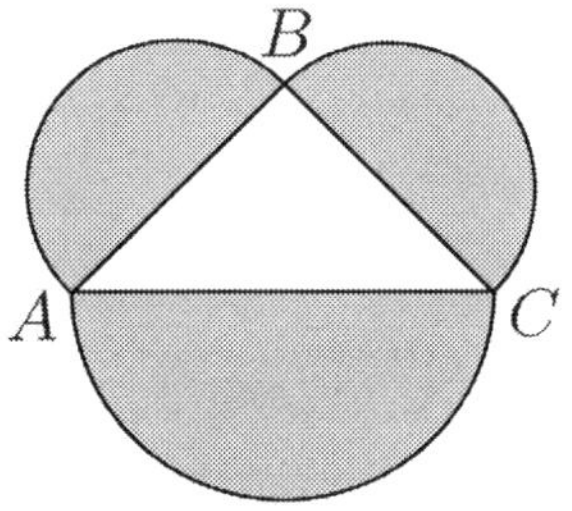

For the following question, enter your answer in the answer box.

54. In $\triangle ABC$ shown above, $AB = 6$, $BC = 8$, and $AC = 10$. There are three semicircles on each side of the triangle. If the total area of the shaded regions is $n\pi$, what is the value of n ?

$n =$ [ ]

55. A function f is said to have a maximum point at $x = c$ if $f(c) \geq f(x)$ for all x on a given interval. Which of the following function has a maximum point in the interval $-2 < x < 2$?

(A) $y = \frac{3}{2}x - 1$

(B) $y = -x^2 + 2$

(C) $y = \sqrt{x + 2}$

(D) $y = x^3 + 1$

56. The tens digit of a two-digit numbers is 3 more than its units digit. If the original number is 2 more than twice the number obtained by reversing the digits of the original number, what is the sum of the digits of the original number?

(A) 5

(B) 6

(C) 7

(D) 8

57. Which of the following is the slope of the tangent line to the graph of $f(x)$ given by $f(x) = \ln(x - x^2)$ at $x = \frac{1}{2}$?

(A) $-\frac{1}{3}$

(B) 0

(C) $\frac{1}{4}$

(D) $\frac{1}{3}$

$$(a_{51} - a_1) + (a_{52} - a_2) + \cdots + (a_{100} - a_{50})$$

58. The nth term of an arithmetic sequence is denoted by a_n. If $a_1 + a_2 + \cdots + a_{50} = 20$, and $a_1 + a_2 + \cdots + a_{100} = 220$, what is the value of the expression above?

(A) 100

(B) 120

(C) 150

(D) 180

59. A line $y = ax + 2$ passes through quadrants I, II, and III. If two lines $y = ax + 2$ and $y = -2x + 8$ intersect at $(t, t + 3)$, what is the value of a ?

(A) $\frac{3}{5}$

(B) $\frac{5}{8}$

(C) $\frac{5}{3}$

(D) $\frac{8}{5}$

60. $\dfrac{x}{x-1} + \dfrac{x}{2x+4} =$

(A) $\dfrac{3x(x+1)}{2(x-1)(x+2)}$

(B) $\dfrac{x^2+x+4}{2(x-1)(x+2)}$

(C) $\dfrac{x^2+3x+3}{2(x-1)(x+2)}$

(D) $\dfrac{3(x+1)}{(x-1)(x+2)}$

STOP

Answers and Solutions

PRAXIS II 5161 PRACTICE TEST 5

Answers

1. C	11. A,B	21. B	31. B	41. D	51. B,C,D
2. C	12. C	22. $\frac{3}{4}$	32. B	42. D	52. A
3. D	13. D	23. B	33. B	43. D	53. A
4. C	14. C	24. B	34. $\frac{5}{12}$	44. A,D	54. 25
5. D	15. B	25. C	35. D	45. B	55. B
6. 50	16. C	26. B	36. D	46. C	56. C
7. B	17. D	27. 20	37. B	47. D	57. B
8. D	18. A	28. B	38. D	48. 9	58. D
9. D	19. C	29. D	39. A	49. C	59. D
10. A	20. D	30. D	40. C	50. D	60. A

Solutions

1. (C) **Number and Quantity**

   In order to solve time problems, use the time $= \frac{\text{distance}}{\text{speed}}$ formula. Since $\frac{220\text{ miles}}{55\text{ miles per hour}} = 4$ hours, it took Sue 4 hours to travel 220 miles. On the return trip, if he travels at 50 miles per hour, it will take him $\frac{220\text{ miles}}{50\text{ miles per hour}} = 4.4$ hours. This means that it will take him 0.4 hour longer on the return trip. Since 0.4 hour is equal to 0.4×60 minutes $= 24$ minutes, it will take Joshua 24 minutes longer on the return trip.

2. (C) **Probability and Statistics**

   To find the median of set B, arrange the numbers from least to greatest. Thus,

   $$B = \{5, 6, 9, 11, 12, 15\}$$

   Since there are six numbers in set B, the median is the average of the 3rd number and 4th number, or $\frac{9+11}{2} = 10$. Therefore, the median of set B is 10.

3. (D) **Algebra**

   Two points $(1, 2)$ and $(1, 8)$ are given. Use the definition of the slope.

   $$\text{Slope} = \frac{y_2 - y_1}{x_2 - x_1} = \frac{8-2}{1-(1)} = \frac{6}{0} = \text{undefined}$$

   Therefore, the slope of the line that passes through the points $(1, 2)$ and $(1, 8)$ is undefined.

4. (C) **Geometry**

In the venn diagram below, let's define A as a set of rectangles, B as a set of rhombuses, $A \cup B$ as a set of parallelograms, and $A \cap B$ as a set of squares since they are both rectangles and rhombuses. Additionally, define $n(A)$, $n(B)$, $n(A \cup B)$, and $n(A \cap B)$ as the number of elements in set A, set B, set $A \cup B$, and set $A \cap B$, respectively.

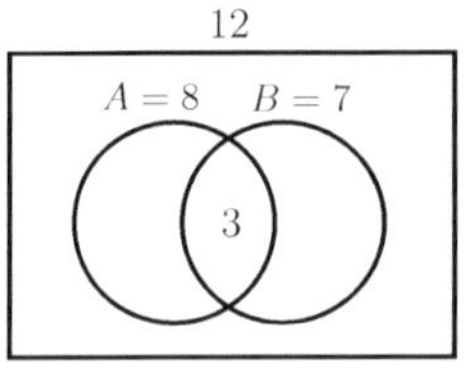

Since there are 12 parallelograms, 8 rectangles, and 7 rhombuses, $n(A \cup B) = 12$, $n(A) = 8$, and $n(B) = 7$. Thus,

$$\begin{aligned} n(A \cup B) &= n(A) + n(B) - n(A \cap B) \\ 12 &= 8 + 7 - n(A \cap B) \\ n(A \cap B) &= 3 \end{aligned}$$

Therefore, three of the parallelograms are squares.

5. (D) **Algebra**

To evaluate $f(k)$ and $f(0)$, substitute k and 0 for x in the function $f(x) = -x^2 + 4x + 5$.

$$\begin{aligned} f(k) &= -(k)^2 + 4(k) + 5 = -k^2 + 4k + 5 \\ f(0) &= -(0)^2 + 4(0) + 5 = 5 \end{aligned}$$

Since $f(k) = f(0)$, set the two expressions shown above equal to each other and solve for k.

$$\begin{aligned} -k^2 + 4k + 5 &= 5 && \text{Subtract 5 from each side} \\ -k^2 + 4k &= 0 && \text{Multiply each side by } -1 \\ k^2 - 4k &= 0 && \text{Use the factoring method} \\ k(k-4) &= 0 && \text{Use the zero product property} \\ k = 0 \quad &\text{or} \quad k = 4 \end{aligned}$$

Therefore, (D) is the correct answer.

6. (50) **Geometry**

A square is a rhombus. To find the area of the square when the length of the diagonal is given, use the area of a rhombus formula: $A = \frac{1}{2}d^2$, where d is the length of the diagonal. Since the length of the diagonal of the square is 10,

$$\text{Area of square} = \frac{1}{2}d^2 = \frac{1}{2}(10)^2 = 50$$

Therefore, the area of the square is 50.

7. (B) **Probability and Statistics**

> Tips $z\text{-score} = \dfrac{x-\mu}{\sigma}$.

Scores on a math test are normally distributed with a mean of 82 and a standard deviation of 6. Therefore, the z-score for a student who received a 94 on the test is $z = \dfrac{x-\mu}{\sigma} = \dfrac{94-82}{6} = 2$.

8. (D) **Number and Quantity**

For simplicity, let $x = \frac{1}{4}$. Thus, Plug in $\frac{1}{4}$ into the value of x for each answer choice to find out which of the following expression has the largest value.

$$(A)\ x = \frac{1}{4} \qquad (B)\ x^2 = \frac{1}{16}$$

$$(C)\ \frac{1}{x} = \frac{1}{\frac{1}{4}} = 4 \qquad (D)\ \frac{1}{x^2} = \frac{1}{\frac{1}{16}} = 16$$

Therefore, (D) is the correct answer.

9. (D) **Algebra**

> Tips The inequality symbol must be reversed when you multiply or divide each side of the inequality by a negative number.

$ax - 2a > 5a$	Add $2a$ to each side
$ax > 7a$	Divide each side by a
$x < 7$	Reverse the inequality symbol since $a < 0$

Therefore, (D) is the correct answer.

10. (A) **Calculus**

$$\int_{\frac{\pi}{4}}^{\frac{3\pi}{4}} \cos x\,dx = \sin x\Big]_{\frac{\pi}{4}}^{\frac{3\pi}{4}} = \sin\frac{3\pi}{4} - \sin\frac{\pi}{4}$$
$$= \frac{\sqrt{2}}{2} - \frac{\sqrt{2}}{2} = 0$$

Therefore, (A) is the correct answer.

11. (A,B) **Algebra**

Let d be the number of dimes. Then $d+3$ is the number of nickels. So $5(d+3)+10d = 270$. Additionally, let n be the number of nickels. Then $n-3$ is the number of dimes. So $5n+10(n-3) = 270$. Therefore, (A) and (B) are the correct answers.

12. (C) **Probability and Statistics**

There are three numbers that are divisible by 3: 3, 6, and 9. Also, there are two numbers that are divisible by 4: 4, and 8. Thus, there are five numbers that are divisible by three or four. Since there are 10 numbers in the hat, five numbers are neither divisibly by 3 nor 4. Therefore, the probability that the number is neither divisible by 3 nor 4 is $\frac{5}{10}$ or $\frac{1}{2}$.

13. (D) **Algebra**

$\|2x+4\| < 6$	Create And compound inequality
$-6 < 2x+4 < 6$	Subtract 4 from each side
$-10 < 2x < 2$	Divide each side by 2
$-5 < x < 1$	

Therefore, (D) is the correct answer.

14. (C) **Functions**

Tips

	Odd functions	Even functions
Definition	$f(-x) = -f(x)$	$f(-x) = f(x)$
Graph	Symmetric with respect to the origin	Symmetric with respect to the y-axis
Example	x^3, $\sin x$, $\tan x$	x^2, $\cos x$

The graphs in answer choices (A), and (D) are graphs of even functions because they are symmetric with respect to the y-axis. So eliminate (A), and (D). Since the graph in answer choice (B) does not pass the vertical line test, it is not the graph of a function. So eliminate (B). Therefore, (C) is the correct answer.

15. (B) **Calculus**

Tips: If the graph of f has either a hole, a jump, a vertical asymptote, a sharp corner, or a vertical tangent at $x = a$, f is **NOT** differentiable at $x = a$.

At $x = -2$, f has a sharp corner. So f is **NOT** differentiable at $x = -2$. At $x = 2$, f has a hole. So f is **NOT** differentiable at $x = 2$. At $x = 3$, f has a vertical tangent. So f is **NOT** differentiable at $x = 3$. Therefore, (B) is the correct answer.

16. (C) **Trigonometry**

$\sin\theta$ is negative in the 3rd and 4th quadrants, and $\cos\theta$ is positive in the 1st and 4th quadrants. Thus, θ must lie in the 4th quadrant. Since $\sin\theta = -\frac{12}{13}$, the length of side opposite to θ is 12 and the length of the hypotenuse is 13. Using the Pythagorean theorem: $13^2 = a^2 + 12^2$, the length of the side adjacent to θ is 5 as shown in the figure below.

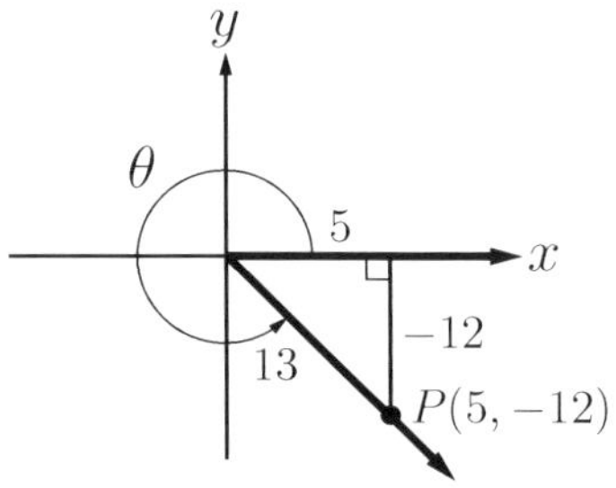

Suppose point $P(x, y)$ is on the terminal side of θ. Since θ lies in the 4th quadrant, the x and y coordinates of point P is $(5, -12)$. Thus,

$$\tan\theta = \frac{\text{opposite side}}{\text{adjacent side}} = -\frac{12}{5}$$

Therefore, the value of $\tan\theta = -\dfrac{12}{5}$.

17. (D) **Number and Quantity**

There are 60 seconds in one minute. Thus, there are $60 \times z$ or $60z$ seconds in z minutes. Define n as the number of feet that Joshua will walk in z minutes. Set up a proportion in terms of feet and seconds and solve for n.

$$x_{\text{feet}} : y_{\text{seconds}} = n_{\text{feet}} : 60z_{\text{seconds}}$$

$$\frac{x}{y} = \frac{n}{60z} \qquad \text{Use cross product property}$$

$$ny = 60xz \qquad \text{Solve for } n$$

$$n = \frac{60xz}{y}$$

Therefore, Joshua will walk $\frac{60xz}{y}$ feet in z minutes.

18. (A) **Functions**

In order to find the vertical asymptote, set the denominator equal to zero and solve for x. Thus, the vertical asymptote of $f(x) = \dfrac{-x+3}{x-1}$ is $x = 1$. In addition, both the numerator and the denominator of $f(x) = \dfrac{-x+3}{x-1}$ are first degree polynomials. Thus, the horizontal asymptote of $f(x) = \dfrac{-x+3}{x-1}$ is the ratio of the leading coefficients, or $y = -1$. Since $g(x) = f(x-1) + 2$, the vertical and horizontal asymptotes of $g(x)$ is obtained by moving the vertical and horizontal asymptotes of $f(x)$ 1 unit to the right and 2 units up. Therefore, the vertical and horizontal asymptotes of $g(x)$ are $x = 2$ and $y = 1$, respectively.

19. (C) **Probability and Statistics**

Of the first 20 nonnegative integers: $0, 1, 2, \cdots, 18, 19$, there are 10 even numbers: $0, 2, 4, 6, 8, 10, 12, 14, 16$, and 18. Therefore, the probability that the number selected is an even number is $\frac{10}{20} = \frac{1}{2}$.

20. (D) **Algebra**

$$\begin{aligned} \sqrt[3]{1-x} + 0.4 &= 1 && \text{Subtract 0.4 from each side} \\ \sqrt[3]{1-x} &= 0.6 && \text{Raise each side to a power of 3} \\ 1 - x &= 0.216 && \text{Solve for } x \\ x &= 0.78 \end{aligned}$$

Therefore, the value of x for which $\sqrt[3]{1-x} + 0.4 = 1$ is 0.78.

21. (B) **Functions**

Tips $\log_a x - \log_a y = \log_a \frac{x}{y}$

$$\begin{aligned} \ln(x^2 + x - 2) - \ln(x - 1) &= \ln \frac{x^2 + x - 2}{x - 1} && \text{Factor} \\ &= \ln \frac{(x+2)(x-1)}{(x-1)} && \text{Cancel } (x-1) \text{ out} \\ &= \ln(x + 2) \end{aligned}$$

Therefore, the logarithmic expression $\ln(x^2 + x - 2) - \ln(x - 1)$ is equivalent to $\ln(x + 2)$.

22. ($\frac{3}{4}$) **Number and Quantity**

If it takes 6 people 4 days to paint a house, the total amount of work required to paint the entire house is equivalent to $6_{\text{ people}} \times 4_{\text{ days}} = 24_{\text{ people}\times\text{days}}$. Since the amount of work provided by 3 people in 6 days is $3_{\text{ people}} \times 6_{\text{ days}} = 18_{\text{ people}\times\text{days}}$, the fractional part of the house painted can be determined by the ratio of the amount of work provided by 3 people in 6 days to the total amount of work required. Thus,

$$\text{What fractional part of the house is painted} = \frac{18_{\text{ people}\times\text{days}}}{24_{\text{ people}\times\text{days}}} = \frac{3}{4}$$

Therefore, 3 people can paint $\frac{3}{4}$ of the house in 6 days.

23. (B) **Geometry**

The surface area A of the rectangular box in terms of x and y is $A = 2x^2 + 4xy$ as shown below.

Top	Bottom	Left	Right	Front	Back	Surface area
x^2	x^2	xy	xy	xy	xy	$2x^2 + 4xy$

The volume V of the rectangular box, $V = x^2y$, is equal to 1000; that is $x^2y = 1000$. Thus, $y = \dfrac{1000}{x^2}$. In order to write the surface area of the box in terms of x, substitute $\dfrac{1000}{x^2}$ for y in $A = 2x^2 + 4xy$.

$$\begin{aligned} A &= 2x^2 + 4xy \\ &= 2x^2 + 4x\left(\frac{1000}{x^2}\right) \\ &= 2x^2 + \frac{4000}{x} \end{aligned}$$

Therefore, the surface area of the box in terms of x is $2x^2 + \dfrac{4000}{x}$.

24. (B) **Algebra**

Tips: The axis of symmetry: $x = -\dfrac{b}{2a}$

The graph of a quadratic function $y = ax^2 + bx + c$ opens down as shown below. Thus, the leading coefficient is negative; that is $a < 0$.

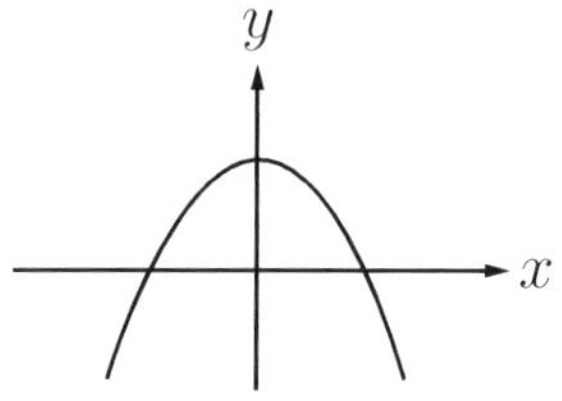

Since the graph is symmetric with respect to the y-axis, the axis of symmetry is zero; that is, $x = -\dfrac{b}{2a} = 0$, which implies that $b = 0$. The y-intercept of the quadratic function, c, lies above the x-axis. Thus, $c > 0$. Therefore, $a < 0$, $b = 0$, and $c > 0$.

25. (C) **Calculus**

Tips:
1. $f'(a)$ means the slope of the tangent line at $x = a$.
2. If the graph of f is concave up at $x = a$, then $f''(a) > 0$.

$f(2) = 0$. The slope of the tangent line to the graph of f at $x = 2$ is negative. So $f'(2) < 0$. The graph of f is concave up at $x = 2$. So $f''(2) > 0$. Therefore, $f'(2) < f(2) < f''(2)$.

26. (B) **Probability and Statistics**

In order to solve this problem, it is not necessary to determine the other terms. In a set of five terms of an arithmetic sequence, the third term is both the mean and the median. For instance, 4, 7, 10, 13, and 16 is an arithmetic sequence in which the third term, 10, is both the mean and the median. Since 5 is added to each element in the set T, the new mean and the median of set T are both 15. Therefore, the sum of the new mean and median of set T is $15 + 15 = 30$.

27. (20) **Geometry**

In figure 1 below, there are 8 lines that connect three points. In figure 2, there are 4 lines that connect two points. In figure 3, there are 8 additional lines that connect other two points.

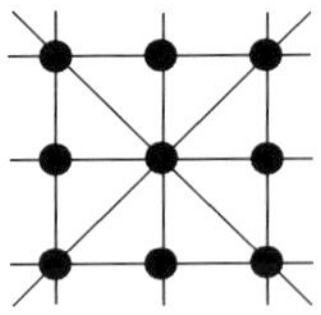
Figure 1

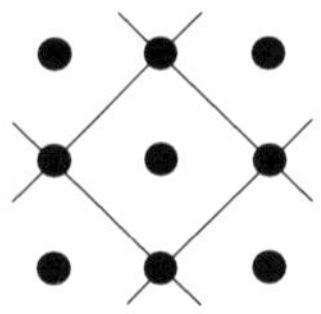
Figure 2

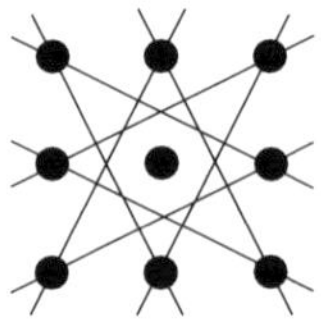
Figure 3

Therefore, there are $8 + 4 + 8 = 20$ different lines that connect at least two points.

28. (B) **Calculus**

Tips
1. The Chain rule: $\left(e^{f(x)}\right)' = e^{f(x)} \cdot f'(x)$
2. The Product rule: $(f \cdot g)' = f' \cdot g + f \cdot g'$

$g(x) = e^{f(x)}$. Differentiate $g(x)$ using the Chain rule.

$$g'(x) = e^{f(x)} \cdot f'(x)$$

Differentiate $g'(x)$ using the Product rule to get $g''(x)$.

$$\begin{aligned} g''(x) &= (e^{f(x)})' \cdot f'(x) + e^{f(x)} \cdot (f'(x))' = e^{f(x)} \cdot \left(f'(x)\right)^2 + e^{f(x)} \cdot f''(x) \\ &= e^{f(x)}\left[\left(f'(x)\right)^2 + f''(x)\right] \end{aligned}$$

Therefore, (B) is the correct answer.

29. (D) **Trigonometry**

Tips

If point $A(x_1, y_1)$ is the initial point and point $B(x_2, y_2)$ is the terminal point, a vector, denoted by $\mathbf{AB}$, is defined as

$$\mathbf{AB} = \langle x_2 - x_1, y_2 - y_1 \rangle$$

and the magnitude of the vector, denoted by $|\mathbf{AB}|$, is defined as

$$|\mathbf{AB}| = \sqrt{(x_2 - x_1)^2 + (y_2 - y_1)^2}$$

The initial point is $(-2, -3)$. If the terminal point is $(6, 3)$, vector $\mathbf{V} = \langle 8, 6 \rangle$ such that $|\mathbf{V}| = 10$. Therefore, the terminal point of vector $\mathbf{V}$ is $(6, 3)$.

30. (D) **Algebra**

Tips

The conjugate pairs theorem states that complex zeros and irrational zeros always occur in conjugate pairs.

If $a + bi$ is a zero of f, $\implies$ $a - bi$ is also a zero of f.

If $a + \sqrt{b}$ is a zero of f, $\implies$ $a - \sqrt{b}$ is also a zero of f.

According to the conjugate pairs theorem, $2 + \sqrt{2}$ and $2 - \sqrt{2}$, and $1 - 3i$ and $1 + 3i$ are the solutions to $ax^4 + bx^3 + cx^2 + dx + e = 0$. Therefore, (D) is the correct answer.

31. (B) **Algebra**

In the figure below, the area of the shaded region equals the area of the triangle. Since the y-intercept of $y = 2x + 8$ is 8, the length of the base of the triangle is 8.

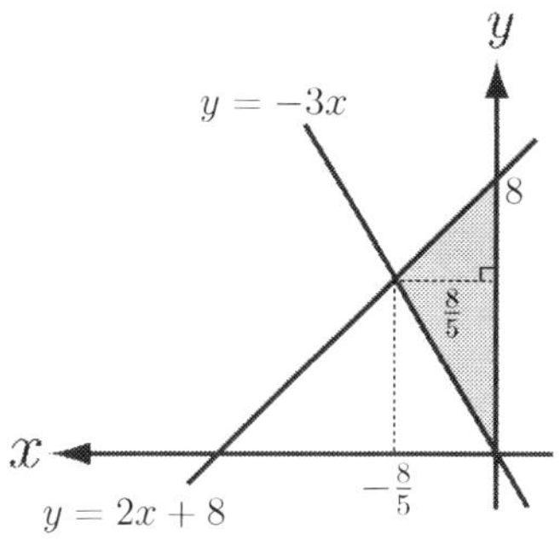

Two lines $y = 2x + 8$ and $y = -3x$ intersect. Set each equation equal to each other. Solve for x, which determines the height of the triangle.

$$\begin{aligned} 2x + 8 &= -3x \\ 5x &= -8 \\ x &= -\frac{8}{5} \end{aligned}$$

Since the x-coordinate of the intersection point is $-\frac{8}{5}$, the height of the triangle is $\frac{8}{5}$. Therefore, the area of the shaded region is $\frac{1}{2} \times 8 \times \frac{8}{5} = \frac{32}{5} = 6.4$.

32. (B) **Discrete Mathematics**

Tips

- Conditional statement: If P, then Q.
- Contrapositive: If Not Q, then Not P.

The contrapositive the conditional statement is "If $x^2 \neq 9$, then $x \neq 3$". Therefore, (B) is the correct answer.

33. (B) **Functions**

The figure below shows the two lines. Let's find the equation of the first line that passes through the two points $(3, 3)$ and $(0, -3)$ when $x \leq 3$. The slope of the line that passes through the two points is $\frac{-3-3}{0-3} = 2$.

Start with the slope-intercept form, $y = mx + b = 2x + b$. Since the point $(0, -3)$ is the y-intercept, $b = -3$. Thus, the equation of the first line that passes through the two points $(3, 3)$ and $(0, -3)$ is $y = 2x - 3,\ x \leq 3$.

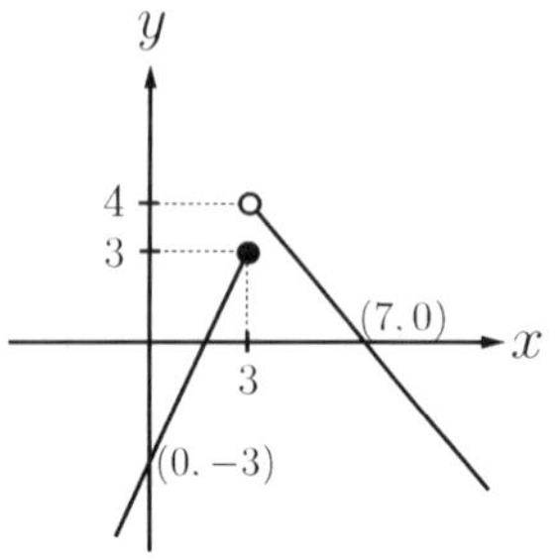

Furthermore, find the equation of the second line that passes through the two points $(3, 4)$ and $(7, 0)$ when $x > 3$. The slope of the line that passes through the two points is $\frac{0-4}{7-3} = -1$.

Start with the slope-intercept form, $y = mx + b = -x + b$. Since the point $(7, 0)$ is on the line, $(7, 0)$ is a solution to the equation $y = -x + b$. Substitute 7 for x and 0 for y in the equation and then solve for b.

$$
\begin{aligned}
& y = -x + b && \text{Substitute 7 for } x \text{ and 0 for } y \\
& 0 = -7 + b && \text{Solve for } b \\
& b = 7 &&
\end{aligned}
$$

Thus, the equation of the second line that passes through the two points $(3, 4)$ and $(7, 0)$ is $y = -x + 7,\ x > 3$. Therefore, the piecewise function that represents the figure above is as follows:

$$
f(x) = \begin{cases} 2x - 3, & x \leq 3 \\ -x + 7, & x > 3 \end{cases}
$$

34. ($\frac{5}{12}$) **Probability and Statistics**

Two numbers are selected at random without replacement from the set $\{1, 2, 3, 4\}$ to form a two-digit number. To find the total number of two-digit numbers, use the fundamental counting principle. Define event 1 and event 2 as selecting a digit for the tens' place, and ones' place, respectively. Event 1 has 4 ways to select a digit out of 4 digits. After one digit is taken, event 2 has 3 ways to select a digit out of the three remaining digits. Thus, there are $4 \times 3 = 12$ possible two-digit numbers using 1, 2, 3, and 4, which are shown below.

12 possible two-digit numbers: 12, 13, 14, 21, 23, 24, 31, 32, 34, 41, 42, and 43

Out of 12 possible two-digit numbers, there are 5 prime numbers: 13, 23, 31, 41, and 43. Therefore, the probability that the two-digit number selected is a prime number is $\frac{5}{12}$.

35. (D) **Algebra**

> Tips: To solve a radical equation, square both sides of the equation to eliminate the square root. Then, solve for the variable. Once you get the solution of the radical equation, you need to substitute the solution into the original equation to check the solution. If the solution doesn't make the equation true, it is called an extraneous solution and is disregarded.

$x-1=\sqrt{2x+22}$	Square both sides
$(x-1)^2=2x+22$	Use the binomial expansion formula
$x^2-2x+1=2x+22$	Subtract $2x+22$ from each side
$x^2-4x-21=0$	Factor the quadratic expression
$(x-7)(x+3)=0$	Use zero product property: If $ab=0$, then $a=0$ or $b=0$.
$x=7$ or $x=-3$	

Substitute 7 and -3 for x in the original equation to check the solutions.

$$7-1=\sqrt{2(7)+22} \qquad -3-1=\sqrt{2(-3)+22}$$
$$6=6 \quad \checkmark \text{ (Solution)} \qquad -4=4 \quad \text{(Not a solution)}$$

Therefore, the solution to $x-1=\sqrt{2x+22}$ is $x=7$.

36. (D) **Discrete Mathematics**

$$\binom{10}{4}=\frac{10!}{6!\times 4!}, \qquad \binom{10}{6}=\frac{10!}{4!\times 6!}$$

Since both $\binom{10}{4}$ and $\binom{10}{6}$ have the same numerator and denominator, $\binom{10}{4}=\binom{10}{6}$.

37. (B) **Number and Quantity**

x, y, and z are positive integers. To write z in terms of y, substitute $3y$ for x in the equation $z=x^2+y^2$.

$$z=x^2+y^2=(3y)^2+y^2=10y^2$$

Since y is a positive integer, $z=10y^2$ implies that z must be a positive integer that is a multiple of 10. Answer choice (B) cannot be equal to z because 36 is not a multiple of 10. Therefore, (B) is the correct answer.

38. (D) **Algebra**

> Tips: Factor Theorem: If the remainder $r = f(k) = 0$, then k is a zero of $f(x)$ and $x - k$ is a factor of $f(x)$.

When $x = -1$, $x = 2$, and $x = 5$, $y = 0$; that is, $f(-1) = 0$, $f(2) = 0$, and $f(5) = 0$. Thus, the polynomial function f has factors of $x + 1$, $x - 2$ and $x - 5$. Since the leading coefficient of f is unknown, let $f(x) = a(x+1)(x-2)(x-5)$. When $x = 0$, $y = -20$. Substitute 0 for x, and -20 for $f(x)$ to solve for a.

$$f(x) = a(x+1)(x-2)(x-5) \quad \text{Substitute 0 for } x\text{, and } -20 \text{ for } f(x)$$
$$-20 = a(0+1)(0-2)(0-5) \quad \text{Solve for } a$$
$$a = -2$$

Therefore, the polynomial function f is $f(x) = -2(x+1)(x-2)(x-5)$.

39. (A) **Trigonometry**

Set the angle mode to Radians in your calculator.

$$2\cos\theta + 0.36 = 1$$
$$\cos\theta = 0.32 \quad \text{Take the inverse cosine of both sides}$$
$$\theta = \cos^{-1}(0.32) = 1.25$$

Therefore, (A) is the correct answer.

40. (C) **Geometry**

In the figure below, points A, C, and D are on the same line. Since $AC : CD = 1 : 2$, let x be the length of $\overline{AC}$ and $2x$ be the length of $\overline{CD}$.

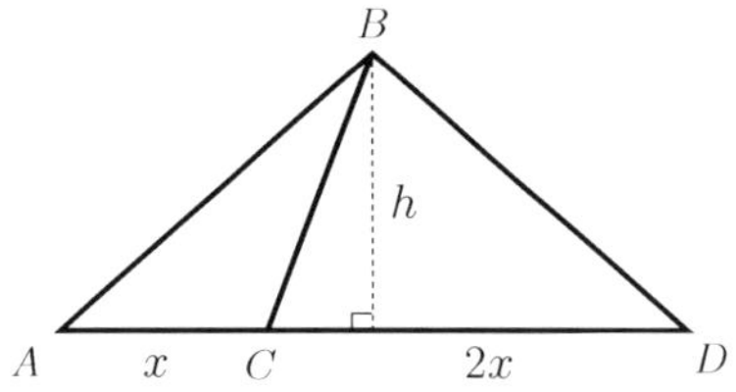

$\triangle ABC$ and $\triangle CBD$ have the same height, h. Thus,

$$\frac{\text{Area of } \triangle ABC}{\text{Area of } \triangle CBD} = \frac{\frac{1}{2} \times AC \times h}{\frac{1}{2} \times CD \times h} \quad \text{Since } AC = x \text{ and } CD = 2x$$
$$= \frac{\frac{1}{2}xh}{\frac{1}{2}(2x)h} \quad \frac{1}{2}xh \text{ cancels out}$$
$$= \frac{1}{2}$$

Therefore, the ratio of the area of $\triangle ABC$ to that of $\triangle CBD$ is $\frac{1}{2}$.

41. (D) **Functions**

The value of the stock increases 20% per year. The value of the stock for the first three years is shown below.

The value of the stock after 1 year: $\$312(1+0.2) = \$374.4$

The value of the stock after 2 years: $\$312(1+0.2)^2 = \$449.28$

The value of the stock after 3 years: $\$312(1+0.2)^3 = \$539.14$

Therefore, the value of the stock after 3 years is \$539.14.

42. (D) **Algebra**

To evaluate the value of $x^2 - y^2$, use the special factoring pattern: $x^2 - y^2 = (x+y)(x-y)$. First, find the value of $x+y$ by squaring each side in the first equation $(x+y)^{\frac{1}{2}} = 4$. Thus, $x+y = 16$. Next, find the value of $x-y$ from the second equation $(x-y)^{\frac{3}{2}} = 8$.

$(x-y)^{\frac{3}{2}} = 8$	Square each side
$(x-y)^3 = 64$	Take the cube root of each side
$x-y = (4^3)^{\frac{1}{3}}$	Use the properties of exponents
$x-y = 4$	

Since $x+y = 16$ and $x-y = 4$,

$$x^2 - y^2 = (x+y)(x-y) = 16(4) = 64$$

Therefore, the value of $x^2 - y^2$ is 64.

43. (D) **Algebra**

Define x, y, and z as the age of Mr. Rhee, Joshua, and Vivian, respectively. Then, the sum of all ages of Mr. Rhee, Joshua, and Vivian can be expressed as $x+y+z$. The sum of the ages of Mr. Rhee and Joshua is 47 which can be expressed as $x+y = 47$. The sum of the ages of Joshua and Vivian is 46 which can be expressed as $y+z = 46$. Additionally, the sum of the ages of Vivian and Mr. Rhee is 79 which can be expressed as $z+x = 79$. To find the sum of all ages of Mr. Rhee, Joshua, and Vivian, add the three equations shown below.

$x+y = 47$	
$y+z = 46$	
$z+x = 79$	Add three equations
$2x+2y+2z = 172$	Divide each side by 2
$x+y+z = 86$	

Therefore, the sum of all ages of Mr. Rhee, Joshua and Vivian, $x+y+z$, is 86.

44. (A,D) **Geometry**

All squares are parallelograms. All squares are rhombuses. Therefore, (A) and (D) are correct answers.

45. (B) **Functions**

In order to find the time at which the temperature of the pizza reaches $85°F$, substitute 85 for $P(t)$ and solve for t.

$P(t) = 72 + (450 - 72)e^{-0.4t}$	Substitute 85 for $P(t)$
$85 = 72 + (450 - 72)e^{-0.4t}$	Subtract 72 from each side
$378e^{-0.4t} = 13$	Divide 378 from each side
$e^{-0.4t} = \dfrac{13}{378}$	Convert the equation to a logarithmic equation
$-0.4t = \ln\left(\dfrac{13}{378}\right)$	Divide each side by -0.4
$t = 8.42$	

Therefore, after the pizza is cooled at room temperature for 8.42 minutes, the temperature of the pizza reaches $85°F$.

46. (C) **Geometry**

Divide each side of the equation $x^2 + 4y^2 = 4$ by 4. We find that $\dfrac{x^2}{2^2} + \dfrac{y^2}{1^2} = 1$.

$$e = \sqrt{1 - \frac{b^2}{a^2}} = \sqrt{1 - \frac{1^2}{2^2}} = 0.87$$

Therefore, the eccentricity of the ellipse $x^2 + 4y^2 = 4$ is 0.87.

47. (D) **Algebra**

> **Tips** Solutions to a system of nonlinear equations are ordered pairs (x, y) that satisfy all equations in the system. In other words, solutions to a system of nonlinear equations are intersection points that lie on all graphs.

$(x - 2)^2 + (y - 2)^2 = 4$ represents a circle with radius 2 as shown in the figure below. The center of the circle is $(2, 2)$.

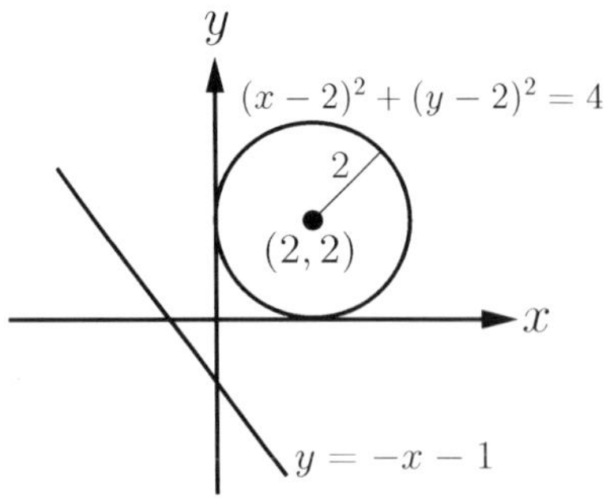

$y = -x - 1$ represents a line that does not intersect the circle $(x - 2)^2 + (y - 2)^2 = 4$. Since there are no intersection points that lie on the two graphs, there are no solutions to a system of nonlinear equations.

48. (9) **Number and Quantity**

Tips
1. $\log_b b = 1$
2. $b^{\log_b a} = a^{\log_b b} = a$

$5^{\log_5 3}$=3. $7^{\log_7 6} = 6$. $2^{\log_2 x} = x$. Thus,

$$2^{\log_2 x} = 5^{\log_5 3} + 7^{\log_7 6} \implies x = 3 + 6 = 9$$

Therefore, the value of x is 9.

49. (C) **Geometry**

In the figure below, $\triangle ABC$ and $\triangle DEC$ are isosceles right triangles. So, they are 45°-45°-90° special right triangles whose sides are in the ratio $1 : 1 : \sqrt{2}$.

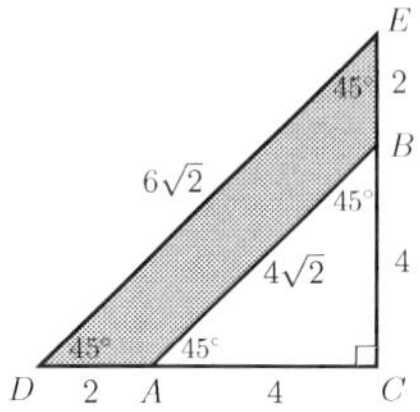

In $\triangle ABC$, $AC = 4$. Thus, $BC = 4$ and $AB = 4\sqrt{2}$. In $\triangle DEC$, $DC = 6$. Thus, $EC = 6$ and $DE = 6\sqrt{2}$.

$$\begin{aligned}\text{Perimeter of shaded region} &= DE + EB + AB + DA \\ &= 6\sqrt{2} + 2 + 4\sqrt{2} + 2 \\ &= 10\sqrt{2} + 4\end{aligned}$$

Therefore, (C) is the correct answer.

50. (D) **Trigonometry**

Tips
1. $(a \pm b)^2 = a^2 \pm 2ab + b^2$
2. $\sin^2\theta + \cos^2\theta = 1$

$$\begin{aligned}(\sin\theta + \cos\theta)^2 - (\sin\theta - \cos\theta)^2 &= \sin^2\theta + 2\sin\theta\cos\theta + \cos^2\theta - (\sin^2\theta - 2\sin\theta\cos\theta + \cos^2\theta) \\ &= 1 + 2\sin\theta\cos\theta - (1 - 2\sin\theta\cos\theta) \\ &= 4\sin\theta\cos\theta\end{aligned}$$

Therefore, (D) is the correct answer.

51. (B,C,D) **Number and Quantity**

The frequency f of a vibrating guitar string can be written as $f = \dfrac{1}{2}\dfrac{\sqrt{T}}{L\sqrt{\mu}}$, which means that f varies directly with $\sqrt{T}$, inversely with L, and inversely with $\sqrt{\mu}$. The statement in (A) is wrong because the larger the linear density μ, the lower the frequency f. The statements in answer choice (B), (C), and (D) are correct.

52. (A) **Number and Quantity**

Tips The absolute value of a complex number $z = a + bi$, denoted by $|z|$, is the distance from the origin to the complex number in the complex plane. The formula for finding the absolute value of a complex number $a+bi$ is as follows:

$$\text{If } z = a + bi, \qquad |z| = \sqrt{a^2 + b^2}$$

(A) If $z = 3i$, $\quad |z| = \sqrt{3^2} = 3$

(B) If $z = \sqrt{3} + i$, $\quad |z| = \sqrt{(\sqrt{3})^2 + 1^2} = 2$

(C) If $z = -\sqrt{3} - 2i$, $\quad |z| = \sqrt{(-\sqrt{3})^2 + (-2)^2} = \sqrt{7}$

(D) If $z = -2 + \sqrt{2}i$, $\quad |z| = \sqrt{(-2)^2 + (\sqrt{2})^2} = \sqrt{6}$

Therefore, the complex number farthest away from the origin is $3i$.

53. (A) **Geometry**

It will take too much time to calculate the distance between Mr. Rhee and the starting position in each move as shown below. Instead, calculate the overall distances for the north and south direction, and the east and west direction. It is easier and faster to calculate the distance between Mr. Rhee and the starting position after the 8th move.

To calculate the overall distances for the north and south direction, assign $+$ to the north direction and $-$ to the south direction. For instance, walk 3 feet due north can be written as $+3$ and walk 1 foot due south as -1. Thus,

$$\text{Overall distances for north and south} = -1 + 3 - 5 + 7 = +4$$

$+4$ indicates that Mr. Rhee has moved 4 feet north overall. Next, calculate the overall distances for the east and west direction. Assign $+$ to the east direction and $-$ to the west direction.

$$\text{Overall distances for east and west} = -2 + 4 - 6 + 8 = +4$$

$+4$ indicates that Mr. Rhee has moved 4 feet east overall. Thus, Mr. Rhee has moved 4 feet north and 4 feet east after the 8th move. In the figure below, O represent the starting position and P represents where Mr. Rhee is after the 8th move.

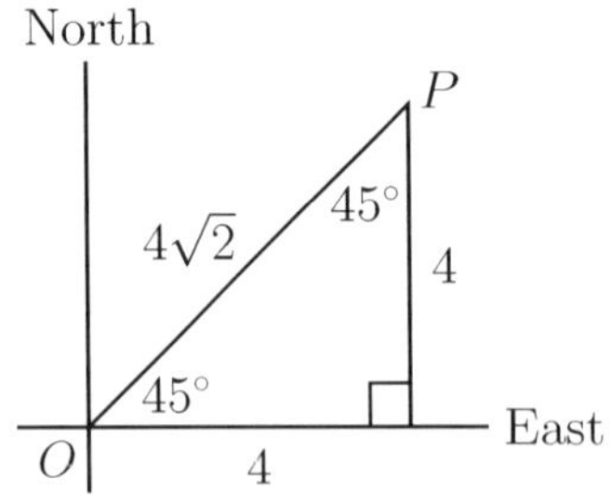

To find the distance between Mr. Rhee and the starting postion, OP, use the 45°-45°-90° special right triangle ratio: $1 : 1 : \sqrt{2}$, or use the Pythagorean theorem: $OP^2 = 4^2 + 4^2$. Thus, $OP = 4\sqrt{2}$. Therefore, Mr. Rhee is $4\sqrt{2}$ feet away from the staring position after the 8th move.

54. (25) **Geometry**

In $\triangle ABC$ shown below, $AB = 6$, $BC = 8$, and $AC = 10$. There are three semicircles on each side of the triangle. Thus, the radii of the three semicircles are 3, 4, and 5.

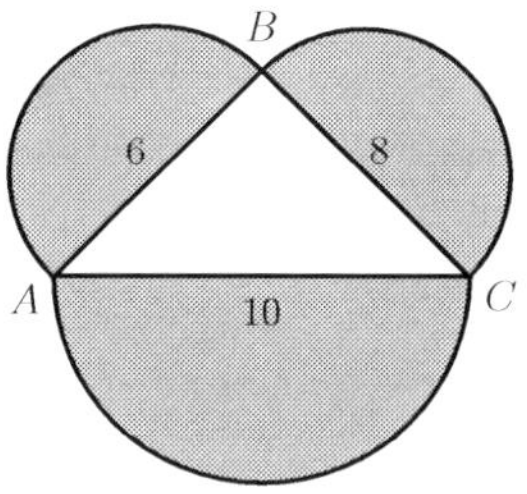

To find the total area of the shaded regions which equals the sum of the areas of the three semicircles, use the area of a semicircle formula: $\frac{1}{2}\pi r^2$.

$$\begin{aligned}\text{Total area of shaded regions} &= \text{Sum of the areas of three semicircles}\\ &= \frac{1}{2}\pi(3)^2 + \frac{1}{2}\pi(4)^2 + \frac{1}{2}\pi(5)^2\\ &= 25\pi\end{aligned}$$

Thus, the total area of the shaded regions is 25π. Therefore, the value of n is 25.

55. (B) **Functions**

The graphs of functions in answer choices are shown below.

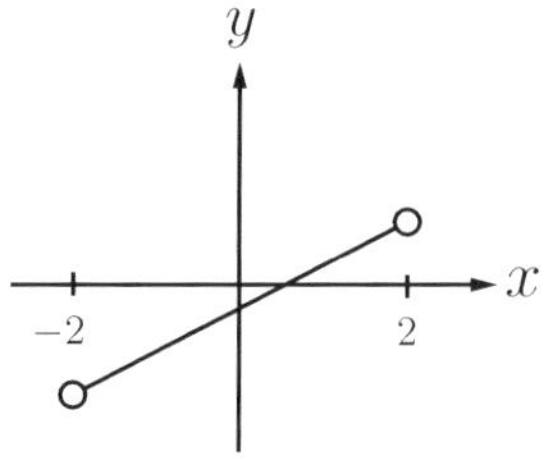

(A) $y = \frac{3}{2}x - 1$

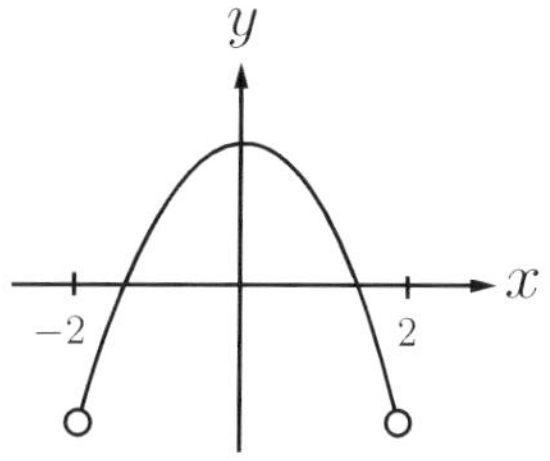

(B) $y = -x^2 + 2$

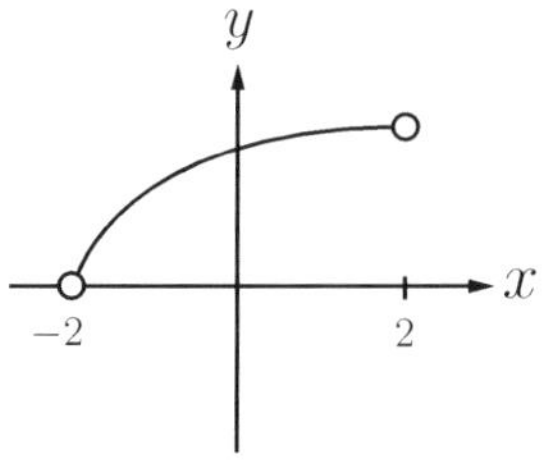

(C) $y = \sqrt{x+2}$

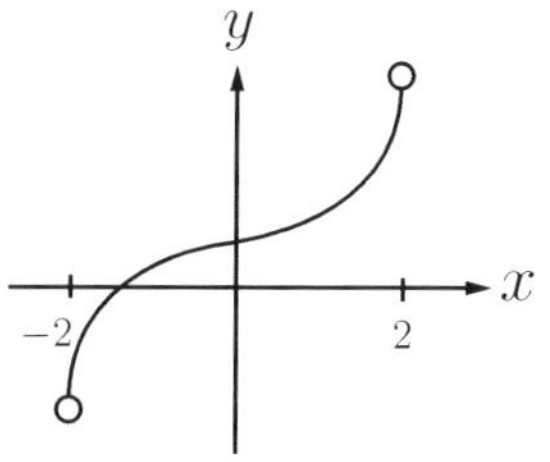

(D) $y = x^3 + 1$

Only function that has a maximum point in the interval $-2 < x < 2$ is $y = -x^2 + 2$. Therefore, (B) is the correct answer.

56. (C) **Algebra**

Let x and y be the tens digit and units digit of the original number, respectively. The tens digit of a two-digit numbers is 3 more than its units digit can be written as $x-y=3$ or $x=y+3$. The value of the original number, xy, can be written as $10x+y$. The value of the number obtained by reversing the digits of the original number, yx, can be written as $10y+x$. Thus, the original number is 2 more than twice the number obtained by reversing the digits of the original number can be written as $10x+y=2(10y+x)+2$, which simplifies to $8x-19y=2$. Substitute $x=y+3$ into $8x-19y=2$ to solve for y.

$$\begin{aligned} 8x-19y &= 2 \\ 8(y+3)-19y &= 2 \\ -11y+24 &= 2 \\ -11y &= -22 \\ y &= 2 \end{aligned}$$

Since $y=2$, $x=y+3=5$. Thus, the original number xy is 52. Therefore, the sum of tens and units digit of 52 is 7.

57. (B) **Calculus**

Tips The Chain rule: If $f(x)=\ln h(x)$, then $f'(x)=\dfrac{h'(x)}{h(x)}$

$f(x)=\ln(x-x^2)$. Differentiate $f(x)$ using the Chain rule to get $f'(x)$.

$$f'(x)=\frac{1-2x}{x-x^2} \quad \Longrightarrow \quad f'\left(\frac{1}{2}\right)=\frac{1-2\cdot\frac{1}{2}}{\frac{1}{2}-\left(\frac{1}{2}\right)^2}=0$$

Therefore, (B) is the correct answer.

58. (D) **Discrete Mathematics**

$a_1+a_2+\cdots+a_{50}=20$, and $a_1+a_2+\cdots+a_{100}=220$ implies that $a_{51}+a_{52}+\cdots+a_{100}=220-20=200$.

$$\begin{aligned} (a_{51}-a_1)+(a_{52}\quad a_2)+\cdots+(a_{100}-a_{50}) &= (a_{51}+a_{52}+\cdots+a_{100})-(a_1+a_2+\cdots+a_{100}) \\ &= 200-20 \\ &= 180 \end{aligned}$$

Therefore, the value of the expression $(a_{51}-a_1)+(a_{52}-a_2)+\cdots+(a_{100}-a_{50})$ is 180.

59. (D) **Algebra**

The two lines $y = ax + 2$ and $y = -2x + 8$ intersect at $(t, t+3)$, which means that the line $y = -2x + 8$ passes through the point $(t, t+3)$. Substitute t for x and $t+3$ for y in the equation $y = -2x + 8$ and solve for t.

$$\begin{aligned} y &= -2x + 8 && \text{Substitute } t \text{ for } x \text{ and } t+3 \text{ for } y \\ t + 3 &= -2t + 8 && \text{Solve for } t \\ t &= \frac{5}{3} \end{aligned}$$

Since $t = \frac{5}{3}$, $t + 3 = \frac{5}{3} + 3 = \frac{14}{3}$. The x and y coordinates of the point $(t, t+3)$ is $(\frac{5}{3}, \frac{14}{3})$.

Additionally, $(\frac{5}{3}, \frac{14}{3})$ is the intersection point between the lines $y = ax+2$ and $y = -2x+8$, which means that the line $y = ax + 2$ also passes through the point $(\frac{5}{3}, \frac{14}{3})$. Substitute $\frac{5}{3}$ for x and $\frac{14}{3}$ for y in the equation $y = ax + 2$ and solve for a.

$$\begin{aligned} y &= ax + 2 && \text{Substitute } \frac{5}{3} \text{ for } x \text{ and } \frac{14}{3} \text{ for } y \\ \frac{14}{3} &= \frac{5}{3}a + 2 && \text{Subtract 2 from each side} \\ \frac{8}{3} &= \frac{5}{3}a && \text{Solve for } a \\ a &= \frac{8}{5} \end{aligned}$$

Therefore, the value of a is $\frac{8}{5}$.

60. (A) **Algebra**

Since the two rational expressions have unlike denominators, find the least common denominator of the rational expressions, which is $2(x-1)(x+2)$.

$$\begin{aligned} \frac{x}{x-1} + \frac{x}{2x+4} &= \frac{2x(x+2)}{2(x-1)(x+2)} + \frac{x(x-1)}{2(x-1)(x+2)} \\ &= \frac{2x^2 + 4x + x^2 - x}{2(x-1)(x+2)} \\ &= \frac{3x^2 + 3x}{2(x-1)(x+2)} \\ &= \frac{3x(x+1)}{2(x-1)(x+2)} \end{aligned}$$

Therefore, $\dfrac{x}{x-1} + \dfrac{x}{2x+4} = \dfrac{3x(x+1)}{2(x-1)(x+2)}$.

PRAXIS II 5161 PRACTICE TEST 6

Time — 150 minutes
Number of questions — 60

Directions: Solve each of the following problems using the available space for scratch work. Choose the best answer among the answer choices given and fill in the corresponding circle on the answer sheet.

1. The price of a pen is \$4.50 in April and is increased by 100% in May. What is the price of the pen in May?

(A) \$5.25

(B) \$6.75

(C) \$7.75

(D) \$9.00

2. Which of the following linear equations are perpendicular to each other?

(A) $y = \frac{1}{2}x + 4$
$x + 2y = 6$

(B) $y = \frac{1}{3}x + 4$
$3x - y = 6$

(C) $y = \frac{1}{3}x + 4$
$3x - y = -6$

(D) $y = \frac{1}{3}x + 4$
$3x + y = 6$

For the following question, enter your answer in the answer box.

3. A ferris wheel with a diameter of 60 feet takes 35 seconds to make a rotation. What angle, in degrees, will the ferris wheel rotate for 1 minute and 24 seconds?

[ ] °

4. One yard of wire is divided into two pieces. The length of the shorter piece is 8 inches, which is $\frac{2}{7}$ of the length of the longer piece. What is the length of the longer piece in inches?

(A) 24 inches

(B) 26 inches

(C) 28 inches

(D) 30 inches

5. How many factors of 96 are odd?

(A) 1

(B) 2

(C) 3

(D) 4

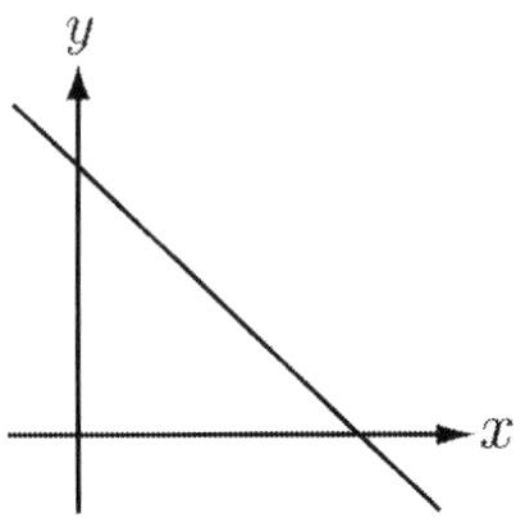

6. The graph above shows the graph of $y = 5 - x$. If $0 < x < 5$, how many points (x, y) are on the graph have integer values of x and y ?

(A) 3

(B) 4

(C) 5

(D) 6

7. $\cos 35° \times \sec 35° =$

(A) $\csc 35°$

(B) $\tan 35°$

(C) $\cot 35°$

(D) 1

8. What value of x is the matrix $\begin{bmatrix} 4 & x \\ 2 & 3 \end{bmatrix}$ **NOT** invertible?

(A) 4

(B) 6

(C) 7

(D) 8

For the following question, enter your answer in the answer box.

9. If $\sqrt{2} + \sqrt{8} + \sqrt{32} = n\sqrt{2}$, what is the value of n ?

$n =$ [ ]

10. Jason borrowed \$20,000 from a bank to purchase a car. The bank charges him 0.5% interest per month on any unpaid balance and he will pay \$300 toward the balance each month. Jason's balance each month after making a \$300 payment is defined by $a_n = 1.005a_{n-1} - 300$, $a_0 = 20,000$, for $n \geq 1$. What is Jason's balance after he makes the third payment?

(A) \$18,784

(B) \$18,990

(C) \$19,194

(D) \$19,397

11. Which of the following residual plot best shows that the independent variable x and dependent variable y are linearly related?

(A)

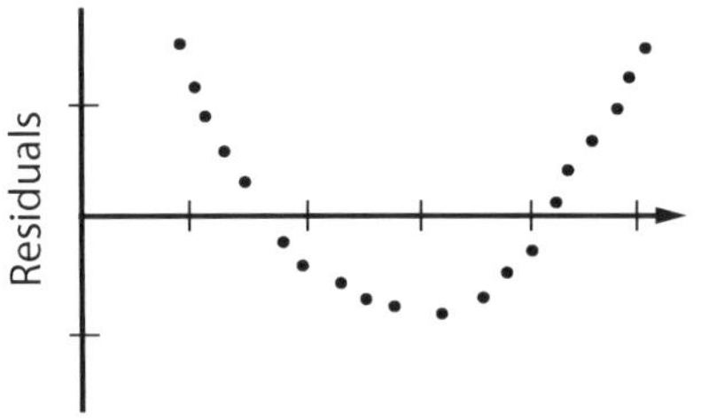

(B)

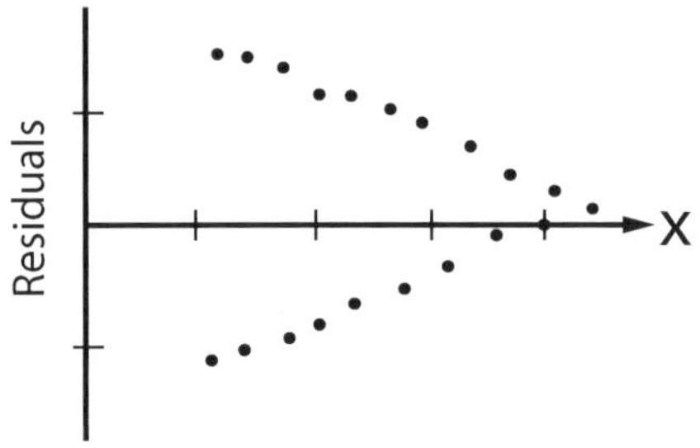

(C)

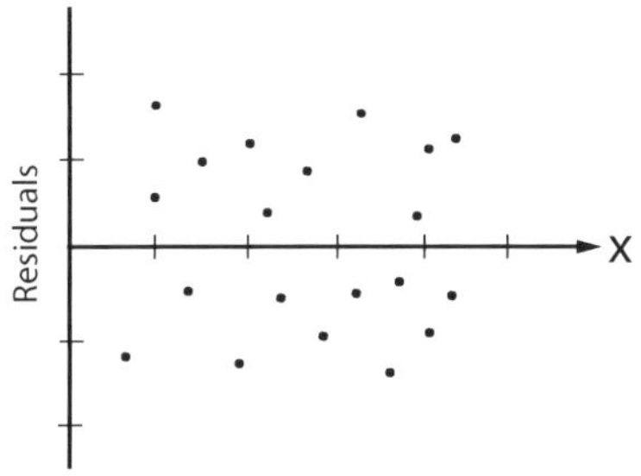

(D)

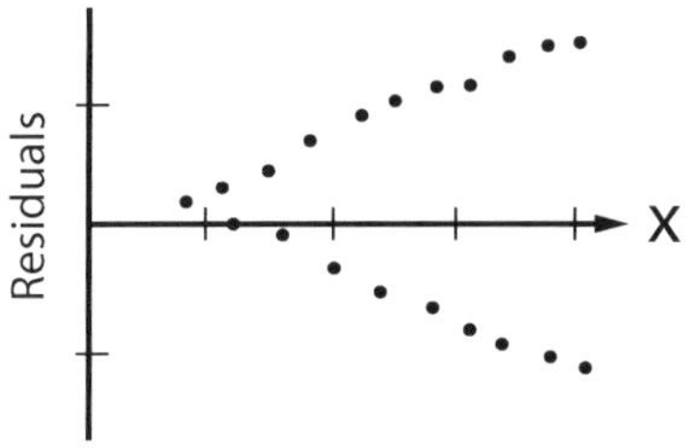

For the following question, enter your answer in the answer box.

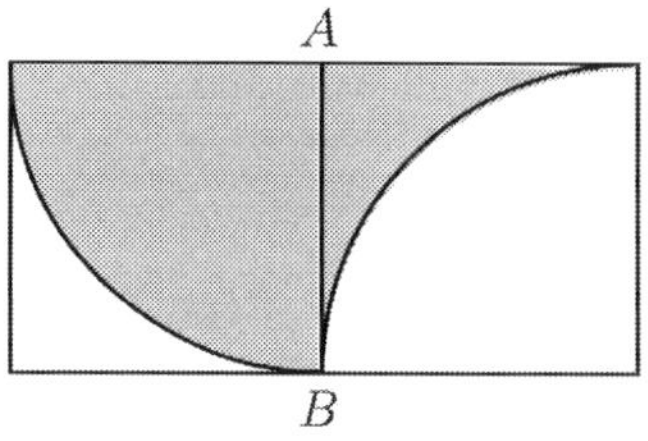

12. In the rectangle above, segment $\overline{AB}$ is drawn so that the rectangle is divided into two smaller squares. If the area of the rectangle is 98, what is the area of the shaded region?

$$g(x) = \begin{cases} \frac{2}{3}x + 2, & x \geq 3 \\ -2x - 1, & x < 3 \end{cases}$$

13. For the following function g above, what is the value of $g(2) + g(3)$?

(A) -1

(B) 0

(C) 2

(D) 3

14. Which of the following is the particular solution to the equation $f'(x) = \dfrac{x+1}{x}$ with the initial condition $f(1) = 3$?

(A) $x + 2$

(B) $x + \ln|x| + 2$

(C) $e^{x-1} + 3$

(D) $\sqrt{x-1} + 3$

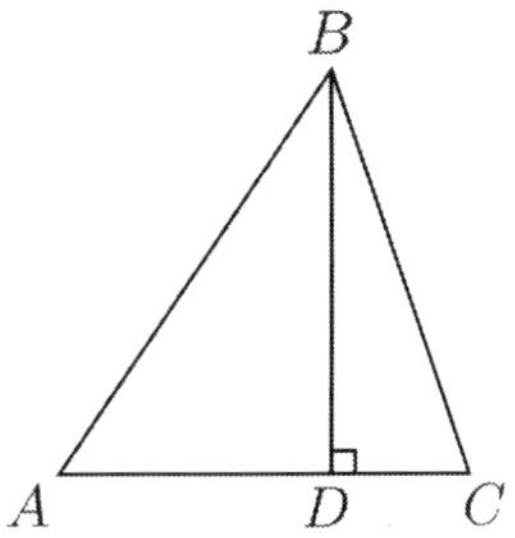

15. In the triangle above, $AB = 15$, $BC = 13$, and $AC = 14$. If CD is four less than AD, what is the area of $\triangle BCD$?

(A) 30

(B) 36

(C) 42

(D) 48

16. In the right triangle ABC, $m\angle C = 90°$. If $AB = 13$ and $AC = 12$, what is the exact value of $\cos B$?

(A) $\frac{1}{5}$

(B) $\frac{5}{13}$

(C) $\frac{5}{12}$

(D) $\frac{12}{13}$

17. If $4^x + 4^x + 4^x + 4^x = 2^k$, which of the following expression is equivalent to k ?

(A) $x + 1$

(B) $2x + 2$

(C) $3x + 1$

(D) $4x + 1$

For the following question, enter your answer in the answer box.

18. If x is a positive integer greater than 1 for which $\sqrt{x}$ and $\sqrt[3]{x}$ are both integers, what is the smallest possible value of x ?

$x = $ ☐

For the following question, select all the answer choices that apply.

19. Which of the followings are the principles of experimental design?

Select all that apply.

(A) Simple random sample

(B) Placebo effect

(C) Replication

(D) Randomization

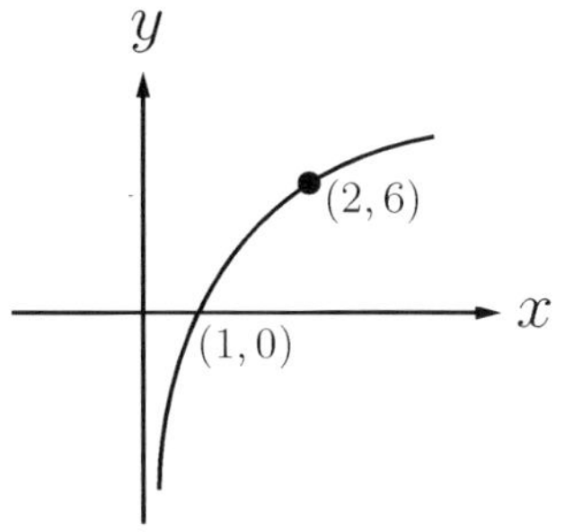

20. The figure above shows the graph of the logarithmic function $y = n\log_4 x$. If the graph contains the point $(2, 6)$, what is the value of n ?

(A) 4

(B) 6

(C) 8

(D) 12

21. In a dog park, there are thirty dogs. Eighteen dogs have short hair and twelve dogs have spots. What is the largest number of dogs that can have both short hair and spots?

(A) 12

(B) 13

(C) 14

(D) 15

x	f	g	f'	g'
-1	2	1	-1	3
1	1	3	0	-2
2	-2	-1	2	1

22. The table above shows values of the differentiable functions f and g and of their derivatives f' and g' for selected values of x. If the function h is defined by $h(x) = f(g(2x))$, which of the following is the slope of the tangent line to the graph of h at $x = 1$?

(A) -5

(B) -2

(C) 3

(D) 4

23. What is the value of x for which $x^2 = 3x$?

(A) $x = 3$ only

(B) $x = 1$ only

(C) $x = 3$ or $x = 0$

(D) $x = 3$ or $x = -3$

24. The number of milligrams A of a certain drug in a patient's bloodstream t hours after the drug has been injected can be modeled by $A(t) = 10e^{-0.2t}$. What is the number of milligrams of the drug in a patient's blood stream after 10 hours?

(A) 1.35 milligrams

(B) 2.23 milligrams

(C) 3.68 milligrams

(D) 5.51 milligrams

For the following question, enter your answer in the answer box.

25. If $0.01 < \frac{1}{k} < 0.1$ and k is an integer, what is the largest possible value of k ?

$k =$ [ ]

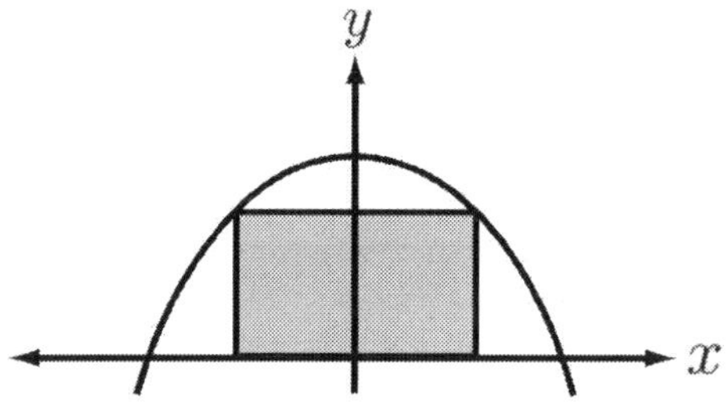

26. In the graph above, the two vertices of a rectangle are on the graph of $y = 9 - x^2$, and the other two vertices are on the x-axis at $x = -2$ and $x = 2$. What is the area of the rectangle?

(A) 10

(B) 20

(C) 30

(D) 40

For the following question, enter your answer in the answer box.

$$S = \frac{1}{3} + \frac{1}{9} + \frac{1}{27} + \cdots$$

27. What is the sum S of the geometric series above?

Give your answer as a fraction.

$$S = \frac{\square}{\square}$$

For the following question, enter your answer in the answer box.

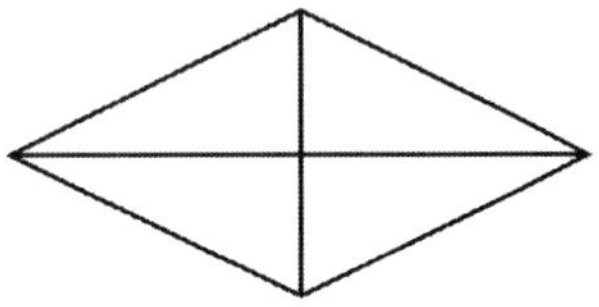

28. In the figure above, the lengths of the diagonals of the rhombus are 12 and 16. What is the perimeter of the rhombus?

Perimeter = $\square$

29. Set A has 5 numbers. The mean and the median of set A are 7 and 10, respectively. If 10 is added to set A to produce set B, which of the following best represents the mean and the median of set B ?

(A) Mean = 7 and Median = 10

(B) Mean = 7 and Median = 13.5

(C) Mean = 7.5 and Median = 10

(D) Mean = 7.5 and Median = 13.5

Blood type	A	B	O	AB
Probability	0.35	0.15	0.38	

30. All human blood can be either A, B, O, or AB. The table above shows the distribution of blood types for a randomly chosen person in a small city. If the small city has a population of 250, how many people in the city have AB as their blood type?

(A) 30

(B) 42

(C) 55

(D) 70

31. What is the period of $y = \sin\left(\frac{2\pi}{3}x - 1\right) + 2$?

(A) 2

(B) 3

(C) 2π

(D) 3π

32. $\int x\,e^x\,dx =$

(A) $-\frac{1}{2}x^2\,e^x + C$

(B) $\frac{1}{2}x^2\,e^x + C$

(C) $x\,e^x - e^x + C$

(D) $x\,e^x + e^x + C$

33. If $f(x) = 2x^3 - 3x + 2$ is divided by $x^2 + 1$, what is the remainder?

(A) $-x + 2$

(B) $-2x + 5$

(C) $-5x - 5$

(D) $-5x + 2$

34. Which of the following statement is logically equivalent to the conditional statement "If the weather is sunny, Joshua goes on a field trip." ?

(A) "If Joshua does not go on a field trip, the weather is not sunny."

(B) "If Joshua goes on a field trip, the weather is sunny."

(C) "If Joshua goes on a field trip, the weather is sometimes sunny."

(D) "If the weather is not sunny, Joshua does not go on a field trip."

x	-2	0	3	5
y	7	3	-3	k

35. The table above shows the four points on a straight line. If the slope of the line is -2, what is the value of k ?

(A) -4

(B) -5

(C) -6

(D) -7

36. If $f(x) = \sqrt[3]{\dfrac{x-1}{2}} + 4$, which of the following is $f^{-1}(x)$?

(A) $f^{-1}(x) = 2(x-4)^3 - 1$

(B) $f^{-1}(x) = 2(x-4)^3 + 1$

(C) $f^{-1}(x) = 2(x+4)^3 - 1$

(D) $f^{-1}(x) = 2(x+4)^3 + 1$

37. Solve the equation: $\cos\theta = \sqrt{3}$, where $0 \leq \theta < 2\pi$.

(A) $x = \dfrac{\pi}{4}$

(B) $x = \dfrac{\pi}{6}$ or $x = \dfrac{11\pi}{6}$

(C) $x = \dfrac{\pi}{3}$ or $x = \dfrac{5\pi}{3}$

(D) No solution

For the following question, enter your answer in the answer box.

x	-2	-1	0	1	2
$f(x)$	3	7	-5	-1	-2

38. The table above shows the function values of f at certain x values. If function p is defined by $p(x) = f(x) + g(x)$ where $g(x) = f(-2x)$ for all values of x, what is the value of $p(-1)$?

$p(-1) =$ ☐

39. Using the substitution $x = \tan\theta$, the definite integral $\int_0^1 \sqrt{1+x^2}\,dx$ is equivalent to

(A) $\int_0^1 \sec^2\theta\,d\theta$

(B) $\int_0^1 \sec\theta\,d\theta$

(C) $\int_0^{\frac{\pi}{4}} \sec\theta\,d\theta$

(D) $\int_0^{\frac{\pi}{4}} \sec^3\theta\,d\theta$

40. How many integers between 100 and 1000 contain only even-numbered digits?

(A) 90

(B) 100

(C) 110

(D) 125

41. Which of the following polar coordinates (r, θ) correspond with the rectangular coordinates $(-\sqrt{3}, -1)$?

(A) $\left(2, \frac{\pi}{6}\right)$

(B) $\left(2, \frac{5\pi}{6}\right)$

(C) $\left(2, \frac{7\pi}{6}\right)$

(D) $\left(2, \frac{4\pi}{3}\right)$

42. If $g(x) = \int_1^{\sqrt{x}} (\ln t)^2\,dt$, which of the following is the value of $g'(e)$?

(A) $\frac{1}{8\sqrt{e}}$

(B) $\frac{1}{2\sqrt{e}}$

(C) $\frac{e}{4}$

(D) $\frac{e}{2}$

For the following question, enter your answer in the answer box.

43. In a triangle ABC, the measure of $\angle C$ is $90°$. If angle A and angle B are complementary and the measure of $\angle A$ is 30 less than twice the measure of $\angle B$, what is the measure of $\angle A$

$m\angle A = \boxed{}\,°$

44. If $f(x) = \log_5 x$ and $g(x) = 5^x$, what is the value of $f(g(3.78))$?

(A) 2.81

(B) 3.43

(C) 3.78

(D) 4.29

For the following question, enter your answer in the answer box.

45. A ladder of 10 feet is leaning against the wall so that the bottom of the ladder is 6 feet away from the wall. If the top of the ladder starts sliding down the wall 1 foot per second, how far away is the bottom of the ladder from the wall after 2 seconds?

[ ] feet

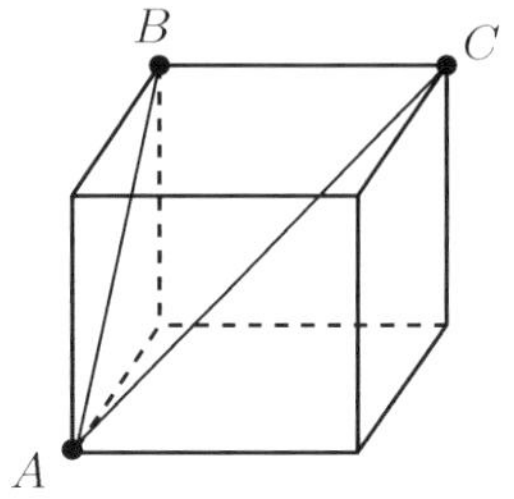

46. Two segments are drawn from point A to point B, and from point A to point C inside or on the surface of a cube as shown in figure above. If the length of the cube is 1, what is the degree measure of $\angle BAC$?

(A) 35.26°

(B) 37.52°

(C) 40.71°

(D) 42.33°

47. If $10^m = 5^n$, what is the value of $\frac{n}{m}$?

(A) 0.85

(B) 0.96

(C) 1.18

(D) 1.43

48. The amount of time spent studying versus test scores for a class of 100 students are graphed. The least-square regression line is $\hat{y} = 24.3x + 11.9$ with a linear correlation of $r = 0.851$. What percent of the variation in test scores can be explained by the amount of time spent studying?

(A) 67.8%

(B) 72.4%

(C) 79.5%

(D) 85.1%

49. If a cube with side length $2\sqrt{3}$ is inscribed in a sphere, what is the volume of the sphere?

(A) 32π

(B) 36π

(C) 42π

(D) 48π

Year	···	9	11	13	···
Amount	···	\$2580	\$2820	\$3060	···

50. The table above shows the amount of money that Vivian has in her savings account over time. If the amount of money increases at a constant rate throughout the years, how much money did Vivian deposit in her savings account in the beginning?

(A) \$1250

(B) \$1500

(C) \$1750

(D) \$2000

51. $\lim_{x\to 4} \dfrac{\sqrt{x+5}}{x-4} =$

(A) 0

(B) 1

(C) 3

(D) The limit does not exist.

52. Set A has 4 numbers. The standard deviation of set A is 4.44. If each number in set A is divided by 2, what is the new standard deviation of set A ?

(A) 1.11

(B) 2.22

(C) 4.44

(D) 8.88

For the following question, enter your answer in the answer box.

53. The length of the shorter side of a rectangle is one less than the length of the longer side of the rectangle. If the area of the rectangle is 110, what is the length of the shorter side?

54. Suppose $f(x) = ax^2 + bx + c$. If $f(-2) = 9$ and $f(-1) = -2$, which of the following is the value of $3a - b$?

(A) 7

(B) 8

(C) 9

(D) 11

55. What is the tens digit of 11^8 ?

(A) 5

(B) 7

(C) 8

(D) 9

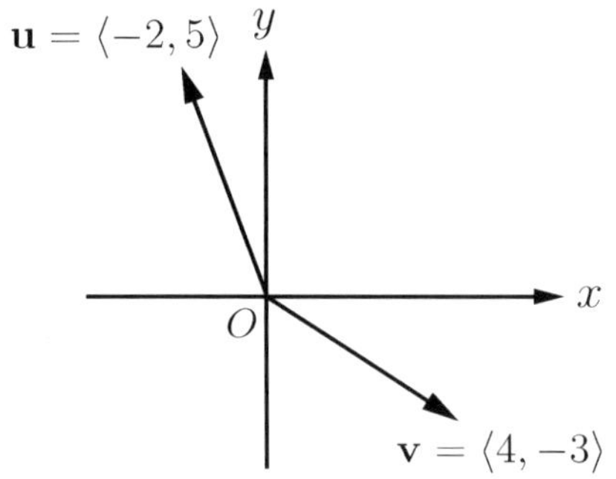

56. If vectors $\mathbf{u}$ and $\mathbf{v}$ are shown above, what is $|2\mathbf{v} - \mathbf{u}|$?

(A) 8.45

(B) 10.24

(C) 14.87

(D) 18.59

57. Which of the following integral best represents the area of the region bounded by $y = x^2$ and $y = \sqrt{x}$?

(A) $\int_0^1 (x^2)^2 - (\sqrt{x})^2 \, dx$

(B) $\int_0^1 (\sqrt{x})^2 - (x^2)^2 \, dx$

(C) $\int_0^1 x^2 - \sqrt{x} \, dx$

(D) $\int_0^1 \sqrt{x} - x^2 \, dx$

58. The rate at which the circumference of a circle is increasing is 4 cm/sec. How fast is the area of the circle increasing when the circumference of the circle is 6π cm ?

(A) 6 cm^2/sec

(B) 8 cm^2/sec

(C) 9 cm^2/sec

(D) 12 cm^2/sec

59. Using the digits 1, 1, 2, and 2 exactly once, how many four-digit numbers can you make?

(A) 2

(B) 4

(C) 6

(D) 12

60. What is the sum of the terms in the arithmetic series $2 + 7 + 12 \cdots + 72$?

(A) 535

(B) 545

(C) 555

(D) 565

STOP

Answers and Solutions

PRAXIS II 5161 PRACTICE TEST 6

Answers

1. D	11. C	21. A	31. B	41. C	51. D
2. D	12. 49	22. B	32. C	42. A	52. B
3. 864	13. A	23. C	33. D	43. 50	53. 10
4. C	14. B	24. A	34. A	44. C	54. D
5. B	15. A	25. 99	35. D	45. 8	55. C
6. B	16. B	26. B	36. B	46. A	56. C
7. D	17. B	27. $\frac{1}{2}$	37. D	47. D	57. D
8. B	18. 64	28. 40	38. 5	48. B	58. D
9. 7	19. C,D	29. C	39. D	49. B	59. C
10. D	20. D	30. A	40. B	50. B	60. C

Solutions

1. (D) **Number and Quantity**

   The price of the pen is increased by 100%, which means that the price of the pen is doubled. Therefore, the price of the pen in May is $2 \times \$4.50 = \$9.00$.

2. (D) **Algebra**

   Perpendicular lines have negative reciprocal slopes. The two linear equations in answer choice (D) show such characteristics.

$$\text{(D)} \quad y = \frac{1}{3}x + 4 \quad \Longrightarrow \quad \text{slope} = \frac{1}{3}$$
$$3x + y = 6 \quad \Longrightarrow \quad y = -3x + 6 \quad \Longrightarrow \quad \text{slope} = -3$$

   Therefore, (D) is the correct answer.

3. (864) **Number and Quantity**

The diameter of the ferris wheel is unnecessary information for this problem. Be sure not to get confused with extra information. There are 60 seconds in one minute. Convert 1 minute and 24 seconds to 84 seconds. Define x as the angle, in degrees, that the ferris wheel will rotate for 84 seconds. Since the ferris wheel rotates 360° every 35 seconds, set up a proportion in terms of degrees (°) and seconds.

$$35_{\text{seconds}} : 360_{\text{degrees}} = 84_{\text{seconds}} : x_{\text{degrees}}$$

$$\frac{35}{360} = \frac{84}{x} \qquad \text{Use cross product property}$$

$$35x = 84(360) \qquad \text{Solve for } x$$

$$x = 864$$

Therefore, the ferris wheel will rotate 864° for one minute and 24 seconds.

4. (C) **Number and Quantity**

There are 12 inches in one foot and 3 feet in one yard. Thus, there are 36 inches in one yard. Since the length of the shorter piece is 8 inches, the length of the longer piece is $36 - 8 = 28$ inches.

5. (B) **Number and Quantity**

List the factors of 96.

$$\text{Factors of } 96 = \{1, 2, 3, 4, 6, 8, 12, 16, 24, 32, 48, 96\}$$

The odd factors of 96 are 1 and 3. Therefore, there are only 2 odd factors of 96.

6. (B) **Algebra**

The possible integer values of x for which $0 < x < 5$ are 1, 2, 3, and 4. As shown in the table below, substitute 1, 2, 3, and 4 for x in $y = 5 - x$ to see if the value of y is an integer. If the value of y is an integer, a point (x, y) is on the graph $y = 5 - x$ and has integer value of x and y.

x	$y = 5 - x$	Point (x, y)
1	$y = 5 - 1 = 4$	$(1, 4)$
2	$y = 5 - 2 = 3$	$(2, 3)$
3	$y = 5 - 3 = 2$	$(3, 2)$
4	$y = 5 - 4 = 1$	$(4, 1)$

Therefore, there are four points $(1, 4)$, $(2, 3)$, $(3, 2)$, and $(4, 1)$ on the graph that have integer values of x and y.

7. (D) **Trigonometry**

Tips $\sec\theta = \dfrac{1}{\cos\theta}$

$$\cos 35^\circ \times \sec 35^\circ = \cos 35^\circ \times \frac{1}{\cos 35^\circ} = 1$$

Therefore, (D) is the correct answer.

8. (B) **Number and Quantity**

The matrix $\begin{bmatrix} 4 & x \\ 2 & 3 \end{bmatrix}$ is not invertible if the determinant of the matrix is zero.

$$\begin{vmatrix} 4 & x \\ 2 & 3 \end{vmatrix} = 0 \quad \Longrightarrow \quad 4(3) - 2x = 0 \quad \Longrightarrow \quad x = 6$$

Therefore, the matrix $\begin{bmatrix} 4 & x \\ 2 & 3 \end{bmatrix}$ is not invertible when $x = 6$.

9. (7) **Number and Quantity**

Tips The product property of the square roots: $\sqrt{ab} = \sqrt{a} \times \sqrt{b}$

Use the product property of the square roots.

$$\sqrt{8} = \sqrt{4} \times \sqrt{2} = 2\sqrt{2}$$
$$\sqrt{32} = \sqrt{16} \times \sqrt{2} = 4\sqrt{2}$$

Thus, $\sqrt{2} + \sqrt{8} + \sqrt{32} = \sqrt{2} + 2\sqrt{2} + 4\sqrt{2} = 7\sqrt{2}$. Therefore, the value of n is 7.

10. (D) **Discrete Mathematics**

Jason's balance each month after making a \$300 payment is defined by $a_n = 1.005a_{n-1} - 300$, $a_0 = 20,000$, for $n \geq 1$. Thus,

Balance after 1st payment: $a_1 = 1.005a_0 - 300 = 1.005(\$20,000) - 300 = \$19,800$
Balance after 2nd payment: $a_2 = 1.005a_1 - 300 = 1.005(\$19,800) - 300 = \$19,599$
Balance after 3rd payment: $a_3 = 1.005a_2 - 300 = 1.005(\$19,599) - 300 = \$19,397$

Therefore, Jason's balance after he makes the third payment is \$19,397.

11. (C) **Probability and Statistics**

The points in a residual plot in answer choice (C) are randomly dispersed around the horizontal axis. This means that the independent variable x and dependent variable y are linearly related. Therefore, (C) is the correct answer.

12. (49) **Geometry**

Move the shaded region of the quarter circle that lies on the left square to the square on the right side as shown below.

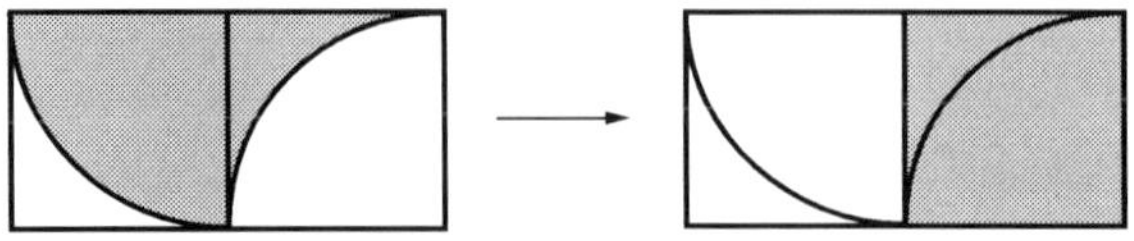

The area of the shaded region equals the area of the smaller square on the right side. Therefore, the area of the smaller square is half the area of the rectangle, or $\frac{1}{2}(98) = 49$.

13. (A) **Functions**

In order to evaluate the piecewise function at $x = 2$ and $x = 3$, check the conditions on the right side of the piecewise function to see where $x = 2$ and $x = 3$ belong. Since $x = 2$ satisfies the condition $x < 3$, the equation for g is $-2x - 1$. Thus, $g(2) = -2(2) - 1 = -5$. Likewise, $x = 3$ satisfies the condition $x \geq 3$, the equation for g is $\frac{2}{3}x + 2$. Thus, $g(3) = \frac{2}{3}(3) + 2 = 4$. Therefore, the value of $g(2) + g(3)$ is $-5 + 4 = -1$.

14. (B) **Calculus**

Tips

1. $\int f'(x)\,dx = f(x) + C$
2. $\int \frac{1}{x}\,dx = \ln|x| + C$

$$\int \frac{x+1}{x}\,dx = \int 1 + \frac{1}{x}\,dx = x + \ln|x| + C$$

Since $f(1) = 3$, substitute 1 for x, and 3 for y to solve for C.

$$\begin{aligned} f(x) &= x + \ln|x| + C \\ 3 &= 1 + \ln|1| + C \\ C &= 2 \end{aligned}$$

Therefore, the particular solution to the equation $f'(x) = \dfrac{x+1}{x}$ with the initial condition $f(1) = 3$ is $f(x) = x + \ln|x| + 2$.

15. (A) **Geometry**

In the figure below, define x as the length of $\overline{AD}$. Then, the length of $\overline{CD}$ is $x - 4$.

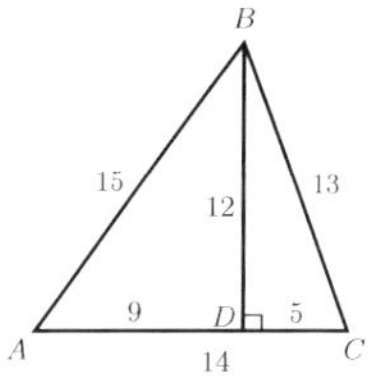

Since $AC = AD + CD$ and $AC = 14$,

$$\begin{aligned} AD + CD &= AC && \text{Substitute 14 for } AC \\ x + x - 4 &= 14 && \text{Solve for } x \\ x &= 9 \end{aligned}$$

Thus, $CD = x - 4 = 5$. $\triangle BCD$ is a right triangle. To find the length of $\overline{BD}$, use the Pythagorean theorem: $13^2 = BD^2 + 5^2$ or use the Pythagorean triple: $5 - 12 - 13$. Thus, $BD = 12$. Therefore, the area of $\triangle BCD$ is $\frac{1}{2}(5)(12) = 30$.

16. (B) **Trigonometry**

Tips $\cos\theta = \dfrac{\text{adjacent side}}{\text{hypotenuse}}$

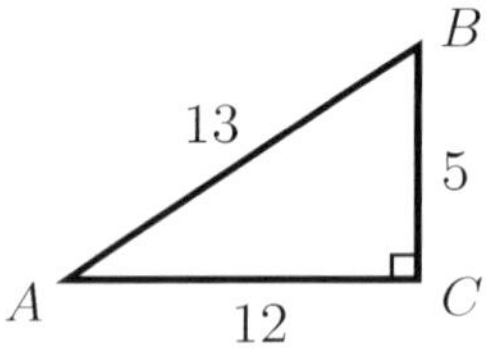

In order to find BC, use the Pythagorean theorem: $13^2 = 12^2 + BC^2$. Thus, $BC = 5$ as shown in the figure above. Therefore, $\cos B = \dfrac{\text{adjacent side}}{\text{hypotenuse}} = \dfrac{5}{13}$.

17. (B) **Number and Quantity**

$$\begin{aligned} 4^x + 4^x + 4^x + 4^x &= 2^k \\ 4 \cdot 4^x &= 2^k \\ 4^{x+1} &= 2^k \\ (2^2)^{x+1} &= 2^k \\ 2^{2x+2} &= 2^k \end{aligned}$$

Therefore, the expression that is equivalent to k is $2x + 2$.

18. (64) **Number and Quantity**

x is a positive integer greater than 1 for which $\sqrt{x}$ and $\sqrt[3]{x}$ are both integers. To obtain integer values for $\sqrt{x} = x^{\frac{1}{2}}$ and $\sqrt[3]{x} = x^{\frac{1}{3}}$, x must be expressed as $x = n^6$, where n is a positive integer. Otherwise, $\sqrt{x}$ and $\sqrt[3]{x}$ cannot be both integers. Since we are looking for the smallest possible value greater than 1 for x, choose $n = 2$. Thus, $x = 2^6 = 64$. Check the answer by substituting 64 for x in both $\sqrt{x}$ and $\sqrt[3]{x}$.

$$\sqrt{64} = 8 \quad \checkmark\text{(Integer)}, \qquad \sqrt[3]{64} = 4 \quad \checkmark\text{(Integer)}$$

Therefore, the smallest possible value of x for which $\sqrt{x}$ and $\sqrt[3]{x}$ that are both integers is $2^6 = 64$.

19. (C,D) **Probability and Statistics**

The three principles of designing an experiment are as follows:

(a) Control: Two or more treatments should be compared.

(b) Randomization: The subjects should be randomly divided into groups in order to avoid selection bias.

(c) Replication: Having enough subjects will decrease the experimental error and increase precision.

Therefore, (C), and (D) are the correct answers.

20. (D) **Functions**

Tips $\log_{a^n} x = \frac{1}{n}\log_a x \implies \log_4 2 = \log_{2^2} 2 = \frac{1}{2}\log_2 2 = \frac{1}{2}$

Since the graph of the logarithmic function $y = n\log_4 x$ contains the point $(2, 6)$ as shown in the figure below, substitute 2 for x and 6 for y to solve for n.

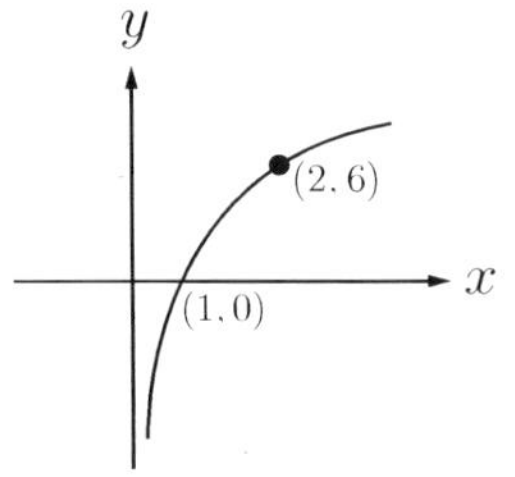

$$y = n\log_4 x \quad \text{Substitute 2 for } x \text{ and 6 for } y$$
$$6 = n\log_4 2 \quad \text{Note that } \log_4 2 = \frac{1}{2}$$
$$6 = \frac{1}{2}n$$
$$n = 12$$

Therefore, the value of n is 12.

21. (A) **Discrete Mathematics**

If all twelve dogs that have spots also have short hair as shown in the diagram below,

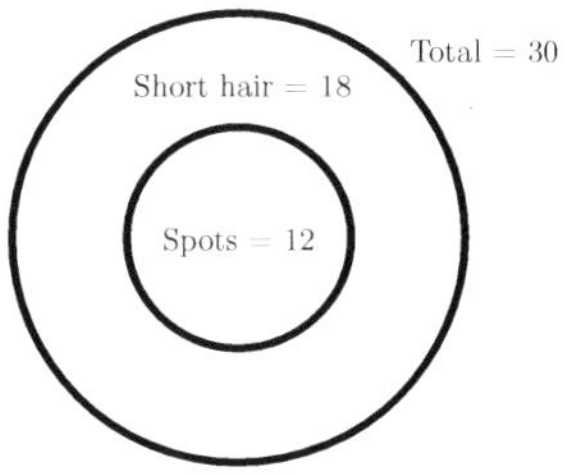

the largest number of dogs that can have short hair and spots is 12.

22. (B) **Calculus**

Tips The Chain rule: If $h(x) = f(g(2x))$, then $h'(x) = f'(g(2x)) \cdot g'(2x) \cdot 2$

Differentiating $h(x) = f(g(2x))$ using the Chain rule gives $h'(x) = f'(g(2x)) \cdot g'(2x) \cdot 2$. Since $g(2) = -1$, $g'(2) = 1$, $f'(-1) = -1$,

$$h'(1) = f'(g(2)) \cdot g'(2) \cdot 2 = f'(-1) \cdot 1 \cdot 2 = -2$$

Therefore, he slope of the tangent line to the graph of h at $x = 1$ is $g'(1) = -2$.

23. (C) **Algebra**

> Tips: When solving an equation, do not divide each side of the equation by a variable, x, because it will eliminate some of the solutions.

$$x^2 = 3x \quad \text{Subtract } 3x \text{ from each side}$$
$$x^2 - 3x = 0 \quad \text{Factor}$$
$$x(x-3) = 0 \quad \text{Solve for } x$$
$$x = 0 \quad \text{or} \quad x = 3$$

Therefore, solutions to $x^2 = 3x$ are $x = 0$ or $x = 3$.

24. (A) **Functions**

In order to find the number of milligrams of the drug in a patient's blood stream after 10 hours, substitute 10 for t in $A(t) = 10e^{-0.2t}$. Thus, $A(10) = 10e^{-0.2(10)} = 1.35$. Therefore, the number of milligrams of the drug in a patient's blood stream after 10 hours is 1.35 milligrams.

25. (99) **Algebra**

Take the reciprocal of each side of the inequality. It's worth noting that the inequality symbol is reversed when taking the reciprocal of each side of the inequality.

$$0.01 < \frac{1}{k} < 0.1 \quad \text{Take the reciprocal of each side}$$
$$\frac{1}{0.01} > k > \frac{1}{0.1} \quad \text{Inequality symbol is reversed}$$
$$10 < k < 100$$

Since k is an integer, the possible values of k for which $10 < k < 100$ is $k = 11, 12, \cdots, 98, 99$. Therefore, the largest possible value of k is 99.

26. (B) **Algebra**

The two vertices of the rectangle are on the x-axis at $x = -2$ and $x = 2$ as shown below. This means that the length of the rectangle is 4.

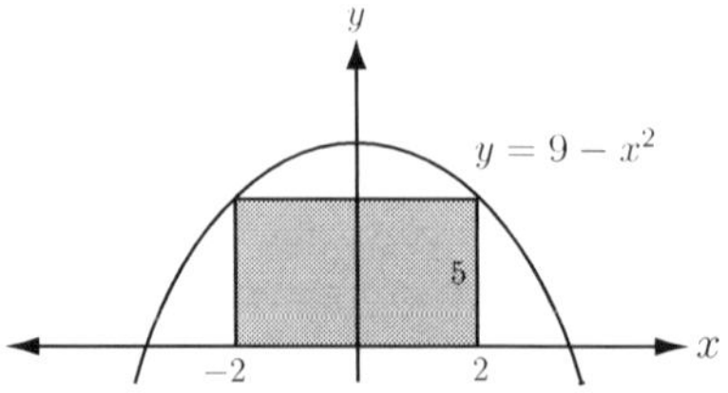

Additionally, the width of the rectangle is determined by the function's value at $x = 2$, or $f(2)$. To evaluate $f(2)$, substitute 2 for x in $f(x) = 9 - x^2$. Thus, $f(2) = 9 - 2^2 = 5$, which means that the width of the rectangle is 5. Therefore, the area of the rectangle is $4 \times 5 = 20$.

27. ($\frac{1}{2}$) **Discrete Mathematics**

Tips: The infinite sum S of a geometric series is $S = \frac{a_1}{1-r}$ if $|r| < 1$, where r is the common ratio of the geometric sequence.

In the geometric series $S = \frac{1}{3} + \frac{1}{9} + \frac{1}{27} + \cdots$, $a_1 = \frac{1}{3}$ and r is $\frac{1}{3}$. Thus,

$$S = \frac{a_1}{1-r} = \frac{\frac{1}{3}}{1-\frac{1}{3}} = \frac{\frac{1}{3}}{\frac{2}{3}} = \frac{1}{2}$$

Therefore, the sum of the geometric series is $S = \frac{1}{3} + \frac{1}{9} + \frac{1}{27} + \cdots = \frac{1}{2}$.

28. (40) **Geometry**

In the figure below, the diagonals of the rhombus are perpendicular and bisect each other. When the rhombus is divided into four congruent right triangles, the lengths of the legs of the triangles are half the lengths of the diagonals: 6 and 8.

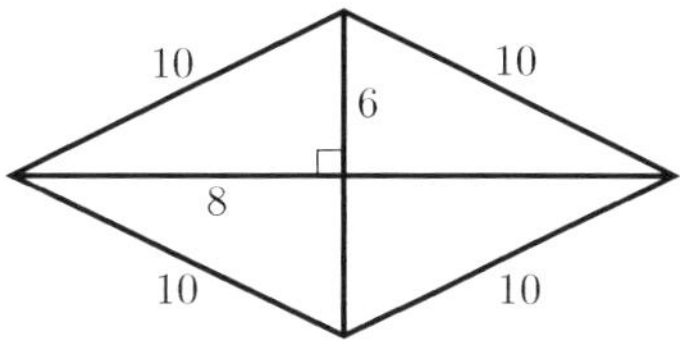

To find the length of the hypotenuse, use the Pythagorean theorem: $c^2 = 6^2 + 8^2$ or use a multiple of the Pythagorean triple: $(3-4-5) \times 2 = 6-8-10$. Thus, the length of the hypotenuse, the length of the rhombus, is 10. Therefore, the perimeter of the rhombus is $10 \times 4 = 40$.

29. (C) **Probability and Statistics**

For simplicity, let set A be $\{1, 1, 10, 11, 12\}$ so that the mean and the median of the set are 7 and 10, respectively. Since 10 is added to set A to produce set B, set $B = \{1, 1, 10, 10, 11, 12\}$. Therefore, the mean and the median of set B are 7.5 and 10, respectively.

30. (A) **Probability and Statistics**

The probability of selecting a blood type AB is $1 - (0.35 + 0.15 + 0.38) = 0.12$ as shown in the table below.

Blood type	A	B	O	AB
Probability	0.35	0.15	0.38	0.12

Since the small city has a population of 250, the number of people who have AB as their blood type is $250 \times 0.12 = 30$.

31. (B) **Trigonometry**

> Tips
>
> The general forms of the sine function and cosine function are as follows:
>
> $$y = A\sin\left(B(x - C)\right) + D \qquad \text{or} \qquad y = A\cos\left(B(x - C)\right) + D$$
>
> where B affects the period. The period, P, is the horizontal length of one complete cycle and is obtained by $P = \dfrac{2\pi}{B}$.

Comparing $y = \sin\left(\dfrac{2\pi}{3}x - 1\right) + 2$ to the general form of $y = A\sin\left(B(x - C)\right) + D$, we found that $B = \dfrac{2\pi}{3}$. Therefore, the period is $P = \dfrac{2\pi}{\frac{2\pi}{3}} = 3$.

32. (C) **Calculus**

> Tips
>
> Integration by Parts: $\displaystyle\int u\, dv = uv - \int v\, du$

According to the list below,

$\ln x$ $(\sin^{-1}x.\tan^{-1}x)$ $(x^n.1)$ $(\sin x.\cos x)$ e^x

u ← easier to differentiate   easier to integrate → dv

x is closer to the left side than e^x. Let $u = x$ and $dv = e^x\, dx$. So $\displaystyle\int xe^x\, dx = \int u\, dv$. Then

$$\begin{aligned} u &= x & v &= e^x \\ du &= dx & dv &= e^x\, dx \end{aligned}$$

Thus,

$$\begin{aligned} \int u\, dv &= uv - \int v\, du \\ &= xe^x - \int e^x\, dx \\ &= xe^x - e^x + C \end{aligned}$$

Therefore, $\displaystyle\int x\, e^x\, dx = xe^x - e^x + C$.

33. (D) **Algebra**

$$\begin{array}{r|l} & \quad 2x \\ \hline x^2 + 1 & \; 2x^3 - 3x + 2 \\ & -\,2x^3 - 2x \\ \cline{2-2} & \qquad -5x + 2 \end{array}$$

When $2x^3 - 3x + 2$ is divided by $x^2 + 1$, the remainder is $-5x + 2$.

34. (A) **Discrete Mathematics**

Tips		
	Conditional statement:	If P, then Q
	Contrapositive:	If not Q, then not P

The conditional statement and its contrapositive are logically equivalent.

The contrapositive of the conditional statement "If the weather is sunny, Joshua goes on a field trip." is "If Joshua does not go on a field trip, the weather is not sunny." Therefore, (A) is the correct answer.

35. (D) **Algebra**

Use the definition of the slope: slope $= \frac{y_2 - y_1}{x_2 - x_1}$. Since the slope of the line is -2, choose two points $(0, 3)$ and $(5, k)$ to set up an equation in term of the slope.

$$\begin{aligned} \text{Slope} &= \frac{k-3}{5-0} = -2 \\ k - 3 &= -10 \\ k &= -7 \end{aligned}$$

Therefore, the value of k is -7.

36. (B) **Functions**

Switch the x and y variables and solve for y.

$$\begin{aligned} y &= \sqrt[3]{\frac{x-1}{2}} + 4 && \text{Switch the } x \text{ and } y \text{ variables} \\ x &= \sqrt[3]{\frac{y-1}{2}} + 4 && \text{Subtract 4 from each side} \\ x - 4 &= \sqrt[3]{\frac{y-1}{2}} && \text{Raise each side to the power of 3} \\ (x-4)^3 &= \frac{y-1}{2} && \text{Multiply each side by 2} \\ y - 1 &= 2(x-4)^3 && \text{Add 1 to each side} \\ y &= 2(x-4)^3 + 1 \end{aligned}$$

Therefore, the inverse function of $f(x) = \sqrt[3]{\frac{x-1}{2}} + 4$ is $f^{-1}(x) = 2(x-4)^3 + 1$.

37. (D) **Trigonometry**

Solving the equation $\cos\theta = \sqrt{3}$ means to find the x-coordinates of the intersection points when two graphs $y = \cos\theta$ and $y = \sqrt{3}$ intersect.

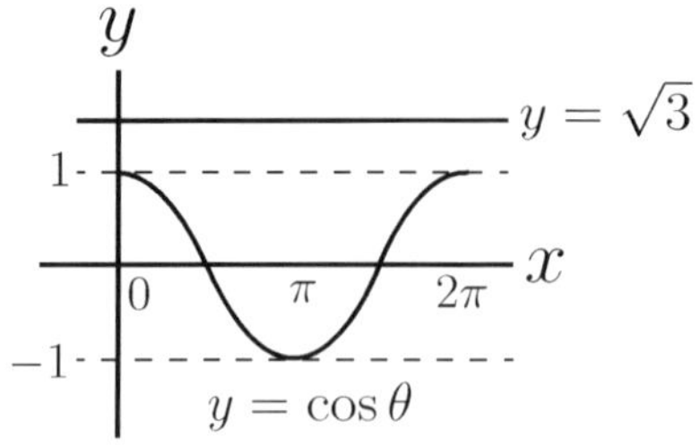

As shown in the figure above, the two graphs $y = \cos\theta$ and $y = \sqrt{3}$ never intersect. Therefore, there are no solutions to $\cos\theta = \sqrt{3}$.

38. (5) **Functions**

Since $g(x) = f(-2x)$, $p(x) = f(x) + f(-2x)$. To evaluate $p(-1)$, substitute -1 for x in $p(x)$.

$$\begin{aligned} p(x) &= f(x) + f(-2x) && \text{Substitute } -1 \text{ for } x \\ p(-1) &= f(-1) + f(2) && f(-1) = 7 \text{ and } f(2) = -2 \\ &= 7 - 2 = 5 \end{aligned}$$

Therefore, the value of $p(-1) = 5$.

39. (D) **Calculus**

Tips $\sqrt{1+\tan^2\theta} = \sqrt{\sec^2\theta} = \sec\theta$.

Let $x = \tan\theta$. Then $dx = \sec^2\theta\, d\theta$. Since $x = \tan\theta$, $\theta = \tan^{-1} x$. Let's find the new lower limit and upper limit for the integration.

$$\text{When } x = 0,\ \theta = \tan^{-1} 0 = 0, \qquad \text{When } x = 1,\ \theta = \tan^{-1} 1 = \frac{\pi}{4}$$

Thus, the new lower limit and upper limit for the integration are 0 and $\frac{\pi}{4}$, respectively.

$$\int_0^1 \sqrt{1+x^2}\, dx = \int_0^{\frac{\pi}{4}} \sqrt{1+\tan^2\theta}\ \sec^2\theta\, d\theta = \int_0^{\frac{\pi}{4}} \sec\theta \cdot \sec^2\theta\, d\theta = \int_0^{\frac{\pi}{4}} \sec^3\theta\, d\theta$$

Therefore, (D) is the correct answer.

40. (B) **Discrete Mathematics**

> Tips — The fundamental counting principle: If one event can occur in m ways and another event can occur in n ways, then the number of ways both events can occur is $m \times n$.

Let event 1 be selecting a digit for the hundreds place. There are 4 possible digits: 2, 4, 6 and 8 since integers must be greater than 100. Let event 2 and event 3 be selecting a digit for the tens place and ones place. Event 2 and event 3 each have 5 possible digits: 0, 2, 4, 6, and 8. According to the fundamental counting principle, the number of integers between 100 and 1000 that contain only even-numbered digits is $4 \times 5 \times 5 = 100$.

41. (C) **Trigonometry**

To convert from the rectangular coordinates $(-\sqrt{3}, -1)$ to the polar coordinates (r, θ), do the following three steps:

- Step 1: Plot the point $(-\sqrt{3}, -1)$ as shown in Figure A. Since the point $(-\sqrt{3}, -1)$ is in the third quadrant, $\pi < \theta < \dfrac{3\pi}{2}$.
- Step 2: Find the distance between the point $(-\sqrt{3}, -1)$ and the origin, r, and the reference angle, β, formed by the positive x-axis and the terminal side as shown in Figure B.

$$r = \sqrt{x^2 + y^2} = \sqrt{(-\sqrt{3})^2 + (-1))^2} = 2$$
$$\beta = \left|\tan^{-1}\frac{y}{x}\right| = \left|\tan^{-1}\left(\frac{-1}{-\sqrt{3}}\right)\right| = \frac{\pi}{6}$$

- Step 3: Find θ using the reference angle based on the quadrant that θ lies in as shown in Figure C. Since $\beta = \dfrac{\pi}{6}$ and θ lies in the third quadrant, $\theta = \pi + \beta = \pi + \dfrac{\pi}{6} = \dfrac{7\pi}{6}$.

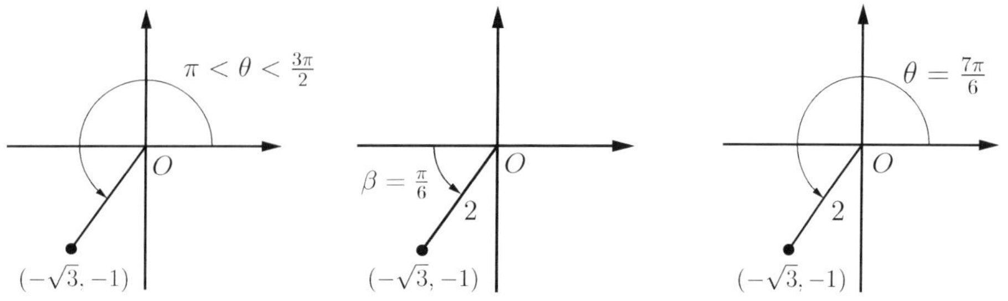

Figure A　　Figure B　　Figure C

Therefore, the polar coordinates that correspond with the rectangular coordinates $(-\sqrt{3}, -1)$ are $\left(2, \dfrac{7\pi}{6}\right)$.

42. (A) **Calculus**

Tips

1. The Fundamental Theorem of Calculus, Part I:

$$g'(x) = \frac{d}{dx}\int_a^{p(x)} f(t)\,dt \implies g'(x) = f(p(x)) \cdot (p(x))'$$

2. $\ln\sqrt{e} = \ln e^{\frac{1}{2}} = \frac{1}{2}\ln e = \frac{1}{2}$

$$g'(x) = \frac{d}{dx}\int_1^{\sqrt{x}} (\ln t)^2\,dt = (\ln\sqrt{x})^2 \cdot (\sqrt{x})' = (\ln\sqrt{x})^2 \cdot \frac{1}{2\sqrt{x}}$$

Thus,

$$g'(e) = (\ln\sqrt{e})^2 \cdot \frac{1}{2\sqrt{e}} = \left(\frac{1}{2}\right)^2 \cdot \frac{1}{2\sqrt{e}} = \frac{1}{8\sqrt{e}}$$

Therefore, the value of $g'(e)$ is $\frac{1}{8\sqrt{e}}$.

43. (50) **Geometry**

Angle A and angle B are complementary angles. Thus, the sum of their measures is 90°. Define x as the measure of $\angle B$. Since the measure of $\angle A$ is 30 less than twice the measure of $\angle B$, the measure of $\angle A$ can be expressed as $2x - 30$.

$$\begin{aligned} m\angle A + m\angle B &= 90 \\ 2x - 30 + x &= 90 \\ x &= 40 \end{aligned}$$

Therefore, the measure of $\angle A$ is $2x - 30 = 50°$.

44. (C) **Functions**

Tips

1. $y = 5^x$ is the inverse function of $y = \log_5 x$.
2. $f\left(f^{-1}(x)\right) = x$

Since $g(x) = 5^x$ is the inverse function of $f(x) = \log_5 x$, $g(x) = f^{-1}(x)$. Thus,

$$f(g(3.78)) = f\left(f^{-1}(3.78)\right) = 3.78$$

Therefore, the value of $f(g(3.78))$ is 3.78.

45. (8) **Geometry**

The length of the ladder is 10 feet. Although the top and bottom of the ladder are sliding down and sliding away, the length of the ladder remains the same. When the bottom of the ladder is 6 feet away from the wall, the top of the ladder is 8 feet above the ground as shown in the diagram below. Use the Pythagorean theorem: $10^2 = a^2 + 6^2$, where a is the height of the wall at which the top of the ladder leans against. It is also possible to use a multiple of the Pythagorean triple: $(3-4-5)\times 2 = 6-8-10$.

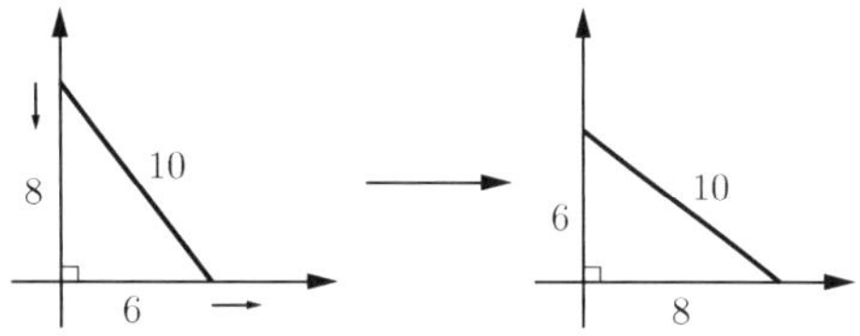

The top of the ladder is sliding down for 2 seconds at a rate of 1 foot per second so it is $8-2=6$ feet above the ground. To determine how far the bottom of the ladder is from the wall, use the same multiple of the Pythagorean triple: $6-8-10$. Therefore, the bottom of the ladder is 8 feet away from the wall after 2 seconds.

46. (A) **Trigonometry**

Tips

1. The length of the longest diagonal of a cube with side lengths x is $x\sqrt{3}$.
2. If triangle ABC shown at the right is a SSS triangle (a, b, and c are known), the measure of angle A can be calculated by the Law of Cosines.

$$m\angle A = \cos^{-1}\left(\frac{a^2-b^2-c^2}{-2bc}\right)$$

Note that side a is opposite angle A.

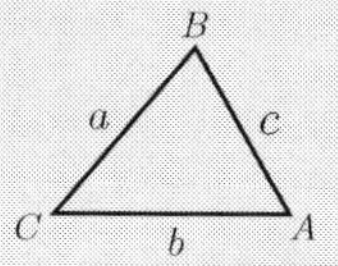

Since the length of the cube is 1, $BC = 1$. $\overline{AB}$ is a diagonal with $AB = \sqrt{2}$, and $\overline{AC}$ is the longest diagonal with $AC = \sqrt{3}$ as shown in Figure A.

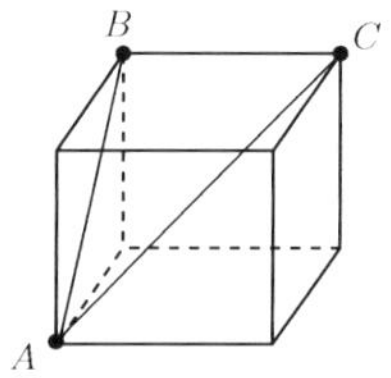

Figure A

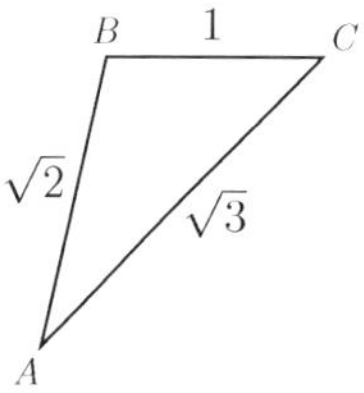

Figure B

$\triangle ABC$ is a SSS triangle (three sides are known) as shown in Figure B. Thus, the degree measure of $\angle BAC$ can be calculated by the Law of Cosines.

$$m\angle BAC = \cos^{-1}\left(\frac{BC^2-AB^2-AC^2}{-2\cdot AB\cdot AC}\right) = \cos^{-1}\left(\frac{1^2-(\sqrt{2})^2-(\sqrt{3})^2}{-2\cdot(\sqrt{2})\cdot(\sqrt{3})}\right) = 35.26^\circ$$

Therefore, the degree measure of $\angle BAC$ is 35.26°.

47. (D) **Functions**

> Tips
>
> When each side of an exponential equation has a different base, convert the exponential equation to a logarithmic equation.
>
> If $a^x = b \implies x = \log_a b$ e.g. If $2^x = 7$, then $x = \log_2 7$

Since each side of the exponential equation has a different base (the left side has a base of 10 and the right side has a base of 5), convert the exponential equation to a logarithmic equation.

$10^m = 5^n$	Convert the equation to a logarithmic equation
$m = \log_{10} 5^n$	Use $\log_a x^n = n \log_a x$
$m = n \log_{10} 5$	Divide each side by n
$\frac{m}{n} = \log_{10} 5 = 0.70$	Take the reciprocal of each side
$\frac{n}{m} = 1.43$	

Therefore, the value of $\frac{n}{m}$ is 1.43.

48. (B) **Probability and Statistics**

> Tips
>
> The coefficient of determination, r^2, is the proportion of the variation in y that is predictable from x. Larger the r^2, better the least square regression model is.

Since $r = 0.851$, $r^2 = (0.851)^2 = 0.724$. Therefore, 72.4% of the variation in test scores can be explained by the amount of time spent studying.

49. (B) **Geometry**

> Tips
>
> 1. The length of the longest diagonal of a cube with side length x is $x\sqrt{3}$.
> 2. When a cube with side length x is inscribed in a sphere, the diameter of the sphere is the same as longest diagonal of the cube. Thus, the diameter of the sphere is $x\sqrt{3}$ and the radius of the sphere is $\frac{x}{2}\sqrt{3}$.
> 3. The volume V of a sphere: $V = \frac{4}{3}\pi r^3$

The length of the cube is $2\sqrt{3}$. Thus, the longest diagonal of the cube and the diameter of the sphere are both $2\sqrt{3} \times \sqrt{3} = 6$. Since the radius of the sphere is 3, the volume of the sphere is $V = \frac{4}{3}\pi r^3 = \frac{4}{3}\pi(3)^3 = 36\pi$.

50. (B) **Algebra**

The amount of money in Vivian's savings account increases at a constant rate throughout the years. This suggests that a linear function best describes the information in the table. Create two ordered pairs, $(9, 2580)$ and $(11, 2820)$ from the table and find the slope of the linear function, which determines the rate at which the amount of money increases per year.

$$\text{Slope} = \frac{y_2 - y_1}{x_2 - x_1} = \frac{2820 - 2580}{11 - 9} = 120$$

Thus, the linear function can be written as $y = 120x + b$, where x represents the number of years, b represents the initial amount of money that Vivian deposited in the beginning, and y represents the total amount of money in the savings account in x years. To find b, substitute 9 for x and 2580 for y.

$$\begin{aligned} y &= 120x + b && \text{Substitute 9 for } x \text{ and 2580 for } y. \\ 2580 &= 120(9) + b && \text{Solve for } b \\ b &= 1500 \end{aligned}$$

Therefore, Vivian deposited \$1500 in her savings account in the beginning.

51. (D) **Calculus**

In order to find the limit of the function $\frac{\sqrt{x+5}}{x-4}$ at $x = 4$, plug-in $x = 4$ to both the numerator and denominator.

$$\lim_{x \to 4} \frac{\sqrt{x+5}}{x-4} = \frac{\sqrt{4+5}}{4-4} = \frac{3}{0} = \text{undefined}$$

Therefore, the limit does not exist.

52. (B) **Probability and Statistics**

Tips: If all numbers in the data set are divided by the same number, k, the standard deviation is divided by k.

Since each number in set A is divided by 2, the new standard deviation of set A is $\frac{4.44}{2} = 2.22$.

53. (10) **Algebra**

Define x as the length of the longer side of the rectangle and $x - 1$ as the length of the shorter side of the rectangle. Then, the area of the rectangle can be expressed as $x(x - 1)$. Since the area of the rectangle is 110,

$$\begin{aligned} x(x-1) &= 110 && \text{Expand } x(x-1) \\ x^2 - x - 110 &= 0 && \text{Use the factoring method} \\ (x+10)(x-11) &= 0 && \text{Use the zero-product property} \\ x = -10 \quad &\text{or} \quad x = 11 \end{aligned}$$

Since x represent the length, x must be positive. Thus, $x = 11$. Therefore, the length of the shorter side of the rectangle is $x - 1 = 10$.

54. (D) **Algebra**

Since $f(-2) = 9$ and $f(-1) = -2$, substitute -2 and -1 for x in $f(x) = ax^2 + bx + c$.

$$f(-2) = 4a - 2b + c = 9, \qquad f(-1) = a - b + c = -2$$

In order to find the value of $3a - b$, subtract $a - b + c = -2$ from $4a - 2b + c = 9$ as shown below.

$$\begin{array}{r} 4a - 2b + c = 9 \\ a - b + c = -2 \\ \hline 3a - b = 11 \end{array} \qquad \text{Subtract the two equations}$$

Therefore, the value of $3a - b$ is 11.

55. (C) **Number and Quantity**

The tens and units digits of the powers of 11 are shown below.

Powers of 11	11^1	11^2	11^3	11^4	11^5	11^6	11^7	11^8
Tens and units digits	11	21	31	41	51	61	71	81

Therefore, the tens digit of 11^8 is 8.

56. (C) **Trigonometry**

Tips The magnitude of a vector $\mathbf{V} = \langle a, b \rangle$, denoted by $|\mathbf{V}|$, is $|\mathbf{V}| = \sqrt{a^2 + b^2}$.

Since $\mathbf{v} = \langle 4, -3 \rangle$ and $\mathbf{u} = \langle -2, 5 \rangle$,

$$\begin{aligned} 2\mathbf{v} - \mathbf{u} &= 2\langle 4, -3 \rangle - \langle -2, 5 \rangle \\ &= \langle 8, -6 \rangle - \langle -2, 5 \rangle \\ &= \langle 10, -11 \rangle \end{aligned}$$

Thus, $2\mathbf{v} - \mathbf{u} = \langle 10, -11 \rangle$. Therefore, $|2\mathbf{v} - \mathbf{u}|$ is $\sqrt{10^2 + (-11)^2} = 14.87$.

57. (D) **Calculus**

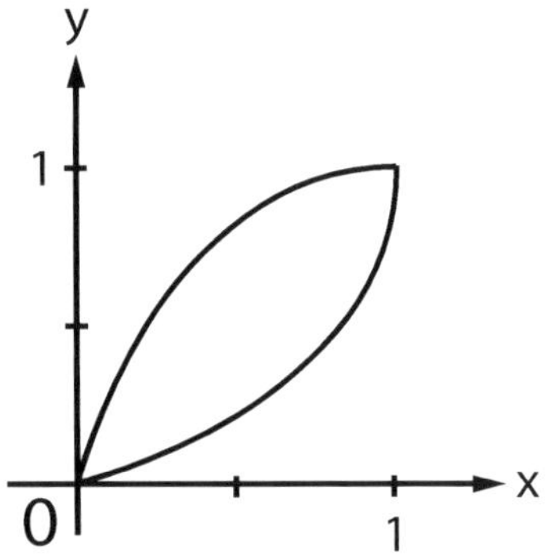

The graphs of $y = \sqrt{x}$ and $y = x^2$ intersect at $x = 0$ and $x = 1$ as shown above. The top curve f_T is $y = \sqrt{x}$, and the bottom curve f_B is $y = x^2$. Thus,

$$A = \int_a^b [f_T - f_B]\, dx = \int_0^1 \sqrt{x} - x^2\, dx$$

Therefore, (D) is the correct answer.

58. (D) **Calculus**

As time t increases, the circumference C, the radius r, and the area A of a circle increase. So the circumference, the radius, and the area are the functions of t. We are given that $\frac{dC}{dt} = 4$ cm/sec, and try to find $\frac{dA}{dt}$ when $C = 6\pi$ cm. Let's set up an equation that relates the area $A = \pi r^2$ and the circumference $C = 2\pi r$.

$$A = \pi r^2 = \pi\left(\frac{C}{2\pi}\right)^2$$

Differentiate both sides with respect to t using the Chain rule and solve for $\frac{dA}{dt}$.

$$\frac{dA}{dt} = \pi \cdot 2\left(\frac{C}{2\pi}\right) \cdot \frac{1}{2\pi} \cdot \frac{dC}{dt} = \frac{C}{2\pi}\frac{dC}{dt}$$

Substituting $C = 6\pi$ cm, and $\frac{dC}{dt} = 4$ cm/sec gives

$$\frac{dA}{dt} = \frac{C}{2\pi}\frac{dC}{dt} = \frac{6\pi}{2\pi}(4) = 12$$

Therefore, the rate at which the area of the circle increasing when the circumference of the circle is 6π is 12 cm^2/sec.

59. (C) **Discrete Mathematics**

Tips

Permutations with repetition: The number of permutations of n objects, where there are n_1 indistinguishable objects of one kind, and n_2 indistinguishable objects of a second kind, is given by

$$\text{Permutations with repetition} = \frac{n!}{n_1! \cdot n_2!}$$

Since 1 and 2 are distinguishable, the order is important. However, there are 2 1's and 2 2's out of 4 numbers.

$$\text{Permutations with repetition} = \frac{4!}{2! \cdot 2!} = \frac{4 \cdot 3 \cdot \cancel{2!}}{2! \cdot \cancel{2!}} = 6$$

Therefore, using the digits 1, 1, 2, and 2 exactly once, the number of four-digit numbers you can make is 6.

60. (C) **Discrete Mathematics**

Tips

The sum of the first n terms S_n of an arithmetic series is

$$S_n = \frac{n}{2}(a_1 + a_n)$$

where a_1 is the first term, and $a_n = a_1 + (n-1)d$ is the nth term of the arithmetic sequence.

$2, 7, 12, \cdots, 72$ is the arithmetic sequence with a common difference $d = 5$. Using the nth term formula $a_n = a_1 + (n-1)d$,

$a_n = a_1 + (n-1)d$	Substitute 72 for a_n, 2 for a_1, and 5 for d
$72 = 2 + (n-1)5$	Subtract 2 from each side
$5(n-1) = 70$	Divide each side by 5
$n - 1 = 14$	Add 1 to each side
$n = 15$	

we found that 72 is the 15th term of the arithmetic sequence. Thus, $2 + 7 + 12 + \cdots + 72$ is the sum of the first 15 terms of the arithmetic series.

$S_n = \frac{n}{2}(a_1 + a_n)$	Substitute 15 for n
$S_{15} = \frac{15}{2}(a_1 + a_{15})$	Substitute 2 for a_1 and 72 for a_{15}
$= \frac{15}{2}(2 + 72) = 555$	

Therefore, $2 + 7 + 12 + \cdots + 72 = 555$.

Made in the USA
Coppell, TX
26 April 2020

22761510R10245